❀ ❀ ❀

How to Read Chinese Drama

HOW TO READ CHINESE LITERATURE SERIES

HOW TO READ CHINESE LITERATURE

ZONG-QI CAI, GENERAL EDITOR
YUAN XINGPEI, EDITORIAL BOARD DIRECTOR

How to Read Chinese Poetry: A Guided Anthology
(2008)

How to Read Chinese Poetry Workbook
(2012)

How to Read Chinese Poetry in Context:
Poetic Culture from Antiquity Through the Tang
(2018)

How to Read Chinese Prose: A Guided Anthology
(2022)

How to Read Chinese Drama

A GUIDED ANTHOLOGY

EDITED BY PATRICIA SIEBER
AND REGINA LLAMAS

Columbia University Press   New York

CENTER FOR LANGUAGE
EDUCATION AND COOPERATION
中外语言交流合作中心

Columbia University Press wishes to express its
appreciation for assistance given by the Center for
Language Education and Cooperation in the publication
of this series.

Columbia University Press
Publishers Since 1893
New York   Chichester, West Sussex
cup.columbia.edu

Library of Congress Cataloging-in-Publication Data
Names: Sieber, Patricia Angela, editor. | Llamas, Regina,
editor.
Title: How to read Chinese drama : a guided anthology /
edited by Patricia Sieber and Regina Llamas.
Description: New York : Columbia University Press,
2022. | Series: How to read Chinese literature | Includes
bibliographical references and index. | Majority of text
in English with snippets from plays in Chinese with
parallel English translations.
Identifiers: LCCN 2021009040 (print) | LCCN
2021009041 (ebook) | ISBN 9780231186483 (hardback)
| ISBN 9780231186490 (trade paperback) | ISBN
9780231546669 (ebook)
Subjects: LCSH: Chinese drama—History and criticism.
| Chinese drama—Translations into English.
Classification: LCC PL2359 .H69 2022 (print) | LCC
PL2359 (ebook) | DDC 895.12009—dc23
LC record available at https://lccn.loc.gov/2021009040
LC ebook record available at https://lccn.loc.gov/2021009041

Columbia University Press books are printed on
permanent and durable acid-free paper.

Printed in the United States of America

Cover design: Milenda Nan Ok Lee
Cover image: Susii © Shutterstock

CONTENTS

* Excerpts from those plays are also featured, accompanied by modern Chinese translation and extensive annotation, in Guo Yingde, Wenbo Chang, Patricia Sieber, and Xiaohui Zhang, eds., *How to Read Chinese Drama in Chinese: A Language Companion*. New York: Columbia University Press (under advance agreement).

THEMATIC CONTENTS

❀ ❀ ❀

7. DRAMATIC ART

PREFACE TO THE HOW TO READ CHINESE LITERATURE SERIES

Welcome to the How to Read Chinese Literature series, a comprehensive collection of literary anthologies and language texts covering all the major genres of Chinese literature. The series will consist of ten volumes: five guided literary anthologies, one book on poetic culture, and four language companions. Together, they will promote the teaching and learning of premodern Chinese poetry, fiction, drama, prose, and literary criticism.

In particular, the five guided anthologies offer innovative ways of overcoming some barriers that have long hindered the teaching and learning of Chinese literature. While fine scholarly monographs on Chinese literature abound, they are usually too specialized for classroom use. To make that scholarship more accessible, guided anthologies present the highlights of scholarship on major genres, subgenres, and writers through commentary on individual texts as well as broad surveys.

Every reader of Chinese literature is aware of the gap between English translations and Chinese originals. Because most existing anthologies offer only an English translation, however, students will find it hard to see how diverse linguistic elements work together in the original. To remedy this, each guided anthology presents the Chinese text alongside an English translation, with detailed remarks on the intricate interplay of word, image, and sound in Chinese.

So far, scant attention has been given to the relation between sound and sense in English-language studies of Chinese literature. As a corrective, the poetry anthology explains in detail the prosodic conventions of all major poetic genres and marks the tonal patterning in regulated verse and *ci* poetry. Samples of reconstructed ancient and medieval pronunciation are also given to show how the poems were probably pronounced when first composed. For the poetry and prose anthologies, we offer a sound recording of selected texts, read in Mandarin. For the drama and fiction anthologies, video clips of traditional storytelling and dramatic performance are also provided free of charge online.

For decades, the study of Chinese literature in the West was a purely intellectual and aesthetic exercise, completely divorced from language learning. To accommodate demand from an ever-increasing number of Chinese-language learners, we provide tone-marked romanizations for all poetry texts, usually accompanied by sound recording. For any text also featured in the accompanying language companion, cross-references allow the reader to quickly proceed to in-depth language study of the original.

Designed to work with the guided anthologies, the four language companions introduce classical Chinese to advanced beginners and above, teaching them how to appreciate Chinese literature in its original form. As stand-alone resources, these texts illustrate China's major literary genres and themes through a variety of examples.

Each language companion presents a select number of works in three different forms—Chinese, English, and tone-marked romanization—while also providing comprehensive vocabulary notes and prose translations in modern Chinese. Subsequent comprehension questions and comments focus on the artistic aspect of the works, while exercises test readers' grasp of both classical and modern Chinese words, phrases, and syntax. An extensive glossary cross-references classical and modern Chinese usage, characters and compounds, and multiple character meanings. A sound recording is provided for each selected text in the poetry and prose companions. Along with other learning aids, a list of literary or grammar issues addressed throughout completes each volume.

To achieve a seamless integration of literary anthologies and language companions, we draw from the same corpus of canonical texts and provide an extensive network of cross-references. Moreover, by presenting the ten books as a coherent set, we aim to help readers cross the divide between literary genres and between literary and language learning, thereby achieving a kind of experience impossible with traditional approaches. Thanks to these innovative features, we hope the series will help to energize the learning and teaching of Chinese literature, language, and culture throughout the English-speaking world for decades to come.

Zong-qi Cai

A NOTE ON HOW TO USE THIS ANTHOLOGY

How to Read Chinese Drama: A Guided Anthology seeks to introduce Chinese drama and theater to a broad audience of undergraduate students, their teachers, and general readers. The volume places a premium on clarity, accessibility, and accuracy, while bringing together leading scholars from around the world who look at Chinese drama within and across the fields of literary studies, cultural and political history, ethnomusicology, art history, and anthropology.

Theater has permeated Chinese society for centuries. It was performed everywhere—in the streets, temples, markets, teahouses, playhouses, and private homes, and on a variety of occasions ranging from religious rituals, temple fairs, banquets, public performances, and small gatherings of family or friends. Whether or not it was originally conceived as entertainment for both divine and mortal audiences, theater quickly acquired many other functions. It transmitted and questioned moral values, celebrated, admonished, and remonstrated with the powers that be, commented on history, and gave voice to people left out of history, while continuously imagining different pasts and possible futures. Theater was also an artistic medium for actors and playwrights alike—the actors showcased their artistry through movement and voice, and the playwrights through their ability to tell a compelling story. The fact that it was musical added to the theater's emotional charge and affective power. In addition, it knitted audiences from vastly different backgrounds into communities of appreciation. The pleasures that theater afforded encompassed the crudest jokes and the most refined sentiments. The many dramatic texts that have survived the ages are some of the most vivid witnesses to the vitality and beauty of Chinese theater.

To quickly access the topics and subtopics addressed in this anthology, we recommend that readers consult the "Thematic Contents." On the one hand, this section makes it easy to identify topical resources for culture, history, theater, and literature courses. On the other hand, it draws attention to the recurrence and subtle distinctions within the dramatic tradition and also highlights the various functions that theater had in society.

If readers are interested in an overview of milestones in the history of theater and major historical episodes discussed in the selected dramatic texts, the "Chronology of Historical Events" provides a dynastic breakdown of key events.

For a general orientation, "Introduction: The Cultural Significance of Chinese Drama" offers a narrative survey of key aspects in the development of Chinese theater, primarily from the Tang (618–907) through the Qing dynasties (1644–1911), while also touching upon some facets of traditional Chinese theater performed in modern times. This is the one element of *A Guided Anthology* that is copiously annotated in order to help curious readers easily locate further scholarship, both for teaching purposes and for the writing of term papers.

The body of the book is divided into four large parts, with chapters roughly organized chronologically and classified according to theatrical genre. *A Guided Anthology* does not strictly list primary sources per se. Instead, each chapter offers close readings of one or two plays, while highlighting one or two salient theatrical and cultural issues. We interpreted "how to read" broadly to include visual, musical, literary, political, and religious approaches to drama. To facilitate accessing the contents of each chapter, we have identified and numbered the headings throughout.

The chapters provide bilingual excerpts from key plays, as well as contextual information and critical analysis. For the most part, we chose plays not only because of their iconic status in the Chinese dramatic canon, but also because of the availability of English translations. For ready identification of reliable translations, we list recommended translations at the end of every chapter.

In the bilingual excerpts, we seek to strike a balance between complexity and readability. We set off different aspects of the dramatic actions with different typographic conventions. On first appearance, we identify the role type of the character; in all subsequent entries, we refer to them by their names. We identify stage directions (italics in English, round parentheses in Chinese) and tune titles. We indicate whether a passage is sung or spoken (italics) and use line breaks for the songs to reflect their poetic structure. The translations are meant to provide something of the literary flavor of the passages, rather than a word-for-word gloss on the original.

To make the connections between individual plays and other forms of writing explicit, the chapters feature a system of cross-referencing. In the body of the chapters, as well as in the occasional note, we refer the reader to related discussions elsewhere in *A Guided Anthology*. Also, because *A Guided Anthology* is part of the multivolume "How to Read Chinese Literature" series, we direct readers to other volumes in that series (e.g., poetry, prose, and fiction).

To place these plays within the living tradition of Chinese theater, the "Visual Resources" section features contemporary theatrical or film adaptations of the plays discussed in *A Guided Anthology*, as well as other relevant visual resources. We plan to house select excerpts from contemporary performances on a webpage housed at Ohio State University under the title "The Chinese Theater Collaborative." As demonstrated in *A Guided Anthology* and other works, traditional Chinese theater in contemporary times thrives on revival and innovation within a framework of traditionality. Thus, these visual materials should not be read as unchanging renditions of classical plays, but rather as creative interpretations within the continuously evolving theatrical tradition in China and elsewhere. Yet we believe that these audiovisual materials, in conjunction with the chapters included here, will help students better understand the plays and their significance.

Finally, the "Glossary-Index" contains Chinese characters for all Chinese terms, phrases, and titles, together with brief English explanations. We homogenized the English translations of important Chinese terms as much as we could, but this was not always possible. We do, however, always provide romanization for the Chinese terms in the main text, and the characters for all the romanized terms and any alternative translations for them used in individual chapters can be easily found and compared by using the "Glossary-Index."

In due course, a companion volume entitled *How to Read Chinese Drama in Chinese: A Language Companion* (edited by Guo Yingde, Wenbo Chang, Patricia Sieber, and Zhang Xiaohui) will be published in the same "How to Read Chinese Literature" series. It will provide scenes from some of the plays discussed in *A Guided Anthology* in the original Chinese, along with copious English-language annotations, translations into modern Chinese, and language and cultural exercises. The plays in question are *The Orphan of Zhao, The Story of the Western Wing, Top Graduate Zhang Xie, The Lute, The Female Mulan Joins the Army in Place of Her Father,* and *The Peony Pavilion.* That future volume can be used in conjunction with *A Guided Anthology* in literature courses with advanced learners and native speakers of Chinese, but it can also be used independently in the Chinese-language classroom for learners of modern and classical Chinese.

Patricia Sieber and Regina Llamas

CHRONOLOGY OF HISTORICAL EVENTS

ZHOU DYNASTY (CA. 1046–256 BCE)

ca. 1046–256 BCE	Emergence of the Great Exorcism rituals (*Da nuo*), often associated with New Year's festivities, where clamorous sound is crucial for ritual purposes (chap. 15; chap. 16)
Late sixth century BCE	The killing of the powerful ministers of the Zhao family in the state of Jin as recorded in the *Zuo Tradition* (*Zuozhuan*), the ultimate source material for the Yuan *zaju* play *The Orphan of Zhao* by Ji Junxiang (fl. thirteenth century) (chap. 5)

HAN DYNASTY (206 BCE–220 CE)

First century BCE	The earliest positive portrait of jesters as an embodiment of a remonstrative tradition associated with Confucian ideals of government service, in *The Records of the Historian* (*Shiji*) by Sima Qian (ca. 135–ca. 85 BCE), China's most influential history (Introduction)

THREE KINGDOMS (SHU, WU, WEI) PERIOD (220–280)
AND THE JIN DYNASTY (265–420)

161–223	Lifetime of Liu Bei, member of the Peach Orchard Brotherhood; founder of the state of Shu Han in the Three Kingdoms period and its first ruler (chap. 16)
Early third century	Death of Guan Yu, member of the Peach Orchard Brotherhood; famed warrior and eventual god of war (chap. 3; chap. 16)
221	Death of Zhang Fei, member of the Peach Orchard Brotherhood; an impetuous warrior (chap. 3; chap. 16)

SOUTHERN AND NORTHERN DYNASTIES (420–589)

Sixth century	Earliest record of the story of Mulan, "Poem of Mulan" ("Mulan shi") (chap. 6)

TANG DYNASTY (618–907)

Early seventh century	The development of entertainment districts catering to aspiring civil service examination candidates (chap. 1)

	Establishment of the Office of Music Instruction (*Jiaofang si*), in charge of songs, dances, and theater for court performances (chap. 13)
712–756	The reign of Emperor Xuanzong of the Tang, whose romance with the Prized Consort Yang (Yang Guifei, Yang Yuhuan, 719–756) became source material for later romantic fiction and drama, including *Palace of Everlasting Life* (*Changsheng dian*) (chap. 12)
	Establishment of the Pear Garden (*liyuan*) by Emperor Xuanzong as a conservatory for the training of musicians and performers at court (chap. 13)
	The Prized Consort Yang creates a dance to "The Melody of Rainbow Skirts and Feathered Robes" (*nichang yuyi qu*) (chap. 12)
755–763	An Lushan instigates a rebellion against the imperial house of Tang that drives Emperor Xuanzong into exile (chap. 12)
756	Sacrificial death of the Prized Consort Yang to quell mutiny during the An Lushan Rebellion (chap. 12)
Late ninth to early tenth centuries	Emergence of "transformation texts" (*bianwen*), a form of storytelling geared toward illiterate lay audiences via images and narrative (Introduction; chap. 3; chap. 15)

(KHITAN) LIAO DYNASTY (907–1125)

Tenth to eleventh centuries	Battles of Chinese generals against the Liao that became source material for Ming court plays (chap. 2)

NORTHERN SONG DYNASTY (960–1127)

960–1127	Skits, farces, and more developed plays are performed as part of the variety shows in urban playhouses known as "Song *zaju*" (chap. 1)
	Transformation of the *nuo* ceremony into a form of dramatic entertainment (*nuoxi*) (chap. 16)
Tenth to eleventh centuries	Chantefable stories (*shuochang cihua*) are told by professional storytellers in urban theaters and by itinerant storytellers traveling through villages (chap. 16)
Twelfth century onward	Emergence of "Wenzhou *zaju*" or "Yongjia *zaju*" (later known as "early southern drama" [*nanxi*, *xiwen*]) in the southern regions of the Yangzi River (Introduction; chap. 1; chap. 7)

Visual records of processions, musical troupes,
and performances, including paintings, murals,
tiles, and reliefs of theatrical role types (chap. 4;
chap. 9)

(TANGUT) XI XIA DYNASTY (1038–1227)

Eleventh to twelfth centuries   Battles of Chinese generals against the Xi Xia
that became source material for Ming court
plays (chap. 2)

(JURCHEN) JIN DYNASTY (1115–1234)

1153   Establishment of the capital of the Jin dynasty
under the name of Zhongdu (Central Capital) in
the area of modern Beijing (chap. 2)

ca. 1200   Composition of *The Story of the Western Wing
in All Keys and Modes* (*Xixiang ji zhugongdiao*)
by Dong Jieyuan (fl. 1200), the only surviving
complete text of an "all keys and modes"
(*zhugongdiao*) ballad (chap. 1; chap. 8)

1215   Mongol invasion of Zhongdu (chap. 3)
Visual records of theater performance, including
paintings, murals, tiles, reliefs, stone carvings,
and figurines of musicians and theatrical role
types found in northern China (chap. 4; chap. 9)

SOUTHERN SONG DYNASTY (1127–1279)

Twelfth to thirteenth centuries   The rise of the backstage in theater architecture
(chap. 9)
Visual records of processions and theater
performance, including paintings, reliefs,
and figurines of theatrical role types found in
southern China (chap. 4; chap. 9)

(MONGOL) YUAN DYNASTY (1271–1368)

1271–1368   The first flowering of full-fledged theater in
dynastic China (Introduction; chap. 2)

ca. 1220–after 1279   Lifetime of Guan Hanqing, the purported
founder of mature *zaju* theater and its most
prolific playwright (chap. 1; chap. 3)

1227–1293   Lifetime of Hu Zhiyu, a scholar-official and
theater aficionado, noted for critical writings on
female performers, including Zhulian xiu
(chap. 3)

ca. 1270–1300   The approximate period when the leading
female *zaju* performer Zhulian xiu was active
(chap. 3)

Late thirteenth century   Composition of *The Story of the Western Wing*
(*Xixiang ji*) by Wang Shifu (fl. second part of

	the thirteenth century), China's most famous love comedy in a modified northern *zaju* drama format (chap. 1; chap. 4; chap. 8)
1324	Publication of the earliest extant treatise on singing, *Discourse of Singing* (*Changlun*) by Yannan zhi'an (fl. early fourteenth century) (Introduction)
	Dated inscription for the mural "Zhongdu xiu from the Great Guild of Roving Troupes Performed Here" ("Dahang sanyue Zhongdu xiu zaici zuochang") in the Hall of Mingying wang in Shanxi province (Introduction; chap. 4; chap. 9)
1330s–1340s	Publication of various recensions of *Rhymes of the Central Plain* (*Zhongyuan yinyun*) by Zhou Deqing (1277–1365), an influential formulary and work of criticism for *zaju* drama and *sanqu* songs (Introduction)
Mid-fourteenth century	Publication of *Register of Ghosts* (*Lugui bu*) by Zhong Sicheng (ca. 1277–after 1345), which included short biographies of over eighty playwrights (chap. 5)
Fourteenth century onward	The genre of the "all keys and modes" (*zhugongdiao*) ballad disappears from performance (chap. 1)
Mid-fourteenth century	Publication of the earliest extant *zaju* recensions later collected in *Thirty Yuan-Printed Zaju Plays* (*Yuankan zaju sanshi zhong*) (Introduction), including *Purple Clouds* (chap. 2), *The Pavilion for Praying to the Moon* (chap. 3), and *The Orphan of Zhao* (chap. 5)
	Composition of *The Lute* (*Pipa ji*) by Gao Ming (ca. 1305–ca. 1370), the first individually authored play in the tradition of southern drama (*nanxi*) (Introduction; chap. 7)
1360s	Compilation of *The Record of the Green Bowers* (*Qinglou ji*) by Xia Tingzhi (ca. 1300–1375), a collection of biographies of female performers (Introduction; chap. 2; chap. 3)

MING DYNASTY (1368–1644)

1384	The official and permanent reinstatement of the civil service examination system of the Ming dynasty (chap. 7)
ca. 1398	Compilation of *Formulary of Correct Prosody of the Era of Great Peace* (*Taihe zhengyin pu*) by Zhu

	Quan (1378–1448), which classifies the then-known *zaju* corpus into "Twelve Categories of Northern Drama" ("Zaju shi'er ke") (chap. 2; chap. 3)
1408	Compilation of the imperial encyclopedia manuscript *Great Canon of the Yongle Era* (*Yongle dadian*) which included the earliest-known versions of early southern *nanxi* drama (Introduction; chap. 1; chap. 2; chap. 7)
1400s–1440s	The successive publication of plays by Zhu Youdun (1379–1439) that shaped later typographic conventions for play imprints (chap. 1)
After 1435	Civil service graduates dominating the politics at court (chap. 7)
1478	Publication of *The Story of Hua Guan Suo in Prose and Song* (*Hua Guan Suo zhuan*), the only extant complete rendition of the story of Hua Guan Suo, the fictional son of the great warrior Guan Yu (chap. 16)
1499	Publication of the earliest preserved complete text of *The Story of the Western Wing*, known as the Hongzhi edition, renowned for its handscroll-like, woodblock-printed illustrations (chap. 1; chap. 4)
ca. 1522–1527	Creation of the "polished" style of music (*shuimo diao*, literally "water mill tunes") by Wei Liangfu (ca. 1489–1566), the foundational music of the Kunqu dramatic tradition, representing a synthesis of northern and southern music (Introduction)
1527–1602	Lifetime of Li Zhi (style name Li Zhuowu), the alleged commentator of many drama and fiction imprints (Introduction; chap. 4)
Sixteenth century	The genre of "southern *nanxi* drama" develops into the form of *chuanqi* drama (Introduction; chap. 1)
1548–1604	Lifetime of Ma Shouzhen, the notable Nanjing-based courtesan, playwright, and owner of a courtesan theater troupe (Introduction)
1558	Composition of *Washing Silk* (*Huansha ji*) by Liang Chenyu (1519–1591), the first drama set in the Kunqu musical style (Introduction; chap. 8)
1550s	Composition of *The Southern Western Wing* by Li Rihua (fl. 1550s?), a seminal adaptation of

	The Story of the Western Wing in the Kunqu style (chap. 8)
1559	Publication of *A Record of Southern Ci* (*Nanci xulu*) by Xu Wei (1521–1593), the first significant discussion of southern drama as an art form (Introduction; chap. 7)
1566	Composition of *The Crying Phoenix* (*Mingfeng ji*) and the emergence of the topical "drama on current affairs" (*shishiju*) as a means to expose malfeasance, attack political rivals, or both (Introduction; chap. 10)
Late sixteenth century	Emergence of a new school of Confucianism, the School of the Mind (*xinxue*), whose followers celebrated human emotions and desires in fiction and drama in what modern scholars term a cult of *qing* (chap. 12)
1570s	Elements of theatrical performance began to appear in book illustrations (chap. 4)
1570s–1640s	Heightened factionalism dominates the Ming government (Introduction; chap. 4; chap. 10)
1580–1644	Lifetime of Ling Mengchu, a well-known editor-publisher of drama and writer of fiction (chap. 4)
1580s	Publication of the first extant version of *The Injustice to Dou E* (*Gantian dongdi Dou E yuan*) (chap. 3) Publication of Xu Wei's collection of four *zaju* plays, *Four Cries of a Gibbon* (*Sisheng yuan*), including *The Female Mulan Joins the Army in Place of Her Father* (*Ci Mulan tifu congjun*) (chap. 6)
1582	Publication of the earliest extant and most influential dramatic version of the Mulian play, a three-volume text written by the Ming-dynasty literatus Zheng Zhizhen (1518–1595) (chap. 15)
ca. 1591–ca. 1671	Lifetime of Li Yu, the most representative and prolific playwright of the Suzhou School dramatists (chap. 14)
1597–1684	Lifetime of Zhang Dai, a well-known literatus and theater aficionado noted for his critical writings on drama criticism and personal experience with dramatic performance (Introduction; chap. 15)

1598	Composition of *The Peony Pavilion* (*Mudan ting*) by Tang Xianzu (1550–1616), the most renowned and influential Chinese *chuanqi* drama (chap. 9)
Early seventeenth century	Full maturity of Kunqu performance, China's oldest continuously performed operatic form (chap. 8)
ca. 1602	Composition of Tang Xianzu's "Epigraph for the Temple for Theater God Master Qingyuan in Yihuang County" ("Yihuang xian xishen Qingyuan shi miao ji"), a powerful literati apologia for the transformative power of theater (Introduction; chap. 3; chap. 9)
1604	The emergence of the Eastern Grove faction (Donglin) as an important force in dynastic politics (chap. 10)
	A documented performance of the complete northern-style *zaju The Story of the Western Wing* by Ma Shouzhen's troupe (Introduction)
1610	The Rongyutang, one of the best-known publishing houses of Hangzhou, brought out an influential literati-flavored version of *The Story of the Western Wing*, combining poetry, painting, and calligraphy (chap. 4)
1611–1680	Lifetime of Li Yu an influential and prolific critic and writer of fiction and drama and theatrical troupe owner (chap. 10; chap. 11)
1615–1616	Compilation of *Select Yuan Plays* (*Yuanqu xuan*) by Zang Maoxun (1550–1620), the most influential anthology of Yuan *zaju* drama (Introduction; chap. 2)
1621–1627	The reign of Emperor Tianqi; dominated by the eunuch Wei Zhongxian (1568–1627) and his associates, who seek to purge members of the Eastern Grove faction (Introduction; chap. 10)
1628–1644	The reign of Emperor Chongzhen; final period of the Ming dynasty, during which the members of the eunuch faction are punished (chap. 10)
ca. 1629	Establishment of the Restoration Society (Fushe), a literary successor to the Eastern Grove faction (chap. 10)
1633	Restoration Society scholars claim that the play *The Green Peony* (*Lü mudan*) mocks its members and petition for an official ban (chap. 10)

1634	Composition of *The Spring Lantern Riddles* (*Chundeng mi*), the earliest play by Ruan Dacheng (1587–1646) (chap. 10)
1639	Circulation of "Proclamation against Treachery in Nanjing" ("Liudu fangluan gongjie"), directed against Ruan Dacheng (chap. 10)
1639–1640	Publication of *The Exclusive Edition* of *Western Wing* designed by Chen Hongshou (1598–1652), who adapts literati painting techniques to woodblock carving and vice versa (chap. 4)
1642	Composition of *Swallow's Letter* (*Yanzi jian*), arguably the best-known play by Ruan Dacheng (chap. 10)
	Mao Xiang (1611–1693) and other Restoration Society scholars gather to watch a performance of *Swallow's Letter* by Ruan Dacheng's family troupe in Nanjing, applauding the performance while condemning the playwright (chap. 10)
1618–1655	Lifetime of Hou Fangyu, a scholar-official, writer, and a respected member of the Restoration Society, whose romance with the courtesan Li Xiangjun (1624–1653) is the source material for the famous historical play *The Peach Blossom Fan* (*Taohua shan*) (Introduction; chap. 12)

QING DYNASTY (1644–1912)

1645	Establishment of the Southern Ming regime in Nanjing, marked by the enthronement of Zhu Yousong (1607–1646) as the Emperor Hongguang (chap. 12)
ca. 1650s	Compilation of *Sixty Plays* (*Liushi zhong qu*) by Mao Jin (1599–1659), an influential compendium of mostly *chuanqi* drama (Introduction; chap. 8)
ca. 1661	Publication of *The Sixth Book of Genius* (*Diliu caizishu*) by Jin Shengtan (1610–1661), the most widely circulated version of *The Story of the Western Wing* in the Qing dynasty, featuring Jin's extensive interlinear commentary (chap. 1)
1671	Publication of Li Yu's *Leisure Notes* (*Xianqing ouji*), the most systematic theatrical treatise in dynastic China (chap. 10; chap. 11; chap. 15)
1671 onward	Imperial edicts are issued to prohibit playhouses from operating within the Inner City and to

	forbid high officials and bannermen from attending performances in commercial theaters (chap. 14)
1688	Composition of *Palace of Everlasting Life* (*Changsheng dian*) by Hong Sheng (1645–1704), a historical *chuanqi* play centered on the romance between Emperor Xuanzong and the Prized Consort Yang, which was so popular that it even traveled to Vietnam (chap. 12)
1699-1708	Composition (1699) and publication (1708) of the famous historical play *The Peach Blossom Fan* by Kong Shangren (1648–1718), which decisively shaped the collective memory of the political history of the Ming-Qing dynastic transition (chap. 10; chap. 12)
1720s	The Jesuit missionary Joseph de Prémare (1666–1736) prepares a partial translation of *The Orphan of Zhao* (*Zhao shi gu'er*) into French, the first such endeavor in a European language (chap. 3; chap. 5)
1735–1736	Publication of the compilation *Description de la Chine* (*The Universal History of China*) by J. B. du Halde (1674–1743) (chap. 1), in which he characterizes *The Orphan of Zhao* as a tragedy (chap. 3; chap. 5)
1736–1796	The reign of Emperor Qianlong, during which Chinese court theater reaches its height, being used for political, ritual, and entertainment purposes (chap. 13)
1746	Publication of *The Formulary of Northern and Southern Tunes in the Great Anthology of the Nine Modes* (*Jiugong dacheng nanbeici gongpu*, alternatively translated as *Great Compilation of Musical Scores from the Southern and Northern Arias in All Nine Modes*), a magisterial comprehensive court-sponsored anthology of both northern and southern musical tunes (chap. 8; chap. 14)
1746–1799	Lifetime of Heshen, the powerful and reputedly corrupt Manchu grand councilor and former imperial guardsman, who is believed to be the inspiration for the lead villain in *The Eight-Court Pearl* (*Bachao zhu*) (chap. 14)

1753	Publication of Voltaire's adaptation of *Orphan of Zhao*, *L'orphelin de la Chine* (*The Orphan of China*) (chap. 5)
Mid-eighteenth century	Rearranged scenes (*zhezixi*) become the norm of Kunqu performance, which prompts the publication of anthologized Kunqu performance scripts (chap. 8)
ca. 1750–ca. 1800	Development of a new "fanzine" literature (*huapu*)—that is, catalogs of star "boy actresses," who cross-dress to perform the young ingenue (*dan*) roles (Introduction; chap. 14)
1772	Emperor Qianlong officially bans all female performers in Beijing (chap. 11)
Early nineteenth century	Performance experimentations of several Hui troupes (*Huiban*) in the capital, including the famous Hechun Troupe, which plant a seed for the eventual development of Peking opera (Introduction; chap. 14)
1814	After suppressing an uprising targeting the imperial palace, Emperor Jiaqing (r. 1796–1820) issues an edict proscribing the commercial theatrical performance of martial plays in the capital (chap. 14)
Late nineteenth century	Emergence of the theatrical form of *jingju* (literally "capital opera," alternatively translated as "Peking opera" and "Beijing opera"), which later advances to the status of a "national theater" (*guoju*) in the twentieth century (Introduction)
1894–1961	Lifetime of Mei Lanfang, the eminent female impersonator in Kunqu performance and Peking opera (Introduction; chap. 8; chap. 14)

MODERN CHINA (1912–PRESENT)

1913–1914	Publication, in installments, of *A Study of Song and Yuan Drama* (*Song Yuan xiqu kao*, also known as *Song Yuan xiqu shi*) by Wang Guowei (1877–1927), the seminal history and criticism of early Chinese song-drama (Introduction; chap. 5)
1914	Collective publication of *Thirty Yuan-Printed Zaju Plays* (*Yuankan zaju sanshi zhong*) (Introduction; chap. 3; chap. 4; chap. 5)
1919–1960	Mei Lanfang tours abroad in Japan (1919), the United States (1930), the Soviet Union (1935, 1952, 1957, 1960), and European countries

SYMBOLS, ABBREVIATIONS, AND TYPOGRAPHICAL USAGE

chap. 8	Chapter 8
C8.4	Chapter 8, the fourth selected text
L01	Lesson 1 in *HTRCDrama—LC*
☛	A cross-reference marker Example: (☛ *HTRCDrama—LC*, L01; *HTRCP*, chap. 8)
Straight underline in a Chinese text	Marking the use of repetitive patterning or a highlight in a Chinese text, unless indicated otherwise. Example: "怕不問時<u>權做弟兄</u>。"
Straight underline in an English text	Marking the corresponding passage underlined in the parallel Chinese text, unless indicated otherwise. Example: "If no one asks, let's resort to being siblings <u>for the time being</u>."
（末云了）	In the Chinese text, round brackets indicate the designation of singing parts and stage directions.
[*The main lead*]	In the English text, square brackets indicate the addition of implied information.
FEMALE LEAD *as* **WANG RUILAN**	In the English text, capital letters indicate the role type (on first appearance) and the name of the protagonist (in first and subsequent appearances).
The male role has spoken.	In the English text, italics indicate stage directions.
[*GHQXQJ* 854]	In the English text, capital letters in square brackets indicate page numbers in primary sources that are listed in alphabetical order at the end of each chapter.
HTRCDrama-LC	Guo Yingde, Wenbo Chang, Patricia Sieber, and Xiaohui Zhang. *How to Read Chinese Drama in Chinese: A Language Companion.* New York: Columbia University Press, under advance agreement.

HTRCProse-CCC	Cui, Jie, Liu Yucai, and Zong-qi Cai. *How to Read Chinese Prose in Chinese: A Course in Classical Chinese.* New York: Columbia University Press, 2022 (forthcoming).
HTRCProse	Cai, Zong-qi, ed. *How to Read Chinese Prose: A Guided Anthology.* New York: Columbia University Press, 2022 (forthcoming).
HTRCP	Cai, Zong-qi, ed. *How to Read Chinese Poetry: A Guided Anthology.* New York: Columbia University Press, 2008.
HTRCPIC	Cai, Zong-qi, ed. *How to Read Chinese Poetry in Context: Poetic Culture from Antiquity through the Tang.* New York: Columbia University Press, 2018.
HTRCFiction	Shang Wei, ed. *How to Read Chinese Fiction: A Guided Anthology.* New York: Columbia University Press, under advance agreement.
HTRCFiction-LC	Pan Jianguo, Jing Chen, and Shang Wei, ed. *How to Read Chinese Fiction in Chinese: A Language Companion.* New York: Columbia University Press, under advance agreement.

How to Read Chinese Drama

Introduction

The Cultural Significance of Chinese Drama

Sometime during the 1620s, Ma Jin, a famous actor who also went by the stage name "Moslem Ma" on account of his Central Asian ancestry, suffered a humiliating defeat in a public competition between two rival theatrical troupes. On a business trip to Nanjing, some well-to-do Cantonese merchants invited Actor Ma's and Actor Li's famed troupes to stage the story of *The Crying Phoenix* (*Mingfeng ji*, 1566), a *chuanqi* drama that turned one of the most notorious cases of political martyrdom in the sixteenth century into a gripping play.[1] At the core of the story were a number of righteous men who, at the cost of their own lives, stood up against the political malfeasance of Yan Song (1480–1567) and Yan Shifan (1513–1565), a ruthless father-son duo who enjoyed the emperor's favor.

In simultaneous performances on opposite sides of a market, both Actor Ma and Actor Li played Yan Song, the archvillain. However, it was Actor Li's performance of that role that riveted the audience, to the point that Actor Ma felt so ashamed, he ran away. Yet, three years later, when a public rematch of the same play was organized at the behest of Actor Ma, his rendition of Yan Song was said to be "the height of perfection," making Actor Li lose his voice midplay. When asked how he came to embody the epitome of a villainous minister so perfectly, Actor Ma reportedly told the following story:

> [After my humiliation three years ago,] I heard that the current minister Gu Bingqian of Kunshan bears a striking resemblance to minister Yan [Song]. So I traveled to the capital where I begged to serve as his doorman for three years. Every day I waited upon the minister from Kunshan in his offices at court. I observed his movements and listened to his speech habits. After a long time, I finally mastered them. This is how I taught myself.[2]

In his performance, Actor Ma reportedly crafted his own rendition of an infamous official out of the playtext of *The Crying Phoenix*, his own life experience, and his autodidactic theatrical training. By all accounts, Ma was haunted by his rival's consummate artistry three years earlier, and his enactment was thus influenced by it, as well as by the historical resonances between the factionalism rampant in Yan Song's and Actor Ma's own time.[3] In this movement between dramatic time (playtext), theatrical time (performance), and historical time (the 1560s and the

1620s), Actor Ma drew upon the social energy gathered in and released by theater to mesmerize the audience and stun his fellow actors. Meanwhile, Hou Fangyu (1618–1655), an antagonist of Gu Bingqian's (1550–1632) faction at court and the author of "Biography of Actor Ma" ("Ma ling zhuan"), could not have anticipated that he himself would eventually become the hero of the dramatic retelling of the factional struggles of Actor Ma's time, as chapters 10 and 12 explore. In short, Actor Ma's story allows us to catch a glimpse of the artistic conception of classical Chinese theater (alternatively called *xiqu* in modern China and "Chinese opera" in the West): it was first and foremost—and continues to be in certain contexts—a theater of affect, designed to conjoin the emotions experienced by the dramatist, the actor, and the audience.[4]

The expressive pillars of Chinese theater—vocal music, poetic songs, and expressive gestures and body movements—all came together to entertain and move audiences. Music, particularly the human voice, had long been thought to be a privileged conduit to externalize feelings, while harmonizing relationships between people and among humans, nature, and otherworldly realms.[5] Rhymed expression made full use of the intrinsic musicality generated by the tonal nature of the Chinese language. Poetry had long served as the preferred vehicle for autobiographical reflection among literate elites (via *shi* poetry); in various forms, poetry had also been used as a versatile medium for popular storytelling (through prosimetric ballads, chantefables, and other types of tales). The manifestation of emotive powers, particularly in poetic genres, had been closely tied to physical movement ever since the canonical preface to the *Book of Songs* (*Shijing*) claimed that when chanting and singing are not sufficient to express one's feelings "unwittingly, one's hands will dance and one's feet will tap" (☞ chap. 9).[6] Further, while literati often wrote poetry for social occasions such as birthday parties, farewell, travels, and so forth, they typically shared their poetically mediated feelings with a small number of intimates (friends, family, other officials) and an unspecified number of future readers (posterity) in mind. By contrast, theater happened in the immediacy of the here and now, with audiences that could number in the thousands.

In the aesthetic realization of Chinese theater, three parties played key roles—the playwrights, the actors, and the audience. The poet-scriptwriters—many individually known, others members of a collective, still others anonymous—wrote lyrics with preexisting tunes in mind as they adapted existing stories or made up new ones. Actor-singers, though socially marginal, nevertheless garnered artistic recognition through their consummate acting and vocal skills in embodying particular characters. An actor's performance could prompt audiences to laugh, sigh with appreciation, cheer, shout, applaud, or cry, among many other reactions. If the acting was successful, as one critic noted, "the admonishments of one hundred Confucian teachers do not compare to the force of a single actor."[7]

If literati were for the most part convinced that theater put people in touch with their deepest, most real feelings, the authorities at times feared its ability to incite audiences to act in unpredictable or rebellious ways. At different points in history, particularly during the Qing dynasty (1644–1911) (☞ chap. 14), such anxieties led to crowd-control measures, proscription of performances, exclusion of certain demographics from theatergoing, the suppression of dramatic texts, and the regulation of costuming.[8] Accordingly, both protheatrical and antitheatrical views shared the belief that theater was a powerful form of social communication.

Importantly, a playwright's expression of a range of feelings in the protagonists—fear, joy, sorrow, longing, disappointment, anger, surprise, and excitement, to name a few—was not channeled into (highbrow) tragedy and (lowbrow) comedy. Instead, from its textual inception in the Yuan dynasty (1234–1368), Chinese theater aimed to represent the totality of human experience onstage. In our view, that element of totality is in fact the most expansive understanding of the Chinese term for the earliest genre of mature theater, the so-called *zaju* drama (literally "variety plays," perhaps better translated as "wide-ranging plays").[9] Rather than segregating the tears from the laughter, the seamless integration of these fundamental forms of human response became one of the distinctive features of Chinese theater. Theater's capacity to be wide-ranging and socially inclusive in terms of subject matter, language use, moral authority, and audience appeal set it apart from other literary forms and made it appealing to playwrights, theater practitioners, publishers, and audiences alike. If music in the classical era was believed to extend and refine the relationships among friends,[10] theater had the potential to transform and enrich all relationships.

However, as one of the world's great theatrical traditions, Chinese theater was neither static nor monolithic. On the contrary, over time, Chinese theater has sported a wide variety of regional and local musical styles.[11] Moreover, as was evident in "Biography of Actor Ma," innovation and individual excellence have been consistently prized, even if different theatrical forms operated (and in some cases continue to operate) within a shared framework of tradition. Such an emphasis on innovation also explains why, ever since the dawn of the modern era, what has come to be called "traditional Chinese theater" (i.e., *xiqu*) has found new audiences despite fierce competition from other media. Rather than letting themselves be relegated to the cultural sidelines by social, commercial, and political pressure, modern practitioners of traditional theater have embraced the challenges and opportunities inherent in the new age of sound recording, radio, film, television, and access to foreign theatrical traditions.[12]

At the same time, traditional theater has left a deep imprint on a range of contemporary media, including modern spoken drama (*huaju*), with which it is often contrasted; film; classical Chinese dance; and theatrical forms within the Chinese diaspora.[13] In the wake of international tours by the iconic actor Mei Lanfang (1894–1961) in Japan, Europe, and the United States between 1919 and 1960, Chinese theater also became a force on the global stage.[14] It is for this reason—that is, the continued viability of traditional Chinese theater as a contemporary art form—that *How to Read Chinese Drama* does not end its coverage with dynastic China, but rather carries it forward into the present, albeit in a selective fashion.[15]

In what follows, we will highlight some of the core elements that characterized dynastic Chinese theatrical culture. Specifically, we will address the presumed origins of Chinese theater, the major regional forms, and the question of roles, language, music, and staging practices. At the same time, we will draw attention to how dramatic texts were transmitted over time. In their dual capacity as theatrical scripts and dramatic literature, full-length plays and anthologies of rearranged scenes (*zhezixi*) had both long and short afterlives—long because certain plays became a fixture in regional repertoires, but short because they were endlessly adapted and revised for new audiences.

However, one thing was for certain—once it attained its mature forms, Chinese theater was ubiquitous. As one nineteenth-century observer noted in his travels through China: "There are theaters everywhere; large cities are full of them and actors perform in them day and night. There is not a single small village that does not have its own theater."[16] We hope that the general observations given here will provide theatrical context for the exploration of the individual plays found in the rest of *How to Read Chinese Drama*.

ON ORIGINS

Chinese theater is as rich in content as its history is long. The book before you draws on this tradition to explore a wide spectrum of forms, themes, and musical genres. Within this spectrum, there are innumerable historical and generic variants that, explained beforehand, will facilitate and assist readers in understanding the chapters of this book. We begin with a puzzle that has intrigued generations of scholars: Just how long *is* the history of Chinese theater? Where did it begin?

There are a number of theories on the origins of Chinese theater; but two dominate the discussion. One argues that theatrical performance originated in ritual, specifically in the early Shang-dynasty dances of shamans who entertained the spirits with dance, songs, and drums. The other theory contends that theater stemmed from a progressive development of the culture of entertainment in China, and more particularly from the One Hundred Entertainments (*baixi*) of antiquity, performed at the palace and in nobles' houses, which included song, dance, various forms of acrobatics, and short narrative skits. Of all the historical approaches to the origins of drama, Wang Guowei's (1877–1927) account remains the most influential.[17] On the one hand, Wang identified two early lines of dramatic development—one in song and dance and the other in comedy; on the other, he argued that the convergence of these two practices resulted in mature theater.

In Wang's schema, song and dance derived from pre–Han dynasty (206 BC–220 AD) descriptions of shamanic performances. He argued that in early Chinese history, shamans were portrayed as uncorrupted, wise people who were chosen by the spirits to come down into them so that the spirits could be served with offerings. Female shamans (*wu*) actively sought to attract and serve the spirits through song, dance, and drum playing.[18] In Wang's view, comedy, by contrast, stemmed from the witty language and actions of early performers (*paiyou*), particularly the court jesters of the Zhou dynasty (1122–256 BC). The earliest historical documents described jesters in negative terms, as depraved characters whose stunts and pranks distracted the ruler from the more serious task of governing; however, the "Biographies of Jesters" ("Guji liezhuan") chapter in China's most influential history, *The Records of the Historian* (*Shiji*) by Sima Qian (ca. 135 BCE–ca. 85 BCE), portrayed jesters in a positive light for the first time. Specifically, they were commended for displaying moral stature, eloquence, and wit in the service of tactfully admonishing rulers for their shortcomings. In their ingenious use of language to reprimand rulers, these jesters embodied a remonstrative tradition associated with Confucian ideals of government service. In the Confucian view, scholar-officials were encouraged to indirectly influence the judgment of their rulers through the use of exemplary and allegorical stories, and to allow the ruler to understand the folly of his ways.

To determine when Chinese theater came into existence, Wang Guowei examined historical documents with a view toward finding the point where they converged to create a new form of artistic performance. Wang concluded that the various arts that eventually defined Chinese theater (song, dance, comedy, dialogue, costumes and face paint, props, and others) came together as a "variety show" sometime during the Song dynasty (960–1279) (known as "Song *zaju*"), but only manifested as full-blown theatrical scripts with overarching storylines in the Yuan dynasty (1271–1368) (known as "Yuan *zaju*"). The difference between these forms, evidently, was such that one astute critic in the Yuan dynasty noted that theatrical offerings from previous dynasties "could not be mentioned in the same breath" as Yuan *zaju*.[19]

A century after Wang published his seminal *A Study of Song and Yuan Drama* (*Song Yuan xiqu kao*) (1913–1914), neither the many textual nor the archeological discoveries that have been made in the interim have changed the timeline. However, what has come into sharper focus is that developments during the Jurchen Jin dynasty (1115–1234), most notably through farcical skits (*yuanben*), also contributed to the maturation of Chinese theater. Thus, while we may call it "Chinese" theater, this designation reflects the fact that mixed-register Chinese (also called "vernacular," "colloquial," or "plain Chinese" writing) served as a literary lingua franca for people with diverse ancestries in Jin and Yuan China.

Only in the twentieth century did the phrase "Chinese theater" come to mean a national tradition defined in contradistinction to theatrical practices current elsewhere in the world.[20] Indeed, as chapter 2 explores in some detail, at its first point of major efflorescence, Chinese theater was mediated by a cultural outlook that embraced people from different parts of Eurasia.[21] If the traces of these polycultural negotiations are less visible in the extant dramatic corpus than we might expect, we have to keep in mind that the textual tradition of northern drama (*zaju*) underwent substantial and targeted editing after the fall of the cosmopolitan Yuan (1271–1368).

NORTHERN DRAMA BETWEEN THE STAGE AND THE PAGE

Most historical texts divide Chinese theater broadly into two traditions—a northern one called *zaju* and a southern one consisting of *nanxi* (literally "southern drama") and its mature successor, known as *chuanqi* (literally "transmission of wonders"). The differences between these two traditions are structural, musical, and social; they will be explained briefly here. Preceded by variety shows in Song China and farces in Jin China, mature *zaju* with full-blown storylines, the so-called Yuan *zaju*, flourished in the thirteenth and fourteenth centuries (☛ chaps. 1, 2, 3, 4, and 5). In the Ming and Qing dynasties, *zaju* became a looser and often shorter form that freely mixed northern and southern conventions (☛ chaps. 6 and 13).[22] Growing out of Song- and Yuan-dynasty southern forms, *chuanqi* gradually came to dominate the stage from the late sixteenth century onward (☛ chaps. 7, 8, 9, 10, 11, 12, 14, and 15). From the Qing dynasty onward, other regional forms began to take hold (☛ chap. 16).

The *zaju* and *chuanqi* traditions generated a substantial number of playtexts, even if the type of information about such texts varies greatly. For so-called Yuan *zaju*, more than 160 plays survive; for Yuan and Ming *nanxi* and *chuanqi*, there are roughly 950 unique titles; and there are many others for Ming and Qing *zaju*, as well as for Qing *chuanqi*. Regional forms such as Beijing opera created countless texts as well.

However, it is important to keep in mind that drama texts are notoriously unstable objects, prone to changes not just as they move from hand to hand, or manuscript to actor, but also from author to editor and editor to print. At each stage, people tinkered with the plays—lengthening and shortening them, fixing mistakes even as they introduced new ones, improving on the plays or sanitizing their language, or adjusting the plot or the lyrics in a subtle or heavy-handed fashion.

While the textual tradition has been in constant flux to this day, some historical playtexts also became prized artifacts cherished by generations of playwrights, theater practitioners, and bibliophiles alike. Most remarkably, perhaps, our earliest glimpse of the *zaju* tradition, a clutch of thirty independent imprints now collectively known as *Thirty Yuan-Printed Zaju Plays* (*Yuankan zaju sanshi zhong*, 1914), owes its transmission to the present to a number of dynastic and modern literati who cherished these materials despite their poor print quality. Some of the most remarkable of these early plays—*Purple Clouds*, *The Pavilion for Praying to the Moon*, and *The Orphan of Zhao*—are discussed in chapters 2, 3, and 5, respectively. In each case, wherever later versions of these texts exist, it is clear that they have been transformed to reflect the exigencies and values of the Ming court, literati, and commercial publishers.

These fourteenth-century *zaju* plays typically consisted of four acts (*zhe*) with an occasional prelude, interlude, or envoi (*xiezi*, literally "wedge"). As noted in chapter 1, each act, ranging from five to twenty arias, was composed in accordance with a particular musical mode (*gongdiao*) that accommodated different song combinations within the suite and was said to connote different emotional flavors.[23] If later instrumental practices are any indication, a *dizi* (a transverse bamboo flute)—and perhaps the *sanxian* (a three-stringed, lute) and the *pipa* (a four-stringed, pear-shaped lute) as well—supplied the melodic line for the singing, while percussion instruments such as the *ban* (wooden clapper), *gu* (drum), and *luo* (hanging gong) may have accentuated the rhythm and meter of the song, provided cues for the actors' stage movements, and drawn the audience's attention to dramatic moments (see figure 9.2 in chap. 9).[24] All the rhyme words within an act were taken from the same rhyme category, thus using prosodic means to underscore the dramatic structure of a "well-made play." In act 1, we are typically introduced to the central dramatic conflict; in act 2, the conflict is developed further; in act 3, the conflict escalates; and in act 4, a denouement is presented.

Generally, the *Thirty Yuan-Printed Zaju Plays*, especially when compared to the Ming versions of Yuan *zaju*, provide only the bare essentials for each act: they give the lyrics of the arias, offer varying amounts of stage directions, and intersperse minimal cues for dialogue. Scholars assume that these early play scripts may have originated as "singing texts" for the lead actor-singers; the fact that someone incurred the expense of printing them, however, strongly suggests that they served as the functional equivalent of subtitles for an educated audience who may have had trouble following the lyrics of the songs or simply did not understand the exact form of Chinese in which they were sung.[25] A single play could feature two (*Tiger Head Plaque*, discussed in chapter 2) or three singing protagonists (*Single Sword Meeting*, discussed in chapter 3; *The Orphan of Zhao*, discussed in chapter 5), but in each instance, a single actor-singer would impersonate all these protagonists. In its focus on a single male or female lead actor, *zaju* theater was designed to showcase the virtuosity of a theatrical troupe's star. As noted in chapter 3, such virtuosic range was further underlined by the fact that female actors were routinely commended for their representation of male roles. At the same time, as explored in chapter 5, such a multiplicity of singing parts also offered a stereoscopic view of a particular dilemma, moral issue, or dramatic conflict.

However, it is the Ming editions of Yuan *zaju* plays that have traditionally been the principal primary sources for the study and discussion of "Yuan drama." The attractive Ming versions were also the ones that were most commonly translated into other languages.[26] These recensions, however, are not entirely representative of what we can reconstruct about *zaju* theater in the Yuan dynasty—in fact, they not only reflect how the Ming court and Ming literati adapted earlier versions of the *zaju* tradition for their own ends but also came into being precisely when northern-style *zaju* performance began to decline. Ming emperors, princes, and their literary coteries and eunuch-staffed offices of music instruction sought to tame the unruly *zaju* tradition and turn it into a site of moral didacticism for others and a lavish spectacle for themselves. Most notably, across the Yuan *zaju* corpus, they greatly diminished the appearance of imperial roles.[27] Meanwhile, under the guise of a "classical form" that had allegedly enjoyed government support in the Yuan dynasty, *zaju* drama offered a vehicle for Ming literati to remonstrate with what they often saw as an unresponsive or outright incompetent imperial bureaucracy in their own times—a subtle version of *Saturday Night Live (SNL)*, one of the premier political comedy shows in the United States today.

Among the Ming anthologies of Yuan *zaju* plays, Zang Maoxun's (1550–1620) *Select Yuan Plays* (*Yuanqu xuan*, 1615–1616), though controversial in its own day, turned out to be the most influential. More perhaps than other Ming editors, Zang took major liberties with the text and freely removed, added, and rewrote songs. The changes that he wrought in these texts were so considerable that he could almost be credited as the author of some of these new recensions. Zang selected what he considered the finest plays, reduced the number of arias while greatly expanding the dialogue; and, for better and sometimes for worse, he corrected the prosody, harmonized the music, and standardized the role designations. In the process, as noted in chapters 2 and 5, Zang also massaged the language to reflect literati values while offering an alternative to Confucian orthodoxy. If the Ming court had done its best to purge any references to imperial protagonists, Zang made the story of an emperor's ill-fated love the opening play of the anthology.[28] All these editorial changes to the early *zaju* plays were designed to transform these texts into reading material for the entertainment of the cultured class, while also serving as a touchstone for the composition of southern drama.[29]

Despite all the tweaking and the makeovers, the preservation of dramatic texts was clearly an important concern among Ming literati and commercial publishers alike. As the literati pondered how to cultivate their own sensibilities in the face of a dangerously factionalized political environment and a relentlessly commercializing economy, theater increasingly presented itself as a viable complement to political service or to other purely monetary ventures. As one Ming playwright put it, in theater's ability to "make all people under heaven happy or sad . . . in absence of this great treasure of the feelings between people, how could the ultimate musical pleasures of the Confucian way be attained?"[30]

In addition, as a remonstrative tool, *zaju* drama could represent historical political intrigue (☞ chap. 5), often interpreted figuratively as reflecting a contemporary political moment. This critical function never ceased to exist, continuing into the early Ming, when it engaged with social injustice (☞ chap. 7), but most prominently in the late Ming and Qing with the emergence of "drama on current affairs" (*shishiju*), in which plays could directly address current political issues onstage. Thus drama came to serve as a platform of political factionalism (☞ chap. 10), as an outlet to vent one's political grievances, and as a tool of subversion (☞ chap. 14). In short, not only could theater "attain the myriad twists of human behavior and gather a thousand transformations of times old and new,"[31] but with a simultaneous boom in print and performance, dramatic texts and their staging became part of an urban mediasphere that was believed to capture the real, the genuine, the authentic, and the one-of-a kind in an age where the well-worn distinctions of gentility and crassness imploded in the face of an increasingly monetized economy.

SOUTHERN DRAMA BETWEEN POPULARITY AND SOPHISTICATION

In the year 1604, Ma Shouzhen (1548–1604), a notable Nanjing-based courtesan-cum–theatrical troupe owner with extant paintings, poetry, and a *chuanqi* play entitled *The Story of Three Lives* (*Sansheng ji*) to her credit, went on a grand performance tour in Suzhou and the West Lake (Hangzhou). The only known female owner of a courtesan troupe, she staged the northern version of *The Western Wing*, the iconic love comedy discussed in chapters 1 and 4, to great acclaim among literati audiences (☛ *HTRCProse-CCC*, L20).[32] Ma herself imagined the success of playacting as follows: "When your singing, dancing, and playing music all become perfect, you will see that beautiful carriages fill the lane to our gate."[33] Meanwhile, on the occasion of Ma's performance of *The Western Wing*, Shen Defu (1578–1642), one of the most astute observers of the cultural trends of this period, noted, "Northern *zaju* plays have almost died out, only in Jinling [present-day Nanjing] are there still such performances."[34] While *zaju* may have lived on at court and in rural areas well into the seventeenth century,[35] Shen's comment points to the fact that the prosperous southern cities had begun to embrace southern-style theater.

The earliest type of southern theater, *nanxi* (also known as *xiwen*, literally "play-texts") or Wenzhou *zaju*, began in southeast China in the area around Wenzhou (Zhejiang province). It is unclear exactly when it first appeared, but since the first extant play in this form, *Top Graduate Zhang Xie* (*Zhang Xie zhuangyuan*, 1408), discussed in chapter 7, was already fully conceptualized, it is likely that this type of theater was already well developed in the Yuan period. While *nanxi* adopted stories from the *zaju* repertoire, as noted in chapter 2, these southern plays tended to be longer and more elaborate. The playtexts included song, spoken dialogue, and declamatory speeches marked by rhyme. The division of acts was based on the entrances and exits of roles, songs were clearly marked, the function of roles was indicated, and spoken, sung, and declaimed parts were differentiated. Typically weaving together two or more plotlines across thirty to fifty interrelated scenes (*zhe, chu*), these plays advanced the plot in a parallel manner, eventually culminating in a grand reunion (*datuanyuan*). Both the primary and the secondary plotlines alternated between serious and comic scenes; in the serious scenes, singing by the main role dominated, while dialogue by funny roles was the focus of the comic scenes. As noted in chapter 7, the balance between the comic and the serious was especially conspicuous in tragic moments like the death of a child, which was immediately followed by the absurd japes of a comic role.

Musically, even though *nanxi* and later *chuanqi* borrowed preexisting heptatonic tunes from the Yuan *zaju* repertoire, the overall musical style favored pentatonic tunes. Songs were not composed in suites, but rather in sequences of two or more songs, and these were not bound together by a single rhyme or a single musical mode, as in northern *zaju*. Yet the choice of tunes was not completely random. Xu Wei (1521–1593), a noted critic and the author of several Ming *zaju* discussed in chapter 6, observed that despite the absence of modes, "the arrangement of tunes in a suite must be carried out according to a proximity of sound," suggesting that southern songs still conformed to hidden rules of harmony in music (☛ chap. 7).[36] In southern drama, potentially all the roles could sing, including the minor ones, but certain tunes were better suited for the leading and more serious roles, and others for comic roles.

Nanxi drama was the precursor of another southern style of drama, called *chuanqi*. The first evidence of such *chuanqi* plays comes from fifteenth-century tombs where some families placed entertainment texts, including *chuanqi* plays, as noted in chapter 16. From the mid-sixteenth century onward, some publishing houses, notably in Nanjing, scaled up and diversified their *chuanqi* imprints to cater to an increasing demand for playtexts among late Ming audiences, as discussed in chapter 4. Lavishly illustrated, such imprints pleased theatergoers and readers alike. By the mid-seventeenth century, a well-known bibliophile and literati publisher, Mao Jin (1599–1659), collected *chuanqi* in an influential compendium called *Sixty Plays* (*Liushi zhong qu*, ca. 1650s) that, while still including plays that would be considered *nanxi* as well as the northern *zaju*-style *The Western Wing*, served as a repository for the *chuanqi* tradition in the Qing dynasty and beyond.

For the better part of the Ming dynasty, southern theater had been considered unsophisticated compared to its northern counterpart. Critics charged that it was composed of loosely constructed plots in an unintelligible local language, accompanied by a regional music that made no use of musical modes. In literary terms, the first play worthy of literati appreciation and an eventual canonical favorite of late Ming playwrights was *The Lute* (*Pipa ji*) by Gao Ming (ca. 1305–ca. 1370), one of the plays discussed in chapter 7. Gao's play demonstrated that southern drama could make full use of the range of written registers on a spectrum ranging from the rigors of parallel prose to the earthiness of common speech. Meanwhile, in musical terms, the perennial problem of how to reconcile literary phrasing and prosody with singability—an abiding concern that had preoccupied influential song critics and formulary compilers like Zhou Deqing (1277–1365) and Zhu Quan (1378–1448)—found a new solution. As noted in chapter 8, evolving out of one of the earlier regional musical styles from Kunshan, Kunqu instituted a manner of singing where the tonal contours of the language were closely matched by the musical notes. Specifically, in terms of articulation, words were broken into their three basic constituents (namely, the initial consonant, the medial vowel, and the final sound), all of which had to be smoothly strung together in the enunciation of sung words. Moreover, detailed methods of sound articulation, together with dynamic shadings and vocal ornaments, began to structure the techniques of Kunqu vocal delivery.[37]

These musical changes are credited to music master Wei Liangfu (ca. 1489–1566). The legend goes that sometime between 1522 and 1527, Wei was walking around Taicang (near Suzhou, in Jiangsu province) and "angered by the error-ridden and vulgar state of southern tunes" (*fen nanqu zhi elou ye*), he was determined to change them. With the help of other musicians, he created the successful polished style of music (*shuimo diao*, literally "water mill tune"), which is considered the foundational music of the Kun dramatic tradition. Mixing elements from northern and southern theater, Wei's main changes were concentrated in the manner of singing and in the introduction of string instruments (traditionally associated with northern music) to the southern musical style.[38] A little later, Liang Chenyu (1519–1591), a Suzhou native, set his play *Washing Silk* (*Huansha ji*, 1558) to this musical style, much to the acclaim of the urban, educated elite. Other playwrights, such as Li Rihua (fl. 1550s), who adapted the *Western Wing*, followed suit as explored in chapter 8. Although commercial theater sung in other musical forms flourished together with Kun theater, Kun music became the preferred musical style for the literati writing for *chuanqi* drama.

As early southern theater transitioned to the later *chuanqi*, almost every facet of dramatic composition became more sophisticated: the language shifted from the more vernacular register of both song and dialogue to a more elaborate and abstract language; many other literati forms (parallel prose, Tang poetry, Song dynasty *ci* song lyrics, among others) were incorporated; the plots became increasingly polished and skillfully put together; the complexity of plots in turn spurred an increase in the number of characters, and thus a subdivision of roles; the new musical arrangements changed the prosody and rhyme of song composition; and the singing became even more melismatic. While *chuanqi* was rooted in early southern *nanxi* drama, after Wei Liangfu's musical reforms and the increased interest of the cultured class in this art, the complexity of this form increased so dramatically that it became almost exclusively an elite pastime, alongside more popular styles of theater. However, for all the elite interest in matters of music, language, and affect, Chinese theater has also been part and parcel of a culture suffused with ritual practices.

EFFICACY AND ENTERTAINMENT IN RITUAL THEATER

Sometime before 1644, Zhang Dai (1597–1684), an avid theater aficionado and accomplished essayist, attended a theater performance. In his account, he described the eye-catching acrobatics that opened the proceedings:

> The actors (*xizi*) offered different kinds of acrobatics on the stage: tightrope walking, dancing ropes, overturned tables, overturned steps, somersaults, dragonflies, flipping tables and spinning mortars with their legs, rope jumping, hoop jumping, fire breathing and sword swallowing—it was all very mind-boggling (*da fei qingli*).[39]

In guessing what kind of play might have occasioned such kinesthetic feats, we might be tempted to think that they formed part of a martial tradition within Chinese theater as discussed in chapter 16, but in fact, as Zhang's title for this vignette, "Mulian Performance," informs us, these displays of physical prowess had become an integral part of what would become one of the most influential ritual play cycles, *Mulian Rescues His Mother* (*Mulian jiumu*).

To investigate the relationship between theater and ritual, historians and anthropologists of the theater have looked at holidays and festivals in both urban and rural contexts. From at least the Song period onward, theatricals were performed in local and village festivals to honor local deities, as evidenced by the common practice of building stages as part of temples and shrines, as well as textual references.[40] As described in a well-known *sanqu* song, when a peasant visited the commercial urban theater for the first time, he stated with amazement that even though this theatrical performance "does not welcome the gods and offer sacrifices (*yingshen saishe*) (☛ chap. 1), [the female musicians] continuously beat the drums and hit the cymbals."[41] One aspect that particularly struck our peasant-observer—the presence of professional female musicians—hints at the fact that such village theatricals were often exclusively staged by men. Such ritual performances, however, were not limited to the countryside. In what may well be one of the earliest mentions of a play title, a mid-twelfth-century account of the cultural practices of the capital of the northern Song dynasty noted that in conjunction with temporary stages set up for the Ghost Festival observed on the seventh day of the seventh lunar month, open-air theatricals in Kaifeng featured *Mulian Rescues His Mother*.

As chapter 15 explores, the story of Mulian is one of a select group of ritual plays that have had remarkable staying power from at least Song times to the present. Endowed with extraordinary magical powers, Mulian, one of the historical Buddha's chief disciples, journeyed through the various hells in search of his sinful mother. The story of Mulian did not originate as a play but as a narrative in a Buddhist sutra. The story was gradually adapted to many genres, narrative and otherwise, including the theatrical tradition. As it spread, it synthesized with the indigenous folk religious traditions and was performed throughout China as a means to send offerings to ancestors, ghosts, and gods, as well as a medium to dispel evil and pacify restless spirits. At the same time, *Mulian* performances also legitimated and enhanced social relations and helped to explain the meaning and value of the rituals to the community.

If *Mulian* seems to be a case of a story adapting to a performance genre, there are also clear cases of the reverse. As examined in chapter 16, the exorcistic plays known as *nuo* performances may have originated as performances enacted as well-wishing rituals for the gods and as requests for protection from evil. The rituals included song and dance and were carried out by specialists wearing costumes and masks. In contrast to the story of Mulian, which reached theater as part of its many generic transformations, the *nuo* ritual performance is regarded by scholars as a fossilized and deritualized performance that came to absorb dramatic narratives. In the process, it slowly moved from being an efficacious ritual to primarily serving as a means of entertaining the public.

Ritual plays such as *Mulian Rescues His Mother* may have been among the earliest kinds of dramatic performances, and among the most long lived within the Chinese theatrical corpus. At the same time, we also have to be mindful of the fact that with the institution of new cultural and religious policies in the People's Republic of China, the form, the meanings, and the functions of such theatricals have been altered. On the one hand, in light of repeated government campaigns against superstition, the supernatural elements of such plays became suspect and were banned. On the other hand, rather than abolishing such performances outright, they were revived under the auspices of "cultural heritage" to promote tourism and bring much needed revenue to less prosperous regions. In official discourse, they have largely lost their ritual significance, even if local practitioners may selectively activate residual ritual connotations. Yet even in their contemporary incarnations, the visually pleasing elements such as acrobatics and colorful costumes have been retained.[42] Hence, all the attempts to trace theater to ritual notwithstanding, the history of these ritual plays hints at one pervasive characteristic of theater: no matter what additional function it is accorded, its value as entertainment is always vital.

THE DYNAMICS OF ACTORS, ROLE TYPES, AND CHARACTERS

In *The Record of the Green Bowers* (*Qinglou ji*, 1360s), a compendium devoted to female performers that its author, Xia Tingzhi (ca. 1300–1375), had personally known or heard about, an entry about a *zaju* actress read as follows: "Tianxi xiu . . . excelled in outlaw plays (*lulin zaju*). Even though her feet were tiny, her martial steps onstage looked very imposing (*zhuang*)."[43] One of the most distinctive aspects of Chinese theater, and one of the hardest to grasp for those new to it, is the distinction between actor, role (*juese, hangdang*), and character (*renwu*). Actors were for the most part theatrical professionals, often drawn from the ranks of hereditary entertainers or servants. Characters were the specific figures represented in the plays. A role is a method of performance that mediates between the actor and the character whom the actor impersonates, and it typically indicates a set of skills and methods required for the onstage realization of that character. In other words, depending on what role a particular character was assigned by the playwright, the same character might turn into a stalwart hero, a comic target of satire, or a mere bystander. Similar to the role-type systems found in the *commedia dell' arte* or the "lines of business" of French theater, Chinese theatrical role systems were a means to an end rather than an end in themselves: they were a rhetorical tool to aid in the realization of relatable characters.

Over the centuries, a complex performative apparatus began to develop around the conception of individual role types, and even around particular protagonists. Broadly, we observe the emergence of different role types from the Song period at the earliest, but how such role types were realized over the course of China's theatrical history is a matter of scholarly debate (☞ chap. 1). In Yuan *zaju* theater, the most important distinction was between the lead actor-singer (the female *dan* and male *mo*, respectively) and various supporting roles (*waijiao*). In general terms, with the growing elaborations of role types, actors needed to acquire specialized knowledge to play particular roles. In northern theater, the leading male or female role determined who would be the lead singer; hence, to have a voice "melodious like a string of pearls" (*leileiran ru guanzhu*) that could sing well enough "to make the dust fall off the rafters" (*sheng zhui liangchen*) or "to arrest the drifting clouds" (*sheng e xingyun*)[44] would be an important skill to possess (☞ chap. 3).

In southern theater, on the other hand, since theoretically all the roles could sing, the role referred to a character type—for example, the young scholar, the ingenue, the comic. It also referred to the skills by which that character was played—a set of gestures, postures, and body movements, makeup, costume, and a type of voice and language—that make the character come alive onstage.

Northern *zaju* plays used three large categories of roles—that is, leads who were male (*zhengmo*) or female (*zhengdan*), comic and villainous roles (*jing*), and a host of minor characters (☞ chap. 1). Because only the lead actor could sing the major song suites, the characters that actor performed were always better developed and more deeply characterized than those who could only engage in dialogue. On occasion, to offer multiple perspectives on the same situation, *zaju* playwrights assigned the lead role to different characters. In fact, fully one-third of the extant corpus called for the main lead actor-singer to represent more than one character in the course of the play. For example, as discussed in chapter 5, in *The Orphan of Zhao*, the male lead (*zhengmo*) plays a stalwart and empathetic general (act 1), a fearless recluse retired from officialdom (acts 2 and 3), and an impulsive grown-up orphan (act 4). Furthermore, as noted in chapter 3, by allowing socially marginal groups to assume the main lead, *zaju* playwrights explored the thoughts and feelings of women from all walks of life with new nuance and depth.

As mentioned previously, the other major role type found in *zaju* is the comic/villain (*jing*), who was readily recognizable onstage by their painted face (see figure 9.2 in chap. 9). Typically conceived as a comic or villainous foil to the main lead, this role encompassed a wide variety of characters who helped to develop the dramatic conflicts at the heart of the play. When there was a need for additional roles, there was a role type whose name basically meant "extra" (*wai*) to employ, or a qualifier such as "second" (*er*), "supporting" (*tie*), or "secondary" (*fu*) to modify one of the more major role types.

Some role types were defined by their theatrical function, such as the "opening male" (*chongmo*), who was the first performer to appear onstage. Some roles referenced official positions, such as the "imperial role" (*jiatou*) and "officials" (*gu*). Some role types were known by generic names given to the characters; for example, the maid (*meixiang*) was both a role type and a name given to maids in plays. Others are referred to by their historical names, such as the powerful Tang dynasty eunuch official Gao Lishi (684–762), who could only play himself in specific historical plays. Some role types stressed the difference in age, such as the old lady (*bu'er*) or the child (*lai'er*), or occupations such as innkeeper (*dian xiao'er*) and executioner (*guizi*).[45] For comic roles, southern theater distinguished between "comic/villain" and "clown" (*chou*), largely according to social status (generally higher for the former) and predilections for comic remarks and actions (generally more developed for the latter); it was under the influence of southern theater that the "clown" role appeared in the Ming recensions of Yuan *zaju*.

Southern *nanxi* plays, on the other hand, have specialized roles from the first texts. Because all the roles can sing, the unique place held by the leading role in northern *zaju* drama dissolves. In southern theater, the male role (*sheng*) and female role (*dan*) typically do not change character at any time in the play. While the specific characters performed by these roles change from play to play, given the importance of romance and marriage in this corpus, the *sheng* is generally a young man and the *dan* a young lady. There were five additional role types: a second female role (*tiedan*) and four role types whose names we have already introduced: an extra (*wai*), a comic (*jing*), a clown (*chou*), and an additional male role (*mo*). In contrast to the *mo* in *zaju*, in southern drama, the *mo* assumed a metatheatrical function. The *mo* mediated between the comic roles onstage and between the characters and the audience. Characters that belong to these four role types can be male or female, and the same actor would often portray more than one character in a play. For example, in *Top Graduate Zhang Xie*, the first extant complete southern play that we have, the *jing* plays a total of thirteen characters, which include figures who are central and minor characters, young and old, male and female, human and divine.

By the late Ming and Qing dynasties, when *chuanqi* plays flourished, the plots of the plays in the southern tradition became more complex and involved more characters. At the same time, we observe an increase in the subdivision of roles, as well as a shift in the function of certain roles. This subdivision of roles may not have done much to generate more subtlety or complexity of character, but it did enable plays to treat more complex subjects and stories. However, in one of the culminations of *chuanqi* theater, *Peach Blossom Fan* (*Taohua shan*, 1699), a sprawling play depicting the fall of the Ming dynasty that features a huge cast, the playwright Kong Shangren (1648–1718) complained that the current role system was still inadequate to capture the full range of his historiographic project. As a result, he made unconventional choices with the role of the *jing*. In contrast to the greedy innkeepers or gluttonous temple gods that populated the *jing* roles of early southern drama, he cast magistrates, generals, and other imposing figures such as the disgraced official and playwright Ruan Dacheng (1587–1646) (☞ chaps. 10 and 12) in that role type, while also grudgingly assigning positive characters to that category.[46]

In a fully formed Chinese play, roles were an important aspect of its composition. As chapter 1 notes in detail, when playwrights such as Wang Shifu adopted earlier genres such as the tale (*chuanqi*) and the ballad (*zhugongdiao*) for his stage rendition of *The Western Wing*, role assignments recalibrated the internal balance and the emphasis of the plot. For instance, the maid Crimson (Hongniang), a subsidiary character in earlier versions of the story, became much more central to the story by virtue of the fact that she was promoted to the position of lead singer. Similarly, as discussed in chapter 6, in Xu Wei's adaptation of the cross-dressed female warrior Mulan for the stage, casting the eponymous protagonist as a "female lead" who deliberately assumed the role of a "he" opened the possibilities of playfully examining the tensions between social and theatrical roles. Hence, in the presentation of a deliberate mismatch between social body (status of character, gender of actor) and theatrical body (role), the theatrical role system facilitated the scrambling of real-life social and gender hierarchies. In that regard, it is important to note that the nonalignment between physical gender (actor) and theatrical gender (role) has been a major practice in Chinese theater, even if the prevalence and meanings of male and female impersonation varied considerably over time.[47] At the same time, not all plays placed a premium on role characterization. In the court-oriented theatricals discussed in chapter 13, for example, role differentiation might be superseded by visual spectacle and literary panegyrics.

In modern times, as Chinese theater came to be defined as part of a distinctly Chinese heritage, the notion of traditionality has often obscured just how creative individual actors could be in their realization of roles and scenes. To be sure, as teachers (whether veteran actors or music masters) transmitted a set of singing techniques and role conventions to their disciples, each performance of a role type would rely on a comparable repertoire of makeup, costume, gestures, poses, body and eye movements, and singing and speaking styles. However, as actors became more proficient, they would not necessarily perform their roles in exactly the same manner as either their teachers or their contemporaries. On the contrary, while roles provided actors with a set of skills as general guidance, as the story of Actor Ma demonstrates, it was often the actors' personal interpretation of their characters that propelled them into stardom. Apart from the performative modalities, language registers constituted one of the important verbal means by which to differentiate roles and the characters they impersonated. As we will see later, critics in dynastic China considered the phrasing, linguistic provenance, and pronounceability of a play, as well as the more elusive matter of literary style, as one of the key considerations of whether to rank a play as a "sublime" (*shen*), "marvelous" (*miao*), "competent" (*neng*), or "able" (*ju*) work.[48]

THE ALLURE OF A NATURAL LANGUAGE

In 1592, the iconoclastic philosopher and literary critic Li Zhi (1527–1602) debated the linguistic merits of what he identified as the representative plays of northern theater (*Moon Pavilion, Western Wing*) and southern theater (*The Lute*):

> *The Story of Praying at the Moon Pavilion* and *The Story of the Western Wing* are works of nature (*huagong1*). *The Lute* is a work of artifice (*huagong2*). Artists [such as the author of *The Lute*] think they can seize the creative powers of heaven and earth, but who among them understands that heaven and earth have neither skill nor technique [as evidenced in *Moon Pavilion* and *Western Wing*]?[49]

Li's essay points to one of the reasons why Chinese literati were fascinated by drama as a literary form.

In fashioning a subtle new expressive medium, Guan Hanqing (ca. 1220–after 1279), the founder of mature *zaju*, and later generations of playwrights laid the foundation for northern *zaju* drama to be credited as the form that had pioneered "artistry without artifice" (*gong er bugong*).[50] As a mixed-register genre that blended popular argot and diverse song traditions, northern *zaju* drama was written in a mixture of northern vernacular and standard classical Chinese. It utilized a mixture of classical poetic language and plain Chinese elements for the arias and a purer vernacular register proximate to modern Mandarin for the dialogue. On the one hand, as discussed in chapter 1, the language of *zaju* plays built on the linguistic dexterity and hybridity of performative genres such as transformation texts (*bianwen*) and ballads (*zhugongdiao*) to range across high and low registers; on the other hand, as noted in chapters 1 and 3, it also followed their cue in borrowing broadly across a range of different oral-connected forms (e.g., songs, proverbs, sayings, oaths, curses, clever doggerel, etc.). In its seemingly easy and much vaunted blend of the poetic and the everyday, *zaju* theater represented a new synthesis of verbal artistry—a kind of mashup and remix of elements elegant and familiar, classical and contemporary. In modern times, Wang Guowei praised the language of *zaju* plays for its "naturalness." In his view, such language could express feelings in a direct and unmediated fashion, while also conveying the complexity of different states of affairs.[51]

Southern theater similarly used different registers from the quasi-spoken vernacular to the more elaborate parallel prose. Discussion of what kind of language was appropriate for drama was important early on: dramatists believed that the correct linguistic register of a play had to be "natural" (*bense*, literally, "original color").[52] It had to be simple enough to be aurally understood by an illiterate audience, yet poetic enough to please the educated classes. If a play utilized very obscure language, if it made extensive use of parallelism, if it employed classical allusions in excess, or if its subject matter was overly didactic, then such a play ran counter to the idea of "natural language." The language of dramatic plays had to convey meaning through simple and lucid language, but what precisely was "simple and lucid" was not always obvious. Just what constituted this perfect blend of natural, yet elegant language was always a subjective judgment. While some believed *The Lute* to be the perfect example of dramatic language (chap. 7), other critics such as Li Zhi considered it too elaborate.

The pronunciation and performability of *chuanqi* drama in performance constituted another area of scholarly debate. The Ming scholar and drama aficionado Wang Jide (1542?–1623) noted how different regional languages created different musical styles and manners of singing: "The musical structure is the song, and the color and patina is in the vocal performance practices. Since the pronunciation is different everywhere, the musical sounds (*sheng*) also differ."[53] For example, the language used in Kun drama was a southern-accented Mandarin (*daiyou Wuyu kouyin de zhongzhou yun nianfa*)[54] based on the rhymes established in Zhu Quan's *Correct Rhymes of the Hongwu Reign* (*Hongwu zhengyun*, 1375) at the beginning of the Ming. Informed by its long history and theatrical practices, the singing and speaking of Kun drama were heavily influenced by Wu pronunciation, the regional language of its place of origin. Lower-class and/or more comic characters appear to have used the local dialect of Suzhou from quite early on, but such dialect usage does not become textualized until around the fall of the Ming dynasty such as in the plays by Li Yu (1591?–1671?) (chap. 14).

Accordingly, Ming and early Qing playwrights frequently debated what it meant to put together a play. Should playwrights simply write the words that expressed what they wanted to say, or should they also be mindful of the underlying prosodic requirements of the musical style in which plays would be performed, making sure that the words they wrote could also be sung in a musically appealing and intelligible fashion? If they were attentive to music, how would they learn what they needed to know? Should they try to fit their words to the music on their own, or should they learn from or collaborate with professional music masters? Or, alternatively, should they directly work with actor-singers in a troupe of their own choosing? In other words, should playwrights "write" plays or "compose" them? Was it possible to mesh words and music seamlessly? To understand these issues, let us turn to the music that underwrote Chinese theater.

THE FORCE OF MUSIC

As noted initially, music has been central to the expressive power of traditional Chinese theater in both the north and south, now and then. The Chinese graph for "music" (*yue*), in an alternative pronunciation, also means "taking pleasure in something" (*le*), culminating in the classical phrase "music is what the sages take pleasure in" (*yuezhe, shengren zhi suo le*). In antiquity, music came predominantly in two flavors—the loud ritual music orchestrated at court and the quiet music performed among like-minded spirits. Such was the connection between the shared appreciation of music that the word "the knower of sound" (*zhiyin*) came to embody the most sublime kind of friendship.[55] From the Yuan period onward, a music-centered discourse of friendship sprang up around the cultivation of the *qin* zither.[56] At the same time, theater was now tasked with the diffusion of the trans-formative resonant response believed to be inherent in music across the broad spectrum of human relations: rulers and ministers, fathers and sons, mothers and sons, husbands and wives, older and younger brothers, and friends.[57] Thus, theater made musical and affective experiences that previously were reserved for homo-social elites available to the broader populace.

Yet for all the discursive elaboration around the affective force of music before the modern era, it is difficult to know what the music of Chinese *zaju* theater sounded like. For the *zaju* plays, we have scripts indicating musical modes and the titles of the tunes, as well as brief remarks written by music masters and theater fans. But we do not have any scores, we know relatively little about the musical ensembles, and we do not know how exactly the songs were sung. Hence, much about early theatrical music—its rhythm, melody, beat, and tone color—has been irretrievably lost. Yet, despite the absence of musical scores, the *zaju* texts found in *Thirty Yuan-Printed Zaju Plays* clearly set the titles of song patterns for all sung passages in black cartouches. From this typographic convention, we can infer that these so-called *qu* songs (also translated as "arias") were the musical building blocks of *zaju* theater.

Qu songs were composed to named tunes called *qupai* (literally "titled song," alternately translated as "tune titles," "song patterns," "melodic models," or "song matrices") (☛ chaps. 1 and 8). The name to which such songs were written was, above all, a tune title that exemplified a musical and prosodic pattern; however, in both literary and musical practice, such tunes could be modified. After deciding which song pattern to use, a playwright would know (or could look up) such things as how many lines the arias should contain, how many words (*zi*) should appear in each line, what lines would rhyme, and where characters of a certain tonal contour had to be used.[58] Within this broad framework, however, playwrights had consid-erable liberty to add what are called "extrametrical" or "padding" words (*chenzi*). Such flexibility allowed playwrights to capture the intrinsically wordier colloquial registers not only in the dialogue but also in the sung parts. Furthermore, if later singing practices are any indication, individual performers could vary the phras-ing, tempo, and ornamentation of a particular tune.

Compared to *zaju* theater, the music of southern theater is better documented. Southern theater as performed in different localities used different tunes, manners of singing, and regional pronunciation to create distinct musical styles. *Chuanqi* theater also used "song patterns" (*qupai*) as their building blocks, but the songs were typically drawn from different musical repertoires. In the southeast, four vocalizing styles of southern theater (*nanxi sida shengqiang*) emerged, which included the Kun musical style discussed previously, as well as the Yiyang, Haiyan, and Yuyao forms (☞ chaps. 8 and 14). Unfortunately, we do not have detailed notations for how the arias were to be sung in any of those four traditions until the eighteenth century. Some were sung in Mandarin, others in local dialect, and as such they could be hard to understand by northerners traveling to the south.

One of the first critics to draw attention to this phenomenon was the Ming prince Zhu Quan. In the preface to his *Refined Rhymes from the Jasper Realm* (*Qionglin yayun*, 1398), a rhyme dictionary for northern *zaju* song-drama, Zhu noted the difficulty of understanding southern dialects: "In the North there are no dialects (*xiangtan*), but the widespread southern drama (*nanxi*) of Wu [present-day Jiangsu province] and Yue [present-day Zhejiang province] . . . all make use of local dialects."[59] At times, literati translated regional plays for their own entertainment, as was the case with Chen Maoren (fl. 1606), from Zhejiang. He noted that wealthy families from Quanzhou (present-day Fujian province) kept their own troupes and trained them, but because they used local language and he could not understand them, he decided to translate their plays. Unfortunately, considering theater nothing more than an amusing pastime, he did not keep his translations.[60]

Given the prestige of the northern *zaju* form in the Ming dynasty, it is perhaps not surprising that some aspects of its music were incorporated into southern drama. To be sure, some partisans of southern drama such Xu Wei, the critic mentioned earlier in this chapter, drew a firm distinction between the effects of listening to northern and southern music:

> Listening to northern tunes makes one's spirit soar and one's hair stand on end. It is enough to build one's determination to proceed with courage. Truly, "northern barbarians" (*huren*) excelled at rousing anger. The expression "Its sounds are pressing and inhibited in order to manifest their resentment" exemplifies this. Southern tunes are slow paced and leisurely, flowing and meandering, elating people who thoughtlessly abandon their composure. Truly, this is the gentle charm of the South. It is exemplified by the phrase "The sounds of the fallen state induce thoughts of sorrow."[61]

However, despite Xu Wei's insistence that northern and southern styles were entirely distinct, Kun-style music actually represented a new synthesis of northern and southern music. While *zaju* theater was eventually lost as an independent art form, it lives on in changed form in later theatrical traditions.[62]

Alongside elite patronage of Kunqu and official tolerance of the popular Yiyang style, new theatrical styles continued to emerge in the Qing dynasty despite official attempts to suppress new "vulgar tunes." Most notably, on the occasion of the Qianlong emperor's eightieth birthday in 1789, four troupes from Anhui (Huiban) began to blend two regional musical styles called *xipi* and *erhuang*.[63] As explored in chapter 14, one of the commercial troupes that formed in the wake of this success, the Hechun troupe, riveted middlebrow audiences in the commercial theaters of Beijing for half a century with its martial arts acrobatic stunts and eclectic musical offerings. As musical experimentation with regional forms evolved into *jingju* (literally "capital opera," a term first used in the late nineteenth century and alternatively translated as "Peking opera" and "Beijing opera"), it became the novel and favored mode of performance in the capital city. Not only did Beijing opera eventually secure Qing court patronage,[64] but in the twentieth century, it advanced to the status of a "national form," which was called "national theater" (*guoju*) in some contexts. However, transformations in musical styles were only one aspect of theatrical change. Different venues and the associated troupes also inspired playwrights to produce different kinds of plays.

THE CHANGING FORTUNES OF PLAY SPACES AND TROUPES

Over the course of dynastic China, Chinese theater was performed on permanent stages, temporary structures, and improvised theatrical spaces delineated by a red felt carpet (*qushu*) (☛ chap. 9).[65] The most popular place for dramatic performances, and perhaps the most long lived, were stages constructed in temple complexes all over China. During festivals, temples of all religious traditions were the gathering places for the community, and weekly or monthly markets were also held there, providing opportunities for touring and local troupes to perform on the temple stages (☛ chap. 1).[66]

Some of the most interesting early material documentation stems from these temple theaters: for example, a mural found in the Water God's Hall (Mingying wang miao) in Shanxi dating from 1324 bears a head banner with the inscription "The Famous Actress of the Grand Guild of Roving Troupes Zhongdu xiu Performed Here," ("Dahang sanyue Zhongdu xiu zaici zuochang") and features both female and male actors, musicians, and stagehands on a brick-paved stage (see figure 9.2 in chap. 9). While some scholars point to this mural to illustrate troupe size and organization (between ten and twenty members), cross-gender performance (three out of five roles being women performing male roles), costumes (both Chinese and Mongolian dress), and musical instruments (e.g., drum, clapper, flute), others place the mural within the larger pictorial program of the temple, arguing that this painting represents the theatrical culmination of a rainmaking ceremony addressed to the resident deity.[67] However, even in this temple setting, it is important to note that the actress hailed from the entertainment district of Pingyao, a small city in Shanxi, and the play that she might have performed there formed part of the urban *zaju* corpus, pointing to the porous boundaries between ritual and commercial forms of entertainment.

Government-sponsored commercial stages provided the backdrop for the emergence of northern *zaju* and southern *nanxi* theater. From the Song dynasty onward, we have detailed descriptions of large theaters (*goulan*) in commercial entertainment districts (*washe*, literally "tiled markets") in urban areas operating under government auspices in an effort to generate tax revenues from wine sales.[68] For example, in mid-twelfth-century Bianliang (present-day Kaifeng), the capital of the northern Song, theaters could hold up to one thousand people. Similar districts and playhouses existed in the southern capital of Lin'an (present-day Hang-zhou), where one source enumerates twenty-three theaters.[69] The introduction to *Top Graduate Zhang Xie*, the early *nanxi* play discussed in chapter 7, described a raucous crowd waiting for a theater competition to begin. Most likely the setting of such a competition would have been one of the numerous theaters in Wenzhou, a town in southeast China and the cradle of *nanxi*. While no exact statistics exist for the Yuan dynasty, one knowledgeable mid-fourteenth-century observer notes that such theaters existed in the capital of Dadu (present-day Beijing), as well as in smaller towns.[70] The performers in these government-sponsored venues were members of family troupes from the hereditary ranks of "musician households" (*yuehu*). The most talented actors and actresses fascinated playwrights and literati alike, in terms of individual ability, as potential paramours, and as a sign of just how resplendent the Yuan dynasty truly was.[71]

In the Ming dynasty, it was small-scale residential troupes made up of inden-tured family servants or concubines that formed the theatrical backbone for the *chuanqi* composed by the literati playwrights discussed in chapter 9 (Tang Xianzu), chapter 10 (Ruan Dacheng), and chapter 11 (Li Yu).[72] In retirement, the Ming offi-cial Ruan Dacheng (1587–1648) wrote plays and trained his troupe with so much care and skill that it became a national phenomenon. Another very successful liter-atus was the cultural impresario Li Yu (1611–1680), who wrote many very popular plays and took his own theater company, which featured two of his concubines, on tour, as such performances were one of the main means of supporting his house-hold. In addition, commercial troupes such as the courtesan troupe of Ma Shou-zhen discussed earlier in this chapter, as well as all-male troupes, performed in a variety of indoor and outdoor settings, popularizing the literati plays originally written for more intimate settings.

In the Qing dynasty, dedicated playhouses inaugurated a new era of commer-cial theater, most notably in the capital of Beijing.[73] In an effort to balance popular appeal and political allegiance, all commercial troupes needed a guarantor from one of the princely households of the Qing dynasty. Similar to the Yuan period, men from all walks of life attended these playhouses, even if the seating structure reflected the social hierarchy. It was during this period that, as noted in chapter 11, women began to be excluded from the stage and restricted from attending pub-lic theaters, but in their place, cross-dressing boy actors (*xianggong*) became the stars of the theater. Such was the fascination with these actors that they generated a "fanzine literature" (*huapu*) that chronicled their fortunes onstage and offstage. Moving between artistic and sexual patronage, the male patron-actor relationships of the commercial Qing stage provided one of the enduring archetypes of male same-sex relationships in modern Chinese culture.[74] As noted in chapter 14, these troupes adapted stories from the existing dramatic repertoire, but they also created new plays to reflect the changing preferences of different subsets of theatergoers.

While the fortunes of commercial and private troupes fluctuated over time, the imperial court and its members and agencies continuously shaped the fortunes of the theatrical arts in dynastic China. In the Song and Yuan dynasty, patronage for the theater involved the occasional requisitioned performance at court.[75] In the Ming dynasty, members of the imperial family—most notably the imperial princes Zhu Quan and Zhu Youdun (1379–1439)—not only engaged in theatrical criticism or playwriting but also supported other courtiers in their dramatic pursuits.[76] At the same time, the Office of Musical Instruction (jiaofang si) revised the zaju corpus and put on very lavish productions, with casts numbering in the hundreds. However, it was probably the Qing court whose interest in theater reached new heights, both in terms of regulating all aspects of the theater, while also playing a very active role in fostering old and new styles.

As explored in chapter 13, extravagant theatricals not only formed part of everyday life at the Qing court but also accompanied imperial tours of the land. These ceremonial and private occasions inside the palace and on travel at large stimulated the production of a vast theatrical corpus that has yet to be systematically explored.[77] These imperially commissioned plays may no longer be performed, but the pageantry and spectacle of Qing imperial theater live on in events such as the opening ceremony of the Beijing Olympics (2008) and the grand celebrations around the four-hundred-year anniversary of the deaths of Tang Xianzu (1550–1616) and William Shakespeare (ca. 1564–1616) (2016) (➮ Visual Resources).

A FINAL WORD ABOUT COVERAGE

How to Read Chinese Drama is the first guided anthology of its kind. Hence, we see the chapters that follow as a beginning rather than as the final word on Chinese drama. Despite the bulk of the resulting volume, we are keenly aware that we have not given due consideration to many other important facets of Chinese theater. In some cases, the omission has occurred because other studies have already addressed them in some detail. In others, we hope that future works will continue to trace the threads of exploration begun here. Taking our cue from the Chinese critic Lü Tiancheng (ca. 1580–ca. 1618),[78] we hope that our combined efforts have yielded a guided anthology that will allow readers to tap into the artistic wellspring of Chinese drama and enjoy these works as part of a very old and very contemporary conversation about how to make sense of the world through theater.

Patricia Sieber and Regina Llamas

NOTES

1. Kenneth J. Hammond, *Pepper Mountain: Life, Death, and the Posthumous Career of Yang Jisheng* (London: Routledge, 2007), 101–122.

2. Hou Fangyu, "Ma ling zhuan" ("Biography of Actor Ma"), *Hou Fangyu quanji xiaojian* (An Annotated Edition of Hou Fangyu's Complete Works), ann. Wang Shulin (Beijing: Renmin wenxue chubanshe, 2013), vol. 1, 297–300; translation from Hou Fangyu, "The Biography of Actor Ma," trans. Victor H. Mair, in *The Shorter Columbia Anthology of Traditional Chinese Literature* (New

York: Columbia University Press, 2000), 462. Our thanks to Ying Zhang and Professor Yan Zinan for arranging access to the Chinese source text.

3. For a modern formulation by a famous *xiqu* director on how to create a *xiqu* character from performance conventions, life experience, and feelings, see Ah Jia, "Xiqu daoyan" ("The Role of the Director in Chinese Theater"), in *Zhongguo dabaike quanshu xiqu quyi* (The Chinese Encyclopedia: Traditional Theater and Storytelling) (Beijing: Zhongguo dabaike quanshu chubanshe, 1983), 444–445, as discussed in Megan Evans, "The Emerging Role of the Director in Chinese *Xiqu*," *Asian Theatre Journal* 24, no. 2 (2007): 488–489.

4. This line of thinking is indebted to Michael Nylan, *The Chinese Pleasure Book* (Brooklyn: Zone Books, 2018), 71; Haiping Yan, "Theatricality in Classical Chinese Drama," in *Theatricality*, ed. Tracy C. Davis and Thomas Postlewait (Cambridge: Cambridge University Press, 2003), 65–89; and Weihong Bao, *Fiery Cinema: The Emergence of an Affective Medium in China, 1915–1945* (Minneapolis: University of Minnesota, 2015). For an affective conception of Chinese theater in contemporary times, see Joseph Lam, "Impulsive Scholars and Sentimental Heroes: Contemporary Kunqu Discourses of Traditional Chinese Masculinities," in *Gender in Chinese Music*, ed. Rachel Harris, Rowan Pease, and Shzr Ee Tan (Rochester, NY: University of Rochester Press, 2013), 87–106. However, in no way do we suggest that this affective structure was uniform over time. On the different ways these affective bonds between dramatist, actor, and audience could be realized in dynastic China, see chap. 9.

5. See Nylan, *The Chinese Pleasure Book*, 66–69; and Judith T. Zeitlin, "From the Natural to the Instrumental: Chinese Theories of the Sounding Voice before the Modern Era," in *The Voice as Something More: Essays toward Materiality*, ed. Martha Feldman and Judith T. Zeitlin (Chicago: University of Chicago Press, 2019), 54–57.

6. See "Mao shi xu" ("Preface to the *Book of Songs* as Annotated by Mr. Mao"), in *Mao shi zhengyi* (The Correct Meanings of the *Book of Songs* as Annotated by Mr. Mao), in *Shisanjing zhushu* (The Annotated Thirteen Classics), ed. Ruan Yuan (Beijing: Zhonghua shuju, 1980), 1.2a (modern pagination 270).

7. Chen Hongshou, " 'Jieyi yuanyang zhong Jiao Hong ji' xu" ("Preface to *The Mistress and the Maid*"), in Meng Chengshun, *Jiao Hong ji* (The Mistress and the Maid) (Shanghai: Shanghai guji chubanshe, 1988), 270.

8. Bernd Eberstein, "Theaterzensur und Aufführungsverbote zur Qing-Zeit" (Theatrical Censorship and Performance Prohibitions in the Qing Period), *Oriens Extremus* 48 (2009): 153–197; Andrea S. Goldman, *Opera and the City: The Politics of Culture in Beijing, 1770–1900* (Stanford, CA: Stanford University Press, 2012); Guojun Wang, *Staging Personhood: Costuming in Early Qing Drama* (New York: Columbia University Press, 2020).

9. The alternative translation is inspired by Hu Zhiyu, "Zhu shi shijuan xu" ("Preface to Ms. Zhu's Poems"), in *Zishan daquan ji* (The Collected Works of [Hu] Zishan) (Taipei: Taiwan Commercial Press, 1973), vol. 292, 8.9a–10b.

10. Nylan, *The Chinese Pleasure Book*, 59–66.

11. For major studies on recent regional styles, see Alexandra B. Bonds, *Beijing Opera Costumes: The Visual Communication of Character and Culture* (Honolulu: University of Hawai'i Press, 2008); Jin Jiang, *Women Playing Men: Yue Opera and Social Change in Twentieth-Century Shanghai* (Seattle: University of Washington Press, 2009); Wing Chung Ng, *The Rise of Cantonese Opera* (Urbana: University of Illinois Press, 2015); Elizabeth Wichmann, *Listening to Theatre: The Aural Dimension of Beijing Opera* (Honolulu: University of Hawai'i Press, 1991). On stories in the contemporary *xiqu* repertoire, see Siu Wang-Ngai with Peter Lovrick, *Chinese Opera: Images and Stories* (Vancouver: University of British Columbia Press, 1997).

12. On early recordings, see Peng Xu, "Hearing the Opera: 'Teahouse Mimesis' and the Aesthetics of Noise in Early *Jingju* Recordings, 1890s–1910s," *CHINOPERL* 36, no. 1 (2017): 1–21; on the genre of opera on film in the 1950s and 1960s, see Paola Iovene, "Chinese Operas on Stage and

Screen: A Short Introduction," *Opera Quarterly* 26, no. 2-3 (2010): 181–199; on television, see Megan Evans, "Chinese *Xiqu* Performance and Moving-Image Media," *Theatre Research International* 34, no. 1 (2009): 21–36; on traditional storytelling and radio, see Carlton Benson, "The Manipulation of *Tanci* in Radio Shanghai during the 1930s," *Republican China* 20 (1995): 117–146; on intercultural *xiqu*, see Alexa Huang, *Chinese Shakespeares: Two Centuries of Cultural Exchange* (New York: Columbia University Press, 2009); and Wei Feng, *Intercultural Aesthetics in Traditional Chinese Theatre: From 1978 to the Present* (New York: Palgrave MacMillan, 2020).

13. On the so-called operatic mode in Chinese film, see Chris Berry and Mary Farquhar, *China on Screen: Cinema and Nation* (New York: Columbia University Press, 2006), 47–74. On *xiqu's* impact on *huaju*, see Ma Junshan, "Huaju biaoyan: Xingshen de pili yu huahe" ("Spoken Drama Performance: The Splitting and Blending of Form and Spirit—A Study of the Professionalization of Theater"), *Xiju yishu* (Theater Arts) 114, no. 4 (2003), 27–42; and Hui Yao, "Acting (as) a Beijing Opera Star: Shi Hui (1915–1957), *Begonia*, and Spoken Drama Performance," unpublished paper (used with permission). On *xiqu's* impact on dance, see Emily Wilcox, *Revolutionary Bodies: Chinese Dance and the Socialist Legacy* (Berkeley: University of California Press, 2018); on *xiqu* in diasporic and transnational contexts, see Daphne P. Lei, *Operatic China: Staging Chinese Identity across the Pacific* (New York: Palgrave MacMillan, 2006).

14. On Mei Lanfang's tours, see Xie Sijin and Sun Lihua, ed., *Mei Lanfang yishu nianpu* (A Chronicle of Mei Lanfang's Artistic Career) (Beijing: Wenhua yishu chubanshe, 2009).

15. For an annotated bibliography of key studies on traditional Chinese drama, see Colin Mackerras and Zhen Hai, "Traditional Chinese Drama (*Xiqu*)," in *Oxford Bibliographies Online* (2015).

16. Évariste Huc, *L'empire chinois: Suite au souvenirs d'un voyage dans la Tartarie et le Thibet* (The Chinese Empire: Recollections of a trip to Tartary and Tibet) (Paris: Éditions OMNIBUS, 2001), 176.

17. Wang Guowei, *Song Yuan xiqu kao* (A Study of Song and Yuan Drama), in *Wang Guowei Xiqu lunwenji: Song Yuan xiqu kao ji qita* (Wang Guowei's Collected Writings on Drama: *A Study of Song and Yuan Drama* and Other Works) (Taipei Liren shuju, 1993).

18. Regina Llamas, "Wang Guowei and the Establishment of Chinese Drama in the Modern Canon of Classical Literature," *T'oung Pao* 96 (2010): 165–201.

19. Xia Tingzhi, "Qinglou ji zhi" ("Preface to *The Record of the Green Bowers*"), in *Qinglou ji jiaozhu* (An Annotated Edition of *The Record of the Green Bowers*), ed. Sun Chongtao and Xu Hongtu (Beijing: Zhongguo xiju chubanshe, 1990), 44.

20. Joshua Goldstein, *Drama Kings: Players and Publics in the Re-Creation of Peking Opera, 1870–1937* (Berkeley: University of California Press, 2007).

21. Paul Jakov Smith, "Impressions of the Song-Yuan-Ming Transition: The Evidence from *Biji* Memoirs," in *The Song-Yuan-Ming Transition*, ed. Paul Jakov Smith and Richard van Glahn (Cambridge, MA: Harvard University Asia Center, 2003), 71–110.

22. For a detailed discussion of the various meanings encompassed by the term *zaju* from the Tang through the Qing periods, see Stephen H. West, "Tsa-chü," in *The Indiana Companion to Traditional Chinese Literature*, ed. William H. Nienhauser (Bloomington: Indiana University Press, 1986), 774–783.

23. A *musical mode* is a term that indicates the pitch around which a basic scale is constructed. Musical modes were considered important in determining the emotional context of a piece of music and may originally have been instrumental for musicians in clarifying pitch (in wind and string instruments) and perhaps for singers as well. See Rulan Chao Pian, *Sonq* [sic] *Dynasty Musical Sources and Their Interpretation* (Hong Kong: Chinese University of Hong Kong Press, 2003), 43–50. In Yuan *zaju*, nine modes were in place, in addition to a Jurchen suite used for Jurchen plays. For an analytical inventory of these modes, see Dale R. Johnson, *Yuarn* [sic] *Music Dramas* (Ann Arbor, MI: Center for Chinese Studies, 1980), 7–24. For the moods associated with particular modes, see Yannan zhi'an, "Changlun" ("Discourse on Singing"), in Yang Chaoying, *Yangchun baixue* (Sunny Spring, Brilliant Snow), ann. Xu Jinbang (Zhengzhou, China: Zhongzhou guji chubanshe, 1991), 2.

24. For the identification of these instruments, see Bell Yung, "Chinese Opera: An Overview," in *Garland Encyclopedia of World Music: East Asia: China, Japan and Korea*, ed. Robert C. Provine, Yosihiko Tokumaru and J. Lawrence Witzleben (Alexandria, VA: Alexander Street Press, 2006), vol. 7, 276.

25. See Stephen H. West and Wilt L. Idema, ed. and trans., "Introduction," in The Orphan of Zhao *and Other Yuan Plays: The Earliest Known Versions* (New York: Columbia University Press, 2015), 3–9.

26. Wilt L. Idema, "From Stage Scripts to Closet Drama: Editions of Early Chinese Drama and the Translation of Yuan *Zaju*," *Journal of Chinese Language and Literature* 3, no. 1 (2016): 175–202.

27. Tian Yuan Tan, "The Sovereign and the Theater: Reconsidering the Impact of Ming Taizu's Prohibitions," in *Long Live the Emperor! Uses of the Ming Founder across Six Centuries of East Asian History*, ed. Sarah Schneewind (Minneapolis: Society for Ming Studies, 2008), 147–163.

28. Patricia Sieber, *Theaters of Desire: Authors, Readers, and the Reproduction of Early Chinese Drama, 1300–2000* (New York: Palgrave, 2003), 103.

29. Zang Maoxun, "Xu'er" ("Second Preface"), *Yuanqu xuan* (Select Yuan Plays) (Beijing: Zhonghua shuju, 1989), vol. 1, 3–4.

30. Tang Xianzu, "Yihuang xian xishen Qingyuan shi miaoji" ("Epigraph for the Theater God Master Qingyuan in the Yihuang County Temple"), in *Lidai quhua huibian: Mingdai* (A Chronological Compendium of Writings on Chinese Drama: The Ming Dynasty, hereafter *LDQH*), ed. Yu Weimin and Sun Rongrong (Hefei, China: Huangshan shushe, 2009), vol. 1, 609. For a substantially different translation, see Tang Xianzu, "Epigraph for the Theater God Master Qingyuan in the Yihuang County Temple," in *Chinese Theories of Theater and Performance from Confucius to the Present*, ed. and trans. Faye Chunfang Fei (Ann Arbor: University of Michigan Press, 1999), 55–56.

31. Tang, "Yihuang xian xishen Qingyuan shi miaoji," 608.

32. Mi Zhao, "Ma Xianglan and Wang Zhideng Onstage and Offstage: Rethinking the Romance of a Courtesan Theatre in Ming-Qing China," *Asian Theatre Journal* 34, no. 1 (2017): 122–151.

33. Quoted in Zhao, "Ma Xianglan and Wang Zhideng Onstage and Offstage," 126.

34. Shen Defu, "Beici chuanshou" ("The Transmission of Northern Drama"), *Wanli yehuobian* (Unofficial Compilations of the Wanli Period) (Beijing: Zhonghua shuju, 1997 [1959]), vol. 2, 646–647.

35. For information on the court, see Li Zhenyu, *Mingdai gongting xiju shi* (A History of Ming-Dynasty Court Theater) (Beijing: Zijincheng chubanshe, 2010); for rural areas, see Liao Ben, *Song Yuan xiqu wenwu yu minsu* (Theater-Related Archeological Remains and Customs of the Song and Yuan Dynasties) (Beijing: Wenhua yishu chubanshe, 1989), 355–421.

36. See Xu Wei, *Nanci xulu* (A Record of Southern Songs), in *Zhongguo gudian xiqu lunzhu jicheng* (A Compendium of Classical Chinese Drama Criticism) (hereafter *LZJC*) (Beijing: Zhongguo xiju chubanshe, 1959), vol. 3, 241.

37. Isabel Wong, "*Kunqu*," *Garland Encyclopedia of World Music: East Asia: China, Japan and Korea*, vol. 7, 315.

38. Shen Chongsui, *Duqu xuzhi* (Essential Knowledge for Song Composition), in *LZJC*, vol. 5, 198.

39. Zhang Dai, "Mulian xi" ("Mulian Performance"), in *Tao'an mengyi* (Dream Memories of Tao'an) (Taipei: Taiwan Kaiming shudian, 1975), 78. On how some of these skills are represented in contemporary *xiqu*, see Siu Wang-Ngai with Peter Lovrick, *Chinese Opera: The Actor's Craft* (Hong Kong: Hong Kong University Press, 2014).

40. Liao Ben, *Zhongguo xiju tushi* (An Illustrated History of Chinese Drama) (Zhengzhou, China: Henan jiaoyu chubanshe, 1999), 168–180; and Liao, *Song Yuan xiqu wenwu yu minsu*, 365–370.

41. Du Shanfu, "Zhuangjia bushi goulan" ("The Country Cousin Is Not Familiar with Urban Theater"), *Quan Yuan sanqu* (Complete Yuan Sanqu), ed. Sui Shusen (Beijing: Zhonghua shuju, 1989), vol. 1, 31. Typically, such "welcoming" involved a public procession of the god's icons and statues, accompanied by troupes dressed up in various costumes.

42. Wei Liu, "Religious Ambiguity, ICH, and a Local Mulian Performance," presented at the CHINOPERL International Conference (Denver, March 21, 2019), unpublished paper (used with permission); and Josh Stenberg, "Rescuing Mulian's Mother in the Xi Era: Reviving Ritual *Xiqu* in Contemporary Fujian," *Asian Theatre Journal* 36, no. 1 (2019): 28–48.

43. Xia, *Qinglou ji jiaozhu*, 142.

44. For the first expression, see Hu Zhiyu, "Huang shi shijuan xu" ("Preface to Ms. Huang's Poems"), in *Zishan da quanji*, vol. 292, 8.13A; for the second and the third, see Xia, *Qinglou ji jiaozhu*, 167 and 141, respectively.

45. For a summary of northern roles, see Stephen H. West and Wilt L. Idema, ed. and trans., "Introduction," in *Monks, Bandits, Lovers, and Immortals: Eleven Early Chinese Plays* (Indianapolis: Hackett Publishing, 2010), xvii–xviii.

46. Maria Franca Sibao, "Maids, Fishermen, and Storytellers: Rewriting Marginal Characters in Early Qing Drama and Fiction," *CHINOPERL* 35, no. 1 (2016): 1–27. This convention can also be seen in the earliest southern plays.

47. For female impersonators (*nandan*) in dynastic China, see Cheng Yu'ang, *Ming shiren yu nandan* (Ming Poets and Female Impersonators) (Shanghai: Shanghai guiji chubanshe, 2012) and Cuncun Wu, *Homoerotic Sensibilities in Late Imperial China* (London and New York: Routledge Curzon, 2004), 111–151. For modern female impersonators, see Goldstein, *Players and Publics*, for modern male impersonators, see Lam, "Impulsive Scholars and Sentimental Heroes," 93–97, and Joseph Lam, "Kunqu Cross-Dressing as Artistic and/or Queer Performance," in *Oxford Handbook on Music and Queerness* (Oxford: Oxford University Press, 2019).

48. Lü Tiancheng, *Qupin jiaozhu* (A Collated and Annotated Edition of *Play Categorizations*), ann. Wu Shuyin (Beijing: Zhonghua shuju, 1990).

49. Li Zhi, "Zashuo" ("On Explaining Miscellaneous Matters"), in *Fenshu Xu Fenshu* (*A Book to Burn*; An Addendum to *A Book to Burn*) (Beijing: Zhonghua shuju, 2009), 96. This translation has been modified from Li Zhi, "On Miscellaneous Matters," trans. Pauline C. Lee, in *A Book to Burn and a Book to Keep (Hidden): Selected Writings*, ed. Pauline C. Lee, Rivi Handler-Spitz, and Haun Saussy (New York: Columbia University Press, 2017), 102. Our thanks to Ying Zhang for providing access to the Chinese text.

50. Zang Maoxun, "Xu" ("First Preface"), in *Yuanqu xuan*, vol. 1, 3.

51. See Wang, *Song Yuan xiqu kao*, 131.

52. Jing Shen, "The Concept of *Bense* in Ming Drama Criticism," *CHINOPERL* 24, no. 1 (2002): 1–33.

53. See Wang Jide, *Qulü* (Rules for Songs), in *LZJC*, vol. 4, 115. Our thanks to Joseph Lam for sharing his insights on this passage.

54. See Wang Zhenglai, *Quyuan zhuoyin* (A String of Flowers from the Garden of Songs) (Nanjing daxue yinwu youxian gongsi, 1962), 150.

55. Nylan, *The Chinese Pleasure Book*, 59–73.

56. Zeyuan Wu, "Becoming Sages: *Qin* Song and Self-Cultivation in Late Imperial China," PhD dissertation, Ohio State University, 2020.

57. Xia, "Qinglou ji zhi," in *Qinglou ji jiaozhu*, 44.

58. *Qupai* have been described as "a repertoire of melodic models" (3), which "in their basic forms, . . . are essentially short structures, with melodies several or more phrases in length" that can be performed at moderate or faster tempos (4). *Qupai* is the shortest unit in Chinese music, while the extended suites of melodies organized in different ways (*taoqu*) are the longest. The *qupai* are typically identified by name, and in some regions by their number of beats as well. See Alan R. Thrasher, "*Qupai* in Theory and Practice," in *Qupai in Chinese Music: Melodic Models in Form and Practice*, ed. Alan R. Thrasher (London: Routledge, 2016), 3–17.

59. Zhu Quan, "Xu" ("Preface"), in *Qionglin yayun* (Refined Rhymes from the Jasper Realm), in SKQS, 4th series (Jinan, China: Qilu chubanshe, 1995), vol. 426, 784.

60. Chen Maoren, *Quannan zazhi* (Miscellaneous Notes on Southern Fujian), in SKQS 2nd series (Jinan, China: Qilu chubanshe, 1996), vol. 247, 858.

61. Xu, *Nanci xulu, LZJC*, vol. 3, 245.

62. For example, in scene 23 of the *Peony Pavilion*, in imitation of Yuan *zaju*, only one actor sings and a northern song suite dominates; scene 55 of that same play mixes northern and southern suites (*nanbei hetao*). See also Wang Ning, *Kunju zhezixi xukao* (A Study of the Rearranged Scenes of Kunqu) (Hefei, China: Huangshan shushe, 2013). We thank David L. Rolston for noting this point.

63. For the musical, linguistic, and instrumental features of these two styles, see Rulan Chao Pian, "Peking Opera: *Jingju*," in *Garland Encyclopedia of World Music East Asia: China, Japan and Korea*, vol. 7, 282–286.

64. Ye Xiaoqing, *Ascendant Peace in the Four Seas: Drama and the Qing Imperial Court* (Hong Kong: Chinese University Press, 2012), 219–257.

65. Sophie Volpp, *The Worldly Stage: Theatricality in Seventeenth-Century China* (Cambridge, MA: Harvard University Asia Center, 2011), 59–88.

66. For a modern account of the revival of such temple performances, see Ziying You, "Entertaining Deities and Humans with Performances of *Puju* (Puzhou Opera) at a Temple Fair in Yangxie Village, Southwestern Shanxi, May 29–June 2, 2013," *CHINOPERL* 34, no. 2 (2015): 139–161.

67. On the first approach, see West and Idema, *Monks, Bandits, Lovers and Immortals*, xv–xvii; on the second, see Anning Jing, *The Water God's Temple of the Guangsheng Monastery: Cosmic Function of Art, Ritual, and Theater* (Leiden, Netherlands: Brill, 2002), 57–60 and 144–199.

68. Hanmo Zhang, "Property of the State, Prisoner of Music: Identity of the Song Drama Players and Their Roles in the *Washe* Pleasure Districts," *Bulletin of the Jao Tsung-i Academy* 2 (2015): 277–326.

69. For Bianliang, see Meng Yuanlao (ca. 1090–1150), *Dongjing menghua lu* (The Eastern Capital: A Record of a Dream of Splendor); and for Lin'an, see Zhou Mi (1232–1298), *Wulin jiushi* (Recollections of Wulin). Both texts are included in *Dongjing menghua lu wai sizhong* (The Eastern Capital: A Record of a Dream of Splendor and Four Other Texts) (Shanghai: Gudian wenxue chubanshe, 1956), 2.14 and 6.440-441, respectively.

70. Xia, "Qinglou ji zhi," in *Qinglou ji jiaozhu*, 43.

71. On the latter point, see Xia, "Qinglou ji zhi," in *Qinglou ji jiaozhu*, 43.

72. Grant Guangren Shen, *Elite Theatre in Ming China, 1368–1644* (London and New York: Routledge, 2005), 36–44.

73. Goldman, *Opera and the City*, 63–87. For a diagram of a typical playhouse, see Goldman, *Opera and the City*, 19.

74. On fan literature, see Goldman, *Opera and the City*, 17–60; on the longevity of this archetype, see Jie Guo, "The Male *Dan* at the Turn of the Twenty-First Century: Wu Jiwen's *Fin-de-siècle Boylove Reader*, *Prism* 18, no. 1 (2021): 70-88.

75. Beverly Bossler, *Courtesans, Concubines, and the Cult of Female Fidelity: Gender and Social Change in China, 1000–1400* (Cambridge, MA: Harvard University Asia Center, 2013), 295–297.

76. Wenbo Chang, "Performing the Role of the Playwright: Jia Zhongmin's *Sanqu* Songs in the Supplement to *The Register of Ghosts*," *Journal of Chinese Literature and Culture* 8, no. 1 (2021): 59–88; Wilt L. Idema, *The Dramatic Oeuvre of Chu Yu-tun* (Leiden, Netherlands: Brill, 1985); Tian Yuan Tan, "Emerging from Anonymity: The First Generation of Writers of Song and Drama in Mid-Ming Nanjing," *T'oung Pao* 96 (2010): 125–164.

77. On theater at the Qing court, see Ye, *Ascendant Peace in the Four Seas*, and Liana Chen, *Staging for the Emperors: A History of Qing Court Theatre, 1683–1923* (Buffalo, NY: Cambria, 2021).

78. "At the beginning of our [Ming] dynasty there were innumerable distinguished playwrights, and their knowledge of song-drama was superior. Writers were unique and the tunes they composed numbered in the hundreds." See Lü, *Qupin*, in *LZJC*, vol. 6, 209.

PART I

Yuan and Ming Dynasties

Zaju Plays

I

The Story of the Western Wing

Tale, Ballad, and Play

The Story of the Western Wing (*Xixiang ji*, hereafter *The Western Wing*)[1] is China's most famous love comedy. Written in the late thirteenth century by Wang Shifu (fl. 1260–1300), it remained a stage favorite for centuries. Originally composed for the northern music of *zaju* variety plays, the story was adapted twice to the southern music of *chuanqi* drama in the sixteenth century (➤ chap. 8) and thereafter became a staple of all genres of local theater throughout China. The story was popular even beyond the stage, as many genres of narrative ballad (in either an alternation of verse and prose or completely in verse) featured the story of the talented student Zhang Junrui (Student Zhang), the beautiful and daring Cui Yingying (Oriole), and the sassy maid Hongniang (Crimson).

Wang's play also became extremely popular in print. A few pages survive from an edition that may have been published in the late fourteenth century, but it is the earliest preserved complete text, entitled *A Newly Printed Deluxe Completely Illustrated and Annotated Story of the Western Wing* (*Xinkan qimiao quanxiang zhushi Xixiang ji*, 1499), the so-called Hongzhi edition or *The Deluxe Edition* (➤ chap. 4), that set a new standard for drama publishing. Illustrated like a graphic novel or a comic strip, the Hongzhi edition transformed *The Western Wing* from a purely theatrical experience into a source of reading pleasure. The Hongzhi edition was followed by a continuous flood of printed editions, most of which were lavishly illustrated, extensively annotated, and supplemented with a wide range of bonus features such as appreciative poetry and satirical songs. The most famous of the later editions was *The Sixth Book of Genius* (*Diliu caizishu*; ca. 1661) by Jin Shengtan (1610–1661), which became the most widely circulated version of the play during the Qing dynasty. In this edition, the text of the play is accompanied not only by extensive essays, but also by a detailed, line-by-line commentary to the text (which Jin had adapted in places to fit his commentary).

From the sixteenth century onward, high-minded moralists time and again condemned the play as unfit for impressionable young readers because of its explicit description of premarital sex. Nevertheless, *The Western Wing* remained a fixture of the cultural landscape of the Ming (1368–1644) and Qing (1644–1911) dynasties and has endured as a popular story into the twenty-first century. Actually, the whiff of scandal that surrounded the play may well have facilitated its reception by China's modern reforming and revolutionary intellectuals during the May Fourth Movement of the 1920s. One aspect of the movement for cultural reform was the call for "free love": following the introduction of romantic love as the ultimate value in the early twentieth century, these intellectuals rejected the traditional system of arranged marriage and insisted on the freedom to choose their own marriage partners on the basis of love. Guo Moruo (1892–1978), an influential revolutionary poet, in his preface to the first modern edition of *The Western Wing* in 1921 (without Jin's commentary), hailed Wang Shifu's play (in his usual grandiloquent style) as "the most beautiful and most extraordinary" of all works of the Yuan dynasty, going so far as to declare, "*The Story of the Western Wing* is a work of art that transcends time and space and has an eternal and universal life. *The Story of the Western Wing* is the song and the monument celebrating the victory of human nature brimming with life over lifeless ritualism" [*GMR* 668–69]. Influenced by his readings in Sigmund Freud's psychoanalytic theories, he even suggested that the composition of the play originated in Wang Shifu's fetishistic obsession with bound feet. *The Western Wing* was also one of the earliest Chinese plays to be adapted for the screen when, in 1927, the husband-and-wife team of Hou Yao (1903–1942) as director and Pu Shunqing (1902–?) as scriptwriter collaborated to make a silent film that creatively used the possibilities of this new technology to come up with a highly original version, the first Chinese movie to be shown abroad (⏵ Visual Resources).

After 1949, in the wake of the reform of the marriage laws in the People's Republic of China, Wang's play came to be viewed as emblematic of the struggle of young people in the so-called feudal society to choose their own marriage partners without interference by their families. But whatever reasons critics in the past and present may invoke to enhance the status of the work, *The Western Wing* is first of all a consummate, lighthearted comedy about young people falling in love, encountering the opposition of the elder generation, but marrying happily in the end with the support of their friends and servants. This is, of course, a theme that has been popular on stage in East and West from earliest times—the Chinese twist to this theme being that the young man may end up not only with the lovely maiden, but also her equally adorable maid.

The Western Wing is set in the Tang dynasty. A short summary of the play reads as follows: On his way to the capital city of Chang'an (modern Xi'an), where Student Zhang plans to take the civil service examinations, he finds lodging at the Temple of Universal Salvation, a Buddhist monastery in southwest Shanxi. There, he catches a glimpse of a girl (Oriole), who is staying in the western wing of the same monastery with her mother and her maid (Crimson), and he falls head over heels in love with her. When he engineers to see her again at a service that the monks conduct for the benefit of Oriole's deceased father, he makes an utter fool of himself, as he is completely bewitched by her charms. Soon thereafter, mutinous soldiers led by Commander Sun Feihu lay siege to the monastery to claim the young woman.

When Oriole's mother promises to treat the man who will save her daughter as kin, Student Zhang writes a letter to his friend Du Que, who serves as a general nearby. Once alerted, Du Que quickly disperses the rebels, but when Student Zhang is invited to a celebratory banquet and expects to be given Oriole as his bride, her mother orders her to greet him as her brother. At the advice of Crimson, Student Zhang returns to his room and tries to seduce Oriole by playing the zither. Oriole indeed comes out to listen, but she disappears before he can speak with her. When, through the good offices of Crimson, he sends Oriole a poem declaring his love, Oriole sends him a poem in return, which he interprets as an invitation to visit her at night in her room in the monastery's western wing. But when he goes there, climbing over a wall to gain access, she sternly rebukes him for his improper behavior.

A desperate Student Zhang now falls ill. This time, it is Oriole who comes to his room and willingly gives herself to him. Their relationship is soon discovered by Oriole's mother, who is infuriated but then is persuaded by Crimson to assent to an engagement on the condition that Student Zhang passes his examinations. He departs for the capital, leaving Oriole behind, full of longing. But when he returns to the monastery after passing the examinations with flying colors, he discovers that Oriole's original fiancé, Zheng Heng, has also arrived to claim his bride. But all ends well when Du Que once again arrives in the nick of time, and the lovers are happily united in wedlock.

In what follows, we will examine three equally famous versions of the story—the early narrative rendition in "The Tale of Oriole" ("Yingying zhuan," alternatively translated as "The Story of Yingying" or "Biography of Yingying") by Yuan Zhen (779–831), a famous scholar-official of the Tang dynasty (617–906) (☛ *HTRCFiction-LC*, L06, *HTRCPIC*, chap. 16); the ballad version by Dong Jieyuan (fl. 1200), an otherwise unknown figure of the Jin dynasty (1115–1234); and Wang Shifu's play of the Yuan dynasty (1260–1368). While sharing a core cast of characters, each form made the plot mean something else: a literati meditation on the emotional toll of romance in the Tang tale, a tender and erotically charged lampooning of love-addled youngsters in the Jin ballad, and a celebration of a woman's transference of her allegiance to her groom's family upon marriage in the Yuan play. In the discussion of the three renditions, we will focus on how the needs of each form—prose narrative for a literate coterie, storytelling for a popular audience, and stage production for urban and court theaters—combined to make *The Western Wing* both a uniquely malleable but also uniquely enduring landmark of China's performative repertoire.

1.1 YUAN ZHEN'S "THE TALE OF ORIOLE"

The ultimate source for the plot of Wang Shifu's *The Western Wing* is the "The Tale of Oriole," by the well-known Tang dynasty poet and bureaucrat Yuan Zhen. Yuan's story does not end well: after Student Zhang finally succeeds in seducing Oriole, he eventually leaves for the capital to take his examinations, and once there, he decides to break up with her, even though he receives a touching letter from her in which she declares her abiding love. When Student Zhang later meets with her husband and asks to see her, she refuses to meet him and sends him a poem in which she urges him to love his current wife. This ending has been one of the most controversial aspects of Yuan's tale ever since it first appeared.

At the beginning of his story, Yuan Zhen stresses Student Zhang's lack of sexual experience even at the relatively advanced age of twenty-three: prior to his encounter with Oriole, whenever friends would ask him to come along to courtesan houses, he declined to join them, telling them that he did not care for mere sex and was waiting to meet his true partner. His high-minded innocence makes falling in love for the first time a very unsettling experience for him. Throughout the story, the focus of perception is on Student Zhang, which makes Oriole's actions all the more puzzling: after her initial shyness, she eventually joins him in his room on her own initiative. In the capital, however, Student Zhang declares that his mental stamina is no match for what he now considers Oriole's life-sapping charms. Ever since Western notions of true love entered China in the early twentieth century, Student Zhang's elaborate defense of his decision to abandon Oriole has been widely condemned by critics as the self-serving hypocrisy of an ambitious young man, eager to enter into a more advantageous marriage match after his examination success.

Yet, despite Student Zhang's ultimate rejection of Oriole, Yuan Zhen's "The Tale of Oriole" was a product of a culture of romance that started to develop in the early ninth century. This was a period in China's history when the development of the examination system, especially the growing prestige of the literary examination in the capital, brought increasing numbers of well-to-do young men to Chang'an to make connections, seek political patronage, and sit for the exams, a sojourn far from home that could extend over many years because the number of successful candidates at each exam was very small. As single young men about town, without parents to rein them in, these examination candidates became eager patrons of Chang'an's many courtesan houses. Previously, in a culture where family elders typically arranged marriages, passion (*qing*) was suspect and generally not viewed as a prerequisite for marriage. By contrast, these young men were now free to indulge in amorous pursuits and hence came to view passion as a positive attribute and a source of poetic inspiration, even if their love affairs with courtesans only rarely had a happy ending.

One of the rare tales of the love of a young examination candidate for a courtesan that ends happily was "The Tale of Li Wa" ("Li Wa zhuan"), written by Bai Xingjian (ca. 776–826), the younger brother of Yuan Zhen's bosom friend Bai Juyi (772–846). In this tale, a rich young man is smitten with the courtesan Li Wa and moves in with her. After he has spent all his money on her, she and her madam ditch him by a complicated house-moving trick. The young man survives first as a professional mourner, but he eventually ends up as a beggar. When by chance he passes by Li Wa's new establishment, she recognizes his voice and, filled with remorse, takes him in. She then nurses him back to health, supervises his studies, and is willing to let him go so he can marry a woman of comparable status after he has obtained an official appointment. But his father, who earlier had beaten his disgraced son almost to death, now insists that they get married because he is impressed by Li Wa's moral behavior. In the case of Yuan Zhen's "The Tale of Oriole," with its detailed descriptions of Student Zhang's emotions at each stage of the story, many readers through the ages have believed that the tale is highly autobiographical—that Student Zhang is only a thinly disguised alter ego of the author, Yuan Zhen. At least one famous modern scholar, Chen Yinke (1890–1969), has argued that the tale does not reflect a love affair of Yuan with a girl of his own class, but with a courtesan, which of course also would make it more understandable why he would feel compelled to abandon her.

1.2 STORY OF THE WESTERN WING IN ALL KEYS AND MODES: "THE TALE OF ORIOLE" IN NARRATIVE BALLADS

As a tale written in classical Chinese that also included an elaborate letter and several poems (one of which is very long), "The Tale of Oriole" was clearly intended by the author for a small reading public of understanding male friends. One of those, Li Shen (772–846), turned the story into a ballad in lines of seven-syllable verse, which likely contributed to the wider dissemination of the tale. By the eleventh century, not only did literati often discuss "The Tale of Oriole," but many entertainers told the story in outline form, often in versions that departed considerably from the original tale. This we learn from the adaptation of "The Tale of Oriole" by Zhao Lingzhi (1051–1134) as a drum song (*guzi ci*). This eleventh-century version alternates excerpts from Yuan Zhen's prose text with twelve lyrics (all to the same tune). It concludes with a short discussion on the propriety of Student Zhang's and Oriole's behavior. Importantly, the final two lyrics clearly censure Student Zhang for his betrayal of Oriole, indicating that performers and their audiences preferred a happy ending.

If it was not yet found before the eleventh century in popular ballads, such a happy reunion was at last offered in Dong Jieyuan's *Story of the Western Wing in All Keys and Modes* (*Xixiang ji zhugongdiao*), alternatively translated as *Master Tung's Western Chamber Romance*. This adaptation turned a short private tale of love and betrayal into a long and involved satiric romance with a happy ending. Whereas Yuan Zhen's text was intended for only a small circle of intimate friends, Dong Jieyuan wrote a script for one of the most demanding musically based performance genres of his time.

All we know about Dong is that he lived around the year 1200 in northern China, most likely in the capital of what was the Jurchen Jin dynasty (1115–1234), in the region of modern Beijing. "Jieyuan" is not his personal name; the expression typically refers to a person who is named first on the list of those who have passed a provincial examination. However, it is not clear whether it truly indicates Dong's examination status—he may also have been a professional entertainer who designated himself in this manner because of his remarkable erudition. Dong's *Story of the Western Wing in All Keys and Modes* is the only surviving complete text of an "all keys and modes" (*zhugongdiao*) ballad. This genre originated in the final years of the eleventh century, flourished in the twelfth and thirteenth centuries, and then disappeared from the stage in the fourteenth century (we know the name of the last person who was able to perform Dong's work in its entirety). The preferred subject matter of the genre was love.

The earliest known (but only partially preserved) "all keys and modes" ballad is the anonymous *Liu Zhiyuan in All Keys and Modes* (*Liu Zhiyuan zhugongdiao*), which deals with the marriage of the down-and-out farmhand Liu Zhiyuan to his employer's daughter, Li Sanniang. Upon the death of his father-in-law, his brothers-in-law chases the good-for-nothing Liu Zhiyuan from the farm, and when he becomes a soldier, he is forced to marry his commander's daughter. But as soon as he has done so, relatives deliver to him the baby that Li Sanniang had borne to him in the meantime. Liu Zhiyuan and Li Sanniang are only reunited twelve years later, when Liu has risen to a high rank.

We also only have extensive fragments of the last-known work in the genre, Wang Bocheng's *Anecdotal History of the Heavenly Treasure Era in All Keys and Modes* (*Tianbao yishi zhugongdiao*), which treats Emperor Xuanzong's (r. 712–756) infatuation with the full-bodied Yang Guifei (d. 756), who in this version of the tale cheats on her elderly patron with the even more portly An Lushan. The two male protagonists of these texts are very much fools for love, putty in the hands of women.

A fourth love story that we know was once adapted as an "all keys and modes" ballad was that of Shuang Jian and Su Xiaoqing. When the poor student Shuang Jian is on his way to the examinations, he falls in love with the courtesan Su Xiaoqing. After his departure for the capital, the madam tells Xiaoqing that her lover has died and sells her off to a rich tea merchant. When the couple's boat passes by Jinshan Monastery, near Zhenjiang, on their way to Jiangxi, Xiaoqing inscribes a lament on the wall of the pagoda. After Shuang Jian succeeds in the exams, he is appointed to a post in Nanchang, in Jiangxi, and, en route to his posting, finds Xiaoqing's lament at the monastery, pursues and catches up with the tea merchant's boat, and promptly abducts her. When the outraged tea merchant appeals to the authorities, they side with their newly appointed junior colleague and award Xiaoqing to Shuang Jian. This romance enjoyed equal billing with the tale of Student Zhang and Oriole between 1100 and 1450, but afterward was dropped from the repertoire, perhaps on account of Shuang Jian's unseemly abduction of someone else's wife.

The genre of the "all keys and modes" ballad derived its awkward name from its demanding musical structure. Traditional China knew a great many genres of prosimetric narrative. In the largest number of genres, prose passages alternate with passages written in verse made up of seven-syllable rhyming lines. The earliest examples of such genres are the so-called transformation texts (*bianwen*) found among the manuscripts discovered at Dunhuang and dating from the ninth and tenth centuries. In a smaller number of genres, including the "all keys and modes" ballad, the verse passages are written to heterometric tunes (so-called *qupai*), melodies that stipulate for each tune a specific number of lines of specific length, featuring a specific rhyme scheme. For its verse sections, the "all keys and modes" ballad used sets of songs (*taoshu*) performed in the same musical key or mode, but sets in the same mode or key could not follow each other. The large number of different melodies, in combination with the requirement to shift constantly from key to key, must have made the "all keys and modes" the most musically demanding genre of its time. This is reflected in its relatively high status; we have more information on this genre in contemporary sources than on all other genres of narrative ballad. As the genre developed, the musical demands on the performers only continued to grow because the song sets tended to become longer and longer. Whereas initially, a song set might be made up of only two stanzas of one melody followed by a coda, later on, the sets could run to ten or more melodies. Consisting of three (rather than four) lines of seven-syllable verse, the codas formally resembled an abbreviated quatrain and often ended on a clear punchline.

Any author of "all keys and modes" not only had to be acquainted with the musical demands of the genre, such as the specific requirements of each of the melodies at his disposal, but he also had to pay attention to the needs of the performance. "All keys and modes" ballads were performed in multiple installments, as a form of public entertainment in the theaters of the time. This meant that the male or female performer needed a cliffhanger at the end of each daily segment to entice audiences to return the next day to listen to the continuation of the story. But they also needed a cliffhanger somewhere in the middle of their daily segment, where they could interrupt their performance to make the round of their audiences to collect contributions—there was no point in trying to collect money at the end because many members of the audience might leave before they could reach them.

This division of cliffhangers is clearly visible in *The Story of the Western Wing in All Keys and Modes*. In the earliest preserved edition, dating from the sixteenth century, Dong's work is divided into eight "scrolls" (*juan*) that all—except for the last one, of course—end on a cliffhanger. Hence, it seems likely that each scroll corresponds to one day's entertainment. Moreover, each scroll contains at least one more cliffhanger, marked by a stereotypical question most often occurring about two-thirds of the way through.

To provide the performers with enough text to fill eight days of performance, Dong Jieyuan greatly expanded the narrative. Incidents such as the siege of the monastery, which had taken only a few words to describe in the classical tale, were developed at great length. Each character in the story was allowed to voice his or her feelings in multiple arias. In doing so, Dong freely drew upon the language of preceding poetic genres such as the poem (*shi*) and the song lyric (*ci*). The greatest beneficiaries of this strategy were the main protagonists, Student Zhang and Oriole, who in their many arias could now express the many and varied emotions that motivated their behavior. But minor characters also came to life in a new way, most notably Oriole's maid, Crimson. The young mistress's maid is a typical character of love comedies of both East and West, and Crimson now came into her own as the outspoken and daring servant. She may not have had a lover of her own in the story (Student Zhang's boy servant remains much of a nobody in all versions of *The Western Wing*), but she may well have an eye on Student Zhang herself (if her mistress ended up marrying Student Zhang, Crimson might have expected to accompany her to her new home and become a concubine of her husband). Other characters who are barely or not at all mentioned in the classical tale, but now acquire personalities of their own, include the monk who befriends Student Zhang at the monastery; Student Zhang's military friend, who now acquires the name of Du Que; and Oriole's original fiancé, Zheng Heng, who arrives at the monastery near the end of the "all keys and modes" ballad and makes a happy ending possible by committing suicide.

Dong Jieyuan further expanded his text by borrowing episodes from other famous love stories. Yuan Zhen's "The Tale of Oriole" did not contain an episode in which Student Zhang tries to seduce Oriole by playing his zither (*guqin*) at night in his room. His tale states that Oriole is an expert player of the zither, but when she performs in front of Student Zhang at his request, her performance is interrupted when she bursts into tears.

Dong Jieyuan clearly borrowed the episode of Student Zhang playing the zither to seduce Oriole from the immensely popular story of Sima Xiangru's seduction of Zhuo Wenjun. When the great poet Sima Xiangru (179–118 BCE) (☞ *HTRCP*, C3.1, *HTRCPIC*, chap. 3) fails in his first attempt to make a career at court and returns penniless to his native Sichuan, a friend of his, who happens to be the local magistrate, hatches a scheme of how he might seduce Zhuo Wenjun, the widowed teenage daughter of Zhuo Wangsun, the richest man in town. After the magistrate urges Zhuo Wangsun to invite the famous Sima Xiangru to his home for a banquet, Sima Xiangru arrives only after repeated requests. When he finally allows himself to be persuaded to play the zither, his performance and his song impress Zhuo Wenjun such that she elopes with him that very night, and when her father refuses to give her the dowry to which she is entitled, the couple shame him into paying up by opening a wine shop in the market of the provincial capital, Chengdu. Soon thereafter, Sima Xiangru is invited to the imperial court, where this time around his poetic talent is greatly admired. But where the cynical Sima succeeds in his seduction, the sincere Student Zhang fails. Oriole does come to the window of his room to listen to him play, but when he rushes out, he catches Crimson in his arms, not her mistress.

Other new plot elements in Dong Jieyuan's *Story of the Western Wing in All Keys and Modes* are borrowed from classical tales of the Tang dynasty. For instance, once Student Zhang has left for the capital to sit for the exams after his affair with Oriole has been discovered by her mother, he hears Oriole knocking at his door after he has taken to bed for the night at an inn. This element is clearly borrowed from "The Tale of the Disembodied Soul" ("Lihun ji"), in which a departing student is followed by his beloved, who will eventually bear him two children—only when the couple visits her natal home does the student learn that he has been living with the girl's soul, while her body has stayed with her parents. As in the case of the borrowed elements of the story of Sima Xiangru and Zhuo Wenjun, Dong Jieyuan provides his audience with a different denouement: as soon as Student Zhang lets Oriole inside and takes her to bed, Sun Feihu's soldiers burst into the room to carry her off, whereupon he wakes up startled, only to realize that Oriole's visit was a dream.

For the final happy ending of his ballad, Dong Jieyuan contrived a story that relied heavily on conventional plot elements. After passing the examinations successfully, Student Zhang falls ill, so he cannot travel. This delay in his return allows Oriole's original fiancé, Zheng Heng, to hasten to the monastery, where he tells the widow that Student Zhang has been forced by the prime minister to marry his daughter when an embroidered ball she threw into a crowd of suitors to select a husband struck him (as far as we know, no high-born young lady in China ever selected a groom in this way except in stories and plays). Convinced by Zheng Heng's story, the widow thereupon once again changes her mind and decides to entrust her daughter to him. When Student Zhang returns to the monastery and is invited to a welcome banquet, he finds that Oriole is seated between her mother and Zheng Heng.

His hopes dashed once again, a frustrated Student Zhang that night shares his room with the monk Facong, who earlier had fought his way through the ranks of the rebels besieging the monastery to deliver his letter to Du Que. Once again willing to come to Student Zhang's aid, Facong now offers to kill the widow and abduct Oriole. This episode reminds one of "The Tale of Lady Willow" ("Liu shi zhuan"), a Tang dynasty tale in which a dashing military man reunites an impecunious poet and his lady love by abducting her from the harem of a mighty general. But before Facong can follow through, Oriole and Crimson enter Student Zhang's room. When the desperate lovers contemplate suicide, Facong suggests that they instead elope and seek the protection of Du Que. The lovers, accompanied by Crimson, follow his advice. When Zheng Heng appears in court early the next day to lay plaint, Du Que shames him into killing himself by dashing his head against the floor and spilling his brains all over. This ghastly denouement sets the scene for Student Zhang and Oriole's wedding celebration. The unsuccessful appeal to a judge by the man who believes that he is the rightful husband of an eloped wife was also found, as we saw earlier in this chapter, in the love story of Shuang Jian and Su Xiaoqing.

In the Chinese classification of genres, the "all keys and modes" ballad may be grouped with *zaju* plays as *qu* songs because both genres employ northern tunes, and because the rules for organizing these tunes into sets within the "all keys and modes" genre in many ways prefigure the later rules of the organization of tunes into sets in *zaju*. But whereas *zaju* plays rely on the actions and dialogue (in prose or in verse) of the actors to present their stories, "all keys and modes" is a genre of performed storytelling: a single narrator tells and sings the story, taking on the different voices (male and female, old and young, high-class and low-born, civil and martial) of the many characters in the narrative. If Dong Jieyuan also performed his own text, we could compare him to Chaucer reading the latest installment of his *Canterbury Tales* to the English court, even if Dong's audience would not have been limited to royalty and their hangers-on.

But as the "all keys and modes" ballad is a narrative, the author also allows the narrator in the text every opportunity to indulge in description and commentary. The descriptive passages are not limited to the actions and feelings of the characters in the narrative; they also detail the setting of the action in time and place to make sure that it harmonizes with the mood of the protagonists. As a narrative, *The Story of the Western Wing in All Keys and Modes* is also not bound to the role system of traditional theater. Dong Jieyuan was at liberty to develop the characterization of his protagonists according to his own vision, unconstrained by any fully developed role system that would greatly affect how Wang Shifu conceived his characters.

As a rule, great lovers tend to be either great heroes or great fools, and Student Zhang is definitely no great hero—his most heroic action is dashing off a note to his friend Du Que. If there is a heroic character in Dong's work, it is not so much Du Que, who only functions as a deus ex machina at crucial points, but the monk Facong, who delivers Student Zhang's letter at the risk of his life. But, as we just saw, Dong denies him the opportunity of a second heroic act by rescuing Oriole from the boorish Zheng Heng. As a lover, Student Zhang is depicted by Dong as a great fool, and he does so in broad strokes.

If Yuan Zhen was very much in sympathy with his Student Zhang, Dong Jieyuan happily holds him up to ridicule. The Japanese scholar Tanaka Kenji, who was one of the first to discuss *The Story of the Western Wing in All Keys and Modes* in detail, even went so far as to call Dong's characterization of Student Zhang a caricature. Once Student Zhang has fallen in love, he makes a fool of himself at every turn and is an easy dupe of Oriole's mother, and of Oriole herself. Not knowing how to go about winning Oriole's heart, he can only follow the suggestions of the wily Crimson, and it is also only this intrepid maid who convinces Oriole's mother that she has no other option but to allow her daughter to marry her lover. Student Zhang may be able to dash off a poem, but even after he has passed the exams, he is at a loss for what to do when, upon his triumphal return to the monastery, he is confronted with Zheng Heng's presence—together with Oriole, he can only contemplate suicide.

Such a satiric portrayal of a student who is utterly unable to manage the problems in his personal life (and so cannot be expected to be of much use in managing the country once appointed as an official) may well have been intended to make fun of literati more in general, but that does not automatically mean that the author was criticizing the social system as such. Depicting those who fall short of the norms of their class may also be understood as emphasizing the value of those very norms: by showing how ludicrous one becomes by forgetting these norms, the audience is only encouraged to uphold them better. If Student Zhang still has much to learn as a student, he may seek a model in his foil, Du Que, who brings order to society as both a general and a judge. But for all the importance of the social satire in this text, which also takes aim at the majority of Buddhist monks portrayed as sex-starved cowards, at the mutinying soldiers out to abduct maidens, at the clever maids that enable affairs and outwit their superiors, and at the smug offspring of high officials, the author may also have hinted at a hidden message in his narrator's self-introduction. Prosimetric narratives often start with an introduction in which the narrator provides a historical survey from the beginning of time to the period in which the story in question supposedly took place. Dong Jieyuan preceded his "all keys and modes" ballad with a highly original self-introduction, in which the narrator claims to be an expert in the art of love:

【醉落魄纏令】   *To the tune* "Zuiluopo chanling"
秦樓謝館鴛鴦幄，   Behind the bed-curtains of the best bordellos
風流稍是有聲價。   My savoir-faire is very much famed.
教惺惺浪兒每都伏咱。   I have the smartest playboys all yield to me.
不曾胡來，   Never once have I made a mess of things—
俏倬是生涯。   Sophistication is my style of life!

[*DXY* 1]

The narrator proceeds to tell China's most famous love story, not shying away from explicit descriptions of sex. It has been suggested that the story, as told in *The Story of the Western Wing in All Keys and Modes*, may even be read as an allegory on the arts of the bedchamber—why else would the narrator vaunt his savoir-faire in the "best bordellos"? One point of note here is that Dong's work, now universally acknowledged as one of the masterworks of traditional Chinese literature, was repeatedly reprinted in the liberal atmosphere of the late Ming dynasty, but it was practically forgotten during the nearly three centuries of the more puritanical Qing dynasty.

1.3 *THE STORY OF THE WESTERN WING*: STUDENT ZHANG AND ORIOLE ON STAGE

Dong Jieyuan's *Story of the Western Wing in All Keys and Modes* invites one to imagine how one would present the text if one were a performer: how to distinguish description from narrative, how to voice the various dialogue, and how to sing the many songs to achieve the maximum impact on one's audience. In the same way, it makes sense to ask oneself how one would stage the play when reading Wang Shifu's *The Western Wing*. But to do so, one must set aside the realistic conventions that have dominated modern theatrical performance in the West. Neither should one think of the over-the-top dramatic acting conventionally associated with Italian opera. More important still, we had better bracket what we know about the performance of traditional Chinese opera in modern and contemporary times—there is no reason to assume that Chinese actors of the thirteenth century performed their plays in the highly stylized manner of contemporary Peking opera or sang their arias in the long, drawn-out manner of contemporary Kunqu opera (☞ chap. 8). This is because the theatrical genre used by Wang Shifu has very much its own characteristics. With its equal emphasis on music and text and its relatively simple acting style, early *zaju* song-drama might be meaningfully compared to nineteenth-century Gilbert and Sullivan operas.

By the time Wang Shifu was writing, theater—that is, the enactment by one or more persons of a narrative through action, gesture, and dialogue before an audience—had a long history in China. A wide range of skits, farces, and more developed plays were performed as part of the variety shows that offered entertainment in the playhouses of big cities during the Song dynasty. Another performance venue, found all over China, were the temple stages where various kinds of entertainments such as song and dance were presented to please the gods on their festival days.

From the twelfth century onward, south of the Yangzi River, we can follow the emergence of a theatrical genre that consisted of long plays, presumably written for performance on temple stages and requiring a large cast. Like all other genres of traditional Chinese theater, this southern genre was a kind of ballad opera, as the text consisted largely of arias sung to well-known local tunes. Whereas ballad opera always remained a very minor mode in the Western tradition, it became the dominant form of theater in the Chinese tradition. Practically all actors in these southern plays would be assigned arias. This genre, first known as "Wenzhou *zaju*" and later as "early southern drama" (*xiwen, nanxi*), would eventually develop into the "mature southern drama" (*chuanqi*) of the sixteenth century and beyond (🖝 chap. 7). Performed in local dialects to local tunes, it took a long time before this genre had any impact north of the Huai River.

In northern China, a major breakthrough occurred somewhere around the middle of the thirteenth century, when local playwrights started to incorporate long sets of songs such as those in the "all keys and modes" ballads into their plays. The man who is credited with that breakthrough is Guan Hanqing, an extremely prolific playwright in the second half of the thirteenth century in Dadu, the capital of the Mongol Yuan dynasty (present-day Beijing; 🖝 chap. 3). In the *zaju* as practiced by Guan, the core of the play consisted of four sets of eight to twenty northern songs; the tunes in each set belonged to the same key or mode, and the songs of a single set would maintain the same rhyme (or at least assonance). These four sets of songs were all assigned to a single male or female performer. As the other actors in the play spoke only in prose, this musical convention created a highly asymmetrical format. Whereas it seems an almost universal rule for stage performances that both parties in the central dramatic conflict get equal time to voice their views, in *zaju*, only one of them will be allowed to express his or her impressions and emotions, feelings and opinions in detail. As a consequence, the action on stage may well have been rather static whenever the actors or actresses who had been assigned the songs availed themselves of the opportunity to showcase their vocal talents.

The song sets defined the overall structure of the *zaju* play as conceived by Guan Hanqing and later playwrights and editors. Each set of songs could be preceded by a so-called wedge (*xiezi*) made up of one or two songs, and on rare occasions, the final set of songs would be followed by two or three more songs. Usually one set of songs would form the core of a major scene, and so later editors divided *zaju* into four acts (*zhe*) on the basis of its musical structure. The 1499 edition of *The Western Wing* was the first *zaju* imprint to explicitly adopt this convention (🖝 chap. 4). In drama scripts, dialogue was, at least initially, only a secondary element. The printed editions of individual *zaju* that have been preserved from the fourteenth century basically limit themselves to the four sets of songs of the lead performer and his or her cue lines, and it is not clear whether the playwrights at this stage already wrote out the full dialogue of all the secondary actors in each play. Most likely, they trusted professional actors to be able to ad-lib their lines once they had been acquainted with the plot. This stage practice was still widely encountered in many genres of traditional local theater in China until quite recently. In terms of print, we have to wait until the early fifteenth century, when an imperial prince had his own plays printed with the advertisement that they came "with the complete dialogues," a practice emulated by the literati editors of drama in the sixteenth and seventeenth centuries who edited earlier plays for reading (☞ Introduction, chaps. 2 and 5).

When Wang Shifu set out to adapt Dong Jieyuan's *Story of the Western Wing in All Keys and Modes* for the stage as a *zaju*, he had several options. For instance, he could have decided to turn Dong's work into a regular *zaju* built around four sets of songs. In doing so, the most logical choice might have been to assign the four sets of songs to Student Zhang, but he also might have chosen to assign them to Oriole, which would have resulted in a quite different play. In both cases, he would have had to decide which scenes were going to be central to the play in such a way that they would allow the full expression of emotion in each scene.

When Wang Shifu adapted the romance of Shuang Jian and Su Xiaoqing, which also circulated as "all keys and modes," we are probably justified in believing that that lost play was a regular *zaju*. But in the case of his adaptation of the story of Student Zhang and Oriole, he took the unprecedented step of turning Dong's work into a series of five full-fledged *zaju*, and in yet another break with convention, he did not assign the four sets of songs in each play to a single performer, instead distributing the twenty sets over three performers who played Student Zhang, Crimson, and Oriole, respectively. Furthermore, in the second play, he inserted a short set of songs to be performed by Huiming, the fighting monk who delivers Student Zhang's letter to Du Que when rebels besiege the monastery. Only in the first and third plays are the sets of songs assigned to a single character (Student Zhang and Crimson, respectively). In yet another break with *zaju* convention, Wang Shifu, having several fine singers on stage, occasionally allowed a second character to sing one or more songs of another character's set. Modern audiences, of course, are acquainted with far more complex and spectacular operatic performances, but for the original audiences, these departures from the rules must have been startlingly original. For all the literary qualities of the texts that have come down to us, especially Wang Shifu's *The Western Wing*, we should bear in mind that in its heyday, *zaju* drama was primarily a genre of musical theater (unfortunately, that music has largely been lost) (☞ Introduction, chap. 8).

We do not know why Wang Shifu made the remarkable decision to turn the story of Student Zhang and Yingying into a series of five *zaju*. Perhaps Dong's work enjoyed such popularity that he wanted to retain as much of its material as possible. Even though Wang Shifu's play closely followed the story as told by Dong Jieyuan, the shift from third-person to first-person narrative in the play required a number of changes. While Wang borrowed heavily from Dong's language, he could not simply take over the songs as written by Dong because despite some similarities, the musical structures of *zaju* and of "all keys and modes" ballads were quite different. In the earlier genre, the length of the song sets was determined by the needs of the plot and the whims of the author, but in *zaju*, each set was of comparable length. And in "all keys and modes" ballads, the only rule that governed the sequence of modes had been that no sets in the same mode could directly follow each other, while in *zaju*, each play started with a set of songs in one specific key, to be followed in the majority of cases by a set of songs in yet another specific key. As a result, even many songs that had been written by Dong in the voice of one of the characters had to be rewritten to fit a different tune, in a different key or mode. Moreover, a *zaju* performance on the bare stages of the Yuan could not do without evocative descriptions of scenery and season, which meant that many of Dong's third-person songs had to be rewritten as the impressions and emotions of the singing role.

Whereas Dong Jieyuan wrote his work as sixteen major sections with all (except the last) ending on a cliff-hanger, Wang had to reorganize that content into twenty major scenes that each formed a more or less coherent whole in terms of central character, action, and mood. While the audience at the end of each of these major scenes was invited to wonder how the action would develop, these scenes did not end on a typical cliffhanger. Such a reorganization of materials was bound to result in a host of changes and transpositions large and small. Wang Shifu also used this opportunity to tighten up the plot, for instance by mentioning both Du Que and Zheng Heng at the earliest opportunity. He greatly cut down the description of the siege of the monastery, probably because the limited size of a traditional stage and of a standard *zaju* company could not accommodate such a massive scene. The most important change in content, however, may well not be due to the form of the play, but to its function.

While we lack all materials on the early staging history of Wang's play, in view of its length, it is highly unlikely that it was intended for performance in the context of the variety shows that were offered by the urban theaters. It appears more likely to me that Wang's play was intended for performance at a large-scale festive event, most likely a wedding in a noble or rich family, a point to which I will return later in this chapter. As an auspicious offering at such a celebration, the play would have to end on a happy note in a grand reunion scene in order to bring good luck to the assembled audience. Under these circumstances, the play could not end with Oriole's elopement and an unhealed rift between mother and daughter. Hence, Wang moved the final scene to the monastery, where Du Que, who earlier had been a witness to Madame Cui's promise to treat Student Zhang as kin, now arrives to attend the wedding. A shamefaced Zheng Heng still commits suicide, but at least Oriole's mother joins the wedding banquet at the end of the play.

In the People's Republic of China, while Wang's play was praised for its socially progressive character by Marxist critics, it was hotly debated whether Dong's ending or Wang's conclusion was more progressive. If the theme of the story is a struggle against the values and conventions of the old society, an elopement would seem to betray more fighting spirit—Tian Han (1898–1968), in his 1958 adaption of *The Western Wing* as a Peking opera, opted to end with the rebellious elopement.

The most important changes in Wang's adaptation, however, result from the need to fit the characters to the available role types in drama. Throughout its long history, traditional Chinese drama has worked with role types (🞂 Introduction) that may be compared to the division of labor in a traditional stock company or the way in which voices are related to roles in the tradition of Italian opera. The basic lineup of role-types in *zaju* is based on the tripartite division of *mo*, *dan*, and *jing*. An actor or actress classified as *mo* (male) plays the roles of positive, young male characters, and therefore this person is the logical choice to play the young lover in a love comedy. An actor or actress who is classified as *dan* (female) is expected to play the roles of positive young women, and therefore this performer is expected to play the lover's object of affection in a love comedy. Women of an elderly generation will be played by a *laodan* (elderly female). Saucy female characters will be played by a *huadan* (flowery female), and bawdy and evil female characters will be performed by a *chadan* (painted female). An actor or actress trained as *jing* was expected to play the roles of clowns and villains (including low-class elderly women like professional matchmakers). Additional characters might be performed by *wai* (extras). If we compare *zaju* to Italian opera, the *mo* shows a certain similarity to the tenor, the *dan* to the soprano, and the *huadan* to the soubrette.

The *dan*, of course, was the logical choice of role type for Oriole, as she is a young woman who will experience all the thralls of passion, ranging from exuberant joy to deepest sorrow. She is assigned three of the four regular sets of songs that make up the second play, which starts with the siege of the monastery by the rebel troops. Upon her first entrance in this second play, Oriole starts by confessing to what extent she has been struck by the sight of Student Zhang, but she is immediately informed that rebel troops are laying siege to the monastery and demanding her person. Following the relief of the siege, the second regular set of songs is assigned to Crimson, who invites Student Zhang to the banquet thrown by Madame Cui to thank him for his assistance, where Oriole's hand, so he believes, will be offered to him in marriage. Oriole then again sings the two final sets of songs of the second play. The first of these two records her reactions when her mother reneges on her promise to give her daughter to the man who would save her and concludes with the scene in which Student Zhang tries to seduce her by playing the zither. Oriole also sings the first set of songs of the fifth act—the final set of songs, officially assigned to Student Zhang, will be jointly performed by the lovers, who, now united in marriage, are singing *unisono*.

The character that benefited most from Wang Shifu's decision to assign the songs to different roles no doubt is Crimson, who sings the four sets of songs of the third play. This turns her into one of the major protagonists of the play, on par with Student Zhang and Oriole. The four acts of this play show her busily going back and forth between Student Zhang and Oriole as a *postilion d'amour*, taking poems from one to the other, and she is there in the third act to witness how the hopeful Student Zhang gets a terrible tongue-lashing from Oriole. As she observes the outpouring of emotions on the part of Student Zhang and the feigned indifference of her mistress, she provides sardonic commentary on the actions of her confounded social betters. In the final act of the third play, she can finally bring Student Zhang the note in which Oriole promises that she will visit him that night in his room. Crimson assumes once again the singing role in the second act of the fourth play—her finest moment in the entire series—when she is questioned by Oriole's mother about her daughter's behavior and manages to convince the old woman that she has no choice but to give Oriole in marriage to Student Zhang. Crimson also takes the singing role in the third act of the fifth play, when she is allowed to tell off the competing suitor, Zheng Heng. All told, Wang Shifu's *The Western Wing* turned Crimson into one of the most beloved characters of the Chinese stage (➤ chap. 4).

The practically unavoidable decision of Wang Shifu to have Student Zhang performed by a *mo* did not work out equally well. Whereas Dong Jieyuan had had a field day in making fun of Student Zhang, the assigned role type in the play of the *mo* militated against such a portrayal. Student Zhang is still often a figure of fun, of course, but the edge of the satire is blunted: if the "all keys and modes" ballad invites an ironic distance in the audience through its third-person narrative, the play invites us to sympathize with Student Zhang as we are swept up by the intensity of the emotions expressed in his songs. If Crimson is allowed to comment on his actions with mordant wit in the second and third plays, she is at the same time shown to assist him in his endeavors to approach Oriole, who may renege on her word at times but is burning with love the whole time. If the women who matter love him so much, Student Zhang must have the endearing traits of a romantic hero. He is allowed all four sets of songs of the first play to gain the audience's sympathy. He sings two sets of songs in the fourth play: the first describes the joy and happiness of the first night he sleeps with Oriole, while the second details his despondency after he has departed for the capital, his joy when Oriole joins him in his room at the inn, his fright when she is next abducted by soldiers, and his relief to find out that it was only a dream. Student Zhang has two more sets of songs in the final play: in the second act, he is still in the capital, where he receives Oriole's letter and her presents; and in the final act, he is reunited with Oriole, this time for good.

1.4 CONTROVERSIES IN THE MING AND QING DYNASTIES

The penultimate song of the final act reads:

【清江引】   *To the tune* "Qing Jiang yin"
謝當今盛明唐聖主。   We thank the Present Sagely and Enlightened ruler of the Tang
勅賜為夫婦。   Who bestowed on us a Decree making us man and wife:
永老無別離。   For all eternity without separation,
萬古常完聚。   For all infinity forever united—
願普天下有情的都成了眷屬。   May lovers of the whole world all be united in wedlock!

[*XXJ* 193; trans. West and Idema (1995), 285]

This concluding wish appears to make this play the perfect choice for a performance in celebration of a wedding. In view of the preceding song (sung to the tune of "Jin shang hua") by Student Zhang in praise of the present imperial administration, one may even wonder whether the play perhaps was originally composed in celebration of a princely wedding, to be performed in the imperial palace, or whether the text as we have it in the Hongzhi edition was based on a revision in preparation for such a performance. To understand why this play might be a suitable choice for such an occasion, we have to realize that a wedding in traditional China did not so much celebrate the union of two young people, but primarily celebrated that the groom's family had acquired a bride. While the young man was expected to continue to live with his parents after marriage, the bride was expected to transfer her filial feelings of allegiance from her own parents to her new kin.

Modern critics in the People's Republic of China often read Wang's play as a subversive text that taught young people to struggle for the freedom to choose their own marriage partner. But if there is any struggle in *The Western Wing*, it occurs in the mind of Oriole, who may fall in love with Student Zhang quickly enough, but who has already been engaged to someone else and wants to be a good daughter. If her behavior may appear contradictory at times, the conflicting emotions are easily understood. Even after her mother has gone back on her promise, she still cannot give in to Zhang's pleas, and even when she seems to have done so, she recoils and sends him off with a stern lecture. But a happy marriage can come about only when the girl freely, and of her own accord, joins her husband to enjoy all the attendant pleasures, and so it is Oriole who has to join Student Zhang in his room. Once that happens, all problems can be solved. As the enactment of a young woman shifting her emotional attachments from her own family to her groom, *The Western Wing* would seem to be a most fitting entertainment when a family welcomed a bride and offered well wishes for a happy marriage.

Admittedly, *The Western Wing* had its detractors in the Ming and Qing dynasties. Moralists of all ages decried Wang's work as "a book that teaches lechery" and claimed to be scandalized by the premarital sex in the play. In his extensive commentary, the seventeenth-century critic Jin Shengtan went to great length to argue that the premarital sex was not actually premarital sex because Student Zhang and Oriole had become man and wife the moment that he saved her from the defiling hands of the bandit Sun Feihu by writing his letter. To support his argument, Jin Shengtan was not beyond adapting the text. It was his sanitized print version of *The Western Wing* that circulated widely during the Qing dynasty (and served as the basis for the earliest Western translations). In this connection, it is interesting to see how the play is discussed in the famous eighteenth-century novel *Dream in the Red Chamber* (*Honglou meng*; also translated as *Story of the Stone*) (➤ HTRCFiction, chap. 12). When Lin Daiyu, one of the young heroines of the novel and the embodiment of unfulfilled passion, becomes totally absorbed in the declarations of love and longing in *The Western Wing* and quotes it in a game, she is chided by Xue Baochai, one of the novel's other young females. The prim and proper Baochai admits that she and her female cousins had read the play behind the backs of her brothers and male cousins—who had in turn read the book behind the backs of their elders—but then she warns Lin Daiyu against reading love stories with the following words:

> As for girls like you and me: pinning and sewing are our proper business. What do we need to be able to read for? But since we can read, let us confine ourselves to good improving books; let us avoid like the plague those pernicious works of fiction, which so undermine the character that in the end it is past reclaiming.
>
> [*HLM* 449; trans. Hawkes, 334]

But when, later in the novel, the same Baochai feigns ignorance of the names of the protagonists of *The Western Wing* and *Peony Pavilion: The Soul's Return*, (☞ chap. 9) she is berated as too "stuffy" by yet another character in the novel, who points out that they all have seen performances of those plays:

> There can't be a man, woman, or child who isn't familiar with them. And even if one knows them from the *books*, it can hardly be said that to have read a few lyrics from *The Western Wing* or *The Soul's Return* is tantamount to reading pornography.
>
> [*HLM* 550; trans. Hawkes, 515]

The fact that *The Western Wing* aroused passions did not mean that it was a prohibited work. Even if the title may have appeared occasionally on lists of obscene books, it continued to circulate freely, often in gorgeously rendered editions.

Theater aficionados of the late imperial period also discussed other issues, such as the play's authorship. All sources of the Yuan and early Ming dynasties agree about crediting the authorship of the play to Wang Shifu. During the sixteenth century, however, when information on Yuan drama was rare and hard to come by, some scholars claimed that the play was the work of Guan Hanqing—after all, it must have made sense to assume that the most famous *zaju* play was written by the most famous *zaju* author (☞ chap. 3, *HTRCP*, C16.7). When other scholars who wished to follow the old ascription to Wang Shifu suggested that the play might have been the work of them both, the division of labor between these two authors became an issue: Had Wang written the first four plays and Guan the final one, or was it the other way around? Those who believed that Guan had authored the first four plays would then argue that the fifth play was only a second-rate sequel.

One theory held that Wang Shifu, overcome by emotion, had dropped the brush in the middle of the parting scene in the third act of the fourth play, and that Guan Hanqing had finished the work. Jin Shengtan, who included the fifth play in his commentary edition, would argue at length that the play actually ended in the final act of the fourth play, when Student Zhang awakes and realizes that not only was his dream of Oriole that night only a figment of passion, but his whole past affair with her was but a flash of passion: as a memory of the past, no more than a dream (☞ chap. 4). Whatever merit Jin Shengtan's reading of *The Western Wing* may have, it was not only a boon to translators, who felt absolved from the duty to translate the fifth play, but also to modern adaptors of the play like playwright Ma Shaobo (1918–2009), who had to fit his Kunqu adaptation into the format of an evening's entertainment (I attended a performance of this adaptation on October 5, 1983, in Beijing) (chap. 8).

One of the many reasons why later scholars have continued to question Wang Shifu's role in the composition of *The Western Wing* is that the Wang who emerges from a reading of his other preserved works is only a rather mediocre author. None of his other works have achieved a status anywhere comparable to that of *The Western Wing*—if Wang Shifu was indeed the author of *The Western Wing*, he was very much a one-hit wonder. A number of modern scholars who doubt Wang's authorship (and realize that none of the early sources credits the work to Guan) have tried to argue that the play cannot be by Wang because it could not have been written during his lifetime, but only a century later, in the late fourteenth century. As most of their arguments are rather subjective, their thesis has not been adopted more generally, and the overwhelming majority of contemporary scholars is willing to accept Wang Shifu as the author of *The Western Wing*.

But we know next to nothing about the life and thought of Wang, so ascribing the play to him provides no clue as to the interpretation of the play. Our earliest catalogue of *zaju* only states that Wang was, like Guan, "a man of Dadu (modern Beijing)," and credits him with fourteen plays besides *The Western Wing*, only two of which are still extant. Most likely, he was, like Guan Hanqing, a highly educated professional playwright who met the urgent need for new material in the burgeoning commercial theater of his time. And if William Shakespeare could write occasionally for the court, why not Wang Shifu?

CONCLUSION

In imperial China, drama was first of all considered as entertainment. When in the final years of the Qing dynasty, an early Japanese history of Chinese literature was adapted for use in Chinese schools, the chapters on drama and fiction were deleted. This occurred because in traditional China, drama and fiction were not considered part of high literature. That changed with the May Fourth movement, when—under Western influence—drama and fiction came to be seen as major genres of literature, on a par with poetry and essayistic prose. This meant not only that modern Chinese authors established their reputation via their fiction and drama, but also that the major works of premodern fiction and drama now were studied and taught in universities at a safe distance from the hurly-burly of the theater. As a consequence, plays more often than not were read in the same way as poetry and fiction, as drama also was read for its literary qualities and—perhaps even more important—as an expression of the moral stature and the thought of the author. Such close readings of the text as a literary artifact are of course extremely important and may result in original insights into almost every aspect of the work.

In this chapter, however, I have tried to stress the nature of *The Western Wing* as a play by showing how the story was shaped by the practical demands of genre as it moved from classical tale, to narrative ballad, to *zaju* play. As Wang Shifu adapted Dong Jieyuan's long ballad for the stage, he confronted many concrete questions.

In solving these problems, he was very much constrained by the conventions of the genre he worked in, but at the same time, he had the daring originality to produce a five-play set of plays rather than a single *zaju*, to assign the song sets to multiple performers, and even to have them perform together.

For all his indebtedness to his predecessors, Wang created a play that would remain hugely popular on stage and in print for seven centuries. *The Western Wing* can be viewed as a formative influence behind every other successful romantic Chinese play of the Ming and Qing dynasties. If the direct influence of *The Western Wing* on the portrayal of love in fiction, drama, and movies may have become less pronounced as the twentieth century proceeded, it gained an eminent position in Chinese literary history as a paean to free love.

Wilt L. Idema

NOTES

  1. The title has also been translated as *The Romance of the Western Chamber* and *Romance of the Western Bower*.

PRIMARY SOURCES

DJY   Dong Jieyuan 董解元. *Dong Jieyuan Xixiang ji* 董解元西廂記 (*Master Dong's* Story of the Western Wing in All Keys and Modes). Ann. Ling Jiangyan 凌景埏. Beijing: Renmin wenxue chubanshe, 1962.

GMR   Guo Moruo 郭沫若. *Guo Moruo gudian wenxue lunwenji* 郭沫若古典文學論文集 (*Guo Moruo's* Collected Essays on Classical Chinese Literature). Shanghai: Shanghai guji wenxue chubanshe, 1985.

HLM   Cao Xueqin 曹雪芹. *Honglou meng bashihui jiaoben* 紅樓夢八十回校本 (*The Collated 80-Chapter Version of* The Dream of the Red Chamber). Coll. Yu Pingbo 俞平伯 and Wang Xishi 王惜時. Beijing: Renmin wenxue chubanshe, 1958.

XXJ   Wang Shifu 王實甫. *Xixiang ji* 西廂記 (*The Story of the Western Wing*). Ann. Wang Jisi 王季思. Shanghai: Shanghai guji chubanshe, 1978.

SUGGESTED READINGS

TRANSLATIONS

Cao Xueqin. *The Story of the Stone: The Crab-flower Club.* Vol. 2. Trans. David Hawkes. Harmondsworth, UK: Penguin Books, 1977.

Dong Jieyuan. *Master Tung's Western Chamber Romance (Tung Hsi-hsiang chu-kung-tiao), A Chinese Chantefable.* Trans. Li-li Ch'en. Cambridge: Cambridge University Press, 1976.

Yuan Zhen. "The Story of Yingying." Trans. James R. Hightower. In James R. Hightower, "Yüan Chen and the 'The Story of Yingying,'" *Harvard Journal of Asiatic Studies* 33 (1975): 90–123.

Yuan Zhen. "*Yingying zhuan*: Biography of Yingying." Trans. Stephen Owen; essays by Pauline Yu, Wai-yee Li, Katherine Carlitz, and Peter Bol. In *Ways with Words: Writing about Reading Texts from Early China*, ed. Pauline Yu, Peter Bol, Stephen Owen, and Willard Peterson, 173–201. Berkeley: University of California Press, 2000.

Wang Shifu. *The Moon and the Zither: The Story of the Western Wing.* Trans. and introd. Stephen H. West and Wilt L. Idema, with a study of the woodblock illustrations by Yao Dajuin. Berkeley: University of California Press, 1991.

Wang Shifu. *The Romance of the Western Chamber (Hsi hsiang chi).* Trans. S.I. Hsiung. Introd. C. T. Hsia. New York: Columbia University Press, 1968.

Wang Shifu. *The Story of the Western Wing.* Trans. and introd. Stephen H. West and Wilt L. Idema. Berkeley: University of California Press, 1995.

ENGLISH

Wang, John Ching-yu. *Chin Sheng-t'an*. New York: Twayne, 1972.

CHINESE

Wang Shifu 王實甫. *Jin Shengtan piping Xixiang ji* 金聖嘆批本西廂記 (*Jin Shengtan's Edition* of The Story of the Western Wing). Ann. Zhang Guoguang 張國光. Shanghai: Shanghai guji chubanshe, 1986.

Wang Shifu 王實甫. *Xinkan qimiao quanxiang zhushi Xixiang ji* 新刊奇妙全相注釋西廂記 (*A Newly Printed, Deluxe, Completely Illustrated and Annotated* Story of the Western Wing). Shanghai: Shangwu yinshuguan, 1955.

Wang Shifu 王實甫. *Xixiang ji* 西廂記 (*The Story of the Western Wing*). Ann. Wu Xiaoling 吳曉鈴. Hong Kong: Zhonghua shuju, 1974.

2

Purple Clouds, Wrong Career,
and *The Tiger Head Plaque*

Jurchen Foreigners in Early Drama

The representation of the foreign in Chinese drama is a largely understudied topic, and perhaps for good reason: it is an interesting but complicated subject. On the one hand, the Yuan dynasty (1271–1368) was a cosmopolitan society with a multi-ethnic and polyglot population that extended across the Mongol world from Europe to India to China to Mongolia. On the other hand, the Yuan ruling elite, the Mongols with their Central Asian administrators and Chinese officials, did not censor the production of texts in any of the written languages in the regions under their rule (Chinese, Uyghur, Mongolian, Persian, etc.). Accordingly, one would expect that the foreign would be well represented in the literary corpus, particularly in a form of drama that catered to urbanites and the court alike. Surprisingly, this is not the case.

There are many reasons for why this is so. Most important perhaps, the majority of shorter stage performances noted as being produced in North China between 1115–1275, as well as those fully formed full texts that appear in historical rather than textual sources and were produced after 1276 in the area of what we now consider the heartland of China, do not represent a linear, unbroken tradition of writing about the foreign. The provenance of dramatic texts—the place of performance and the people who participated in staging the productions—changed radically over time, which had a demonstrable effect on leaving the foreign underrepresented. To complicate matters, no scripts or imprints of drama survive from the theater of the Jin and early Yuan periods, except as titles. Ranging from the mid-to-late fourteenth to the mid-seventeenth centuries, the extant print and manuscript editions were to a greater or lesser extent also subject to the pressures exerted by historical forces at any particular time.

Broadly speaking, we can differentiate between four strata of extant texts. The first comprises the mid- to late-fourteenth-century copies of sometimes shoddily printed scripts produced in the large cities of Dadu (present-day Beijing) and Gu Hang (present-day Hangzhou), which clearly stem from stage performances. They are scripts written for either the male or female lead. Their appearance in print, however, suggests they were (like modern visual displays of the aria texts during performances or on video) meant for an audience of readers and aficionados. Second are a group of plays written by literati and princes in the late fourteenth and early fifteenth centuries (which are largely outside the scope of this chapter). These plays demonstrate increasing literati involvement with colloquial forms. Some of these earliest Ming plays include full stage directions, plain-speech dialogue, and clearly marked arias. Third are Ming court plays, which were subject to heavy-handed censorship and designed to promote the cultural and political agendas of the state. No doubt because of the editing and censorship that these court plays underwent, they tend to be remarkably similar in their portrayal of the foreign. Finally come the commercial editions of the late sixteenth and early seventeenth centuries, produced by the hands of literati editors eager to reshape quotidian, popular texts into literary works that more purely reflect the values of Confucianism. In many places, these works were rewritten to remove the possibility of conflict between the universal ethical relationships of Confucianism (the so-called Five Basic Relationships)[1] and the more particularistic relationships based on friendship and economic transactions.

Among the corpus of extant plays, three distinct groups address the foreign. First, a relatively early stratum of stories concerns the Jurchens, the tribe that conquered and ruled North China from 1115 to 1234; all of these treat in some way a documented Jurchen interest in performance. A second group of plays lionizes foreigners who are either in service to or offer diplomatic tribute to an ethically and materially superior Chinese civilization; all of these are plays that were performed before Ming officials or the emperor at the Ming court. A third set of stories deals with the great Chinese families of generals who fought either the Tangut Xi Xia dynasty (1038–1227) in the west or the Khitan Liao dynasty (907–1125) located north of the Song state. Other plays lie on the periphery or outside of these three thematic domains, but they are similar in character to the three strata that we will discuss here. Importantly, the further one moves from the performance texts dated to the mid- and late-fourteenth century, the pressures exerted by the later Ming theatrical and publishing milieus brought foreign figures more and more in line with stereotyped caricatures that conformed either to the interests of the Ming state or to a level of general condescension or disdain that was matched in other popular texts, particularly the sections on foreigners in everyday-life encyclopedias.

In this chapter, we will focus on three plays from the earliest strata (the so-called Jurchen plays) to explore the particular relationship between the foreign and Chinese. As we shall see, in the world of these plays, love and performance are central to that relationship.

2.1 APPROACHES TO THE FOREIGN

Scholars generally agree that the Yuan period saw the first flowering of full-fledged theater in China. Modern studies of the development of early Chinese northern drama (*zaju*) have debunked the early-twentieth-century argument that this dramatic form arose because of the following three factors: the Mongol conquest; the subsequent dispossession of the elite meritocracy (both ethical and literary) as the primary means to recruit officials; and the desire to express "the people's resentment against the Mongols." But little subsequent attention has been paid to the actual role of the foreign in drama.

What studies there are primarily treat two areas. The first are linguistic forays into a lexicon of foreign words from Mongol, Jurchen, and—to a lesser extent—Persian and Arabic, which appear as part of the everyday language (*koine*), with which characters communicated on stage and which seem to have been part of the patois of the urban areas of the fourteenth century. The second area is more ethnographic in nature and uses the texts of the plays as verifiable evidence for reconstituting a so-called authentic culture of the predecessors of modern China's ethnic minorities (*shaoshu minzu*). These latter scholarly works invariably also denote the highly successful conquerors of parts or all of China—Shatuo Turks (Five Dynasties), Jurchen (Jin dynasty), Khitan (Liao dynasty), Mongols (Yuan dynasty), and Manchus (Qing dynasty)—as "ethnic minorities." This is an act of dehistoricizing that imposes a modern political term on groups of people who, at that time, could not possibly have conceived of themselves as ethnic minorities. By all accounts, they saw themselves as elite groups who controlled the landmass we now call "China." Moreover, many of these ethnographic studies simply accept the literary portrayal of foreigners in dramas, based on Chinese observations, as true representations of the observed rather than as a carefully fashioned view of the foreign that served the interests of the writers and producers.

Yet, a question remains. Why, in a time when Chinese society was more cosmopolitan than ever, is the foreign such a minor part of the corpus? One way to explain the relative scarcity of such portrayals may be the Chinese roots of much of the material that found its way into drama: from the biographies of the dynastic histories (Han through Song) (➳ *HTRCProse*, C.6), short fictional tales (Six Dynasties through Tang) (➳ *HTRCFiction*, chaps. 1, 2, and 3), to Song-through-Yuan proto-dramatic forms and prosimetric ballads (➳ chap. 1), these stories derived from Chinese history or the Chinese literary corpus and from the common experience of people living under Chinese dynastic rule. In the Ming prince Zhu Quan's (1378–1448) famous "Twelve Categories of Northern Drama" ("Zaju shi'er ke"), he does not reserve a place for anything beyond the norms of Chinese domestic literature. Here is a numbered list of his categories:

1. Stories about people led to enlightenment by the teachings of Daoist immortals (*shenxian daohua*)
2. Stories about people who live as hermits in perfect harmony with the Way (*yinju ledao*), also called "forest springs and mountain valleys" (*linquan qiuhe*)
3. Stories about lords and ministers (literally, "wearing court robes and holding the plaque of office" [*pipao binghu*]), also known as *zaju* dramas about lords and ministers (*junchen zaju*)
4. Stories of upright and loyal ministers and ardent martyrs (*zhongchen lieshi*)
5. Stories about ethical exemplars of filial piety, loyalty, integrity, and purity (*xiao yi lian jie*)
6. Stories of cursing the treacherous and reviling those who slander (*chijian machan*)
7. Stories of expelled ministers and orphaned sons (*zhuchen guzi*)

8. Stories of bandits and martial exploits (literally "knife pikes and clubs for expelling" [*bodao ganbang*]), also known as "bare-shouldered *zaju* plays" (*tuobo zaju*)

9. Love stories between talented men and pure maidens (literally, "blossoms in the breeze and moonlight on the snow" [*fenghua xueyue*])

10. Stories of the grief of parting and the happiness of reunions (*beihuan lihe*)

11. Love stories between young men and beguiling courtesans (literally, "blossoms of the mist and powder and kohl" [*yanhua fendai*]); also called "*zaju* with a flowery female role" (*huadan zaju*)

12. Holy figures and ghost faces (*shentou guimian*); that is, "*zaju* on the holy Buddha" (*shenfo zaju*)

[*THZYP* 38–45]

No system of categorization could possibly encompass the entirety of *zaju* thematic material then circulating, but as a conceptual shorthand for that corpus, we can see that this list centers on both the substance and historical moments of Daoist conversion (1–2); ethics in politics as an extension of the virtues of family interaction (3–7); on bandits (8); love stories in which young men of good families are matched at two levels of society (8–11); the partings of friends, lovers, and family (10); and Buddhism. There is no special place for plays that deal with the foreign. Any representation of life outside China would (and this is borne out by the extant plays on the foreign) have to be incorporated into a local category, mostly in either the arena of family or history plays. Of the three Jurchen plays that we will discuss next, *A Playboy from a Noble House Opts for the Wrong Career* (*Huanmen zidi cuo lishen*) and *Moonlight and Breezes in the Courtyard of Purple Clouds* (*Fengyue ziyunting*) fall within the "love stories between young men and beguiling courtesans," while *The Tiger Head Plaque That Authorizes Its Bearer to Act on His Own Judgment* (*Bianyi xingshi hutou pai*) roughly aligns with the category of loyal ministers or examples of loyalty.

Interestingly, however, despite the lack of a "foreign category" per se, one theme that runs through a cluster of family and history plays is the Jurchen love for music and dance. Song dynasty travel accounts describe the Jurchen as nomads who were exceptionally fond of singing and dancing and of drink.[2] Of the three Jurchen dramas we will consider here, two were written by Jurchen descendants and the third was demonstrably inspired by an earlier Jurchen-authored play. While these plays may show some fashioning of that culture through Chinese eyes—the infatuation with song and dance and its use for pleasure rather than ritual—it seems that we must recognize that this obsession with performance runs through all the dramas we will cover. We have no way of judging the actual knowledge that these dramatists had about the culture of their families' origins; that remains imponderable. However, given that the portrayals are consistent from the earliest performance texts through the desktop reading dramas some three hundred years later, we should perhaps accept them as accurate, if idealized, representations of some aspects of Jurchen culture. This marks this set of plays as radically different from those that would follow later, all of which stemmed from Ming dynasty court performances.

2.2 *WRONG CAREER* AND *PURPLE CLOUDS*: JURCHEN PERFORMERS IN THE WORLD OF ENTERTAINMENT

In this chapter, we are discussing three plays, two early and one late, that have either a significant character or a singing lead who is a Jurchen and ends up as a professional performer in the floating world of entertainment. The first is *Moonlight and Breezes in the Courtyard of Purple Clouds* (hereafter *Purple Clouds*), found in a mid-late-fourteenth-century print edition from Hangzhou and attributed to a Jurchen descendant, Shizhan Deyu (1192–1256?), better known by his Chinese name, Shi Junbao. The second, *A Playboy from a Noble House Opts for the Wrong Career* (hereafter *Wrong Career*), is a southern play copied into an early-fifteenth-century encyclopedia too big to print, the *Great Canon of the Yongle Era* (*Yongle dadian*) (☛ chap. 7). It is anonymous but follows the same general story line as *Purple Clouds*. In two of its scenes (5 and 12), it incorporates either partially or entirely song suites, each of which stems from an earlier *zaju*. This *zaju*, which had also prompted a second play by that name in the north, is simply named *Opts for the Wrong Career* (*Cuo lishen*) and is now lost. But in early bio-bibliographical works, it is attributed to a second- or third-generation Jurchen called Pucha Li Wu, better known by his Chinese name as Li Zhifu (ca. 1294–1320).[3]

The third play, *The Tiger Head Plaque That Authorizes Its Bearer to Act on His Own Judgment* (hereafter *The Tiger Head Plaque*), is also attributed to the same Li Zhifu. Found only in the *Select Yuan Plays* (*Yuanqu xuan*) edition printed in 1615, this drama is different in kind than the other two, but as we will see, it is bound to them by the portrayal of Jurchens as performers. It is also noteworthy because it contains a sequence of songs that occur only in dramas about Jurchens, and these songs have traditionally been thought to have been authentic Jurchen music.

These first two dramas are actually a subset of domestic plays that deal with a traditionally Chinese love quadrangle: a young man of high breeding but financially dependent on his family falls in love with a singsong girl—a professional entertainer cum prostitute; his father, usually a high official, opposes the relationship. Her mother, actually a procuress, also protests because the girl's earning power is crucial to maintaining the family of entertainers. In the madam's eyes, if the girl is going to quit the business, she must be married to a rich merchant who can redeem her from her indentured state by paying off an amount equivalent to the girl's presumed lifetime income. This general pattern of conflict appears in both *Wrong Career* and in *Purple Clouds*, the single change from the general pattern being that it is a young Jurchen nobleman who wants to become an actor and who falls in love with an entertainer. His father, a high official who wants him to be a good Confucian and future official, is adamantly opposed. In the typical Chinese setting, the girl, the star of her troupe and main money-earner, falls for the young man and wants to quit her trade. But in these Jurchen plays, the lovers opt to continue their relationship by him joining the low-status ranks of entertainers, against the initial wishes of their elders.

The plays are domestic in nature because they focus on two different sets of conflicts between sons or daughters and their parents. On the one hand, the interference of the father is seen as a lack of compassion or a failure of parenting—that is, the absence of true paternal feeling or the oppressive exercise of control in response to unfilial decisions on the part of the son. The ethics of the Confucian family system are shown to suffer a breakdown when they are subject to a willful pursuit of self-determination that conflicts with familial expectations (☞ chap. 3). On the other hand, the intercession of the mother revolves much more around the issue of economic exploitation, both of the actress by her mother and of male customers who become destitute playboys. This sets out another conflict with the traditional hierarchies of the patriarchal system that is the ideological basis of the family, the clan, and even the state, which is metaphorically defined as a family with the emperor as father. When carnal desire is pursued outside of familial systems of marriage or concubinage, it moves from ethical considerations to a realm of economics and exploitation. On the one hand, the feelings that the young people involved have for each other encounter resistance when they have to confront the entrenched force of economic exploitation of the woman. Her mother needs the female entertainer to remain active as a sex worker. Authentic human feelings and love interests threaten the control that the mother exercises over the woman. On the other hand, in a society where arranged marriages are the norm, that same freely chosen love of a person, particularly one who is not a match in terms of family status, cannot be contained within the ideal compass of the ethics of Confucian parenthood—compassion on the part of the father and filial piety on the part of the young man.

Arguments and actions against the youngsters enlist either ethical cautions about personal failures or physical punishment. Compassion on the part of those who are elders may be a philosophical ideal espoused by Confucianism, but in real terms, it grants unlimited license to parents to repress their children by any means necessary, including beating, banishment, and even filicide, all without suffering any legal repercussions. All these harsh actions refer to the ethical failures of the young as excuses: the lack of filial piety, the lack of care and support of parents, and particularly going against the wishes of an elder. In such a case, whether it is a family like the girl's, an economic unit built on kinship ties created through adoption, or a Confucian family of the elite class, the ideology of hierarchies that always places power in the hands of the elder is enlisted as a way to quell private love interests. Confronted with this conflict between the economic or ethical needs of the family and the expression of one's personal love, the young also abandon filial piety and their willing support of the family. This failure turns the ethical categories by which families are constructed into empty shells as the status-oriented mentality of the elder clashes with the personal feeling and romantic desires of the younger (☞ chap. 3).

In *Wrong Career*, a young Jurchen nobleman, the male lead (*sheng*), Wanyan Shouma, falls for the actress Wang Jinbang (hereafter Starlet Wang), and he begins practicing plays and farces with her with the intent of joining her family's itiner-ant troupe. Caught by his father, the Vice-prefect of Luoyang, and confined to his study, Shouma escapes, tracks down Starlet Wang's troupe, and is reunited with her. But by the time he reaches her, he has lost all his money, has pawned his extra clothes, and is roundly abused by her family. He is allowed to join the troupe only after proving his expertise in various types of theater work and Starlet recognizes him as her lover again. He thereafter shares the troupe's hardships on the road. His father, meanwhile, has been appointed as a traveling censor and summons the troupe one night to alleviate his weariness and depression. He recognizes his son, and the play ends in an act of reunion, with the young man receiving his father's blessing to marry Starlet Wang.

　　As mentioned previously, in scenes 5 and 12 of this southern play (*nanxi*) (☛ Introduction), a song suite from a northern *zaju* drama, presumably *Wrong Career* by Li Zhifu, is incorporated wholly or partially. Scene 5 incorporates four northern songs and intersperses them with southern tunes; scene 12 lifts an entire northern suite, most probably from the second or third act of the *zaju* version of the story. In both cases, the incorporated songs are composed of lists of either dramas or farce skits that Shouma is able to perform. For instance, in scene 5, he recites the names of plays that he has at hand:

（旦唱）	YOUNG FEMALE *as* STARLET WANG *sings*:
【賞花時】	*To the tune* "Shanghua shi"
憔悴容顏只為你，	My face haggard and worn, all because of you,
每日在書房攻甚詩書！	And just which classics do you apply yourself to in your study every day?
（生）	YOUNG MALE *as* WANYAN SHOUMA [*sings*]:
閒話且休提，	Don't waste time on idle talk,
你把這時行的傳奇。	Bring out those popular musical plays!
（旦）	STARLET WANG [*sings*]:
看掌記。	Look at the scripts,
你從頭與我再溫習。	And rehearse them all for me right from the start!
（旦白）你直待要唱曲，相公知道，不是耍處。	STARLET WANG *speaks*: All you want to do is to sing. If your father finds out, it'll be no laughing matter.
（生）不妨，你帶得掌記來，敷演一番。	SHOUMA [*speaks*]: No problem. Let's practice the scripts that you've brought along.
（旦）這裏有分付：（淨看門介）	STARLET WANG [*speaks*]: I'm turning them over to you now. COMIC *as* MANSERVANT *acts out guarding the door.*
（旦）	STARLET WANG [*sings*]:
【排歌】	*To the tune* "Paige"
聽說因依，	Listen as I explain
其中就裏：	In every detail:
一個負王魁；	There is one *Cold-Hearted Top Graduate Wang Kui*

孟姜女千里送寒衣;	*Meng Jiangnü Brings Winter Clothing from a Thousand Miles Away,*
脫像云卿鬼做媒;	*With Fading Image, Yunqing's Ghost Acts the Matchmaker,*
鴛鴦會，卓氏女;	*A Reunion of Mandarin Ducks, Daughter of Zhuo Family,*
郭華因為買胭脂;	Just because *Guo Hua Bought Rouge,*
瓊蓮女,	The girl Qionglian,
船浪舉,	Her boat tossed by waves,
臨江驛內再相會。	Meets her father again at Linjiang Posthouse.
（又）	[*Sings*] *again:*
【那吒令】	*To the tune "Nezha ling"*
這一本傳奇,	This story
是《大周孛太尉》;	Is *Commander Zhou Bo;*
這一本傳奇,	This story
是《崔護覓水》;	Is *Cui Hu Looking for a Drink;*
這一本傳奇,	This story
是《秋胡戲妻》;	Is *Qiu Hu Flirts with his Wife;*
這一本是《關大王獨赴單刀會》;	This one here is *Great King Guan Goes Alone to the Single Sword Meeting;*
這一本是《馬踐楊妃》。	And this one here, *Horses Trample the Precious Consort.*
（又）	[*Sings*] *again:*
【排歌】	*To the tune "Paige"*
柳耆卿《樂城驛》;	Liu Shiqing and *The Luan City Posthouse,*
張珙《西廂記》;	Zhang Gong and *The Story of the Western Wing,*
《殺狗勸夫婿》;	*She Kills a Dog to Set Her Husband Straight,*
《京娘四不知》;	*Four Things Jingniang Didn't Know,*
《張協斬貧女》;	*Zhang Xie Beheads Poorlass,*
《樂昌公主》;	*Princess Lechang,*
《牆頭馬上》擲青梅,	*From Walltop to Horseback,* she tosses a green apricot,
《錦香亭上》賦新詩,	*At Jinxiang Pavilion,* he composes new poetry,
契合皆因手帕兒;	A perfect match was all because of a handkerchief,
《洪和尚，錯下書》;	*Monk Hong, A Letter Wrongly Delivered,*
《呂蒙正風雪破窯記》;	*Lü Mengzheng Braves a Winter Storm in a Broken-Down Kiln,*
楊寔遇，韓瓊兒;	*Yang Shi meets Han Chong'er,*
《冤冤相報趙氏孤兒》。	*Injustice Requited with Injustice: The Orphan of Zhao*
（又：）	[*Sings*] *again:*
【鵲踏枝】	*To the tune "Que ta zhi"*
劉先主，跳檀溪;	*First Ruler Liu Bei Jumps Sandalwood Creek,*
雷轟了薦福碑;	*Thunder Destroys the Jianfu Stele,*
丙吉教子立起宣帝;	*Bing Ji Instructs His Son and Sets up Emperor Xuan,*
老萊子斑衣;	*Laolaizi and His Colored Clothes,*
包待制上陳州糶米;	*Rescriptor in Waiting Bao Travels to Chenzhou to Issue Rice,*
這一本是《孟母三移》。	And this one is *Mother Meng Thrice Moves House.*

[*HMZD* 231–232]

This long sequence of song titles rhymes on the final -*i* (the *qi-wei* rhyme class in early Mandarin) in its main lines, with a secondary rhyme of -*u* or -*ü* (the *yu-mo* rhyme class; and notably on the word "female" or "woman," *nü*). The list contains a variety of dramas, including historical plays on the Three Kingdoms and legal cases, but the majority are about love, a fitting topic in this context because several of them feature faithless men and loving women. In these plays, of course, the main male characters are Chinese, often men of poetic talent and deep romantic sentiment, who will eventually become well known in real and fictional, social and literary worlds.

A similar plot with the same central conflicts underlies *Purple Clouds*, but it focuses exclusively on the entertainer-mother conflict. Such a singular emphasis is easy to understand because northern drama has only one singing role and only one point of view in any one act through which the action of the play and its meaning are refracted (which is all the more true when we don't see the dialogue of the other characters, as in our only edition of this play). Using a female lead ensures that it is her reactions that we will witness (☛ chap. 3). Interestingly, however, in both plays the actress is much more outspoken and has more agency than the male, who appears quite passive and often fearful. In the aria here, the female lead dwells on the fact that it was her actions that shaped the course of their lives together:

（旦）	FEMALE LEAD *as* HAN CHULAN [*sings*]:
【哨遍】	*To the tune* "Shaobian"
送的人赤手空拳難過，	What sent him to his troubles, empty-handed and broke,
都是俺舌尖上一點砂糖唾。	Was that little drop of sugary saliva from the tip of my tongue—
越精細的越著他，	The more I worked it, the further he went—
怎出俺這打多情地網天羅。	There was no way to escape the net that I stretched over Heaven and Earth to capture those full of feeling.
且說俺這小哥哥，	Let's talk about my little older brother now,
為俺耽驚受怕，	Who, frightened and scared on my account,
波進流移，	Was set adrift on the waves to float on their currents
冷落了讀書院，	And, after deserting his study,
一就把功名懶墮。	At once casually let drop away all interest in a meritorious name.
自盡教萱堂有夢，	He might have worked with all his might to cause "the lily chamber"[4] to have dreams,
並不想蘭省登科。	But he never considered taking the examinations at the "orchid hall."[5]
幾時得兩扶紅日上青天，	When can we expect two red suns to be raised aloft in the blue heavens?[6]
空望著一片白云隔黃河。	In vain he gazes at a layer of white clouds that keep the Yellow River from view.[7]

則共我這般攜手兒相將，　　But holding hands with me like this, supporting each other,

舉步兒同行，　　And walking stride for stride with me,

他想所事滿心兒快活。　　He believes everything will cause a heart full of joy.

[*ZYT* 9a]

Each of the two plays features a set of "recognition" scenes that exploit the tensions around social status and individual feeling. In the first, the male appears in rags and is made fun of before showing off his acting skills and being accepted by his female lover. In the second, the male is reunited and reconciled with his father through the girl's good graces. In scene 12 in *Wrong Career*, Shouma has been drifting about, cold and hungry, and he gazes into a river, takes some of the water to slick his hair back, treks into town, and sees a broadside that announces a performance by Starlet Wang and her troupe. This recognition scene is prefaced by an exchange of sarcastic comments:

（見生不認介）　　STARLET WANG *acts out seeing* SHOUMA *without letting on that she recognizes him.*

（旦）莊家調判，難看區老。　　STARLET WANG [*speaks*]: A farm boy dancing the infernal judge[8]—a body really hard to look at.

（生）老鼠咬了葫蘆藤，小姐好快嘴。　　SHOUMA [*speaks*]: A rat gnawing through a squash vine—you've got a sharp tongue.

（旦）鸚鵡回言，這鳥敢來應口。　　STARLET WANG [*speaks*]: Well, the parrot echoes what is said, but does this bird dare try and keep up with me?

（生）耐打鼓兒，我較得你兩片。　　SHOUMA [*speaks*]: I'm a drum that can take any beating; I'm the equal of your two lips!

（旦）你課牙比不得杜善甫，串仗卻似鄭元和。　　STARLET WANG [*speaks*]: You can't clack your teeth together as well as Du Shanfu, but you're dressed up just like Zheng Yuanhe!

（生）姐姐，使錢不問家豪富，風流不在著衣多。　　SHOUMA [*speaks*]: Sister, if somebody has money to spend, you don't ask if they are rich or poor, having real sophistication doesn't come from how many clothes you have.

[*HMZD* 242–243]

She comments first that he looks like an unwashed, ragged farm boy trying to do the dance of the infernal judge that was common on the stage; he retorts that she is a sharp-tongued shrew. Then an interesting exchange takes place that has a clear second level of meaning. As in modern Chinese, "bird" (*niao*) is a rhyming pun on "penis" (*diao*), roughly meaning "this damned guy," but slightly stronger. This leads to the obvious pun in the following lines, which might be understood at a second level as "I can match whatever your two netherlips can dish out!" She retorts that he is no equal to the famous wit Du Shanfu (➤ Introduction), but rather looks like a broken-down beggar. In the next aria, he begins by chiding her for taking so long to come to the teahouse:

（生）	SHOUMA [sings]:
【駐雲飛】	*To the tune* "Zhu yun fei"
你款步難擡，	Your slow steps must have been hard to lift,
便做天仙難見你來；	Even if I were an immortal in heaven, no way I'd have seen you coming.
我把你相看待，	I have treated you well,
它把我相杪壞。	But you have tortured me.
猜。	Guess!
緣何在花街，	Why, there in the flowery lanes
共人歡愛？	Did you so freely share your pleasure and love?
說又不偢，	I speak, she pays no attention,
罵又佯不采。	I curse, she pretends to turn a deaf ear.
正是，本性難移山河易改，	True it is, "One's basic nature is hard to budge, [in comparison] mountains and rivers are easy to change,"
山河易改。	Mountains and rivers are easy to change.

[HMZD 243]

As the sequence of the aria moves on to Starlet Wang, she starts by telling him that no matter how good he is, there is no way she would follow him through life. We are, of course, missing the action on stage, but the last "Aha!" that she says clearly signals her notice of some action or act on the male's part that she recalls as his alone, something that she recognizes:

（旦）	STARLET WANG [sings]:
【同前】	*Reprise*
便做眞龍，	Even if you were a true dragon,
我也難從你逐浪波。	I would find it hard to follow you through the waves and billows.
訊口胡應和，	You answer off the top of your head in some idiotic way,
譯話喫不過。	I really can't stomach that gibberish you dish out.
嗏。	Aha!
一剗是舊特科，	Now, there's that whole flavor that is his special talent!
我把它瞧[瞧]破，	I can see him clearly now for what he is!
誰慣得如今膽似天來大？	Who could ever get used to such gall, as big as Heaven itself?
你向咱行說箇甚麼？	What do you have to say for yourself, right here in front of me?
你向咱行說箇甚麼？	What do you have to say for yourself, right here in front of me?

[HMZD 243]

In the next scene, the owner of the teahouse appears to wrap up the scene with his comments. The description of the beggarlike appearance is used to comment on the playboy's supposed new status as the man beneath the clothes. That is, before, his rundown appearance had been a key to his status—a scruffy, dirty farm boy, an unsuitable mate, someone who does not know his place. But the next lines comment on the incommensurability of appearance and presumed status. From the objective stance of the teahouse owner, the comment can be seen as an expression of learned common sense: "Don't believe a word he says because there is no outer sign he is what he says he is." This concludes a metaphorical undertone running through the entire section: clothes and appearance both reveal social identity, but they also can mask the real person; it depends solely on the perceiver to be able to see the real person:

（淨）	COMIC *as* TEAHOUSE OWNER [*sings*]:
【同前】	*Reprise*
仔細思之，	If you think about it carefully,
你是何人它是誰？	What kind of person are you, and who is she?
姐姐多嬌媚，	Elder sister is just so full of charm,
你卻身藍縷。	You, on the other hand, are a walking jumble of tattered rags.
嗏。	Phew!
模樣似乞的，	With the looks of a beggar,
盖紙被，	Covered with a paper cloak,
日裏去街頭教他求衣食，	Out on the street during the day, we can suppose he begs for clothes and food,
夜裏彎跧樓下睡，	At night, he curls up under the eaves of a tower to sleep,
夜裏彎跧樓下睡。	At night, he curls up under the eaves of a tower to sleep.
（生）	SHOUMA [*sings*]:
【同前】	*Reprise*
覆水難收，	Spilled water is hard to recover,[9]
一度思量珠淚流，	Just thinking about it all makes tears like pearls flow.
指望長相守，	I just wanted us to be together forever,
誰信不成就？	Whoever believed it wouldn't happen?
（旦）	STARLET WANG [*sings*]:
嗏。	Aha!
一筆盡都勾，	A single brush stroke wipes it all away—
免喫僝僽，	Let's not curse or fret anymore.
剪髮拈香，	I'll cut my hair and burn incense,
共你同說呪。	And together we will speak our oath.[10]

[*HMZD* 243]

A similar recognition scene is found in *Purple Clouds*, unfolding under similar circumstances. Despite the fact that the dialogue is missing from this play, what happens is clearly analogous. First, the actress does not immediately recognize her former lover when they meet again. And, as we can see next, the prelude to the recognition scene also includes a comment on the beggar's daytime and nighttime activities, a repeat of the adage about sophistication not being a matter of dress (exterior appearance), and her consternation about the contentious way that he responds. These elements seem to be part of a fairly set sequence that involves a fair amount of expected and clichéd banter:

（旦）	FEMALE LEAD *as* HAN CHULAN [*sings*]:
【堯民歌】	*To the tune* "Yaomin ge"
你則是風流不在著衣多，	You are a perfect fit: "Sophistication is not about how many clothes you wear."
你這般浪子何須自開呵？	Why does a wastrel like you need to make your own "opening announcement?"[11]
嘩！	Well damn!
這廝白日街上打呆歌，	This guy sings his begging songs on the street in broad daylight—
卻怎生到晚人前逞僂儸？	So how dare he show off his smarts in front of others when evening comes?
哎！	Ai!
哥哥！你明日吃甚末？	What are you going to eat tomorrow, brother?
兀自忍不到那十分餓！	You won't be able to stand starving hunger!
【快活三】	*To the tune* "Kuaihuo san"
無明火怎收撮，	How can I control my anger, this fire without light?
摑打會看如何？	Let me box his ears and then see how it goes.
則教我烘地了半晌口難合，	Well, this makes me stand awhile with my mouth agape,
不覺我這身起是多來大。	All unaware of how much I have worked myself up!
【鮑老兒】	*To the tune* "Baolao'er"
從來撒欠颺風愛恁末，	Why, it's that love of mine who has made me so addlepated and crazy all this time!
敲才兀自不改動些兒個。	You ought-to-be-beaten lover, you have not changed a whit.
你這般忍冷耽饑覓著我，	And that you have borne cold and suffered such hunger to find me
越引起我那色膽天來大。	Stirs up an appetite for sex as big as heaven itself.
我每日千思萬想，	I thought about you a thousand, ten thousand times a day,
行眠立盹，	I walked as though asleep, stood as if in a slumber,
不是存活。	That was no way to live!
這般山長水遠，	With mountains so far and the rivers so distant,
天遙地闊，	Heaven so expansive, Earth so wide,
不想你直來呵。	I never thought you would come straight to me.

[*ZYT* 4a]

It is these recognition scenes that provide a key to understanding the ultimate source of these two dramas: the narrative structure derives from the well-known Tang dynasty story, "The Tale of Li Wa" ("Li Wa zhuan") (☞ chap. 1), in which a young man of good family (who is called Zheng Yuanhe in later versions) goes to the capital to take the metropolitan exams and meets and falls for a young courtesan, Li Wa. He becomes her live-in lover, but when the large amount of money that he brought with him has all been spent on her, Li Wa's "mother" gets rid of him, with Li Wa's silent contrivance, by moving their residence after he has been tricked into leaving their old place. Unable to find his beloved, he first falls so ill that he gets prematurely dumped at an undertaker's, but instead of dying, he becomes their star singer of dirges at funerals. Meanwhile, his father, who thinks his son is dead, comes to the capital on official business; his servant notices and points out that the dirge singer is Yuanhe. Yuanhe's father is so mad at how low his son has fallen that he beats him severely, leaving him for dead. Yuanhe slowly recovers and becomes a beggar who sings very moving beggar songs about his misfortunes. On a cold winter's night, Li Wa recognizes his singing, takes him in, gradually nurtures him back to health, and helps him prepare for the examinations. Passing with high marks, he is appointed an official and wants to take Li Wa home with him. She objects, but in the end it is his father who praises what she has done and accepts both of them into the family. Yuanhe has a successful official career, and she ends up with a title.

But the proximate source for the plot of *Purple Clouds* is clearly Shi Junbao's *Li Yaxian: Flowers and Wine at Serpentine Pond* (*Li Yaxian huajiu qujiang chi*, hereafter *Serpentine*), a dramatic retelling of the original short story as a *zaju*, albeit minus the recognition scene. Not only is the plot of what transpires in Shi Junbao's play nearly the same as the two Jurchen dramas, but much of the actual language in *Purple Clouds* is shared with *Serpentine*. Nevertheless, one of the signal differences between *Serpentine* on the one hand, and *Wrong Career* and *Purple Clouds* on the other, is that in the latter two, the young man is not restored to his place in society. Both plays end with him continuing as part of the actress's troupe. For instance, if we consider the following passage from *Purple Clouds*, which occurs when the father acknowledges his son, we note that the woman pleads *not* to have her man restored to his elite status, for that would mean either separation or a second-class status as a concubine for her. The actress recounts how the father had split the young lovers apart and sent the young man back to his study under guard and the acting troupe off to their hometown:

（旦）　　HAN CHULAN [*sings*]:

【水仙子】　*To the tune* "Shuixianzi"

相公那日正暴雷急雨怒在書房，　On that day in the study, My Lord, you were as angry as pounding thunder and driving rain,

幾曾這般和氣春風滿畫堂？　We never saw any "harmonious ethers of spring zephyrs filling the painted hall."

（孤云）   OFFICIAL ROLE *as* FATHER [*speaks*]:

（旦）   HAN CHULAN [*sings*]:

舍人也沒那五陵豪氣三千丈，   My man—he had no "high bravado of the Five Tumuli,"[12]

脖項上連鐵索兩托長！   But did have two spans of iron chain around his neck [as he was led away under guard].

卻雖是妾煩惱歡喜殺家堂，   And, even though my own troubles delighted our parents to no end,

路岐人生死心難忘。   This itinerant performer's desire is with me through life and death.

謝相公齎發覷當，   And thank you, My Lord, for being concerned enough then to provide us with travel funds,

直把俺牒配還鄉。   To send us straight back to our homeland![13]

【雁兒落】   *To the tune* "Yan'er luo"

相公把孩兒呵腹內想，   You, My Lord, begin to think how you feel at heart about your child,

越教妾小鹿兒心頭撞，   And this makes the little deer of my heart pound even more.[14]

我如今引來這園圃中，   If I lead him through the garden now

莫不是賺到這筵席上？   Isn't it just to trick him into joining the feast mat?[15]

【得勝令】   *To the tune* "Desheng ling"

卻又休金殿鎖鴛鴦，   Don't lock up this mandarin duck pair in the golden hall,

一似書幃中拆鸞凰。   That would be exactly like when you split apart simurgh and phoenix in the study.

恁那秀才憑學藝，   Your young scholar still relies on talent for learning,

他卻也男兒當自強。   And is proof that "a man should make himself strong."

他如今難當，   He is now without peer—

日寫在招兒上。   Every day his name is writ on our playbills.

相公試參詳，   Think clearly about this, My Lordship,

這的喚功名紙半張！   This can be called "half of the sheet of that paper of merit and fame!"[16]

[*ZYT* 6a-b]

What is interesting here (and replicated in *Wrong Career*) is the desire for an equal union between man and woman that may be possible only within the world of actors, and as mentioned previously, perhaps only for non-Chinese males who willingly give up the quest for the cultural capital that came from passing the examinations, not just temporarily but permanently. If the playboy were restored to his original place in society, the disparity between them in terms of social and ethical hierarchies of status probably would end their relationship. The same tension that existed at the beginning of the play, the quadrangle of conflict, would reassert itself. Han Chulan goes to great lengths to persuade the boy's father of his son's literary talent, boasting that it is demonstrated in a public environment (albeit a different one), and that it represents an achievement that can be counted as having at least a portion of the literary merit that normal success in the examination would hold. This ameliorates the father's concerns but, just as important, it also raises her merit in the father's eyes because she is making arguments in his own terms of how he understands the world.

It also acknowledges that the romantic ending of *Serpentine* and its rescuing of a prostitute from the red dust of the world to elite status as a model of female virtue may be unrealistic to achieve in the real world. This is not to say that these two Jurchen plays are any more real than *Serpentine*, but that they demonstrate how playwrights can offer two distinct versions of a possible ending without placing a necessary test of truthfulness on either one. In the case of *Purple Clouds* and *Serpentine*, for instance, while Shi Junbao does not have to believe either scenario he creates as an ending, it is probably likely that his own experience as playwright (he wrote ten plays) and theater person would suggest that, of the two options, that of the Jurchen plays might be more likely. From what we can glean from the only source from the fourteenth century that discusses actresses, *The Record of the Green Bowers* (*Qinglou ji*, hereafter *Record*), many were brought into the households of the powerful. But they were classified as "adjacent to the actual household" (*cefang*)—their real status was probably much lower than that of a concubine, and the position certainly came with severe strictures on some of the freedoms they had previously enjoyed as actresses. That same *Record* also contains stories of women disfiguring themselves as a way to maintain a way of life they had chosen, rather than prove themselves appealing to the powerful.

Still, placing the narrative structure of Li Wa in the acting world and disguising its original design allowed the playwrights to escape the expectations of the "talent and beauty" archetype, and at the same time (consciously or unconsciously) vaunt the acting profession as a place where gender equality is not only desired but expected. Both *Wrong Career* and *Purple Clouds* are incomplete; they were not part of any major anthology or collection of dramas and were saved only through serendipity. The particular model of gender equality implied in the ending of these plays does not seem to appear in other Yuan and Ming *zaju* about actresses, whose quest for love is most often intermixed with a desire for elevation of status (*congliang*, to be granted the tax status of a "good family").

There are two points to consider here. One is that perhaps it takes a Jurchen character, a non-Chinese, to impart an appearance of reality to the assumption of a role at the very bottom of the social ladder, on par with servants and slaves, and to the relinquishing of all desire for a successful social and political career and all the cultural capital that it entails. Or it may be that once drama became a literati fetish, both the dramatic performances recorded in an expanding literati discourse on theater and the production of dramatic text moved upward in the social scale; such an idea was simply too radical to sustain in such an environment.

Both *Wrong Career* and *Purple Clouds* were clearly closer to the urban commercial theater, which was free of such concerns. We can surmise that, even though not recorded in any great detail in the selective records from the hands of elite writers, such commercial theater continued unabated and unnoticed. But we have no no textual record by which to know if such endings remained possible in the real world of popular performance.

2.3 *THE TIGER HEAD PLAQUE*: JURCHEN PERFORMERS IN THEIR NATIVE LANDS

The third play that we will discuss, *The Tiger Head Plaque*, is quite different from the first two. It does not involve a professional performer; instead, it features, in act 2, a once highly placed Jurchen, Jinzhuma, who sings at clan banquets and celebrations in a postconquest Jurchen world (i.e., after the fall of the northern Song in 1126) that was still primarily constituted of nomadic, tribal, and clan affiliations. The portrayal is of a down-and-out member of the ruling clan who has lost his money, position, and self-respect. We are never told the reason why this happened because he appears only in act 2, in an interlude within an otherwise tightly woven plot of the conflict between duty and family loyalty.

The play was selected for inclusion in what is perhaps the most famous anthology of Chinese drama, the *Select Yuan Plays*, edited by the literatus Zang Maoxun (1550–1620) (☞ Introduction). In putting together his hand-picked collection of 100 plays, Zang freely revised the plays that he selected, so we must approach this later version of *The Tiger Head Plaque* with some caution. However, we cannot discount the fact that it certainly stems from a much earlier tradition, and it may well stem from a Ming dynasty court edition. As we shall see, thanks to extant mid-Ming excerpts from an earlier version of the play, some of that earlier tradition can be reconstructed.

The play has a relatively simple plot line. A Jurchen character by the name of Wanyan Shanshouma holds a critical pass between what is now North China and the northern steppe, keeping border incursions by northern tribes at bay thanks to his martial prowess and attention to military training. By virtue of his position as a superior chiliarch in the Jurchen army, he carries a silver tally of office. On a hunt, he is interrupted by news that his uncle Yinzhuma and his aunt, who raised him from infancy, have arrived. He spreads a feast for them but is soon interrupted by an envoy from the emperor, who appoints him to the high position of grand marshal and director of the Bureau of Military Affairs. He is also allowed to grant the silver plaque of the superior chiliarch to anyone under his command. After a considerable amount of wheedling on the part of his family, he grants the silver plaque and the position of defender of the pass to his uncle. This decision takes up a considerable part of act 1, as it turns out that his uncle is an unrepentant drunkard. But Yinzhuma swears that he will drink no more if given the command, and Shanshouma relents despite his misgivings.

The second act, which we will turn to in detail next, takes place in Yinzhuma's home district as he prepares to leave the clan village to take up his command. The act is a long and emotional parting from his elder brother, Jinzhuma. Jinzhuma recounts his descent into poverty from a once-opulent lifestyle, the disappearance of his son into the netherworld of entertainment, and his own desirability as a singer and dancer in clan celebrations such as weddings.

In the third act, the foreshadowed disaster happens: while Yinzhuma is drunk, foreign troops invade the pass and capture livestock and people. He manages to recapture the lot from the invading troops, but the crime of losing the pass cannot be overlooked. Several runners from Shanshouma's court are sent to bring Yinzhuma to court to adjudicate his crime and mete out justice. Yinzhuma has them all beaten, claiming that because he is Shanshouma's uncle, he is untouchable. He is finally brought to court in chains, but he still refuses to believe that his nephew will go through with any punishment. But Shanshouma reads an edict of accusation and then sentences Yinzhuma to decapitation. Again, the family members plead on his behalf, and his sentence is reduced to 100 strokes of the cane. The exact number he is allotted is changed both by Shanshouma and by a servant who takes a share in Yinzhuma's stead. He is released and sent back home. In the final act of the play, Shanshouma takes some food and wine to Yinzhuma's place to hold a banquet of celebration, ostensibly to assuage his uncle's pain, but in reality, it is to make the family whole again.

Most critical work on this play points to the clash between the demands of the state and those of filial piety. This is certainly one understanding of the conflict that Shanshouma feels in sentencing his foster father to such severe punishment. But another way of thinking about this conflict is that it may also reflect a period in which the Jin was being established as a Chinese dynasty and was changing from a clan-based military aristocracy to a Chinese-style government. Originally, centarchs (*baihu*), chiliarchs (*qianhu*), and myriarchs (*wanhu*), all members of a military aristocracy, had overseen different-sized military units as part of the nomadic administration. In the play, Chinese titles, like those bestowed on Shanshouma, and the act of locating his authority within one of the major branches of the government (i.e., the head of the Bureau of Military Affairs), metonymically symbolizes the shift from an aristocratic to a bureaucratic style of governance.

This change in the locus of governmental authority is also represented by a specific line (marked with **) in the translation given here of the aria "Yue'er wan," a tune pattern found in this play alone. In this line from the second act, Jinzhuma laments his son's disappearance into the pleasure districts of the capital, where he fritters away his time in the company of ne'er-do-wells:

（[正末] 唱）	[MALE LEAD *as* JINZHUMA] *sings:*
【月兒彎】	*To the tune* "Yue'er wan"
則俺那生忿懺逆的醜生，	That willful and disobedient beast of mine—
** 有人向中都相見，	Someone saw him in the Central Capital,**
伴著火潑男也那潑女，	Hanging around with a group of trashy men and women
茶房也那灑肆，	In tea houses and taverns,

在那瓦市里穿，　　Threading back and forth through the pleasure precincts;
幾年間再沒個信兒傳。　No letter from him for several years.
有句話舌尖上挑著，　I have something to say, hovering right here on the tip of
　　　　　　　　　my tongue,
我去那喉嚨裏咽.　　That I'm just about to swallow down my throat.

[*HTP* 197c]

The use of the geonome of "Central Capital" is quite anachronistic. For instance, when Shanshouma departs in the first act to take up his position, he says that he is going to Zhongxing Prefecture (Zhongxing fu), the name of the area of modern Beijing before the Jin central capital was established there in 1153 under the name of Central Capital (Zhongdu) (☞ Visual Resources). The use of "Central Capital" as a place name seems to be a later addition. Earlier mid-Ming texts on rhyme and scansion that cite the song "Yue'er wan" from *The Tiger Head Plaque* simply give the name of the area as "Yanjing," a holdover of the city's name when it was the former Liao capital, or simply call it by the general term "capital" (*jingshi*). If we are to recognize from these earlier sources that the action of the play takes place before 1153, a mere forty years from the establishment of the Jin dynasty, then the play reflects a period when the switch from a nomadic coalition of family lineages to a state-centered Confucian government was still in progress. One of the ways that we might understand the conflict between Shanshouma and his uncle may be to think of it as a generational rift. In other words, while the older generation was accustomed to the use of aristocratic clan privilege as the fundamental principle of governance, the younger Jurchen leaders operated in a Confucian model of a state authority based on selection through merit.

The previous aria takes place in act 2, which holds much interest because it also contains a set of songs that since the Ming dynasty has commonly been called "the Jurchen suite." Because this act is clearly an interlude, there is some debate as to whether this whole act in fact belongs to *The Tiger Head Plaque*, or whether some of or all the arias are lifted from another play or plays. But there is enough internal evidence, such as the foreshadowing in it of Yinzhuma's loss of the pass and the consequent punishment by his nephew, to convince us that the dialogue that surrounds the arias makes them an integral part of this particular play.

The action also makes more sense if we look at an aria that was deleted from Zang Maoxun's edition and found only in the earlier works on rhyme and scansion mentioned previously. In act 2, Jinzhuma assumes the role of the lead singer. By doing so, he becomes the voice and the mirror of action. The scene represents the rituals of parting between Jurchen brothers and the worshipping of the cardinal directions of east and west, the exact opposite of the Chinese north-south axis. As he pours out the sacrificial wine, Jinzhuma utters his prayer wishing that brothers are able meet again in this life:

（正末做遞酒科唱）　JINZHUMA *acts out passing the wine and sings*:
　　【落梅風】　*To the tune* "Luomei feng"
抹的這瓶口兒淨，　I've wiped the lip of this jug until it is clean,
斟的這盞面兒圓。　And filled this cup until it is full.
望著那碧天邊太陽澆奠。　Gazing far away at the sun at blue heaven's edge, I pour out a sacrifice.

則俺這女真人無什麼別咒願，　"Let me, this Jurchen man, have no other prayer of need
則願的俺兄弟每能勾相見。　Than wishing that we brothers will be able to see each other once again."

[*BCGZP* 278]

The missing aria reflects two aspects that are slightly dissonant in the overall suite. The first is expressed in the opening three lines, where there is a hint of jealousy and envy in Jinzhuma's tone. This is followed by a slight resentment that he must remain behind, fettered to duty at home to tend the estate and the family plot:

（正末唱）　JINZHUMA *sings*:
　　【早香詞】　*To the tune* "Zao xiang ci"
你如今掌着軍權，　Now you control military authority,
　　蒙着帝喧，　And bear the emperor's command,
誰似你叔侄每稱心滿意？　Who is as content and pleased as you and your nephew?
離了家鄉住在別地面。　You are leaving home to live in some other place,
我與你覷着莊園守着坟院，　While I watch the estate for you and guard the graves;
可憐見俺正值着暮景衰年。　Have pity on me, directly confronted by these scenes of fading light and declining years.

[*BCGZP* 278]

This makes his statement about his lost fortune (shown next) more understandable to the reader. It certainly adds a little dimension to Jinzhuma:

（正末）　JINZHUMA [*sings*]:
　　【阿那忽】　*To the tune* "Anahu"
若得我往日固家緣，　Were I to have my family fortune of days gone by,
可也多齎發你些盤纏。　Then would I be able to provide you much traveling money.
有鰾接來的兩根家竹箭，　But I have these two arrows of bamboo homegrown joined with fish glue,
　　更有那蠟打弓弦。　And this bow string struck with beeswax.

[*BCGZP* 278]

The *Select Yuan Plays* version of the text shortens this passage to two arias, but it is fleshed out with dialogue that books on rhyme and scansion often delete. In this version, the younger brother, Yinzhuma, is all too eager to drink the wine, creating a scene of contrast between hasty indulgence and cautious respect for ritual that is indicative of the respective personalities of each brother:

（老千戶云）看你這般艱難，你那裏得這錢來買酒？教哥哥費心。	OLD CHILIARCH *speaks*: You are in such difficulty, how in the world did you get the money to buy wine? I've caused such distress for you.
（正末做遞酒科，唱）	JINZHUMA *acts out passing him wine and sings*:
【落梅風】	*To the tune of* "Luomei feng"
我抹的這瓶口兒淨，	I've wiped the lip of this jug until it is clean,
我斟的這盞面兒圓。	And filled this cup until it is full.
（老千戶做接盞科）	OLD CHILIARCH *acts out accepting the cup.*
（正末云）兄弟，且休便吃。	JINZHUMA *speaks*: Brother, don't drink it yet.
（正末唱）	JINZHUMA *sings*:
待我望著那碧天邊太陽澆奠。	Wait until I gaze at the sun at blue heaven's edge and sprinkle a sacrifice.
則俺這窮人家又不會別咒願，	"Let me, this poverty-stricken person, have no other prayer of desire
則願的俺兄弟海每可便早能勾相見。	Than wishing that we brothers will be able to see each other once again."

[HTP 196c]

Note that the phrase uttered in Jinzhuma's prayer in the earlier version of "Luomei feng" "Let me, this Jurchen, have no other wish" has been changed here to "Let me, this poverty-stricken person." This makes this particular aria less about Jurchen and Jinzhuma's particular condition and more about a general notion of poverty; what was specific to one person of one ethnicity now becomes a comment that can apply to any such situation:

（做澆奠、再遞酒科，云）兄弟滿飲一杯。	JINZHUMA *acts out pouring out a sacrifice, presents the wine again, and speaks*: Drink to the full, brother.
（老千戶云）哥哥先飲。	OLD CHILIARCH *speaks*: Brother, you go first.
（正末云）好波，我先吃了。兄弟飲。	JINZHUMA *speaks*: All right, I'll drink first, and then you drink.
（老千戶云）待你兄弟吃。	OLD CHILIARCH *speaks*: Let me drink first then.
（正末云）兄弟再飲一杯。	JINZHUMA *speaks*: Have another cup.

（老千戶云）只我今日見了哥哥，吃幾杯
酒；到了夾山口子，我一點酒也不吃了。

OLD CHILIARCH *speaks*: I'm only having a few today because of seeing you, but I won't drink even a single drop when I reach Mountain Narrows Pass.

（正末云）兄弟，你哥哥無甚麼與你。

JINZHUMA *speaks*: I have nothing to give you as a going-away present, brother.

（老千戶云）我今日辭哥哥去，敢問哥哥要
甚麼？

OLD CHILIARCH *speaks*: I'm taking my leave of you today. What would I dare ask you for?

（正末唱）

JINZHUMA *sings*:

【阿那忽】

To the tune "Anahu"

再得我往日家緣，

Were I but to have my family fortune of earlier days,

可敢齎發與你些個盤纏。

Then would I be able to provide you some traveling money.

有他這鰾接來的兩根兒家竹箭。

But I have these two arrows of homegrown bamboo joined with fish glue—

（老千戶云）你兄弟收了者。

OLD CHILIARCH *speaks*: I will accept them.

（正末云）還有哩。

JINZHUMA *speaks*: I have more.

（正末唱）

JINZHUMA *sings*:

更有條蠟打來的這弓弦。

And this bow string struck with beeswax.

[*HTP* 196c–197a]

In the dialogue about Jinzhuma's past, Yinzhuma constantly contrasts Jinzhuma's opulent lifestyle of the past with the present, including his presence in people's lives as a performer. This is not a performer in a Chinese setting, and surely not one subject to the same opprobrium and lack of status. He is a clan musician and dancer, who is an important figure in the rituals of life—birth, death, and marriage—when proper ritual music is desired. In the next few songs in the suite, Yinzhuma mentions this role:

（老千戶云）想哥哥那往日。也曾受用快活
來。

OLD CHILIARCH *speaks*: Thinking back on days past, you were happy then and full of joy.

（正末唱）

JINZHUMA *sings*:

【大拜門】

To the tune of "Da baimen"

我可也不想今朝，

I cannot think about today,

常記的往年，

But always recall years past,

到處裏追陪下些親眷。

When I was companion everywhere to my kith and kin,

我也曾吹彈那管弦，

And played those pipes and plucked the strings—

快活了萬千，

There were infinite joys then,

可便是大拜門撒敦家的筵宴。

At the childbirth-visit celebrations of our family.

[*HTP* 197a–197b]

Yinzhuma then brings up Jinzhuma's clothes. While we can understand this as a general comment on his hard times, it may also speak to the special costumes that

YUAN AND MING DYNASTIES

Jinzhuma wore when he was performing. In either case, Yinzhuma's statements act as a continual prodding to make Jinzhuma confront his own decline and feel the pain of his current situation:

（老千戶云）我想哥哥幼年間，穿著那等樣的衣服，今日便怎生這等窮暴了？

OLD CHILIARCH *speaks*: Thinking back on the beautiful clothes you wore when young, how can you now be so poor?

（正末唱）

JINZHUMA *sings*:

【山石榴】

To the tune "Shanshiliu"

往常我便打扮的別，
流妝的善，
幹皂靴鹿皮綿團也似軟，
那一領家夾襖子是藍腰線。

Back then I dressed distinctly,
And groomed myself finely.
The deerskin of my black boots was as soft as a ball of silk,
And my padded housecoat was sashed with blue at the waist.

【醉娘子】

To the tune "Zui niangzi"

則我那珍珠豌豆也似圓，
我尚兀自揀擇穿。
頭巾上砌的粉花兒現，

我系的那一條玉兔鶻是餘廂面。

And my real pearls were as round as peas,
And still, from among those, I chose the best to wear.
The scarf I wore layered upon my head revealed plum flower patterns,
The jade belt that I tightened was inlaid with gold.

（老千戶云）哥哥，你那幼年間中注模樣，如今便怎生老的這等了？

OLD CHILIARCH *speaks*: Your former looks, how they have changed!

（正末唱）

JINZHUMA *sings*:

【相公愛】

To the tune "Xianggong ai"

則我那銀盆也似龐兒膩粉鈿。
墨錠也似髭須著絨繩兒纏。

Like a silver bowl, my face was laid thick with paint,[17]
As black as inksticks, my beard was twined with colored yarn.

對著這官員，
親將那籌箸傳，
等的個安筵盞初巡遍。

Facing these many officials,
I personally handed about the wine tallies
In anticipation of the first round's circulation that set the feast.

【不拜門】

To the tune "Bu baimen"

則聽的這者刺骨笛兒悠悠聒耳喧，

那駝皮鼓冬冬的似春雷健。

I just listened until the drawn out wavering flute of the *zhelagu* song grated on my ears,
And that camel-skin drum boomed and rumbled like strong spring thunder—

我向這筵前，
筵前，
我也曾舞蹁躚，
舞罷呵誰不把咱來誇羨！

Then, I moved before the feast mat,
Before the feast mat
I, too, once danced the whirl,
And when the dance was done, who among them did not laud me?

[*HTP* 197b]

CONCLUSION

The representations of performance in the three plays discussed in this chapter give us a sense of the importance of music and performance in Jurchen life, whether in China or in their native lands. Such representations are fictional, but they are based on perceptions of nomadic lives found in a variety of Chinese texts from the eighth to the twelfth centuries, including travel literature, monographs, and poems.

Of course, an interest in the musical talents of foreigners is an old trope in Chinese literature, but there seems to be some deeper connection in this case. We might ask: What is it that ties together the insubordinate sons who give up a life of ease and officialdom and the lone performer of *The Tiger Head Plaque*? Two are set in the commercial world of the urban theater in China, while the other is based on the function of music in quotidian rituals of life that mark its passage. Both Li Zhifu and Shi Junbao were Jurchen descendants, although removed by several generations from the culture of their homeland, and cultural lore would have continued in their family, even as rituals that had no understandable meaning in their own lives. (At this point, one is reminded of people of Mexican descent in New Mexico who are Catholics, but who still turn statues toward the wall on Friday nights, blithely unaware of their own Jewish ancestry.) Of course, we must never exclude the possibility that Li and Shi had to operate in a Chinese environment, where their own livelihood rested on the performance of their plays, and so they manufactured plays that would meet the Chinese stereotype of foreign tribes—loving to dance and sing, allowing marital practices that violated Chinese ethical norms, and being generally difficult to control—that would bring them an audience. A less cynical view would argue that this love of music and performance, stereotyped in Chinese sources, was real enough in their culture to make it worthwhile for them to explore it in different environments.

Certainly, Li Zhifu's inclusion of the "Jurchen suite" in his play (whether lifted from another source or not) is a clue that this music continued into the thirteenth century and was popular enough to remain in the repertoire. We should keep in mind that the audience in North China, before and after the Mongol invasion, would have included a considerable number of Jurchens. It is also interesting that in all three plays, the performer is free from any constraints or expectations of the culture in which they operate. Shouma and Lingchunma, by becoming actors and two denizens of the theater world, escaped the heavy responsibility of social and official life, while Jinzhuma once enjoyed an opulent way of life by virtue of his talents. While the scenes of performance are in two different cultural domains, it is the love of music and of performing music that binds the plays together in often unsuspected ways.

Stephen H. West

NOTES

1. The Five Basic Relationships are the hierarchical ethical relationships that obtained between lord and minister, father and son, husband and wife, elder and younger brothers, and friend and friend.

2. See Herbert Franke, "Chinese Texts on the Jurchen: A Translation of the Jurchen Monograph in the *San-ch'ao pei-meng hui-pien*," *Zentralasiatische Studien* 9 (1975): 125, 137, and passim.

3. Li was the Chinese surname adopted by the Pucha clan.

4. "Lily chamber" was originally a name for the mother's chamber; later it designated the mother.

5. The term "orchid offices" referred from the Tang onward to the Palace Library and, by extension, to any of the places involved in collecting, editing, or collating books, occasionally including the Bureau of History.

6. That is, when will father and son both hold high positions?

7. This is a reference to a story about the famous Di Renjie (630–700; known better in the West as Judge Dee), who was sent to a post in Shanxi. He passed over the Taihang Mountains and looked toward his home in northern Hebei, but he saw only white clouds, and he said, "My parents live below these." From this, people take the image of white clouds to mean "thinking of one's parents."

8. The dance of the infernal judge was performed on stage from at least as early as the Song dynasty. The judge was costumed in a mask, a long beard, and black boots. He decided in which of the ten courts of hell humans might spend their afterlives. Here, Starlet Wang is making sarcastic remarks about his haggard looks and ratty clothes.

9. The relationship cannot be recovered.

10. An engaged woman would cut her long hair and present it to her man as a token of love; the incense and oath sealed the pact forever.

11. The opening announcement of a play usually vaunted the skill of the performers.

12. Many rich and powerful families lived near the five tumuli of the Han emperors on the outskirts of Chang'an. In later times, it simply became a metaphor for important and powerful young dandies—a polite way of saying, "someone who has it made."

13. These lines are meant to be sarcastic.

14. I.e., for fear that fatherly love will force Lingchunma to abandon her and return home.

15. That is, to reunite father and son, despite how she personally feels.

16. The "sheet of that paper" is a list that announces the successful graduates of the Advanced Scholar examination.

17. Jurchen men painted their faces silver.

PRIMARY SOURCES

BCGZP   Li Yu 李玉, comp. *Beici guang zhengpu* 北詞廣正譜 (*The Expanded and Accurate Formulary of Northern Songs*). In *Xuxiu Siku quanshu* 續修四庫全書 (*The Sequel to* The Complete Books of the Four Treasuries). Shanghai: Shanghai guji chubanshe, 2002.

HMZD   Talents from Old Hangzhou 古杭才人. *Huanmen zidi cuo lishen* 宦門子弟錯立身 (*A Playboy from a Noble House Opts for the Wrong Career*). In *Yongle dadian xiwen sanzhong jiaozhu* 永樂大典戲文三種校注 (*An Annotated Edition of Three Southern Plays from* The Great Canon of the Yongle Era). Ann. Qian Nanyang 錢南揚. Beijing: Zhonghua shuju, 1979.

HTP   Li Zhifu 李直夫. *Bianyi xingshi hutou pai* 便宜行事虎頭牌 (*The Tiger Head Plaque That Authorizes Its Bearer to Act on His Own Judgment*). In Zang Maoxun 臧懋循, ed. *Yuanqu xuan* 元曲選 (*Select Yuan Plays*). Hangzhou, China: Zhejiang guji chubanshe, 1998.

THZYP   Zhu Quan 朱權. *Taihe zhengyin pu jianping* 太和正音譜箋評 (*An Annotated Edition of* The Formulary of Correct Prosody of the Era of Great Peace). Ann. Yao Pinwen 姚品文. Zhongguo wenxue yanjiu dianji congkan 中國文學研究典籍叢刊 (*A Compiled Series of Classics for Research on Chinese Literature*), ed. Luo Di 洛地. Beijing: Zhonghua shuju, 2010.

ZYT   Shi Junbao 石君寶. *Fengyue ziyunting* 風月紫雲庭 (*Breezes and Moonlight in the Courtyard of Purple Clouds*). In *Yuankan zaju sanshi zhong* 元刊雜劇三十種 (*Thirty Yuan Printed Zaju Plays*). *Guben xiqu congkan siji* 古本戲曲叢刊四集 (*The Fourth Set of the Collectanea of Ancient Editions of Plays*). Vol. 2. Shanghai: Commercial Press, 1958.

SUGGESTED READINGS

TRANSLATIONS

Li Zhifu. *The Tiger Head Plaque.* Trans. Yoram Szekely, C. T. Hsia, Wai-yee Li, and George Kao. In *The Columbia Anthology of Yuan Drama*, ed. C. T. Hsia, Wai-yee Li, and George Kao, 233–266. New York: Columbia University Press, 2014.

Talents from Old Hangzhou. *Grandee's Son Takes the Wrong Career.* Trans. William Dolby. In *Eight Chinese Plays: From the Thirteenth Century to the Present Day*, ed. William Dolby, 30–52. London: Elek, 1976.

Shi Junbao. *Breezes and Moonlight in the Courtyard of Purple Clouds.* Trans. Wilt L. Idema and Stephen H. West. In *Chinese Theater, 1100–1450: A Source Book*, ed. Wilt L. Idema and Stephen H. West, 236–278. Wiesbaden, Germany: Franz Steiner Verlag, 1982.

Shi Junbao. *A Playboy from a Noble House Takes the Wrong Career.* Trans. Wilt L. Idema and Stephen H. West. In *Chinese Theater, 1100–1450*, ed. Wilt L. Idema and Stephen H. West, 205–235. Wiesbaden, Germany: Franz Steiner Verlag, 1982.

ENGLISH

Franke, Herbert. "Chinese Texts on the Jurchen: A Translation of the Jurchen Monograph in the *San-ch'ao pei-meng hui-pien.*" *Zentralasiatische Studien* 9 (1975): 119–186.

Tillman, Hoyt Cleveland, and Stephen H. West, ed. *China under Jurchen Rule: Essays on Chin Intellectual and Cultural History.* Albany, NY: SUNY Press, 1995.

West, Stephen H. "Jurchen Elements in the Northern Drama *Hu-t'ou-p'ai.*" *T'oung Pao* 69, no. 4 (1977): 273–295.

CHINESE

Che Xilun 車錫倫, and Yuan Aiguo 袁愛國. "Qianlun Nüzhen zu juzuo jia Li Zhifu de zaju Hutou pai" 淺論女真族劇作家李直夫的雜劇《虎頭牌》 (An Exploration of the *Zaju The Tiger Head Plaque* by Jurchen Author Li Zhifu). *Nei Menggu daxue xuebao* (*Journal of the University of Inner Mongolia, Philosophy and Social Sciences*) 4 (1983): 91–96.

Li Zhanpeng 李占鵬. "Shaoshu minzu yu Yuanqu chuangzuo" 少數民族與元曲創作 (Ethnic Minorities and the Creation of Yuan Songs and Drama). *Hubei minzu xueyuan xuebao* (*zhexue shehui kexue ban*) 湖北民族學院學報（哲學社會科學版) (*Journal of the Hubei Nationalities College, Philosophy and Social Sciences*) 30, no. 1 (2012): 92–98.

Wang Fang 王方. "*Hutou pai* zhong Nüzhen yinyue tese ji sixiang zhuti tanjiu" 《虎頭牌》中女真音樂特色及思想主題探究 (A Study of the Characteristics of Jurchen Music and Themes in *The Tiger Head Plaque*). *Weifang jiaoyu xueyuan xuebao* 濰坊教育學院學報 (*Journal of the Weifang Teacher's College*) 24, no. 3 (2011): 45–47.

Wang Peng 王鵬. "Yuan zaju zhongde Nüzhen zu tese" 元雜劇中的女真族特色 (The Characteristics of the Jurchens in Yuan *Zaju* Plays). *Hebei minzu shifan xueyuan xuebao* 河北民族師範學院學報 (*Journal of the Hebei Province Nationalities Teacher College*) 32, no. 2 (2012): 9–11.

3

The Pavilion for Praying to the Moon and *The Injustice to Dou E*

The Innovation of the Female Lead

As the purported "father of Yuan *zaju* drama," with a corpus of more than sixty plays attributed to him, Guan Hanqing (ca. 1220–after 1279) is best remembered for his spirited female protagonists. Among his eighteen extant song-dramas that have come to us in fourteenth-century or in late-sixteenth/early-seventeenth-century imprints, no fewer than eleven feature female leads in courtroom, domestic, romantic, and history plays. Availing themselves of the singing part of a "female lead" (*zhengdan*), Guan's plays crafted female characters structured around a dramatic conflict, and as such they had no precise analog in earlier male- or female-authored writings about women. The notion of a "female lead" not only indicated the importance of that part relative to all the other characters in a play, but the lead singer, no matter the gender, was invariably conceived as a sympathetic figure. Hence, singing the lead part allowed a woman to inhabit the moral center of the play. In short, these plays do not feature one-dimensional, stock characters; rather, they invest the female lead with moral dilemmas, conflicting emotions, and rhetorical versatility.[1]

In Guan Hanqing's extant female lead plays, community norms are in crisis within the family or within the body politic at large, and it falls to the female lead to make morally defensible decisions amid acts of war, official corruption, sexual aggression, or the selfish behavior perpetrated by others. Rather than being confronted with a single predicament, Guan's heroines routinely face a battery of successive challenges, each of which prompts the protagonist to grapple with her stated aspirations and the unforeseen consequences of her decisions. However, instead of simply defaulting to gendered expectations of proper behavior, Guan's heroines champion improvisation—that is, they choose a course of action that may violate the expectations of their elders or their social betters—but at the same time, they do not act impulsively. Rather, they go to great lengths to justify their decisions in accordance with their own moral principles. To express their evolving thoughts and emotions to themselves, to other protagonists, or to the audience within the span of four short acts, Guan's female leads engage in many forms of verbal display, but whether such verbal expression takes the form of tender care or pointed cursing, their utterances are grounded in their belief that the impartial judgment of Heaven (*tian*) will vindicate them.

In contrast to earlier literature on female moral exemplars, these plays do not simply show us a snapshot of a single moment of absolute devotion to a Confucian ideal, but rather let the audience experience the unfolding of a series of "good enough" moral choices in the face of the unpredictable and often conflicting exigencies of everyday life. When the plays resolve the heroine's unconventional actions within the framework of broader social norms, it is the female lead's moral choices that are publicly vindicated, not those of her elders. In some plays, the deeds of the female lead are explicitly validated by Heaven. In others, coincidences are deployed as a means to endorse the heroine's conduct. In crafting female leads who struggle to make their own moral reasoning socially legible within the world of the play, Guan Hanqing's song-dramas prize a dynamic and deeply affecting form of moral integrity.

In what follows, we will examine how Guan Hanqing's plays help us understand three aspects of early Chinese theatrical culture. In doing so, we will pay particular attention to two female lead plays (*danben*): *A Beauty's Boudoir Lament: The Pavilion for Praying to the Moon* (*Guiyuan jiaren Baiyueting*, extant in a fourteenth-century recension known as *Thirty Yuan-Printed Zaju Plays* [*Yuankan zaju sanshi zhong*], hereafter *Moon Pavilion*) and *Moving Heaven and Earth: The Injustice to Dou E* (*Gantian dongdi Dou E yuan*, extant in late-sixteenth-century and early-seventeenth-century versions, hereafter *Injustice*). First, we will explore how the structure of Guan's *zaju* plays draws attention to the fact that Chinese drama is not organized around a differentiation between tragedy and comedy. As we shall demonstrate, plays instead revolve around an ideal of creating a rhetorical vehicle (e.g., a play) that is capacious enough to accommodate a range of affects, emotions, and moods across a broad spectrum of experiences—joy and sorrow, separations and reunions (*beihuan lihe*). As we read Guan's plays against what we can reconstruct about the artistic demands placed upon Yuan-dynasty actresses, we will see that the theatrical culture of the time similarly favored virtuosic range.

Second, we will analyze how *Moon Pavilion* uses stage directions and songs to characterize the female lead. In particular, we will explore how the decisions of the female lead neither blindly followed prevailing social norms nor reflected the frowned-upon behavior to which women were said to be prone (e.g., premarital liaisons, adulterous relationships, and hasty widow remarriages, among others). Instead, through the skillful use of morally tinged language, the lead is able to prevail against formidable odds arrayed against her.

Finally, we will examine *Injustice*, another of Guan Hanqing's signature plays, in light of what it tells us about the rhetorical power of female virtue. Far from being exclusively a reactionary force designed to stabilize social hierarchies, extreme acts of virtue—as demonstrated by *Injustice's* heroine, Dou E—can be deeply disruptive of the social status quo. In fact, so powerful has Dou E's appeal been that she remains a household name in the Chinese-speaking world to this day.

3.1 GUAN HANQING, ZHULIAN XIU, AND THE ACTING CULTURE OF YUAN *ZAJU* THEATER

The question of what to call Chinese song-drama has been a point of lively discussion ever since Chinese theatrical texts came to the attention of foreign critics. In the 1720s, when the Jesuit missionary Joseph de Prémare (1666–1736), who was knowledgeable about and enamored of Chinese literature, first translated *The Orphan of Zhao* (*Zhao shi gu'er*, ➤ chap. 5) into French, he observed that the Chinese did not distinguish between comedy and tragedy. However, J. B. du Halde (1674–1743), the editor who published Prémare's partial translation, pitched the play as a tragedy in an attempt to secure more attention for his monumental and highly influential compilation, *Description de la Chine* (The Universal History of China) (1735–1736). Ever since, the question as to whether or not certain *zaju* plays qualify as tragedy—the perceived pinnacle of dramatic expression in Western culture—has absorbed a lot of scholarly energy in both Europe and China. Here, I will suggest that *zaju* plays, rather than limiting themselves to people of high station (French tragedy), irresolvable conflicts (German tragedy), or unfortunate events (modern tragedy), featured people from all walks of life, who, though beset by difficult choices, nevertheless found means to resolve conflicts in unexpected and yet morally resonant ways. In short, Yuan-dynasty acting stage practices, acting appreciation, and playtexts all showcased affective breadth and nuance.

Prolific and versatile, Guan Hanqing wrote for the urban commercial stage in the Yuan capital of Beijing, where female performers had come to occupy a place of note. Most prominent among these was one of Guan Hanqing's literary acquaintances, a performer who went by the stage name Zhulian xiu ("Pearl Curtain Beauty"), an epithet that played on an ancient trope that likened sublime singing to a "string of pearls"[2] (➤ Introduction). From Zhulian xiu's entry in the famous biographical compendium of female Yuan dynasty performers, *The Record of the Green Bowers* (*Qinglou ji*, ca. 1360s) (➤ chap. 2), we infer that she was as important to the rise of *zaju* acting as Guan Hanqing was to the creation of the written *zaju* repertoire:

> Zhulian xiu's surname was Zhu and she was the fourth in the familial birth order. In the realm of *zaju* plays, she was unrivalled in her time. In terms of role types, she was able to bring out the subtleties of imperial roles (*jiatou*), coquettish female roles (*huadan*), and soft male leads (*ruan moni*) among others. . . . Later generations of actors revered her [as their tutelary patron deity] under the name "Foremother Zhu" (Zhu niangniang).

> [*QLJJZ* 82]

Literate to the point of compiling a poetry collection of her own, Zhulian xiu attracted the attention of many literati who worked in or frequented the world of the urban theater. First and foremost, they appreciated the enormous versatility evident in her many performances. The mastery of singing parts enumerated thus far spanned gender (both male and female roles), social status (emperors and courtesans), and disposition (romantic versus serious). Hu Zhiyu (1227–1293), an eminent scholar-official and theater aficionado, repeatedly raved about Zhulian xiu's ability to assume every conceivable theatrical guise: "When one concentrates one's efforts for a long time in any given field, one can get old just studying that one craft or profession or skill (*yi*). Previously, all the crafts, professions, or skills could not be united in one woman [such as Zhulian xiu has done]!" [*ZSDQJ* 8.9b–10a]. In his view, gifted performers—situated as they were between the lyrical self-expression of the songs and the narrative exigencies of the plot—could potentially capture the dynamic nature of the world through the many-splendored prism of a lead part. Guan Hanqing, for another, also composed a highly laudatory song about Zhulian xiu's simultaneously "noble and elegant" (*fugui*) and "stylish and romantic" (*fengliu*) qualities [*GHQXQJ* 948], two sets of attributes that were often thought to be mutually exclusive (☞ *HTRCP*, C16.7). Given her talent, their documented acquaintance, and his explicit regret over her retirement from the stage, it is very likely that Guan may have written some of his female lead plays as star vehicles for Zhulian xiu.

A closer look at the extant corpus of Yuan *zaju* plays also demonstrates how the role distribution, the stage directions, and the plotline sought to capitalize on a main lead's performative virtuosity. Among a total of more than 160 extant Yuan and Yuan-inspired *zaju* plays, about 50 feature a main singing role who assumes the voice and perspective of more than one character in the course of four (or occasionally five) acts and of the occasional demi-act or wedge. Moreover, the characters portrayed by the lead singer in the course of a single play are often people with vastly different temperaments. Guan Hanqing's paired Three Kingdoms plays are an excellent case in point. In *The Great King Guan and the Single Sword Meeting* (*Guan Dawang dandaohui*, hereafter *Single Sword Meeting*), the awe-inspiring military prowess of Guan Yu (d. 220), China's fieriest warrior and eventual god of war, is eloquently invoked by the singing lead in three capacities: the arc of the play requires that the main lead be able to perform a level-headed civil service official (a minister, act 1), a free-spirited, but politically seasoned recluse (a Daoist, act 2), and an imposing, godlike military figure (Guan Yu, acts 3 and 4) (☞ chap. 16).[3] *In a Dream Zhang Fei and Guan Yu, a Pair, Rush to Western Shu* (*Guan Zhang shuangfu Xi Shu meng*), the main lead assumes the identities of three similarly diverse protagonists, who reminiscence about the glory days of China's most famous sworn brotherhood. First, the main lead plays an eloquent imperial envoy (act 1), and then a famously cool-headed strategist (Zhuge Liang, act 2) (☞ *HTRCProse*, C7.1), before impersonating a notoriously impetuous warrior (Zhang Fei, acts 3 and 4) (☞ chap. 16).[4]

The performative demands for protean nuance were reflected not only in the role distribution for plays, but also found their way into the stage directions. Fourteenth-century *zaju* plays vary widely in terms of how many stage directions they provide, but typically, such directions touch upon timing and manner of entrances (e.g., regular pace versus fast pace), as well as exits (e.g., actual versus apparent); costume (e.g., full costume versus plain or casual dress, specific accessories, changing clothes); physical actions (e.g., sitting in a boat, kneeling, slipping and falling, running, opening a door, changing clothes, carrying wine, greeting another character, assisting others); and the precise manner of oral delivery. In that regard, the most basic distinction is whether to sing (songs), to recite (poetry), or to speak (dialogue, different forms of announcements). Speaking, in particular, is frequently further characterized by more specific suggestions on the manner of delivery. For example, stage directions may indicate that the actor should make a declaration or confession (*gao*), make a formal report (*bao*), officially proclaim something (*xuan*), offer remonstration or censure (*jian*), submit a memorial to the throne (*zou*), or recite the Amituo Buddha's name (*nianfo*). Stage directions may also include cues about the emotional tenor of the remarks in instructions, such as speaking as if pondering a question (*xunsi yun*), speaking with a smile (*xiaoyun*), saying something angrily (*nuyun*), or cursing (*ma*).

As Wilt L. Idema has observed, Guan Hanqing's *Moon Pavilion* contains more stage directions than any other early *zaju* play, numbering close to seventy for the female lead alone.[5] In contrast to other plays, where the majority of stage directions concern physical actions, over half of the ones in *Moon Pavilion* address the expression of diverse, mixed, and occasionally conflicting emotions. During the play, the stage directions direct the main lead to express deep sorrow and steadfast concern (wedge), panic, shame, and resolve (act 1); wifely concern, grief, embarrassment, panic, and distress (act 2); sorrow, embarrassment, and joy (act 3); and resolve and steadfastness (act 4). For instance, in act 1, over the course of three songs, when the main lead is looking for her mother among a stream of war refugees and happens to chance upon a scholar, the performer is enjoined to act out the following emotions in quick succession: being panicked (*zuo moluan ke*), fiercely glaring at the male role (*mengjian mo*), being scared and embarrassed (*da can haixiu ke*), being resolute (*zuo zhu*), making up one's mind (*zuo yi*), and smiling in a conciliatory fashion (*zuo peixiao ke*). The admixture of different states, together with the rapid succession from one state to the next, challenged the skills of the actors as they were attempting to "speak with eloquence and make every sentence and every word ring true and clear" while "employing expressive gestures and visual cues to aid the audience's understanding."[6]

Such quick shifts from one emotional extreme to another were also reflected in the plotlines of individual acts. A single act could contain a spectrum of verbal actions with very different emotional resonances. Specifically, descriptions of physically embodied vocal forms such as public wailing (*ku*), generally associated with wrongful or premature death, lamentation/sighing (*yuan, tan*), associated with the dissonance between one's innate potential and the actuality of one's situation, oaths (*shi*), associated with contracting and shoring up bonds among people, remonstration (*jian*), associated with making the moral shortcomings of superiors public, cursing (*ma*), associated with public shaming of people below or above one's station, or battle cries (*jiao, he*), associated with intimidating one's enemies, could be placed side by side with evocations of joyous singing (*ge*), associated with happy reclusion away from politics, boasting/praise (*zan*), associated with military prowess (☞ chap. 16), mockery (*chao*), associated with spirited satire and wit, and banter (*xiaotan*), associated with feasting at banquets.

For instance, in act 2 of the *Single Sword Meeting*, the Daoist recluse juxtaposes his idyllic life in rustic retirement full of joyous singing with the imagined horrors of the sound of war drums and the resulting bloodshed from a drunken court feast gone awry. Similarly, in act 1 of Guan Hanqing's other fourteenth-century female lead play, *The Clever Maid Arranges a Match for Herself* (*Zha nizi tiao fengyue*), the main female lead, a personal maid in a noble household who prides herself on her own steadfast integrity, expresses many misgivings about male lovers who swear oaths of eternal fidelity but casually abandon women beneath their stations. Yet when the nobleman whom she serves asks her for a night of romance, she hesitatingly consents to sexual relations in the hope of eventually becoming his concubine. Thus, in a single act, torn between caution and longing, the main lead chooses the risky route of sexual intimacy after having outlined every possible reason to forego such a commitment. In short, rather than requiring that an actress or an actor specialize in a stock character linked to a single mood or a single mode of delivery, Yuan plays offered a platform for demonstrating a wide range of sentiments and associated expressive practices.

In contrast to Western theater with its Aristotelian distinction between (high-brow) tragic and (lowbrow) comic characters, Chinese *zaju* drama aimed to be theater that could capture all social strata with equal gravitas. As Hu Zhiyu, our astute Yuan theater buff, put it in his etymology of *zaju* theater: "As *zaju* plays are called 'mixed and wide-ranging' (*za*), . . . there is not a single scenario, of which the emotions are not represented and the outward appearance is not captured" [*ZSDQJ* 8.57a]. In Hu's view, the fullness of theatrical representation across social strata, moral sensibilities, gender, religion, professions, and people from native and foreign lands was the distinguishing feature of the form and of its most accomplished practitioners: "In terms of outward appearance, [Zhulian xiu's *zaju* performances] can fully capture [everyone's] demeanor (*tai*), in terms of inner lives, [her acting] details the nuances of [everyone's] feelings (*qing*)" [*ZSDQJ* 8.11a].[7]

In that sense, mature Chinese *zaju* drama was, for all its commitments to performative stylization and to ritual conventions, a realistic kind of theater from its inception. However, in contrast to modern forms of realism that are underwritten by a psychologically driven secularism, Chinese plays had deep roots in a highly moral, if not outright religious view of the world. Hence, as we shall see in our analysis of *Moon Pavilion*, *zaju* theater did not feature virtuoso displays of feelings and movements simply for the sake of individual characterization—rather, it tied such virtuosity to the exploration of ethical dilemmas in an imperfect society.

3.2 *THE PAVILION FOR PRAYING TO THE MOON:* THE MORAL SUASION OF SITUATIONAL ETHICS

The protagonists of Yuan *zaju* found themselves in a rough-and-tumble world where they often were at the mercy of forces beyond their control. Such contingencies could take many forms—historical events such as war; personal misfortune such as illness or sudden death of loved ones; violence in the form of sexual assault, banditry, and miscarriage of justice; or coincidences such as unexpected encounters or involuntary separations. Accordingly, whatever high-minded moral ambitions the protagonists might have, such moral resolve was challenged, more often than not, by the trials and tribulations of everyday life. Hence, rather than hewing to a singular moral stance, the protagonists of Yuan *zaju* were forced to improvise and devise impromptu solutions to the many practical and moral dilemmas that they found themselves confronted with. To differentiate such actions from mere convenience or opportunism (*suiji er bian*), the heroine's unconventional choices often exacted a toll of suffering from her before she was rewarded with a satisfactory resolution.

Zaju drama developed a variety of tools to allow for the main lead's moral agonizing to become a process that an audience could relate to. First and foremost, the main leads expressed themselves through a series of songs that performed a wide variety of functions. Key among them was to offer a subjective perspective on a set of moral issues. In their attempt to forge a practically efficacious and morally defensible course of action, the main lead could address themselves to different people both inside and outside the play. Such a multipronged approach to communication was all the more important because *zaju* heroines often acted in ways that invited skepticism and potential censure from their social superiors within the play and the audience outside the play. In interpreting the moral significance of her own behavior and that of the other characters in the play, female lead characters—drawn from the humble ranks of servants, courtesans, commoners, and genteel women under pressure—considerably enlarged the moral authority that a female persona could occupy in Chinese literary writings. In what follows, we will examine how one *zaju* play attributed to Guan Hanqing, *Moon Pavilion*, explores the nuances of such morality under duress. While the female lead played the same character throughout the story, it will become clear that she assumed many emotional modes and stances over the course of the play.

As a play whose story lacks documented antecedents, *Moon Pavilion* showcases a female lead who, amid all the messy trials of everyday life (war, family separations, the threat of sexual violence and abduction, illness, and the emotional toll of male careerism), is in principle devoted to the notion of female sexual restraint and the ritual propriety of arranged marriage. At the same time, she seeks to persuade the other protagonists—and, by extension, the audience—of the righteousness of her decision to modify such behavior in the face of external threats. Specifically, the play examines the decisions of a young woman from a prominent Jurchen family by the name of Wang Ruilan in the chaos following the Mongol invasion of the Jin-dynasty capital Zhongdu (present-day Beijing) (☛ chap. 2). First, Ruilan and her mother bid farewell to Wang Zhen, the head of their family and a Jurchen military official, as he departs on official business amid news of invading armies advancing from the Western frontier (wedge). As the capital is about to fall, Ruilan flees along with her mother, but she loses sight of her in the melee of a battle skirmish. When

Ruilan suddenly finds herself all alone, she agrees to a nominal marriage with an aspiring Chinese scholar, Jiang Shilong, who offers to protect her against the sexual predation of other men—a threat made vivid by the subsequent appearance of Tuoman Xingfu, a bandit and sworn brother of Jiang Shilong's (act 1).

Later, we learn that what started out as a pseudomarriage of convenience has flowered into a full-fledged husband-and-wife bond; however, what prompts such an unexpected turn of events is not the pursuit of romance, but rather Jiang Shilong's sudden, life-threatening illness. In a reversal of the roles of protection, Wang Ruilan painstakingly takes care of her languishing common-law spouse and seeks medical help. By coincidence, Ruilan encounters her father in the inn where they have sought refuge, but what should have been a happy reunion quickly turns into a taut standoff. Appalled that his daughter has contracted a marriage on her own, her father has his soldiers grab Ruilan and coerces her to abandon Jiang Shilong (act 2).

After being sequestered in her father's residence in the southern capital of Bianliang (modern-day Kaifeng), Ruilan rants against her father and pines for her scholar paramour, while getting acquainted with Ruilian, a war refugee recently adopted by her family. Torn between treating Ruilian as a tattletale, rival, or confidante, Ruilan finds out that Ruilian is in fact Jiang Shilong's long-lost sister. Thereupon, Ruilan recaps her grievances about the man whom she considers "a brute of a father," while confessing her deep love for Jiang Shilong, whom she fears has died in the interim (act 3).

When subsequently pressed by her father to marry the top graduate of the military examinations, Ruilan extols the virtues of a scholarly spouse compared with the crassness of a military husband. When it turns out that Jiang Shilong is the top civil service graduate, and as such is not eligible to marry his would-be betrothed Ruilian, Ruilan finds herself reunited with Jiang. However, his readiness to simply consent to a marriage occasioned by his examination success gives her sufficient pause to doubt whether her deep attachment to him had been warranted, or whether he is just another opportunist. They make up in the end, however, and she agrees to marry him. Meanwhile, Ruilian, after some hemming and hewing, is married to the top graduate of the military examination, who turns out to be none other than the former bandit Tuoman Xingfu (act 4).

The play uses a variety of rhetorical techniques to reconcile the female lead's own breeches of conventional morality with her strident critique of other people's moral lapses. For starters, it makes extensive use of morally tinged speech codes, with roots in the earlier philosophical, poetic, and performative literature. In the course of the play, Ruilan deploys the following forms of expressive language:

The language of filial tenderness ("Father, you are so advanced in years, as you ride on the horse, please be careful!" [*GHQXQJ* 713])

The language of filial counsel ("Although during this military campaign you bear the burden of [keeping] Heaven and Earth from collapsing, you must think of Mother and me and come home soon!" [*GHQXQJ* 713])

The language of female decorum ("With Heaven and Earth in turmoil, I cannot
keep to the straight and narrow [*GHQXQJ* 716]);

The language of pointed wifely counsel ("If you [Jiang Shilong] think of it in this
way, haven't you gotten it all wrong?!" [*GHQXQJ* 716])

The language of wifely care and worry ("It is just me, this lone woman, who,
day and night, passes him the medicine and prepares some broth" [*GHQXQJ*
717])

The impassioned invective against her father ("It is as though I have chanced
upon a wild beast, . . . hoping for the warmth and ease of spring weather,
suddenly on top of the frozen snow, more frost has settled" [*GHQXQJ* 719])

The language of wifely fidelity ("You here at this inn—a lonesome traveler
detained by illness, me there on the post road, all distraught . . . I'd rather be
a widow [than marry somebody else]! [*GHQXQJ* 720])

The language of social satire ("My senile father, when he hears talk of ancient
books, he hates it so much his skull seems to burst" [*GHQXQJ* 721])

The poetic language of female longing ("When will my stomach not be in knots?
When will my heart be free from such vexation?" [*GHQXQJ* 721])

The invocation of Heaven ("I often had you in my thoughts, but you did not pine
after me, luckily there is Heaven above." [*GHQXQJ* 717])

In addition to deploying various literary stances, the main lead's songs also shift
between general pronouncements addressed to the audience, inner monologues,
and morally charged comments directed toward a particular person. General pronouncements elucidate moral principles or situational constraints, often presented
from an omniscient point of view, devoid of any personal pronouns ("As lances and
spears have shaken the Earth, sundry misfortunes have descended from Heaven"
[*GHQXQJ* 717]). Or, alternatively, a song may summarize the prevailing social
norms ("If you are overly attached to your groom, that will promptly stir talk in the
extended family, and it is said that if you are very affectionate with your husband,
you will become less mindful of your parents" [*GHQXQJ* 722]). By contrast, inner
monologues shed light on how the protagonist sees herself relative to moral principles, with frequent occurrences of subjective pronouns such as "I" (*wo*) or "we"
(*an*) marking the subjective nature of the observations ("With Heaven and Earth
in turmoil, I cannot keep within the straight and narrow" [*GHQXQJ* 716]). Finally,
dialogic songs directed toward others serve to explain the lead's own actions, while
also offering insight on what she may think of other people's behavior. Quite often,
such dialogic song passages not only comment on present circumstances, but also
anticipate future occurrences or reminisce about past events. Importantly, such
songs can feature an explicit relational form of self-address ("I, your child" [*anzi*],
"me, this wife of yours" [*nin zhe qi'er*]) or a direct address for another person to
indicate to whom the main lead is singing or speaking (e.g., "Husband" [*nan'er*],
"Father" [*fuqin*], "Papa" [*ama*]). Thus, the content of the songs is embedded within
that particular social relationship, and as such, subject to different possibilities
and constraints.

Such a differentiated system of address lays the foundation for the deployment of the notion of "situational compromise" or "moral expediency" (*quan*), a long-standing philosophical concept that authorized the nonobservance of conventional gender norms under extraordinary circumstances.[8] In one of the major turning points in the play, when Ruilan first encounters the scholar Jiang Shilong in act 1, she uses the first aria shown here to work through for herself how she feels (monologue mode), while in the second aria, she responds to two separate things that Jiang says, quoting Jiang Shilong's words as a general principle of the changed ways of the world (dialogue mode). Both of her songs culminate by invoking the character *quan* for its literal meaning of "for the time being," while also alluding to its more profound philosophical connotation of "expediency" (underlined in the following):

（正旦）	FEMALE LEAD *as* WANG RUILAN [*sings*]:
【後庭花】	*To the tune* "Houting hua"
每常我聽得綽的說箇女婿，	In the past, whenever the subject of a groom unexpectedly came up,
我早豁地離了坐位，	I abruptly got up from my seat,
悄地低了咽脛，	Silently lowering my head,
緼地紅了面皮。	And my face would flush bright red.
如今索強支持，	Now in search of support
如何迴避？	How can I avoid [such contact]?
藉不的那羞共耻。	I have no [longer any] use for such embarrassment or shame.
（末云了）（做陪笑科）	*The male role has spoken.* [*The female lead*] *acts out smiling in a conciliatory fashion.*
（正旦）	WANG RUILAN [*sings*]:
【金盞兒】	*To the tune* "Jinzhan'er"
您昆仲各東西，	You and your esteemed sister have gone East and West,
俺子母兩分離，	Me and my mother have likewise been separated from each other.
怕哥哥不嫌相辱呵,權為箇妹。	If you, esteemed Elder Brother, do not consider it too humiliating, how about if, <u>for the time being</u>, we resort to me being a Younger Sister?
（末云了）（尋思了）	*The male role has spoken.* [*The female lead*] *has thought about it.*
哥哥道做軍中男女相隨，	You, esteemed Elder Brother, said that in wartime if men and women accompany each other,
有兒夫的不擄掠，	Then those [women] who have a husband will not be abducted,
無家長的落便宜。	Whereas those without a male head of household will come to grief.

（做意了）　　　　　 *The [female lead] conveys [having made up her mind].*[9]

這般者波，怕不問時權做弟兄。　Under these circumstances, if no one asks, let's resort to
being siblings <u>for the time being</u>,

問着後道做夫妻。　　And only if asked, let's claim that we are husband and wife.

[*GHQXQJ* 715]

However, the play goes beyond a simple defensive stance for its female protagonist; instead, it grants Wang Ruilan the authority to judge behavior (both her
own and that of the other protagonists), regardless of whether they are her social
peers (Jiang Shilong's sister Jiang Ruilian); her social superiors (her father, her
mother, her common-law spouse); or her social inferiors (Tuoman Xingfu). As
the play pits a young woman from a respectable family against the various men in
her life (her father first and foremost, but also the scholar-cum–top graduate Jiang
Shilong and the bandit-cum–military top graduate Tuoman Xingfu), while engi-
neering a happy ending for everyone, the young woman sets the terms of what is
appropriate behavior for herself (act 1), for her common-law husband (act 1, act 4),
for her husband's sworn brother (act 1, act 4), and for her father (act 2, act 3). In so
doing, Ruilan's behavior appears to run counter to the expectation of social mod-
esty required of a proper daughter and wife, but the play takes great pains to couch
Ruilan's observations and decisions in morally grounded reasoning. Furthermore,
as Heaven appears to intercede on her behalf in aligning her impromptu marriage
choices with the outcome of the civil service examinations, her social defiance ultimately presents itself as a moral triumph for the female lead rather than as an ethical failure.

Such a moral basis for attempting to sway the people with more authority and
power in her life is most apparent in Ruilan's interactions with her father, Wang
Zhen, as the play casts both her tenderness and her pointed rants about him as
expressions of moral reasoning. A dutiful military man of Jurchen descent, Ruilan's father is full of political ambition, a trait that culminates in his quest to marry
both his daughters (Ruilan and Ruilian) to the top graduates of the civil and military examinations, respectively. However, in Ruilan's view, from the play's inception, her father is in danger of neglecting his paternal love in favor of political
pursuits (chap. 2). As the play begins, Ruilan outlines these competing Confucian concerns and makes no secret of the fact that she considers his parental
duties more important than his professional obligations. When her father is about
to embark on a military campaign, Ruilan reminds him of his parental obligations:
"Even though during this military campaign you shoulder the burden of [keeping]
Heaven and Earth from collapsing, you must think of us, your child and Mother,
and return home soon" [*GHQXQJ* 713]. Implicit in this remark is a reminder that
in his capacity as a father, he should offer her protection, something that he fails to
do, as she and her mother must flee the capital in his absence. When Ruilan later
chances upon him at the inn, she is quick to point out that she was left to fend for

herself, especially after she and her mother lost sight of each other in the terrifying chaos of battle: "I, your child, had no one to depend on and no one to turn to—this man really helped me out!" [*GHQXQJ* 718]. When her father orders his retinue to drag her off against her will and leave her sick, common-law husband behind, she vents her frustration in a song directed at her father: "Seeing someone on the brink of death, who would not be upset? But you are not prepared to show any compassion or concern. How could I not sigh and be heartbroken?" [*GHQXQJ* 719].

It is at this point in the play that Wang Ruilan begins to resort to invective against her father, but importantly, the pertinent songs are directed toward her husband, herself, or her adoptive sister, Ruilian. None of them are addressed toward her father, thus allowing the possibility of a reconciliation at the end. In her words of farewell to her husband, she observes, "Husband, these are the evil machinations of my Father, please don't bear a grudge against me, your wife" [*GHQXQJ* 719]. When she promises Jiang that she will remain faithful to him, she exclaims in exasperation that her "prick" (*na hua'er*) of a father better not even think about arranging another match. At her family's residence, she rants against her father, both for his refusal to recognize her marriage and for his heedless pursuit of the military arts and of social advancement. The epithet that she reserves for him is "my senile old man" (*an zhege beihui ye*), while repeatedly characterizing him as "brutal" (*henxin*), "savage" (*henqie*), and "cruel and vile" (*chezhe lieque*). She likens him to "a fierce tiger, a vicious wolf, a poisonous scorpion, a venomous viper" [*GHQXQJ* 724] and "a raging firestorm—mean-spirited and heartless" [*GHQXQJ* 724]. She feels that everyone else has a paterfamilias (*laofu*), an esteemed head of family (*zunjun*), and an affectionate daddy (*qinye*), but her vicious father (*hen diedie*) does not measure up to any of these paternal exemplars, but instead is unrivaled among crass strongmen (*cuhao*) [*GHQXQJ* 724]. In short, she concludes that "he has swept up and gathered the world's noxiousness in himself, while I have become entangled in all the woes under Heaven" [*GHQXQJ* 725]. While these are harsh words that at first glance may not seem compatible with filial behavior, Ruilan makes clear that her censure rests in what she sees as her father's failure to live up to his paternal responsibilities. In the final act, Ruilan spells out the conflict at the heart of the play in a climatic declaration to her sister-in-law:

（正旦）	WANG RUILAN [*sings*]:
【慶東原】	*To the tune* "Qing dongyuan"
他則圖今生貴，	All he aspires to is to attain status in this life.
豈問咱夙世緣？	What does he care about my karmic marriage bond?
違着孩兒心只要遂他家願。	He goes against the wishes of his child and only wants to indulge his own family ambitions.
則怕他夫妻白年。	In the hopes of a long-lived union of a hundred years,
召了這文武兩圓，	he has summoned the civil and martial top graduates for a double wedding

他家里要將相雙權。	In order to concentrate the power of both top general and prime minister in his family.
不雇自家嫌。	He disregards the objections of his own family members.
則要傍人羨。	He just wants to be the envy of everyone else.

[GHQXQJ 726]

Moon Pavilion features a feisty heroine who is not shy about speaking her mind. However, her utterances do not amount to a static subject position; instead, they are animated by an underlying conflict that propels her into a new set of circumstances and associated feelings. Rather than tending toward a single referent—a perfect fusion of subjective feeling and natural phenomenon in the manner of the short forms of classical poetry (☞ *HTRCP*, chap. 8)—the successive songs continuously destabilize each other as unexpected events disrupts the temporary accommodations that the main lead has chosen to embrace.

When the Yuan *zaju* corpus traveled through the hands of the many Ming editors, Guan's *Moon Pavilion* dropped out of the *zaju* drama corpus, perhaps eclipsed by the slightly less edgy *chuanqi* adaptation of the story that appeared under the title *The Story of the Secluded Boudoir* (*Yougui ji*) (☞ Visual Resources). Guan Hanqing's most famous play, *Injustice*, another story centered on a daughter left to fend for herself while her father pursues an official career, survives only in late-sixteenth- and early-seventeenth-century recensions.[10] However, despite the lateness of the first available scripts for many plays, some features of Guan's female lead plays are still visible, the likely editorial modifications notwithstanding (☞ Introduction, chap. 2, chap. 5).

For example, in contrast to *Moon Pavilion*, in the extant *Injustice*, stage directions are few and far between, and emotional cues tend to be reserved for secondary characters rather than the female lead. Furthermore, in contrast to Wang Ruilan's breadth of sentiment, Dou E is cast in a more consistently somber mood. Moreover, while *Moon Pavilion* never explicitly names the moral lodestars of Ruilan's behavior, *Injustice* repeatedly and explicitly invokes "filial piety" and "widow chastity" as Dou E's guiding principles. However, in at least one regard, Dou E's versatility rivals that of Wang Ruilan: the linguistic registers that Dou E taps into range from pointed cursing to high-minded remonstration to efficacious prophesy. In contrast to the domestic scope of Wang's plaints, *Injustice* turns Dou E's grievances into a matter of public concern, as the play hinges on a major miscarriage of legal justice that Dou E seeks to redress. It is through distinct speech acts, primarily delivered in song, that Dou E is able to defy the social odds and turn the moral capital of her virtue into a powerful lever for the righteousness of her cause.

3.3 *THE INJUSTICE TO DOU E*: THE DISRUPTIVE POWER OF FILIAL REMONSTRATION

In some ways, *Injustice* illustrates what Jiang Shilong alluded to in *Moon Pavilion*: women without male protection easily come to grief. Many Yuan *zaju* plays, as well as some Ming *chuanqi* (☛ chap. 7), exploit the dramatic potential inherent in the precarious position of young women who, for one reason or another, find themselves without the support of male protectors, whether it be because the father or husband pursues success far from home in the civil service, in the military, or in commerce; or that the wife is left a widow at an early age. More often than not, the vulnerability of the women is compounded by the precarious socioeconomic standing of their families of origin or the family that they have married into. Situated among impoverished scholars, farmers aspiring to officialdom, or itinerant merchants, the women in such plays hover on the threshold between being able to hold on to a modicum of respectability, becoming a pawn in a villain's quest for sexual gratification or ill-gotten financial gains, or both. What distinguishes *Injustice*'s female lead Dou E from other imperiled heroines is her ability to mobilize different forms of verbal expression to make up for the male protection that she lacks.

Dou E is on the receiving end of many misfortunes. Her mother dies when she is only three years old. Her father surrenders her to Madam Cai, a widowed moneylender, as a child bride-to-be, in exchange for travel funds for him so he can take the examinations. While her relationship with her mother-in-law is so tender that it has overtones of a mother/daughter bond, Dou E has already lost her husband by the time the play's main action begins. Her mother-in-law, in an attempt to collect a debt from a quack, is nearly strangled to death. Two drifters, Old Man Zhang and his son, Donkey Zhang, rescue Madam Cai, only to threaten her with strangulation in turn unless she accedes to a dual marriage, along with Dou E. When Dou E learns of this arrangement, she firmly refuses to entertain the possibility of a second marriage and takes her mother-in-law to task for turning her back on her erstwhile husband (act 1).

Undeterred by Dou E's resistance, young Donkey Zhang blackmails the quack into selling him poison, with which he plans to murder Dou E's mother-in-law in order to put more pressure on Dou E to accept his marriage proposal. When Madam Cai happens to fall ill and Dou E fixes her some mutton tripe soup, Donkey Zhang slips the poison into it. The plan backfires, however, as Old Man Zhang tastes the soup first and dies shortly thereafter. Unfazed by this unforeseen turn of events, Donkey Zhang promptly accuses Dou E of having murdered his father and gives her an ultimatum: either marry him or be dragged off to court. Certain of her innocence, Dou E agrees to go to court, but the incompetent and corrupt prefect tortures her to extract an admission. She resists as best she can, but when the prefect threatens to torture her mother-in-law as well, she quickly offers a false confession in the hopes that Heaven will eventually vindicate her. She is sentenced for the supreme crime of killing her father-in-law (act 2).

As Dou E is being led to the execution ground in midsummer, she calls out "Injustice," but she is now doubting whether even Heaven and Earth are as incorruptible as she had previously believed. At the execution ground, she issues a trifold prophesy: if she is unjustly executed, her blood will not spill onto the ground, snow will start to fall, and the county will suffer three years of draught. As Dou E is on the verge of being beheaded, it indeed starts to snow, which restores her confidence in the moral power of Heaven and Earth (act 3).

Three years later, after being dispatched as a surveillance commissioner with extraordinary powers to punish official malfeasance, Dou E's father arrives at the district yamen where Dou E was executed. As he is poring over the records of local court cases at night, Dou E's ghost appears to him and seeks to impel him to get to the bottom of her case. After initially doubting the righteousness of her claims, her father champions her case in light of another unjustly executed filial daughter-in-law whose oath caused a severe drought many centuries ago. He overturns the earlier judgment to restore Dou E's good name, and at Dou E's request, punishes Donkey Zhang and the physician with execution and canes and dismisses all the other officials and clerks involved. He promises to take care of Madam Cai and arranges for proper funerary rites for his deceased daughter (act 4).

If we seek to place this play within the framework of the "Twelve Categories of Northern Drama" ("Zaju shi'er ke") dating to the early Ming period (☞ chap. 2), we might say that it is a cross between plays about "ethical exemplars of filial piety, loyalty, integrity, and purity" and those that involve "cursing the treacherous and reviling those who slander" [*THZYP* 38–45]. By choosing a woman as the main protagonist for *Injustice*, Guan Hanqing could exploit the fact that women were associated with certain speech acts: in oral culture, on certain ritual occasions, women were expected (or at least allowed) to present extended lamentations; and in other cases, women engaged willy-nilly in extended forms of swearing and cursing (☞ *HTRCFiction-LC*, L16). At the same time, in classical sources and story collections, women could express themselves in the formal language with a certain reticence and decorum. Such formal expressions often took the form of remonstration, an act of seeking to remind the social betters to act in accordance with the code of ethics upon which their claim to authority rested in the first place. In a combination found in other female lead plays by Guan Hanqing and other Yuan playwrights, Dou E's songs draw on the sacrificial language of tales of marital devotion, the remonstrative language of the Confucian idealism, and a ritualized rhetoric of cursing and prophesy.

Most interestingly, perhaps, in contrast to *Moon Pavilion*, where Wang's father is the sole target of Ruilan's privately uttered criticism, *Injustice* directs Dou E's recriminations not only against other characters in the play (Old Zhang, Donkey Zhang, Madam Cai), but also against entire groups of people (faithless men, casual women) and against the pillars of morality (Heaven and Earth). Moreover, the play divorces such comments from simple one-on-one interchanges between protagonists; instead, Dou E's songs take on a public quality, either within the diegetic frame of the story (e.g., the courtroom and the execution ground) or within an extradiegetic world of viewers and readers (e.g., through commonly known allusions to history). Not only does *Injustice*'s story unfold in public settings, but many of the songs that Dou E sings throughout the play are not addressed to anyone in particular, but instead appear to be delivered as general pronouncements for the benefit of the audience. Moreover, in contrast to *Moon Pavilion*'s self-contained world of family life, *Injustice* embeds its main lead in a discursive web of female and—to a lesser degree—male exemplars. Most notably, whereas Ruilan ponders her predicament strictly in relation to herself, Dou E sees herself as part of the sociomoral category of "women." As such, she views her own conduct and that of her mother-in-law not simply as being their own, but broadly reflecting what women in general ought to do (or not do).

Such explicit identification with newly normative gender codes—particularly the notion of widow chastity—tempers the situational ethics so prominent in *Moon Pavilion*. In the Ming period in particular, we witness a substantial uptick in support for and in the actual practice of widow chastity among elite communities. Such a shift toward a more prescriptive view of female behavior at the expense of moral improvisation is seen in Dou E's response to her mother-in-law's impromptu marriage. Dou E acknowledges that Madam Cai agreed to the marriage with Old Zhang under duress. However, rather than sympathizing with her mother-in-law's plight, Dou E repeatedly chides her for dishonoring the memory of her deceased husband and begrudges what comfort the old woman might find in her new beau. In fact, Dou E sees her mother-in-law as part of a broader social trend of unfaithful widows. After her mother-in-law has fallen ill—perhaps implicitly as a result of her sexual exertions with Old Zhang—Dou E prepares the fateful soup while singing about the "immoral, lamentable, and shameful women" she considers typical of the current generation:

（旦）	FEMALE LEAD *as* DOU E [*sings*]:
【一枝花】	*To the tune of* "Yizhi hua"
…有一等婦女每相隨，	… There is a certain type of woman who, when following a man [into marriage],
並不說家克計，	Does not discuss how to properly run a household,
則打聽些是非，	But instead seeks out gossip,
說一會丈夫打鳳的機關，	Tells stories about the outlandish exploits of her husband,
使了些不着調虛嚚的見識。	And makes up preposterous stuff devoid of rhyme and reason.

[GHQXQJ 854]

However, if such a categorical censure may reflect elite concerns, Dou E subsequently contrasts such empty posturing with the heroic steadfastness and sense of purpose exhibited by exemplary women of yore:

【梁州】	*To the tune* of "Liangzhou"
…那裡有走邊廷哭倒長城？	Where are those who would travel to a border region [to bring winter clothes to their conscripted husband] and topple the Great Wall with their public wailing [because the husband is already dead]?

| 那裡有浣紗處甘投大水？ | Where are those women washing silk who would willingly throw themselves into the Great River [in order to keep the whereabouts of a fugitive hero a secret]? |
| 那裡有上青山便化頑石？ | Where are those who would climb up the Green Mountain [to look out for the return of their conscripted husbands] and turn into an adamantine stone? |

[*GHQXQJ* 855]

Dou E's female paragons—all of them commoners—are single-minded in their devotion to those who suffer at the hands of a capricious and willful state. The first line of the song refers to Mengjiangnü, who traveled great distances to deliver winter clothes to her husband conscripted to build the Great Wall, only to find out that he had perished. As she wailed, the wall crumbled and exposed the bones of her husband, which she then miraculously identified and gave a proper burial. The second line invokes a young woman who offered a meal to the unjustly perse-cuted official Wu Zixu (ca. 559–484 BCE) and then drowned herself in the nearby river so as not to betray his whereabouts to his pursuers. The third line retells the legend of an unnamed wife who so intently looked out from a mountain as she waited for her conscripted husband's return that she was transformed into an indestructible stone. The stories of Mengjiangnü and Wu Zixu in particular occu-pied a prominent place in the storytelling tradition, particularly within the corpus of so-called transformation texts (*bianwen*); they were also frequently referenced in the fourteenth-century theatrical corpus. In each case, the female protagonists stretched the boundaries of everyday expectations through extreme acts—repeated public wailing in the case of Mengjiangnü, intentional drowning in the case of the young woman at the river, and the self-petrification of the faithful wife. Public wailing (*ku*) in particular runs as a leitmotif through these stories, suggesting that community-oriented grievance was an efficacious and widely circulated modality of female expression to draw attention to injustices within the body politic.[11]

Through these allusions, Dou E places herself in a long line of women whose resolve and persistence in the face of adversity earned them a place in the collec-tive memory. But perhaps more so than the female paragons that she invokes, Dou E distinguishes herself through her verbal actions rather than through physical fortitude or protracted lamentation. Her story can be viewed as a series of different types of speech acts—cursing, making a fateful confession, public remonstration, taking an oath, and voicing an extended plea—all uttered in the pursuit of collective recognition of her moral integrity. In contrast to Ruilan, Dou E does not stray from the "straight and narrow" at any point in the play, but her incantatory speech acts prove more disruptive to community life than Wang's moral improvisation.

As the female lead, Dou E is conceived to offer pointed assessments of all the other characters in the play. In the face of Donkey Zhang's violence, Dou E resorts to invective to first keep him at bay, next to single him out as someone to haunt after her unjust death, and finally to make him an object of legal action. Hence, he becomes a veritable magnet for unflattering epithets from his very first appearance in the play: "a head case" (*bulütou*), "a depraved and shameless gangster" (*haose huangyin loumian zei*), and, repeatedly, a "bastard" (*nasi*).

Such uniformly barbed insults directed against Donkey Zhang contrast with the range of expressions that Dou E adopts regarding her mother-in-law. However, even with her mother-in-law, Dou offers anything but blind obedience. Instead, she shifts between the language of care, sacrifice, and remonstration. In keeping with Confucian stories of filial exemplars who mutilate themselves to save their ailing parents, Dou E does everything within her power to spare her mother-in-law physical and emotional suffering, even at the cost of her own life. Most important, Dou E makes a false confession (*quzhao*) to save her mother-in-law from certain torture and death ("If I don't die, how can I save you?" [*GHQXQJ* 859]). However, Dou E also publicly takes her mother-in-law to task for her foolishness in acceding to the sexual demands of the Zhang father-and-son duo. While Dou E is being tortured, she bemoans her mother-in-law's ill-considered actions:

(旦)	DOU E [*sings*]:
【罵玉郎】	*To the tune* of "Ma yulang"
這無情棍棒教我挨不的。	This heartless club is making it impossible for me to hold out.
婆婆也。	Oh, Mother-in-Law.
須是你自做下。	This must be something you yourself brought on.
怨他誰？	Who else is there to blame?
勸普天下前婚後嫁婆娘每	I urge all women under heaven who might consider remarriage
都看取我這般傍州例。	To look upon me as a precedent.

[*GHQXQJ* 858]

In a poignant scene often dramatized in modern productions of *Injustice*, Dou E's mother-in-law concurs with her daughter-in-law's assessment as she regretfully gazes upon Dou E's bloodied body and laments: "Oh, Dou E, my child, how could this not pain me to death! I am the one who has brought about your untimely demise" [*GHQXQJ* 859]!

Furthermore, in keeping with this spirit of "cursing the treacherous and reviling those who slander," *Injustice* does not stop at doubting even the most sacred pillars of the traditional Chinese belief system—that is, Heaven and Earth themselves. In contrast to Dou E's initial certainty that Heaven and Earth would intercede on her behalf, when faced with the imminent prospect of execution, she is less sanguine about whether Heaven and Earth will in fact come to her rescue. In a song that is perhaps without parallel in other Yuan plays, Dou E begins to direct her recriminations against Heaven and Earth:

（旦）   DOU E [*sings*]:

【滚秀毬】   *To the tune of "Gunxiuqiu"*

...天也。却不把清濁分辨。   . . . Heaven! Contrary to [popular] belief, you do not distinguish between those who have integrity and those who are corrupt.

可知道錯看了盜跖顏淵。   It is obvious that you have confused [the notorious] Bandit Zhi with [the principled and high-minded disciple] Yan Yuan!

有德的受貧窮更命短。   The virtuous ones are poor and have their lives cut short.
造惡的亨富貴又壽延。   The evildoers enjoy wealth and fame and a long life to boot.

天也。做得箇怕硬欺軟。   Heaven! All you do is fear the bullies and harass the meek.
不想天地也順水推船。   I never thought that Heaven and Earth would just let the boat drift in the current.

地也。你不分好歹難為地。 Earth! If you cannot tell apart good and evil, how can you call yourself Earth?

我今日負屈銜冤哀告天。   On this day, as I harbor this grievous injustice, I grieve and lay plaint against Heaven:

空教我獨語獨言。   In vain it compels me to hold forth all on my own.

[*GHQXQJ* 860]

Bandit Zhi led a small army of outlaws known for abducting women, but he enjoyed a long life nevertheless. Yan Hui was the student whom Confucius lauded most highly, but, in defiance of the Confucian idea that virtue resulted in longevity, he died at a very young age. On the one hand, Dou E compares Donkey Zhang to the long-lived Bandit Zhi and herself to the short-lived Yan Hui. On the other hand, Dou E takes the act of remonstration to new heights: rather than simply cursing a scoundrel like Donkey Zhang, she maligns the very foundations upon which the traditional Chinese belief system was built. She indicts Heaven and Earth for what she views as their utter abdication of their moral responsibilities. If Heaven and Earth are as obtuse and indifferent as she fears, then—as she is keenly aware—laying plaint, no matter how pointedly, will fall on deaf ears.

After the feverish pitch of her disillusionment with Heaven, at the execution ground, Dou E proceeds to lay bare her grievances in her threefold challenge to Heaven—her blood flying upward, the sudden snow fall, and the three-year drought. As soon as she has uttered her predictions, the Executioner promptly calls upon her "to shut up," deeming such words unbecoming of a criminal. As the snow starts to fall, Dou E concludes her incantatory invocation of a heavenly response with the following lines:

（旦）　　DOU E [*sings*]:

【尾聲】　　*Coda*

...霜降始知說鄒衍，　　... When the frost descended, they first became aware that it spoke of Zou Yan['s innocence].

雪飛方表竇娥冤。　　As the snow twirls, it finally makes manifest the injustice to Dou E.

[*GHQXQJ* 862]

Dou E's prophetic curse is crafted from two different historical traditions dealing with injustice, one surrounding an unjustly executed widow, the other concerning a political advisor imprisoned on false charges. Specifically, the gravity-defying gushing of blood and the three-year drought are derived from an early story known as "Filial Woman of Donghai" ("Donghai xiaofu") about a widow whom Dou Tianzhang remembers in act 4. According to that tale, the widow took exemplary care of her mother-in-law, but to lighten the burden on her daughter-in-law, the mother-in-law decided to hang herself—the customary form of suicide for women in dynastic China. The daughter of the woman lodged an official complaint with the court, alleging that the daughter-in-law had murdered her mother-in-law in order to shirk her duties. Under torture, the young woman confessed to a crime that she had not committed. It was said that the elders of the county orally communicated that when the widow was about to be executed, she "spoke an oath to the multitude: 'If I am guilty, I submit to being slain and my blood will drop to the ground. If I have died wrongly, then my blood will stream upward in defiance of what would be normally the case.' Her blood then flew upward and stained the banners hanging from bamboo poles."[12] Meanwhile, the symbol of unseasonal frost in midsummer reworked a legend about Zou Yan (ca. 305–ca. 240), a well-known early Chinese philosopher and political advisor. When Zou was thrown in jail on baseless accusations, his grievous lamentations were said to have moved Heaven to send frost in the summer to reveal his innocence.[13]

In fusing elements from a story about a widow ("Filial Woman of Donghai") with those about a Chinese statesman (Zou Yan), *Injustice* strengthened its appeal as a riveting drama about injustice for women and men alike. By framing a family drama with allusions to legendary precedents, *Injustice* turned Dou E into more than just another steadfast heroine in a world of fickle women, depraved would-be husbands, and greedy judges: she moved from the social margins (as a child bride, a widow, a criminal convict sentenced for a heinous crime) to the center of moral authority, becoming a female lead role who dared to challenge even Heaven and Earth. Such moral gravitas was likely one of the key reasons why Yuan critic Xia Tingzhi (fl. 1340–1366) noted that Yuan-dynasty *zaju* plays "could not be mentioned in the same breath" as the old comic forms of Song and Jin theater.[14]

CONCLUSION

Playing to urban audiences with an appetite for novelty, *zaju* theater broke new cultural ground. Guan Hanqing, together with other Yuan playwrights, fashioned a new kind of play from the elements of theatrical slapstick characteristic of Song-dynasty variety shows (*zaju*) and Jin-dynasty farces (*yuanben*), the linguistically versatile tradition of storytelling, and the high-minded tales of the Confucian classics and histories. Situated at the confluence of different cultural practices, such plays seamlessly blended comic aspects, different vocal modes, and affective concerns into "well-made plays." Animated by a dramatic conflict, such plays were not simply didactic exposés of Confucian virtues: instead, they presented moral dilemmas from new perspectives. In contrast to earlier poetry, where literati often appropriated a female subject position to explore their own political predicaments (☞ *HTRCP*, chap. 2), *zaju* theater leaves little doubt that these plays are not meant to be read as allegories, but rather as stories about plausible female (or male) subjects. One of the major innovations to drive home that possibility was the rhetorical device of a female lead.

What is remarkable about northern *zaju* theater is the social breadth of protagonists encompassed by the female lead—imperial concubines, maids, courtesans (☞ chap. 2), young respectable women, or old women could all occupy the diegetic space of a major female role. This social free-for-all leveled customary social hierarchies: the musings of a serving maid might be as interesting as the reflections of an empress; the trials of a courtesan might be as heartrending as the tribulations of a young widow. Affective range in a protagonist was no longer the prerogative of the socially privileged. Thus, the conception of the "female lead" did not create "stock characters"; instead, with unprecedented nuance, it explored moral dilemmas that women from different walks of life might encounter. Accordingly, the stuff of ordinary women's lives was no longer too trivial or too mundane for public consideration. The idea that female figures who had little authority in the offstage "real" world could become reliable narrators, keen observers, and astute commentators in the diegetic world of *zaju* theater gives many of these plays a distinctly modern feel.

Patricia Sieber

NOTES

1. This chapter has benefited from the critical acumen of many audiences and readers. I am particularly indebted to the following individuals: Shih-pe Wang, Regina Llamas, S. E. Kile, David L. Rolston, Hunter Klie, Yawei Li, Junquan Pan, and Joey Smith.

2. Hu Zhiyu, "Huang shi shijuan xu" ("Preface to Ms. Huang's Poems"), *ZSDQJ*, 8.31a. All translations are my own unless otherwise noted. For a translation of the trope apropos Zhulian xiu herself, see Chunfang Fei, *Chinese Theories of Theater and Performance from Confucius to the Present* (Ann Arbor: University of Michigan Press, 2002 [1999]), 35; and Wilt L. Idema and Stephen West, *Chinese Theater, 1100–1450: A Source Book* (Wiesbaden, Germany: Franz Steiner, 1982), 201.

3. For the play, see Guan Hanqing, *Guan Dawang dandao hui* (The Great King Guan and the Single Sword Meeting), in *Jiaoding Yuankan sanshi zhong* (The Thirty Yuan-Printed Plays, Annotated and Edited), ann. Zheng Qian (Taipei: Shijie shuju, 1962), 1–10. On how these two Three Kingdom plays form a pair and invite performative virtuosity, see Wilt L. Idema, "Traditional Dramatic Literature," in *The Columbia History of Chinese Literature*, ed. Victor H. Mair (New York: Columbia University Press, 2001), 807.

4. For the play, see Guan Hanqing, *Guan Zhang shuangfu Xi Shu meng* (In a Dream, Guan and Zhang, a Pair, Rush to Western Shu), in *Jiaoding Yuankan sanshi zhong*, 17–27.

5. Wilt L. Idema, "Some Aspects of *Pai-yüeh-t'ing*: Script and Performance," *Proceedings of the International Conference on Kuan Han-ch'ing* (Taipei: Xingzhen yuan wenhua jianshe weiyuanhui, 1993), 57–77; and Idema, "Traditional Dramatic Literature," 801.

6. Hu, "Huang shi shijuan xu," 8.31a. For other translations of this passage, see Fei, *Chinese Theories of Theater and Performance*, 35; and West and Idema, *Chinese Theater, 1100–1450*, 201.

7. For a more extensive translation of Hu's tribute to Zhulian xiu's artistry, see Beverly Bossler, *Courtesans, Concubines, and the Cult of Female Fidelity: Gender and Social Change in China, 1000–1400* (Cambridge, MA: Harvard University Asia Center, 2013), 293–295.

8. In a famous anecdote, Mencius noted that while it is not proper for a man to touch his sister-in-law under normal circumstances, it would go against moral norms not to touch her if she needed to be rescued from drowning in a well (*Mengzi* 4A.17).

9. It has been suggested that the Yuan usage of the term (*zuoyi*) implies that the actor uses her body and face to express either an external action or an inner state. See Min Tian, "Stage Directions in the Performance of Yuan Drama," *Comparative Drama* 39, no. 3–4 (2005–2006): 428–429.

10. In my discussion given here, I follow the earliest extant rendition of the play.

11. For the story of Mengjiangnü in the transformation text tradition, see Wang Zhongmin et al., ed., "Mengjiangnü bianwen" ("The Transformation Text of Mengjiangnü"), in *Dunhuang bianwen ji* (An Anthology of Transformation Texts from Dunhuang) (Beijing: Renmin wenxue chubanshe, 1984), vol. 1, 32–35. For the story of Wu Zixu, see Wang et al., "Wu Zixu bianwen" ("The Transformation Text of Wu Zixu"), *Dunhuang bianwen ji*, 1–31. For translations of these legends, see Arthur Waley, *Ballads and Stories from Dunhuang: An Anthology* (London: George Allen and Unwin, 1960), 25–52 and 145–149.

12. Quoted and translated in Stephen H. West and Wilt L. Idema, *Monks, Bandits, Lovers, and Immortals: Eleven Early Chinese Plays* (Indianapolis: Hackett, 2010), 5.

13. For a Han-dynasty reference to Zou Yan's legend of having brought about frost in early summer, see the highly critical account in Wang Chong, *Lun heng zhushi* (Annotated Edition of the Deliberations on the Proper Measure [of Truth]), ed. Beijing University History Department (Beijing: Zhonghua shuju, 1979), vol. 2, 858–862. The story about the drought induced by the "Filial Woman of Donghai" and the one about the untimely frost precipitated by Zou Yan are both listed as entries under "Unjust Imprisonment" ("Yuanyu") in a well-known medieval encyclopedia among other sources. See Bai Juyi, *Bai shi Liu tie shilei ji* (Bai Juyi's Collection of Topically Arranged Matters in Six Sheets) (Taipei: Xingxin shuju, 1969), vol. 2, 578.

14. Xia Tingzhi, "Qinglouji zhi," *QLJJZ*, 44.

PRIMARY SOURCES

GHQXQJ Guan Hanqing 關漢卿. *Guan Hanqing xiqu ji* 關漢卿戲曲集 (*Guan Hanqing's Collected Plays*). Ed. Wu Xiaoling 吳曉鈴. Beijing: Zhonghua shuju, 1958.

QLJJZ Xia Tingzhi 夏庭芝. *Qinglou ji jianzhu* 青樓集箋注 (*An Annotated Edition of* The Record of the Green Bowers). Ann. Sun Chongtao 孫崇濤 and Xu Hongtu 徐宏圖. Beijing: Zhongguo xiju chubanshe, 1990.

THZYP Zhu Quan 朱權. *Taihe zhengyin pu jianping* 太和正音譜箋評 (*An Annotated Edition of* The Formulary of Correct Prosody of the Era of Great Peace). Ann. Yao Pinwen 姚品文. Zhongguo wenxue yanjiu dianji congkan 中國文學研究典籍叢刊 (*A Compiled Series of Classics for Research on Chinese Literature*), ed. Luo Di 洛地. Beijing: Zhonghua shuju, 2010.

ZSDQJ Hu Zhiyu 胡祇遹. *Zishan daquan ji* 紫山大全集 (*The Comprehensive Collected Works of [Hu] Zishan*). Siku quanshu zhenben siji 四庫全書珍本四集 (*The Fourth Collection of the Complete Rare Editions of The Four Treasuries*), vols. 291–296. Taipei: Taiwan shangwu yinshu guan, 1973.

SUGGESTED READINGS

TRANSLATIONS

Guan Hanqing. *Gold Thread Pond*, trans. Dale R. Johnson. In Dale R. Johnson, "Courtesans, Lover, and 'Gold Thread Pond' in Guan Hanqing's Music Dramas." *Journal of Song-Yuan Studies*, 33 (2003): 124–154.

Guan Hanqing. *The Great King Guan and the Single Sword Meeting*. In *Battles, Betrayals, and Brotherhood: Early Chinese Plays on the Three Kingdoms*, ed. and trans. by Wilt L. Idema and Stephen H. West, 236–265. Indianapolis: Hackett Publishing, 2012.

Guan Hanqing. *In a Dream, Guan and Zhang, a Pair, Rush to Western Shu*. In *Battles, Betrayals, and Brotherhood: Early Chinese Plays on the Three Kingdoms*, ed. and trans. by Wilt L. Idema and Stephen H. West, 296–315. Indianapolis: Hackett Publishing, 2012.

Guan Hanqing. *Injustice to Tou O (Tou O Yüan)*. Trans. and introd. Chung-wen Shih. Cambridge: Cambridge University Press, 1972.

Guan Hanqing. *Moving Heaven and Shaking Earth: The Injustice to Dou E*. In *Monks, Bandits, Lovers, and Immortals: Eleven Early Chinese Plays*, trans. and introd. Stephen H. West and Wilt L. Idema, 1–36. Indianapolis: Hackett Publishing Company, 2010.

Guan Hanqing. *Pining in Her Boudoir: The Pavilion for Praying to the Moon*. In *Monks, Bandits, Lovers, and Immortals: Eleven Early Chinese Plays*, trans. and introd. Stephen H. West and Wilt L. Idema, 77–104. Indianapolis: Hackett Publishing Company, 2010.

Guan Hanqing. *Rescuing a Sister*, trans. George Kao and Wai-yee Li. In *The Columbia Anthology of Yuan Drama*, ed. by C.T. Hsia et al., 269–297. New York: Columbia University Press, 2014.

ENGLISH

Ao, Yumin. *A Study on the Thematic, Narrative, and Musical Structure of Guan Hanqing's Yuan Zaju*, Injustice to Dou E. New York: Peter Lang, 2015.

Harbsmeier, Christopher. "Weeping and Wailing in Ancient China." In *Minds and Mentalities in Traditional Chinese Literature*, ed. Halvor Eifring, 317–422. Beijing: Culture and Art Publishing House, 1999.

Idema, Wilt L. "Traditional Dramatic Literature." In *The Columbia History of Chinese Literature*, ed. Victor H. Mair, 785–818. New York: Columbia University Press, 2001.

Sieber, Patricia. *Theaters of Desire: Authors, Readers, and the Reproduction of Early Chinese Song-Drama, 1300–2000*. New York: Palgrave MacMillan, 2003.

West, Stephen H. "Zang Maoxun's *Injustice to Dou E*," *Journal of the American Oriental Society* III, no. 2 (1991): 283–302.

CHINESE

Luo Di 洛地. "Yizheng zhong wai, Yi jiao zhong jiao": Yuan zaju fei jiaose zhi lun" 〈一正眾外，一角眾腳〉：元雜劇非角色論 (One Main Part, Many Minor Parts, One Part, Many Types: Why Yuan *Zaju* Did Not Feature Roles). In *Luo Di xiqu lunji* 洛地戲曲論集 (*Luo Di's Essays on Traditional Chinese Drama*), 39–70. Taipei: Guojia chubanshe, 2006.

Wang Shih-pe 汪詩珮. "Suming, pingfan, jiaohua guan: Lun liangben Dou E yuan 宿命，平反，教化觀：論兩本 《竇娥冤》(Fate, Vindication, Morality: A Comparison of Two Editions of *The Injustice to Dou E*)," *Xiju xuekan* 戲劇學刊 (*Taipei Theatre Journal*) II (2010): 129–161.

Wang Xueqi 王學奇 et al., ed. *Guan Hanqing quanji jiaozhu* 關漢卿全集校注 (*An Annotated Edition of the Complete Works of Guan Hanqing*). Beijing: Hebei jiaoyu chubanshe, 1988.

Zheng Qian 鄭騫. "Zang Maoxun gaiding Yuan zaju pingyi," 臧懋循改定元雜劇評議 (A Critique of Zang Maoxun's Emendations to Yuan Drama). In his *Jingwu congbian* 景午叢編 (*The Collected Essays of Jingwu*), vol. 1, 408–421. Taipei: Taiwan Zhonghua shuju, 1972.

4

The Story of the Western Wing

Theater and the Printed Image

Illustrated drama texts in late imperial China offered a multimedia experience for their readers.[1] Each book provided its own particular mix of media, but typically, such works drew on stage performance, poetry, painting, the decorative arts, and the art of bookmaking to generate images. How books weighted elements from the stage, poetry, and the visual arts varied, but readers increasingly found that drama publications not only delivered playtexts but offered entry into sensory realms full of textual, visual, haptic, and musical experiences. In the case of *The Story of the Western Wing* (*Xixiang ji*, hereafter *The Western Wing*) (🖙 chap. 1), publishers continuously egged each other on to issue yet another inventive release, turning that particular play into the most frequently illustrated text in the history of Chinese woodblock printing. According to one count, there were more than sixty editions of *The Western Wing* published in the Ming dynasty alone, more than half of which were illustrated.[2] The publishers' decision to include images could expose them to charges of pandering to popular taste, but many seemed to agree with Ling Meng-chu (1580–1644), a well-known editor-publisher and writer in his own right, that pictures were a must. In his prefatory remarks to his edition of *The Western Wing*, he described the dilemma that publishers confronted:

> This imprint is truly meant as an aid to broad learning (*boya*) and ought to be considered a literary work (*wenzhang*). It should not be approached as [mere] song-drama (*xiqu*). In this light, it would not be necessary to include images (*tuhua*), but because people these days value "rouge" (*zhifen*), I fear that if we omit images from our edition, it will be considered a shortcoming.
>
> [*XXJ* 3]

While Ling was clearly aware of the potential criticism that the incorporation of illustrations might cause, he still felt compelled to cater to new tastes.[3] Given the competitive pressures faced by publishers, it may not be entirely surprising that not only was *The Western Wing* the most frequently published playtext in China, but some of the most famous Chinese illustrated imprints were in fact editions of that play.

Technological factors played a part in this happy symbiosis between playtexts and images. Compared to European-style letterpress printing, woodblock printing offered several major advantages: for one, text and images were carved out of the same woodblocks. Thus, it was possible to seamlessly integrate textual and visual elements, even if different carvers might specialize in one or the other type of carving. Furthermore, from the sixteenth century onward, cheaper paper and a standardized form of calligraphy known as *jiangti* ("artisanal style") helped to spur a boom in books. Even though the added expense of carving illustrations and the sheer length of plays could make drama imprints more costly, the increased price did not necessarily put them beyond the reach of common readers. As Matteo Ricci (1552–1610), the Jesuit missionary and keen observer of Chinese book culture, noted with astonishment, "The simplicity of Chinese printing is what accounts for the exceedingly large numbers of books in circulation here and the ridiculously low prices at which they are sold."[4] Thanks to the wider availability of books, such imprints made cultural experiences that had previously been restricted to certain groups, certain occasions, or certain media more accessible to a wider range of people. For example, thanks to these printed playtexts, song-drama could now be enjoyed at will, anytime and anywhere, by anyone with an appetite for theater. Furthermore, in mixing elements from theater, poetry, the visual arts, and woodblock printing, drama imprints not only transformed what people could do by themselves but also affected how people thought of themselves in relation to others. For the cultural avant-garde, theater had the performative power to embody the deepest and most authentic feelings amid widespread political disillusionment; for the nostalgically inclined segments of the elite, conversely, theater's central conceit— the art of impersonation—pointed to the deplorable currency of deceit, fakery, and fraud in an era of unprecedented social mobility. In short, not only was drama something that one went to see on temple stages or enjoyed at intimate gatherings in private settings, but it became a mirror that reflected inner and outer worlds.

In this chapter, we will explore how some of the landmark editions of *The Western Wing* positioned themselves as "apps" in the brave new world of drama publishing. In borrowing the contemporary term "app," we mean to highlight the fact that readers of these imprints did not passively consume texts; rather, they could actively use them to enrich their real or imaginary lives. To illustrate the diverse functionalities embodied in these works, we will discuss three outstanding examples in chronological order:

1. *The Deluxe Edition* (1499):[5] The first complete version of *The Western Wing*, typically called the "Hongzhi edition" after the reign period in which it appeared in Beijing, and renowned for its cinematic, handscroll-like illustrations (☞ chap. 1) [QMQX]
2. *The Glossed Edition* (c. 1609): The so-called Liu Longtian edition, named for its Fujian-based publisher and well known for its invocation of stage performance [YBTPYS]
3. *The Exclusive Edition* (1639–1640):[6] The Zhang Shenzhi edition printed in Hangzhou, named for the military patron who paid for its publication, and acclaimed for its images, designed by one of the most innovative painters of the period, Chen Hongshou (1598–1652) [ZSZMB]

Before analyzing how each of these versions of *The Western Wing* aimed to create new experiences for successive generations of readers, we will first address how two particular forms of image-making—that is, the world of paintings signed by well-known literati and the often-anonymous artisanal art of woodblock printing—entered into a closer dialogue with each other from the mid-Ming period onward.

4.1 IMAGE-MAKING BETWEEN SELF-EXPRESSION AND COMMERCE

Thanks to the nonalphabetic nature of the Chinese writing system, image and text have long been considered closely allied arts. Chinese literati regarded calligraphy, painting, and poetry as the "fine arts," referring to them as "the three perfections (*sanjue*)." In their view, images and writing shared the same roots in a mythical past when Fu Xi, a creator figure, created the Eight Trigrams (*bagua*), presumably the earliest writing system, to represent Heaven, Earth, thunder, wind, water, fire, mountains, and rivers. Further, all three of these arts involved writing with a brush, and as such, they shared the visual appeal of good brushwork. For instance, Zhang Yanyuan (815–907), the literati author of the earliest-known history of painting, maintained that painting and calligraphy have different names, but they do not differ in spirit.[7] By the eleventh century, other critics equated poetry and painting with one another. Su Shi (1037–1101), the leading scholar of the late Northern Song dynasty, first advocated that there is "poetry in painting and painting in poetry."[8] Writing poetry and creating a painting could be understood as being parallel to each other, partly because poetry made extensive use of conventionalized tropes from nature (☛ *HTRCP*, chap. 6), and so did the favored form of painting among literati—that is, landscape painting.

Moreover, from the eleventh century onward, the sister arts of poetry, calligraphy, and literati painting hewed closely to the idea of "self-expression." According to this literati ideal, painting was meant to manifest the inner qualities of the person wielding the brush rather than to depict the physical world with a high degree of verisimilitude. Accordingly, the expressive concerns of a picture could be partially or completely independent of what was represented; strictly representational content was thought to be the province of the professional painters active at court, in religious institutions, or in the open market. The emphasis on the communication of aspirations and sensibilities went hand in hand with a self-professed "amateur ideal." To exemplify a lofty spirit of detachment and refinement, literati took care to create the appearance that they did not paint, compose, or write for financial gain. To compound this sense of leisured sophistication, literati shared their work only on certain social occasions with like-minded friends. In other words, most people never got to see what the literati considered artistic masterpieces because they circulated among only a very small group of people, and even among the elite, it was difficult to gain firsthand access to fine painting and calligraphy. The literatus Zhou Mi (1232–1298), an avid art enthusiast and keen cultural observer, wistfully noted that "I have heard that the painting scrolls collected [by Mr. Zhang, the Commander of Songjiang] are quite numerous. . . . None is not a marvelous work. I have only seen the following [five] items."[9]

The art form of woodblock printing, by contrast, addressed itself to a broader public. Making woodblock-printed illustrations was a collective effort involving draftsmen, carvers, and printers. Printing was a complex technical process that consisted of three main steps (namely, drawing preparation, woodcarving, and ink-ing/imprinting). As a first step, a draftsman used black ink and a fine brush to make the initial design with an outline on paper. To ensure that the design in the next step could be transferred onto the wooden board exactly as it was, it required a type of paper with a higher degree of transparency such as semitransparent "goose paper" or "goose-skin paper." In the second step, a carver transferred this design onto a block of hardwood such as pear, jujube, or catalpa.[10] The carver usually pasted the original drawing facedown on the woodblock [figure 4.1(a)]. The paper was then made transparent by either treating it with oil or by peeling off a thin layer of paper fibers with the fingertips, thus leaving the ink drawing visible to guide the cutting knife. The ink drawing transferred onto the woodblock was the mirror image of the original drawing on tracing paper. Next, the carver chiseled away portions of the wood block using a set of knives, gouges, and chisels espe-cially made for this task [figures 4.1(b), 4.1(c)]. The remaining raised surfaces of the woodblock were inked [figure 4.1(d)]. Typically, the woodblock prints were mono-chrome, which required only a single block. In the next step, the printer placed a piece of paper facedown on the block for texts and images. A traditional printing burnisher (a piece of wood wrapped in paper and palm fibers) was used to firmly

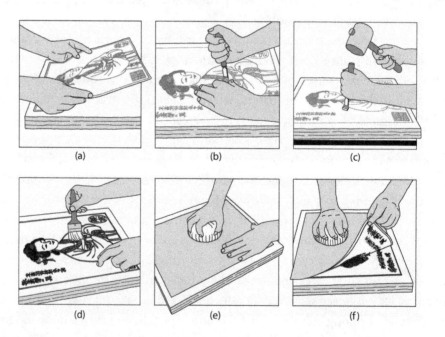

FIGURE 4.1 The process of making woodblock prints, modified from an illustration in Penelope Mason, *History of Japanese Art*, 2nd ed. (Upper Saddle River, NJ: Pearson Prentice Hall, 2005), 283. This illustration uses a portrait of Cui Yingying in *Xixiang ji zalu* (Miscella-neous Notes on *The Story of the Western Wing*, 1569) as an example.
Diagram: Courtesy of Yongfeng Zhang.

rub the back of the paper, transferring ink from the block [figure 4.1(e)]. In doing so, the reversed writing and image carved on the block was reversed again to its correct orientation and appeared as a black imprint against the background of the uncolored paper [figure 4.1(f)].

The practitioners associated with woodblock carving, including draftsmen, woodcarvers, and printers, were by and large professional artisans who often remained anonymous. In the Tang dynasty, they worked under the auspices of Buddhist patrons aiming for greater religious merit, but with the establishment of commercial printing in the Song dynasty, such artisans also began to work for businesses concerned with financial profit, a practice that continued into the Yuan dynasty and beyond. By the late Ming dynasty, artisans produced a wide variety of images, including loose leaves of single-sheet pictorial prints, stationery (*jianzhi*), book illustrations, painting manuals, and printed versions of painting albums. Unlike the so-called fine arts, these kinds of images could reach broad segments of viewers beyond the literati. Moreover, woodblock-printed images did not seek to constitute a self-contained world of poetry, painting, and calligraphy, but they were in open dialogue with these and many other forms of artistic expression, including the theater and decorative arts such as porcelain, lacquer, cloisonné, textiles, and woodcarving. Thus, even though woodblock-generated images have only recently begun to capture the attention of modern scholars, they were widely disseminated throughout Chinese society through religious institutions, bookshops, and itinerant peddlers.

Nevertheless, during the course of the late Ming dynasty (1550–1644), the boundaries between "fine art" and "commercial art" began to blur. In the wake of intensified interactions between and among literati arts and the popular arts, poetry, pictures, and drama texts combined to form a new synthesis of elite and popular forms. For example, the first complete edition of *The Western Wing*, which we call *The Deluxe Edition* (1499) and will discuss in greater detail later in this chapter (see section 4.2), united continuous, cross-page illustration in the style of narrative handscrolls with captions explaining the plot in language simple enough to be accessible to novice readers. At the same time, among its prefatorial materials, *The Deluxe Edition* contained both witty songs that presupposed prior knowledge of the story and plot-driven, poetic digests that may have helped familiarize other readers with the ins and outs of the story. In another instance of boundary crossing, elements of stage performance found their way into book illustration. In the Song, Jin, and Yuan dynasties, theatrical imagery of actors, musicians, and troupes was featured in temples and tombs, but they had yet to be represented in print. Resonating with the emphasis on verisimilitude and likeness found in such figure-oriented visual traditions, some drama publications, such as *The Glossed Edition* that we will discuss later (see section 4.3), expanded the dialogue between the language of the theater and the evolving platform of book illustration. Eventually, the format of full-page figures allowed the stylized gestures and choreographed body movements of theatrical stage action and accompanying facial expressions to come into focus.

In the social realm, the boundaries between literati artists and commercial artisans also began to break down. For one, faced with intense competition at the examinations, a dangerously factionalized environment, and eventually the collapse of the Ming dynasty, an increasing number of literati sought alternative forms of livelihood that, by dint of their cultural cachet, could still be considered socially acceptable (⟶ chaps. 10 and 11). Some literati produced occasional writing for their communities in exchange for gifts and money; others engaged in the commercial book market through composing, editing, and publishing; while still others openly embraced the status of professional painters.[11] This trend of literati professionalization paved the way for a number of prominent literati artists to become involved in commercial book publishing. For example, Chen Hongshou, whom we will discuss later (see section 4.4), brought paintings and woodblock printing into artistic dialogue with one another. For another, woodblock carvers gained more respect and recognition for their artistic talents. Certain families of artisans rose to prominence as they perfected the art of woodblock-engraved images. Most notably, through their meticulous craftsmanship, the Huang family from the mountainous region of Huizhou (then known as Xin'an in today's Anhui province) turned book illustrations into a versatile and vibrant art form. For instance, when Ling Mengchu issued his illustrated edition of *The Western Wing*, he insisted on employing members of that family to carve the blocks.

Like many of his late Ming contemporaries, Ling credited the carver by name ("Huang Yibin from Xin'an") in the published edition [*XXJ* 5]. Inscribing their names on the prints imitated the forms of authorship of the literati, which suggested that the product expressed the producer's personality. One modern scholar has pointed out that "the commercial possibilities of the claim to authorship count among the great economic discoveries of late Ming craftsmen and designers," and "artisanal trademarks came to . . . convey an upwardly mobile aspiration to literati self-expression."[12] Thus, instead of being relegated to the status of anonymous artisans, certain woodblock carvers achieved individual fame.

Furthermore, artisan families also expanded the overall artistic repertoire of image-making, most notably in the domain of polychrome printing. Two-color block printing (in red and black) was first invented in the Northern Song dynasty (960–1127), when it was mainly used in the production of Buddhist works and paper currency. The technique was widely applied to the book industry in the Ming dynasty because examination aids with color annotations that indicated punctuation and differentiated between main text and commentaries were in great demand. The polychrome printing of images was achieved through various methods. The Cheng family in Huizhou applied differently colored ink to the same block to produce the famous compendium of ink stick designs done by the artist Ding Yunpeng (1547–after 1628), *The Ink Garden of the Cheng Family* (*Cheng shi moyuan*, 1606). Other publishers refined the technique of polychrome printing through the method called "assembled blocks" (*douban*). In this elaborate process, a separate woodblock was cut for each color, which was then printed on the same piece of paper to create a polychrome print similar to the "brocade picture" (*nishiki-e*) in

Edo-period Japan (1603–1868). In inking the blocks to create gradations that mimicked brushwork, the printer contributed to the artistic effect of the print and could also exploit blockcutting itself for visual effects unique to that medium. The Ling and the Min families in Wuxing county (Zhejiang province) were among the most notable publishers in the arena of polychrome printing. According to incomplete statistics, these two families issued more than 140 books, some of which, like Ling Mengchu's *The Western Wing*, were produced in two colors (red and black), while others featured four or five colors.

Among the most famous of these polychrome works is the Min Qiji album of *The Western Wing* (1640), named for Min Qiji (1580–after 1661), the publisher who signed some of the prints with his seal. Printed in as many as eight colors (primarily black, red, blue, green, and yellow), a single copy exists in Cologne, Germany.[13] The rich use of color found in these prints further enhanced the sensory pleasures associated with *The Western Wing*. Consisting of twenty loose, album-like leaves, the pictures represented scenes from the play through the prism of twenty different media, ranging from different types of painting (handscroll, hanging scroll, fan, screen) to decorative arts (porcelain, bronzes, moving lanterns, stationery, jade rings) to theater (human actors, puppet theater). The resulting effect is a visual extravaganza that scholars have variously described as "metapictures" (i.e., pictures that seek to delineate what could be considered appropriate to frame as a picture), as pictures that playfully undermine the certainty of what a picture is, or as pictures that foreground a range of visual experiences.[14]

In what follows, we will examine in greater detail how three editions of *The Western Wing* that combined text and images mediated between the audiences' experiences of the page, the stage, and other media. Our contention is that woodblock imprints offered unprecedented access to sensory and mental experiences that previously more likely than not had been reserved for social elites, special occasions, or special media. Thus, the hybrid nature of book illustrations not only conspired to produce a multimedia experience within the confines of the two covers of a book, but it did so for audiences beyond the charmed circles of literati, scholar-officials, and the court.

4.2 THE STORY OF THE WESTERN WING: THE DELUXE EDITION (1499)—AN APP FOR SINGING

The advent of illustrations in dramatic texts transformed how Chinese plays were read and understood. The very earliest surviving imprints relating to the theater did not include any images. Instead, in the earliest texts of the northern tradition, the so-called *Thirty Yuan-Printed Zaju Plays* (*Yuankan zaju sanshi zhong*, 1914) (☛ Introduction, chaps. 2, 3, and 5), they primarily featured the arias sung by the lead performer without visually subdividing the text into acts or scenes. Modern scholars surmise that these shoddily produced imprints enabled the audience to more readily comprehend the arias sung on stage (i.e., the Yuan equivalent of subtitles). The manuscripts of the earliest texts of the southern tradition likewise provide few visual cues (☛ Introduction, chap. 7).

While these southern texts contain arias, dialogue, and declamatory verse set off by blank spaces and names for song patterns (*qupai*), they do not visually distinguish among scenes. Modern editors have divided these early plays into acts or scenes based on the entrances and exits of characters, their melodic structure, later texts, or their own understanding, but the absence of segmentation in the original should not be thought of simply as an oversight on the part of the Yuan/Ming compilers of song-drama; they could also indicate that the idea of "scenes" as a narrative (as opposed to a theatrical or musical) unit had yet to take hold in the world of the theater.

From the Song through the early Ming periods, observers emphasized different facets of Chinese theater. It might have served as a potentially efficacious form of ritual practice, as exemplified by plays revolving around the filial Buddhist disciple and son by the name of Mulian (☞ chap. 15). It was a form of entertainment reliant on slapstick comedy ("Country Cousin Is Not Familiar with Urban Theater"). It was an art of creating the aesthetic personae of particular roles through sublime singing and body movements (*Record of the Green Bowers*) (☞ chaps. 2 and 3).[15] It was a vehicle for comic routines, singing, and communal sportsmanship (prologue and act 2 of the play *Top Graduate Zhang Xie*) (☞ chap. 7). Importantly, it was also construed as an affective experience, as is evident from the observations of the Yuan official and theater aficionado Hu Zhiyu (1227–1293), who noted that if "a single young female [actor] can combine the actions of a myriad [different] people [onstage], then this can delight the ear and eye even more and ease the worries of the heart"[16] (☞ Introduction, chap. 3).

Less conspicuous was the notion that plays were composed of a series of discreet narrative scenes that were, either implicitly or explicitly, propelled forward by a dramatic conflict. By the Ming dynasty, however, the appearance of illustrations in playtexts signaled a clearer sense that plays also began to be viewed as "stories" rather than primarily as an extended form of "sung poetry." In other words, the inclusion of images and their specific layout points to the possibility that song-drama was beginning to be assimilated to the narrative modes of history and fiction.

In that vein, *The Deluxe Edition* took the blending of different formats to new aesthetic heights. Published in 1499 by the otherwise obscure Yue family of Jintai in Beijing under the full title *The Western Wing: A Newly Printed, Large-Character, Deluxe-Sized, Fully Illustrated, Expanded, and Marvelously Annotated Edition*, the lavishly produced edition combined extensive prefatory paratexts, including poems and *sanqu* songs about the story, the characters, and the playwrights of *The Western Wing* with a richly annotated text of the play in the bottom register of the page. Continuous illustrations were featured across the top register. A total of 255 pages of pictures were divided among 150 scenes; some of these occupy a single full page, while others run between two and eight pages, depending on the length of the playtext and the notes explaining allusions and pronunciation.[17] Keenly aware of the novelty of this arrangement, the publisher promoted their work in an advertisement at the back of the book:

Among those people who reside in the back alleys and transmit [*The Western Wing*] as a family tradition through recitation (*yong*), staged singing (*zuoxi*), or costumed playacting (*banyan*), they all need for the characters and lines to be accurate. Now that the songs and the pictures match, it is possible to circulate this edition in the marketplace (e.g., the realm of less educated people). . . . [Furthermore], we have diligently relied on [the format of the illustrated] classics (*jingshu*)[18] to re-create the images (*huitu*), and we have corrected their order. In this sumptuous deluxe edition with large characters, the singing [parts] and the images (*tu*) match and so those who lodge in inns, travel in boats, or roam in their minds, can take it all in at a glance and sing it from beginning to end and in doing so refresh everyone's heart.

[*QMQX* 316]

The advertisement suggests that this edition was suitable for different audiences. For one, commoners, and perhaps actors residing in the middling parts of town, could chant, sing, or enact *The Western Wing*. For them, accuracy in terms of characters, lines, and sound glosses was paramount in order to enhance the singability of the arias. Because many of these readers may not have been sufficiently literate to know the texts of the arias, which they may have learned through oral channels of transmission, having extensive notes on the meaning of characters and on allusions immediately following individual arias would have helped them to acquire a greater understanding of the text. At the same time, the advertisement also had pretensions to appeal to well-to-do merchants, scholar-officials, and literati, who had the necessary resources to lodge in inns, use boats for professional travel or leisure excursions, or engage in armchair travel. This audience was exhorted to "sing" (*qingchang*) the songs rather than watch them as part of a collective appreciation of drama on certain commercial, religious, ceremonial, or festive occasions, together with a community of fellow viewers. Hence, as one modern scholar has noted, such songs were now a portable experience that could be re-created anytime and anywhere by amateur aficionados to gladden themselves and their fellow listeners.[19] The advertisement also repeatedly underscores the importance of the proper correlation between songs and images as a crucial aid in the replication of the text for both types of audiences.

Interestingly, *The Deluxe Edition* offered a unique blend of the popular "picture above/text below" (*shangtu xiawen*) configuration, with the alternation of text and image found in some narrative handscrolls (see figure 4.2). As a result of this innovative hybridization of formats, the text can be read in a variety of ways. On the one hand, the "picture above/text below" layout suggests a synchronic and cooperative relationship between image and playtext. In the numerous single-image scenes, the arias typically correspond to the characters depicted in the image. For the sophisticated reader, the dual modality of "printed painting" and "narrated verse" in what was a relatively appealing calligraphic style would have enabled them to enjoy various sensory experiences all at once. On the other hand, the continuous pictorial sequencing of the illustrations in the manner of a handscroll also points

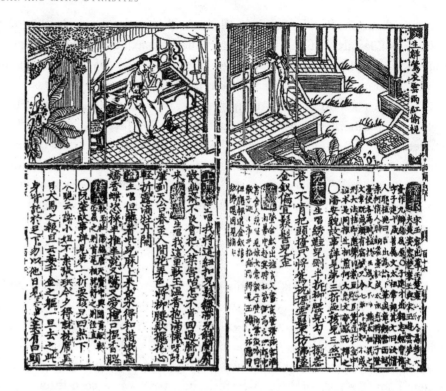

FIGURE 4.2 The "picture above, text below" format found in *The Deluxe Edition*. The scene represents "Crimson eavesdropping on Scholar Zhang and Oriole" [*QMQX, juan* 4, act 1, "The Secret Tryst" ("Yuyun youhui") 226–227].

to the relative autonomy of image and playtext (i.e., they could be read independent of one another).

This was especially the case in *The Deluxe Edition* because boxes with short, plot-oriented captions in extremely simple Chinese preceded virtually every pictorial scene. For example, among the first few scenes, the captions read as follows: "Student Zhang asks about and is told by the innkeeper about the local sights;" "Student Zhang together with monk Facong stroll around the Temple of Universal Salvation;" "While strolling around the Temple of Universal Salvation with monk Facong, Student Zhang encounters Oriole." Thus, it was possible to follow the details of the play without necessarily reading the much more demanding playtext below. Various types of captions (right-margin or left-margin scene caption boxes, in-picture name/character caption boxes) had been common in the fictionalized histories printed in Fujian in the Yuan dynasty.[20] However, *The Deluxe Edition* modified this convention in several innovative ways. For one, it consolidated all the relevant text into a single box on the right side that was clearly demarcated from the visual field of the image. Moreover, by consistently putting them before the pictorial sequences, the regularity of the captions' positioning underscored the narrative rather than the merely illustrative function of the text. For another—a first in the corpus of extant song-dramas—the play was broken into minute, action-centered units that offered a detailed digest of all the major events in the story. Finally, the captions indicated the names and titles of the characters (e.g., Student Zhang, Oriole) rather than referencing them by their role types as the playtext, albeit inconsistently, did in the lower register (e.g, male lead, female lead). This naming strategy allowed the characters to be read as protagonists in a simple prose narrative rather than exclusively as dramatic roles on stage.

The Deluxe Edition also adapted and played with the conventions of the painted handscroll. In narrative handscrolls of painting, segments were typically delineated by either related text or landscape elements, architectural elements, furniture, or empty space, as the action unfolded in the same direction as the unfolding of the scroll—that is, right to left. In such narrative scrolls, characters usually do not look directly at the viewer and are represented at a scale proportionate to their social importance. However, *The Deluxe Edition* visually acknowledged that Crimson, Oriole's female servant, occupied a place in the social world of the play far above that of a "mere maid" (☛ chap. 1). In Student Zhang's first encounter with Oriole, the maid, Crimson, is considerably smaller in size than Oriole or Student Zhang. However, importantly, Crimson does not simply follow Oriole; rather, she actively motions her to move away from Student Zhang [QMQX 68]. Later in the play, the images invert these tropes: when a desperate Student Zhang kneels before Crimson to enlist her assistance, she is taller than he is, as is the case in a later scene when he bows down to further solicit her help [QMQX 157; 197; 205; 225]. Notably, once Crimson shifts her allegiance to the match between Oriole and Student Zhang instead of to Madam Cui, she is the one leading the way as Oriole embarks on meetings with Zhang [QMQX 147; 161; 163; 166; 201; 220]. Moreover, rather than turning her back to the viewer, once she assumes the role of intermediary between the couple, she is typically portrayed in side view or three-quarter view [QMQX 173; 182; 193; 287].

Interestingly, Crimson is also most frequently portrayed as the lone figure in a frame [QMQX 182; 211, 212; 216], most memorably perhaps in the two images where she spies on Student Zhang to assess his true feelings and when she secretly observes the couple's lovemaking [QMQX 177 and 226] (☛ chap. 8). By contrast, Oriole appears by herself only once—namely, when Student Zhang dreams of her after he journeys to the capital [QMQX 256]. At the end of the play, Crimson is the one who reconciles Madam Cui to the prospect of Oriole's match with Student Zhang, a proposal then seconded by the male elders (the abbot and the general) [QMQX 307]. In contrast to the conventions of painted handscrolls, the humblest character within the Cui family, Crimson, assumes outsized importance in the "printed handscroll" of *The Deluxe Edition*, thus upending customary social hierarchies.

In sum, the genius of *The Deluxe Edition* lay in its recalibration of various kinds of media experiences within the covers of a single book. For the price of one carefully produced book, a modestly well-heeled buyer could re-create what might otherwise have been a communal occasion (theater performance), a socially exclusive experience (the viewing of painted handscrolls), or a literati art (the chanting or singing of verse) in everyday life. Meanwhile, for minimally literate commoners or actors, in blending the format of the painting handscroll with the detailed plot cartouches commonly found in historical tales, the "pictorial narration" of *The Deluxe Edition* may have made it the most accessible retelling of *The Western Wing* available. Thus, *The Deluxe Edition* hints at a range of possible ways of using drama imprints: as something that was not simply read, but sung as part of professional, popular, and elite transmission of songs along an oral/written continuum; as a picture book that unfolds with its own distinct emphases, much as films, graphic novels, and comic strips do now; as a prose primer about iconic protagonists distinct from the actors who impersonated them on stage and separate from the audience who watched or read them; and, last but not least, as a story that blends the lyrical vision of sung poetry with the focalizing, action-driven power of narrative.

From the mid-sixteenth century onward, other editions of *The Western Wing* picked up on the multimedia nature of *The Deluxe Edition* and experimented with different combinations. One new approach brought the visual culture of the theater itself in conversation with the images found in drama imprints. As we shall see next, such an invocation of the stage formed part of a multimedia experience designed to allow the reader to have vicarious emotional experiences.

4.3 *THE STORY OF THE WESTERN WING: THE GLOSSED EDITION* (C. 1609)—AN APP FOR ROLE-PLAYING

Our earliest visual records of theater performance are found in several kinds of media. For one, we have what are either Southern Song or Yuan paintings that depict actors and actresses impersonating comic roles against the backdrop of drums used for accompanying stage action.[21] For another, starting in the twelfth century under the Southern Song and the Jin dynasties, well-to-do families began to commission the placement of murals, reliefs, coffins, and figurines of theatrical role types in their tombs (➤ chap. 9).[22] In yet another vein, theater-related images also entered the repertoire of temple decorations. Most famous among these is the mural with the inscription "Zhongdu xiu, Actress of the Grand Guild of Roving Troupes, Performed Here" ("Dahang sanyue Zhongdu xiu zaici zuochang") found in the Hall of Mingying wang (a local water deity) (Mingying wang miao) that belonged to a major religious complex known as the Guangsheng Temple (Hongtong county, Shanxi province) (➤ Introduction, chap. 9, figure 9.2).

What these several media—paintings, tomb decorations, and temple murals, among others—share, however, is that access to them was rather limited. Paintings were typically circulated within only a small group of people, tomb decorations were mainly made for the owner of the tomb/deceased person(s), and temple murals were accessible only to people who visited that specific location. In short, despite the ubiquity of theater performances, visualized representations of the theater did not become available to a larger group of viewers until the late Ming period.

It was only when a boom in publishing in the late Ming dynasty coincided with the heyday of southern *chuanqi* drama that the visual conventions of theatrical staging began to intrude into drama illustrations.[23] The secondary capital of the Ming dynasty, Nanjing, played a key role in marrying the arts of the theater with those of print. Not only was the city a major center for the performance of the newly popular southern *chuanqi* drama, but the city grew into one of the largest publishing centers in China. We catch a glimpse of this vibrant market in books and its diverse offerings in the character of the bookseller Cai Yisuo, who appears in Kong Shangren's (1648–1718) play *The Peach Blossom Fan* (*Taohua shan*) (👉 chap. 12):

（丑扮書客蔡益所）天下書籍之富，無過俺金陵。這金陵書鋪之多，無過俺三山街。這三山街書客之大，無過俺蔡益所。（指介）

你看十三經，廿一史，九流三教，諸子百家，腐爛時文，新奇小說，上下充箱盈架，高低列肆連樓。

CLOWN *as* BOOKSELLER CAI YISUO [*speaks*]: When it comes to the abundance of books, no city surpasses our Nanjing. And among the many bookstores here, no place surpasses our Three Mountain Street. And among the businesses on that street, none is larger than mine. *Acts pointing* (*to books*). You see that the Thirteen Classics, the Twenty-Four Histories, the learning of the Nine Philosophical Schools and the Three Religions, the assorted texts of the Hundred Thinkers together with hackneyed examination essays and the innovative works of fiction fill boxes and overflow shelves, high and low, in room after room, story after story.

[*THS* 189, Scene 29 "Suppressing the Club" ("Daishe")]

Interestingly, Cai reserves his most positive comments for the "innovative works of fiction," which he contrasts favorably against the "hackneyed examination essays." Indeed, if we turn to what we know about the actual books printed in Nanjing during that period, narrative and dramatic works of the imagination constitute close to 30 percent of the total extant output. Drama amounts anywhere from 100 to perhaps as many as 300 separate play titles. Of all the plays issued and reissued in Nanjing, *The Western Wing* was the most popular, followed by *The Lute* (👉 chap. 7) and *The Peony Pavilion* (👉 chap. 9). Among the close to 200 commercial publishers in Nanjing, a handful of them dominated the market of drama publishing, most notably the Tang family's several firms—Fuchuntang (about 45 plays), Shidetang (about 15 plays), Wenlin'ge (about 27 plays), and Guangqingtang (around 8 plays)—as well as Chen Bangtai's (fl. 1598–1608) Jizhizhai (around 30 titles), Wang Tingna's (1573–1619) Huancuitang (around 20 titles), and Wang Yunpeng's (fl. 1593–1600) Wanhuxuan (around 6 titles). Thanks to the close ties among publishers in Nanjing and Fujian, certain titles and their illustrations also found their way into drama publications from Fujian.[24]

The majority of drama imprints issued by these Nanjing firms feature page-spread or single-page illustrations,[25] and many of these images allude to stage performance and the architectural elements of a stage in one way or another. Not only do figures dominate the image, but they are roughly all the same size. Furthermore, figures adopt poses and make gestures (*ke* or *jie*) that resonate with what we can retrospectively reconstruct as conventions of traditional performance (e.g., gestures of entering the stage; symbolic journeying on the stage; gestures of

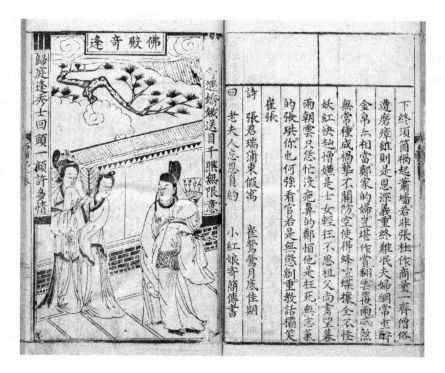

FIGURE 4.3 "The Marvelous Encounter at the Buddhist Hall" ("Fodian qifeng"), in Wang Shifu, *Chongke Yuanben tiping yinshi Xixiang ji* (The Reprinted, Original Yuan Edition of *The Story of the Western Wing* with Annotations and Phonetic Glosses) (Jianyang: Liu Longtian, 1609). Woodblock print. Beijing: National Library of China. Reprinted in *YBTPYS* 3.

greeting and speaking; gestures of crying; gesture of serving drinks; gestures of shyness; comic gestures). Occasionally, the facial design of clownish roles appears in the image. The image may also contain objects that could serve as stage props, such as curtains, screens, draped tables, wine cups, batons, and the like. In the Qing dynasty, when single-sheet color prints of popular plays came to prominence, such printed images often featured color-coded theatrical costumes, role-specific makeup and facial designs, and symbolic stage props.[26]

Such theatrical referentiality could serve at least two purposes. On the one hand, a small number of publishers explicitly note that these theatrical elements are meant to instruct prospective performers. Implicitly, such images might also have initiated theatergoing audiences to some of the gestures that they would encounter on stage; for example, when Oriole first encounters Student Zhang (see figure 4.3), she not only conceals her face behind a fan but also raises her left hand to cover her face with long "water sleeves" (*shuixiu*), a gesture of shyness in the modern repertoire of Chinese *xiqu*-style acting.[27] Meanwhile, the movements of both the monk Facong's left hand and Oriole's right hand suggest a stylized gesture characteristic of stage performance rather than the casual hand movements of daily life. Thus, such texts could help readers to either better prepare for their own performance or, more commonly, to better appreciate the performances of others. On the other hand, for all their invocation of the actuality of the stage, such images also point to the gap between the event-time of the play and the present moment of the viewer/ reader, thus underscoring the fictional nature of drama. This mediated divergence between self and other—or, to put it another way, how the self experiences itself relative to a mediatized outside world in accordance with what Ling Hon Lam calls "face-off" (☞ chap. 9)—becomes especially clear if we also take other aspects of these drama imprints into account, such as the location of the images in the text, the inscriptions in the images, and the overall organization of the text.

Here, it is instructive to examine *The Reprinted, Original Yuan Edition of The Story of the Western Wing with Annotations and Phonetic Glosses* (hereafter *The Glossed Edition*).[28] While *The Glossed Edition* adopted a great deal of the paratextual material of *The Deluxe Edition*, it organized both its text and its images in fundamentally different ways and addressed itself explicitly to "readers" (*kanguan*) in the prologue. Moreover, despite *The Glossed Edition's* claim to be a "Yuan Edition" (i.e., an "original edition,") the influence of southern drama can be strongly felt throughout (☞ chap. 8). For instance, instead of the continuous handscroll format of *The Deluxe Edition*, *The Glossed Edition* divided the text into twenty continuous "scenes" (*chu*) in the manner of a southern *chuanqi* and preceded each of them with a full-page illustration. Rather than offering running explanations after each aria, all the notes were relegated to the end of each scene, thus further reinforcing the sense of a "scene" being a distinct unit. Furthermore, each scene was given a four-character title, which encapsulated the play as follows:

Prologue	"The Troupe Leader Comes on Stage and Presents the Opening Recitation"	"Moshang shouyin"
Scene 1	"The Marvelous Encounter at the Buddhist Hall"	"Fodian qifeng"
Scene 2	"Renting Monk's Quarters Under False Pretenses"	"Sengfang jiayu"
Scene 3	"Matching Poetry at the Wall"	"Qiangjiao lianyin"
Scene 4	"Upstaging the Funerary Mass"	"Zhaitan naohui"
Scene 5	"General White Horse Lifts the Siege"	"Baima jiewei"
Scene 6	"Crimson Delivers an Invitation to the Banquet"	"Hongniang qing yan"
Scene 7	"Mother Calls Off the Marriage"	"Mushi tinghun"
Scene 8	"Expressing Sentiments Through Zither Playing"	"Qinxin xiehuai"
Scene 9	"Brocade Words Transmit Feelings"	"Jinzi chuanqing"
Scene 10	"Espying the Missive at the Jade Terrace"	"Yutai kuijian"
Scene 11	"Seizing the Night to Jump across the Wall"	"Chengye yuqiang"
Scene 12	"Dispatching Crimson to Inquire after His Illness"	"Qian Hong wenbing"
Scene 13	"The Happy Tryst on a Moonlit Night"	"Yuexia jiaqi"
Scene 14	"Clever Parsing [of the Facts] before Her Ladyship"	"Tangqian qiaobian"
Scene 15	"Feelings of Farewell on an Autumn Evening"	"Qiumu lihuai"
Scene 16	"The Interrupted Dream at Grass Bridge"	"Caoqiao jingmeng"
Scene 17	"Happy Tidings of Examination Success"	"Nijin jiebao"
Scene 18	"The Missive That Brings Sorrow"	"Chisu jianchou"
Scene 19	"Insidiously Plotting a Marriage Match"	"Guimou qiupei"
Scene 20	"Returning Home in Glory"	"Yijin huanxiang"

The titles offered a third-person perspective on the plot of the play, but it was by no means neutral: the qualifications of "marvelous encounters," "happy trysts," and "clever reasoning" all invited the reader to side with the young lovers rather than with the older authority figures.

The prominence of these four-character titles was underscored in that they appeared not only in the text proper next to the numbered scene in question, but they were emblazoned across the top of each image in the manner of a horizontal cartouche that mimicked both the inscribed valences found above actual stages and the calligraphic boards (*bian'e*) that adorned residential and public buildings. At the same time, each image was bounded by two calligraphic "hanging scrolls" on either side. Such an arrangement echoed how interior focal points such as altars, niches, and rooms were decorated, while also alluding to the practice of inscribing the frontal pillars of stages with matching poetic couplets.

Moving between first- and third-person perspectives, the inscriptions in the simulated vertical "scrolls" did not relay action in the manner of *The Deluxe Edition*; instead they created an emotional interiority for the characters portrayed in the image. For instance, in *The Glossed Edition's* image for the first scene (figure 4.3), the vertical "scroll" on the right—positioned next to Student Zhang, who is accompanied by a monk with a flywhisk—reads: "As I roamed around the temple, I chanced upon female beauty and charm—parting eyes intimate a thousand glances full of boundless meaning." Located on the left next to Oriole, who was a little tempted but still behaved modestly as a genteel female, the vertical "scroll" reads: "Upon returning to the garden, I happened upon a refined scholar, and as I turned my head to leave, in a single glance, so much longing!" Perfectly parallel in wording, grammar, and length, the couplet not only points to the dramatic potential inherent in this "marvelous encounter," but invites the viewer to identify with the feelings of one or more of the characters, despite the fact that the prologue to *The Glossed Edition* issued a tongue-in-cheek exhortation to make fun of the lovers. Such an invitation is even more keenly felt, as all the images in *The Glossed Edition* featured at least two characters, and some of them contained an explicit voyeur [*YBTPXXJ* 118 and 164]. In all cases, the vertical "scrolls" tease out the sentiments of at least two characters, who are invariably addressed by their names rather than their role type.

Thus, the images in *The Glossed Edition* began to distill and coalesce scenes around a central idea, contrast, or conflict rather than illustrate an action per se. While other scholars have pointed to the theatrical language referenced in these images, it is also important to take note of the ways in which text and image conspired to entangle the reader in an imaginary world of multiple affective possibilities. Such an affective invitation into a self-created—yet mediatized—world of fiction becomes especially clear if we compare *The Glossed Edition*'s cartouches with the action-centered cartouches in *The Deluxe Edition* ("While strolling around the Temple of Universal Salvation with monk Facong, Student Zhang encounters Oriole"). Such images did not offer iconic constructs that called for a viewer's worship or reverence, nor did they present themselves as a self-contained narrative

THE STORY OF THE WESTERN WING 117

about distant others to be contemplated by a detached viewer.²⁹ Instead, in what may well have been a new viewing position for readers, such images appear to function more as gateways into an imaginary world of "playable characters," with whom one could choose to identify or not, depending on whether one wanted to laugh at them as love-addled fools or embrace them as romantic catalysts for one's own feelings. As we shall see, by the end of the Ming dynasty, the three-way dialogue between the stage, painting, and woodblock images culminated in yet another configuration—that is, the celebration of virtual dream worlds in what a modern historian has called one of the world's great "dream blooms."³⁰

4.4 *THE STORY OF THE WESTERN WING: THE EXCLUSIVE EDITION* (1639–1640)—AN APP FOR VIRTUAL REALITY

As noted initially, the late Ming era witnessed greater permeability among the three perfections of literati arts (poetry, painting, calligraphy) and the popular arts (woodblock printing, song-drama). Many of these new kinds of hybrid artifacts stemmed from the city of Hangzhou and its environs. As the capital of the Southern Song and an important cultural crossroads during the Yuan dynasty, Hangzhou had long prided itself on its cultural output. From the Song dynasty onward, Hangzhou had been a center of fine publishing, a reputation that was intact in the late Ming. Partly, Hangzhou was able to uphold this reputation because it became home to carvers from Huizhou (Anhui province)—that is, members of the Huang family, who, as noted previously, from the late sixteenth century onward were among the most innovative blockcutters.³¹

Several editions of *The Western Wing* from Hangzhou and environs speak to the rapprochement between artistic styles and subjects favored by the literati and the increasingly sophisticated craftsmanship of woodblock printing. In 1610, one of the best-known publishing houses of Hangzhou, the Rongyutang, brought out an influential *The Western Wing* as part of a set of six plays [*LZWXXJ*].³² In contrast to *The Deluxe Edition* and *The Glossed Edition*, this *The Western Wing* invoked the literati taste of uniting poetry, painting, and calligraphy. For one, it claimed to have been annotated by Li Zhi (1527–1602; literary name Li Zhuowu), one of the most controversial critics and an avowed proponent of literature like *The Western Wing*. In the wake of the success of *Li Zhuowu's Commented Edition*, many publishers recruited other well-known literati, dead and alive, to serve as figureheads for their own new *The Western Wing* editions. As far as the accompanying images went, *Li Zhuowu's Commented Edition* borrowed from the iconography of literati painting and calligraphy, an endeavor enabled by the skills of the famous carver named in the edition, Huang Yingguang (1592–unknown). First, instead of the continuous or interspersed format of *The Deluxe* and *Glossed Editions*, respectively, *Li Zhuowu's Commented Edition* grouped all the images together in the manner of a painting album placed at the beginning of the text. Rather than illustrating the actions or emotions of individual scenes, the images centered on poetic lines of the playtext, with only passing reference to the plot of the scenes from which they were derived. Furthermore, in the manner of literati painting, the excerpted lines were inscribed in the image itself as a form of poetic inscription. Finally, in contrast to the focus on figures found in *The Deluxe* and *Glossed Editions*, Li Zhuowu's *Commented Edition* highlighted landscapes as the backdrop of scholarly pursuits or devoid of any figures, while making the elements of nature (e.g., trees, rivers, mountains, rocks) come alive with the detailed brushwork characteristic of literati painting. Such images focused more on poetic atmosphere than on the plot or any dramatic conflict. Aided by the rise of printed painting manuals, this style of image-making echoed through many later imprints of *The Western Wing* and other plays.[33]

At the same time, figures did not disappear from the repertoire of literati-flavored illustrations. However, rather than focusing on figures in action, such editions honed in on the theme of female beauty. Arguably, female beauties had long been featured in painted and printed images, but the late Ming witnessed a burgeoning of such works in painting and print alike. For example, a long handscroll titled *Peerless Beauties throughout the Ages* (*Qianqiu jueyan*) featured fifty lovely women (including Oriole) engaged in various activities. *The Classical Edition of The Western Wing* (1614), issued by one of the most knowledgeable late Ming connoisseurs of song-drama, Wang Jide (1550–1620), a native of Shaoxing, exemplified this fascination with female beauty. On the one hand, Wang carefully collated the text against other texts associated with both the historical and the fictional Cui Yingying; on the other hand, *The Classical Edition* included a portrait of Oriole attributed to a Song-dynasty academy painter, together with a calligraphic rendition of a newly coined alternate title for *The Western Wing*, *A Beauty Unrivalled in*

FIGURE 4.4 Crimson is spying on Oriole reading a love letter from Student Zhang [*ZSZMB* 224–225].

FIGURE 4.5 Student Zhang is dreaming at an inn [*ZSZMB* 226-227].

a *Thousand Years* (*Qianqiu jueyan*) [*GBXXJ* 339–345]. In the wake of *The Classical Edition*, many other versions of *The Western Wing* made a point of featuring either this or other newly commissioned portraits of the play's gentry heroine. Thus, in contrast to the plebeian emphasis that *The Deluxe Edition* placed on Crimson, these late Ming editions redirected the viewer's attention to the socially prominent female character of the play, Cui Yingying. However, set against the Confucian notion that respectable women should be invisible to the public eye, such sustained visual exposure broke taboos of its own (☛ *HTRCProse*, C14.2).

The images in *The Exclusive Edition* (1639–1640), designed by Chen Hongshou, one of the most idiosyncratic painters of the seventeenth century, forged a distinctive visual synthesis out of these various trends. Born into a scholarly family near Hangzhou, Chen pursued training for the civil service, but when that proved a dead end, he increasingly relied on his gift as a painter to make his mark in the world. Apprenticed to a well-known professional painter in Hangzhou in his youth, Chen embraced painting as his livelihood after the fall of the Ming dynasty in 1644, on account of his unwillingness to serve in the new regime. While living on the family estate early on, he eventually moved to Hangzhou proper to drum up more business.

One of the distinctive aspects of Chen Hongshou's oeuvre is that he not only treated woodblock printing as a full-fledged medium for artistic creation, but he also transferred techniques from woodblock printing to painting and vice versa.[34] Furthermore, more than any other known painter, he simultaneously engaged with the world of the theater and the world of fiction and drama illustrations.[35]

Chen Hongshou was involved in two editions of *The Western Wing*, as well as the play *The Mistress and the Maid* (*Jiao Hong ji*), which he illustrated for his friend, the playwright Meng Chengshun (1599–1684). For both *Western Wing* versions, he collaborated with a well-known contemporary engraver, Xiang Nanzhou (ca. 1615–1670), who would go on to work on an edition of *The Swallow's Letter* (*Yanzi jian*, 1643) by Ruan Dacheng (1587–1646) (☛ chap. 10).

Of Chen's *Western Wing* illustrations, the most famous was the one conventionally called the "Zhang Shenzhi edition," which was named for the military patron who paid for its publication and was published under the full title of *The Exclusive Edition of the Correct Northern Western Wing Commissioned by Zhang Shenzhi*. Chen's exquisite mastery of lines can be seen in *The Exclusive Edition*. It contained only six images: a newly drawn portrait of Oriole that took up a single page, and five page-spreads referencing distinct scenes (namely, the funeral mass, the imminent victory of White Horse General over the bandit Sun Feihu, Crimson spying on Oriole reading a love letter from Student Zhang, Student Zhang dreaming at an inn, and Oriole and Crimson sending presents to Student Zhang in the capital). Three of those images feature the signature of the carver, Xiang Nanzhou. Chen's inscription was carved on the following pages.

The play scene titled "Peeking at the Letter" ("Kuijian") represents a key moment in the play (see figure 4.4). In the background, a four-fold screen highlighted Chen Hongshou's skills as a master of "flower-and-bird painting," with each panel representing a different season (from left to right: autumn, winter, spring, and summer) that used the language of poetry to allude to the courtship between Oriole and Student Zhang. In the foreground, Oriole reads a love letter from Student Zhang without noticing that Crimson is hiding behind the screen and peeping at her. Oriole's facial expression is too vague to express her inner thoughts, but Crimson's anxiety and suspense can be detected in her pose of putting a finger to her lips.

As a master of lines, Chen adopted the plain-drawing (*baimiao*) technique, which was favored by literati painters for its elegant simplicity, but was also well suited to the production of monochrome woodblock printing. Both Oriole and Crimson are rendered in delicate and exquisite line drawings that convey a sense of antiqueness.[36] This archaizing linear style, showing figures and landscape elements in angular contours and parallel folds, lent itself to woodblock cutting.[37] This achievement also depended on the consummate craftsmanship of the carver Xiang Nanzhou, who skillfully rendered the contour of the clothing with his knives by retaining the graceful fluidity of the brushstrokes. The unusual design derived from the painter's idiosyncratic combination of motifs: the summer scene depicts both butterflies (signifying light amorous dalliance) and lotuses (symbolizing moral purity but also invoking the homophonous notion of "love"), while the winter scene represents banana palms (a summer plant) covered by snow (winter), a trope first conceived by the Tang poet-painter Wang Wei (699–761) to declare his freedom from realistic conventions. By borrowing this theme, Chen seemed to wittily invoke the literati tradition while also expressing his own sensibilities and underscoring the fictionality of the image.

All the images play with the blending of the iconography of various media, often having the effect of blurring the boundaries between what is "real" and what is "imaginary." The scene "Interrupted Dream" ("Jingmeng") represents what Student Zhang dreams of while he is napping at an inn on his way to the capital (see figure 4.5). In Zhang's dream, Oriole overcomes many difficulties and dangers to meet Student Zhang again at the Grass Bridge, but she is chased by a bandit, who tries to abduct her—at the precise moment when Student Zhang suddenly wakes. In printed illustrations, "dream bubbles" were a standard convention to represent a person's dream. However, the unique part of Chen Hongshou's design is the relation between dream and reality. To represent a dreamland, designers would usually situate the figures against a blank background, emphasizing the visional quality of their experience. By contrast, Chen Hongshou creatively endowed the virtual dreamspace with the detail typically reserved for "reality." At the same time, however, the theatrical pose and costuming of the bandit within the dream implodes the very duality of "real" and "imagined." Hence, the reversal of representational conventions not only challenged viewers' common sense of what is real and what is imagined, but it also infused the scene with the virtual power of dreams so memorably articulated in *The Peony Pavilion* and other contemporary media (☞ chap. 9).

CONCLUSION

When scholars discuss images in books, we are tempted to refer to them as "illustrations." However, that term suggests that images and text relate to each other in a fixed, stable fashion: the images are subordinate to the text and explain it in some way. In this chapter, we have sought to show some of the inherent plurality of text/image relations in a Ming context in China in order to highlight what Pierre Bourdieu has called the "co-possibles" inherent in cultural artifacts.[38]

Such malleability could take many forms. First, as we have seen, the format varied greatly among the imprints that we examined. Not only did such varying displays engage different visual conventions, but they communicated very different things about both the text and the images. Second, the content of such images differed greatly as well. If some images hewed closely to the text itself, others made only passing reference to the plot of the play. Thus, rather than simply explaining the text, these images point to the fact that the text itself is subject to vastly different interpretations. Third, as books began to address themselves to a broader spectrum of readers, they also began to define more explicitly how they spoke to different audiences. Instead of offering a single vantage point from which to engage the story, such works made different appeals to different kinds of readers. Finally, as we observed, such images were in dialogue not only with the text, but also with many other media, such as painting, poetry, the decorative arts, and the theater. Thus, these images can help us see that these works were not isolated products, but rather that they traversed the protean late Ming cultural space in ways old and new.[39]

Insofar as such books evoked, in the words of a contemporary media scholar, a "convergence culture," they pointed to the desirability of having multiple functionalities embodied in a single edition while also foregrounding the ability of readers to make connections among dispersed media content.[40] In this regard, such books may well offer new ways for us to think about how the early modern media landscape relates to and differs from its modern counterparts in China and elsewhere.

Patricia Sieber and Gillian Yanzhuang Zhang

NOTES

1. The early research represented here profited from Julia Murray's and Eugene Wang's insights and encouragement. In its current form, this chapter benefited from extensive and incisive comments offered by Wilt L. Idema and S. E. Kile, as well as the thoughtful observations of Regina Llamas, Mengjun Li, and David L. Rolston. Translations are our own unless otherwise noted.

2. Denda Akira, *Minkan Gen zatsugeki Seishôki mokuroku* (A Bibliography of the Ming Dynasty Imprints of the Yuan Dynasty *Zaju* Play *The Story of the Western Wing*) (Tokyo: Tôyô bunko, 1970); and Chen Xuyao, *Xiancun Mingkan Xixiang ji zonglu* (An Annotated List of Currently Extant Ming Dynasty Imprints of *The Story of the Western Wing*) (Shanghai: Shanghai guji chubanshe, 2007).

3. J. P. Park, "The Publisher's Dilemma: A Study of 'Editorial Statements' on Late Ming Book Illustrations (1550–1644)," *Chinese Historical Review* 15, no. 1 (Spring 2008): 25–49.

4. Louis J. Gallagher, ed. and trans., *China in the Sixteenth Century: The Journals of Matthew Ricci, 1583–1610* (New York: Random House, 1953), 21.

5. The publisher's colophon indicates that it was written in the twelfth lunar month of the *wuwu* year of the Hongzhi reign. In that lunar calendar year, the twelfth month starts from January 12, 1499 (hence our date).

6. The preface of this edition notes that it was written in the twelfth month of the *jimao* year. In that lunar calendar year, the twelfth month straddles the years of 1639 and 1640, lasting from December 24, 1639 to January 22, 1640 (hence our dual-year reference).

7. Susan Bush and Hsio-yen Shih, ed. and trans., *Early Chinese Texts on Painting* (Hong Kong: Hong Kong University Press, 2012 [1985]), 50.

8. Alfreda Murck and Wen C. Fong, "Introduction: The Three Perfections—Poetry, Calligraphy, and Painting," in *Words and Images: Chinese Poetry, Calligraphy, and Painting* (New York and Princeton, NJ: Metropolitan Museum of Art and Princeton University Press, 1991), xv.

9. Zhou Mi, *Yunyan guoyan lu* (Records of Clouds and Mist Passing before One's Eyes), trans. Ankeney Weitz (Leiden, Netherlands: Brill, 2002), 124.

10. David Barker, *Traditional Techniques in Contemporary Chinese Printmaking* (Honolulu: University of Hawai'i Press, 2005), 19.

11. Jerome Silbergeld, "Kung Hsien: A Professional Chinese Artist and His Patronage," *The Burlington Magazine*, 123: 940 (July 1981): 400–410.

12. Jonathan Hay, *Sensuous Surfaces: The Decorative Object in Early Modern China* (Honolulu: University of Hawai'i Press, 2010), 60.

13. For this particular edition, see Museum für Ostasiatische Kunst, Cologne (https://mok .kulturelles-erbe-koeln.de/documents/obj/05161815/rba_d040420_01). One study of this version mentions that a single page uses a total of eight colors. See Dong Jie, "De cang ben Xixiang ji banhua ji qi kanke zhe" (The Woodblock-Printed Illustrations of *The Story of the Western Wing* held in Germany), *Xin meishu* (Journal of the China Academy of Art) 5 (2009): 17.

14. For these three interpretations, see Wu Hung, *The Double Screen: Medium and Representation in Chinese Painting* (Chicago: University of Chicago Press, 1996), 241; Craig Clunas, *Pictures and Visuality in Early Modern China* (Princeton, NJ: Princeton University Press, 1997), 56–57; and Jennifer Purtle, "Scopic Frames: Devices for Seeing China, c. 1640," *Art History* 33, no. 1 (2010): 59.

15. For the first, see Du Renjie (also known as Du Shanfu), "Zhuangjia bu shi goulan" ("Country Cousin Is Not Familiar with Urban Theater"), in *Quan Yuan sanqu* (The Complete *Sanqu* Songs of the Yuan Dynasty), ed. Sui Shusen (Beijing: Zhonghua shuju, 1989 [1964]), vol. 1, 31–32. For the second, see Xia Tingzhi, *Qinglou ji jiaozhu* (An Annotated Edition of *The Record of the Green Bowers*), ann. Sun Chongtao and Xu Hongtu (Beijing: Beijing xiju chubanshe, 1990).

16. Hu Zhiyu, "Zeng Song shi xu" ("A Preface [Bestowed] to Ms. Song"), *ZSDQJ*, v. 292, 8.57a. Translation modified from Wilt L. Idema and Stephen H. West, ed. and trans., "A Preface [Bestowed] to Ms. Sung," in their *Chinese Theater, 1100–1450: A Source Book* (Wiesbaden, Germany: Franz Steiner Verlag, 1982), 156–157.

17. Yao Dajuin, "The Pleasure of Reading Drama: Illustrations to the Hongzhi Edition of *The Story of the Western Wing*," in Stephen H. West and Wilt L. Idema, ed. and trans., *The Moon and the Zither: The Story of the Western Wing* (Berkeley: University of California Press, 1991), 440.

18. For the existence of "illustrated classics" in nonreligious contexts from the Song period onward, see Lucille Chia, *Printing for Profit: The Commercial Publishers of Jianyang, Fujian (11th–17th Centuries)* (Cambridge, MA: Harvard University Asia Center, 2002), 40. *The Classic of Filial Piety, The Great Learning,* and *The Doctrine of the Mean* were issued in this format in the early Ming dynasty. See Anne E. McLaren, *Chinese Popular Culture and Ming Chantefables* (Leiden, Netherlands: Brill, 1998), 59. Narrative texts and song-related texts illustrated in this format include the classical-language tale collections (*Jiandeng xinhua* [*New Stories Told While Trimming the Wick*] and *Jiandeng yuhua* [*Additional Stories Told While Trimming the Wick*]), plays (*Lijing ji* [*The Story of the Litchi and Mirror*]), song collections (*Fengyue jinnang* [*The Brocade Pouch of Romance*]), and many works of fiction from Fujian.

19. Yao, "The Pleasure of Reading Drama," 465.

20. See the digitized versions of the five extant "plain tales" (*pinghua*) in the National Diet Library, Tokyo: https://www.digital.archives.go.jp/DAS/pickup/view/detail/detailArchivesEn/0503000000 /0000000807/00. *The Story of Hua Guansuo* chantefable also uses a box of text in the manner of *The Deluxe Edition* (☞ chap. 16).

21. For the painting entitled *The Eyedrop Quack* (*Yanyaosuan*), see Liao Ben, *Zhongguo xiju tushi* (Zhengzhou: Henan jiaoyu chubanshe, 1996), 78. For the painting entitled *Actresses Playing the Flower Drum* (*Zaju: Da huagu*), see Ankeney Weitz, "Two Tales of Song-Dynasty Painted Fans," *Archives of Asian Art* 69, no. 1 (2019): 77.

22. Jeehee Hong, "Virtual Theater of the Dead: Actor Figurines and Their Stage in Houma Tomb No. 1, Shanxi Province," *Artibus Asiae* 71, no. 1 (2011): 75–114.

23. Anne McLaren notes that theatrical poses had made their way into the chantefable images dating to the Chenghua period (1465–1487). See McLaren, *Chinese Popular Culture*, 64–67. On the growth of drama illustrations in the late Ming period and their connection to theatrical performances, see Li-ling Hsiao, *The Eternal Present of the Past: Illustration, Theatre, and Reading in the Wanli Period, 1573–1619* (Leiden, Netherlands: Brill, 2007).

24. For the findings on Nanjing drama publishing, see Lucille Chia, "Of Three Mountain Street: The Commercial Publishers of Ming Nanjing," in *Printing and Book Culture in Late Imperial China*, ed. Cynthia J. Brokaw and Kai-wing Chow (Berkeley: University of California Press, 2005), 107–151.

25. We use the terms "single page" and "page spread" for readers who are familiar with Western books. However, in traditional Chinese thread-binding books, the definition of "page" is different from that of Western books. Chinese woodblocks used only one side of a sheet of paper. After being folded down the middle and stitched together along the cut edge, the printed side faced out, acting as a leaf in a book with two pages (recto and verso), whereas the unprinted sides faced inward. For more details, see Jesse Munn, "Side-Stitched Books of China, Korea and Japan in Western Collections," *Journal of the Institute of Conservation* 32, no. 1 (March 2009): 103–127.

26. The abovementioned inventory is based on Li-ling Hsiao, *The Eternal Present of the Past*, 38–175; and Catherine Pagani, "The Theme of *Three Kingdoms* in Chinese Popular Woodblock Prints," in *Three Kingdoms and Chinese Culture*, ed. Kimberly Besio and Constantine Tung (Albany, NY: SUNY Press, 2007), 87–109.

27. Cecilia S. L. Zung, *Secrets of the Chinese Drama: A Guide to Its Theatre Techniques* (New York: Benjamin Blom, 1964 [1937]), 78–81.

28. The extant editions of *The Glossed Edition* appeared as an imprint of Xiong Longfeng (fl. 1592) and of Liu Longtian (c. 1609), both of which were likely published in Fujian, but we base

our discussion here solely on Liu Longtian's edition. In terms of text, these two editions took much of their inspiration from the Xu Shifan edition (1580), but their titles are different. The full title of the Liu Longtian edition is *Chongke Yuanben tiping yinshi Xixiang ji* (The Reprinted, Original Yuan Edition of *The Story of the Western Wing* with Annotations and Phonetic Glosses), and the Xiong Longfeng edition is *Chongqie chuxiang yinshi Xixiang pinglin daquan* (The Recarved, Illustrated *Western Wing* with Phonetic Glosses and Complete Annotations). As opposed to *The Deluxe Edition*, *The Glossed Edition* enhanced the affective dimension of the text (e.g., creating more explicitly emotional overtones for scene titles) and strengthened the association with performance (e.g., adding a section on stage directions in the explanatory apparatus appended to each scene). In terms of the images, the style mirrors that of Fuchuntang and Shidetang, the leading late-Ming drama publishing houses in Nanjing. None of the other extant imprints by Xiong Longfeng adopt the exact visual format of his *The Western Wing*. Hence, we are inclined to believe that the stylistic influence was transmitted from the two Nanjing publishers to the Fujian-based Xiong Longfeng and then to Liu Longtian rather than the other way around, especially because prior to 1592, Fuchuntang had already published two datable and illustrated drama imprints (*Yujue ji* [*The Story of the Jade Pendant*, 1581] and *Zhufa ji* [*The Story of the Shaven Head*, 1583]), as had Shidetang (*Jingchai ji* [*The Thorn Hairpin*, 1585] and *Duanfa ji* [*The Story of Cutting Hair*, 1586]).

29. Wu Hung terms "episodic" those narrative images with action elements set in specific places and times and calls "iconic" frontal and hieratic images without those features, but stresses that they need to be completed by the viewer (through acts of worship and other actions). See Julia K. Murray, *Mirror of Morality: Chinese Narrative Illustration and Confucian Ideology* (Honolulu: University of Hawai'i Press, 2007), 8.

30.   Lynn Struve, *The Dreaming Mind and the End of the Ming World* (Honolulu: University of Hawai'i Press, 2019).

31.   Hiromitsu Kobayashi, "Printed Beauties," in *Repentant Monk: Illusion and Disillusion in the Art of Chen Hongshou*, ed. Julia M. White (Berkeley: University of California Press, 2017), 25.

32.   The existing imprints of the Rongyutang publishing house with Li Zhuowu annotations were in all likelihood not written by Li Zhi (style name Zhuowu), but by a relatively obscure literatus by the name of Ye Zhou (fl. 1594–1625). See Huang Lin, "Lun Rongyutang ben Li Zhuwo xiansheng piping *Bei Xixiang ji*" (A Study of the Rongyutang Edition of *Li Zhuowu's Commented Edition of the Northern Western Wing*), *Fudan xuebao (shehui kexue ban)* (Fudan Journal (Social Science)) 44, no. 2 (2002): 119–125.

33.   Ma Meng-ching, "Linking Poetry, Painting, and Prints: The Mode of Poetic Pictures in Late Ming Illustrations to *The Story of the Western Wing*," *International Journal of Asian Studies* 5, no. 1 (2008): 1–51.

34.   Kobayashi, "Printed Beauties," 29.

35.   Chen Hongshou obtained inspiration from and even incorporated contemporary theatrical conventions into his rendition of figures. See Shi-Yee Liu, "The World's a Stage: The Theatricality of Chen Hongshou's Figure Painting," *Ars Orientalis* 35 (2008): 155–191; Patricia Berger, "Living in a World of Regret: Buddhist Painting," in *Repentant Monk*, 47 and Julia M. White, "Bodhisattva Guanyin in the Form of Buddha-Mother Zhunti," in *Repentant Monk*, 89.

36.   Hiromitsu Kobayashi argues that Chen Hongshou's innovative portrayal of female figures is based on his studies from ancient masters like Zhou Fang (c. 730–800), a Tang-dynasty master. Wen C. Fong believes that Chen's unique painting style could be attributed to his frequent access to "traditions and forms of craft—woodblock illustrations, tapestries, lacquer and ceramic decorations—and, imbuing these forms with a new life and emotion, to turn them into a highly expressive style." See Kobayashi, "Printed Beauties," 30; and Wen C. Fong, "Archaism as a 'Primitive Style,'" in *Artists and Traditions: Uses of the Past in Chinese Culture*, ed. Christian F. Murck (Princeton, NJ: Princeton University Press, 1976), 103.

37.   Fong, "Archaism as a 'Primitive Style,'" 103.

38. For "co-possibles" in the context of Chinese drama, see Patricia Sieber, *Theaters of Desire: Authors, Readers, and the Reproduction of Chinese Song-Drama, 1300-2000* (New York: Palgrave MacMillan, 2003), 2.

39. He Yuming, *Home and the World: Editing the "Glorious Ming" in Woodblock-Printed Books of the Sixteenth and Seventeenth Centuries* (Cambridge, MA: Harvard University Asia Center, 2013).

40. Henry Jenkins, *Convergence Culture: Where Old and New Media Collide* (New York: New York University Press, 2008).

PRIMARY SOURCES

GBXXJ   Wang Shifu 王實甫. *Xin jiaozhu guben Xixiang ji* 新校注古本西廂記 (*The Ancient Edition of* The Story of the Western Wing *Newly Annotated, referred to as* The Classical Edition), ed. Wang Jide 王驥德. In *Guben Xixiang ji huiji chuji* 古本《西廂記》彙集初集 (*First Set of the Collection of Old Editions of* The Story of the Western Wing), vols. 1 and 2. Beijing: Guojia tushuguan, 2011.

LZWXXJ   Wang Shifu 王實甫. *Li Zhuowu xiansheng piping bei Xixiang ji* 李卓吾先生批評北西廂記 (*Li Zhuowu's Commented Edition of the* Northern Story of the Western Wing, *referred to as* Li Zhuowu's Commented Edition). Attr. Li Zhuowu 李卓吾. In *Guben Xixiang ji huiji erji* 古本《西廂記》彙集二集 (*Second Set of the Collection of Old Editions of* The Story of the Western Wing), vol. 4. Beijing: Guojia tushuguan, 2011.

QMQX   Wang Shifu 王實甫. *Xinkan qimiao quanxiang zhushi Xixiang ji* 新刊奇妙全相注釋西廂記 (*The Newly Printed, Exquisite, Fully Illustrated and Annotated* Story of the Western Wing, *referred to as* The Deluxe Edition). In *Guben Xixiang ji huiji chuji* 古本《西廂記》彙集初集 (*First Set of the Collection of Old Editions of* The Story of the Western Wing), vol. 1. Beijing: Guojia tushuguan, 2011.

THS   Kong Shangren 孔尚任. *Taohua shan* 桃花扇 (*The Peach Blossom Fan*). Ann. Wang Jisi 王季思, Su Huanzhong 蘇寰中, and Yang Deping 楊德平. Beijing: Renmin wenxue, 1997.

XXJ   Wang Shifu 王實甫. *Xixiang ji* 西廂記 (*The Story of the Western Wing*). Ann. Kong Xiangyi 孔祥義. In Ling Mengchu 凌濛初. *Ling Mengchu quanji* 凌濛初全集 (*The Complete Works of Ling Mengchu*), ed. Wei Tongxian 魏同賢 and An Pingqiu 安平秋, vol. 10. Nanjing: Fenghuang chubanshe, 2010.

YBTPYS   Wang Shifu 王實甫. *Chongke Yuanben tiping yinshi Xixiang ji* 重刻元本題評音釋西廂記 (*The Reprinted, Original Yuan Edition of* The Story of the Western Wing *with Annotations and Phonetic Glosses, referred to as* The Glossed Edition). In *Guben Xixiang ji huiji chuji* 古本《西廂記》彙集初集 (*First Set of the Collection of Old Editions of* The Story of the Western Wing), vol. 3. Beijing: Guojia tushuguan, 2011.

ZSZMB   Wang Shifu 王實甫. *Zhang Shenzhi Zheng Bei Xixiang miben* 張深之正北西廂秘本 (*The Exclusive Edition of the Correct* Northern Western Wing *Commissioned by Zhang Shenzhi, referred to as* The Exclusive Edition). In *Guben Xixiang ji huiji chuji* 古本《西廂記》彙集初集 (*First Set of the Collection of Old Editions of* The Story of the Western Wing), vol. 4. Beijing: Guojia tushuguan, 2011. See also the World Digital Library site at https://www.wdl.org/zh/item/3022/.

SUGGESTED READINGS

ENGLISH

Cahill, James. *Pictures for Use and Pleasure: Vernacular Painting in High Qing China.* Berkeley and Los Angeles: University of California Press, 2010.

Clunas, Craig. *Pictures and Visuality in Early Modern China.* Princeton, NJ: Princeton University Press, 1997.

He Yuming. *Home and the World: Editing the "Glorious Ming" in Woodblock-Printed Books of the Sixteenth and Seventeenth Centuries*. Cambridge, MA: Harvard University Asia Center, 2013.

Hsiao, Li-ling. *The Eternal Present of the Past: Illustration, Theatre, and Reading in the Wanli Period, 1573–1619*. Leiden, Netherlands: E. J. Brill, 2007.

Hsu, Wen-chin. "Illustrations of 'Romance of the Western Chamber' on Chinese Porcelains: Iconography, Style, and Development." *Ars Orientalis* 40 (2011): 39–107.

Murray, Julia K. *Mirror of Morality: Chinese Narrative Illustration and Confucian Ideology*. Honolulu: University of Hawai'i Press, 2007.

White, Julia M, ed. *Repentant Monk: Illusion and Disillusion in the Art of Chen Hongshou*. Berkeley: UC Berkeley Art Museum and Pacific Film Archive and University of California Press, 2017.

Zeitlin, Judith, and Yuhang Li, eds. *Performing Images: Opera in Chinese Visual Culture*. Chicago: Smart Museum of Art, University of Chicago, 2014.

CHINESE AND JAPANESE

Chen, Pao-chen 陳葆真. *Luoshen fu tu yu Zhongguo gudai gushi hua* 洛神賦圖與中國古代故事畫 (*The Goddess of the Luo River: A Study of Early Chinese Narrative Handscrolls*). Taipei: Shitou chubanshe, 2011.

Dong Jie 董捷. "De cang ben Xixiang ji banhua ji qi kanke zhe 德藏本西廂記版畫及其刊刻者 (The Woodblock-Printed Illustrations of *The Story of the Western Wing* Held in Germany)," *Xin meishu* 新美術 (*Journal of the China Academy of Art*) 5 (2009): 16–25.

Kobayashi, Hiromitsu 小林宏光. *Chūgoku Hanga Shiron* 中國版畫史論 (*Discourse on the History of Chinese Pictorial Printmaking*). Tokyo: Bensei shuppan, 2017.

Wu, Hung 巫鴻. *Zhongguo huihua zhong de nüxing kongjian* 中國繪畫中的 "女性空間" (*Feminine Space in Chinese Painting*). Beijing: Shenghuo, dushu, xinzhi sanlian shudian, 2018.

5

The Orphan of Zhao

The Meaning of Loyalty and Filiality

The Orphan of Zhao (*Zhao shi gu'er*) is a story of political intrigue, murder, and revenge. Based on an episode from China's early history, it was transformed into a riveting and enduring literary classic. The earliest extant copy of the full story is a fourteenth-century printing of a *zaju* play; it was later adapted for performance as a *nanxi* southern drama (*nanxi*) and then for the *chuanqi* play genre in the Ming dynasty; and it finally made its way into the repertoire of local operas no later than the Qing dynasty. In the early eighteenth century, when European interest in China ran high, the play had the distinction of being the first drama to be translated into a European language. This play not only allowed Europeans to get a first glimpse of Chinese drama and of its moral aesthetics, but in a variety of adaptations, it became a hit on stages across Europe and in England and inspired further relay translations throughout the eighteenth century. So profound was the impact of this play in Europe, and then spreading out to Japan, that in the early twentieth century, Wang Guowei (1877–1927), the founding figure of the study of Chinese drama, proposed that the play should be considered one of the great tragedies of world literature (➳ Introduction).

If we had to choose among the three most frequently performed Chinese plays on the world's stages in the early twenty-first century, *The Orphan of Zhao* would definitely figure on this list. This play has promoted much intercultural dialogue between China and the world. Two well-known Chinese stage directors, Lin Zhaohua and Tian Qinxin, adapted it for modern spoken drama in October 2003.[1] In 2010, the famous film director Chen Kaige turned it into a movie, *Sacrifice*, which was released in the United States, stirring up controversy over the story's moral message. In Britain, the Royal Shakespeare Company (RSC) staged it in 2012 as their first stab at staging a classical Chinese play. In South Korea, in 2015, the National Theater Company adapted it as a modern Korean spoken drama, garnering great acclaim in both South Korea and China.

Given these diverse adaptations, we may well wonder what has made this story a perennial favorite among audiences around the globe. Superficially, this play does have the hallmarks of a blockbuster Hollywood-style drama: blood and violence, undercover machinations, secrecy, and, finally, revenge. But more profoundly, it is the search for balance among loyalty, self-sacrifice, and filial love that renders this play a humane, gripping, and thought-provoking story to this day. In what follows,

we will first examine the historical background of the story; then we will compare
[the two major] extant *zaju* editions of the first-known dramatic adaptations of the
[... re]viewing contemporary renditions on stage and in film, in China and

5.1 HISTORICAL BACKGROUND

[...] the story first appeared in the *Zuo Tradition* (*Zuozhuan*), a narrative
[... o]n the *Spring and Autumn Annals* (*Chunqiu*), one of the five Confu-
[...] HTRCProse, chap. 2).² According to the *Zuo Tradition*, the story
[...] the Spring and Autumn Period during the late sixth century BCE
[...] Jin. The main event is the well-known massacre of the Zhao clan,
[... pro]duced powerful ministers. The first important minister of this fam-
[...] Cui, and his successor was his elder son, Zhao Dun. This prominent
[...] was torn apart in 587 BCE after it was discovered that Zhao Dun's
[... broth]er, Zhao Yingqi, had intercourse with Zhao Zhuangji, a princess of
[... Ji]n who was also the wife of Zhao Dun's son, Zhao Shuo. By that time,
Zhao Dun and Zhao Shuo had long been dead, and Zhao Dun's two other young
brothers, Zhao Tung and Zhao Kuo, decided to send Zhao Yingqi into exile (in
586 BCE). After three years (in 583 BCE), Zhao Zhuangji, angry at her lover's banishment, together with two other powerful families of the state ministers, accused
the Zhao family of rebellion against her brother, the duke of Jin, so Zhao Tong and
Zhao Kuo were killed. Throughout the process, the reputation of the Zhao family for loyalty to the country was besmirched. According to the *Zuo Tradition*, the
direct causes of the Zhao family's downfall resulted from one powerful woman's
passion and revenge, as well as political intrigue.

This historical event was later refashioned by the Han dynasty historian Sima
Qian (145 or 135–90 BCE) in his *Records of the Historian* (*Shiji*) (HTRCProse,
chap. 6). Based on historical documents of the state of Zhao from the Warring
States Period, Sima gave this story a new focus on loyalty and righteousness. He
glossed over the adultery and its aftermath and turned it into a story of high morality instead. To accomplish this transformation, he concentrated on one villain and
two heroes in the plot. He made the original adulteress, Zhao Zhuangji, loyal to
her husband, Zhao Shuo, but she was forced to leave him. Zhao Shuo and the
other family members were all loyal to the country. Rather than fleeing Jin, they
resolutely stayed on, only to die at the hands of the villain, the minister Tu'an
Gu, who had a deep grudge against Zhao Dun. The sole survivor was the unborn
baby of Zhao Zhuangji, who was hidden in the palace. After his birth, to protect
this last heir of the family, a friend and a retainer (*ke₂*) of Zhao Shuo, Cheng Ying
and Gongsun Chujiu, respectively, decided to sacrifice themselves for the orphan:
one would die, and the other would live to raise him to adulthood. Taking a baby
boy from another family, they disguised him as the orphan and housed him with
Gongsun Chujiu, while the real Zhao orphan was secretly sent away. As part of the
ruse, Cheng Ying then led an assault on Gongsun Chujiu's house. In the ensuing
confrontation, Gongsun declared his friend Cheng Ying a traitor, after which both

Gongsun and the substitute baby were slain. The true orphan was then raised secretly by Cheng Ying in the countryside.

Fifteen years later, because of the illness of the duke of Jin, the oracle gave Cheng Ying and the orphan, Zhao Wu, a chance to be summoned and authorized to lead an army to slaughter the Tu'an clan and recover the Zhaos' hereditary position and their lands. The narration of *Records* does not end here. When Zhao Wu turned twenty years old, Cheng Ying insisted on committing suicide so he could go to the netherworld to report this turn of events to Zhao Dun and Gongsun Chujiu.[3] Zhao Wu asked him to stay alive, but Cheng Ying replied, "I had a commitment to Gongsun to assist with the final revenge and revival. Now it is the best time for me to die and to report to him myself, or he will think I failed!"[4] The narration implies that the two heroes, Cheng and Gongsun, represent a glimmer of morality in a dark age of villainy.

In this account, we can perceive three types of loyalty: that of the Zhao family, who are loyal to the state, the duke of Jin, and their countrymen; that of Zhao Zhuangji, who is also a wife and a mother to her husband's family; and that of the friend and retainer of Lord Zhao. All these cases exemplify the Confucian ideal of righteousness. Contrary to the detached tone of the narration recorded in the *Zuo Tradition*, Sima Qian chose to refashion the story from the viewpoint of the Zhao family, producing an account that is sympathetic to the historical figures that it describes—a "history with feeling."

It is likely that in recounting the downfall of the Zhaos, Sima Qian was recalling his own sufferings. In 99 BCE, he had angered Emperor Wu of the Han (Han Wudi, r. 141–87 BCE) when he advocated patience with regard to General Li Ling, who had been captured and suspected of being a traitor. The emperor condemned Sima to death—a fate that Sima was able to avoid only in exchange for accepting the humiliating penalty of castration, leaving him mutilated and without a male heir, but giving him time to continue writing his monumental history (➤ *HTRCProse*, C7.4). Against this background, the figures of Cheng Ying and Gongsun Chujiu would have resonated with Sima Qian for their willingness to sacrifice themselves to preserve a family line. Sima Qian's poignant rendition of the story, with its rich dramatic twists and strong personalities, laid the foundation for the play.

5.2 *THE ORPHAN OF ZHAO*: HOW THE YUAN *ZAJU* PLAY DRAMATIZES THE STORY

According to Zhong Sicheng's (ca. 1279–after 1345) *Register of Ghosts* (*Lugui bu*), Ji Junxiang is the author of the Yuan play *The Orphan of Zhao*. Because most Yuan playwrights were not scholar-officials, there is typically very little biographical information about them, and this is the case for Ji Junxiang as well. We only know that he lived in Dadu, the capital of the Yuan dynasty, in roughly the second half of the thirteenth century. He is said to have written at least six plays, but among these, only *The Orphan of Zhao* still exists. Today, we have two early printed editions, one from the fourteenth century (known as the "Yuan edition" hereafter), and one from the late Ming (1615–1616). They differ in form, content, and intention

(☛ chap. 2). Although the acts in the Yuan edition (which contains nothing but the arias for the play) are not explicitly marked, later scholars divide the play into four acts and a wedge before act 1 on the basis of its short song suite, which is appropriate for a wedge, and the four major song suites, each appropriate for an act in a *zaju* play. The late Ming edition, which is included in the famous *Select Yuan Plays* (*Yuanqu xuan*) by Zang Maoxun (1550–1620) in heavily revised form, consists of a wedge and five acts. The additional fifth act appearing at the end of the play reflects Zang's or his Ming palace source's desire to transform the ending of the play to fit the ideology of the times by eliminating private violence in the pursuit of revenge in favor of state violence (☛ Introduction).⁵ Because of these differences, we have to treat these two editions separately in order to understand and compare their different strategies for adapting the story for the stage and for print.

Generally, *The Orphan of Zhao* (hereafter *Orphan*) condenses the historical timeline and simplifies the complicated relationships between family members and state officials, so the plot concentrates on a single dramatic action. At the core of the story is the effort to ensure the survival of the orphan. In contrast to Sima Qian, whose narrator almost always adopts an omniscient point of view, and his readers, who can reread a chapter or look elsewhere in the history or fill in any needed context as they read any single chapter, the knowledge of spectators watching the play in real time is limited to what they know of the story from other sources (which might be contradicted by the play) and what they learn from the characters in the play, whose points of view are limited. So, the question is: how does the playwright develop one dramatic action at a time while retaining the broader sweep of the story? To address this problem, *Orphan* has a single actor, whose job is to sing all the major song suites, portray three protagonists—that is, General Han Jue in act 1, the retainer Gongsun Chujiu in acts 2 and 3, and the mature orphan, Zhao Wu, in act 4 of the Yuan edition and acts 4–5 of the late Ming one. In this way, *Orphan* presents the story in a more three-dimensional form than would have been the case if the main actor had performed the same character throughout (☛ chap. 3).

In both editions, the leading male in act 1 is Han Jue, the general ordered by Tu'an Gu to guard the court gate. However, he eventually lets Cheng Ying take the baby orphan and leave the palace. Han then commits suicide to maintain the secret of the orphan's survival. In acts 2 and 3, the leading male role changes to Gongsun Chujiu, who, like Han, sacrifices himself to save the orphan. In act 4 (and in the late-Ming edition also act 5), the leading male changes to Zhao Wu, the adult orphan. From acts 1 to 3, we see two martyrs give up their lives for the orphan's survival, while in act 4, the orphan they protected eventually learns the truth and plans revenge, and in act 5 (late Ming edition only), the orphan helps in the arrest of Tu'an Gu and gains his revenge. Thus, the audience sees the unfolding of events from three perspectives.

In addition to the three lead characters, both Cheng Ying, played by the male supporting role (*wai*) and central to every aspect of the protection and preparation of the orphan, and Tu'an Gu, played by the villainous/comic role type (*jing*) and continuously threatening the safety of the orphan, appear in every act in both editions. This adds two contrasting perspectives on justice and evil. All these inter-woven voices form a grand picture of the personae of the historic saga. The elim-ination of the Zhao family is not the main point of the play; what matters is the struggle and sacrifice of the heroes and martyrs who each, at the urging of Cheng Ying, become part of an invisible network that protects the life of the last heir of the Zhao family.

The printed Yuan edition served primarily as a "songbook," providing only the names of the tune patterns and the lyrics for the arias, with no dialogue (*bai*) or stage directions (*ke*). This means that we get to read only what the three characters played by the lead actor sing. The late-Ming edition includes dialogue and stage directions and is a more complete play, and it has been edited to produce a text suitable for reading by literati. Next, we will analyze the play act by act and compare the two edi-tions if needed to appreciate the text and identify the underlying significance.

5.3 *THE ORPHAN OF ZHAO*, WEDGE: THE CONFRONTATION BETWEEN GOOD AND EVIL

The opening wedge of the Yuan edition consists of two arias by Zhao Shuo. He blames Tu'an Gu for the massacre of his family and asks his wife to allow their unborn child to live so that he can one day avenge the family. If we compare this with the form that it takes in the late Ming edition, what has brought this situa-tion about becomes clearer. Tu'an Gu, the first character to come onstage, tells us in an extended monologue of his feud with Zhao Dun and his intrigues against him, borne out of his jealousy and desire for preeminence. Tu'an Gu's schemes failed three times. First, he assigned an assassin named Chu Ni to kill Zhao Dun in the middle of the night, but Chu Ni found Zhao Dun to be a loyal minister, so he decided instead to commit suicide by smashing his head against a tree rather than kill Zhao. Then Tu'an trained a dog to attack and kill Zhao Dun at the sight of him, and then claimed at court that this hound could sniff out evil ministers. Lord Ling of Jin (Jin Ling gong) excitedly asked for a test. Just as the hound was about to attack Zhao Dun, the court guard Ti Miming stepped in to kill it. When Zhao Dun attempted to flee the scene in his carriage, he discovered that Tu'an Gu had removed one of the wheels and released two of the four horses. At this critical moment, Ling Zhe, a man whom Zhao Dun had previously helped, came forward to replace the missing wheel so that Zhao Dum was able to escape.

In other words, Tu'an Gu's schemes failed because three righteous men were willing to sacrifice themselves to stop the attacks on Zhao Dun's life. Although they were persons of no status in themselves, the combined efforts of these three marginal figures foiled the murderous plans of an extremely powerful villain (in the play, Tu'an Gu is presented as the head of the military). Tu'an Gu then goes on to relate that he got the lord to agree to mercilessly exterminate the 300-odd mem-bers of the Zhao clan.

That ends Tu'an Gu's account of what happened in the past. In real time, he then forges an edict demanding that Zhao Shuo, who is living in the palace with the princess, commit suicide. It is hard to imagine that Tu'an Gu's long monologue recounting in detail what has already happened would be very effective acted out as it is written. We can perhaps think that Zang Maoxun, if he was responsible, was depending on the indulgence of the reader. A contemporary Korean adaptation, introduced later in this chapter, enacted these events—including the hound and the horse—on stage, greatly enriching the visual effects of the original dialogue.

5.4 *THE ORPHAN OF ZHAO*, ACT 1: HOW THE ORPHAN WAS SMUGGLED OUT

Because the Yuan edition provides only the song suites, which are designed to convey emotion rather than the details of the plot, we have to turn to the dialogue of the late Ming edition to understand the crisis at court. At the beginning of act 1, Zhao Shuo's wife, the princess, has given birth to a baby boy, the last heir of the Zhao clan destined to become the orphan of the title. Outside the court gates, Han Jue, the male lead of this act, who is serving under Tu'an Gu, stands guard, ready to prevent the baby from leaving the palace. The princess trusts only one person— the commoner Cheng Ying, a doctor as well as one of her husband's retainers, who is not on the register of the family. The princess calls him to come and see her, and beseeches him to save the baby. Once Cheng has accepted this charge and hidden the child inside his medicine box, the princess commits suicide and Cheng leaves the stage.

Han Jue enters the stage and informs us that he disapproves of Tu'an Gu's evil behavior but does not dare to rebel against him. His true sentiments and moral outrage are revealed only when he is symbolically alone; he sings as an aside:

（元刊本）　[From the Yuan edition]
（正末）　MALE LEAD *as* HAN JUE [*sings*]:
【混江龍】　*To the tune* "Hun Jiang long"
晉靈公偏順，　Lord Ling of Jin is a perversely compliant type—
朝廷重用這般人。　The court is giving all the power to people of this stripe!
忠正的市朝中斬首，　The loyal and righteous are beheaded in the marketplace,
讒佞的省府內安身。　While slanderers and flatterers are secure in their official base.
為王有功的當重刑，　Those accomplishing great things for the ruler submit to grievous malevolence,
於民無益的受君恩。　Those bringing no benefit to the people receive the lord's beneficence.
縱得交欺凌天子，　He gets to browbeat the Son of Heaven,
恐嚇諸侯。　Intimidate the lords.
但違他的都誅盡，　All who oppose him have been eradicated.
誅盡些朝中宰相，　Eradicated are the highest ministers of the realm
闕外將軍。　And the generals at the helm.

[YKSSZ 169; trans. Li, 56]

Here, we see Han Jue's feelings about the present rule of terror, which he blames on Lord Ling's blind compliance with the wishes of Tu'an. However, in the late Ming edition, this sharp critique of the lord was modified to avoid associating the Ming emperor with these evil traits or offending him by calling his authority into question. If we compare the two versions, we will see that the late Ming edition weakened Lord Ling's responsibility and strengthened Tu'an Gu's absolute power. Back at the court gates, Han Jue meets Cheng Ying with his medicine box. Cheng Ying knows Han Jue to be a merciful man who owes his promotion to Zhao Dun. When he discovers the orphan, Han Jue is sympathetic, feeling a sense of compassion:

（元曲選本）	[From the late Ming edition]
（正末做揭箱子見科，云）程嬰，你道是桔梗、甘草、薄荷，我可搜出人參來也。	HAN JUE *opens the medicine chest and speaks*: You said there were only balloon flower root, licorice, and mint. Now I've found ginseng![6]
（程嬰做慌跪伏科）	CHENG YING *appears frightened, kneels down, and cowers.*
（正末唱）	HAN JUE *sings:*
【金盞兒】	*To the tune* "Jinzhan'er"
見孤兒額顱上汗津津，	I see on the orphan's forehead sweat in streaks.
口角頭乳食歅。	From the corner of his mouth, milk leaks.
骨碌碌睜一雙小眼兒將咱認，	His little shining, wide-open eyes try to recognize the guest.
悄促促箱兒裡似把聲吞。	All quiet, he seems to be swallowing his voice in the chest—
緊綁綁難展足，	It's so tight: he can't stretch his feet.
窄狹狹怎翻身？	It's so narrow; how can he turn?
他正是成人不自在，	In truth, "To become a man is to not have it easy,
自在不成人。	Having it easy is to not become a man."
	[*YQX* 3723; trans. Huang and Li, 28]

Taking advantage of this opportunity, Cheng Ying persuades Han Jue to act with morality and sympathy. Moved, Han Jue makes his choice:

（元曲選本）	[From the late Ming edition]
（正末云）程嬰，我若把這孤兒獻將出去，可不是一身富貴？但我韓厥是一個頂天立地的男兒，怎肯做這般勾當！	HAN JUE *speaks*: Cheng Ying, if I were to hand the baby over to Tu'an Gu, wouldn't it mean riches and high position? But I, Han Jue, am a man, good and true. How can I do a thing so base!
	[*YQX* 3723; trans. Huang and Li, 28]

Han Jue is depicted as a man of righteousness, choosing to stand on the side of loyalty to the state rather than to his villainous master and the gullible ruler. Cheng Ying's loyalty, above all, is to the Zhao clan, who represent the people and the state—in this way disclosing two expressions of the same loyalty. Out of a sense of moral righteousness, Han Jue not only lets the orphan go, but also commits suicide to keep the details of this event secret. For him, death is the only way to achieve moral justice, but ultimately revenge must be taken to render his sacrifice worthwhile. Therefore, Han Jue's last song before his death ends with the expectation of future revenge by the orphan:

（元刊本）	[From the Yuan edition]
（正末唱）	HAN JUE sings:
【賺煞】	To the tune "Coda"
...	...
這孩兒近初旬，	When this child approaches ten,
便交他演武修文。	Let him take up learning literary and martial.
若學得文武雙全那時分，	By the time he gets to excel in both,
將有讐的記恨，	He is to remember the enemy to loathe,
把有恩人尋趁。	And seek out the benefactors who pledged their troth.
若殺了有讐人，	When he kills his enemy,
休忘了有恩人。	He must not forget his benefactors!

[*YKSSZ* 171; trans. Li, 58]

5.5 *THE ORPHAN OF ZHAO*, ACT 2: TO DIE OR TO LIVE ON

In the opening of act 2, when Tu'an Gu hears of the deaths of the princess and of Han Jue, he knows that the baby has been spirited away. In order to "cut the grass and remove the roots," he orders the killing of all babies from one to six months old until the orphan of Zhao is found. This is an ingenious plot designed to enhance the dramatic tension—in the play, Cheng Ying has an only son of similar age to the orphan. Recalling that Gongsun Chujiu, a retired minister and Zhao Dun's good friend, is now living in Peace Village, Cheng Ying goes to him for help. Gongsun is the male lead in acts 2 and 3. He opposes Tu'an Gu's autocracy and despises Lord Ling's cowardice and incompetence. Upon learning that the orphan is alive, Gongsun is relieved, taking full pity on him. Cheng Ying proposes a plan: Gongsun will raise the true orphan, while he will offer himself and his son to Tu'an Gu in the child's place. Gongsun rejects this plan, claiming that his raising a son at the advanced age of seventy would raise suspicion. Rather, Gongsun argues, Cheng Ying is just the right man to take on this responsibility because he is only forty-four. Gongsun insists that the best plan is to exchange the two babies. Gongsun will die with Cheng Ying's son, who will be disguised as the orphan. Thus, people will think that Cheng Ying is raising his own son, while, in reality, he is acting as the caretaker of the orphan. Now the sacrifice involves not only the life of a righteous old man, but also that of an innocent child.

By accepting this proposal, Cheng Ying commits what Mencius considered the greatest act of unfiliality—the failure to provide an heir for one's family. To save the Zhao line of transmission, Cheng Ying sacrifices that of his own family. Herein lies the paradox: what kind of loyalty to another family deserves such a huge personal cost to one's own family? Cheng Ying does not express himself, while Gongsun Chujiu sings songs on the fate of the baby, the father, and himself to express the indescribable emotion at this time. The father did not hesitate to sacrifice his own son's life. However, readers might ask how his wife, the baby's mother, felt about this decision. The absence of attention to this point shows the cleverness of the play: not only does Cheng Ying's wife not take any part in the decision, she is not even mentioned; this avoids the complication of considering whether a mother, who brought forth a son from her own body, would be as willing to sacrifice him as the baby's father is. However, when a later playwright adapted this story in the Ming dynasty as a Southern play (*nanxi*), the role of Cheng's wife was added, and she gave up her dear son after her husband persuaded her to do so. Such a plot element, which must end with the negation of the mother's maternal instincts, is not very attractive—this is perhaps why the Yuan playwright avoided it—but otherwise, it has dramatic potential, so modern adaptations bring this question back to the fore.

5.6 *THE ORPHAN OF ZHAO*, ACT 3: A PLAY PERFORMED FOR THE EYES OF THE VILLAIN

Act 3 presents the first climax of the play, in which the hero, Cheng Ying, has to justify turning in his friend for harboring the orphan, and Gongsun Chujiu has to suffer torture without revealing the truth, all before the eyes of the villain, Tu'an Gu. At the beginning of the act, Cheng Ying goes to see Tu'an Gu to inform him that Gongsun is concealing the orphan. Cheng explains to the suspicious Tu'an Gu that he is providing this information in order to protect his own son and all the other innocent babies faced with death. Convinced by the ruse, Tu'an Gu leads a raid on Gongsun Chujiu's house, culminating in a key scene in which Cheng and Gongsun have to successfully perform their assumed roles before the eyes of the enemy. Gongsun refuses to "confess" that he has hidden the orphan, and Tu'an Gu commands the soldiers to beat Gongsun, who still does not give in. This makes Tu'an furious:

（元曲選本）	[From the late Ming edition]
（屠岸賈云）…這老匹夫賴肉頑皮，不肯招承，可惱可惱！程嬰，這原是你出首的，就著你替我行杖者！	TU'AN GU *speaks*: . . . The old wretch is really stubborn and refuses to confess. How very maddening! Cheng Ying, since it's you who is informing on him, I want you to wield the rod for me.
（程嬰）元帥，小人是個草澤醫士，撮藥尚然腕弱，怎生行的杖？	CHENG YING [*speaks*]: Marshal, I am but a commoner physician. My wrist is too weak even for measuring medicine, let alone beating a man!

（屠岸賈）程嬰，你不行杖，敢怕指攀出你麼？

（程嬰）元帥，小人行杖便了。（做拿杖子科）

（屠岸賈）程嬰，我見你把棍子揀了又揀，只揀著那細棍子，敢怕打的他疼了，要指攀下你來？

（程嬰）我就拿大棍子打者。

（屠岸賈）住者。你頭裡只揀著那細棍子打，如今你卻拿起大棍子來，三兩下打死了呵，你就做的個死無招對。

（程嬰）著我拿細棍子又不是，拿大棍子又不是，好教我兩下做人難也。

（屠岸賈）程嬰，你只拿著那中等棍子打。公孫杵臼老匹夫，你可知道行杖的就是程嬰麼？

（程嬰行杖科）快招了者！（三科了）

（正末）哎喲！打了這一日，不似這幾棍子打的我疼。是誰打我來？

（屠岸賈）是程嬰打你來。

（正末）程嬰，你剗的打我哪！

（程嬰）元帥，打的這老頭兒兀的不胡說哩。

TU'AN GU [*speaks*]: Cheng Ying, you won't beat him. Is it because you fear that he might implicate you?

CHENG YING [*speaks*]: I'll do it then, Marshal. *Fumbles among the rods.*

TU'AN GU [*speaks*]: Cheng Ying, I see you fumble among the rods trying to pick a thin one. You must be afraid that if you hit him hard he will give you away.

CHENG YING [*speaks*]: I'll use a thick one then.

TU'AN GU [*speaks*]: Stop. First you chose a thin one and now a thick one. You think if you can finish him off in two or three strokes, there will then be no witness against you?

CHENG YING [*speaks*]: You didn't like it when I picked a thin rod. Now you blame me for picking a thick one; I'm really in a quandary.

TU'AN GU [*speaks*]: Cheng Ying, you can simply use a medium-sized one. Gongsun Chujiu, you old wretch, do you realize Cheng Ying is the one who's beating you?

CHENG YING *beats* GONGSUN [*and speaks*]: Now confess! CHENG YING *beats* GONGSUN *three times.*

MALE LEAD *as* GONGSUN CHUJIU [*speaks*]: Ah! They've been beating me all day, but none of the strokes I suffered hurt as much as these! Who's beating me?

TU'AN GU [*speaks*]: It's Cheng Ying.

GONGSUN CHUJIU [*speaks*]: So it's you, Cheng Ying! How come you are beating me?

CHENG YING [*speaks*]: Marshal, after a good beating the old fellow should stop talking nonsense now.

[*YQX* 3739–3740; trans. Huang and Li, 39]

Left with no choice, Cheng Ying beats Gongsun Chujiu savagely, but as a result of the pain, Gongsun keeps getting close to implicating Cheng Ying and revealing the plot. At this point, soldiers bring out Cheng Ying's son, disguised as the orphan (and surely placed right where he would be easily found), and Tu'an Gu gleefully slices the baby into three parts. At this heartbreaking juncture, Cheng Ying cannot let on how he feels, so Gongsun sings on his behalf:

（元刊本）　　[From the Yuan edition]

（正末）　　GONGSUN CHUJIU [*sings*]:

【梅花酒】　*To the tune* "Meihua jiu"

呀！　　Alas!

可早臥血泊，	He is already lying in a pool of blood.
訴生長劬勞。	You can tell the story of toil raising a child.
他天數難逃，	He cannot escape his heaven-allotted fare,
你子嗣難消。	You cannot dispel regrets about your heir.
程嬰！	Cheng Ying!
你可甚養子防備老。	How to prepare for old age? For raising sons you toil—
不信你不煩惱。	I don't believe you are not in turmoil!
這孩兒離蓐草，	From the time the child left his birth mat
和今日卻十朝，	Till now—ten days have passed.
磣可可剁三刀。	He endured three strikes of the sword, aghast.
【收江南】	*To the tune* "Shou Jiangnan"
早難道家富小兒嬌？	Isn't it said that in a rich family, a child is treasured!
見他傍邊廂心癢難揉，	I see him, on the side, unable to salve his heart's gall.
雙眸中不敢把淚珠拋。	His eyes did not dare let tears fall.
背背地搵了，	Stealthily wiped off—tears to hide,
滿腹內有似熱油澆。	It is as if boiling oil were poured all over his insides.

[YKSSZ 174; trans. Li, 63–64]

In contrast to the elated Tu'an Gu, Cheng Ying is forced to conceal his emotion—his heartbreaking grief—so completely that only Gongsun knows how he feels. To make sure that their plan will not be forced out of him, Gongsun kills himself by dashing himself against the steps. He shows himself a righteous man, not related by blood to the Zhao clan yet willing to die to enable the survival of the orphan. However, even more touching is the case of the retainer Cheng Ying, who sacrifices the life of his only heir in the hope of saving the orphan, as well as the other infants of the state. He has lost everyone he loved and respected: master and mistress, friend, and son. Moreover, his seeming betrayal of Gongsun Chujiu and the Zhao family is enough to make every righteous person despise him and doom him to live a lie.

Just before his death, Gongsun pleads for vengeance. Thinking that the orphan and the man who dared to protect him are now dead, Tu'an Gu is content. Here, the playwright, Ji Junxiang, introduces a wrinkle not found in Sima Qian's account of the story. To thank Cheng Ying, Tu'an Gu makes Cheng his retainer and adopts Cheng's child (the disguised orphan) as his son. In this way, the hero becomes an "undercover agent" serving his archenemy, while Tu'an Gu becomes the "father" of the heir of the clan that he had slaughtered. The truth has to be disclosed to the orphan, but that must wait until he is old enough to understand and act on it.

5.7 THE ORPHAN OF ZHAO, ACTS 4 (AND 5): TRUTH AND REVENGE

As act 4 opens, twenty years have passed, and the orphan has grown into a brave and handsome youth. Ignorant of his real identity, the orphan believes that his biological father is Cheng Ying and his original name is Cheng Bo. His adopted father, Tu'an Gu, gave him the name Tu Cheng. However, what the orphan still does not know is that his real name is Zhao Wu (literally "martialism"), and that he is the last remaining heir of the Zhao clan. Given these circumstances, the disclosure of his identity is the key point of this act. Our male lead actor-singer is now the orphan, Cheng Bo. Interestingly, the Yuan edition presents Cheng Bo as a very different character than that of the late Ming edition. We begin with two arias performed to the same tune pattern, but with quite different lyrics:

（元刊本）	[From the Yuan edition]
（正末）	MALE LEAD *as* CHENG BO [*sings*]:
【醉春風】	*To the tune* "Zui chunfeng"
俺待反故主晉靈公，	About to turn against my old master Lord Ling of Jin,
助新君屠岸賈。	I will assist the new ruler Tu'an Gu.
交平天冠，	Exchange for him the royal crown,
碧玉帶，	The green jade belt,
袞龍服。	The dragon robes.
別換個主，主。	Change to another ruler, another ruler!
問甚君聖臣賢？	What is all this talk of "sage ruler and worthy subjects"?
既然父慈子孝，	If "the father is loving and the son is filial,"
管甚主憂臣辱。	Why bother about "the subjects shamed by their ruler in distress"?

[*YKSSZ* 174; trans. Li, 64–65]

Obviously, Cheng Bo has been led astray by Tu'an Gu, who plans to usurp the throne. Ironically, the heir of the loyal Zhao clan has become a traitor. This plot design has great potential for an eventual dramatic reversal because it increases the distance Cheng Bo has to travel to become aware of his true identity. However, this aspect of the earlier version was greatly modified in the late Ming edition:

（元曲選本）	[From the late Ming edition]
（正末）	CHENG BO [*sings*]:
【醉春風】	*To the tune* "Zui chunfeng"
我則待扶明主晉靈公，	The sage ruler Lord Ling of Jin I serve,
助賢臣屠岸賈。	The worthy minister Tu'an Gu I assist with verve.
憑著我能文善武萬人敵，	For prowess civil and martial that let me confront ten thousand foes,
俺父親將我來許、許。	My father on me praise bestows, praise bestows.
可不道馬壯人強，	As the sayings go, "The horses are strong, the soldiers brave,"
父慈子孝，	"The father is loving, the son filial,"
怕甚麼主憂臣辱。	Why should we fear "subjects shamed by their ruler in distress!"

[*YQX* 3747; trans. Huang and Li, 44]

Accordingly, in the late Ming edition, Cheng Bo views his loving adopted father, Tu'an Gu, as a good minister, and Lord Ling as a sage ruler. Cheng Bo naively believes that he is a filial son assisting his virtuous father and his lord for the good of the country, so he never knows of Tu'an's intrigue of sedition. The late Ming edition purges the play of Cheng Bo's original seditious thoughts, while couching the orphan's observations in the language of Confucian morality and obedience. However, in both versions, the orphan's blind, filial respect for his adopted father results in the most unfilial behavior to his true family.

Regardless of how much Cheng Bo is willing to side with Tu'an Gu, he is destined to encounter a powerful moment of disclosure and reversal in both versions of the play. After Cheng Ying creates a drawing on a scroll that illustrates the characters and scenes of the story of the Zhao clan to progressively fill the gaps in Cheng Bo's knowledge, he finally recognizes that that story is also his story, and so he is consumed by an unbearable anguish and fury. The Yuan edition allows him to voice his grief for the loss of his true family, as well as acknowledge his debt to Cheng Ying:

（元刊本）　[From the Yuan edition]

（正末）　CHENG BO [sings]:

【普天樂】　To the tune "Putian le"

我待問從初，　I was to ask what happened, tracing the story from its source,

拔刀相助。　I was to pull out my sword, ready to assist the wronged by force.

交我愁縈心腹，　How this affects me! Sorrow entwines my vital organs,

氣夯胸脯。　Anger besieges my insides.

元來這壞了的是俺父親，　It turns out that the fallen victims of treachery are my father

咱家宗祖。　And the ancestors of my clan!

說到淒涼傷心處，　When the story is told to its heartbreaking point,

便是鐵頭人也放聲啼哭。　Even a man of iron or stone will wail in lamentation!

屠岸賈！你為帝王，　If you, Tu'an Gu, become the king,

咱為宰輔，　And I become your minister—

天意何如？　What about the will of heaven?

[YKSSZ 175; trans. Li, 65–66]

Cheng Bo swears a vow of bloody vengeance, and provides a verbal description of what he intends to do to Tu'an Gu:

（元刊本）　[From the Yuan edition]

（正末）　CHENG BO [sings]:

【二煞】　To the tune "Penultimate Coda"

把那廝剜了眼睛，	Gouge out that villain's eyes,
豁開肚皮，	Slit open his belly,
摘了心肝，	Rip out his heart,
卸了手足。	Lop off his limbs.
乞支支拋折那廝腰截骨。	Crack! Break that scoundrel's spine.
常言恨小非君子，	As the saying goes, not too little rancor—a noble man's at stake.
無毒不丈夫。	It has always been so: without venom a true man you cannot make.
難遮護，	It will be hard to cover him up!
我不怕前遮侍從，	I am not afraid of the guards shielding him in front,
左右軍卒。	Nor of the soldiers to his left and right.

[YKSSZ 176; trans. Li, 67]

This edition ends with a short final coda that is also in the future tense, so we do not know if this version of the play included the actual revenge on stage. This is a typical ending for the fourth act of Yuan edition historical plays: it ends on a note of grief and fury over an unsolved problem. This allows space for the readers and the audience members who are familiar with the historical account to imagine the consequences that will occur in the future. This seemingly truncated or unsatisfactory ending reflects the complexity of the true history, and on the other hand, the suspension of the final act extends the storyline and is better than a simple and fast solution.

By the late Ming era, theatergoers and play readers had been accustomed to seeing a final reunion and a happy ending, something that occurs in almost every *chuanqi* play. Zang Maoxun's decision to add a fifth act to allow the enactment of Tu'an Gu's arrest must be understood in this context, but we also need to note that in the process, his version avoids establishing the shift that Cheng Bo has to make between being a filial son to Tu'an and his true identity as a filial descendant of the Zhaos.

In act 5, there is an unreasonable time leap: the lord of Jin is changed from Lord Ling to Lord Dao, but the time sequence from act 4 to act 5 seems to be continuous. Cheng Bo does not act on his own; rather, he has informed the lord that he will arrest Tu'an Gu, an endeavor overseen from start to finish by a high state official, Wei Jiang, at the orders of the lord. After waiting in ambush for Tu'an Gu in the marketplace, Cheng Bo confronts him, reveals that he is the orphan of Zhao, captures him easily, and turns him over for punishment. Wei Jiang announces Tu'an Gu's punishment: he will "suffer three thousand wounds by fine slicing" and "only when all his skin and flesh are gone can you chop off his head and open up his chest."

In response to this cruel torture about to be inflicted on his adopted father, Cheng Bo expresses full satisfaction. What is bizarre is that Cheng Bo shows no signs of emotional struggle with his previous feelings of filiality and kindness toward Tu'an Gu. In this respect, the bad temper of the orphan in the Yuan edition is more convincing; it also shows that sometimes on stage, words are better than actions in solving a dilemma in the end. Meanwhile, the late Ming edition, intent on satisfying the demands of its audience and readers by explicitly punishing evil and rewarding good, ends up sacrificing the humanity and depth of the orphan's character.

In sum, the Yuan edition is seemingly a revenge play; everyone discusses vengeance, but when the play ends, it has yet to be achieved. Its plot centers on how to preserve the life of the orphan through the selfless acts of many men who stand on the side of loyalty and justice. The play highlights the heroics of martyrs who must choose between mere survival and a momentous death. The only path for recovering the reputations of the victims is a series of great personal sacrifices to save the orphan so he can enact vengeance and achieve justice. The unfinished ending of the earlier edition creates an atmosphere of dark suspense during a time of dynastic transition under the Mongol Yuan. Neither the playwrights nor the audience insisted on harmony and reunion. In other words, the dynastic background contributed to the unique writing style of Yuan drama. As Wang Guowei said in his *History of Song and Yuan Drama* (*Song Yuan xiqu shi*), Yuan playwrights "just expressed their inner feelings as well as the circumstances of the times. But in the process [of writing about their times], they reveal their principles of sincerity and their exceptional talent."[7]

Nevertheless, under the weight of imperial authority and Confucian orthodoxy, late Ming playwrights introduced poetic justice and practical action. In the same vein, subsequent adaptations such as *The Story of the Orphan of Zhao* (*Zhao shi gu'er ji*), a southern *nanxi* play, and *The Story of Eight Righteous Ones* (*Bayi ji*), a *chuanqi* play, pushed the plots to the extreme while interweaving the story with popular didacticism. In these works, not only is the revenge spelled out, but in addition the princess and Zhao Shuo are rescued, setting the stage for a happy family reunion and transforming tragedy into comedy. *The Story of Eight Righteous Ones* was subsequently adapted into a variety of regional plays. These adaptations were not usually performed in their entirety; instead, they were often performed in the form of "rearranged scenes" or "playlets" (*zhezixi*). One of the most popular excerpts performed on the stage in the twentieth century was the Peking Opera version, *Searching for the Orphan and Saving the Orphan* (*Sougu jiugu*).

The late Ming edition of *The Orphan of Zhao* was the first play to be translated and introduced to Europe. The Jesuit missionary Joseph Henri Marie de Prémare (1666–1735) translated its dialogue, stage directions, and a few song lyrics into French in 1731 as *Tchao Chi cou ell ou Le petit orphelin de la maison de Tchao, tragédie chinoise* (*Tchao Chi cou ell, or The Little Orphan of the Family of Tchao, Chinese tragedy*), calling it a "Chinese tragedy." This version was published in *Description de la Chine* (1735) by Jean-Baptiste du Halde (1674–1743), which contributed to Europe's fascination with China. It was soon translated and adapted into English, Italian, and German. Its best-known revision is *The Orphan of China* (*L'orphelin de la Chine*, 1753) by Voltaire (1694–1778) (☞ chap. 3).

Because Europeans recognized *The Orphan of Zhao* as a tragedy, this interpretation influenced Japanese scholars such as Kano Naoki at Kyoto University, who studied in Europe at the turn of the twentieth century. Wang Guowei, who studied in Kyoto between 1911 and 1916 and interacted with Japanese scholars, proposed that Chinese drama included tragedies, which influenced many subsequent scholars:

> After the Ming dynasty, *chuanqi* plays are all comedies, but among Yuan plays, there are some tragedies. . . . Those that are most tragic are Guan Hanqing's *Injustice to Dou E* and Ji Junxiang's *The Orphan of Zhao*. Although these plays contain villains with their intrigues, the acts of great personal sacrifice stem from the determination of the leading characters. These two plays rank among the world's great tragedies.[8]

It is likely that, mediated by Japanese scholarship, Wang's evaluation of the play was indirectly influenced by du Halde's claim that the play was a tragedy.[9]

5.8 *THE ORPHAN OF ZHAO*: TWENTY-FIRST-CENTURY ADAPTATIONS

All the versions of *Orphan* discussed in this chapter provide the potential to expand upon or deepen the tension between loyalty and filial piety, the love of an adopted son for his adopted father, and the issue of revenge. For example, what does Cheng Ying think before and after his own son's death? If there had been a role for Cheng Ying's wife, what would she have done when she heard of the plan of swapping her baby for the orphan? When the secret identity of the orphan is disclosed and he learns that he has three fathers and three names, how does he deal with such a complex situation? Is it reasonable for the orphan to take revenge without a second thought about how well his adopted father has treated him for twenty years? These questions have the potential to push the development of the plot in different directions, and this indeed is what has guided the twenty-first-century adaptations of the piece. Since 2003, there has been a revival of full-scale performances of *Orphan* across various nations, cultures, and media. Next, we will consider three adaptations done in contemporary China, one from England, and one from South Korea, each of which reflects a different approach to these questions.

TWO CHINESE SPOKEN-DRAMA (*HUAJU*) VERSIONS OF THE PLAY: ABANDONING VENGEANCE

Two spoken-drama plays, one directed by Lin Zhaohua and the other by Tian Qinxin, premiered at almost the same time in 2003. They adopted totally different approaches to the story, but both opted for an ending without revenge. Lin's version changed almost the entire plot, reimagining the relationships between characters, although the original names were kept the same. It added new twists to the story, making it more complex, dark, and packed with intrigue. From the late 1980s, Chinese historical plays have become exceptionally popular in the genres of classical drama (*xiqu*), spoken drama, and television miniseries. Most of them tend to emphasize accounts of deceptions, schemes and court intrigue, and infighting, reflecting a general sense of distrust and cynicism. In Lin's play, the orphan grows up at Tu'an Gu's house and becomes a rich playboy who refuses to face the truth that Cheng Ying reveals to him, so he refuses to take revenge. At the end of this version, when Lord Ling takes the orphan back to court for his own political purposes, the orphan says goodbye to his two fathers with callous disregard, leaving them stunned. With no hope of achieving final revenge, Cheng Ying kills himself by drinking poison, while Tu'an Gu sinks into a state of depression. Lin's version is a subversive rewriting of the play, ignoring traditional morality and values in an expression of postmodern indifference that departs radically from the ideals of former generations.

Tian Qinxin's version combines the storylines of the Yuan play and that of the *Zuo Tradition*. Drawing on the *Zuo Tradition*, it depicts Zhao Shuo's wife, the princess, as a licentious woman whose adultery eventually leads to the extermination of the Zhao family. The play is told through a dream of the orphan, as well as flashbacks from the points of view of Cheng Ying and Tu'an Gu. This results in the interweaving of past and present events, and fluctuations in time and space that present the dramatic reality as an illusion. A touching moment comes in the scene when the baby is smuggled out of the palace. Moved by Cheng Ying's words, Han Jue decides to make friends with this doctor. Killing the guards one by one before committing suicide, Han creates even more victims. This addition paradoxically produces both a sense of horror and respect for Han's commitment. In the scene in which Gongsun Chujiu and Cheng Ying exchange infants, the play includes the heartbreaking cry of Cheng Ying's wife, who, unable to accept her baby's death, dies in her husband's arms. Eventually, Cheng Ying dies in a pool of blood after having been stabbed (accidentally) by Lord Ling and (intentionally) by Tu'an Gu.

In the end, faced with the accusations of the orphan, Tu'an Gu, who is dying of an illness, grabs the hand of his adopted son and uses it to plunge a sword into his own heart, saying: "Let my blood stain your sword to prove you are a brave man."[10] In this way, Tu'an Gu kills himself at the orphan's hands in an attempt to expose him as an unscrupulous young man. However, in the end, we do not know what kind of man the orphan becomes. What we do know, though, is that his three fathers, his mother, and all the people with whom he came into contact are now dead. The orphan of Zhao is now truly alone in the world—a real orphan, lost and abandoned to wander. Thus, the play does not end in true revenge, but rather with a meditation on humanity's destiny achieved through poetic dialogue and visual effects on stage. Tian directed this tragedy with an open ending that eventually deconstructs the motif of morality, loyalty, and revenge.

THE RSC VERSION: THE CHINESE *HAMLET*

In 2012, a version was performed by the RSC in Britain, adapted by James Fenton and directed by Gregory Doran. During the rehearsal period, this production caused controversy because among its seventeen actors, only three Asians were cast, all in relatively unimportant roles.[11] Still, it premiered to great success. Aside from its artistic merit, its popularity was partially due to a current fascination with China and a sense of novelty for British audiences.

Fenton's script remained loyal to the late Ming edition in plot, character, and subject, but he rewrote the plotline of the second half of the play to render it more coherent and thrilling. Fenton preserved some conventions of Chinese theater; for instance, the characters introduce themselves upon the first appearance on stage. He also wrote four independent songs in an attempt to reflect some of the importance of the arias in the original and to serve as a bridge between scenes. In the revenge scene, owing to a scheme devised by Cheng Ying, Cheng Bo, and General Wei Jiang, Tu'an Gu is trapped in the audience room in the palace. He has lost his weapons and his soldiers, and an angry crowd is closing in on him. Frightened by the noise of the crowds outside the gate, Tu'an pleads with his adopted son: "Kill me. I am afraid. I dare not kill myself. Kill me quickly if you ever loved me" [*RSC* 65]. His cowardice and the orphan's kindness form a strong contrast, and Fenton thus solves the dilemma the orphan faced between his lingering affection for his adopted father and his desire for revenge.

The most touching moment in the play is the final scene, the grave scene. There, Cheng Ying comes to his child's grave, where he meets the ghost of his son. Having waited eighteen years, the ghost asks why his father despised and betrayed him, and he contrasts his father's lack of love for him with his love for the orphan of Zhao. Cheng Ying tells the ghost that he never despised his son. In their dialogue, Cheng shows how sorry he felt for his child and shares his wish that he had died along with his son eighteen years ago. He asks the ghost to stab him in the chest with a knife, and when he does so, he dies in the arms of his son. The ghost, tasting the blood of his father's heart, says to the dead man: "You love me. You always did love me. And now you belong to me for ever" [*RSC* 70]. This haunting ending amounts to a lyrical and tragic apology for the sacrificed infant. In addition to the element of revenge, Fenton adds some Shakespearean elements, such as the ghost as well as comic dialogue and gestures, and interweaves them with tragic scenes, such that the director and some British critics called this play a "Chinese *Hamlet*."[12]

A CHINESE FILM: THE OTHER AVENGER

Of all the contemporary versions, the film *Sacrifice* (*Zhao shi gu'er*, 2010), directed by Chen Kaige, is the most famous among U.S. audiences (➤ Visual Resources). It raises a fundamental question: How can Cheng Ying sacrifice the lives of his wife and his only child? This film gives the audience a cynical answer that subverts the standard of value from selflessness to selfishness. To do this, the film changes some key parts of the play. First, Cheng Ying does not accept the smuggling mission out of a sense of loyalty, but instead because he is compelled by the princess, the orphan's mother, to do so. Second, Han Jue does not allow the orphan to escape out of a sense of righteousness, but because he accidentally throws the medicine box (where the infant is) out to Cheng, and then is moved by the princess' insistent begging and committing suicide in front of his eyes. Moreover, Han does not commit suicide but is instead blinded in one eye by Tu'an Gu. Later, when Cheng Ying reluctantly brings the orphan home, neither he nor his wife considers giving up their own child. However, when Tu'an Gu orders a search for all the infants of the state, Cheng Ying leaves in order to ask Gongsun Chujiu what to do next. At this point, Cheng Ying's wife hands the orphan over to the soldiers. This turns out to be a mistake: now her child is the only baby in the state that remains hidden, which means that this baby would be taken to be the real Zhao orphan. In the ensuing tragedy of errors, Gongsun Chujiu, along with Cheng Ying's wife and son, are all killed by Tu'an Gu. Cheng Ying then brings the orphan back home, and the child becomes Tu'an Gu's adopted son.

The second part of the film depicts the hardships that Cheng Ying endures over the years and his burning desire for revenge. At the same time, the film shows the affectionate relationship between Tu'an Gu and the orphan as Tu'an Gu trains his adopted son in martial arts and teaches him to be a brave man. Even when Cheng Ying eventually reveals to him the truth behind his birth family's massacre, Cheng Bo is still reluctant to kill his loving adopted father. When the orphan finally decides to take action, he is too weak to overcome Tu'an Gu. At this moment, Cheng Ying places himself between Tu'an Gu and the boy. As the distracted Tu'an Gu stabs Cheng Ying, Cheng Bo simultaneously kills Tu'an Gu.

The last scene of the film is symbolic: the dying Cheng Ying walks down a market street, where he sees his wife with their baby in her arms, smiling at him. Chen Kaige depicts Cheng as a cowardly and passive character, compelled to acts of self-sacrifice even though his true desire is to take revenge. In other words, the final vengeance of the play belongs to Cheng rather than to the orphan. This film adaptation is the tragedy of a common man.

A KOREAN VERSION: CHENG YING'S INNER WORLD

In 2015, the National Theater Company of Korea performed a brilliant, cross-cultural revision of *The Orphan of Zhao: The Seed of Revenge*, adapted and directed by Sunwoong Koh. Soo Kyung Oh, a scholar of Chinese drama, was responsible for translating the Chinese source text and for creating the dramaturgy of the new Korean script.[13] This version is quite loyal to the plot of the Yuan play, while at the same time introducing Korean elements into the performance. The stage is designed as an empty space with only simple props—an approach characteristic of not only of Chinese theater, but also of East Asian theater more generally. Actors dressed in black perform metaphoric actions representing abstractions such as death. This borrows from the use and appearance of *kuroko*, the stagehands in traditional Japanese theatre who dress all in black and come out freely on stage when needed.

The Korean rendition emphasizes the effect of juxtaposing comic and tragic tones. For example, the monologue of Tu'an Gu in the wedge before the beginning of act 1 tells the audience of his three previous attempts to kill his rival. In this version, these three events are performed as comedy—even the hound and the horse, played by men, are funny. The dialogue and action in this rendition are punctuated by puns, jokes, and buffoonery, notwithstanding the overriding themes of hardship and grief. In fact, this sort of comic relief, used to offset serious or tragic scenes, is characteristic of traditional Chinese theater (➤ Introduction, chap. 7) as well as traditional Korean theater.

This play also highlights the leading role of Cheng Ying. The portrayal of his commitment to the survival of the orphan is loyal to the Yuan play, but there is one slight adjustment that influences the whole spirit of this version: the reaction of his wife. Cheng Ying's wife, confronted unexpectedly with her husband's plan of exchanging their child for the orphan, responds with fury, spitting at Cheng Ying and declaring his plan insane, exclaiming: "You go so far as to kill your own child for the other man's child!" As Cheng Ying pulls the baby away from her, she cries out: "The neck will be cracked, and the waist will be broken!"[14] In the end, she has no choice but to let go.

This scene is reminiscent of another Yuan play, *The Chalk Circle* (*Huilan ji*), which was adapted by the German modernist playwright Bertolt Brecht as *The Caucasian Chalk Circle* (1944) and which also involves tensions between a birth mother and an adopted mother. When their child is killed by Tu'an Gu in place of the orphan of Zhao, the devastated Cheng Ying quietly brings the tiny corpse home. His wife holds their dead child tightly, sings a lullaby for him, and then buries him with her own hands. Cheng Ying, now with the little orphan in his arms, attempts to comfort her, but she pulls out a knife, and, threatening him to come no closer, abruptly commits suicide in an act of voiceless protest. Hence, in one scene, Cheng Ying loses both his loving wife and son, not to mention enduring his wife's rebuke just before her death. The grief-stricken Cheng bursts into tears, lifting the orphan above his head and asking Heaven why he has been fated to suffer so, tempted even to throw down this child, the source of his family tragedy. This tableau of Cheng lifting the baby, together with the infant's cries, builds a strong and tragic spectacle right before the intermission. This is the first time that an adaptation gives us a glimpse of Cheng Ying's inner rage before he starts to raise the orphan, and it is a powerful dramatic moment.

Another particularly violent moment happens twenty years later, when Cheng Ying, now an old man, reveals the true identity of the young orphan, again by the use of illustrations. At first, the orphan does not believe him. To convince the young man of the bloody truth, Cheng decides to cut off one of his arms as proof of his sincerity. This act convinces the orphan of the need for vengeance. Moreover, this scene reminds us of the story of *Wang Zuo Cuts off His Arm* (*Wang Zuo duanbi*) from the *The Complete Saga of Yue Fei* (*Shuoyue quanzhuan*), which tells a similar story.[15] In this way, the director and the scriptwriter infused this play with familiar Chinese motifs.

In the end, after the orphan has avenged his clan, the director leaves space for reflection. In a move similar to that of the RSC play, but different from Chen Kaige's film, Cheng Ying is not content. In the Korean version, Cheng is left empty, bitter, and hollow. After the vengeance is achieved, he loses his purpose and kills himself. However, in the darkness of the netherworld, he encounters the ghosts of those victims who had died twenty years earlier, including his wife with their son in her arms, but they pass by without noticing him. Thus, this version of the play ends with Cheng Ying's everlasting loneliness—a metaphor for the interminable wars and sufferings in human history. It could even be considered a parable of the Korean War, an antiwar adaptation that questions and reflects on the cost of vengeance. Arguably, the play deserves a place among the best adaptations of *The Orphan of Zhao* in our times.

CONCLUSION

At their core, many Chinese classical plays are "old stories retold," and their various sources derive from historical records, poems, short stories, anecdotes, and other tales. As described in this chapter, *Orphan* evolved from the historical records of *Zuo Tradition* and *Records of the Historian*, fully developed in the Yuan dynasty as *zaju* drama, added details and length in the Ming dynasty as *nanxi* and *chuanqi*, and enriched the stage performance of regional styles and Peking opera during the Qing dynasty and Republican era. The play showcases a route of a story retold, refined, and reinterpreted. Each time the story was adapted, it also underwent a process of transformation shaped by the circumstances and times of its adaptation. Hence the plot, characters, and motifs were viewed with new eyes.

This play has continued to be reshaped into diverse dramatic genres across nations and cultures in contemporary times. Through the creativity of playwrights, producers, and actors, new significance is produced for different audiences. Not only is *Orphan* related to loyalty, filiality, sacrifice, and revenge, it also gives us a glimpse of human solitude surrounded by love, hatred, grief, and suffering, which exists in everyone's deep unconscious across time and space. Therefore, the orphan is not just a member of the Zhao family—he belongs to all readers willing to delve into and understand his tragedy.

Shih-pe Wang

NOTES

1. See Shiao-Ling Yu, "To Revenge or Not to Revenge? Seven Hundred Years of Transformations of *The Orphan of Zhao*," CHINOPERL 26, no. 1 (2005): 138–147.

2. See Stephen Durrant, Wai-yee Li, and David Schaberg, trans., *Zuo Tradition (Zuozhuan)* (Seattle and London: University of Washington Press, 2016), 748–761, 768–773.

3. Wai-yee Li describes this act 下報 (*xiabao*) as "repaying the dead." See Wai-yee Li, "*The Zhao Orphan*: Introduction," in *The Columbia Anthology of Yuan Drama*, ed. C.T. Hsia, Wai-yee Li, and George Kao (New York: Columbia University Press, 2014), 5. In the context of *Shiji*, the word *bao* involves a pun with a dual meaning—"repay" and "report." Because Cheng Ying later expressed his concern that "the dead would think this a failure if I would have not gone to the underworld to inform them," I translate it as "report" here.

4. Sima Qian, *Shiji* (The Records of the Historian), ed. Yang Jialuo (Taipei: Dingwen shuju, 1985), 43.1785.

5. See Stephen H. West and Wilt L. Idema, ed. and trans., "Introduction," in The Orphan of Zhao *and Other Yuan Plays: The Earliest Known Versions* (New York: Columbia University Press, 2014), 54.

6. The word for "ginseng" (*renshen*, 人參) is homophonic with that for "human body" (*renshen*, 人身); see Pi-twan Huang and Wai-yee Li, trans., *The Zhao Orphan*, 70, footnote 26. Also, the shape of ginseng sometimes is analogized as a baby in the Chinese narratives, like the description

of "ginseng fruit" in chapter 24 of *The Journey to The West*: "The shape of the fruit was exactly that of a newborn infant not yet three days old, complete with the four limbs and the five senses." See Anthony C. Yu, trans., *The Journey to The West* (Chicago: University of Chicago Press, 1977), 464.

7. Wang Guowei, *Song Yuan xiqu shi* (History of Song and Yuan Drama), ann. Huang Shizhong (Nanjing, China: Fenghuang chubanshe, 2010), 116.

8. Wang, *Song Yuan xiqu shi*, 117.

9. Patricia Sieber, *Theaters of Desire: Authors, Readers, and the Reproductions of Early Chinese Song-Drama, 1300–2000* (New York: Palgrave Macmillan, 2003), 15–27.

10. Tian Qinxin, *Zhao shi gu'er* (The Orphan of Zhao), in *Tian Qinxin de xijuben* (Tian Qinxin's Drama Scripts) (Beijing: Beijing University Press, 2010), 121–67, esp. 166.

11. See the special issue, "A Controversial Company: Debating the Casting of the RSC's *The Orphan of Zhao*," *Contemporary Theatre Review* 24, no. 4 (2014).

12. See the webpage of the RSC (https://www.rsc.org.uk/the-orphan-of-zhao); James Fenton, "The Orphan of Zhao at the RSC: A Very Modern Massacre," *Guardian*, https://www.theguardian .com/stage/2012/oct/30/orphan-of-zhao-rsc; and Vincent Dowd, "The Orphan of Zhao comes to RSC," *BBC News*, https://www.bbc.com/news/entertainment-arts-20242623.

13. See Soo Kyung Oh, "Ershiyi shiji zai Hanguo wutai shang de *Zhao shi gu'er*—Zhongguo gudian xiju de dangdaihua yu zaidihua" (*The Orphan of Zhao* on the 21st-Century Korean Stage—Contemporary Interpretation and Localization of Chinese Classical Opera), *Xiju yanjiu* (Journal of Theatre Studies) 20 (2017): 103–134.

14. See Oh, "Ershiyi shiji zai Hanguo wutai shang de *Zhao shi gu'er*," 118.

15. The story of *Wang Zuo Cuts Off His Arm* originates from chapters 54–57 of *Shuo Yue quan-zhuan* (The Complete Saga of Yue Fei), a novel edited by Qian Cai in the Qing dynasty, which narrates the story about the famous military general Yue Fei during the war between the Jurchen-ruled Jin dynasty and the Southern Song dynasty. The plot of the story runs as follows. There is a young general in the Jin camp called Lu Wenlong, the son of Chinese official Lu Deng, who died when the city he governed was raided. Wenlong was abducted and raised by the Jin commander Wuzhu. Wenlong does not know his real identity, and he defeats many Song generals with his great martial skills, which makes Yue Fei worried. One of his generals, Wang Zuo, is eager to make a contribution, and he recalls a historical story from *Wuyue chunqiu* (The Historical Records of Wu and Yue) about an assassin named Yao Li, who cut off his arm in order to be a spy. Wang Zuo cuts off one of his own arms and pretends to flee to the Jin camp, claiming that he was mistreated by Yue Fei. In the Jin camp, he finds out from Wenlong's nanny Wenlong's true identity. Wang Zuo eventually reveals Wenlong's true identity to him using visual aids, and then he persuades him to fight for the Song dynasty. The plot of this story obviously borrows from *The Orphan of Zhao*. In the late Qing dynasty, the story was adapted into a Beijing opera named *Ba dachui* (*Eight Big Ham-mers*), which is still popular today, and it also was readapted by the Taiwanese playwright Wang Anqi in 1985 as a new version of the *Ba dachui* Peking opera entitled *Lu Wenlong*.

PRIMARY SOURCES

LZH   Lin Zhaohua 林兆華 (director) and Jin Haishu 金海曙 (playwright). *Zhao shi gu'er* 趙氏孤兒 (The Orphan of Zhao), *Juben* 劇本 (Play Monthly) 2003.9: 2–33.

OZ   Sun-woong Koh 高宣雄. *Zhao shi gu'er, Fuchou de Zhongzi* 趙氏孤兒，復仇 的種子 (The Orphan of Zhao: The Seed of Revenge). National Theater of Korea. 2015. Video recording of the performance provided courtesy of National Theater of Korea.

RSC   Fenton, James. *The Orphan of Zhao*. London: Faber & Faber, 2012.

TQX   Tian Qinxin 田沁鑫. *Zhao shi gu'er* 趙氏孤兒 (The Orphan of Zhao). In Tian Qinxin, *Tian Qinxin de xijuben* 田沁鑫的戲劇本 (Tian Qinxin's Drama Scripts), 121–67. Beijing: Beijing University Press, 2010.

YKSSZ Zheng Qian 鄭騫, ed. *Jiaoding Yuankan zaju sanshi zhong* 校訂元刊雜劇三
十種 (*A Collated Text of the* Thirty Yuan-Printed *Zaju* Plays). Taipei: Shijie
shuju, 1962.

YXQ Zang Maoxun 臧懋循. *Yuanqu xuan jiaozhu* 元曲選校注 (*An Annotated Text
of* Select Yuan Plays). Ann. Wang Xueqi 王學奇. Shijiazhuang, China: Hebei
jiaoyu chubanshe, 1994.

ZSGE Chen Kaige 陳凱歌. *Zhao shi gu'er* 趙氏孤兒 (*Sacrifice*). DVD. Taipei:
Caichang International Multimedia Company, 2011.

SUGGESTED READINGS

TRANSLATIONS

1. Yuan Version, *Thirty Yuan Printed Zaju Plays*:

Ji Junxiang. *The Orphan of Zhao*, A Fourteenth-Century Edition. In *The Orphan of Zhao and Other
Yuan Plays: The Earliest Known Versions*, ed. and trans. Stephen H. West and Wilt L. Idema,
57–77. New York: Columbia University Press, 2015.

Ji Junxiang. *The Zhao Orphan in Yuan Editions*. Trans. Wai-yee Li. In *The Columbia Anthology
of Yuan Drama*, ed. C.T. Hsia, Wai-yee Li and George Kao, 55–72. New York: Columbia
University Press, 2014.

2. Ming Version, *Select Yuan Plays*:

Ji Junxiang. *The Orphan of Zhao Greatly Wreaks Vengeance*. In The Orphan of Zhao *and Other
Yuan Plays: The Earliest Known Versions*, ed. and trans. Stephen H. West and Wilt L. Idema,
73–111. New York: Columbia University Press, 2015.

Ji Junxiang. *The Zhao Orphan*. Trans. Pi-Twan Huang and Wai-yee Li. In *The Columbia Anthology
of Yuan Drama*, ed. C. T. Hsia, Wai-yee Li, and George Kao, 17–55. New York: Columbia
University Press, 2014.

ENGLISH

He Yuming. "Adopting *The Orphan*: Theater and Urban Culture in Ming China." In *The Ming
World*, ed. Kenneth M. Swope, 161–184. London and New York: Routledge, 2020.

Idema, Wilt L. "*The Orphan of Zhao*: Self-Sacrifice, Tragic Choice and Revenge and the
Confucianization of Mongol Drama at the Ming Court." *Cina* 21 (1988): 159–190.

Sieber, Patricia. *Theaters of Desire: Authors, Readers, and the Reproductions of Early Chinese Song-
Drama, 1300–2000*. New York: Palgrave Macmillan, 2003.

Yu, Shiao-Ling. "*The Orphan of Zhao*: Chinese Revenge Drama and European Adaptations."
Comparative Literature Studies 55, no. 1 (2018): 144–171.

Yu, Shiao-Ling. "To Revenge or Not to Revenge? Seven Hundred Years of Transformations of *The
Orphan of Zhao*." *CHINOPERL* 26, no. 1 (2005): 129–147.

CHINESE

Deng Shaoji 鄧紹基 and Yao Shuyi 么書儀. "Ji Junxiang de *Zhao shi gu'er*" 紀君祥的《趙氏孤
兒》(Ji Junxiang's *The Orphan of Zhao*). *Zhonghua xiqu* 中華戲曲 (*Chinese Drama*), 2 (1986):
194–209.

Lee, Chi-hsiang 李紀祥. "*Zhao shi gu'er* de 'shi' yu 'ju:' wenshu yu yanshu" 《趙氏孤兒》
的「史」與「劇」：文述與演述 (*The Orphan of Zhao* in History and Drama: Text and
Performance). *Hanxue yanjiu* 漢學研究 (*Chinese Studies*) 18, no. 1 (2000): 209–36.

Li Sher-shiueh 李奭學, and Hsieh Pei-hsuan 謝佩璇. "Ma Ruose yu Zhongguo chuantong
xiqu—Cong Mayi *Zhao shi gu'er* tanqi; Fulu: 1731 nian Ma Ruose zhi Fu'ermeng han" 馬若瑟
與中國傳統戲曲—從馬譯《趙氏孤兒》談起；附錄：1731年馬若瑟致傅爾蒙函 (*The Orphan
of Zhao* in the Context of Joseph de Prémare's Knowledge of Chinese Drama; Appendix:
Joseph de Prémare's Letter to Étienne Fourmont, December 4, 1731). *Zhongguo wen zhe yanjiu*

tongxun 中國文哲研究通訊 (*Newsletter of the Institute of Chinese Literature and Philosophy*) 28, no. 4 (2018): 155–205.

Oh, Soo Kyung 吳秀卿. "Ershiyi shiji zai Hanguo wutai shang de *Zhao shi gu'er*—Zhongguo gudian xiju de dangdaihua yu zaidihua" 二十一世紀在韓國舞台上的《趙氏孤兒》—中國古典戲劇的當代化與在地化 (*The Orphan of Zhao* on the 21st-Century Korean Stage—Contemporary Interpretation and Localization of Chinese Classical Opera). *Xiju yanjiu* 戲劇研究 (*Journal of Theatre Studies*), 20 (2017): 103–134.

Tu, Hsin-Hsin 杜欣欣. "Wenxue, fanyi, piping: Cong Bei'erman fanyi pinglun kan Ma Ruose zhi *Zhao shi gu'er*" 文學、翻譯、批評：從貝爾曼翻譯評論看馬若瑟之《趙氏孤兒》(Literature, Translation, and the Critics: On Prémare's Translation of *Le petit orphelin de la maison de Tchao*). *Fanyi luncong* 翻譯論叢 (*Translation Review*) 3, no. 2 (2010): 61–99.

Wang Guowei 王國維. *Song Yuan xiqu shi* 宋元戲曲史 (*The History of Song and Yuan Drama*). Ann. Huang Shizhong 黃仕忠. Nanjing, China: Fenghuang chubanshe, 2010.

6

The Female Mulan Joins the Army in Place of Her Father

Gender and Performance

"Don't judge a book by its cover." "All that glitters is not gold." Aphorisms like these warn about the dangers of making judgments about people and situations based on how they appear. The beast or frog can turn out to be a handsome prince. The dull, misshapen rock, when polished, is transformed into a precious piece of jade. Although we accept the wisdom of these warnings, the same wisdom could apply to the prince or the shining piece of jade: Are they what they appear to be? Is this their final form, or might another twist occur that again reveals the flaws in our judgment? Warnings about appearances are a favorite subject in the theatrical world, a world in which appearances inform knowledge of a character. In traditional Chinese theater, where role types were signified by specific costumes and gestures, the appearance of the character on stage already tells us so much before a single word is spoken: the young girl role is unmistakably distinguished from that of the male warrior. While he discusses choosing a fine steed to ride into battle, she puts flowers in her hair and pines for a young man who seeks her hand in marriage. We see the character arrive, played by a specific role type, and we expect that the range of that characterization will remain consistent with those role expectations. Those expectations are precisely what Xu Wei (1521–1593) relies on—and yet also plays with—when his heroine, Mulan, transforms herself from a young girl into a brave warrior, all with a simple change of dress.

The tale of Mulan has a story arc that contains surprising reversals and contradictions—the kinds of surprising reversals and contradictions that describe Xu Wei and his own life story. He, too, was a true original. An expert in southern drama, he chose to write in a northern form. His calligraphy was fiercely individualistic and defined by its originality, and yet it was effusively copied by multitudes of admirers who imitated his style. He was an accomplished poet and brilliant essayist, but he made his living as an official military strategist. He was a painter and a dramatist, a scholar and a rogue. He created strong-willed, accomplished, and admirable women on stage; meanwhile, off stage, he was given to erratic and unhinged behavior, even murdering his wife. He appeared as one thing at one moment and its polar opposite at the next. This describes Xu Wei, and it describes the theater pieces he authored. It is perhaps fitting that someone whose life contained such contradictions would be drawn to figures who are similarly conflicted.

The plays he composed are centered on characters who respond to extraordinary challenges with creativity, independence, versatility, and a remarkable confidence in the strength of their own personal qualities.

6.1 XU WEI AND HIS QUARTET OF MING *ZAJU* PLAYS

The Female Mulan Joins the Army in Place of Her Father (*Ci Mulan tifu congjun,* hereafter *Mulan*) is one of a quartet of plays composed by Xu Wei, *Four Cries of a Gibbon* (*Sisheng yuan*). The plays, which vary in length, do not restrict the singing role to a single character and freely alternate between northern and southern song modes. In terms of subject matter, they focus on highly dramatic situations possible only in the world of fiction. Each one describes a different unusual scenario. In *The Mad Drummer Plays the Yuyang Triple Rolls* (*Kuanggushi Yuyang sannong,* hereafter *Mi Heng*), the hero is a wronged man who, in a postmortem trial that takes place in the spirit underworld (a literal "show trial" that is performed to entertain the demons and spirits), challenges and triumphs over his enemy Cao Cao, one of the most famous generals in imperial China (➤ *HTRCPIC,* chap. 6). In *The Zen Master Yu Has a Dream of Cuixiang* (*Yu chanshi Cuixiang yimeng,* hereafter *Zen Master Yu*), the eponymous monk is seduced into violating his vows of chastity and reincarnated in the next act so he can get his revenge. In *The Girl Graduate Rejects the Female Phoenix and Gains the Male Phoenix* (*Nü zhuangyuan ci huang de feng,* hereafter *Girl Graduate*), an orphaned and destitute woman dresses up in her father's scholar gown to take part in the male-only imperial bureaucratic examinations—and wins first place.

However, among Xu Wei's four plays, the best-known plot today is *Mulan.* Mulan's fame in world literature no doubt owes something to the Disney's animated version of *Mulan* (1998), which made her a household name to American children; to Maxine Hong Kingston's text, *The Woman Warrior,* which used Mulan as one of the protagonist's alter egos; and, most recently to the live-action Hollywood film released by Disney in 2020. But even before the story was remade in the United States, Mulan enjoyed a robust adaptation history in China that has featured dozens of stage, screen, digital, and textual versions and continues to evolve to this day. This popularity can be ascribed to a number of factors, foremost among which is a seemingly universal interest in the comedy of inverting entrenched gender stereotypes. The inversion of stereotypes is made even more pointedly in a stage world where gender, like role type, was defined by strict conventions.

The story of Mulan is documented as far back as the sixth century, in a ballad that describes a dutiful daughter who puts on her father's armor to successfully defend her country. Xu Wei's play was the first extant adaptation to exploit the potential for comedy and drama in Mulan's situation, and its treatment of the way that Mulan used costume changes to highlight role-playing became a touchstone for later adaptations. The comedic potential for gender-bending plots is particularly salient when viewed against the single-gender casts that constituted standard performance practice at the time in Xu Wei's China (☞ Introduction) and in the Elizabethan theater world of his near-contemporary, William Shakespeare (1564–1616). The theatrical convention of having an actor playing one gender—frequently the opposite gender—and then proceeding to take on yet another disguise of the "opposite" gender allows the playwright to manipulate wordplay and poke fun at gender stereotypes, all while letting the audience share in the dramatic irony of feeling that they know something that the characters on stage do not. Audiences are thus invited to reflect on their own presumptions about gender. By watching a male actor playing a woman thrust in the position of playing a man and directly discussing how "she" can heighten her performance of maleness, the viewers are aware of an extra layer of performance—the actor's—that the diegetic participants in the story lack. Inviting the audience to tease out what parts of gender are natural and what parts are performance accounts for some of a scene's entertainment value.

Furthermore, having a female character flout the traditional expectations generally applied to young women of her time was also an opportunity to entertain by poking fun at social conventions. In the case of Xu Wei's play, this should be understood less as a form of pointed social commentary—an approach taken by many later adaptations of "Mulan"—than as an opportunity for some unusual stage work, adding opportunities for the skilled actor to show off physical comedy and martial arts skills. A talented actor can display a full range of talents with such a role, from bashful maiden to ferocious commander of troops (☞ chap. 3). Part of the charm of *Mulan* is its main character's awareness of the power of performance. Just as the actor who plays Mulan demonstrates incredible breadth, the character Mulan embraces the opportunity to display the full diversity of her talents; equally facile inside and outside the house, Mulan shows her adeptness at knowing how to dress the part. Mulan, as well as her Shakespearean counterparts, is a character onstage who has the advantage of knowing that she is performing.

When Mulan determines to take her father's place, she references other female paragons in her self-introduction as she goes onstage. These predecessors are Qin Xiu, who earned the death penalty (which was later pardoned) when she avenged her father by killing his assassins, and Tiying, who begged to become a slave in Emperor Han Wendi's court as a substitute for her father, who had been sentenced to death. These allusions gesture to a history of filial daughters distinguishing themselves by taking on active roles typically assigned to men. But Mulan considers those accomplishments lesser still in comparison to what she is going to do—she is about to do these things undercover, in disguise as a man. In the following section, Mulan has just appeared onstage to give the conventional self-introduction, in which she details her name and a bit of her family history. She also introduces her predicament, which follows the general outlines of the original ballad: her father has been drafted, but neither of her siblings is fit to serve as his replacement. She looks to the earlier female paragons as models and declares:

（旦）

妾身姓花名木蘭，祖上在西漢時以六郡良家子，世住河北魏郡。俺父親名弧字桑之，平生好武能文，舊時也做一個有名的千夫長。娶過俺母親賈氏，生下妾身，今年才一十七歲。雖有一個妹子木難和小兄弟咬兒，可都不曾成人長大。

昨日聞得黑山賊首豹子皮，領著十來萬人馬，造反稱王。俺大魏拓跋克汗下郡徵兵，軍書絡繹，有十二捲來的，卷卷有俺家爺的名字。俺想起來，俺爺又老了，以下又再沒一人。況且俺小時節一了有些小氣力，又有些小聰明，就隨著俺的爺也讀過書，學過些武藝。這就是俺今日該替爺的報頭了。

你且看那書上說，秦休和那緹縈兩個，一個拚着死，一個拚着入官為奴，都只為着父親。終不然，這兩個都是包網兒，戴帽兒，不穿兩截裙襖的麼？

只是一件，若要替呵，這弓馬槍刀衣鞋等項，却須索從新另做一番，也要略的演習一二纔好。把這要替的情由，告愬他們得知。

FEMALE LEAD *as* MULAN [*speaks*]:

My surname is Hua, my given name is Mulan. Generations ago, in the time of the Western Han, my ancestors, being among those descended from good families of the six prefectures, settled here in Wei. My father's name is Hu, and his courtesy name is Sangzhi. All his life he has been skilled in literature and in martial arts, and he was at one time a famous "commander of a thousand." He married my mother, of the Jia family, and then she gave birth to me. This year, I am barely seventeen years old. Neither my little sister, Munan, nor my little brother, Yao'er, has reached adulthood.

Yesterday I heard that Black Mountain's bandit chief, Leopard Skin, led hundreds of thousands of men on horseback in rebellion and is now calling himself king. Our great Wei's Tuoba Khan has sent down to our district, calling up troops. The army rolls have been arriving, twelve in a row, scroll after scroll bearing my father's name. I realize that my father is not only old, but has no descendants to carry on for him. When I was young, I was not only the strong one, but had a lot of smarts, too, so I accompanied my father in studying books and martial arts. Now here is my opportunity to repay him.

Just take a look at what it says in the books about Qin Xiu and Tiying, one of them willing to die, the other one willing to go to court to be a slave, both for their father's sake. But, weren't those two still putting their buns in hairnets instead of wearing male caps? Didn't they go on wearing their girls' skirts and jackets?

There's just one thing: if I am to stand in for him, I must have a new set of a bow, horse, spear, sword, gown, and boots—all prepared from scratch. And I'd better go over my martial arts once or twice. Only then can I tell my family about my aim to take dad's place.

[*XWJ* 4:1198; trans. Kwa, 169–170]

As a dramatic convention of Chinese drama, the self-introduction functions as an opportunity for the character to detail her name and background, and, in some cases, to present the exposition for the play. It is also our first indication of the way that Xu Wei uses the interplay of form and content, making the mechanics of performance a subject to be exploited and considered. While all plays use such conventions as a matter of course, Mulan's introduction is an opportunity for her to fold her anticipated actions into a tradition of other girls' performances. Outside the frame of the story, she nonchalantly announces to the audience and/or the readers what kind of role she is going to play. Even more interestingly, she acknowledges her plan to dress as a man within the framework of the play's world. She then lets us know how her performance goes beyond the antecedents of several other outstanding women to reach even greater heights. In contemplating the main character's conscious adoption of a role alongside a frank discussion of why the pretense is necessary, we are asked to remember that we are watching a play. This preamble prepares the way for the actions that follow, highlighting the way that clothes can do much of the work of framing others' expectations.

6.2 *MULAN*: THE TWO-ACT STRUCTURE

Traditional Yuan *zaju* have four acts and are defined by strict conventions (☞ Introduction, chap. 1). By contrast, Xu Wei's *Mulan zaju* play, like the other plays in his quartet, flouts those conventions. *Mulan* is composed of two acts, which lends a binary structure to a play about female and male distinctions. Xu took this artistic license in the construction of *Four Cries of a Gibbon*, limiting *Mi Heng* to one act, expanding *Girl Graduate* to five, and keeping both *Zen Master Yu* and *Mulan* to two acts each. The two-act structure was manipulated remarkably well in *Zen Master Yu*, allowing the second act to function as a mirror reversal of the first; the eponymous Zen Master Yu from the first act is reborn as a prostitute, Liu Cui, in the second act, and her path to enlightenment in the second half reverses the order of the monk's path to degradation in the first.

While Mulan's role reversals are not as dramatic as that of a monk who reincarnates himself as his enemy's daughter, the parallelisms and inversions enabled by the two acts in *Mulan* invite us to think of individual events or roles as being somehow partnered elsewhere in the play. *Mulan* shows the folly of believing that one thing or person necessarily comes with a list of fixed and inalterable conditions. Xu Wei's play suggests instead that identity is always encumbered by layers of codes that can be deciphered only when compared exactingly, and only under specific conditions. Because human actors are involved, these conditions are constantly in flux. The codes are too often misread not only by the characters on stage, but by the audience as well. When those codes are overturned, we recognize our mistake and laugh at ourselves.

Mulan is played by a *dan*, and when we first meet her, she is a character who is consistent with the conventional young female type typically expected from a *dan*. This role designation does not tell us whether the actor playing the *dan* is male or female, which already inserts a layer of gender performance. All the songs in the first act are reserved for the *dan* playing Mulan. In the arias, she sings mostly about how she will prepare herself for battle. These songs give us a picture of her transformation from Mulan the daughter into her assumed identity of Hua Hu the warrior. Significantly, once she has transitioned into the new identity of a male warrior, the fact that she is played by a *dan*-specialized actor is complicated by those role expectations. Singing as a conventionally feminine *dan* would undermine her successful disguise, after all.

In the second act, different characters are given songs to perform: Mulan's commanding general, Xin Ping, presents songs that alternate with a chorus of soldiers, in which they describe their attempts to flush out the bandit king known as Leopard Skin. Mulan is congratulated for the role she has played in the army's victory, as well. The combination of singing parts in the second act draws attention to the fact that the united actions taken together by an army composed of men—and Mulan—are crucial to their success. The first act lingered on Mulan's transformation into a man, but once she has effected that change, her actions—even those that make her stand out among the men she fights with—are less about individual glory than they are about fulfilling the responsibilities germane to anyone (i.e., any man) in the role that she has claimed. That this is a role reserved exclusively for men is unquestioned; however, once Mulan has acquired that status, her accomplishments are praised and rewarded but hardly treated as anything out of the ordinary.

Questions of concealment and disguise are central to both the play's action and comedy. The interchange of aria and chorus between Xin Ping and his men underscores the similarities between Mulan's concealment of her true identity and Leopard Skin's concealment from her fellow troops. She has to work equally hard to keep her identity hidden as she works to draw him out. Xin Ping sings:

（外）	EXTRA MALE *as* XIN PING [*sings*]:
【清江引】	*To the tune* "Qing Jiang yin"
黑山小寇真見淺。	Black Mountain's little bandit is truly shortsighted!
躲住了成何幹？	He continues to hide himself—what can he accomplish?
花開蝶滿枝，樹倒猢猻散。	When the flower opens, butterflies fill the branches, when the tree falls, the monkeys scatter off.
你越躲着，	The more you hide,
我越尋你見。	The more I'll seek the sight of you.
（眾）	CHORUS OF SOLDIERS [*sings*]:
【前腔】	*Reprise*
黑山小寇真高見，	Black Mountain's little bandit is truly farsighted!
左右他輸得慣。	Left or right, he's used to defeat.
一日不害羞，	All day long he feels no shame,
三餐吃飽飯。	And at all three meals, gobbles his fill.
你越尋他，他越躲著看。	The more you seek him out, the more he hides and waits.

[*XWJ* 4:1202–1203; trans. Kwa, 179–180]

We are struck again by the irony of knowing something that these men do not. This is highlighted by the puns that emerge in what they sing and what we know about Hua Mulan's identity. While they are celebrating their success at having found the bandit chief in his hiding place, they counter with a challenge: "The more you hide, the more I'll seek the sight of you." They are right, of course, but they are also unaware of the comrade concealing herself among them. Indeed, she precisely seeks to prevent the instance of a flower (*hua*, which happens to be her surname in Xu Wei's play) becoming exposed to the butterflies around it. Similarly, when the tree falls, the macaques (the first part of the compound *husun* for macaque, *hu*, is homonymous with Mulan's assumed first name) scatter off, exposed.

As she explains to them later, when she reveals herself as a woman:

（旦）	MULAN [*sings*]:
【三煞】	*To the tune* "Third from Coda"
論男女席不沾,	It is said that between men and women, even their mats shouldn't touch,
沒奈何才用權。	But when there's no other option, one must use expedient means.
巧花枝穩躲過蝴蝶戀。	The clever blossom hid securely from the butterflies' ardor.
	[*XWJ* 4:1205; trans. Kwa, 185]

The clever flower (the clever "Hua") successfully hid herself from the butterflies. The most radical message of Xu Wei's *Mulan* may be this: Mulan did not undergo any special training or magical transformation (unbound feet notwithstanding) in her transition from being "Mulan" to being "Hua Hu." This is mirrored by the fact that the actor playing both Mulan and Hua Hu presumably remains the *dan* actor, although the father in the first act was played by the "extra male" (*wai*) role. We in the audience are able to see this as the *dan* continues to perform as Hua Hu, even though all the characters on stage treat the *dan* as a man, creating situational comedy at every exchange. The actor playing the "extra male" role, on the other hand, goes from playing Hua Hua in the first act to the commanding general Xin Ping in the second. All Mulan did was change her name and costume.

The two-act structure of the play, then, also draws our attention to the possibility of an equivalence in effort in the first act and the second. The elaborate military tactics, the invasion of the Leopard's lair, and the successful capture of the nation's dreaded enemy are set on an axis against a first act that focuses on Mulan changing out of her girl's clothes, reacquainting herself with the martial arts that she learned from her father, and embarking on a campaign alongside men, while taking pains to guard her true identity from her traveling companions and being mindful of her mother's concerns about her maidenhood.

This structural balance that localizes the fierce defender of country and the gentle defender of chastity in the same performer comments on the relative costs of two situations that seem heavily unequal to our twenty-first-century eyes. This is especially true from the perspective of an audience that has watched the same actor play Mulan and Hua Hu with equal facility over the course of the play. Mulan, however, suggests to us that both are roles that she had put on, and that her essential "I" was not affected at all:

（旦）	MULAN [*sings*]:
【前腔】	*Reprise*
萬般想來都是幻，	Everything is—when I think of it—an illusion, after all;
誇什麼吾成算。	Why should I boast that I succeeded in this scheme?
我殺賊把王擒，	The "I" who killed bandits, and captured their king,
是女將男換。	Was a female officer who had turned into a man.
這功勞得將來不費星兒汗。	After all, these feats did not cost me a drop of sweat.

[*XWJ* 4:1204; trans. Kwa, 182]

6.3 *MULAN*: CHANGING CLOTHES

If these feats did not cost Mulan a drop of sweat, who did all the work? The play, in particular, makes work an undeniable aspect of the plot, with its emphasis on the actions that Mulan has to undertake to perform as she knows her father would have done when he was younger. In earlier versions of the Mulan story, there is little question of an identity crisis. The earliest version of the Mulan story is recorded in the "Poem of Mulan" ("Mulan shi"), thought to date from the sixth century CE. The dating of the poem inspired Xu Wei to set *Mulan* during the northern (Tuoba) Wei dynasty (386–533). In the poem, Mulan's sighs drown out the sounds of the loom and shuttle, where she sits doing the traditional woman's work of weaving, as she is consumed with thoughts about the prospect of her elderly father's conscription. Faced with this predicament, she quickly comes to a solution: "I want to buy a saddle and a horse,/To take my father's place and join the army. The eastern market: there she bought a horse;/The western market: there she bought a saddle./ The southern market: there she bought a bridle;/The northern market: there she bought a whip."[1] This announcement is immediately followed by a send-off from her aged parents as Mulan goes off to Black Mountain to fight in her father's stead.

When adapted for performance in drama, however, the scenes of preparation and training leading up to Mulan's departure can be expanded, both in the songs performed by the actors and in the wordless actions performed on stage. As noted previously, the first act is focused on the complex business of transforming Mulan into just "one of the guys." Writing in the Ming dynasty, when bound feet would have been customary for women in families like Mulan's, Xu Wei could have easily stressed the historical context, where women's feet were not bound, or the cultural context in which non-Han women did not bind their feet. Instead, he seizes on the challenge of using this dramatic moment as an opportunity. Here, Mulan has to resolve this anachronously "unavoidable" and immobilizing complication. His solution is literally a liquid solution—one that returns feet to the size of little lotuses even after they have been unfurled into awkward and unattractive (but more boot-friendly) feet.

A note on an early printed edition of the play, which is not included in the later printed edition, hints at the entertainment value of such a scene: "Let the changing of clothes and shoes be performed [for the audience] to watch for a while."[2] Considering the erotic associations of the bound foot, this scene had the potential to be both titillating—a woman unbinding and exposing her feet!—and comedic—a man pretending to be a woman unbinding and revealing *his*, naturally, big and ugly feet! The stage direction implied that a talented physical actor could milk this scene for laughs, reminding us that scripts cannot always fully represent the experience of watching a play on stage. Wordless stage work can communicate just as much as the words themselves, and physical actions that range from athletic displays to comedic pratfalls are frequently what draw audiences to live performances.

This aspect is seen again when Mulan, with her feet now liberated from their bondage, performs a series of acrobatic moves. As she prepares herself to go to battle, she undertakes a series of martial arts routines that allow elaborate stage performance, but which are designated with only terse stage directions:

（旦）	MULAN [*sings*]:
【天下樂】	*To the tune "Tianxia le"*
穿起來怕不是從軍一長官，	Dressed up, I daresay I *am* a senior campaigning officer,
行間，正好瞞。	Among their ranks, it will be easy to hide.
緊縧鈎廂稱細褶子系刀環。	Hook the belt tightly—I shall hang my sword on the plates.
軟噥噥襯鎖子甲，	The chain mail is pliant and supple,
暖烘烘當夾被單，	Its quilted lining is comfy and warm.
帶回來又好與咬兒穿。	I'll bring this armor back, and it will still be good enough for my brother to wear.
衣鞋都換了，試演一會刀看。	Clothes and boots are all changed, and now I've got to practice some swordplay for a bit.
（演刀介）	*Performs swordplay.*
這刀呵，	This sword!
這多時不拈，	How long it's been since I've drawn it,
俺則道不便；	I've got to say, I thought it wouldn't be easy.
才提起一翻，	But hoisting it up and giving it a whirl,
也比舊一般。	Well, it's just like old times.
為何的手不酸，	Why aren't my hands sore with pain,
習慣了錦梭穿。	Used as they are to threading the loom's shuttle?

[*XWJ* 4:1199; trans. Kwa, 172–173]

The scene continues with Mulan lovingly admiring aloud a lance, a bow, and the accessories associated with riding on horseback:

（旦）   MULAN [*sings*]:

【么】   *Reprise*

繡裲襠坐馬衣，	Embroidered front and back, my horse-riding vest,
嵌珊瑚掉馬鞭，	Inlaid with coral, my horse-urging whip.
這行裝不是俺兵家辦。	This costume is not army issue,
則與他兩條皮生捆出麒麟汗，	So with these two leather reins I'll firmly lead my unicorns,
萬山中活捉個猢猻伴，	Through millions of mountains I'll catch a macaque,
一彎頭平端了狐狸塹。	With this one bit and bridle, I'll trample out the foxes from their den.
到門庭才顯出女多嬌，坐鞍橋，	I will only reveal it was a beautiful girl in the saddle when I return home.
誰不道英雄漢。	Everyone shall call me a great hero! . . .

[*XWJ* 4:1200; trans. Kwa, 175]

In these two examples, the reader will find that much of the process of transformation from Mulan to Hua Hu involves putting on appropriately male-signifying accessories. This cataloguing of each part of Mulan's costume may seem laborious, especially to a reader of the play, but it is an important device that fulfills several functions. The transformation, as detailed step by step by the performer, suggests a step-by-step passage from one persona to another.

Foremost, such scenes underscore the largely cosmetic and gestural nature of the distinctions between male and female, where costume and vocal register reliably designate the gender of the speaker on stage. Mulan's description of her actions when taking on her father's persona are largely occupied with the materials that effect this change: whereas the costume is easy to put on, voice represents a greater challenge, and audiences will be reminded of the physical presence of one actor relying on dress and gesture to convey gender. This sentiment is expressed as well in Shakespeare's *Merchant of Venice*, when Portia, about to dress up as a man to intercede in a trial on her husband's behalf, says:

> I'll hold thee any wager,
> When we are both accoutered like young men,
> I'll prove the prettier fellow of the two,
> And wear my dagger with the braver grace,
> And speak between the change of man and boy
> With a reed voice, and turn two mincing steps
> Into a manly stride,
> . . .
> I have within my mind
> A thousand raw tricks of these bragging Jacks,
> Which I will practise. [act III, scene 4, 62–68, 76–78)][3]

Physical demeanor, and especially clothing and accessories, are crucial in designing how gender is comprehended and assigned by the viewer. Clothing emphasizes the notion of gender as something that can be put on, first by concealing the wearer's actual anatomy, and then by functioning as a sort of exoskeleton that transmits coded information about gender in culturally specific associations with costume, whether through daggers or boots. Stage costumes in both Xu Wei's and Shakespeare's traditions were heavily coded by necessity; audiences could not rely on facial features or body habitus to identify male from female. Drama relied on costume and basic props such as weapons or headdresses to tell audiences whether the actor was playing an old man or a young girl. When these conventions were subverted by, for example, the situation of a cross-dressed actor once again cross-dressing, in character, to further trick the other characters on stage, it achieved comedic value, lending added irony to Mulan's or Portia's pointed verbal commentaries. It also, as Marjorie Garber has argued, can raise larger questions about the anxieties of the culture in which it emerges.[4] Mulan's performance suggests the fine details of how actors prepare for their stage entrance; character is something that they put on to make the identity they perform seem credible.

Mulan's elaborate detailing of weaponry in the first act also allows the skilled performer to show off the skills involved in performing intricate displays of martial arts, which were no doubt a critical skill for Xu Wei's intended performer when considering an audience's enjoyment. Where the stage directions merely say "performs swordplay," "acts out practicing with lance," or "acts pulling on a bow," the reader skips over in a blink of an eye what would have likely been scenes of silent improvisation, based on the actor's own expertise, experience, and skills. In the 1939 film *Mulan Joins the Army* (*Mulan congjun*), directed by Bu Wancang (1903–1974), for example, a full minute is allotted to Mulan's demonstration of her sword and spear skills (Visual Resources). In the Shaw brothers' 1964 film *Hua Mulan*, performed in the Huangmei opera movie genre popular in Hong Kong, Taiwan, Singapore, and elsewhere in southeast Asia, Mulan engages in an extended fight scene with her father, who does not recognize that he is fighting his own daughter. At the end of the scene, when he understands that he has been fighting with Mulan, he holds back tears as he tells her that her fighting skills have surpassed his own.

In a film script, such scenes would similarly have been simply abbreviated as "performs swordplay." While these much later versions of course cannot speak to Xu Wei's own intentions centuries ago, with very different dramatic conventions, they serve as reminders of the distance between a script and an actual live performance. The stage directions in Xu Wei's *Mulan* may thus similarly point to opportunities for virtuoso performances. A trained actor who specialized in these roles would surely have dazzled audiences with displays of swordsmanship and acrobatics between arias that lovingly described the items as they are added to Mulan's battery of armor. Mulan performs these tasks so ably, and with such accomplishment, as both Mulan and Hua Hu. This echoes an image in the original poem, discussed next, of male and female rabbits running side by side. Who can tell if it is male or female? More important, the play asks: Should we even care?

6.4 *MULAN*: GENTLE MEN

Mistaken identity is a standard dramatic situation, and a subset within it comes from a disappointed lover who has mistaken a man for a woman or a woman for a man. This is helped by the lover's overdependence on how things look and how easily gender identities can be created with props and gestures. This is noted by Rosalind in Shakespeare's *As You Like It*. Rosalind, escaping the threats of an uncle who has turned against her, is masquerading as a young man by the name of Ganymede. The name Ganymede already draws attention to gender fluidity by evoking the beautiful boy who was Zeus's favorite in Greek mythology, just as Mulan's surname Hua hinted at the feminine flower hidden among a swarm of lusty butterflies. Although on the inside, Rosalind/Ganymede may tremble with the frailties of her fear, she also believes that the exterior she presents will make her no different from any number of similar men who, frail in spirit, exercise the bluster of performed maleness to those around them:

> Were it not better,
> Because that I am more than common tall,
> That I did suit me all points like a man?
> A gallant curtle-axe upon my thigh,
> A boar-spear in my hand; and—in my heart
> Lie there what hidden woman's fear there will—
> We'll have a swashing and a martial outside,
> As many other mannish cowards have
> That do outface it with their semblances [act 1, scene 3, 114–122].[5]

While it may be acceptable to assume that height and the presence of a curtle-axe and a boar spear would immediately identify their bearers as male, is it reasonable to assume that, without such easy referents, men and women would be indistinguishable? Is it that difficult to tell men and women apart? In these theatrical worlds at least, the players suggest that it is indeed a surprisingly difficult task. How you appear in dress and gesture is more important than any essential qualities that may exist, especially in the world of the theater, where single-sex casts were the norm. This problem of reliance on appearances is also expressed in the final four lines of the "Poem of Mulan," which notes that, while there may in fact be physical characteristics that reveal which is male and which female, these slight and marginally expressed characteristics are obscured in action. The male and female hare run equally fast, side by side, and are indistinguishable, just as Mulan fighting in a male army is not identified as a woman: "The male hare wildly kicks its feet; the female hare has shifty eyes,/But when a pair of hares runs side by side,/Who can distinguish whether I in fact am male or female?"[6] This sentiment, and the use of animal imagery to make the point, is echoed in Mulan's closing song at the play's end:

（旦）　MULAN [*sings*]:

【尾】　*Coda*

我做女兒則十七歲，　I was a woman till I was seventeen,

做男兒倒十二年。　Was a man another twelve years.

經過了萬千瞧，　I passed under thousands of glances,

那一個解雌雄辨？　Who among them could tell cock from hen?

方信道辨雌雄的不靠眼。　Now I know that to tell cock from hen, don't trust your eyes.

黑山尖是誰霸佔，　Who was it that really occupied Black Mountain top?

木蘭女替爺徵戰。　The girl Mulan went to war for her Pop.

世間事多少糊塗，　The affairs of the world are all such a mess,

院本打雌雄不辨。　This comedy mixed cock and hen all up!

[*XWJ* 4:1206; trans. Kwa, 186–187]

Rosalind exploited the homoerotic potentials afforded by a history of conventional types. Ganymede represents the barely mature and feminine young man, who could be admired without censure by the men around him. When Malvolio looks at Viola, dressed up as a man and calling herself Cesario, in Shakespeare's comedy *Twelfth Night*, he, too, notes that Cesario is

Not yet old enough for a man, nor young
enough for a boy; as a squash is before 'tis a peascod, or
a codling when 'tis almost an apple: 'tis with him in
standing water, between boy and man. He is very well-
favoured and he speaks very shrewishly; one would
think his mother's milk were scarce out of him [act 1, scene 5, 156–161].[7]

The homoerotic potential of the beautiful boy is suggested in Xu Wei's play as well. Mulan, disguised as a young man who calls herself by her father's name, Hua Hu, joins two young men to journey to the battlefield. Although the men do not suspect that she is a woman, they nonetheless think of her as a potential sexual object. "Hua Hu" is thus subjected to the leering scrutiny of her fellow soldiers, who see "him" as a potential dalliance. The two traveling companions remark to each other:

（二軍私云）這花弧，倒生得好個模樣兒，倒不像個長官，倒是個秫秫，明日倒好拿來應應急。

TWO SOLDIERS *speak privately*: This Hua Hu doesn't look bad at all. He doesn't look like a senior officer, but he'd be a nice morsel. Tomorrow we can take him to meet our needs.

[*XWJ* 4:1201; trans. Kwa, 176]

Fortunately, over the course of the play, they never manage to do so. Mulan laments her constant peril in the following excerpt:

（旦）	MULAN [*sings*]:
【六么序】	*To the tune "Liuyao xu"*
百忙裡跨馬登鞍，	In great haste, I mount my horse, astride the saddle.
靴插金鞭，	In my boots I plant a golden whip,
腳踹銅環，	My feet push against the bronze rings,
丟下針尖，	Dropping the needle's point,
掛上弓弦。	I've slung on my strung bow.
未逢人先準備彎腰見，	Before I meet anyone, I first prepare to bow to him with a bend at the waist,
使不得站堂堂矬倒裙邊。	No more curtsying like I did in women's skirts.
不怕他鴛鴦作對求姻眷，	I don't fear the mandarin ducks becoming a pair and asking for marriage,
只愁這水火熬煎，	I'm only concerned about the bother of bathroom needs,
這些兒要使機關。	I need a ruse.

[*XWJ* 4:1201; trans. Kwa, 177]

The difficulties of masquerading as a man are ever present, and most dangerous of all is the potential of exposing her body to her male companions, as when using the toilet. Later, in act 2, before Mulan has revealed her true identity, the soldiers remark upon the strange behavior of Hua Hu and his refusal to relieve himself in front of them. Instead of assuming that their fellow soldier has something to hide, however, they interpret the behavior in a different context, assuming that this is the mark of "Brother Hua's" gentility. Class, then, is a way of understanding why Mulan would hide herself from the others. Although the men had congratulated themselves for their ability to reveal Leopard Skin, the more uncomfortable provocations of Mulan's sex remain hidden among them.

6.5 MULAN: HAPPILY EVER AFTER

The armor that Mulan wears to serve as "Hua Hu" in battle not only protects her from the enemy and allows her to present herself as a man, but it also works to preserve her so-called true identity as the young and maidenly girl whom we first meet at the beginning of the play. Mulan mysteriously hints at the true reason for her concealment, but she succeeds in returning to her home village without revealing anything about her true sex. As with her earlier references to Qin Xiu and Tiying, she invokes earlier exemplars to simultaneously disavow the radical nature of her actions while acknowledging her unusual behavior, when she responds to her peers who find it queer that they have never seen Hua Hu urinate:

（旦）　　　MULAN [*sings*]:

【前腔】　　*Reprise*

我花弧有什麼真希罕，　　How am I, Hua Hu, so queer?

希罕的還有一件。　　Of queer things, I only know of one!

俺家緊隔壁那廟兒里，　　Right next to my home, in a temple,

泥塑一金剛，　　There is a fearsome guardian statue whose face

忽變做嫦娥面。　　Suddenly changed into Chang'e's!

你不信到家時我引你去看。　　If you don't believe me, when we reach my home I will take you to see it.

[*XWJ* 4:1204; trans. Kwa, 182]

By comparing herself first to historical precedents who took on heroic roles on behalf of their fathers, and finally comparing herself to a religious icon possessing magical abilities, Mulan adopts the pose of what nowadays we call the "humble-brag." The soldiers who have traveled home with her are amazed and cry out:

（二軍忙跑上）花大爺，你原來是個女兒。俺們與你過活十二年，都不知道一些兒。原來你路上說的金剛變嫦娥，就是這個謎子，此豈不是千古的奇事，留與四海揚名，萬人作念麼。

TWO SOLDIERS *hurriedly running enter* [*and speak*]: Sir Hua! You were a girl all along! We lived with you for a dozen years, and none of us found you out. So! It turns out that this was the riddle of the fearsome guardian statue who turned into Chang'e that you spoke of on the road! You are a great wonder for all time, and your story will be known the world over. Everyone will remember you!

[*XWJ* 4:1205; trans. Kwa, 184]

Mulan sanguinely claims that, after all, these remarkable actions were not really her own. They are merely an illusion that did not cost her a drop of sweat. So, too, is the guardian statue in her hometown temple an illusion. Whether legends about that statue exist at all is never pursued in the slightest because her companions know that, in fact, Mulan herself is this miraculous transformer.

The play's conclusion, in which Mulan is betrothed to the village's most eligible bachelor, is, like the marriages at the end of her Shakespearean counterparts' plays, the only possible satisfying ending according to the conventions of comedy. A young male lead (*sheng*) enters, playing the neighbor, Mr. Wang. He wears the official cap and girdle that Mulan herself had been awarded when she was assumed to be a man. Unlike Mulan, however, he does not get a word in edgewise. Apart from bowing in greeting, he is treated like just another prop in the play. Mulan's mother quickly intercedes: "Mr. Wang, . . . please hold your greetings! I have just looked at the almanac for an auspicious day. You two are as old as cast bronze and elephants,[8] so let's make ourselves a family today! Quick, quick, bow and greet each other!" [*XWJ* 4:1205, trans. Kwa, 185–186]. The haste with which this resolution is performed speaks greater volumes than Mulan's sanguine take on her lack of accomplishments. While marriage may be the expected outcome of comedies such as these, what the playwright and his audiences choose to dwell on are the feats of physical and mental prowess demonstrated by the girl Mulan, who went to war in her father's place. The clothes may change, but Mulan stays the same—and so does our enjoyment and appreciation.

Shiamin Kwa

NOTES

1. Anonymous, "Mulan shi" ("Poem of Mulan"), in *Yuefu shiji* (The Poetry Collection of the Music Bureau) (Beijing: Zhonghua shuju, 1979), 373–375. It is translated in Shiamin Kwa and Wilt L. Idema, eds., *Mulan: Five Versions of a Classic Chinese Legend with Related Texts* (Indianapolis: Hackett, 2010), 1.

2. Xu Wei, *Ci Mulan ti fu cong jun* (The Female Mulan Joins the Army in Place of Her Father), *Sisheng yuan* (Four Cries of a Gibbon), *Guben xiqu congkan chuji* (First Set of the Collectanea of Classical Chinese Plays), vol. 77 (Shanghai: Shangwu yinshiguan, 1954), 30.

3. William Shakespeare, *The Merchant of Venice*, in *Oxford Shakespeare* (Oxford: Oxford University Press, 1993), 183.

4. Marjorie Garber, *Vested Interests: Cross-dressing and Cultural Anxiety* (New York: Routledge, 1992).

5. William Shakespeare, *As You Like It*, in *The Cambridge Dover Wilson Shakespeare* (Cambridge: Cambridge University Press, 2009), 21.

6. Anonymous, "Mulan shi," 375, trans. Kwa and Idema, *Mulan*, 3.

7. William Shakespeare, *Twelfth Night*, in *The Cambridge Dover Wilson Shakespeare*, 17.

8. "As old as cast bronze and elephants" is a contemporary turn of phrase indicating that someone is already past marrying age.

PRIMARY SOURCES

GXCC   Xu Wei 徐渭. *Ci Mulan ti fu cong jun* 雌木蘭替父從軍 (*The Female Mulan Joins the Army in Place of Her Father*). In *Sisheng yuan* 四聲猿 (*Four Cries of a Gibbon*), *Guben xiqu congkan chuji* 古本戲曲叢刊初集 (*First Set of the Collectanea of Classical Chinese Plays*), vol. 77, 27–37. Shanghai: Shangwu yinshuguan, 1954.

SSY   Xu Wei 徐渭. *Sisheng yuan, Gedai xiao (fu)* 四聲猿歌代嘯付 (*Four Cries of a Gibbon with the Play* Singing Instead of Whistling *Appended*). Ed. Zhou Zhongming 周中明. Shanghai: Shanghai guji chubanshe, 1984.

XWJ   Xu Wei 徐渭. *Xu Wei ji* 徐渭集 (*The Collected Works of Xu Wei*). 4 vols. Beijing: Zhonghua shuju, 1983.

SUGGESTED READINGS

TRANSLATIONS

Kwa, Shiamin, and Wilt L. Idema, ed. and trans. *Mulan: Five Versions of a Classic Chinese Legend, with Related Texts.* Indianapolis: Hackett, 2010.

Xu Wei. *The Female Mulan Joins the Army in Place of Her Father.* In *Strange Eventful Histories: Identity, Performance, and Xu Wei's Four Cries of a Gibbon,* introd. and trans. Shiamin Kwa, 169–187. Cambridge, MA: Harvard University Asia Center, 2012.

Xu Wei. *The Girl Graduate Rejects the Female Phoenix and Gains the Male Phoenix.* In *Strange Eventful Histories: Identity, Performance, and Xu Wei's Four Cries of a Gibbon,* introd. and trans. Shiamin Kwa, 189–239. Cambridge, MA: Harvard University Asia Center, 2012.

Xu Wei. *The Mad Drummer Plays the Yuyang Triple Rolls*. In *Strange Eventful Histories: Identity, Performance, and Xu Wei's* Four Cries of a Gibbon, introd. and trans. Shiamin Kwa, 117–138. Cambridge, MA: Harvard University Asia Center, 2012.

Xu Wei. *Zen Master Yu Has a Dream of Cuixiang*. In *Strange Eventful Histories: Identity, Performance, and Xu Wei's* Four Cries of a Gibbon, introd. and trans. Shiamin Kwa, 139–167. Cambridge, MA: Harvard University Asia Center, 2012.

ENGLISH

Garber, Marjorie. *Vested Interests: Cross-Dressing and Cultural Anxiety*. New York: Routledge, 1992.

Goldstein, Joshua. *Drama Kings: Players and Publics in the Re-creation of Peking Opera, 1870–1937*. Berkeley: University of California Press, 2007.

Li, Siu Leung. *Cross-Dressing in Chinese Opera*. Hong Kong: Hong Kong University Press, 2003.

CHINESE

Hu Ji 胡忌. "Beiqu zaju yanchangren xingbie de taolun" 北曲雜劇演唱人性別的討論 (On the Gender of Northern *Zaju* Drama Singers). *Wenxue yichan zengkan* 文學遺產增刊 (Literary Heritage Series Supplementary Issue). Vol. 1, 297–303. Beijing: Zuojia chubanshe, 1955.

Qi Shijun 戚世隽. *Mingdai zaju yanjiu* 明代雜劇研究 (*A Study of Ming Dynasty* Zaju *Plays*). Guangzhou, China: Guangdong gaoji jiaoyu chubanshe, 2001.

Xu Zifang 徐子方. *Ming zaju shi* 明雜劇史 (*A History of Ming* Zaju *Plays*). Beijing: Zhonghua shuju, 2003.

PART II

Ming Dynasty and Early Qing Dynasty

Nanxi and *Chuanqi* Plays

Top Graduate Zhang Xie and *The Lute*

Scholar, Family, and State

In 1920, the scholar Ye Gongchuo (1881–1968), rummaging through a secondhand bookstore in London, discovered a copy of an earlier, long-lost volume of the *Great Canon of the Yongle Era* (*Yongle dadian*), a compendium of texts assembled by imperial commission and finished in 1408.[1] This was an extraordinary find: this volume contained what turned out to be the three oldest extant southern dramas (*nanxi*). Two of them, *Little Butcher Sun* (*Xiao Sun tu*) and *A Playboy from a Noble House Opts for the Wrong Career* (☞ chap. 2), were adaptations of northern plays; the remaining one, *Top Graduate Zhang Xie* (*Zhang Xie zhuangyuan*, hereafter *Top Graduate*), proved to be the earliest complete text composed in the southern tradition.[2]

While *Top Graduate* is the first *complete* text of southern drama, we have snippets of information from earlier periods that hint at the emergence of this new form of entertainment. From the late Song and early Yuan dynasties onward, we find offhand remarks by music aficionados regarding a musical form in the area around the thriving city of Wenzhou (Zhejiang province), alternatively called Yongjia[3] song-drama (Yongjia *xiqu*) and playtexts (*xiwen*). According to these remarks, this musical form used a distinctive manner of singing, breathing, and pronunciation. It also told a complete story and required specialized performers.[4] These earlier references inform us that from the late Song or early Yuan dynasty onward, in the southeastern region of China, a popular musical and narrative art was on the rise. However, such incidental observations tell us little else about the form: How was it performed? Did it use role-types, characters, and dialogue, or did it utilize costumes? All of these are essential elements of what we now call Chinese theater.

The first significant discussion of southern drama as an art form is a mid-sixteenth-century study entitled *A Record of Southern Songs* (*Nanci xulu*, 1559, hereafter *Record*), attributed to the playwright and painter Xu Wei (1521–1593) (☞ chap. 6). *Record*, already far removed from the three plays under consideration, is a synthesis of observations about a variety of aspects of southern drama, including its origins, canonical texts, authors, musical organization, play composition, prosody, singing and pronunciation, and linguistic register. It also includes a glossary of terms and an explanation of differences from other styles. It is, in essence, an attempt at establishing southern drama as an independent genre, with its own set of distinctive musical and literary values. That Xu Wei felt the need to write such a work to vindicate southern drama as a high art suggests that, at least by the mid-sixteenth century, it was a popular art form that had not yet captured the interest of the literati as a whole.

7.1 *TOP GRADUATE* AND *THE LUTE*: BACKGROUND

In this chapter, I will discuss and compare two plays. The first, *Top Graduate Zhang Xie*, was written by members of a writing club in Wenzhou called the Nine Mountain Society (Jiushan shuhui). These urban writing clubs were composed of educated members of society, such as entry-level licentiates, clerks, and so forth, about whom we know very little. Its members were known as men of talent (*cairen*) and were believed to work in close relation with performers.[5] The date for this text is contested: because of internal references in the play to the Imperial Music Academy (*Jiaofang*) and to the famed Crimson and Green Troupe (Feilü she) of Hangzhou comedians, as well as certain linguistic uses, scholars have placed the date of this play in the Southern Song period.[6] But other scholars, while accepting that the story may have circulated in some form at an earlier date, demonstrate—on the basis of its tune composition (i.e., tunes that did not appear elsewhere before the Yuan)—that the play was thoroughly revised, if not entirely composed, in the Yuan dynasty. The other play under consideration here is *The Lute* (*Pipa ji*), by the playwright Gao Ming (ca. 1305–ca. 1370), an official from Rui'an (Zhejiang province). This is the first individually authored play in the southern tradition and is considered *the* foundational work of southern *chuanqi* theater.

While we do not know the precise date of composition of either play, scholars have assumed that *Top Graduate*, the less refined play, came first. The evidence for this order of precedence is shaky, but for simplicity's sake, I will follow suit and treat these two plays in that order.

Both plays belong to a type of story known as the "ungrateful scholar story." Generally, in these stories, an ambitious and talented young scholar goes to the capital to take the imperial exams, leaving his family and recently married wife behind. Once he passes the exams as top graduate, he becomes the most desirable husband for the young daughters of marriageable age among the political elite in the capital. Lured by the beauty of these young girls and excited by the favorable political prospects of such an alliance, the young scholar remarries, abandoning his former wife and aging parents to their fate.

But both *Top Graduate* and *The Lute* diverge from the standard story in important ways. Zhang Xie is not yet married when he leaves his home. On the way to the capital, he is robbed and beaten by a bandit and is forced to spend some time in a village temple to recover. There, he meets Pinnü (Poorlass), an orphaned girl of elite birth who takes care of him with the assistance of two villagers, the Lis. In a moment of gratitude, Zhang Xie marries her, but he immediately regrets it, mumbling to himself that this was not part of his original plan. When he is restored to health, Pinnü sells her hair to raise money so that he can continue his journey to the capital to take the exams. Zhang Xie passes the exams as top graduate and is asked by Prime Minister Wang Deyong to marry his daughter, Shenghua, but he refuses, explaining that he must first consult with his parents. His decision has terrible consequences for both the daughter of the prime minister, who dies of shame, and for himself, because the prime minister swears to avenge his daughter.

The Lute, on the other hand, introduces us to Cai Bojie, an extremely talented scholar and a paragon of filiality and righteousness. Cai has been married for only two months when the imperial exams are announced. Because his parents are both in their eighties, he decides to stay home to care for them, but his father pressures him to go to the capital and take the exams to eventually improve their status in life. Once Cai passes as top graduate, Prime Minister Niu coerces him into marrying his daughter and, with some assistance from the emperor himself, to take up an official post at court. Cai tries to decline both marriage and office, arguing that he needs to fulfill his filial duties and return home to his aging parents and first wife, but he is not allowed to do so and becomes downhearted. Meanwhile, a great famine ravages his hometown, and despite the many efforts of his first wife, Zhao Wuniang, to feed her parents-in-law, they both die. After she buries them, and with no more familial responsibilities to attend to, she resolves to go to the capital to find her husband, playing the lute along the way to provide for herself. Eventually, Wuniang finds him. Mistress Niu (Niu shi), who now knows what has been troubling Cai Bojie, accepts his former wife, and they all return to Cai Bojie's natal village to pay their respects to Cai's dead parents.

Top Graduate is important because as the precursor of *chuanqi*, the mature southern tradition, it includes all the basic structural elements of what we now consider fully formed theater: the performance of a story by an actor through song and dance (gestures) and by means of dialogue.[7] *Top Graduate* is also important for its treatment of the ungrateful scholar theme and for what it can tell us about early depictions of scholars and their ambitions. *The Lute*, on the other hand, became the quintessential model for later *chuanqi* playwrights. Its function as an archetype sparked long debates over the literary and performing functions of drama, most notably on drama's power to disseminate ideas and promote specific values, but also on the aural nature of its dramatic language—that is, how language had to sound to be understood by all. *The Lute* introduced in its prologue the correct moral tenor of a dramatic piece, shifting the aim of southern drama from a leisurely activity intended to entertain, to one where entertainment was fused with instruction, such that the characters in the play became virtuous models held up for emulation for elites and commoners alike. As the first southern play to be associated with an individual author's name, *The Lute* also reflects the values of a group of men of letters more directly, including a defense of theater as a legitimate form of elite entertainment.

Comparing *Top Graduate* to *The Lute* is useful because it allows us to see the transformation from *Top Graduate*, a play that presents itself as urban and urbane, to *The Lute*, exalted and admired by the literati for the propagation of Confucian values and its aesthetic refinement. To be sure, *Top Graduate* was a play included in an imperial encyclopedia, and it most likely underwent editorial changes to make it conform to then-current editorial practices and, to an extent, ideological principles. But its imperial pedigree notwithstanding, the values that this play propounds in its observations of the literati class, the principles of education, its commentary on the examination system, and the imperfect moral acumen of the scholar are very different from those exemplified in *The Lute*.

These texts, however, are also rather similar in two respects. Thematically, the plays homogeneously depict women (especially the main female role) as models of exemplary virtue and endurance on the one hand and as the victims of male ambition on the other (☛ chap. 3). They are also very similar in structure, specifically in the balance between serious and comic scenes, the musical organization of the arias, and the use of the role system. Thus, two ways to read *Top Graduate* and *The Lute* are to trace their literary function and value from "leisure" to "leisure-plus-moral," and from a critique of the scholar to an art that includes social critique and reflects the aesthetic preferences of the literati.

7.2 *TOP GRADUATE* AND *THE LUTE*: THE PROLOGUES

The prologues—the two declaimed poems of introduction—to both *Top Graduate* and *The Lute* are important, as they establish the intention and theme of the plays. These are recited by an additional male *mo* role (at times called *fumo*), who, in addition to playing a number of characters, has the function of mediating with other roles. This role can be patronizing, expressing a sense of moral superiority, especially in the comic sections. In *Top Graduate*, the male *mo* role enters the stage and addresses the audience to deliver—through a series of images on nature—the ubiquitous trope on the transience of life and humanity's inescapable fate, while encouraging the company to make the most of this moment of leisure to fully enjoy the play:

末（上）白	ADDITIONAL MALE *as* TROUPE LEADER *enters and declaims*:
【水調歌頭】	*To the tune* "Shuidiao getou"
韶華催白髮，	The passing of youth hastens the onset of white hair,
光景改朱容。	And time dims our rosy cheeks.
人生浮世，	Our lives float by,
渾如萍梗逐東西。	Like duckweed stems drifting east and west.

[*ZXZY* 1, scene 1; trans. Llamas, 89]

In the second stanza of the same poem, we are informed that it is not a performance by professional actors, but rather a show put on by "sons of good families" and theater aficionados. Although amateur actors could be excellent performers, and their status as "sons of good families" is no proof of deficiency, their nonprofessional standing could still be one reason why the troupe stresses the proficiency of the actors and the resources of the troupe:

（末）	TROUPE LEADER [*declaims*]:
【水調歌頭】	*To the tune* "Shuidiao getou"
但咱們雖宦裔，	Although we are sons of good families,
總皆通。	We can do it all.

彈絲品竹，	We are equally versed in the plucking of strings and the blowing of pipes,
那堪咏月與嘲風。	And even sing of the moon and jest with the wind.[8]
苦會插科使砌，	We are especially good at inserting comic skits and cracking jokes,
何吝搽灰抹土，	And we are not stingy with the white powder and lime,
歌笑滿堂中。	So, our songs fill the hall with laughter.
一似長江千尺浪，	Yes, exactly like the Yangzi with its thousand-foot rolling waves,
別是一家風。	We have our own particular style of performance.[9]

[*ZXZY* 1, scene 1; trans. Llamas, 90]

The male *mo* role addresses a boisterous public, calling on them to quiet down in order to promote the benchmark by which the troupe is to be judged. They promise to entertain their audience with an "endless flow of songs and jokes," thus delineating the core elements of their performance. The troupe's appeal to the audience is based on three elements: their virtuoso instrumental abilities, their novel songs in a repertoire of romantic stories, and their cutting-edge comic skills. Despite their amateur status, they promise that their musical performance will be on a par with the professional musicians of the Imperial Music Bureau, and that their production of comedy will rival that of the Crimson and Green, the famous Song dynasty troupe of comedians from the then-capital of Hangzhou. The generous application of face paint (white powder and lime) indicates the excellence of their facial designs, but it perhaps also denotes higher standards of costuming and props or a more spectacular performance overall. Above all, the introduction is conceived *as if* it were a marketing ploy designed to attract the audience not to a new play, but to a novel and better version of a familiar one:

末(再)白	TROUPE LEADER *declaims again*:
【滿庭芳】	*To the tune* "Manting fang"
暫息喧嘩，	Let this hubbub rest for a while,
略停笑語，	Hold your laughing banter,
試看別樣門庭。	And fix your attention on this distinctive tradition.
教坊格范，	We play in the style of the Music Bureau,
緋綠可同聲。	And are really comparable to the Crimson and Green.
酬酢詞源譚砌。	We promise to entertain you with our endless flow of songs and jokes;
聽談論四座皆驚。	All of you will marvel at our disquisition.

[*ZXZY* 2, scene 1; trans. Llamas, 90]

The male *mo* role notes that this is not a new play, but a newer and more recent version of an older and probably well known version of the same one: "Your people have performed the *Biography of Top Graduate Zhang Xie (Zhuangyuan Zhang Xie zhuan)*, and performed it successfully" [ZXZY 2, scene 1; trans. Llamas, 90]. And he adds that the performance is part of a competition between groups of amateur performers. These statements on musical competence, comic inventiveness, better makeup, and creative revision of a familiar play are all repeated again in a second prologue in scene 2 by the main male role (*sheng*) as he assumes the character of Zhang Xie.

The similarity of the material of these two first prologues certainly indicates revision—that one prologue (probably the former) is drawing on the other. Both the reiteration of skills in the prologue and the retelling of a past familiar tale also illustrate that already in *Top Graduate*, great importance was placed on the aesthetics of *performance* (music and comedy), perhaps to the detriment of the fashioning of a new narrative. In sum, the prologue to *Top Graduate* clearly professes to present the audience with a familiar story while reassuring them of its originality and variation. It describes a troupe in an urban competition promoting a spectacle to an audience that cheerfully awaits the beginning of a performance that promises, above all else, to keep them entertained. But whether this prologue describes the reality of the play's own staging or whether it was something added later for aesthetic effect is unknown to us.

The preface to *The Lute*, on the other hand, presents a very different vision of the theatrical experience. In contrast to *Top Graduate's* raucous opening scene, where the *mo* asks the audience to quiet down, *The Lute* introduces us to a serene autumnal scene, where a scholar is sitting undisturbed in his studio by the night lamp, perusing volumes of stories:

副（末）上　ADDITIONAL MALE *as* TROUPE LEADER *enters [and declaims]*:

【水調歌頭】　*To the tune* "Shuidiao getou"

秋燈明翠幕，　The autumn lantern illuminates the emerald-colored curtains;

夜案覽芸編。　By my night table, I browse through the rue-scented volumes.

今來古往，　From ancient times to this day,

期間故事幾多般。　There have been countless types of stories.

少甚佳人才子，　Mostly concerned with beautiful ladies and talented men,

也有神仙幽怪，　But also with gods and immortals and the mysterious and strange,

瑣碎不堪觀。　All of them of little importance and not worth reading.

正是:不關風化體，　Indeed, a genre unconcerned with moral teachings,

縱好也徒然。　No matter how good it may be, is of little worth.

論傳奇，	As for plays,
樂人易，	It is easy to please people,
動人難。	But hard to move them.
知音君子，	Discerning gentlemen,
這般另作眼兒看。	In this instance, look at the play with new eyes.
休論插科打諢，	Let us not discuss slapstick or jokes,
也不尋宮數調，	And search not for the keys or the various modes.
只看子孝共妻賢。	Just look at the filial son and his virtuous wife.
正是驊騮方獨步，	Truly, the fine steed Hualiu walks alone,
萬馬敢爭先。	For the ten thousand horses would not dare outpace it.

[*PPJ* 1–2, scene 1, "Prologue" ("Fumo kaichang")]

The scholar, reflecting on the nature of past and present stories on romance, gods and the supernatural—all literary writings designed to amuse—reaches the conclusion that stories read for pleasure also need to illustrate moral principle. All stories must serve as models to their readers and instruct on how to improve human conduct. In both plays, the story, together with music and comedy, are the three pillars around which the performance is built and what the audience enthusiastically anticipates as the core of their entertainment. But *The Lute*, in its Confucian discomfort with amoral forms of leisure, forewarns its audience against taking pleasure in or paying excessive attention to music. In the classical Confucian view, music was precariously positioned: if restrained, it could act as an instrument of moral education and as a means to harmonize society, but if excessive and dissolute, it became a corrupting and decadent influence. If the principal aspiration of the playwright was to sway the moral behavior of the audience through an exemplary tale of filial piety and loyalty, then overt attention to music, like comedy, detracted from this goal. In this way, the prologue established a division between the message conveyed through the language and performance of roles and characters in the play and the other two stalwarts of dramatic entertainment: music and comedy. In contrast to *Top Graduate*, where music and comedy were promoted as pure amusement, *The Lute* cajoled the audience to take pleasure in moral paragons, thus giving pride of place to edifying subject matter.

The Lute's prologue was instrumental in formulating the principles underlying the function of drama as a moral force designed to move the audience and influence social and popular customs. Charged with such lofty ideals, a good play was to recount stories with a virtuous subject matter that illustrated values such as filial piety, righteousness, chastity, and loyalty. If the story was successful and its audience moved, it showed that the moral principle had penetrated the innermost recesses of the human heart. Because theater was one medium through which these stories could be transmitted and reach a large segment of the population, plays like *The Lute* exhorted the audience to be more attentive to the virtues of the main protagonists, reminding them not to be remiss in their observance of

Confucian standards and consistently abide by such ideals. In other words, moral teachings could effectively constitute the highest aim of drama.

The differences between *Top Graduate* and *The Lute* mark a transformation in southern dramatic values from drama as entertainment with a critical perspective to drama as entertainment with a critical perspective plus instruction. While southern theater never stopped providing pleasure and distraction where a tired audience could forget the worries of everyday life, it also became a place of reflection, where this same audience could learn about human nature and correct behavior. When *The Lute* succinctly informs the audience that unless a play transmits Confucian values, it is unworthy of attention, it exposes the uneasy relationship between the popular pleasures of comic indulgence and the edifying pleasures of Confucian morality. What made the moral aspects of such a play particularly compelling were the Confucian dilemmas that the characters had to confront (➨ chap. 3).

7.3 *TOP GRADUATE* AND *THE LUTE*: THE UNGRATEFUL SCHOLAR

Top Graduate and *The Lute* form part of a group of southern plays that deal with the competing demands placed on the imperial examination candidates by family and state, respectively. The stories typically begin when the scholar, having expressed his desire to hold office and to serve the emperor, is prepared to leave for the capital to take the imperial examination. As he is about to depart, his parents send him off with words of caution and advice, urging him to be alert on the dangerous road to the capital. They also warn the scholar not to be distracted from his studies by the lure of the capital's excitement and entertainment.

It is interesting to read these plays in terms of how they present the conflicting demands placed on the figure of the scholar. On the one hand, the civil service examination required well-prepared students to administer the state. This path entailed an investment by the scholar and his parents of many years of dedicated learning. If the scholar succeeded in the imperial examination, he would become part of a small elite of influential men who assisted the ruler in government. High office brought the scholar social prestige, as well as some wealth and access to power, but the family also benefited from a young graduate's success. For example, immediately after the initial prologue of *Top Graduate*, there is an introductory chantefable (*zhugongdiao*)[10] (➨ chap. 1), in which Zhang Xie informs his parents of his desire to go to the capital to take the exams. As soon as the parents hear of their son's intentions, they react with disconsolate tears, much to the dismay of their son: "Their son said: 'After ten years of mastering the civil and military arts, this year I finally get to sell them to the imperial house. I want to change your status in life and requite your kindness, so why must you weep!' " [ZXZY 2, scene 1; trans. Llamas, 91-92].

The son's undertone of exasperation reflects the weight of contractual relationships inherent in filial piety. The parents have nurtured their son and supported him in his studies, and they in turn hope that their son's success will raise the family status (*huan menlü*) and bring the family honor and fame. Filial duty in these two plays is undisputed: Zhang Xie will turn out to be an unscrupulous rogue, but even he remains a filial and devoted son. Cai Bojie, the scholar in *The Lute*, meets with powerful forces beyond his control and tragically cannot take care of his parents, but he aspired to be a filial son.

Familial obligations placed on the scholar were not limited to bringing distinction to the family; the son was also responsible for the continuation of the lineage, as well as caring for his aging parents. If anything happened to the scholar on the way to the capital or if he were diverted from his studies, the family fortunes would decline. Indeed, limiting the families in these plays to this one single son amplified quite effectively the hopes and expectations, as well as the burden, placed on these figures. This one scholar was the family's only chance at improving its standing, and he was the catalyst of all aspirations, familial and otherwise.

While the plots of the stories may differ, most plays show this tension between public duty and familial interests. For example, in *The Lute*, the scholar Cai Bojie is recommended by local officials to go to the capital and take his exams. While his father and neighbor support the officials' suggestion—after all, this is the purpose of his studies and the occasion that they have all been waiting for—Cai is torn between leaving and staying, concerned about the advanced age of his parents (who are in their eighties). So, after some consideration, he resolves to stay home and take care of them. Cai Bojie is aware of this conflict when he notes:

（生）蔡邕沈酣六籍，貫串百家。。。幼而學，壯而行，雖望青雲之萬里；入則孝，出則弟，怎離白髮之雙親？到不如盡菽水之歡，甘虀鹽之分。

YOUNG MALE *as* CAI BOJIE [*speaks*]: Steeped in the Six Classics, I have mastered the philosophy of the Hundred Schools of Thought. . . . It is said that when young one should study, and in maturity one should put it into practice, thus I long for those far away azure clouds [of high office]. But it is also said that in the home we should be filial to our parents, and in the community, deferential to our elders, so how could I leave the side of my white-haired parents? It is better to remain here and enjoy the simple pleasures of water and beans, and to willingly accept my meager lot of pickles and salt.

[*PPJ* 6–7, scene 2, "Celebrating the Longevity of the Parents" ("Gaotang chengshou")]

But his father insists he sit for the exams: "Son,/I only hope that those yellowing books and that dark green lamp/will soon be exchanged for a golden seal and purple ribbons" [*PPJ* 8, scene 2]. The mother frets over safety, stability, and the continuation of the family line: "Daughter-in-law,/I only hope that those linked branches of your glorious spring years,/will soon put forth new buds and flourish" [*PPJ* 8, scene 2]. Yet both parents are equally aware of the benefits should their son pass the exams, as the mother notes:

（淨上唱）	COMIC *as* MOTHER *enters and sings:*
【吳小四】	*To the tune* "Wu Xiaosi"
眼兒昏，	My sight is dim,
耳又聾，	And my ears are deaf;
家私空又空。	Our family owns no property, none.
只有孩兒肚內聰，	All we have is our son's abundant cleverness,
他若做得官時運通，	So when he becomes an official our fate will take a turn,
我兩人不怕窮。	And we will never fear poverty again![11]

[*YBPPJ* 37, scene 4, "Father Cai Presses His Son to Take the Examinations" ("Caigong bishi")]

In the end, the scholar leaves for the capital, with devastating consequences for the family and the subsequent destabilization of harmonious social relations.

The most interesting aspect in the comparison of the figure of the scholar in these two plays is the critique of the scholar that appears in *Top Graduate*. Judging from extant fragments of information, there was a great degree of homogeneity in the description of the ungrateful scholar in earlier theater, where the scholar was often portrayed in a negative light. One reason why the denunciation of the scholar may have been so prominent in these earlier plays could be the fact that at the time when *Top Graduate* was included in the *Great Canon*, the civil service elite was not established (the examination system was permanently reinstated in 1384), and the literati shared their power with a military nobility.[12] It is open to question if a text like *Top Graduate*—no matter how popular the story was or how representative of a popular literary genre—with its audacious condemnation of the immoral and uncivil scholar, would have been accepted in an imperial collectanea any time after 1435, when civil service graduates dominated court politics. In all probability, it would have been considered a provocation of the civil elite. Thus, *Top Graduate* is a textual gem for drama historians, in that it affords a glimpse of the representation of the scholar before such satire was expunged (though never entirely) from the theatrical corpus.

There are two instances in this play that are representative of the characterization of the ungrateful scholar: on the road to the capital to take his exams, Zhang Xie is robbed by a bandit who beats him unconscious. When he comes to, the mountain gods direct him to a temple where the main female role in the play (*dan*), Pinnü, a young orphan from a good family, resides. Pinnü nurtures him back to health, and in gratitude for her care and devotion, Zhang Xie marries her. To help him cover the cost of his trip to the capital, Pinnü cuts her hair and sells it to her neighbor, Grandma Li, who offers her a glass of wine to alleviate her distress. When she returns to the temple, Zhang Xie, impatient and angry, accuses her of indulging in wine and the pursuit of pleasure and beats her mercilessly. As she explains the circumstances to Zhang Xie, Pinnü comments: "Husband, you are a person in search of success and fame; don't act like this" [*ZXZY* 104-111, scene 20; trans. Llamas, 206], implying that scholars should be constrained by higher moral standards and control their temper.

Once Zhang Xie passes the exams and becomes the top graduate, he is sought after as son-in-law to the prime minister for his only daughter, Shenghua. However, Zhang Xie refuses to marry her and complains of the abuse of the weak by the powerful:

(生唱)	YOUNG MALE *as* ZHANG XIE *sings:*
【同前】	*Reprise*
求名我不在求妻，	I am looking for fame, not for a wife,
歡諧事心未喜。	And my heart is not yet inclined toward the joys of marriage.
豪家謾把絲鞭刺。	When a powerful house rudely thrusts the silk whip upon us,[13]
甚嬌媚又入人意。	How can any beauty appeal to a man's fancy!

[*ZXZY* 135, scene 27; trans. Llamas, 242]

When the prime minister's daughter learns that she has been rejected, she dies of shame. In the meantime, Pinnü hears of Zhang Xie's success and travels to the capital, only to be rejected by the now-successful Zhang Xie, who, humiliated by Pinnü's appearance, has her thrown out of the *yamen*. When he is later appointed to the post of notary of Zizhou, he resolves to pass through the old temple and kill Pinnü in order to "pull up trouble by the roots, lest it sprouts again next spring [*ZXZY* 174, scene 40; trans. Llamas, 295]." But Zhang Xie's plans do not entirely succeed, and matters take an unexpected turn.

While *Top Graduate* presents the imperial exams as the legitimate means of access to power, it also questions whether education serves any purpose other than as an instrument of government, as a means to an end. In the Confucian view, learning served to realize one's moral nature and study was a lifelong process by which one improved one's mind for the sake of individual growth, not social advancement. But if learning the classics was a means to improve a person's principled behavior, many of these "ungrateful scholar" plays represent study not as an instrument of moral self-cultivation, but as a means to a more practical end: power, status, and fame. Zhang Xie's actions do not reflect the standards of behavior or responsibility expected of the ideal scholar; on the contrary, the play presents a scholar solely interested in fame and status.

This utilitarian view of education is not evident in *The Lute*, where ethical incompatibilities of the sociopolitical code create insurmountable frictions. In what is popularly known as the "Three Objections" (*san bucong*), Cai Bojie is reluctant to leave his parents and wife to attend the examinations, but male ambition and familial duty compel him to do so; once he becomes a laureate, he is unwilling to take up his post, but imperial command forces him to do so; and when he resists the pressure to marry the daughter of the prime minister, once again, political pressure forces his hand:

（生唱）	YOUNG MALE *as* CAI BOJIE *sings*:
【二犯漁家傲】	*To the tune* "Erfan yujia ao"
被親強來赴選場，	Forced by father to attend the examinations,
被君強官為議郎，	Forced by ruler to serve as counselor,
被婚強傚鸞凰。	Forced to marry and to follow the example of the phoenix and simurgh.
三被強，	Forced against my will three times,
我衷腸事說與誰行？	But to whom can I bare my innermost thoughts?

[*PPJ* 169, scene 24, "Fretting in the Official Mansion" ("Huandi yousi")]

The play illustrates the scholar's paragon—the filial and dutiful son, talented scholar, principled administrator, loyal official, and responsible husband—showing not just that the conflicting familial and sociopolitical demands placed on the scholar were impracticable, but that when competing against imperial power, the government's demands take precedence. The moral scholar's resistance to the strong-arm tactics of the state was not effective, and there were critics who viewed Cai not as the fulcrum of societal demands or the epitome of morality and filial conduct, but simply as weak.

Criticism of *The Lute* often centers on the flaws in the plot (the strangely advanced old age of the parents, Cai's inability to send a letter, and so forth), and we can never be sure if the critique is leveled at Cai or if it is a by-product of the story's deficiencies.[14] But the fragility of the main male character may well have been Gao Ming's intention all along, as Cai notes at the beginning of scene 4, perhaps in reference to his own struggle: "In this world, good things are never strong;/ rainbow clouds are easily scattered and porcelain is fragile" [*PPJ* 31, scene 4]. While scholars are either remiss or conflicted with regard to their performance of moral duties, the women in their lives were singularly consistent in their moral conduct.

7.4 *THE LUTE:* THE HUSK WIFE

Women are the scholar's match and are used in contrast to their male counterparts, as a means to call attention to the moral qualities distinctive to both roles. Typically, there are three dominant women in these plays and a host of other minor female roles in the form of servants, innkeepers, and the like: the main female role (*dan*), the second female role (*tie*), and the mother or mother-in-law (a comic *jing*). The character played by the second female role is an only daughter, a young eligible woman of high social status, great beauty, elevated moral principles, and delicate refinement. She is the passive tool of male aspirations—of her father, who wishes to marry his only offspring to the top imperial candidate; and of the scholar, intent on shortening his ascent to power through marriage to the daughter of the highest-ranking official. They are as much the victims of competing ambitions as the first wives of scholars. Mothers, mothers-in-law, and old women are in most cases performed by comic roles (a *jing* in *The Lute*, and a *jing* for Grandmother Li in *Top Graduate*, but Shenghua's mother is a *wai*) and deployed to voice the underlying tensions—often of a commercial or practical nature—of male/female decisions, such as the benefits of the son changing the family status. But by far, the most important female role in these plays is the main wife (*dan*).

The main female role is an archetype of virtue and endurance, and as the protagonist, she is also the backbone of the play (☞ chap. 3). It is her predicament that we follow, her cause that we advocate, and in the denouement to the story, it is her gain that we seek. Her plight is established from the beginning by contrasting male ambitions and their desire for status and fame, which generally disrupts the familial order and imperils the family lineage, with the female order, which seeks to guard the stability and continuation of the family lineage. She has been married to the scholar for only a short time before he has to leave for the capital. She is known as the "husk wife" (*zaokang fu*), named after Zhao Wuniang in *The Lute*: at a time of great famine, when grain was scarce, Wuniang fed her parents-in-law the grains of white rice while she ate the husks to avoid starvation. In this iconic act (☞ Visual Resources), Wuniang addresses and identifies with the husks:

（旦 喫吐介）	YOUNG FEMALE *as* ZHAO WUNIANG *acts out the gesture of eating and vomiting* [*and sings*]:
【孝順歌】	*To the tune* "Xiaoshun ge"
嘔得我肝腸痛，	I vomited until my stomach hurt,
珠淚垂，	Shedding pearly rows of tears,
喉嚨尚兀自牢嘎住。	My throat is blocked up and chokes.
糠那！	Ah, you chaff![15]
你遭礱被舂杵，	As soon as you reach the mill, you are pounded by a pestle,
篩你簸颺你，	Then you are winnowed out,
喫盡控持。	And you suffer every torment.
好似奴家身狼狽，	It is just like this haggard body of mine,
千辛萬苦皆經歷。	That has borne ten thousand hardships.
苦人敕著苦味，	The bitter one eats the bitter taste,
兩苦相逢，	And the two in bitterness meet.
可知難欲吞不去。	Ah, no wonder I cannot swallow you.

[*PPJ* 149, scene 21, "Detesting the Husks" ("Zaokang ziyan")]

Zhao Wuniang endures the initial hardships of the scholar. And when Cai departs, she is expected to continue to carry out her filial duties, which she performs with firmness of purpose. In the central acts of the play, as famine begins to limit her family's resources, domestic drudgery and personal renunciation to preserve the welfare of her in-laws take on deeper meaning. These central acts juxtapose her poverty and hardship with Cai's recently achieved material well-being;

her determination to carry out her filial duties is contrasted with his feeble complaints at not being able to perform his. Zhao's assumption of Cai's duties results in enhancing her virtue while exposing his weakness of will. But because Cai's plight originated in obeying his parents' wishes, does this make him an unfilial son and ungrateful scholar? Or is this simply a manifestation of the contradictions of a social and political system?

Setting the scholar's ambition against the virtue of the wife calls further attention to the question of whether virtue is inborn or acquired through education. This question, raised in *Top Graduate* and other early plays, does not have a simple answer, and it is further complicated by the flaws in the plots of these plays. Zhang Xie does have moral virtue: he is a filial son and shows that he is not ungrateful when he marries Pinnü. When he refuses to marry the daughter of the prime minister, he does so through opposition to political coercion. Trapped in this web of social and moral constraints, Zhang Xie has little room to maneuver. In contrast, while in these plays, women have little agency and the demands placed on them are not comparable to the opposing public and familial exigencies placed on scholars, the qualities ascribed to them are almost superhuman. Their remarkable endurance in embodying the values of filiality, chastity, and loyalty are as absolute as they are seemingly implausibly heroic models to emulate.

Chinese plays demand a happy ending, or at least a just one. In *The Lute*, in line with the overall rendering of Confucian values, the plot leads inexorably to the reunion of husband and first wife and to the reinstatement of Zhao Wuniang as the principal wife. *Top Graduate*, however, presents a more complicated resolution to a story of ignominy, blind ambition, and attempted murder. In the foundational "ungrateful scholar" plays, when the scholar repudiates his "husk wife" (or courtesan) in favor of a daughter of the elite, retribution is meted out either by divine authority, where the male role is killed by a bolt of lightning, or ghostly retaliation, when the ghost of the jilted woman returns from the netherworld to seek revenge. But in *Top Graduate*, retribution and death are no longer vital to the resolution of the story, which turns instead to a form of earthly compensation. Once the prime minister settles into office, all local officials come to pay their respects, but he refuses to give an audience to Zhang Xie. Finally comprehending the magnitude of the political consequences of his earlier refusal to marry Shenghua, Zhang seeks help from a senior official, who suggests he marry the current prime minister's daughter, a proposal to which Zhang consents. As it happens, this daughter is none other than Pinnü, who has been adopted by the prime minister and his wife, and the two are married once again. The marriage solution, in fact, acknowledges the incontestable power that political elites exerted over new officials, and it also serves to establish and elevate Zhang Xie's status. It is also a functional solution for the main female role, who is thus recompensed for her sufferings with family, status, and wealth. Nonetheless, the happy reunion is hard to reconcile with Zhang Xie's earlier cruel and dishonorable conduct—certainly not the conduct expected from a scholar. But what made this imperfect marriage solution possible? Was it to counter the earlier plays, where the wives' misfortunes found no resolution? Or was it a desire to improve the material fate of the heroines? While we cannot adequately answer these questions, we can safely conjecture that the wretched fate of the "husk wife" would have required some form of positive resolution, and audiences saw status and wealth as a just requital.

7.5 *TOP GRADUATE* AND *THE LUTE*: LANGUAGE AND COMEDY

Top Graduate is written in a mixture of classical Chinese and plain language sprinkled with local dialect and idiomatic expressions. Although southern theater is native to the southeast and may have, in an earlier period, used local language, *Top Graduate* is not written in local dialect and makes very little use of local dialect even in the spoken and comic parts, where in later theater, local dialect became standard. One reason for this relative lack of dialect could be that our version of the play was edited when included in an imperial encyclopedia. But it is also entirely possible that this type of theater produced in larger cities was intended for an educated elite versed in a standardized northern written vernacular. *The Lute* is written in a more elaborate language, but it uses a wide variety of registers, ranging from the more terse language of songs, to short sections in parallel prose, to the semicolloquial spoken parts. As such, the play is important because it established the linguistic parameters that southern drama was to follow. During the late Ming, once drama had become a common pastime of educated elites, a discussion arose centering on what aural register should be used, such that all would understand it without descending into vulgarity. In trying to define an approximation to what a play had to *sound* like, playwrights and critics borrowed the term *bense* (literally, "original color") from Song-dynasty poetics to define the capacity of a play to convey meaning through simple and clear language. Because plays were often performed for a general public that included both literate and illiterate men, women, and children, language had to be accessible to all of them. Thus, the obscure and terse language of the classics, parallelism, and the excessive use of classical allusions were all contrary to the "natural" quality sought in the language of drama. However, exactly what playwrights and aficionados meant by this term was never clearly defined. Some considered *The Lute* to be a perfect example of "naturalness" in its mode of expression, while others thought it too erudite and hence devoid of the unaffected language that a dramatic play was supposed to possess (☞ Introduction).

In the eyes of some later critics, the scene called "Playing the Zither" from *The Lute*—a favorite among later generations—superbly exemplifies the pleasure of playful and witty language, another desirable aspect of the concept of "naturalness." In this scene, Cai is trying to dispel his vexation over his predicament by playing the zither when Mistress Niu enters and asks him to play "The Pheasant Flies in the Morning" ("Zhi chao fei"). Cai declines, noting that the tune is intended for a wifeless man (not him), and in the end, he agrees to play "Wind Entering Pines" ("Feng ru song"). Overcome by his own feelings, he plays "Longing to Return" ("Si gui yin") instead. This is repeated twice more, until Cai explains in a passage full of double meanings that play on the analogy between strings and wives:

（生）。。。只是這絃不中用。(貼) 這絃怎的不中用？(生) 俺只彈得舊絃慣，這是新絃，俺彈不慣。(貼) 舊絃在那裡？(生) 舊絃撇下多時了。(貼) 為甚撇了？(生) 只為有了這新絃，便撇了那舊絃。(貼) 相公何不撇了新絃，用那舊絃？(生) 夫人，我心裡豈不想那舊絃？只是新絃又撇不下。(貼) 你新絃既撇不下，還思量那舊絃怎的？我想起來，只是你心不在焉，特地有許多說話。

YOUNG MALE *as* CAI BOJIE [*speaks*]: . . . It's just that I cannot play this string. SECOND FEMALE *as* MISTRESS NIU [*speaks*]. Why can't you use it? CAI: I was accustomed to the old one, but this one is new and I am not used to it. MISTRESS NIU: Where is the old one? CAI: I threw it away some time ago. MISTRESS NIU: Why did you throw it away? CAI: Since I had a new one, I threw away the old one. MISTRESS NIU: Sir, so why don't you throw away the new string and use the old one? CAI: Madam, how can I not long for that old string? Yet how can I throw away the new one!? MISTRESS NIU: You can't throw away the new one, but you are still thinking about the old? I know, you have a lot on your mind.

（生 唱）	CAI BOJIE *sings*:
【桂枝香】	*To the tune* "Guizhi xiang"
夫人，	Madam,
舊絃已斷，	The old string has broken,
新絃不慣。	And I'm not yet used to the new.
舊絃再上不能，	I cannot restring the old one;
待撇了新絃難拚。	I would throw it away, but it is hard to part with the new string!
我一彈再鼓，	I pluck and I thrum,
一彈再鼓，	I pluck and I thrum,
又被宮商錯亂。	And the various keys confuse me.

[*PPJ* 156–157, scene 22, "The Plaint of the Zither at the Lotus Pond" ("Qinsu hechi")]

In this act, Mistress Niu, through the broken string metaphor, finally realizes what is troubling her husband. But it is the double entendre that has won the admiration of generations of readers.

Beyond such spirited playfulness, comedy in general is an essential component of Chinese plays, and no play could do without it. The object of the comedy and its aesthetic intent are to provide respite from the more emotional and serious moralizing parts of the play. *Top Graduate* is fundamentally a comedy, and its comic routine is structured, clear, and, although extremely varied, also very repetitive. The type of comedy performed in *Top Graduate* is for the most part farce—both physical, exemplified by a series of acrobatic feats performed in the form of fighting matches or mimicry, and verbal, through a routine commonly shared with the male *mo* role. The verbal repertoire of the comics uses the ambiguity of language, puns, homophones, and quips on the formation of characters and the correctness of the rhyme, as well as on riddles and onomatopoeia. There are also metatheatrical jokes on the inherent nature of the theater, such as jokes that refer to male actors playing female roles, much absurd nonsense, and even scatological humor (☛ Visual Resources). All of this is intended to overturn social taboos of propriety, ritual conduct, and social decorum. While all comedy is to an extent intended as a social corrective, much of the comedy in this play is either expressions of basic human striving, wordplay, or simply nonsensical buffoonery.

Typically, a comic scene includes a routine played by one or two of the comic roles (*jing* and *chou*), with the arbitration of the male *mo* role. The following example shows both the play on words and the interactions among the three roles. In scene 2 of *Top Graduate*, the main male role (*sheng*) and two friends in the roles of a *mo* and a *jing* come onstage. The *sheng* and the *mo* introduce themselves with a quatrain, after which the *jing* prepares to introduce himself with a quatrain of his own:

（淨）尊兄開談了。（末）亂道。（淨）尊兄也開談了。（生）亂道。（淨）小子正是潭，正是潭。（末）到來這裏打仗鼓。（淨）噯！（末）吃得多少，便飽了。（淨）昨夜燈前正讀書。（末）奇哉！（淨）讀書直讀到雞鳴。（末）一夜睡不著。（淨）外面囉唣。（末）莫是報捷來？（淨）不是。外面囉唣開門看。（末）見其底？（淨）老鼠拖個䭾貓兒。（末）只見貓兒拖老鼠。（淨）老鼠拖貓兒。（三合）（末爭）（淨笑）韻腳難押，胡亂便了。（末）杜工部後代。（生）尊兄高經？（淨）小子詩賦。（末）默記得一部《韻略》。（淨）《韻略》有甚難，一東，二冬。（末）三和四？（淨）三文將，四文蔥。（末）那得是市賣帳。

COMIC *as* FRIEND ONE [*speaks*]: Brother you started talking. ADDITIONAL MALE *as* FRIEND TWO [*speaks*]: Nonsense. FRIEND ONE: You too brother, spoke up. YOUNG MALE *as* ZHANG XIE [*speaks*]: Sheer nonsense. FRIEND ONE: I'll also speak, also speak! FRIEND TWO: At this point we beat the drums.[16] FRIEND ONE: Blurp! FRIEND TWO: How much can you eat before you're stuffed! FRIEND ONE: Last night I was reading in front of the lamp. FRIEND TWO: Strange! FRIEND ONE: I studied until the cock crowed. FRIEND TWO: You didn't sleep the whole night! FRIEND ONE: It was too noisy outside. FRIEND TWO: Perhaps they were celebrating your success? FRIEND ONE: No, there was such a racket outside that I opened the door to check. FRIEND TWO: What did you see? FRIEND ONE: A rat dragging a big old cat along. FRIEND TWO: You mean a cat dragging a rat. FRIEND ONE: A rat dragging a cat. *The three repeat the sentence in unison.* FRIEND TWO *questions it and* FRIEND ONE *laughs.* Never mind, it is a hard word to rhyme with. I did the best I could. FRIEND TWO: One could say you are a modern-day Du Fu![17] ZHANG XIE: What are your literary achievements? FRIEND ONE: I can compose poems. FRIEND TWO: I've memorized the whole *Treatise on Rhymes*.[18] FRIEND ONE: *The Treatise on Rhymes*? What's so hard about that? One toes, two foes.[19] FRIEND TWO: What about three and four? FRIEND ONE: Three cash of sauce; four of tomatoes.[20] FRIEND TWO: Why bring up the market bill?

[*ZXZY* 14, scene 2; trans. Llamas, 98-99][21]

This passage can be divided into three sets, all using the same pattern: Friend One (*jing*) initiates and carries out a joke, and Friend Two (*mo*) caps it by making a remark restating the obvious or invoking some conventional wisdom. This routine is repeated throughout the play when one or two of the comics and the *mo* role are together, showing how the formulaic nature of the language determines the interactions among the roles. For example, the exchange between Friend One (*jing*) and Friend Two (*mo*) given here is very similar to the dialogues carried out between Grandma (*jing*) and Grandpa Li (*mo*) throughout the play. The two comics (*jing* and *chou*) are the real taboo-breakers, the ones attempting to flout social conventions and break free of social inhibition. The *mo* role, on the other hand, upholds at all moments a restraining function, keeping the comedy within bounds but also showing the audience the inane nature of the comics. By pointing out to the spectators the irrational nature of the comics, the *mo*, who stands at the threshold between the stage and the audience, also incorporates them into his point of view, enticing them to assimilate his position. Thus, while the audience laughs at the jokes and antics of these roles, they are also being reminded that the absurdities are socially proscribed. The *mo* not only reins in comedy, but he also keeps the play within acceptable moral bounds.

The organization of the comic routine found in *Top Graduate* is also evident in the comic acts of *The Lute*, but it is more refined there, with fewer comic acts. *The Lute* uses similar bantering between the two comic roles, which generally play secondary characters such as servants, stewards, and go-betweens. But while these sections are inserted into many acts, they do not dominate, as in *Top Graduate*. Besides the "Playing the Zither" scene discussed previously, another popular exchange in *The Lute* appears in a later act, when Mistress Niu, having found out that Cai's parents have died, decides (against her father's wishes) to go to her husband's town in the southeast to pay obeisance to her deceased in-laws and fulfill her mourning duties. In this act, the exchange between Mistress Niu and her father is peppered with references to dictums of wifely propriety from the classics. She wins the argument, eventually forcing her father's hand and having her own way.

CONCLUSION

Top Graduate and *The Lute* are crucial points of reference in the cultural history of Chinese drama. They describe the social tensions created by the demands placed on the scholar by society, both by the family (private) and the government (public), and in the process, they appraise both the means by which scholars were educated and the culture in which they were formed. Both plays offer a social critique. In *Top Graduate*, it is a critique of the moral failure of education to reconcile ethical norms with behavioral standards or, to put it more succinctly, the normative with the instrumental. *The Lute* points out the failure of a system that demanded two virtues—duty to the state and filial conduct to one's parents—that were almost impossible to reconcile.

One process by which the plays manage to highlight these problems was through the contrast of the masculine desire for status and power with the female longing for stability and continuum—a curious contrasting effect, given that those educated to manage the empire were also those destabilizing familial harmony and breaking the ethical code. Setting aside these broad social themes, the two plays can also be read for what they reveal about the craft of playwriting, whether it be the balance between profound moral commentary and entertainment—with the latter represented by comic banter—or the mastery of a full range of linguistic registers, from rough vernacular dialogue to the refined musing of the scholar in his studio.

Regina Llamas

NOTES

1. The copy that Ye found was a copy of the original *Great Canon*, which may have been recopied if the original were misplaced or lost. Two copies were made of the *Great Canon;* one was kept in Beijing and the other in Nanjing. The *Great Canon* was very large and was never printed.

2. *Little Butcher* was translated by Stephen H. West and Wilt L. Idema in their *Monks, Bandits, Lovers, and Immortals* (Indianapolis: Hackett, 2010), 389–456.

3. At the time, Yongjia was another name for Wenzhou.

4. See Regina S. Llamas, *Top Graduate Zhang Xie: The Earliest Extant Southern Play* (New York: Columbia University Press, 2020), 1–7.

5. The term "writing club" (*shuhui*) is first used in Guanpu Naideweng (pseud.), "Sanjiao waidi" ("The Three Religions in the Outskirts of the City"), *Ducheng jisheng* (A Record of the Splendid Scenery of the Capital, preface 1235), in *Dongjing menghua lu wai si zhong* (The Eastern Capital: A Record of a Dream of Splendor *and Four Other Works*) (Beijing: Wenhua yishu chubanshe, 1998), 101 (☛ *HTRCProse*, C12.2).

6. The Imperial Music Academy was the imperial office in charge of palace entertainment. The Crimson and Green was a well-known troupe of comedians active during the Southern Song era in Hangzhou known as "Crimson and Green Association of Pure Music." The troupe is mentioned in two texts that describe the city life of Hangzhou, the Southern Song capital, the *Ducheng jisheng*, and the *Wulin jiushi* (Recollections of Wulin, ca. 1280).

7. See Zeng Yongyi, "Xiqu de benzhi" ("The Nature of Chinese Theater"), in his *Xiqu benzhi yu qiangdiao xintan* (New Explorations of the Nature and Musical Styles of Chinese Theater) (Taipei: Guojia chubanshe, 2007), 23–95.

8. That is, sing songs of romance.

9. These actors were not professionals, but they were playing in a competition between amateur troupes. "Powder" and "lime" refer to facial makeup.

10. This is, to my knowledge, a unique instance in which a *zhugongdiao* is placed as part of the introduction to the play. This *zhugongdiao* includes songs, but there is no indication that it used musical modes.

11. In Qian's edition of *The Lute*, this introductory song is sung by a *jing* (comic) role playing the character of the mother. In Yu's edition, this song does not exist. The mother, as is the norm in these stories, insists that the son stay to take care of the family. See *PPJ*, 32.

12. Edward L. Dreyer, *Early Ming China: A Political History (1355–1425)*, (Stanford, CA: Stanford University Press, 1982), 7–8.

13. The silk whip was given to the prospective son-in-law. If he accepted it, it meant that he accepted the marriage contract.

14. See, for example, Li Yu, *Li Yu quanji* (The Complete Works of Li Yu)(Taipei: Chengwen chubanshe, 1970), vol. 5, 1952–1953.

15. This line is spoken.

16. *Tan1* ("deep," "profound") is also a homophone for *tan2* ("to speak"), so perhaps the idea implied is that Friend One (*jing*) will now say something deep, which is contrary to the buffoonish nature of the role. Because Friend Two (*mo*) and Zhang Xie (*sheng*) have already composed their quatrains, it is now Friend One's turn to make one up. The humor of the section that follows is based on

the incapacity of Friend One to find the correct rhyme. Friend One repeats the word twice, making the sound of a drum, "tam, tam"; hence Friend's Two comment. See *ZXZY*, 20, n. 43.

    17. This refers to the famous Tang poet Du Fu (712–770). There is a pun here on the meaning of du_4 in the compound $duzhuan_4$ ("to fabricate"). See *ZXZY*, 21, n. 50.

    18. The *Treatise on Rhymes* (*Yunlüe*) was compiled by Dingdu in the Song dynasty and was used as the standard rhyming text for the examinations.

    19. This is *yidong* (literally, "one east") and *er dong* (literally, "two winters").

    20. Literally, "three cash of sauce and four cash of onions." The rhymes here are inverted to show the incompetence of the *jing*.

    21. The names of roles have been modified to fit the format of the current text.

PRIMARY SOURCES

PPJ   Gao Ming 高明. *Pipa ji* 琵琶記 (*The Lute*). Ann. Yu Weimin 俞為民. Taipei: Huazheng shuju, 1994.

YBPPJ   Gao Ming 高明. *Yuan ben Pipa ji* 元本琵琶記 (*The Lute: A Yuan Dynasty Edition*). Ann. Qian Nanyang 錢南楊 and Li Tiankui 李殿魁. Taipei: Liren shuju, 1998.

ZXZY   Qian Nanyang 錢南楊, ed. *Zhang Xie Zhuangyuan* 張協狀元 (*Top Graduate Zhang Xie*). In *Yongle dadian xiwen sanzhong jiaozhu* 永樂大典戲文三種校注 (*An Annotated Edition of Three* Nanxi *Playtexts from the* Great Canon *of the Yongle Era*), 1–217. Taipei: Huazheng shuju, 1985.

ZZZYJS *Zhang Xie zhuangyuan jiaoshi* 張協狀元校釋 (*An Annotated Edition of* Top Graduate Zhang Xie). Ann. Hu Xuegang 胡雪岡. Wenzhou wenxian congshu 溫州文獻叢書 (*The Collectanea of Documents from Wenzhou*). Shanghai: Shanghai shehui kexueyuan, 2006.

SUGGESTED READINGS

TRANSLATIONS

Gao Ming. *The Lute*. Trans. Jean Mulligan. New York: Columbia University Press, 1980.

Nine Mountain Society. *Top Graduate Zhang Xie: The Earliest Extant Chinese Southern Play*. Introd. and trans. Regina Llamas. New York: Columbia University Press, 2021.

ENGLISH

Llamas, Regina. "Retribution, Revenge and the Ungrateful Scholar in Early Chinese Southern Drama." *Asia Major*, Third Series, 20, no. 2 (2007): 75–101.

Mei Sun. "Exploring the Historical Development of *Nanxi* Southern Theater." *CHINOPERL* 24 (2002): 35–68.

Xu Peng. "Editing *Pipa ji* for Late-Ming Popular Theater: The Identity of the "Singing Hermit" and His Editorial Work." *Late Imperial China* 41, no. 1 (2020): 159–201.

CHINESE

Guo Zuofei 郭作飛. "Nanxi *Zhang Xie zhuangyuan* yanjiu bashi nian" 南戲《張協狀元》研究八十年 (*Eighty Years of Research on the* Nanxi *Play* Top Graduate Zhang Xie), *Lanzhou xuekan* 6 (2012): 93–97.

Hou Baipeng 候百朋. *Pipa ji ziliao huibian* 琵琶記資料彙編 (*A Collection of Research Materials on* The Lute). Beijing: Shumu wenxian chubanshe, 1989.

Qian Nanyang 錢南揚. *Xiwen gailun* 戲文概論 (*An Introduction to* Nanxi). Shanghai: Shanghai guji chubanshe, 1981.

Yang Baochun 楊寶春. *Pipa ji de changshang yanbian yanjiu* 琵琶記的場上演變研究 (*The Development of the Performance of* The Lute). Shanghai: Sanlian shuju, 2009.

Yu Weimin 俞為民. *Song Yuan nanxi kaolun* 宋元南戲考論 (*A Study of Song and Yuan* Nanxi *Drama*). Taipei: Shangwu yinshu guan, 1994.

8

The Southern Story of the Western Wing (Nan Xixiang)

Traditional Kunqu Composition, Interpretation, and Performance

Since the sixteenth century, Kunqu, a genre of Chinese opera (*xiqu*) that tells stories with words, music, and dance, has dramatized emotions and memories, enriching the imagination and the lived realities of performers and audiences alike. Currently, China presents Kunqu as a Masterpiece of Oral and Intangible Heritage of Humanity by the United Nations Educational, Scientific, and Cultural Organization (UNESCO), as well as a classical opera of China. Kunqu practitioners believe that the repertory they perform, as well as the associated script-writing/editing, music composing/rearranging, dancing, and other practices, are traditional and representative of what their predecessors have done since the 1850s at the latest. To be sure, some current Kunqu works and performance practices are obvious innovations, but for the most part, the practitioners' thesis of traditionality makes it possible to study the works created before the 1850s from a historical-ethnographic point of view.

This chapter presents a case study of the "Happy Time" ("Jiaqi") scene from Li Rihua's (fl. 1550s?) *The Southern Story of the Western Wing* (*Nan Xixiang*, hereafter *Southern Western Wing*) to demonstrate the dynamic ways with which traditional Kunqu operas are written, read, and realized with composed music and choreographed gesture-dances (*shenduan*).[1] In addition, it argues that like Western opera, as a multimedia performing art, Kunqu is driven by music. As realized on stage, scripted Kunqu texts are musically spoken, chanted, and sung with or without instrumental accompaniment; Kunqu acts and dances are performed with vocal music, instrumental music, or both.

To discuss the "Happy Time" scene of *Southern Western Wing* as a representative sample of traditional Kunqu creative and performance practices, this chapter unfolds in five sections: first, an introduction to Kunqu history and its practitioners' tradition of composing, reading, and realizing scripts into multimedia operas; second, an account of the genesis and reception history of *Southern Western Wing*; third, a description of the dramatic content and structure of the "Happy Time" scene and its core aria, the "Twelve Shades of Rouge" ("Shi'er hong," hereafter "Twelve Shades"); fourth, a heuristic analysis of Li Rihua's composition of "Happy Time" and the appreciations that it elicited; and finally, a musicological analysis of "Twelve Shades" as a nexus of Kunqu composition, reading, performance, and audience appreciation.

8.1 STORIED KUNQU AND ITS TRADITIONAL PRACTITIONERS

With historical roots traceable to the transition period between Yuan (1271–1368) and Ming China (1368–1644), Kunqu fully matured by the early seventeenth century; then it dominated the Chinese operatic and entertainment world until the mid-eighteenth century, when it began to decline, losing its audience to younger genres of operas and other multimedia entertainment. From the 1880s through the 1920s, Kunqu practically ceased to operate as a commercially viable genre of Chinese opera and entertainment. In the following seventy or eighty years, the genre precariously survived, with an ebb and flow of creative and performance activities by a national but smallish community of dedicated practitioners. Since the late 1990s, however, Kunqu has revived and become popular again, a result of contemporary China's cultural, economic, and political investment in its cultural heritage and international interest in China and Chinese performing arts. A community of Kunqu practitioners and audiences is gradually expanding both inside and outside China.

Traditional Kunqu practitioners engage in the genre's creative and performance activities with specialized interests and skills. Most assume single roles as dramatists/scriptwriters, music composers, pedagogues, performers who act, sing, and dance, and fans; but some do play multiple roles. Indicative of specialized Kunqu tasks and skills are traditional terms that categorize various types of practitioners, underscoring their verbal, musical, choreographic, and staging practices in traditional Kunqu.

Traditional Kunqu lionizes dramatists (*juzuo jia*), elite and literati authors of Ming and Qing China, who wrote *chuanqi* dramas for reading as literature, for performance on stage, or both. Kunqu performance scripts literally or freely realize *chuanqi* texts, which unfold in scenes, each of which is structured as one or more sequences (*liantao*) of arias and dialogue. Most dramatists would know Kunqu musical and dance practices intimately, and many would seek advice from—if not active collaboration with—other practitioners. They could be either professionals or avocational performers; members of the former group are mostly commoners, while many in the latter group came from elite and privileged families. Kunqu practitioners' social standing and artistry have been intricately intertwined.

Traditionally, in terms of what they create and perform, Kunqu practitioners are divided into the following major types. "Experts" (*qujia*) are elite and erudite practitioners who operate sequentially or simultaneously as generous patrons, virtuoso performers, erudite scholars of Kunqu history and theory, critical readers and commentators, and admired pedagogues who nurture disciples through person-to-person teaching. Many experts perpetuate their Kunqu artistry and scholarship by authoring writings in diverse formats ranging from biographical notes and historical-theoretical writings to detailed descriptions of gesture-dances, as well as notated scores of Kunqu arias that they have personally composed or rearranged. Experts who specialize in linguistic-musical (*yinyun*) matters in Kunqu composition and performance would either advise dramatists on their writing or edit or adjust their texts so that they can be effectively realized onstage. The fact that these experts contributed much to Kunqu composition and performance is routinely acknowledged; however, what they actually created or revised, and how they did so, is only sketchily documented.

Kunqu performers can be professionals or avocational players. Creative and skilled amateurs are generously applauded. Those who regularly perform with professionals are called "featured performers" (*chuanjia, chuanke*). Not infrequently, they turn professional by joining commercial troupes. Most Kunqu practitioners are, however, aficionados (*quyou*) who practice Kunqu as a hobby and whose creative and performance skills are relatively limited. They all would meticulously read performance scripts and notated scores, however. In addition, all would diligently study Kunqu biography, history, repertory, and performance. Many would regularly perform in noncommercial, private, and semiprivate gatherings (*yaji*), entertaining themselves and their friends. Then and there, they would only sing arias that they have selected from Kunqu opera favorites, skipping both oral deliveries of scripted dialogues and kinetic performance of gesture-dances.

Professional Kunqu performers who actively engage in Kunqu music composition and performance are called "music masters" (*qushi*). They would create distinctive melodies for singing newly written lyrics or adjust melodic and rhythmic details in known tunes for singing old and new lyrics. Many music masters, particularly those who have retired from the commercial stage, are hired as music coaches (*paixian*), whose duties are to teach what they have musically realized to professional and avocational performers who would act, sing, and dance onstage. Many music coaches also teach gesture-dances—Kunqu singing, acting, and dancing are inseparable performance practices and modes of expressions. Those who specialize in gesture-dance coaching are called *taxian*.

Regardless of the single or multiple roles they specialize in, traditional Kunqu practitioners are actively involved in all creative and performance aspects of Kunqu operas. In other words, they are acutely concerned with the ways in which scripted speeches and lyrics are written, read, or performed with music and dance. And to read critically and perform expressively, the practitioners would fastidiously pursue the correct enunciation of words in the lyrics and stylized execution of melodies, rhythms, timbres, and gesture-dances. They strive to seamlessly integrate verbal, musical, and choreographic expressions into their Kunqu presentations. Further, they critically comment on all live or recorded Kunqu shows that they witness.

8.2 A HISTORICAL ACCOUNT OF LI RIHUA'S
SOUTHERN WESTERN WING

When Kunqu practitioners approach Li Rihua's *Southern Western Wing* as a Kunqu opera, they know that its story is historically derived from *The Story of the Western Wing* (*Xixiang ji*), a romance that has been told many times since Tang China in the ninth century.[2] They also know that many performance scripts of the story have been creatively produced, continuously transmitted, and strategically revised or rewritten for operatic performances.

As Wilt L. Idema explains (☞ chap. 1), there are four seminal versions of *The Story of the Western Wing*, a love story about Oriole (Cui Yingying), her maid, Crimson (Hongniang), and Student Zhang (Zhang Junrui). The first is Yuan Zhen's (779–831) "The Tale of Oriole" ("Yingying zhuan"), which is written in classical Chinese prose designed for reading, not stage performance. The second is *The Story of the Western Wing in All Keys and Modes* (*Xixiang ji zhugongdiao*), a prosimetric work by Dong Jieyuan (fl. 1190–1208) that tells the love story via suites of songs (*taoshu*) sung in different musical modes (*gongdiao*). As performed, Dong's work presents a historical sample of Chinese narrative singing (*shuochang*); its performers entertain audiences with talks and songs, but a minimum of bodily gestures to illustrate what they tell.

The third version is *The Story of the Western Wing* (hereafter *Northern Western Wing*) by Wang Shifu (1260–1336), a set of five *zaju* (variety) plays with a total of twenty-one acts and four introductory wedges (*xiezi*). Traditionally esteemed and consulted as the version par excellence of the story about Oriole, Crimson, and Student Zhang, Wang's script is praised for not only its dramatically effective narrative, but also its realistic dialogue and literary lyrics. Wang's version is representative of *zaju* as a classical genre of Chinese drama or theater—one that blossomed in Yuan China and boasts many distinctive expressive features and compositional and performance rules. *Zaju* has its dialogues and arias composed, spoken, chanted, and sung in northern Chinese dialects. *Zaju* arias, or northern songs (*beiqu*), have lyrics written according to song patterns (*qupai*) with defined linguistic-literary-musical features such as rhyme schemes, distinctive melodic turns and rhythms, a relatively fixed number of textual lines, and a set number of base and linguistically-tonally specified characters (*zhengzi*) for every line. All characters in *zaju* lyrics are classified and employed as words of the level (*ping*) or oblique (*ze*) categories, and all should be accurately enunciated with their level (*pingsheng*), rising (*shangsheng*), and descending (*qusheng*) linguistic tones. Strict observance of the rules about aria patterns and linguistic tones is practical and expressive. Lyrics that are written according to the rules can be readily sung with the known tunes of the emulated song patterns; however, to make the tunes flow effectively, melodic and rhythmic adjustments are necessary. Arias sung with recognizable tunes can be promptly appreciated with references to cultural, historical, and musical data about the known aria patterns. Many *zaju* musical and staging features are carried over to Kunqu operas. Many northern songs are still sung in Kunqu operas/*chuanqi* texts that emulate *zaju* scripts (☞ Introduction).

The fourth seminal version in *The Story of the Western Wing* tradition is Li Rihua's *Southern Western Wing*, a sixteenth-century *chuanqi* (southern opera) with thirty-six scenes that is a rewrite of Wang's *zaju* play.[3] When performed as a Kunqu opera, the speeches and lyrics in Li's script are enunciated in the Wu dialect: individual words are uttered with one of eight southern linguistic tones (namely, the level, rising, descending, and entering [*rusheng*] linguistic tones, each of which can be enunciated at either the high or low pitch levels [*yinyang basheng*]).

Composed according to southern aria patterns, Li's southern songs (*nanqu*) are sung with pentatonic melodies and elastic rhythms and tempi.

Li's rewriting of Wang Shifu's *zaju* into *Southern Western Wing* is a complex and extensive process, one that is broadly comparable to transforming *Aida*, the classical nineteenth-century Italian grand opera by Giuseppe Verdi (music) and Antonio Ghislanzoni (lyrics), into *Aida*, the twentieth-century Broadway musical by Elton John (music) and Tim Rice (lyrics).[4] Both works tell essentially the same story, but their dramatic aesthetics and structures, musical expressions, and performance practices are substantively different. Any comparison of Wang's *zaju* and Li's southern opera will show that they are significantly different works of dramatic and multimedia performing arts.

Little about Li's biography and career is known, but he has been described as a dramatist and an occasional performer. The allusion to his occasional performances is significant because they help explain the stage success of Li's work. Allegedly, Li's *Southern Western Wing* appeals to performers and audiences because it can be effectively staged, a result of Li's practical knowledge about operatic performance which guided his writing of the opera's performance script. History tells us that Li was probably not the first person to transform *Northern Western Wing* into a southern opera. In fact, some scholars have argued that the original author of *Southern Western Wing* was not Li, but a dramatist called Cui Shipei,[5] a figure whose biography is even more obscure than Li's. Reportedly, Li produced his *Southern Western Wing* by rewriting Cui's libretto. Li was also not the last person to attempt to transform *Northern Western Wing* into a southern opera. Finding Li's version literarily and musically lacking, Lu Cai (1497–1537), one of his contemporaries, produced his own version, but to little effect: it was not popular on the stage and soon was forgotten by both Kunqu performers and audiences.

When it first appeared, Li's *Southern Western Wing* was not well received among contemporary drama connoisseurs; in fact, it was summarily dismissed.[6] For instance, Liang Chenyu (1519–1591), the author of *Washing Silk* (*Huansha ji*), the first *chuanqi* written for performance as a Kunqu opera, found the ways that Li appropriated materials from Cui's text contemptible (*chileng*). Similarly, Qi Biaojia (1602–1645) (➤ chap. 15), another Ming literatus and drama connoisseur, described *Southern Western Wing* as a crippled and incoherent version of *Northern Western Wing*. However, such critical aspersions notwithstanding, by the late seventeenth century, Tu Long (1543–1605), another late-Ming opera enthusiast, observed that by his time, only Li's version was known or staged by contemporary theater performers and audiences.

Among all the criticism whirling around *Southern Western Wing*, an informative and objective verdict came from Li Yu (1611–1680), a prominent Ming-Qing dramatist-producer (➤ chap. 11). Li Yu claimed that Li Rihua had quoted Wang Shifu's literary phrases out of context and interspersed them with vernacular words, generating a southern opera script that is erotically explicit, and thus vulgar. Li Yu, however, also noted that Li Rihua had successfully transformed Wang's *zaju* into a southern opera—one that could be expressively and stylishly sung with contemporary and southern music, to the delight of its regional audience.

Nowadays, little is known about how Li Rihua and his contemporaries performed *Southern Western Wing*. At the time, there were four major styles of southern operatic music (*qiang*), named after their regions of origin: Kunshan (in Jiangsu province), Haiyan (in Zhejiang province), Yuyao (in Zhejiang province) and Yiyang (in Jiangxi province). *Kunshan qiang* (i.e., Kunqu) and *Yiyang qiang* were the most influential, garnering patronage first from the Ming court and then the Qing court (☛ chap. 14). *Southern Western Wing* has been predominantly sung in the Kunqu style since the turn of the sixteenth and seventeenth centuries.

Since the late eighteenth century, four scenes from *Southern Western Wing* have been popularly staged as rearranged scenes (*zhezixi*): "Touring the Temple" ("Youdian"), "Listening to Student Zhang Play the Qin" ("Tingqin"), "Interrogating Crimson" ("Kao Hong"), and "Happy Time." Rearranged scenes in Kunqu are short and dramatically self-contained shows, featuring performance scripts selectively adapted from original *chuanqi* dramas, many of which have thirty or more scenes. Adaptation methods vary, ranging from substituting literary expressions in the original *chuanqi* script with vernacular and stereotyped phrases to the cutting, reordering, and even rewriting of dialogues or arias.

The Kunqu practice of rearranged scenes results from performance and practical goals. Scripts of rearranged scenes are changed whenever performance contexts, performers' needs, and audience preferences change. To become successful shows, rearranged scenes have to satisfy many requirements. Their dramatic narratives should be coherent and entertaining; their multimedia expressions of dances, sounds, sights, and words should be coordinated such that actor-singers have the tools to showcase their virtuoso skills, and audiences should find what they perform appealing and meaningful. Rearranged scenes cannot be too long or too short: currently, most rearranged scenes have a performance time of approximately thirty minutes. If rearranged scenes are unnecessarily short, they might not afford actor-singers enough stage time and space to creatively and expressively bring characters alive (*yanhuole*) on stage. In contrast, rearranged scenes that are narratively opaque and performatively lengthy would tax the audience's attention and even invite their disapproval. In short, the processes and techniques of the Kunqu practice of rearranged scenes are technically multifarious; singularly or collectively, all are, however, employed to render realization of the scripted stories more operatic and entertaining.

By the mid-eighteenth-century, rearranged scenes became the norm in Kunqu performance. Since then, many anthologies of performance scripts, with or without illustrations or musical notation, have been published. All are treasured and studied by Kunqu practitioners. To cite only a few, authoritative references for Kunqu composition and performance include *The Standard Anthology of Southern Arias* (*Nanci dinglü*, 1720); *The Formulary of Northern and Southern Arias in the Comprehensive Anthology of the Nine Modes* (*Jiugong dacheng nanbei ci gongpu*, 1746, hereafter *Comprehensive Anthology*); *The Notated Kunqu Music from Mr. Ye Tang's Library* (*Nashuying qupu*, 1780s–1790s); *The Critical Listening and Viewing of Historical Operas* (*Shenyin jiangu lu*, 1834); *The Notated Kunqu Music from the Studio of*

Superb Singing (*Eyunge qupu*, 1893, hereafter *Superb Singing*); and *The All-Inclusive Collection of Kunqu Performance Scripts and Notated Music* (*Jicheng qupu*, hereafter *All-Inclusive Collection*).⁷ Singularly or collectively, these historical anthologies delineate and sustain Kunqu composition, reading, and performance practices from the mid-eighteenth century to the present day.

8.3 READING LI RIHUA'S "HAPPY TIME" AND "TWELVE SHADES" AS KUNQU

Southern Western Wing makes for a dramatic script—a fact that a traditional reading of the popular "Happy Time" scene will illustrate. Li's text is still an authoritative source for contemporary Kunqu productions of the Oriole and Student Zhang story.⁸ As preserved in *Sixty Plays* (*Liushi zhong qu*, ca. 1650s), Li's "Happy Time" scene begins with Student Zhang coming onstage, a mise-en-scène of a moonlit garden outside a scholar's study located in the western wing of an expansive monastery compound. There, Student Zhang waits in the middle of the night for Oriole and Crimson to come. When they arrive, Zhang welcomes the beauty into his study but has Crimson wait outside, charging her to keep an eye out for potential trouble. Crimson begins her watch by happily noting how the couple is well matched. Then, she begins to feel the night chill, realizes that she is lonely and being ignored, and confesses her desire for company. "Happy Time" concludes with Student Zhang teasing Crimson after he has bidden farewell to Oriole.

As a performance script, Li's "Happy Time" includes nine rounds of arias and dialogue. Eight of the arias are standard vocal compositions (*guoqu*) composed according to distinctive song patterns; and one is an atypical piece—namely, a composite aria (*jiqu*) that is composed according to not any one song pattern, but instead to distinctive lines selected from twelve song patterns. Each line embodies specific prosodic and musical attributes and affords different expressive potential. In terms of their song patterns, aria 1 is composed according to a song pattern called "Offerings" ("Gongyang yin"), one that always serves as an introduction. Arias 2 and 3 share a song pattern entitled "By the Mirror" ("Linjing xu"), one that appears in many Kunqu scenes. Arias 4 and 5 are composed according to the "Gauging Fragrance" ("Luoxiang ling"), a commonly used song pattern. Aria 6 is an atypical vocal composition now known as the "Twelve Shades." Arias 7 and 8 are structured after a commonly used song pattern called "Climbing Higher and Higher" ("Jiejie gao"). Aria 9 is a coda ("Weisheng").

In terms of dramatic narrative and Kunqu performance, Li's script offers many opportunities for expressive singing and dancing. In aria 1, Zhang describes his feelings waiting for Oriole, his object of desire, in a moonlit garden. Then he gives a short monologue, asking whether he has been tricked again by Oriole. Their last meeting was a disaster for him; acting on a supposed invitation to visit her in her room at night, he only got dressed down for his presumption.

In aria 2, Zhang describes how he sees clouds in the sky breaking up and the Moon beginning to shine. The moonlight prompts him to hear sounds and see shadows of people moving in the dark, but he wonders whether Oriole is coming. Confessing that he thinks of Oriole every hour of the day, he asks if Oriole will ever know.

In aria 3, he describes how confused his lovesickness has made him and asks if he is better off not meeting her at all. Mixing spoken and sung phrases, he tries to be sanguine, telling himself that Oriole is late because she could not promptly get away from her mother.

Then, he notices Crimson, but not Oriole. He asks her if Oriole is coming and then jokes with the maid that if her mistress does not come, she will have to take her place. She tells him to behave in a more gentlemanly fashion, and then she asks him how she will be rewarded for delivering Oriole. He swears that he will grant her whatever she desires, even if he is reborn a dog or horse in his next life. Then Zhang notices Oriole, so he kneels in front of her, singing aria 4. He declares that he did not expect to see her and does not deserve her; and then he thanks her for coming and showing pity on him.

In response to Zhang's words, Oriole sings the first half of aria 5, telling him how she pities his forlorn and sick state. Then, Crimson sings the rest of aria 5, congratulating Zhang and telling him how his loyalty and persistence have changed Oriole's mind. A three-way dialogue follows. Oriole stresses how consequential her decision to give herself to Zhang is, and she implores him not to betray her. Zhang says that he would not dare do so. Crimson tells the two of them to go to sleep, saying that she will check if Madam Cui, Oriole's mother, is sleeping. The lovers take this as their cue to enter Zhang's study; hand in hand, reciting a couplet together, they exit the stage. With the stage to herself, Crimson notes how lucky Zhang is and how the two of them are "openly" (gongran) showing their affection for one another; until then, Oriole has not been forthcoming about her desire for Zhang. Crimson then complains about the couple's leaving her behind, and how melancholic she feels.

Aria 6 is the long "Twelve Shades" that Crimson sings. In thirty-four lines, she relays her rapidly developing feelings and thoughts. First, she exclaims how Student Zhang and Oriole perfectly suit one another. Then, she reveals her feelings of being lonely and ignored and asks when and how she will find someone to love her and share her bed as her mistress and Student Zhang are doing. Remembering that her duty is to watch out for the lovers and to make sure that their rendezvous does not turn into a disaster, she knocks on the door of the study, urging the lovers to throw on some clothes so that Oriole can promptly leave and return to her boudoir. (For the musical and choreographic realization of this aria, see the next section 8.4 and musical example 1, in section 8.5.)

Aria 7 is short. Student Zhang sings its first five phrases, confessing how great he feels after having sex with Oriole. He and Oriole sing the last two phrases of the aria together, asking when and how they will meet again. Aria 8, which is also sung by the couple, describes that they feel amorous like the legendary dalliance between ancient King Xiang and the Goddess of Mt. Wu (Wushan shennü). Aria 9 is a coda that Student Zhang sings, noting how the love between him and Oriole is precious and asking her to come again the next evening. Following this aria is the couple's farewell to one another and a flirtatious dialogue between Student Zhang and Crimson. She asks how he feels and whether his love-sickness has been cured. He responds by saying that he is 90 percent cured, but he asks Crimson to take care of the remaining 10 percent. Crimson responds, "Phooey!" ("pei").

8.4 LI RIHUA'S COMPOSITION OF "HAPPY TIME" AND THE REACTIONS IT ELICITED

How and why Li Rihua actually created the "Happy Time" scene in the way he did are historical questions that cannot be fully answered until further information about his biography and career is discovered. But the fact that Li added many dramatic details not found in Wang's text and operated as a traditional dramatist and/or music composer is clear. The processes and goals for Li's traditional composition of "Happy Time" as an operatic scene can be heuristically reconstructed as follows.

To create "Happy Time," Li studied Wang's exemplary *Northern Western Wing* and selectively took what he admired and what served his compositional needs. As a result, Li's script for the scene includes many direct quotations or paraphrases of Wang's words. It also includes central images from the centuries-old story of Oriole and Student Zhang. From Yuan Zhen's work, for example, comes the opening image of the "Happy Time" scene: Student Zhang stands outside his study waiting for Oriole, noticing shadows of flowers moving in the moonlit garden and wondering when and if she would come to his abode. And, to produce a dramatic script that Kunqu performers could effectively stage and southern and commoner audiences would find intelligible and entertaining, Li introduced many vernacular words and phrases into his text.

Li faced many challenges in his attempt to make "Happy Time" entertaining. He had to make maximum use of an unmistakably erotic and precarious situation. This is what makes the scene operatically appealing and what moralistic critics wanted to ban. To make an operatic show of the lover's intimate acts, Li needed more than suggestive words, but he could not have performers do a realistic pantomime of lovemaking on the traditional Kunqu stage. Li's solution was to write the long and atypical composite aria of "Twelve Shades" and have Crimson sing it, presenting a third-person account of the couple's intimate acts.

To make that account a musical and choreographic tease, Li composed the aria as an atypical literary-musical composition—one that brings the sexually aroused Crimson alive (*yanhuole*) onstage. By composing "Twelve Shades" as a structurally complex and unique southern song, Li presented his performers and the audience with a musical "tease"—one that had neither any preexistent musical identity nor any known meanings; it had to be heard and interpreted as a new musical composition and on its own terms. In other words, Li demanded that Kunqu aficionados pay attention to every melodic and rhythmic nuance in his aria, ask how it can be enhanced with dance-gestures, and how all can be coordinated into a multimedia and dramatic expression.[9] As such, "Twelve Shades" can be sung, heard, and interpreted again and again.

When traditional Kunqu practitioners read Li's "Happy Time" as a historical source or as a performance script, their reactions vary. Elite and morally conservative Kunqu practitioners find Li's text vernacular, if not vulgar. Comparing Li's script with that of Wang Shifu's, many informed Kunqu readers find the *zaju* version literarily more ornate and its description of sex more poetic than graphic.[10] In contrast, they consider Li's dramatization of sex and desire more salacious. Crimson's description of her mistress' lovemaking with Student Zhang is voyeuristic, and thus sexually and socially aggressive (for further elaboration of this point, see the English translation and performance annotation of "Twelve Shades" presented in the section entitled "Performing the Twelve Shades" later in section 8.5). Blatantly, it exposes the sexual being of a young household maid in Ming and Qing China, a historical reality that traditional Kunqu practitioners tend to gloss over in their operatic presentations. Above all, the exposé undermines the traditional and elitist aesthetics that Kunqu is proper music (*yayue*), refined (*dianya*) entertainment, or both.

However, despite moralists' efforts to ban it, Li's "Happy Time" has been continuously performed since the late sixteenth century, and its "Twelve Shades" is popularly sung as a self-contained aria. This fact underscores Kunqu's function as a musical and expressive practice. Staging *chuanqi* drama as Kunqu opera was (and still is) an expensive, labor-intensive activity. Until the advance of audiovisual recording and playback technology in modern times (➤ Introduction), Kunqu aficionados could hardly enjoy fully staged presentations as often as they wanted. To satisfy their desire for operatic entertainment, many aficionados studied Kunqu performance scripts and notated scores so that they can learn to sing arias, the focus of their musical and leisurely activities. As a self-contained aesthetic activity or as a personalized substitute for attending multimedia operatic presentations, singing "Twelve Shades" is in principle comparable to the self-expressive games that Patricia Sieber and Gillian Yanzhuang Zhang argue for in the context of the *Story of the Western Wing* illustrations (➤ chap. 4).

As Kunqu aficionados read, perform, and imagine "Happy Time"/"Twelve Shades" with different perspectives and to meet diverse needs, they locate different expressions and meanings. If some get sensory and vicarious pleasure from the scene and the aria, others find cathartic relief or moral challenges. Whereas they know that love and sex are favorite topics in the Chinese performing arts, they have been taught to avoid morally corrosive and vulgar music (*zhengsheng, yinsheng*), particularly when performed by licentious women. Their moralist fathers, mothers, and teachers have made them believe that indulgence in erotic entertainment and carnal pleasure would put their moral standing and sociopolitical status at risk. In other words, Li's "Twelve Shades" is a Kunqu gem that elicits conflicted reactions from its audiences.

It is no accident that some creative Kunqu practitioners strive to find ways to artistically and socially discipline "Happy Time"/"Twelve Shades." For example, in the late 1950s, Shen Shihua (b. 1941), a leading Kunqu performer of twentieth-century China, produced a sanitized version of the scene with all the erotic references deleted.[11] And in the early 1980s, when socialist China lifted its ban on sociopolitically aggressive operas, Liang Guyin (b. 1941), then a young and creative Kunqu performer, promptly produced her pleasurable but not licentious rendition of the scene, winning her both critical and popular acclaim.[12] Liang succeeded by "covering up" suggestive phrases with "innocent" gesture-dances (for further discussion of this point, see the annotations on a video recording of a performance by her in the next section; also ☛ Visual Resources). But enthusiasts who are informed, inquisitive, and sensitive still notice the camouflaged eroticism and are intellectually, visually, and musically pleased.

8.5 PERFORMING "TWELVE SHADES"

The ability to decode overtones and undercurrents is common among those traditional practitioners who sing and listen critically and realize that music is what renders Kunqu operas expressive and entertaining—erotic tones and rhythms in operatic performances are unmistakable to those with experienced ears. On account of its musicality and expressiveness, "Twelve Shades" has become one of the most frequently performed and discussed arias of the genre.

To comprehensively understand the celebrated aria, and to expressively perform it, traditional Kunqu practitioners would explore who, when, why, and how its melodies, rhythms, and gesture-dances of the aria have been created, transmitted, and enjoyed in the past, as well as how they can be performed in the present. History has not comprehensively documented how Li Rihua and later Qing-dynasty music masters created and re-created the music of "Twelve Shades." Judging from the available historical data, the process can be hypothetically compared to a twenty-first-century preparation of a book, or aria lyrics, for a movie on youth culture in the 1960s and 1970s. To give a historical-musical gloss to a scene of reminiscence in the movie, the scriptwriter of the hypothetical movie makes its protagonist sing a theme song that summarizes/flashes back on his life story with a medley of memorable musical phrases from celebrated and popular songs of the era, such as the Beatles' "Yesterday" (1965), Simon and Garfunkel's "The Sound of Silence" (1965), Roberta Flack's "Killing Me Softly with His Song" (1973), and Gloria Gaynor's "I Will Survive" (1978). The theme song produced, a creatively crafted musical composite, would, needless to say, trigger all kinds of cultural-historical memories and associations.

Reading the movie's script and lyrics, and noticing the titles of the quoted songs, an informed actor or reader would promptly find out what the script signifies and how its melodies and rhythms can be affectively performed. Viewing the completed movie, and identifying familiar melodic turns in the theme song, moviegoers/music-lovers who grew up in the 1960s and 1970s would intuitively grasp what it communicated and could critically argue how and why the song/movie was aesthetically pleasurable and historically convincing. What the audience does in this instance is, in principle, comparable to how traditional Kunqu aficionados intertextually create, read, and perform Kunqu rearranged scenes and arias with not only what they know about the genre, but also with their personal feelings and memories.

The process through which historical Kunqu music masters composed and transmitted the composite aria of "Twelve Shades" has not been documented. What is clear for the time being is, however, that a notated version of the aria appears in the magisterial *Comprehensive Anthology* that Prince Yunlu and a group of music masters compiled and published in 1746. Because the music masters could not have composed anew the tunes for the 4,466 arias gathered in the anthology, the music score for "Twelve Shades" preserved in the publication is representative of mid-eighteenth-century Kunqu. It is in all likelihood an adjusted version of "Twelve Shades" that Li Rihua and his music masters composed and performed. What is germane here is that the lyrics and notated music of "Twelve Shades" preserved in the anthology are essentially the same as what is now commonly performed. In other words, the aria has been standardized since the 1740s at least—a fact that renders the aria a representative sample of traditional Kunqu creative and performance practices.

This transmission and canonization of "Twelve Shades" underscores the ways that Kunqu practitioners read and perform their favorite Kunqu arias. Any comparative survey of historically preserved Kunqu scripts and notated scores will show that while masterpieces like "Twelve Shades" are faithfully transmitted, less celebrated rearranged scenes and arias are freely altered to fit specific performances by individual performers. Only Kunqu arias with seamlessly aligned verbal and musical features are treasured, and thus less susceptible to arbitrary changes.

This does not mean that "Happy Time" has been performed without changes since 1746. As a matter of fact, since the turn of the nineteenth and twentieth centuries, "Happy Time" has been rearranged and performed in varying ways. Most nineteenth-century versions of "Happy Time" are abridged scripts of Li's text; those preserved in *Superb Singing* and *All-Inclusive Collection*, for example, have only five arias.[13] Despite the cuts and changes, most traditional versions of "Happy Time" not only keep everything that is dramatically and musically essential in Li's version, but also highlight the dramatic and musical expressions of "Twelve Shades."

Such a process and result of dramatic-musical distillation becomes apparent with a critical reading of the traditional performance script in *Superb Singing*. Aria 1 in the abridged version is identical to Li Rihua's aria 2, which is composed to the song pattern called "By the Mirror;" Li's aria 1, the conventional introductory scene, has been cut. The second aria is a new vocal piece. Composed as a "Dynamic Aria" ("Zhuan"), it summarizes key ideas of Li Rihua's arias 3 through 5: Student Zhang waiting for Oriole's coming and expressing his feelings, and Crimson's ushering her mistress to his studio while flirting with him. The third is practically identical to "Twelve Shades" as it is musically preserved in *Comprehensive Anthology* (1746). The only discrepancy is that phrase 31 in the abridged version is phrase 28 in the

1746 version. The fourth and fifth arias are identical to Li's arias 8 and 9, which are "Gauging Fragrance" and "Climbing Higher and Higher," respectively.

The reasons for singing "Twelve Shades" as it has been standardized since the 1740s and continuously performed are obvious. Virtuoso actor-singers like to perform the atypically long and technically demanding aria to show off their musical and dance prowess. Novice performers learn it to practice and develop their vocal and choreographic skills. Audiences love to hear it again and again, savoring a musical expressiveness that exquisite melodic turns and rhythmic twists in the composite aria convey. Aficionados' engagement with the aria is in all likelihood more aesthetic and musical than erotic.[14] In their occasional and noncommercial recitals or elegant gatherings, they often only sing the aria, skipping the dialogue and gestures, and wear no theatrical makeup or costumes. Discussing their musical interest in the aria, they often focus on its extraordinary length, unique melodic lines, dramatic fermatas, and other musical features.

For example, Wang Zhenglai (1948–2003), a twentieth-century Kunqu expert and a prolific Kunqu music theorist, declared as a defining feature (wutou) the dramatic jump of a twelfth in phrase 20, from the c# to g1, the highest note of the aria. It is at that exact point that Crimson complains about being ignored and left waiting outside the door (phrase 21), and reveals that she is sexually aroused (phrase 22).[15] Mei Lanfang (1894–1961), the legendary Peking opera and Kunqu performer, commented that when actor-singers sing the unusually long aria expressively, they do not need to do any titillating gesture-dances in order to make it entertaining.[16]

To discuss traditional readings and multimedia performances of "Twelve Shades," a representative realization (1984) by Liang Guyin, one with readily accessible online audiovisual recording, will suffice (⋙ Visual Resources). To demonstrate verbal meanings of the aria, its Chinese lyrics and English translations are presented phrase by phrase in the following pages. To evoke the ways in which Li Rihua literally appropriated the verbal expressions from Wang's zaju script, words that he took from arias 11 and 12 of act 1 of volume IV of Northern Western Wing are put inside quotation marks. To demonstrate the linguistic-musical rhyme scheme of Li's aria, characters that are required to rhyme and their pronunciation in modern, standard Chinese is given, italicized, within curly brackets; when the sung pronunciation rhymes but standard pronunciation does not, the former is given in regular brackets.

To evoke the choreography that actresses might realize while singing, short descriptions of the gesture-dances that Liang Guyin did in her recorded performance are included as well. To indicate when the phrases and gesture-dances occur in her audiovisual recording, time markings showing when singing of the phrases begins are included. To identify the source of music sung and what associations it might evoke, the names of the song patterns referenced in the constituent phrases are noted. To notationally demonstrate the musical features of the aria as performed by Liang Guyin, music example 1 is presented next.

"TWELVE SHADES"

（六旦）想他二人哦！　　YOUNG FEMALE as CRIMSON [*chants*]: Talking about those two!

Coming on stage, Crimson presents herself and strikes a pose of a person getting ready to tell something.

（六旦）　　CRIMSON [*sings*]:
【醉扶歸】　*To the tune "Zui fu gui"*[17]

Phrase 1; 20"　　小姐小姐多豐彩{*cai*}，　My lady, my lady, so full of charm;

Crimson performs gesture-dance of looking around, makes feminine poses, and then frames her face with her hands to evoke Oriole's beauty.

Phrase 2; 59"　　君瑞君瑞濟川才{*cai*}，　Student Zhang, Student Zhang, with talent flowing like a river;

Crimson makes masculine poses, and then walks like a man, with feet raised relatively high.

Phrase 3; 1'28"　　一雙才貌世無賽{*sai*}．　His pairing of talents and looks is peerless in the world.

Crimson turns, makes pose of declaring that the couple has no competition.

【雙蝴蝶】　*To the tune "Shuang hudie"*
Phrase 4; 1'55"　　堪愛{*ai*}！　How lovely!

Crimson walks in a circle, swings the tip of her sash fast and high like she is proud of the couple.

【沉醉東風】　*To the tune "Chenzui dongfeng"*
Phrase 5; 2'18"　　愛他們兩意和諧{*xie* [*hai*]}．　I love them so harmoniously matched.

Crimson slowly makes a cross with her left and right index fingers, kinetically suggesting that the couple have found one another; claps her hands to applaud their getting together.

Phrase 6; 3'02"　　一個"半推半就"，　This one is "half resistant, half willing";

Crimson makes facial expression of being shy, and half stretches her arms out to suggest resistance.

Phrase 7; 3'30"　　一個"又驚又愛"{*ai*}。　That one is "now alarmed, now full of love".

Crimson swings two tips of her sash, makes facial expression of surprise and hand gestures of welcoming, making a smile, and hiding.

【桃花紅】　*To the tune "Taohua hong"*
Phrase 8; 3'57"　　一個嬌羞滿面；　This one's face overflows with fetching shyness;

Crimson raises her sash high, covering her face, and then drops the sash slowly and playfully peeping out from under it.

Phrase 9; 4'23"　　一個春意滿懷{*huai*}。　That one's breast overflows with carnal thoughts.

Crimson slowly shakes her head left and right to project Student Zhang's excitement and claps her hands.

Phrase 10; 4'38"　　好似襄王神女會陽台{*tai*}。　They are like King Xiang and the Goddess of Mt. Wu trysting at Yang Terrace.

Crimson makes hand gestures like a royal man, walks a circle, spins her sash, and then drops her body to the floor, showing her back to the audience with her right arm raised high, outlining a fish.

【滴滴金】　　*To the tune "Didi jin"*

Phrase 11; 5'23"　　"花心"摘，　　The heart of her flower is plucked,

Crimson plays with her sash, throws its tips out, and frames her waist with her hands, outlining a flower/a beauty.

Phrase 12; 5'50"　　柳腰擺{*bai*}。　　Her willowy waist undulates.

Crimson tilts her body backward, shakes her torso a bit, suggesting a willow swaying, then crouches.

【洞仙歌】　　*To the tune "Dongxian ge"*

Phrase 13; 6'15"　　似"露滴牡丹"開 {*kai*}，　　It's like "dew dripping; the peony opening,"

Crimson plays with her sash and makes an arm gesture of flowers blossoming.

Phrase 14; 6'40"　　香恣遊蜂採{*cai*}。　　Wandering bee gathers pollen from fragrant beauty.

Crimson spreads the tips of her sash as if they were flapping wings.

【皂羅袍】　　*To the tune "Zao luopao"*

Phrase 15; 7'00"　　一個斜欹雲鬢。　　That one reclines, cloud-like hair disarrayed;

Crimson waves her arms up and down, drawing attention to her head and head ornaments, while walking in a circle backwards.

Phrase 16; 7'27"　　也不管墜折寶釵{*chai*}。　　Unperturbed that her bejeweled hairpin has fallen and gotten bent.

Crimsons makes expansive gestures with the tips of her sash, suggesting Oriole's care-free nature; makes a facial expression like Oriole forgetting her hairpin.

Phrase 17; 7'50"　　一個掀翻錦被，　　That one throws back the embroidered quilt,

Crimson's hands hold the tips of her sash tight in front of her chest, as if she is feeling cold; then she does a gesture-dance of taking a quilt off a sleeping person; she sticks the tip of her tongue out to suggest surprise at what she finds.

Phrase 18; 8'14"　　也不管凍却瘦骸{*hai*}。　　His slender body unperturbed by the cold.

Crimson steps back, shows a facial expression of having no worries, crosses her arms and raises them almost as high as her cheek.

【漁父第一】　　*To the tune "Yufu diyi"*

Phrase 19; 8'33"　　今宵鈎却相思債{*zhai*}。　　Settling their love debts tonight,

Crimson makes gestures of love and then one of a woman mischievously teasing her partner.

Phrase 20; 9'08"　　竟不管　　They are not even perturbed that

Crimson acts like she suddenly realizes that the loving couple has forgotten her.

Phrase 21; 9'19"　　紅娘在門外待{*dai*}，　　Crimson waits outside the door.

Crimson acts like she is lonely, frustrated, and sad, while dutifully waiting for her mistress.

【好姐姐】　　*To the tune "Hao jiejie"*

Phrase 22; 9'45"　　教我無端春興倩誰排 {*pai*}。　　This causes, suddenly, my carnal thoughts to rise, but there's no one to help deal with them.

Crimson acts reflective, turns, bending her head and torso backwards and then turning them left and right.

【傍粧臺】　　*To the tune "Bang zhuangtai"*

Phrase 23; 10'22"　　　　　只得咬定羅衫耐{nai}。　I can only try to bear it by biting my silk tunic.

Crimson plays with the tips of her sash before biting a corner of it; biting a sash or handkerchief is often used in traditional Chinese opera to show a woman trying to deal with erotic thoughts.

Phrase 24; 10'46"　　　　　猶恐夫人睡覺來{lai}。　I also fear that Her Ladyship will wake,

Crimson looks left and right to check if Her Ladyship approaches and shows a facial expression of being worried.

Phrase 25; 11'12"　　　　　將好事翻成害。　And turn a fine thing into a disaster.

Crimson swings the tips of her sash left and right and then makes gestures of warning.

Phrase 26; 11'34"　　　　　將門扣，　I will knock on the door,

Crimson watches and listens for unexpected sounds and then does the knocking-on-the-door gesture.

Phrase 27; 11'45"　　　　　叫秀才{cai}。　and call "Scholar."

Crimson makes a gesture of calling Student Zhang.

　　　　　　　　　　　　　　【排歌】　*To the tune "Paige"*
Phrase 28; 11'52"　　　　　喂秀才{cai}，　Hey, Scholar,
　　　　　　你忙披衣服把門開{kai}。　Hurry up, throw on some clothes, and open the door.

Crimson swings the tips of her sash over her shoulders like she is putting on clothes, and then she does a gesture-dance of pushing the door open.

Phrase 29; 12'17"　　　　　低低叫，　Softly, I call,

Crimson hesitates, and then makes gestures to call her mistress.

Phrase 30; 12'28"　　　　　叫小姐，　I call Missy,

Crimson acts like she is calling her mistress by the door.

Phrase 31; 12'36"　　　　　小姐呀，　Missy,
　　　　　　你莫貪餘樂惹飛災{zai}。　Don't, coveting more pleasure, invite disaster.

Crimson swings the tips of her sash fast, suggesting that she knows what bad things might happen.

13'03"　　（六旦）哎呀，不不,不好了，呀！　CRIMSON [*speaks*]: Ai! This is not, not, not good!

Crimson acts like something bad has happened.

　　　　　　　　　　　　（六旦）　CRIMSON [*sings*]:
　　　　　　　　　　　　【賀新郎】　*To the tune "Hexinlang"*
Phrase 32; 13'14"　　　　　看看月上粉牆來 {lai}。　See the moonlight has risen high on the painted wall.

Crimson makes gestures of looking up to the moon.

Phrase 33; 13'40"　　　　　莫怪　Don't blame me

Crimson shows her sense of being right and will take no blame.

Phrase 34; 13'43"　　　　　再三催。　For rushing you again and again.

Crimson leaves the stage.

Witnessing an expressive performance of "Twelve Shades" by master performers like Liang Guyin, Kunqu practitioners realize that while the aria is a musical attraction by itself, it also affords plenty of room for actor-singers to perform all kinds of gesture-dances that kinetically suggest Crimson's shifting emotions and thoughts. Analyzing the music and gesture-dances of the aria as they are sung and enacted, one realizes that in Kunqu, the interrelationships among words, music, and dance are dynamic.

As a through-composed vocal composition, "Twelve Shades" displays deliberate and expressive manipulations of vocal ranges, melodic contours and directions, and modal cadences and pillar tones.[18] Sung in a large range of two octaves, from low G to high g1, the melodies of the aria go up and down like Crimson's shifting emotions. Melodic directions often change when musical-verbal phrases get close to the lowest or the highest notes of the set vocal range, and/or when ideas or emotions are introduced. Many phrases ending with rhyme-words approach cadences on the first, fifth, or sixth of the tune's modal scale—namely, e, b, and c# and their octaves. The cadences not only highlight key words, but also underscore the modal and structural musicality of the tune composed to sing the lyrics. The same musicality also shines through when melodic turns largely match tonal contours of individual characters (*zidiao*) in the lyrics. For example, characters with the descending linguistic tone, such as *sài* (competition) and *ài* (love) in phrases 3 and 4, respectively, are often sung with descending melodies. The matching of tonal and musical contours creates musical delights that Kunqu enthusiasts savor (☞ Introduction).

In terms of musical rhythm, the aria highlights key words in the lyrics by having them begin on the first beats of the 4/8 and 4/4 measures, and/or sung with melismas or long fermatas. For example, the key words in phrase 1—namely, "*duo/* plenty" and "*cai*/charm"—fall on the first beats of measures. Similarly, the key words of "*chuan*/river" in phrase 2 and "*wu*/no" in phrase 3 are presented with melismas that stretch over beats. Phrase 4, which includes only two monosyllabic words, "How lovely" (*kan'ai*), is sung with a melodic phrase of thirteen beats—a most atypical and unmistakable length for a sung phrase of two monosyllabic words. The ten-beat-long fermata and cadential descent for the word *ai* make a musical expression that no critical listener would miss. Rhythmic setting of words in "Twelve Shades" is musical and structural. Except for key words, "regular" words are sung within the time of two beats. Padding words (*chenzi, xuzi*), such as "*yige*/one," found at the beginning of phrases 7 and 8, would get the rhythmic time of only one beat.

Despite being a through-composed aria, "Twelve Shades" shows a two-part and developing musical structure—one that complements the dramatic development that the lyrics tell. The first part, which ends by phrase 19, portrays Crimson describing Student Zhang and Oriole and their love. The music for this part is ornate, with melodic melismas and rhythmically expansive fermatas. The second part, which begins at phrase 20, when Crimson announces her own erotic and agitated feelings is melodically less ornate and develops more dramatically—words in this second part are sung with relatively short notes. From measure 55 or the end of phrase 26 on, the music shifts from 8/4 time to that of 4/4, and it unfolds with a faster tempo; this musical adjustment underscores the dramatic transition from Crimson's reflexive thoughts to taking action to get Oriole out of Student Zhang's study.

As analyzed here, the musical structure of "Twelve Shades" creates ample time and space for actors to perform gesture-dances that draw the audience to or away from what its lyrics tell. As demonstrated by Liang Guyin's gesture-dances, some of the meanings of scripted words are kinetically highlighted. For example, the verbal portrayal of Student Zhang as a proud and virile man is kinetically illustrated by Crimson's masculine poses and gestures (phrase 2). Similarly, Crimson's happiness for the couple is choreographically projected by her confident bodily turns and swings (phrase 5), the kinetic meanings and symbolic associations of which are contextualized and amplified by Crimson's donning a maid's dress and her playful use of a sash.

Explicitly erotic phrases in the lyrics can be kinetically acted out or suppressed. As Mei Lanfang and some historical records reported, some early-twentieth-century actor-singers did suggestive acts and dances. But twenty-first-century actors like Liang Guyin do not perform any sexually explicit or seductive gestures or dances. Liang, however, has created, or kept, distinctive gesture-dances that simultaneously underscore and cover up erotic messages in "Twelve Shades." For example, while singing phrase 10, which alludes to the myth of King Xiang's rendezvous with the Goddess of Mt. Wu, Liang performs the "resting fish" (*woyu*), an act that involves her dramatically dropping her body onto the stage floor. Kinetically and visually stunning, this gesture-dance is an attraction by itself—one that might make casual audiences forget the suggestive words that the actor is singing. However, for enthusiasts familiar with Chinese cultural-historical tropes, the act is nothing but a subtle symbol of love and sex—a traditional Chinese aphorism declares that lovers would happily embrace one another like fish playing in the water (*yushui zhi huan*).

CONCLUSION

Liang Guyin's interpretation and performance of "Happy Time" is now a model for twenty-first-century performances of this rearranged scene. Her interpretative performance does not, however, stop other performers from creating their own renditions, introducing ornamental and substantive changes in the process. Kunqu practitioners are active, creative, and informed dramatists, composers, readers, singers, dancers, instrumentalists, and fans. Operating in changing times and places, they have evolving identities and needs, and they perform their Kunqu to serve diverse aesthetic, expressive, and practical needs. Reading and performing masterpieces of Kunqu scenes and arias like "Happy Time" and "Twelve Shades," they find many meanings and pleasures to define their Chinese selves. This is perhaps why they creatively compose, critically read, and masterfully perform Kunqu, constructing and negotiating their own identities in the process and sustaining the genre as China's centuries-old-but-still-thriving classical opera and intangible cultural heritage.

Joseph S. C. Lam

NOTES

1. The data and interpretations presented in this chapter are based on the author's fieldwork and library studies since 2006. Basic facts on Kunqu biographies, history, theories, and repertory are either sourced from or confirmed by the following five standard references: Wu Xinlei, ed., *Zhongguo Kunju da cidian/ A Dictionary of Chinese Kunqu Opera* (Nanjing, China: Nanjing daxue chubanshe, 2002); Hong Weizhu, ed., *Kunqu cidian* (A Kunqu Dictionary), 2 vols. (Yilan, Taiwan: Guoli chuantong yishu zhongxin, 2002); Lu Eting, *Kunqu yanchu shigao* (A Draft History of Kunqu Performance) (Shanghai: Shanghai wenyi chubanshe, 1980); Wang Ning, *Kunju zhezixi yanjiu* (A Study of Kunqu Rearranged Scenes)(Hefei, China: Huangshan chubanshe, 2013); Wu Xinlei, *Chatuben Kunqu shishi biannian* (An Illustrated Chronology of Kunqu Activities)(Shanghai: Shanghai guji chubanshe, 2015); and William Dolby, *A History of Chinese Drama* (London: Paul Elek, 1976).

2. This discussion of *The Story of the Western Wing* (*Xixiang ji*) is based on the following Chinese and English editions and studies: Wang Shifu and Zhang Yanjin, ann., *Xixiang ji* (Beijing: Renmin wenxue chubanshe, 1995); Jin Shengtan, ed. and comment., *Xixiang ji, Diliu caizi shu* (The Story of the Western Wing: The Sixth Book of Genius), 2nd ed. (Taipei: Sanmin shuju, 2015); Stephen H. West and Wilt L. Idema, eds. and trans., *The Story of the Western Wing* (Berkeley and Los Angeles: University of California Press, 1995); Fu Dixiu and Fu Mengmeng, comp., *Xixiang ji ziliao huibian* (Collected Documents on *The Story of the Western Wing*), 2 vols. (Hefei, China: Huangshan shushe, 2012); and Huang Jihong, *Xixiang ji yanjiu shi (Yuan Ming juan)* (A History of Scholarship on the *Story of the Western Wing*: The Yuan and Ming Dynasty Volume) (Beijing: Zhonghua shuju, 2013).

3. This is clear with any reading of preserved scripts of "Happy Time." See Li Rihua, "Xixiang youhui" ("Rendezvous at the Western Wing"), in *Qunyin leixuan* (Selective Collection of Arias from Different Operas), compiled by Hu Wenhuan (fl. 1590s?) (Beijing: Zhonghua shuju, 1980), 1367–1370; and Li Rihua, "Yuexia jiaqi" ("Happy Time on a Moonlit Night"), in *LSZQ* (Beijing: Zhonghua shuju, 1982 [1650s?]), vol. 11, 76–79.

4. For Verdi's *Aida*, see "Aida," s.v. *New Grove Dictionary of Music and Musicians*, online edition. For the Broadway musical, see "Elton John and Tim Rice's *Aida*—Wikipedia," https://en.wikipedia .org/wiki/Elton_John_and_Tim_Rice%27s_Aida; accessed on May 11, 2021. I would like to acknowledge Professor Mark Clague for drawing my attention to the two works on the *Aida* story.

5. Su Ziyu, "*Nan Xixiang ji* zuozhe Cui Shipei shengping kao," ("A Study on *Southern Western Wing* and the Biography of Its Author, Cui Shipei") *Xiju* 3 (2005): 96–100.

6. For summaries and bibliographic information on these historical comments on Li Rihua's *Southern Western Wing*, see Fu and Fu, *Xixiang ji ziliao huibian*, 749–773.

7. For concise descriptions and bibliographic information on these Kunqu documents, see their entries in Wu, *Kunju da cidian*, 896–899, 920.

8. While there is ample data on how Chinese elite read *chuanqi* as literature in Ming and Qing times, there is little documentation on how Kunqu practitioners of the same historical period read and realize performance scripts into multimedia operas. For the purposes of the discussion here, the "Happy Time" scene will be read in the way traditional Kunqu practitioners do. Judging from my experiences with them, they would read various versions of the Kunqu operas that they perform, including those that they consider historical and would not literally realize onstage. As they read, they focus on how the unfolding dramatic situations and characters' developing emotions and actions can be realized with singing and dancing.

9. Kunqu experts have made many comments on the complex structure and atypical length of this aria. For an analytical discussion, see Huang Sichao, *Jiqu yanjiu: Yi Wanli zhi Kangxi qupu di jiqu wei lunshu fanchou* (A Study of Composite Arias Preserved in Kunqu Anthologies Published between 1572–1722), 2 vols. (Taipei: Huamulan wenhua chubanshe, 2016), 56–58, 411–414.

10. For a contemporary edition of Wang's Chinese text that corresponds to "Happy Time," see Wang Shifu, *Xixiang ji* (*The Story of the Western Wing*), ann. Zhang Yanjin (Beijing: Zhongguo

guojia tushuguan chubanshe, 2019), 171–174; for English translations of arias 11 and 12, see West and Idema, *The Story of the Western Wing*, 228.

11. Sheng Yuanyuan, "*Nan Xixiang ji Jiaqi*," in *Kuntan qiuyi liushi nian: Shen Shihua Kunju shengya* (Sixty Years of Persuing Kunqu Performance Artistry: Shen Shihua's Kunqu Career), Shen Shihua, dict.; Zhang Yifan, rec/ed. (Beijing: Beijing chuben jituan gongsi and Beijing chubanshe, 2016), 305–317.

12. For a biographical account on her performance of "Happy Time," see Liang Guyin, "*Xixiang ji Jiaqi*," in *Kunqu baizhong dashi shuoxi* (One Hundred Pieces of Kunqu, Master Performers Talk about Their Scenes), (Changsha, China: Hunan dianzi yinxiang chubanshe and Yuelu shushe, 2014), vol. 1, 40–53.

13. Wang Xichun, comp., "*Jiaqi*," in *Eyunge qupu* (Notated Kunqu Music from the Studio of Superb Singing), (Shanghai: Zhuyitang, 1920), vol. 11, n.p.; and Wang Jilie, *Jicheng qupu* (The All-Inclusive Collection of Kunqu Performance Scripts and Notated Music), (Shanghai, 1925), *jin ji juan* 7, n.p. This early twentieth-century version is essentially the same as the current "Happy Time" rearranged scene. A standardized 21st century version appears in Shanghai xiju xueyuan fushu xiqu xuexiao, comp., *Kunqu jingbian jumu diancang* (A Treasure of Critically Edited Kunqu Rearranged Scenes Performance Scripts) (Shanghai: Zhongxi shuju, 2007), vol. 5, 166–171.

14. In our discussions, my Kunqu research partners tend to talk about the aria's musical features much more than its eroticism, which they fully acknowledge.

15. Wang Zhenglai, "*Shuoming*," in *Zhongguo kunju da cidian*, 689.

16. Mei Lanfang and Xu Jichuan, *Wutai shenghuo sishi nian* (Forty Years of Living and Performing on the Stage), Zhonghe chuban ed. (Hong Kong: Open Page Publishing, 2017), 466.

17. Literary-musical phrases/units of the aria are divided according to semantic and rhyme breaks marked in *JGDC*, juan 4, folio 9b–11a; 7:9.312 1 and 4 vol. 88, 618–621. Phrases drawn from the arias featured in the excerpt are as indicated in the text.

18. For concise explanations of technical terms on music styles and structures referenced in this discussion, see Don Michael Randel, *The Harvard Dictionary of Music*, 4th ed. (Cambridge, MA: Harvard University Press, 2003).

PRIMARY SOURCES

CXSWQP   Zhou Qin 周秦, ed. *Cunxin shuwu qupu* 寸心書屋曲譜 ([*Kunqu*] *Music Scores from the Sincere Simple Heart Studio*), vol. 1, 208–215; vol. 2, 126–129. 2 vols. Suzhou, China: Suzhou daxue chubanshe, 1993.

EYG   Wang Xichun 王錫純, comp. *Eyunge qupu* (*The Notated* [*Kunqu*] *Music from the Studio of Superb Singing*). Reprint. Shanghai: Zhuyitang, 1920.

JGDC   Yunlu 允祿 and Wang Qiugui 王秋桂, comp. *Jiugong dacheng nanbei ci gongpu* 九宮大成南北詞宮譜 (*The Formulary of Northern and Southern Arias in the Great Anthology of the Nine Modes*). In *Shanban xiqu congkan* 善本戲曲叢刊 (*The Printed Collectanea of Rare Editions of Drama*), ed. Wang Qiugui 王秋桂, vol. 88, 618–621. Taipei: Xuesheng shuju, 1987.

LSZQ   Li Rihua 李日華. *Xixiang ji* 西廂記 (*The* [*Southern*] *Story of the Western Wing*). In *Liushi zhong qu* 六十種曲 (*Sixty Plays*), comp. Mao Jin 毛晉, v. 11, 1–109. Beijing: Zhonghua shuju, 1982.

SUGGESTED READINGS

ENGLISH

Dolby, William. *A History of Chinese Drama*. London: Paul Elek, 1976.

Fu, Jin. *Chinese Theater: Happiness and Sorrows on the Stage*. Trans. Wang Wenliang, Wang Huan, and Zhang Lina. Beijing: China Intercontinental Press, 2010.

Li, Xiao. *Chinese Kunqu Opera*. San Francisco: Long River Press, 2005.

Picard, François and Lau, Kar Lun Alan. "*Qupai* in Kunqu: Text-Music Issues." In *Qupai in Chinese Music: Melodic Models in Form and Practice*, ed. Alan Thrasher, 119–154. New York: Routledge, 2016.

Swatek, Catherine C. Peony Pavilion *Onstage: Four Centuries in the Career of a Chinese Drama*. Ann Arbor: Center for Chinese Studies, University of Michigan, 2002.

CHINESE

Lu Eting 陸萼庭. *Kunqu yanchu shigao* 昆曲演出史稿 (*A Draft History of Kunqu Performance*). Shanghai: Shanghai wenyi chubanshe, 1980.

Wang Ning 王寧. *Kunju zhezixi yanjiu* 昆劇折子戲研究 (*A Study of Rearranged Scenes in Kunqu*). Hefei, China: Huangshan chubanshe, 2013.

Wu Xinlei 吳新雷. *Chatuben Kunqu shishi biannian* 插圖本崑曲史事編年 (*An Illustrated Chronicle of the History of Kunqu*). Shanghai: Shanghai guji chubanshe, 2015.

9

The Peony Pavilion

Emotions, Dreams, and Spectatorship

As the most renowned work among the "four dream plays" (*si meng*) of Tang Xianzu (1550–1616), *The Peony Pavilion* (*Mudan ting*, 1598) is often taken as the Chinese counterpart to *Romeo and Juliet*, written one year earlier. A still more intriguing point of reference might be *Sleepless in Seattle*, a 1993 movie famous for not having Tom Hanks and Meg Ryan's characters really meet until the end. *The Peony Pavilion* does not go that far—the young scholar, Liu Mengmei, and the prefect's daughter, Du Liniang, have dream encounters early in scenes 2 and 10—but it was unprecedented in its time for the romantic personae not to have met in person halfway through such a long play. The "person" who comes to visit Mengmei in scene 28 is the specter of Liniang, who had already died three years earlier, consumed by her erotic dream.

The second half of the play follows a more conventional development—the revival of Liniang, her marriage to Mengmei, Mengmei's victory in the examinations, and the ultimate approval, taking the form of an imperial edict. It is the first half that has startled people then and now, as noted by the Infernal Judge, who reviews Liniang's cause of death in disbelief: "How on earth would there be such things as dying of a dream" without her even knowing who and where the dreamt lover is [*MDT* 123]?[1] In this regard, *The Peony Pavilion* breaks from the timeworn tableau of love at first sight (exemplified by the late-thirteenth-century *The Story of the Western Wing;* ☛ chaps. 1 and 4) and ushers in a new species of romance in the seventeenth century, in which the lovers hardly make each other's acquaintance until very late; what they keep running into are itinerant artifacts in various media—most prominently, poems and paintings—in lieu of the persons behind such creations (☛ chaps. 10 and 11).

This new species of romance stemming from *The Peony Pavilion*, therefore, is less about the absence and deferral of the encounter than about the mediated encounter, or better still, the encounter with and among media, which in Tang Xianzu's play hinges on the changing meaning of the dream. The dream is no longer a transcendent plane to bring the lovers together, as in ancient and medieval literature; neither is it simply a figment of a wish-fulfilling imagination that expresses one's inner state of mind, as modern readers after Freud tend to think. Rather, this chapter will argue, dreams in *The Peony Pavilion* configure a media environment interfacing images and desires—a mediating space that structures emotion and subject positions.

In *Sleepless in Seattle*, such an environment distends among three moments of media economy: the throwback to the old medium (radio) still lingering with American car culture (Meg Ryan first hears Tom Hanks on air while driving back from a road trip); the heyday of the VHS prominently featured in Ryan's living room (which explains why characters living across the country can watch the 1957 Hollywood classic *An Affair to Remember* in their homes on separate occasions); and a nod toward the nascent Internet (thanks to which a mysterious voice from Seattle can be tracked down and an eight-year-old boy can book himself a flight ticket, sealing the happy ending on the top of the Empire State Building), foreshadowing Hanks and Ryan's next blockbuster *You've Got Mail* (1998) being a brazen placement for America Online. By contrast, the historical significance of *The Peony Pavilion* lies less in registering the transition between old and new media, but more fundamentally, in heralding the emergence of media per se as an issue when theater and print increasingly intersected in late-sixteenth-century China and generated a new subject position available to viewers and readers—namely, spectatorship. In other words, medium is foregrounded as an issue when dreamers stop meeting each other in the dream but turn into spectators confronting the dream as an interface of their proliferating images.

To fully understand the transfiguration of the dream into a media environment and the metamorphosis from dreamer to spectator, we need to push the argument one step further: rather than saying that a mediating space structures emotion and subject positions, we have to reconceive of emotion itself as a historically varied spatial structure, of which the emergence of spectatorship and medium is one of its corollaries. To account for the historical transfiguration of the dream, therefore, is to uncover and follow a genealogy of "emotion-realms" (*qingjing*), by which I stress the spatiality rather than the interiority of emotion.

If *The Peony Pavilion* is the romantic play par excellence, it is not because, as many assume, the play upholds emotion as the innermost essence of the individual liberated in a new social and media environment. Rather, I will argue, it is because the play eloquently encapsulates the three major regimes of the spatiality of emotion—namely, winds, dreamscapes, and theatricality—each predicated on a particular way that we are moved. By "moved," I refer not to a stirred state of mind, but rather by turns to a universal motion within which my body is immersed and swayed as one of the relay spots, or to an endless trajectory through which one is transported from one realm of existence to another, or to the remove at which we are distanced from ourselves as well as the others. It is these three ways of being moved, not the static measurements (length, width, height), that constitute the three dimensions (embedment, deliverance, face-off) of an emotion realm. While these dimensions are always coeval and inseparable, each historical regime of spatiality privileges a different dimension around which the interdimensional relationship is particularly rewired.

As a capsule of these various regimes, *The Peony Pavilion* has deployed them in an anachronistic juxtaposition, obliterating their timeline and structural differences. My reading of the play, therefore, is an archaeological one, sorting out the layers of sedimentation through which we can glimpse into the subtle transformation of Chinese theater—of which the transfiguration of the dream and the rise of the media environment are telling symptoms—as an aspect of the genealogy of emotion realms.

9.1 UNDER THE WEATHER

"Out of *qing* forms the dream; out of the dream forms drama" [*TXZQJ* 2:1464]. Thus is explained the genesis of drama in a letter from Tang Xianzu, whose *The Peony Pavilion* did more than any other work to define the cult of *qing*—a polyvalent word meaning emotion, feeling, sentiment, passion, and love—at the turn of the seventeenth century. Depicting a young woman, Du Liniang, who dies dreaming of a lover she never met and then revives thanks to her ineradicable passion, the play has gained unrivaled fame for celebrating the power of emotion to transcend life and death. In Tang's own words, however, emotion and dreams are not just themes or leitmotifs of the play, but also the origin of theater in a profound sense. He seems to suggest that drama is traceable all the way to the innermost site of the human psyche where emotion resides, with the dream as the intermediate, inner "stage" on which intangible emotions take a visual form for the mind's eye, providing the prototype for theatrical performance.

The implications of this genesis for our understanding of Chinese literary history and of the history of emotion are intertwined. For the former, modern scholars regard drama as deriving from the grand tradition of lyricism at the core of Chinese culture—a tradition allegedly predicated on expressing the emotive interior rather than mimicking external actions, just as poetry has been defined ever since the "Great Preface" to the *Book of Songs* (*Shijing*) as "emotions being stirred within and taking form in words" [*MSZY* 1:270] (➥ Introduction, *HTRCP*, chap. 1). For the latter, since emotion is understood as the interior awaiting expression, our modern account of emotion in traditional China can only be a story of suppression and emancipation.

Tang Xianzu is thus often portrayed as the liberator of emotion battling a conservative ethos, and modern critics frequently invoke the playwright's defense of his romantic plays, in which he is alleged to contrast his Neo-Confucian mentor's advocacy of moral nature (*xing*) with his own advocacy of emotion (*qing*).[2] By the same token, *The Peony Pavilion* is celebrated for the "awakening" of human desire and women's subjectivity, as emblematized by Du Liniang's erotic dream that takes and gives life. Our modern understanding of emotion and its historical unfolding have affected how we understand Chinese drama, and vice versa; both spring from the premise about a continual exteriorization of the emotive interior.

However, Tang Xianzu's foreword to *The Peony Pavilion* casts a different light on this premise. Instead of presuming emotion as the inner origin of dreams and drama, he calls into question whether we can successfully locate the source of emotion itself:

Emotion, of source unknown, runs ever deeper. The living may die of it, and the dead may be brought back to life.

[*MDT* 1]

Pan Zhiheng (1556–1622), a drama aficionado associated with Tang, came to a similar conclusion upon watching a performance of *The Peony Pavilion*. Emotion, as Pan traces it, lies less in the self than in the uncharted beyond:

It is not known where the trajectory of emotion begins, where it ends, from what it separates itself, and with what it rejoins. Somewhere between being and nonbeing, between what's faraway and what's nearby, between existence and extinction—that is perhaps where emotion certainly goes, but it is not known why it is so.[3]

Such an ontologically uncanny and spatially unbounded notion of emotion complicates the classical view that emotion is anchored in the heart, stirred up inside, and emitted from within.

These complications do not so much break with the classical view of emotion as underscore within ancient sources a much broader horizon of emotion than the innermost site of the subject. The unbound nature of emotion is already suggested by the related trope of "winds" or "airs" (*feng*) in the "Great Preface," which opens the section of a poetic genre also called "Airs" ("Feng") in the *Book of Songs*. Notably, the "Great Preface" does not start with its locus classicus for literary expression of the stirred interior. Preceding what is "stirred within" is the encompassing atmosphere, the pervasive "winds" that stir things up:

"Winds/Airs" (*feng*) means "admonition" (*feng*) or "teaching." Winds are that with which things are stirred up. Teaching is that with which people are cultivated.

[*MSZY* 1:269]

Short-circuiting any distance between input and feedback, winds were not seen as external things causing one's emotive reactions, but a motion inseparable from its own medium and effects.[4] In this light, therefore, emotion is not a psychological state; rather, as affective winds, it manifests as a spatial structure constituted by this continuum of motion, in which things in the cosmos resonate with each other. The flip side of this cosmology is that the body, itself never a self-contained substance, is susceptible to being harmed by cosmic energies. Conceived as saturating every corner and penetrating all thresholds, the winds from the second century BCE came to be seen as a pathological agent of malady in medical discourse or melancholy in sentimental lyrics.[5] Just as the otherwise self-enclosed body is diffused by the currents of air permeating its porous surfaces, the melancholic feeling is not an inner state of mind to be expressed in verbal form, but rather an enveloping "mood" or atmosphere we suddenly find ourselves embedded in. Refuting the reductive notion of psychological interiority, the topos of winds discloses emotion as a spatial structure of sphere—an emotion realm—whose defining dimension can be summed up with the word "embedment." In short, the human subject is embedded in the mood, not the other way around.

In his inscription for a temple in Yihuang county paying tribute to the drama god Erlang shen (written between 1598 and 1606), Tang Xianzu clearly has that cosmological force in mind when he mystifies the powers of theater to the extent that it is alleged to arouse "phoenixes, birds, beasts, and even barbarian spirits of Ba and Yu" as well [*TXZQJ* 2:1188]. Exercised on the human body, such powers can even reactivate lost functions and wipe out pestilence:

> The blind wants to see, the deaf wants to hear, the dumb wants to sigh, the crippled wants to rise, the emotionless can be made emotional, and the voice-less can be given a voice. . . . If every household has this art, no plague and malady would break out.
>
> [*TXZQJ* 2:1188]

The entire model of how drama overwhelms its audience with penetrating affects is a pathological one. The affected subject under the sway of winds should be called the "patient."

This understanding of emotion as a field of dubious cosmological energies helps explain why, in *The Peony Pavilion*, a poem that Liniang reads in the "Airs" section of the *Book of Songs* would affect her so deeply—"for the verse, her senti-mental viscera were stirred over its explication" [*MDT* 43]; that her condition is compared to contracting an "embarrassing disease" (*gan'ga bing*) from the "rear garden" (*hou huayuan*), a euphemism for anal sex [*MDT* 93], or to possession by evil spirits, as her mother laments: "Her body, I fear, was contaminated by the Wil-low Spirit" [*MDT* 81]. By the same token, her poetry tutor Chen Zuiliang's tongue-in-cheek attempt to cure her with the same *Book of Songs* ("use the *Book of Songs* to cure the *Book of Songs* disease" [*MDT* 92]) wittily reactivates this ancient view of powerful words as winds that physically impact the body, for better or worse, in an unmediated fashion. The homeopathy of the affecting wind continues into Liniang's afterlife. The same powerful cosmological forces that consume her to death also transform her into a ghost, a congestion of *yin* ether, so the stage direc-tions repeatedly accompany Liniang's apparition with a chilly breeze [*MDT* 147, 149, 153, 165]. And what brings her back to life ultimately is the cosmological energy of *yang*, hilariously preserved in "the machismo's underwear" (*zhuang nanzi de kudang*) donated by Tutor Chen and used in the ritual of resurrection [*MDT* 184].

How Liniang is "moved" by the *Book of Songs* is correlative to how the audience is "moved" by *The Peony Pavilion*. The differences between reading poetry and watching a play are obliterated if we approach these two kinds of experiences on the plane of winds, precisely because permeating all boundaries, winds short-cir-cuit the source and end, the means and effect, vehicle and content. In the "Great Preface" to the *Book of Songs*, distinctions among media—speech, music, danc-ing—are simply leveled by the cosmic forces that spill from one medium to another without calling attention to any media specificity of each one of them [*MSZY* 1:270].

Early Chinese performance venues—plazas and roofless raised platforms (*lutai*) since the Han dynasty (see figure 9.1), or Tang-Song dancing pavilions (*wuting*)—opened up on all four sides for this omnidirectional flow of affective forces pervading the world,[6] facilitating the direct communication with and emotive impact upon the audience, as exemplified by a public performance scene of the First Full-Moon Festival in Kaifeng, the early-twelfth-century capital of the Northern Song: "tens of thousands of commoners were watching [the variety plays] at the foot of the roofless stage, and the performers from time to time induced them to hurray."[7]

This relatively free structure of playgrounds—characterized by a directly addressed audience with vocal presence and mobile orientation—continued to inform certain layers of latter-day stage performance on varied scales (full play, extracted scenes, pure singing) and settings (public/domestic, ad hoc/permanent), and is often highlighted by modern scholars as something quintessentially Chinese, in contrast to the silenced, stationary, and segregated spectatorship that is rendered inconspicuous in the shadow and "absent" from the fictive world on the Western proscenium stage. It is noteworthy that Pan Zhiheng penned his comment on the unbounded trajectory of emotion after he saw two separate performances at his friends' places by their private troupes, which most likely just

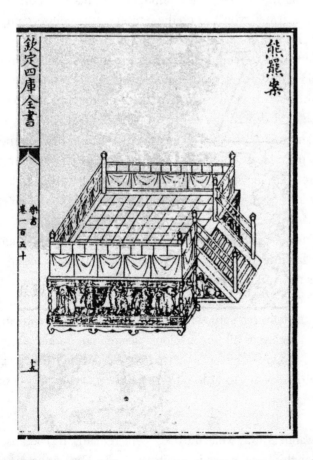

FIGURE 9.1 A roofless, raised platform depicted in the *Book on Music* (*Yueshu*) by Chen Yang (1064–1128), from Che Wenming, *Ershi shiji xiqu wenwu de faxian yu quxue yanjiu* (Beijing: Wenhua yishu chubanshe, 2001), 27.

performed on the carpets in the dining halls. His experience with the play must partially be informed with such kinds of casually structured space quite common in early-seventeenth-century China (▶ Introduction).

9.2 WAKING TO DREAMS

And yet, the topos of winds as an electrifying sphere of cosmological forces bespeaks just one of the dimensions of the emotion realm in *The Peony Pavilion*; that particular dimension, though perhaps with the longest history, hardly exhausts the nature of Chinese theater or the audience's experience in Tang Xianzu's times. Beside the topos of winds, which permeate all boundaries and make experience present and immediate to the human subject embedded within, there lies in the play another topos, which goes in a different direction by stressing layered demarcation over diffusion, alternation over immediacy, retrospection over presence—or in short, a dimension of deliverance over that of embedment. It is the topos of what I propose to call "dreamscape." Just as emotion does not come from the heart, but the moving heart itself is part of the motion in the air, a dream in traditional Chinese discourse is not a Cartesian theater for the mind's eye, but rather what delivers us outside in the world. In his *Rhapsodies of the South* (*Chuci*), the exiled poet Qu Yuan (ca. 340 BCE–ca. 278 BCE) frequently takes flight in his dreams (▶ *HTRCP*, chap. 2).[8]

This journeying motif formed as a subgenre of dream lore under the heading of "Dream Travel" ("Mengyou") when the tenth-century editors compiled the Tang tales (▶ *HTRCFiction*, chap. 2).[9] Wandering out there in the world rather than being trapped in their own minds, dreamers (a married couple, for instance) in such tales could "run into each other in dreams" (*liang xiang tongmeng*).[10] These two spatial features—dreaming as deliverance and the dreamscape as a common ground into which dreamers get delivered—thus provide the very conditions for Liniang and Mengmei to meet in their dreams. As if to drive home the primacy of this conceit, the adaptation of *The Peony Pavilion* by rival playwright Shen Jing (1553–1610) is retitled *The Story of Shared Dreams* (*Tongmeng ji*).[11]

For Liniang and Mengmei to be delivered into each other's dream, one may ask, isn't it already presumed that they each have already harbored certain hidden desires for a mate, just as the Chinese idiom goes, "One dreams at night of what one ponders in the daytime" (*ri you suo si, ye you suo meng*)? But for the ancient Chinese, a dreamer does not fulfill his or her wish by retiring into the innermost phantasm called "dream"; quite the contrary, in fact driven by what the thought is pointing to, the dreamer is delivered somewhere else. The ancient interpretation of dreams is therefore not analysis of unconscious desire, but rather prognostication— the deciphering of divine messages that are gathered from heavenly gods precisely when one is spirited away. According to *A Manual of Dreams* (*Meng shu*), quoted in the late tenth century:

> The spirit wanders away while the body alone remains. It is because the heart has something to think about that it forgets the body. [The wandering spirit] receives a premonition from heavenly gods and comes back to announce it to people.[12]

But if prognostication literature is by default forward-looking in telling one's fortune by deducing the true message from the dream, the early Daoist philosopher
Zhuangzi (ca. 369–286 BCE) looks *back* on the spatial structure of the dream as the
ontological condition that undercuts the whole business of dream interpretation.
We think that we are in the position of clarifying the meaning of our dreams on the
ground that we are already awakened, without knowing that "one is divining one's
dream yet within another dream" [*ZZJS* 1:104], as Zhuangzi contends. There is no
ground or position outside the dream that can serve as an Archimedean point, simply because we realize that we were in a dream only *retrospectively*—that is, only after
we are delivered to a waking reality, which then will be belatedly demystified as just
another layer of the dream after one more round of deliverance. Demarcated into
the layered realms of existence that the dreamer is incessantly delivered through,
the topos of dreamscapes emblematizes a vastly different set of spatial structuration
and problematics for emotion than does the topos of winds. Rather than a saturated
field of unfiltered energies by which the human body is precariously permeated,
emotions are now territorialized as an endless layering of real and unreal, subjecting
dreamers to recurrent cycles of disillusion and reenchantment: "Those drinking in
dreams at dawn find themselves crying; those crying in dreams at dawn find themselves going out to hunt" [*ZZJS* 1:104]. These two topoi of emotion also entail differences in temporal orientation: whereas the embedding winds make *present* both the
patient's body and the instant sensations of affect, the dreamscape is structured in
such a way that the only thing the dreamer could anticipate when incessantly delivered forth is a belated retrospect on how deeply one has already been thrown into an
ever-receding background, whose veiled past could strip off only one layer at a time.

Ensnarled in the nascent dreamscape back in the fourth century BCE, Zhuangzi
was left with what he called a "paradox in suspense" (*diaogui*)—that awakening
collapses into dreams and postpones forever the ultimate reality until "we run
into an ultimate sage who knows its solution tens of thousands of years later—
that is just a matter of time' " [*ZZJS* 1:105]. The solution arrived much earlier than
expected when the Madhyamaka School of Mahayana Buddhism introduced into
fourth-century China the influential Two Truths or Middle Way doctrine, which
advocates taking illusions, sensations, and dreams as expedient means (*upāya*) for
attaining heightened understanding. Rather than an obstacle to awakening, the
dream itself was now valorized as the "provisional" truth without which the ultimate truth of the world—emptiness (*śūnyatā*)—alone cannot be accessed.[13] It was
through the cross-fertilization between Buddhism and Daoism during medieval
times that the dreamscape was fully developed as the underlying topos of theatrical culture at every level.

As early as the Tianbao era (742–756), dramatic performance, characterized as
provisional and suppositional, was taken as an analogy of life as dream. Puppet
plays, for instance, were compared to evanescent dreams: "In an instant the play
was over, silence befalls,/Just like a life in a dream."[14] The analogy continued into
the eleventh and twelfth centuries, usually focused on the ephemerality of worldly
success manifested by performers costumed as mock officials.[15]

Drama as dream further took a concretized form in theater architecture. To the open structure of earlier roofless stages and dancing pavilions, a major overhaul took place around the twelfth and thirteenth centuries—namely, the rise of the backstage, which created extra layers of existence by marking out a *threshold* across which characters were transported from an otherworldly realm through what is called the "ghost gateway" (*guimen guan*). It was the demarcation not between audience and performers, but between stage and backstage that ontologically grounded this kind of early theater (figure 9.2). Moreover, since the mid-Ming era, there emerged another set of new architectural features applying the same operation

FIGURE 9.2 Division between the stage and backstage, portrayed in a 1324 mural painting in Mingying Wang Hall, Shanxi, from Liao Ben, *Zhongguo xiju tushi*, rev. ed. (Zhengzhou, China: Daxiang chubanshe, 2000), 76.

FIGURE 9.3 Early extant passage stage, in Hejin City, Shanxi, late fifteenth century. From Feng Junjie, *Shanxi shenmiao juchang kao* (Beijing: Zhonghua shuju, 2006), 230.

of deliverance to the audience as well. First recorded around the Chenghua era (1465–1487), what modern scholars would later term "passage stage" (*guolu tai*) comprises an elevated stage and its backstage,[16] both of which are established on the top of a passage to the courtyard where hundreds to more than a thousand people can be accommodated (figure 9.3). Worshippers would first go through the gateway, and sounds of music coming from behind would motivate them to turn around and find the performance on stage towering over their heads.

By piling the stage on the theater's entrance, this composite structure literally has the two thresholds that define the theater as dreamscape overlap—one across which the actor delivered a character on- and off-stage, and another across which worshippers, and indeed the temple god, entered and left the theater. The performer, the audience, and the god—none of them actually constituted the vantage point around which the spatial configuration of the temple theater was structured; on the contrary, each of them was constituted as a *dreamer*, by being delivered across the overlapped thresholds whose prominence is underscored with the architectonics of the passage stage.

The dreamscape also manifests in the subgenre of the "deliverance play" (*dutuo ju*) flourishing since the Yuan dynasty (1271–1368). In this type of play, a protagonist is spirited away by a Buddhist or Daoist master into a series of nightmarish scenes called "dreadful realms" (*e jingtou*), only to wake up and realize that life at large is no more than a brief dream.[17] The device of the dreadful realm was so powerful that it was circulated across genre boundaries into courtroom and romantic plays. For instance, in *The Story of the Western Wing* (☞ chap. 1), the scene of love at first sight at the Buddhist temple in act 1, play 1, not only depicts the beauty Cui Yingying as the immortal Bodhisattva Guanyin in apparition, but also delivers the infatuated Student Zhang to an entirely different realm, and he has to remind himself: "This is certainly a Tuṣita Palace;/Don't suspect it to be the Heaven of Separation" [XXJ 7]. But eventually, after Yingying has left, he embraces the changed realm: "What should I do with the jade maiden now gone?/The palace of Brahma I suspect to be the Wuling Spring" [XXJ 9].

The relationship between the goddess and the male mortal is reversed in the final act of play 1, however, where Student Zhang appropriates a Buddhist ceremony meant for Yingying's deceased father so that he can see her again; symbolically, it is as if he is using the power of the ritual to summon and deliver the celestial beauty back to Earth, only to sadly see the woman retreat from his sight again once the ritual is over [XXJ 38–41]. This motif of deliverance culminates in one of the most memorable dream scenes in Chinese literature, in which the beauty is delivered to her journeying lover, who then wakes to a bleak condition of solitude at the end of play 4, which was rumored to have been the "original" ending of the whole play [XXJ 158–161] (☞ chaps. 1 and 4).

The more philosophical usage of the dreamscape in Tang Xianzu's romantic play was probably related to his Buddhist acquaintance, Master Zibo Zhenke (courtesy name Daguan, 1543–1603). Zhenke took dreams to be a gradual procedure heralding sudden enlightenment, an intermediate step that can neither be dispensed with nor be hurried through. That is why he regards "awakening in dreams" (mengwu)—"the more one dreams, the more one becomes awake" (yu meng er yu jue)—as being superior to "delusion awake" (xingmi).[18] It is, therefore, no coincidence that Tang Xianzu, whose friendship and poetic correspondence with Zhenke are well documented, adopted a similar rhetoric of reversal, putting Zhuangzi's paradox on its head: "Why must emotion in the dream not be real? Is there ever a shortage of people living in dreams [MDT 1]?

While, in 1598, this dream of emotion stood as the ultimate plane transcending anything else in The Peony Pavilion, the infinite operation of deliverance—thanks to which all dreams turn into a series of demystification ad infinitum—seemed to eventually subject emotion to prostration and spell the end of Tang's career as a playwright. He devoted his last two works, The Dream of the South Branch (Nanke meng ji, 1600) and The Dream of Handan (Handan meng ji, 1606), to the "deliverance play" genre. The former delivers the protagonist to the exhaustion of emotion (qing jin) [TXZQJ 4:2430–2436]; the latter finishes the task by "burning up the remnant brushwood of emotion" [TXZQJ 4:2563]. One might be tempted to infer that the trajectory of Tang's "four dream plays" as a whole (including the 1590 romantic comedy The Purple Hairpin [Zichai ji]) somehow followed Zhenke's spiritual program.

And yet, just like winds, the dreamscape was a timeworn topos lingering into late imperial periods, and it was not what pertinently defined Tang Xianzu's times. As a closer examination of the dream scenes in The Peony Pavilion will show, that play was ultimately not so much a product of the dreamscape, but rather its modification predicated on a different dimension of the emotion realm.

9.3 IN FACE OF THE PAGE

At first glance, Tang Xianzu's "four dream plays" rearticulate the conventional dream-life-drama analogy and redeploy the terms of real/unreal and enchantment/disillusion that by then were familiar and typical of the dreamscape. More than just a "relay" play amid the trajectory of interminable deliverance, *The Peony Pavilion* can be said to occupy a central position as a "shared dream" not only for the romantic couple (hence continuing the tradition of Tang tales) but also for the late imperial performers and the audience (both of whom were conjured across the overlapped thresholds on and under the passage stage). However, precisely at this critical juncture, the play frustrated the expectation of its more acute readers so much that Feng Menglong (1574–1646) was motivated to redact Tang Xianzu's play into *The Romantic Dream* (*Fengliu meng*). The very first thing that Feng's "General Commentary" ("Zongping") complains of is that Liniang's and Mengmei's dreams, at a closer look, are temporally set apart rather than articulated as a single shared dream:

> Even without prior collaboration, two dreams tally with each other—that is what makes them extraordinary. But in the original play, the male lead makes the first entry and explains his change of name on account of his dream, whereas the female lead does not enter her dream until several scenes later [in "The Interrupted Dream" ("Jingmeng")]. The two dreams appear so disconnected that they taste awful. Now this redaction has the male lead change his name only after the female lead's dream in order to show the resonance of the love karma. The scene "[Husband and Wife] Match Dreams" is the point of convergence.
>
> [*FMLQJ* 12:1049]

By putting Mengmei's dream account right after Liniang's dream scene—and by suppressing all the details in Mengmei's original account that are downright incompatible with "The Interrupted Dream" (scene 10)[19]—Feng tries to reassure us that the couple have gone through one and the same dream. But the problem presented by *The Peony Pavilion* is not really that there are two different dreams rather than one—no matter how many dreams there were, the couple could still have *shared* all of them, as the Flower God apparently suggests by explaining to us that he has had Mengmei delivered into Liniang's dream. Rather, the real problem is that neither Liniang nor Mengmei has any recollection of entering the other's dream. The "point of convergence" that Feng Menglong highlights in his adaptation, in which the protagonists finally "match" their dreams and realize that they have met in a shared dreamscape, is fundamentally at odds with Tang's original design.[20]

With this ruptured dreamscape that is at once shared and jarringly disjunctive, does this mean that we are falling back on the notion of dream as expression of the individual interior, leading to the familiar conclusion that Mengmei and Liniang are each just obsessed with their own inner fantasies, in which the dream lovers they meet are no more than the projected shadows of their desires? And yet, despite his misguided attempt to squeeze *The Peony Pavilion* back into the medie-val model of one shared dream, Feng Menglong unwittingly shows us, in his com-ments to the classical tale collection *History of Emotion* (*Qing shi*) that he compiled in the 1630s, how the dreamscape actually metamorphosed into a different spatial structure of emotion at the turn of the seventeenth century:

> Dreams are the roaming of the ethereal soul. The humic soul is nothing mirac-ulous but the ethereal soul is, and hence the body is nothing miraculous but a dream is. A dream can reach what has not yet happened and inspire what has not yet been thought. If it does not turn out to be accurate, we call it "dream"; if it turns out to be accurate, we call it "not-a-dream." A dream that turns out to be a dream is the unreal that looks real; a dream that turns out to be not a dream is a reality that looks more unreal! Others cannot be aware of my dream, of which only I am aware; I cannot see my ethereal soul, but others perhaps see it. I am aware of my dream but cannot understand it myself—this is because the ethereal soul cannot be interrogated; others might see my ethereal soul but my ethereal soul is not self-aware—that is just like the case of a dream. [The ethereal soul] can be detached from a living person, but can be called back even if the person has been dead. It can even possess another person's body. Is it that the ethereal soul takes the body as a tavern?
>
> [*FMLQJ*]

Underneath the "roaming" and "real-unreal" commonplace, Feng Menglong articulates a new language of the outsider in order to make sense of dream experi-ences. Dreaming is a form of roaming, no longer just because spirit, as the locus of consciousness, departs from the immobile body, as traditional prognostication liter-ature describes, but more fundamentally because of the bipartite structure of spir-it-consciousness itself, which is split into ethereal (*hun*, the lighter half that ascends and wanders away) and humic souls (*po*, the turbid half that sinks and stays). This revamped origin of dreams in the splitting of the soul in turn modifies the reason for skepticism about dreams: dreams are impossible to understand, not because the very ground of reality for us to do interpretation keeps collapsing into dreams, as Zhuangzi contends, but because the split soul undercuts self-consciousness per se. In place of a well-informed spirit that would return and communicate to humanity the divine message, Feng sees a detached and aloof "ethereal soul," which, like an undutiful child, comes home and does not feel like being asked where, how, and for what purpose it has spent the night. This communication breakdown with my som-nambulant half-soul renders me an outsider of my dream. Most important, such an "outsider" position that I occupy vis-à-vis my own dream mirrors the symmet-rically opposite position occupied by "other people" vis-à-vis a dream of mine. The two positions mirror each other: whereas I, as an outsider of my dream, cannot see my own ethereal soul when it sneaks out—and even the ethereal soul is unable to see or be aware of itself because it is somnambulant—other people, outsiders as well by default, stand a chance to *see* my ethereal soul. The previous problematic of being, delivered across infinitely layered realms of realities and illusions, is displaced with the early modern one of trying to see and understand a dream from an outside position—that is, the position of the spectator.

The shift from dreamer to spectator marks the subtle modification of the dreamscape into theatricality as the newly emergent mode of spatiality of emotion at the turn of the seventeenth century. The historical change has for the most part been glossed over under the aegis of the same old drama-dream analogy, and yet a closer look can detect it, for instance, between the lines of Tang's contemporary Xie Zhaozhe (1567–1624):

> Drama and dreams are the same. Sorrow and joy upon separation and reunion—none of these emotions is real; affluence or poverty, high or low status—none of these situations is genuine. The transient world is just like this. Nonetheless, the unwise cheer in auspicious dreams and worry in nightmares; their countenance would be saddened over a play of torment but lit up over a play of prosperity. Overall, people rarely avoid their vulgar view of life. Recently men of letters love picking on dramas for their deviation from historical facts. This is just as the idiom goes: "Telling a dream in front of an idiot."[21]

Apparently, Xie only reproduces the familiar structure of a dreamscape as demarcated layering into and through which the dreamer is transported out there experiencing passions and their nullification alternately; hence "the transient world" is just a dream at large. And yet the threefold analogy of dream/drama/world established by a couple of forthright assertions—"drama and dreams are the same" and "the transient world is just like this"—conceals the significant shift in the way that drama conjoins with dreams. The point of convergence no longer hinges on the protagonist undergoing ephemeral states of passion like a dreamer or a performer (along with the audience) crossing a threshold into the theater as a dreamlike realm, but rather on a new analogy between dreamer and spectator: "The unwise cheer in auspicious dreams and worry in nightmares; their countenance would be saddened over a play of torment but lit up over a play of prosperity." Less than experiencing passions *within and through* layers of a dreamscape, the dreamer is now reconstituted as a spectator *in front of* the dreamscape.

Here, we see the old idiom "Never tell a dream in front of an idiot" (*chiren qian bu de shuo meng*) acquire a brand-new meaning.[22] The "idiot," *in front of* whom we cannot relate a dream, lest he should take it to be real, actually maps out the paradigmatic position for the dreamer-spectator. The point is no longer that the idiot has to be doubly removed as an underprivileged outsider (he is denied access to another person's dream) because he is too stupid to appreciate the unreal as what it is; quite the contrary, it is the insider—the dreamer himself—who is now strangely sidelined as an onlooker to his own dream, and he does not so much immediately experience the dream as trying to recuperate it at a distance.

The curious rupture of shared dreams in *The Peony Pavilion*—which is doubly ironical for a scene of intimacy—should now be understood in the light of the emergence of theatricality. To use Feng Menglong's terms, dreams are shared, but in the most disjunctive fashion, precisely because Liniang and Mengmei are the outsiders of their own dreams and the spectators to the other's wandering soul. Since those who truly make love and get intimate in "The Interrupted Dream" are not their persons, but rather the alienated half-souls of theirs who would not fully inform the persons of what has been experienced, one has to take the position of the Other and be a spectator to one's own ethereal soul's dream. This is an especially poignant issue for Liniang compared to Mengmei, since, in Pan Zhiheng's words, "the former takes for real her dream, while the latter takes for real his life";[23] that is, the man cares about the worldly success in mundane life—a beautiful spouse and an official title—promised in his dream, rather than the dream per se. That is why, after waking up, only Liniang tries to retrieve what has been left behind from the bygone dream.

The defining moment for the play, therefore, is not "Interrupted Dream"—the best-known and most frequently performed scene, which is already laid out in the classical tale "The Story of Du Liniang" ("Du Liniang ji") published in 1594,[24] the immediate source for Tang Xianzu's play—but scene 12, "Pursuing the Dream" ("Xunmeng"), which was Tang's original creation without much precedent to fall back on. Liniang revisits the peony pavilion where the dream scene of lovemaking took place. At first, she finds no trace of the encounter in the desolate corner of the garden, but then things start to come back on:

（旦）	YOUNG FEMALE as DU LINIANG [sings]:
【玉交枝】	To the tune of "Yujiaozhi"
是這等荒涼地面，	Such a forlorn vicinity
沒多半亭臺靠邊，	Without other kiosks and terrains nearby.
好是咱睒暝色眼尋難見。	My squinted eyes seek but hardly find a trace.
明放著白日青天，	Clearly the blazing sun is up in the bright blue sky,
猛教人抓不到魂夢前。	Momentarily making one unable to grasp things to the front of the soul's dream.
霎時間有如活現！	But all of a sudden they seem to vividly emerge!
打方旋再得俄延。	I circle the area just to gain some more time.
呀，是這答兒壓黃金釧匾。	Ah, this is precisely where my gold bracelet was pressed to the ground.

[MDT 60]

From then on, images are flooding in, and in the next aria, she sings:

| 眼下心前， | Right under my eyes and before my mind, |
| 陽臺一座登時變。 | A terrain of love comes into being in a flash. |

[MDT 60]

An elusive object of desire before one's eyes, as suggested toward the end of this quote—these are leitmotifs traceable all the way to the *Book of Songs* and popular throughout the medieval and late imperial periods. But what makes Du Liniang the icon from the late sixteenth century is the strange lament she makes earlier in the passage. Although using her eyes as the means of seeking, she does not simply want to put things before her eyes, nor does she really say that she wishes to grasp what was *in* the dream (as all other available translations, including English subtitles on video, have misleadingly suggested), which would be still in the language of dreamscapes. She could have tried getting back to the dream (since the playwright maintains that it would be even truer than the waking life) or turning it into reality (which happens only in the later parts of the play, but not at this point). Instead, what Liniang actually laments here is: she is "unable to grasp things to the front of the soul's dream."

If deliverance through the ancient and medieval dreamscape turns any way out into just another inside of the dream, and hence repeatedly doubles emotion into an endless interfold of truth and falsehood, Liniang's attempt to retrieve the oneiric experience of emotion and stay with it *in front of* (rather than inside, outside, or through) the dream suggests a revised spatial morphology. An interstitial strand that arrests (however briefly) the otherwise incessant deliverance, this "front" (*qian*) is actually where the postdreamer (the spectator to the dream) stands, and it is therefore at first glance outside the dream, but more important, it is by being situated in the newly delineated space—the "front"—that the outside is at once bordered on, reconnected to, and yet decisively split from the inside. In this deeper sense, the front is less an outside than an interface; the spectatorial position itself would be naught without this mediating surface that at once flattens, articulates, and divides the inside and the outside of the dream. The spatiality of emotion is now restructured and orchestrated among this being "in front of," "bordered on," "reconnected to," and "split from," altogether forming a dimension that I call "face-off," as distinct from the dimensions of embedment and deliverance.

In this face-off dimension, emotion is neither a stream of motion presently synchronized with the embedding winds nor an infinite recess of some preceding background whose unveiling is ever belated and partial; rather, it is what lies ahead and is yet to be identified with. It is this particular dimension that distinguishes theatricality from other historical modes of the spatiality of emotion such as winds and dreamscapes. The pertinent subject position (namely, spectatorship)—as distinct from being a patient or a dreamer—is the locus not of an emotive interior but of the mediating surface itself, underscoring at once the indelible distance from and imaginary reconnection to emotion that lies in the yonder. Diametrically opposite the overflowing force of immediate presence that obliterates media differences in the topos of winds, spectatorship foregrounds the issues of medium and mediated identification, both of which converge at the notion of interface.

Liniang's mediated rapport to the dream from a spectatorial position underlies, but is not reducible to, her narcissistic relationship to herself, which is most flaunted in the "Painting the Self-Portrait" ("Xiezhen") scene. Recoiling from her withering mirror reflection ("How could my enticing litheness of yesterday all succumb to such emaciation?") [*MDT* 69], she proceeds to transfigure it with the paintbrush: "As anticipated, the picture comes to look great halfway through,/As if reborn into quite a different kind of charm" [*MDT* 70]. Neither to recuperate her beauty from memory nor to duplicate the ailing look in the mirror, she is making up by brushwork and speech act, on silk and metaphorically on her face, an ideal image in anticipation (figure 9.4). To say that this image is just a narcissistic projection of her fantasy, insulated from reality (what she actually looks and looked like), would again evoke the specter of interiority; instead, what this image production empathetically relies on is a series of material interface—the mirror, the canvas, as well as the face—in which the spectator's body is an integral part of the whole media environment.

Hence, spectatorship entails not passive recipients, but an assemblage of mediated relationships to self and other through media production, distribution, and

FIGURE 9.4 Huang Mingqi, "Painting the Self-Portrait"; illustration to *The Peony Pavilion* (1617 edition), from Carlos Rojas, *The Naked Gaze: Reflections on Chinese Modernity* (Cambridge, MA: Harvard University Asia Center, 2008), 37.

exchange of assorted images. The dream versions of Liniang that hardly match foreshadow the symptomatic proliferation of her other images, incongruous with one another. Mengmei fails to connect his dream lady, the portrait, and later the revenant to one another, misrecognizing them at every turn as something else.[25] This dispersal of conflicting images undermines any possibility of a unitary identity,[26] but this identity crisis itself should be ascribed as one of the effects of the transmutation of the dreamscape into theatricality. The wandering half-soul is a peel of resemblance coming off the person. In this regard, the modified dreamscape is shared not by the dreamers themselves, but by their detached images. Romance commences when one image encounters another, and to them, the so-called lovers are spectators whose disjunctive interconnection is mediated by the communion of avatars and simulacra. A modern analogy would be the "friends" that we make and become nowadays on Facebook, a cybernetic dreamscape where nothing meets anything except for pictures, videos, and textual postings altogether, taken as our "faces" on display.

Back in early modern China, this universe of simulacra already came into being on printed pages. The disjunctive yet somehow shared dreams thematized in *The Peony Pavilion* turn out to be most appropriate to describe the very milieu in which it was disseminated among the expanded reading public newly augmented with a strong sense of women's presence, as testified to by a slew of sentimental female readers reportedly moved to death and by their published works related to the play that incited further passionate responses and imaginings. The one who earns the most sympathy, and whose story is included in Feng Menglong's *History of Emotion*, Feng Xiaoqing (1595–1612), might not even be a real person, as betrayed by her allegory-ridden name that suggests by sound and in shape "romantic charm" (*fengqing*). However, her imaginary status is precisely what goes with the traffic in the detached images propelled by the play, as well as the entire industry of reading surrounding it [FMLQJ 14:496–501].[27]

Another case in point is the so-called Three Wives' Commentary to the play, a work initiated by Chen Tong (d. 1665)—Wu Ren's (b. 1647) betrothed who died before the wedding—completed by Wu's second and third wives, Tan Ze (d. 1674) and Qian Yi (b. 1671). The three female commentators never met, separated by death and conjoined only by the play that they ardently identified with. Their virtual communion was opened up for more to join when the commentary was published in 1694, which symptomatically features a portrait depicting the "Du Liniang" that Qian Yi claimed to have met in her dream, but turns out to be another simulacrum—namely, a ripoff of an illustration of Cui Yingying from the 1676 edition of *The Story of the Western Wing* (☞ chap. 4).[28]

As one of the most frequently reprinted Chinese plays (second only to *The Western Wing*), *The Peony Pavilion* has also been one of the most beloved ones on the Chinese stage. These two prized aspects come into conflict, however, as people have complained ever since Tang Xianzu's time that the play was written in such a way that it was better for reading than for performance, as reported by Zang Maoxun (1560–1620) (☞ Introduction): "The four plays including *The Peony Pavilion* by Tang [Xianzu] of Linchuan, some critics said, 'are books for the desktop, not operas sung at a banquet.' "[29] Attempts to redact *The Peony Pavilion* and to make it "performable" were made, starting with the aforementioned Shen Jing's *The Story of Shared Dreams* and Zang Maoxun's *The Soul's Return* (*Huanhun ji*, 1616). The complaints always converged on the play's disagreeability to the ears as a result of Tang Xianzu's alleged failure to abide by the prosodic rules of the Kun music that was rising to predominance at the time, although scholars today are still debating whether Tang intended to write in Kun style at all, and whether that prosodic criticism against him was fair. Another line of attack, raised by the early Qing dramatist Li Yu (1611–1680) (☞ chap. 11), was more intrinsic to Tang's lyrics themselves, and therefore harder to refute—namely, that the fancy compositions were too complicated for the audience's ears to understand:

> Not that Yuan people never read, but the arias they wrote convey no bookish air. . . . Even though the two scenes ["The Interrupted Dream" and "Pursuing the Dream" from *The Peony Pavilion*] are well-written, they are simply contemporary drama, not Yuan drama. The first line of "The Interrupted Dream" reads: "The lithe sunlit gossamer is borne across the idle court, / And the spring is whiffling like a thread." Here "gossamer" is used to signify the gossamer of passion (*qingsi*). How much energy has the writer spent on this one opening line! We can call it an exertion of refinement. Yet out of a hundred people who listen to *The Peony Pavilion*, do even one or two really get this intent? If this verse doesn't really harbor the author's original intent but was merely incited from what he happened to see, he could have said he saw the rippling thread; but why did he have to go through a double convolution from the "sunlit gossamer" to the "spring," and then from the "spring" and the "sunlit gossamer" to the final realization that the spring is like a "thread"? If the author does have a deep intent here, I'm afraid those who can understand it are difficult to find. If those who understand are so rare, why should we perform the play in a singing banquet for the delectation of both gentlemen and commoners? . . . This kind of fabulous language can only be taken as writing, not as a *chuanqi* play.[30]

Ironically, Tang's original text came to be justified on prosodic grounds within the circle of Kun-style aficionados. Music notations of the play published in the seventeenth and eighteenth centuries elected to change his tunes but preserve his lyrics rather than the other way around. And even when the performance of extracted scenes from the play became increasingly influenced by professional actors during the Qing dynasty, Tang's idiosyncratic language outlasted their heavy-handed adaptations and continued to enchant audiences. The changes made in the extracted scenes mostly involved dialogue and stage directions, leaving intact the arias from the original (☞ chap. 8). Audiences were thus required to adapt their ears to the inscrutable arias. Li Yu might be right about the aural incomprehensibility of *The Peony Pavilion*, but that did not stop the play from being performed, as the history of its reception shows. As Mao Xianshu (1620–1688) noted in a letter to Li Yu,

"Posterity loves the sophistication of Tang Xianzu's original text, so instead of using Zang Maoxun's adaptation, people insist on having the original sung."[31]

Composed in the spirit of print matter, the "bookish" text of *The Peony Pavilion* was preserved not so much at the expense of the audience's ears, but rather it can be said to have perverted listening per se into a form of *reading*. This synesthetic experience was first articulated by Tang Xianzu's associate Zhang Dafu (1554–1630): "I seldom go deep in songs; what I get from them is merely sound. Yet when I listen to *The Soul's Return* [*The Peony Pavilion*], I worry about whether I have got its meaning clearly."[32] Rather than dismissing the aurally incomprehensible text as inappropriate, Zhang Dafu instead takes it as an intriguing challenge to the ears, which now are required to do the kind of close reading normally reserved for the eyes. This challenge is particularly acute for Zhang Dafu, who went blind in 1593. In 1617, having someone recite *The Peony Pavilion*, Zhang Dafu copied some segments into *Recording What My Ears Received* (*Ershou lu*). His ears literally came to stand in for his eyes in "reading" the play.[33]

Zhang Dafu's synesthetic experience testifies to one important point: if *The Peony Pavilion* as a disjunctive dreamscape entails a media environment embodied by the surface of printed pages on which detached images are produced, circulated, and exchanged, that surface does not dichotomize reading and performance, eyes and ears, as the critics of Tang Xianzu presume. Rather, it interfaces between print and theater and generates a new sensorium. The locale of theatricality is therefore not the theater, but the intersection between page and stage; the first spectator in the nascent regime of theatricality was a blind man reading with his ears.

CONCLUSION

The Peony Pavilion was pivotal at the end of the sixteenth century not because it precipitated the cult of emotion, but because it sedimented various modes of spatiality. In this light, we should revisit Tang Xianzu's explanation of the origin of drama that was cited at the beginning of the chapter: "Out of *qing* forms the dream; out of the dream forms drama." Too often reduced to a statement of psychological genesis of dreams and drama, Tang's remark should now be clarified as a mapping schema that outlines a genealogy of emotion realms: winds, dreamscapes, and theatricality, each of which presents a different mode of spatiality.

Rather than obliterating previous regimes of spatiality, theatricality traverses them, redeploying their symbolisms with their meaning altered. Ironically, the apparent anachronism of this juxtaposition in return has obscured the historical specificity of theatricality. Hence, either theatricality is generalized for the entire "classical Chinese drama," but it is allegedly characterized by the forces of human feeling whose "energy 'moves Heaven and Earth' "; or when studied in the context of later periods, theatricality tends to be absorbed into the question of whether one obsesses with or (in so doing) transcends the illusion of phantasmagoria in analogy of the dreaming-awakening experience, a medieval motif still reverberating in sixteenth- and seventeenth-century discourse. These accounts—the former reminiscent of the spatial mode of winds, the latter of the dreamscape—are insightful on their own. And yet without sorting out the mode of spatiality pertaining to each period in question, we have not yet captured the distinctiveness of early Chinese theater (that began around the twelfth century) and of theatricality (as a late sixteenth-century phenomenon), respectively. The subtle transition from dreamscapes to theatricality, as demonstrated by our preceding reading of *The Peony Pavilion*, suggests that the spectator is neither a natural given nor a universal category for any kind of theatrical performance; rather, as the front of the dream, it came into being only when the dreamscape was modified into theatricality in late-sixteenth-century China.

Ling Hon Lam

NOTES

An earlier version of this chapter appears in Ling Hon Lam, *The Spatiality of Emotion in Early Modern China: From Dreamscape to Theatricality* (New York: Columbia University Press, 2018), 19–52.

1. All translations are mine. For a full translation of the play, see Tang Xianzu, *The Peony Pavilion*, trans. Cyril Birch, rev. ed. (Bloomington: Indiana University Press, 2002).

2. Chen Jiru, "Pidian *Mudan ting* tici" ("Foreword to the Commentary to *The Peony Pavilion*"), in *Tang Xianzu yanjiu ziliao huibian* (A Sourcebook of Tang Xianzu Studies), ed. Mao Xiaotong (Shanghai: Shanghai guji chubanshe, 1986), vol. 2, 855–856.

3. Pan Zhiheng, "Qing chi: Guan yan *Mudan ting huanhun ji* shu zeng er ru" ("Infatuation: Written for Two Boy Actors After Watching Their Performance of the *Peony Pavilion*, aka the *Soul's Return*"), in *Pan Zhiheng quhua* (Pan Zhiheng's Discourse on Opera), ed. Wang Xiaoyi (Beijing: Zhongguo xiqu chubanshe, 1988), 72.

4. That is why *feng* here not only refers to the underlying forces and the verbal vehicle (the *feng* poetry) that carry the forces, but it also names the very act of oral recitation by which poems are delivered, the effect of poetry for admonition (which in Chinese is written variably as *feng2*, with the same sound), as well as the ultimate object to which that effect is applied (i.e., social customs or *fengsu*).

5. Shigehisa Kuriyama, "The Imagination of Winds and the Development of the Chinese Conception of the Body," in *Body, Subject, and Power in China*, ed. Angela Zito and Tani E. Barlow (Chicago: University of Chicago Press, 1994), 23–41; Ogawa Tamaki, "Kaze to kumo: Kanshoo bungaku no kigen" (Wind and Cloud: Origins of Sentimental Literature), in *Ogawa Tamaki choshakushū* (Ogawa Tamaki's Collected Writings) (Tokyo: Chikuma Shobō, 1997), vol. 1, 235–258.

6. Liao Ben, *Zhongguo gudai juchang shi* (History of Theater in Ancient China) (Zhengzhou, China: Zhongzhou guji chubanshe, 1997), 21.

7. Meng Yuanlao, *Dongjing meng Hua lu* (Dreaming of "Huaxu," the Eastern Capital) (Beijing: Zhonghua shuju, 2006), vol. 2, 542.

8. Hong Xingzu, comp., *Chuci buzhu* (Supplementary Commentary to *The Songs of the South*) (Beijing: Zhonghua shuju, 2001), 134.

9. Li Fang et al., comp., *Taiping guangji* (Extensive Records Compiled in the Taiping Era) (Beijing: Zhonghua shuju, 1961), 2241–2252.

10. Bai Xingjian, "Sanmeng ji" ("A Record of Three Dreams"), in *Tang Song chuanqi zongji: Tang Wudai* (Complete Collection of Tang Song *Chuanqi* Stories: The Tang and Five Dynasties), ed. Yuan Lukun and Xue Hongji (Zhengzhou, China: Henan renmin chubanshe, 2001), vol. 1, 198–199.

11. Xu Shuofang, ed., *Shen Jing ji* (Collected Works of Shen Jing) (Shanghai: Shanghai guji chubanshe, 1991), 819–820.

12. Li Fang et al., comp., *Taiping yulan* (The Imperial Reader of the Taiping Era) (Beijing: Zhonghua shuju, 1960), vol. 2, 1835. For dream prognostication in traditional China, see *Wandering*

Spirits: Chen Shiyuan's Encyclopedia of Dreams, trans. Richard E. Strassberg (Berkeley: University of California Press, 2004).

13. Qiancheng Li, *Fictions of Enlightenment: Journey to the West, Tower of Myriad Mirrors, and Dream of the Red Chamber* (Honolulu: University of Hawai'i Press, 2004), 35–43.

14. Liang Huang, "Yong mu laoren shi" ("A Verse on the Puppet Old Man"), in *Quan Tang shi* (Complete Tang Poetry), comp. Peng Dingqiu et al. (Beijing: Zhonghua shuju, 1960), vol. 3, 2116.

15. Wang Anshi, "Xiangguosi qi Tongtianjiedaochang Xingxiangyuan guan xizhe" ("Watching the Performers in the Xingxiang Yard During the Rite of the Tongtian Festival Held at the Xiangguo Temple"), in *Linchuan xiansheng wenji* (Collected Works of Wang Anshi) (Beijing: Zhonghua shuju, 1959), 156.

16. Che Wenming, *Ershi shiji xiqu wenwu de faxian yu quxue yanjiu* (Theater Archaeological Findings and Opera Studies in the Twentieth Century) (Beijing: Wenhua yishu chubanshe, 2001), 36–38.

17. Wang Jisi, ed., *Quan Yuan xiqu* (Complete Yuan Plays) (Beijing: Renmin wenxue chubanshe, 1999), vol. 2, 43, 451; vol. 7, 120, 122.

18. Mingxue, ed., *Zibo dashi quanji* (The Complete Works of Zibo Zhenke) (Shanghai: Shanghai guji chubanshe, 2013), 153.

19. The woman dreamed by Mengmei promises him the prospect of marriage and high office [*MDT* 3], which never comes up in Liniang's dream. Conversely, in Liniang's dream, she makes love with a young scholar at a peony pavilion [*MDT* 51–53], but the consummation and its singular locale are left out of Mengmei's account, which only registers a plum tree under which he sees the woman [*MDT* 3]. The plum tree prominently featured in Mengmei's dream does not appear in Liniang's oneiric vision either; she sees the tree only on her second visit to the garden, and thereupon decides to be buried underneath it.

20. Catherine Swatek, Peony Pavilion *Onstage: Four Centuries in the Career of a Chinese Drama* (Ann Arbor: Center for Chinese Studies at the University of Michigan, 2002), 56.

21. Xie Zhaozhe, *Wu zazu* (Five Assorted Tapestries), in *Xuxiu Siku quanshu* (Continued Series of the Complete Writings of the Four Repositories) (Shanghai: Shanghai guji chubanshe, 1995), vol. 1130, *juan* 15, 313.

22. It can be traced to Huang Tingjian's (1045–1105) "Shu Tao Yuanming zezi shi hou" ("Postscript to Tao Yuanming's 'Poem of Reprimanding My Sons,'"), in *Yuzhang Huang xiansheng wenji* (Collected Essays of Mister Huang of Yuzhang), in Sibu congkan, 1st series, *juan* 26, 3b.

23. Pan, "Qing chi," 73.

24. Hu Wenhuan, "Du Liniang ji" ("The Story of Du Liniang"), in *Baijia cuibian* (An Essential Compilation of Tales), ed. Xiang Zhizhu (Beijing: Zhonghua shuju, 2010), 109–114.

25. In scene 26, Mengmei falls for the portrait the moment he lays eyes on it, but he has a hard time identifying it as his dream lady back in scene 2. If there is any connection he can find, it is through his own name suggested both in that early dream and in the poetic inscription on the portrait rather than through the woman figure itself. Liniang's specter shows herself just two scenes later, but again, Mengmei sees no resemblance in her to his dream lady or to the portrait, and hence he easily accepts the lie that she is from next door.

26. Tina Lu, *Persons, Roles, and Minds: Identity in Peony Pavilion and Peach Blossom Fan* (Stanford, CA: Stanford University Press, 2001), 34–35, 38–39, 67.

27. Ellen Widmer, "Xiaoqing's Literary Legacy and the Place of the Woman Writer," *Late Imperial China* 13, no. 1 (June 1992): 111–155.

28. Judith T. Zeitlin, "Shared Dreams: The Story of the *Three Wives Commentary* on *The Peony Pavilion*," *Harvard Journal of Asiatic Studies* 54 (1994): 127–179.

29. Zang Maoxun, "Yuming tang chuanqi yin" ("Preface to Tang Xianzu's *Chuanqi* Drama"), in *Tang Xianzu yanjiu ziliao huibian*, vol. 2, 776.

30. Li Yu, *Xianqing ouji* (A Casual Refuge for Leisurely Feelings), ed. Jiang Jurong and Lu Shourong (Shanghai: Shanghai guji chubanshe, 2000), 34.

31. Mao Xianshu, "Yu Li Liweng lun ge shu" ("A Letter of Discussing Singing with Li Yu"), in *Tang Xianzu yanjiu ziliao huibian*, vol. 2, 881.

32. Zhang Dafu, *Meihua caotang bitan* (Jottings of the Plum Flower Straw Hut) (Shanghai: Shanghai zaji gongsi, 1935), 6.127.

33. Zhang Dafu, "Ti *Ershou lu*" ("Foreword to *Recording What My Ears Received*"), in *Meihua caotang ji* (Collected Works of the Plum Flower Straw Hut), in *Xuxiu Siku quanshu*, vol. 1380, 557.

PRIMARY SOURCES

FMLQJ   Wei Tongxian 魏同賢, ed. *Feng Menglong quanji* 馮夢龍全集 (*Complete Works of Feng Menglong*). 18 vols. Nanjing, China: Jiangsu guji chubanshe, 1993.

MDT   Tang Xianzu 湯顯祖. *Mudan ting* 牡丹亭 (*The Peony Pavilion*), ed. Xu Shuofang 徐朔方 and Yang Xiaomei 楊笑梅. Beijing: Renmin wenxue chubanshe, 1997.

MSZY   *Mao shi zhengyi* 毛詩正義 (*The Mao Text of the* Book of Songs). In *Shisanjing zhushu* 十三經註疏 (*Commentaries and Subcommentaries on the Thirteen Classics*), comp. Ruan Yuan 阮元, vol. 1, 259–630. 2 vols. Beijing: Zhonghua shuju, 1977.

TXZQJ   Xu Shuofang 徐朔方, ed. *Tang Xianzu quanji* 湯顯祖全集 (*Complete Works of Tang Xianzu*). 4 vols. Beijing: Beijing guji chubanshe, 1999.

XXJ   Wang Shifu 王實甫. *Xixiang ji* 西廂記 (*The Story of the Western Wing*), ed. Wang Jisi 王季思. Shanghai: Shanghai guji chubanshe, 1978.

ZZJS   Guo Qingfang 郭慶藩, comp. *Zhuangzi jishi* 莊子集釋 (*Collated Commentaries to Zhuangzi*). 4 vols. Beijing: Zhonghua shuju, 1961.

SUGGESTED READINGS

TRANSLATION

Tang Xianzu. *The Peony Pavilion, Mudan ting*. Trans. Cyril Birch. 2nd ed. Introd. Catherine Swatek. Bloomington: Indiana University Press, 2002 [1980].

ENGLISH

Lam, Ling Hon. *The Spatiality of Emotion in Early Modern China: From Dreamscapes to Theatricality*. New York: Columbia University Press, 2018.

Li, Wai-yee. *Enchantment and Disenchantment: Love and Illusion in Chinese Literature*. Princeton, NJ: Princeton University Press, 1992.

Lu, Tina. *Persons, Roles, and Minds: Identity in* Peony Pavilion *and* Peach Blossom Fan. Stanford, CA: Stanford University Press, 2001.

Swatek, Catherine. Peony Pavilion *Onstage: Four Centuries in the Career of a Chinese Drama*. Ann Arbor: Center for Chinese Studies at the University of Michigan, 2002.

Volpp, Sophie. *Worldly Stage: Theatricality in Seventeenth-Century China*. Cambridge, MA: Harvard University Asia Center, 2011.

CHINESE

Cai Mengzhen 蔡孟珍. *Chongdu jingdian Mudan ting* 重讀經典牡丹亭 (*Rereading the Classic*: The Peony Pavilion). Taipei: Taiwan Shangwu yinshuguang, 2015.

Cheng Yun 程芸. *Tang Xianzu yu wan Ming xiqu de shanbian* 湯顯祖與晚明戲曲的嬗變 (*Tang Xianzu and the Transformation of Late Ming Drama*). Beijing: Zhonghua shuju, 2006.

Hua Wei 華瑋, ed. *Tang Xianzu yu Mudan ting* 湯顯祖與牡丹亭 (*Tang Xianzu and* The Peony Pavilion), 2 vols. Taipei: Zhongyang yanjiu yuan Zhongguo wenzhe yanjiusuo, 2005.

Ke Qingming 柯慶明 and Xiao Chi 蕭馳. *Zhongguo shuqing chuantong de zaifaxian* 中國抒情傳統的再發現 (*Rediscovering Chinese Lyrical Traditions*), 2 vols. Taipei: Taida chuban zhongxin, 2009.

Mao Xiaotong 毛效同, ed. *Tang Xianzu yanjiu ziliao huibian* 湯顯祖研究資料匯編 (*A Sourcebook of Tang Xianzu Studies*). 2 vols. Shanghai: Shanghai guji chubanshe, 1986.

The Green Peony and *The Swallow's Letter*

Drama and Politics

This chapter explores how politics and drama intersected in the Ming dynasty (1368–1644). During this period, the literarily and musically sophisticated *chuanqi* drama saw a surge in its engagement with contemporary political and social issues. Various developments in the cultural sphere—a flourishing print culture, a growing readership, faster and wider transmission of information, and an expanded entertainment sector—had created a competitive but exciting environment for the literati to spend their creative energy on *chuanqi* drama. In their hands, *chuanqi* became a form of artistic production, a means of socializing, and a tool for sociopolitical mobilization. Through theater, members of the literati class strove to make sense of and adapt to the political, social, and cultural transformations in the empire. Increasingly, literati inside and outside the government began to compose dramas specifically to advocate for distinct political camps and associated policy positions. Thus, the production and consumption of drama directly and indirectly intervened in power struggles at and beyond the court. Playwrights could count on an engaged, energized, and experienced audience ready to be entertained, influenced, and roused by what they read in playtexts and saw on stage.

The literati enthusiasm for theater intersected with epistemological and spiritual shifts in the early modern era when socioeconomic and cultural changes caused both anxiety and excitement. On multiple levels, and in every corner of the world including Ming China, social and cultural orders were reconfigured. Elites struggled to reach a reasonable consensus on "authority" of any kind, ranging from scholarly interpretations of the classics to sources of political information. Which public figures were truly superior in moral character, and hence deserved more political authority? Whose judgments about art, literature, religion, and all aspects of everyday life were correct? These were some of the most pressing questions of the time. Because drama could shape perceptions of truth from the stage and affect political, social, and cultural realities, plays and theatrical productions could have extremely high importance. By writing plays about political issues, and by trying to control how the public accessed drama, Ming literati exploited the potential of drama as a medium of political communication and negotiation. Such political endeavors in turn raised new questions about the art of drama.

The stories of the two famous plays examined in this chapter, *The Green Peony* (*Lü mudan*, hereafter *Green Peony*) and *The Swallow's Letter* (*Yanzi jian*, hereafter

Swallow's Letter), reveal some of the conventional as well as the new ways to make *chuanqi* drama politically meaningful in the seventeenth century. Their performances created occasions for the literati and their official allies to mobilize against and to attack their factional enemies in what were often life-and-death struggles over governance and historical memory. To understand how plays operated as part of the political arena, we will consider the following questions: What determined whether literati viewed a play as political? What were the social consequences for the playwright if their play had a certain political agenda? Would the perception of a play as politically significant affect the assessment of its aesthetic value? In this chapter, we consider three intersecting factors that could determine the answers to the abovementioned questions: the content, the playwright, and the literati theater as a space of emotions.

10.1 NEW DRAMAS AND OLD INTERPRETIVE TECHNIQUES

Ming China saw the emergence of "drama on current affairs" (*shishiju*), a new category of the *chuanqi* drama that addressed contemporary politics head on by representing recent political events onstage.[1] Many dramas on current affairs were anonymous, but their political intentions and stance were so unambiguous that the identity of the author was not of paramount concern. For instance, *The Crying Phoenix* (*Mingfeng ji*, 1581?), arguably the first drama of this kind, portrayed in vivid detail a sixteenth-century grand secretary's corruption and murderous persecution of officials.[2] Its popularity in literati theater persisted in the late Ming, partly because the eternal battles between the so-called gentlemen and small men resonated strongly at a time of escalating factionalism (➤ Introduction). Drama on current affairs also reflected and contributed to a strong sense of contemporaneity in the consciousness of Ming audiences by incorporating contemporary sociocultural phenomena into the plots of plays, especially the ubiquitous presence of news in everyday life—from official channels, rumors, and gossip. While the rise of this new type of *chuanqi* drama and its explicit engagement with official power struggles satisfied the audience's interest in contemporary affairs and could create a "politically engaged" sense of unified community on and off the stage,[3] it is unclear to what extent this political consciousness might have played a decisive role in shaping policymaking among officials at court or to what degree it heightened the desire to take political action among the elite or the commoner class.[4]

Important for our purposes here in terms of the connection between drama and politics, drama on current affairs was not the only theatrical means to communicate political messages. Potentially, any play could be political. Literati employed and looked for insinuation and revisionist presentation of history or legends in plays that did not depict current affairs. Further, many insisted on factoring in the dramatist's moral reputation in assessing the political agenda and the aesthetic quality of their plays. The latter point in particular merits some extra explanation.

We cannot overestimate the degree to which the audience's perception of the author determined how they evaluated a play's contents during this period. For modern audiences, a playwright's identity is often understood to be artistic, and hence apolitical. He or she *becomes* political when attempting to insert particular emotions and views into a theatrical production in order to inspire actions. In Ming China, as we will see later in this chapter, some literati indeed made a case for separating a playwright's life as a scholar-official—and by extension, a politician in the premodern Chinese sense—from his artistic accomplishments. But typically, it was difficult for the early modern literati to look at a play without thinking about its author's moral-political reputation. In their public careers and their lives more generally, the literati pursued their ambitions more or less in accordance with a Confucian emphasis on moral cultivation. The following words from the Confucian classic *Great Learning* (*Daxue*) describe the life trajectory of a properly educated man. This formula fundamentally structured the state institutions, intellectual priorities, and the entanglement of the personal and the political in early modern China:

> Rectify the mind, and subsequently the self is cultivated. Cultivate the self, and subsequently the household is regulated. Regulate the household, and subsequently the state is brought to good order. Bring good order to the state, and subsequently the world is at peace. From the Son of Heaven down to the ordinary people, everyone without exception should take cultivation of the self as the root.[5]

After spending many years studying the Confucian classics that illuminated an ethical understanding of the universe—from the abstract Heavenly Principle to specific behavioral norms in everyday life—the literati aspired to pass the civil service examinations and to become government officials to fulfill their Confucian commitment to public service. They gained prestige and power in this way but were also subject to high ethical standards. Failure to abide by such standards might result in being dismissed from office or worse. Hence, moral judgment played a significant role in evaluating not only an official's career performance, but also his place in official historical records and in the collective memory.

Paradoxically, and probably because of the intimate connection between morality and politics, the premodern Chinese political elite had sought to maintain certain boundaries for moral and political attacks in the government to shield officials from groundless personal accusations.[6] Still, in politics, moral attacks and counterattacks were legitimate and prevalent. In the seventeenth century, for example, the moral performance of public figures assumed utmost political importance. Brutal factionalism put their personal lives under closer scrutiny, subjecting their claims of authority to intense questioning not only in official political spaces, but also in society through print and theater. As the performing arts matured as an art form by and for literati, a playwright's creation, irrespective of his intentions, was inevitably assumed to harbor political overtones. As the case of Li Yu discussed next demonstrates, this interpretive practice was as pervasive as it was potentially unwelcome.

10.2 A DRAMATIST'S DILEMMA

Comments on satire by Li Yu (1611–1680), a renowned playwright and theorist who lived through the Ming-Qing dynastic transition (☞ chap. 11, *HTRCP*, C17.5), offer a glimpse at the intensely contested boundaries between art and politics in the world of theater. In "Forgo Satire" ("Jie fengci"), an important section of his famous treatise on drama, Li Yu warns against satire in dramatic writing, for, in his view, dramatists should concern themselves with illuminating moral ideals but refrain from misrepresenting social realities on stage or engaging in explicit or implicit insinuation [*XQOJ* 20–22]. Some scholars have suggested that Li, for fear of Qing literary persecution, used this essay to publicly announce his disinterest in using the power of theater for political purposes, implying that he really might not have meant to denounce the use of insinuation.[7] However, it is also possible that Li's opposition to weaponizing drama by both the playwrights and the audience derived from his observation that the use of drama to target a rival had become pervasive—and tasteless—by midcentury.

Li's experience revealed a dilemma in theatrical practices parallel to the one faced by the political elite, who were struggling to gain more authority at court by claiming moral superiority. They insisted on the fundamental priority of moral cultivation. However, although they understood the practical importance of maintaining reasonable boundaries between the official and personal lives, they did not share a consensus—other than a few well-known historical precedents—on who could draw or reinforce the boundaries between politics and morality. Hence, debates about policy and personal morality were often intertwined, with disputes about certain officials' moral performance—in particular their filial piety and sexual behavior—significantly affecting the perception and reception of their policy stances. Similarly, the literati world had no consensus on critical questions such as: Who among them had the literary authority to decide whether or how playwrights should intervene in power struggles? Were there established criteria to help the audience determine if a play served to illuminate moral ideals or to intervene in contemporary politics?

Further, like a politician unable to harness his message and public image in the seventeenth century, a dramatist could not control how his work would be interpreted by the literati public and what kind of emotions might be stimulated at its performance. Li Yu's own experience attested to this dilemma. In an announcement supposedly printed with his published plays, Li made an unusually serious pledge:

> When I honor persons cast in the roles of hero and heroine, it is not to lay the ground for ingratiating myself. When I give painted faces to persons cast as underhand or clownish characters, it is without intention to mock them. In all cases the purpose is to adorn the stage, give it color and life, nothing more. But I have to bear in mind that human affections and desires give rise to all sorts of situations, and the world is so large that any place I can think of will be found in it. If I dream up an incident I find there is a real incident to match it,

if I fabricate a name, there is a real name to coincide with it. *How can I be sure that no one will take a figment of my imagination as a veiled criticism of himself? I hereby bare my heart and take an oath in blood, if there is the slightest sly reference in my work, I am willing to be struck dumb for three lifetimes; even if I am spared retribution in the visible world, I will not escape punishment in the netherworld!*

[*XQOJ* 21; trans. Pollard, 39; emphasis added]

In spite of Li Yu's efforts to keep politics at arm's length, he could not prevent others from reading politics into some of his plays. He was dismayed: "This heart-felt pledge has long since appeared in print, and experience has confirmed its veracity. Yet meddlesome individuals, that is, people who have not forgiven me, still ask with every play of mine they see whom the characters allude to" [*XQOJ* 21; trans. Pollard, 39]. He felt so strongly about this matter that he commented at length on the dangers of satire:

The swords of the warrior and the pen of the literary man are both instruments for killing people. Everybody knows that swords can kill. It is not widely known that pens can kill, but still some do know. However, the fact that the pen is a hundred times sharper and crueler than the sword as an instrument for killing has never been plainly stated, and the world thus warned against it.

[*XQOJ* 20; trans. Pollard, 37]

Li Yu's words here might not specifically target art and high politics, but they nonetheless reveal a few important points regarding drama and politics in the seventeenth century that we will discuss more carefully later in this chapter. First, it was a widespread practice among the literati—official and nonofficial—to claim that a drama(tist) was politically motivated based on slim or no evidence. For instance, a character's name could be interpreted in the wildest way to imply that it alluded to a certain political or social rival. Second, no one, not even the playwright himself, could control how a play would be interpreted. A political reading of a given play could be stretched indefinitely, even if the play presented little more than a conventional romantic story. Finally, irresponsible satire and overreading could lead to serious consequences and cause damage to the playwright. All these meant that factors outside the playwright's control, especially in terms of the emotions that his work triggered and how it might be invoked by politicians arbitrarily in power struggles, seemed to play a more important role than the content of the work in determining its political significance.

In the remaining sections of this chapter, we will look at two famous seventeenth-century plays, Ruan Dacheng's *Swallow's Letter* and Wu Bing's *Green Peony*, as examples of two related modes of political interpretation. In the case of *Swallow's Letter*, the moral-political reputation of the author looms large over the seemingly innocuous particulars of the play. By contrast, in the case of *Green Peony*, the innocuousness of the reputed author notwithstanding, the social particulars of the play could be read as pointed political satire. To think through these two trajectories, we will first review the political environment in which they were produced, performed, and given political meaning. We will think about how this context shaped the interpretation of the contents of these plays and their authors' intentions. In addition, we will explore how all these factors made theater a highly volatile and emotionally charged space in which strong expression of political sentiments might erupt unexpectedly.

10.3 WU BING, RUAN DACHENG, AND THE FACTIONAL STRUGGLES IN A NEW POLITICAL CULTURE

During the last decades of the Ming dynasty, from the 1570s to the 1640s, conflicts among political cliques dominated the government. This period of heightened factionalism coincided with the golden age of drama on current affairs, which produced many plays on the battles between the gentlemen and small men in politics, and of the *chuanqi* drama more generally. Two rival factions are particularly pertinent to our discussion in this chapter: the Eastern Grove (Donglin) faction and the so-called eunuch faction. The Eastern Grove has been remembered in Ming historiography as a camp of righteous men—that is, officials who were exemplary in their moral integrity. And this was an image that the Eastern Grove and its supporters were eager to fashion and embrace, sometimes even by distancing themselves from officials in the same political camp whose reputations had been tarnished.[8]

The other major faction was the eunuch faction, a label that included officials who had allied with a eunuch named Wei Zhongxian (1568–1627), who was at the peak of his power during the reign of Emperor Tianqi (r. 1621–1627). Many officials associated with this faction participated in persecuting their political rivals in the government, especially those in the Eastern Grove camp. The power struggle between these two groups—namely, the bloody suppression of the defiant Eastern Grove by the eunuch faction and the subsequent punishment of this faction during the reign of the new emperor, Chongzhen (r. 1628–1644)—came to define the political character of the last years of the Ming. This struggle became so deeply personal and emotional for those identified with the "righteous" Eastern Grove camp that they sought a relentless, and often disproportional, punishment of the individuals formerly connected with the eunuch faction.

This struggle continued to evolve and involved literati outside court politics. In the late Ming, a large, empirewide literary organization called the Restoration Society (Fushe) emerged. The Restoration Society identified with the Eastern Grove politically. It was often called the "Little Eastern Grove," partly because some of the Restoration Society leaders lost their Eastern Grove–identified fathers at the hands of the eunuch faction during the Tianqi reign. Although only officials—literati who had passed the civil service examinations and obtained positions in the government—could participate in court policy debates, literati in general formed a significant political force by engaging in local affairs and using their voice to influence officials. Restoration Society scholars were particularly familiar with and effective at utilizing the expanding transportation system, print culture, and entertainment for their organizational purposes.

The power struggle between these groups became one of the most frequently depicted subjects of contemporary novels and the drama on current affairs.[9] It affected the reception of other *chuanqi* plays as well. The playwrights focused on in this chapter lived in this volatile political climate and became entangled, voluntarily or involuntarily, in complicated relationships with the abovementioned groups.

Ruan Dacheng (1587–1646), a successful examination graduate in 1616, became a metropolitan official and socialized with colleagues in the Eastern Grove circle. However, in the early 1620s, disagreement on personnel decisions with one of the Eastern Grove officials, Wei Dazhong (1575–1625), led him to seek support from the eunuch faction, an action that many believed to have played a role in the de facto murder of Wei Dazhong in prison. For this reason, Ruan was identified as a member of the eunuch faction upon its downfall and eventually expelled from government service. Although he was not a leader or particularly committed to factionalist causes, his entanglement with the death of Wei Dazhong during the eunuch persecution of the Eastern Grove resulted in intense hostility toward Ruan from the literati identified with the Eastern Grove and the Restoration Society. This hostility did not recede even after he retired and moved to Nanjing, the cultural center of the south, where he sought to make peace with the partisans and form his own literary circle to enjoy some kind of cultural leadership. He was successful for a while in his efforts to organize a literary club and socialize with some widely respected scholar-officials through their shared passion for theater. Ruan composed several *chuanqi* dramas during retirement, all of which received high marks from the literati audience for their exceptional artistic sophistication, but also invited fierce criticism for allegedly having hidden political agendas.

Swallow's Letter is perhaps Ruan's best-known play. In this story, the scholar Huo Duliang meets and marries a courtesan, Hua Xingyun. When he travels to the capital to take the civil service examinations, he makes a painting of himself with the courtesan and sends it to a framer. Li Feiyun, the daughter of an official, happens to send an image of the Bodhisattva Guanyin to the same framer. The framer confuses the two and returns them to the wrong owners. Meanwhile, Li Feiyun falls in love with Huo's image in the painting and writes a poem that is plucked by a swallow, eventually reaching Huo. Just as Huo succeeds in the civil service examinations, a rebellion causes all the characters in the play to disperse across the empire. While participating in a military campaign, Huo meets and marries Li Feiyun, and Li Feiyun's parents encounter the dislocated Hua Xingyun and adopt her. The play ends when Huo is officially commended for his excellent performance on the exams, honored for his military prowess against the An Lushan Rebellion, and finally reunited with the two women. Conventionally set in the Tang dynasty, this play does not engage contemporary people or matters at all. But some people at the time believed Ruan used the play to mock the Eastern Grove, as we will see later in this chapter.

While *Swallow's Letter* creates some supposedly historical events to develop the characters and plot throughout the play, the other play, *Green Peony*, makes no such effort. Set in the Song dynasty, its two references to the time period are neg-ligible.[10] On its face, *Green Peony* is simply a light comedy about the love stories of two talented scholars and two talented women. It begins with the retired official Shen Zhong's plan to select a son-in-law for his daughter. He sets up a literary club and invites the sons of the local elite to participate in a poetry contest. Much of the play depicts how some rich and ignorant men in this contest try to present them-selves as talented scholars by cheating and relying on ghostwriters. Eventually, the real talented scholars, who are also the morally upright, prove themselves not only in this contest, but also in the imperial civil service examinations. One of them marries Shen's daughter, and the other marries the female ghostwriter and sister of one of the cheaters. In this time of "fakes," truly talented and morally upright men prevail, earn the hearts of the women they desire, and attain career success.[11] Thus, by making issues such as authentic talent, literary clubs, and empirewide literati networking and publishing central to its storyline, *Green Peony* turns out to keenly engage the social and cultural phenomena of its own time.

The extant version of *Green Peony* is attributed to Wu Bing (1595–1648), who served in the government in the 1620s and 1630s. He resigned from service due to frustration with a governor-general during a military campaign. He was not asso-ciated with any factions while in government, but he remained friendly with some members of the Restoration Society during his retirement, and might have even sympathized with their stance. Although he was not known to have befriended any groups hostile to the Restoration Society, according to some late Ming sources, the play named *Green Peony* was written by an enemy of the Restoration Society, whose request to join the organization met with firm rejection because his brother, the leading grand secretary at court at the time, had engaged in factional fights against the Eastern Grove and the Restoration Society. These historical sources document that the play was so slanderous of the Restoration Society that the society's leaders petitioned for it to be officially banned. Since the late Ming period, many have iden-tified Wu as the author of the extant *Green Peony* without adequately addressing the apparent discrepancy between his biography and the political controversy sur-rounding this play. Curiously, the contents of the extant playtext ostensibly contain nothing controversial, and thus can hardly substantiate the Restoration Society's claims about the political agenda of the playwright and the serious consequences of this dramatic production.

This brief review of the playwrights' backgrounds and the plots of the two plays shows that the understanding of a *chuanqi* play was fluid and conditioned by the volatility characteristic of late Ming political culture. Neither of these plays was written as drama on current affairs. However, as we shall see next, their production and reception reveal the two most prevalent practices of politicizing theater in the late Ming—that is, ad hominem readings and out-of-context innuendo.

10.4 WEAPONIZING DRAMA

In 1633, Society scholars claimed that because they had rejected the request of the leading grand secretary's brother to join their organization, the latter had *Green*

Peony written to ridicule them. "At the time, people all wanted to put on [the play],"
one Society insider documented. Portraying themselves as victims of vicious slander by a play that mocked its members for their fake talents and their opportu-
nistic networking activities, Society scholars asked their two leaders to intervene.
The leaders subsequently paid a special visit to the local government and garnered
substantial support from an allied official sympathetic to their cause. This official
"banned bookshops from selling the play, had the woodblocks destroyed, charged
the author, and imprisoned someone from the Wen family," thereby completely
squashing the local challengers of the Restoration Society.[12] It can be established
that a play entitled *Green Peony*, quite well written and entertaining enough for it to
become an instant hit, painted a clownish picture of some of the prominent members of the Restoration Society and its major initiatives.[13] Its success testified to the
fact that rival literati groups—with their powerful patrons in the government—
remained active and effectively challenged the claims of superiority by the Restoration Society. Eventually the Society had to rely on its own official-patrons to
suppress the play.

None of these records can be found in biographical accounts about Wu Bing.
But let us assume for a moment that the extant version of *Green Peony* authored
by Wu indeed provoked the Restoration Society uproar. How might its depictions
of the literati activities in the play have invited audiences to imagine a connection between the play and the most famous contemporary literary society in the
empire? And how might they have been seen as satirizing this organization?

To answer these questions, let's look at some potential "evidence" in the scenes
of the play itself. In scene 2, "Composition under Duress" ("Qiangyin"), we get a
look at the inner workings of the publishing activities of literati; and in scene 3, "An
Ode in the Manner of Xie" ("Xie yong"), we are introduced to the selfish reasons
for founding a literary society. Neither of these scenes paints a particularly flatter-
ing view of such scholarly endeavors. In scene 2, Gu Can and Xie Ying, two truly
talented scholars, talk about poetry and literary networking, which attracts interest
from two fake ones, Liu Xiqiang and Che Bengao.

（小生看生文介）是一首《牡丹賦》。妙，妙！芬芳燦爛，允稱名花。宙合大社中，當以此作為冠，即付梓便了。（作袖去介）	SECONDARY YOUNG MALE *as* GU CAN *acts out reading the literary work of male lead Xie Ying [and speaks]:* This is a "Rhapsody on the Peony." Excellent! Excellent! Like a peony, its intensive fragrance and splendid flowers have earned peony its fame. This piece should cap the entire Literary Collection of the Great Zhouhe Literary Society. I shall immediately arrange to have it put to print. *He puts away the rhapsody.*
（生）惶恐。	YOUNG MALE *as* XIE YING [*speaks*]: I am humbled.

（淨）甚麼宙合大社？

COMIC *as* LIU XIQIANG [*speaks*]: What is this Great Zhouhe Literary Society?

（小生）小弟徧訪天下名士，徵其文章，彙選大社，以公同好。

GU CAN [*speaks*]: I pay visits to famous literati all over the country. I compile their writings into this great collection and print them to share.

. . .

（淨）小弟有幾篇胡說，一定求刻上去。

LIU XIQIANG [*speaks*]: I have a few nonsensical essays. Please make sure to have them printed in this collection.

（丑）小弟也求附一兩篇。

CLOWN *as* CHE BENGAO [*speaks*]: I would like to submit one or two pieces, too.

（小生）這却使不得，目錄已刻定了。

GU CAN [*speaks*]: This is impossible. The table of contents has already been decided on and printed.

（淨）方纔謝兄的，怎又袖去？

LIU XIQIANG [*speaks*]: But you just took Mr. Xie's writing!

（生）拙作原不通，千萬莫刻。

XIE YING [*speaks*]: My work is really not exemplary. Please don't print it.

（丑）多送些刻費來便是。

CHE BENGAO [*speaks*]: I can offer some more money toward the printing fees.

（小生笑介）那個為此？

GU CAN *laughs* [*and speaks*]: Who does this for money?

（淨笑介）小顧，你也忒氣傲了。

LIU XIQIANG *laughs* [*and speaks*]: Mr. Gu, you are too lofty.

. . .

（生）二兄不必性急，待續集出來，收些人情文字便了。

XIE YING [*speaks*]: Don't worry. When we put forth the second volume, we can include some compositions to make everyone happy.

[*LMD* 7–8, scene 2, "Composition under Duress" ("Qiangyin")][14]

In scene 3, the retired official Shen Zhong plans to start a literary club to find a good match for his daughter, Winsome:

（外看介）原來是顧粲姪兒新選社刻，求我作序。

EXTRA MALE *as* SHEN ZHONG *reads* [*the letter and speaks*]: It says Gu Can has compiled a new collection of essays for his literary society and will have it printed. He is requesting a preface from me.

（小旦）孩兒且先告退了。

SECONDARY YOUNG FEMALE *as* WINSOME [*speaks*]: I will now excuse myself.

（外）小鳳，剪一枝綠牡丹，與小姐房中供養。

SHEN ZHONG [*speaks*]: Maid Phoenix, cut a green peony flower and place it in your mistress's room.

（小丑）曉得。

SECONDARY CLOWN *as* PHOENIX [*speaks*]: I will.

. . .

（同下）

WINSOME *and* PHOENIX *exit together.*

（外）女兒如此才質，豈配庸流？外面朋友家都有文會，老夫如今也創立小社，一來挈引後生，二來訪求快壻。顧生原係通家，不消說了；還有柳希潛、車本高，皆舊家子弟，不免邀來同社。

SHEN ZHONG [*speaks*]: My daughter possesses such good qualities and talents. She should not be married to a mediocre man. My friends all organize literary gatherings at home. I should establish a small literary club myself. With this I can promote younger scholars. In the meantime, I can find a wonderful son-in-law. Mr. Gu is the son of an old acquaintance of mine and should definitely be invited. Liu Xiqiang and Che Bengao are also sons of established families. Of course, they should be asked to join, too.

[*LMD* 15, scene 3, "An Ode in the Manner of Xie" ("Xie yong")]

This scene establishes a context for the development of the storyline: the popularity of organizing literary clubs, which unmistakably was a defining feature of late Ming literati society. It also reveals the complex agendas of literary society organizers and members. Some hoped to network and socialize; some aimed to advance their literary and professional careers; and some had very personal reasons. As a result, even if a literary organization adopted lofty ideals, it might still include members who could not live up to them. As the story unfolds, it turns out that Liu and Che used others' writings to fake their literary reputations. Notably, in a similar vein, in the late Ming era, the Restoration Society faced accusations that their pretensions to exemplariness were but a farce. Thus, these two scenes could be easily taken out of context and interpreted as satirizing the Society.

Now we return to the unsettled question of the authorship of *Green Peony* and the political controversies that it purportedly provoked. First, in the highly divisive environment of late Ming politics, had Wu acted as a conspirator against the Restoration Society, he would likely have been mentioned—if not outright condemned—by literati publications. Second, the extant version of the play does not contain the kind of sensational material that deserved an official ban. The late Ming is not known for literary censorship; the official decision to ban the play, to the point of even destroying the woodblock of its text, was extraordinary. Was it possible, then, that two authors wrote two different plays with the title *Green Peony*? Some scholarship suggests that *Green Peony* was rewritten by Wu Bing after an earlier version by the factional enemies of the Eastern Grove and Restoration Society had been banned.[15] The play's criticism of contemporary literati's social and cultural practices may indeed reflect Wu's own concerns about these matters. But it might not be the banned play.

Earlier, in the case of Ruan Dacheng and his *Swallow's Letter*, we saw an author's reputation overshadow his work and shape the perception of the play. Here, in Wu Bing's questionable authorship of *Green Peony*, we find an example of another trajectory: the identity of the playwright became a less important question than the political incidents around the play itself. Curiously, literati at the time were eager to document this title as a political satire, but they did not have coherent or accurate records about the author (or authors). Drama commentators chose not to clarify whether Wu Bing's play was the same as the one produced as a political weapon and suppressed by the Restoration Society. It almost seems that evidence of authorship mattered little in this case.

Even though we do not have convincing answers to some key questions about the history of the title *Green Peony*, the story around it nonetheless shows that weaponizing drama was a familiar practice. Not only could a drama be written to launch a specific political attack, the audience also could weaponize it by imposing a particular political meaning on a play and then using this point to attack its author or some political enemy.

10.5 THE SUSPECT AUTHOR

Whereas Wu Bing's involvement with the *Green Peony* remains unclear, Ruan Dacheng's futile attempt to separate his art from politics is symptomatic of a time when literary works by officials inevitably invited a political reading as the literati public closely followed political issues—in particular, far-reaching debates about institutional reform, border security, and factionalism. As we will see in the following discussion, Ruan's identity and image as a controversial official always prompted speculation that his plays were politically motivated and rife with specific political messages.

Ruan's four famous plays—*The Spring Lantern Riddles* (*Chundeng mi*), *Reunion by Mouni Beads* (*Mouni he*), *Double Examination Success* (*Shuang jinbang*), and *Swallow's Letter*—were all composed after his forced departure from the court as a former member of the eunuch faction. But no matter how lighthearted the plays might have appeared on the surface, due to Ruan's infamous history, they could not escape being read in a politically charged fashion. For instance, the earliest of these plays, *Spring Lantern Riddles*, appeared in 1634, a few years after his retirement. Ruan himself had initially claimed that this play aimed to be purely entertaining. But according to a scholar in the Restoration Society, at one performance, Ruan confessed that the trope of mistaken identity (*cuo ren*), a central theme of this play, was meant to highlight the messiness and severe consequences of factional identification during the chaotic Tianqi reign. Thus, in this view, the play could be seen as an expression of remorse over having been too close to some officials in the eunuch faction, as well as self-defense, arguing that he had not intentionally engaged in factional persecution against the Eastern Grove.[16] In short, Ruan could be understood to be defending his innocence and reiterating his intention to reconnect with the righteous men in the government.[17] Aware that factional identities were often loosely applied to officials and led to unfair treatment, some literati, at least for the time being, were willing to accept Ruan's gesture of reconciliation.

Still, Ruan's past made him a constant suspect and an easy target for the opinionated factionalists. In 1639, some Restoration Society scholars decided that Ruan's successful cultural networking in retirement was political in nature, threatening to relaunch the careers of some officials previously associated with the eunuch faction. They took immediate action against him. In a widely circulated "Proclamation against Treachery in Nanjing," they listed writing slanderous plays as one of Ruan's reprehensible acts. They cited and denounced *Spring Lantern Riddles* for libeling the sages and satirizing contemporary affairs. The "Proclamation" insisted that the two plays that Ruan had written by then, *Spring Lantern Riddles* and *Reunion*, though not dramas on current affairs, had a vicious agenda: they employed insinuation to degrade good men and questioned the emperor's decision to purge the eunuch faction. They made these accusations by liberally interpreting the plots and names in the plays.[18] With this public proclamation, Society scholars turned Ruan into the perennial enemy of the "righteous camp." After that, few wanted to openly express sympathy toward him; nothing written by Ruan could be innocent in either their eyes or those of the broader literati public. The *chuanqi* dramas that he composed afterward were always closely scrutinized for any hidden political messages.

For instance, when Ruan completed and produced *Swallow's Letter* a few years after the sensational anti-Ruan movement organized by the Restoration Society, it was suggested that the ending of the play, where the protagonist married two women as official wives, mocked a particular Eastern Grove–identified official whose domestic problems had been brought up in political debates at court and subsequently ruined his career. We will look at this incident more closely in the next section. Suffice it here to point out that the identities and public lives of certain playwrights played a key role in determining whether the audience considered their works "political."

10.6 EVIDENCE OF INSINUATION

Playwrights with political baggage could not escape accusations of insinuation, one of the most common methods used in premodern Chinese literature (from poetry to drama) to convey political messages. Among other things, insinuation could take the forms of allegory and pun. It is no exaggeration to say that reading for evidence of insinuation was an everyday exercise for literati, who were schooled in the art of decoding hidden messages through their training in the Confucian classics. By virtue of the fact that Ming literati had turned *chuanqi* into a form of elite literature,[19] they continued this habit in their reading of dramatic texts. Their speculations on insinuation involved close examination of the linguistic and literary aspects of a dramatic text, especially word games.

Determining whether an element of a play functioned as a politically meaningful insinuation often depends on what sources we have access to besides the play itself. Unlike the case of Wu Bing, for Ruan Dacheng, we have a rich corpus of biographical, political, and historical sources. These materials help us decide whether his plays may or may not have been as innocent as their light comedy might suggest. In fact, Ruan sometimes voluntarily revealed the use of insinuation. For instance, he explicitly admitted that the play *Double Examination Success* allowed him to illustrate how an innocent man was wronged, and the work was inspired by his own political experience of factionalism. This play was a response to the intense antagonism that Ruan encountered in the wake of the "Proclamation" incident instigated by the Restoration Society in 1639. In the preface of the play, Ruan recalled when his political enemies cornered him by spreading base-less claims against him, and stated that the depiction of some characters in this play represented the factional chaos to which he fell victim.[20] But Ruan was not equally forthright about the use of insinuation in some of his other plays, so his attackers imagined them freely. The history of *Swallow's Letter* allows us to get a glimpse at how the literati audience looked for evidence of insinuation, some-times at the risk of misinterpreting the author's intentions, but at times justly picking up on subtle clues.

As briefly noted earlier in this chapter, the playwright arranged for the protag-onist of this play to marry two women. The conflict between these two women suddenly surfaces at the very end of the play, as the male main protagonist, Huo Duliang, is named the Optimus (Top Graduate) in the civil service examinations, which means that his official wife—and only her—will receive an imperial honor-ific. The conflict over who is the official wife entitled to the flowery headdress is vividly captured in scene 42, "Investiture Completed,"[21] where the protagonist and the two women, as well as the parents of the women, have to confront the issue at the ceremony for receiving the imperial honors:

（小旦問生介）相公你纔說花冠有幾副麼。	SECONDARY YOUNG FEMALE as WANDERING CLOUD *questions* YOUNG MALE as HUO DULIANG [*and speaks*]: Sir, how many sets of flowery headdress did you mention?
（生）怎麼有幾副。只有一副。	YOUNG MALE *as* HUO DULIANG [*speaks*]: "How many sets?" Of course there is only one set.
（小旦）畫上像兩個共得。不知那花冠兒可共戴得麼。	WANDERING CLOUD [*speaks*]: Two women can look alike in paintings. Could we share one set of a flowery headdress?
（生笑介）這卻怎生共戴得。下官不好說。（指旦介）這個讓飛。 . . .	HUO DULIANG [*speaks*]: How could it be shared? I really don't know. *He points to the* YOUNG FEMALE *as* FLYING CLOUD [*and speaks*]: Let Flying . . .
（小旦）甚麼飛。	WANDERING CLOUD [*speaks*]: "Flying" what?
（生指旦介）權讓飛雲小姐戴罷。	HUO DULIANG *points at* FLYING CLOUD [*and speaks*]: For the time being just let Flying Cloud wear it.
（旦）相公。此是正經道理。怎麼說權讓。	FLYING CLOUD [*speaks*]: Sir, I am entitled to have the headdress. What do you mean by "for the time being"?
. . .	. . .
（外驚介）今日錦堂佳宴。正該大家歡喜纔是。怎麼兩個孩兒這般樣別調。是何緣故。	EXTRA MALE as LI ANDAO [*startled speaks*]: Today we are holding a banquet in this beautifully decorated hall. Every-one should be joyful. Why are these two girls so upset?
（旦上前跪介）稟告爹爹。	FLYING CLOUD *steps forward, kneels before him,* [*and speaks*]: Father, I plead my case with you.
（外）我兒起來。	LI ANDAO [*speaks*]: Stand up, my dear.

（旦）孩兒幼生閨閣。長效于歸。與霍郎合 FLYING CLOUD [*speaks*]: Your daughter was born to the
卺軍中，節度為媒。原非野合。今日華行雲 boudoir and had aspired to be married to Sir Huo Duliang.
要硬奪孩兒誥封。于理固是不通。說來甚是 The general-governor arranged for my marriage with Sir
　　　　　　　　　　　　　　　　可笑。 Huo. Our marriage is not contrary to rites. But today Wandering Cloud wants to take away my official title of investiture. This violates the norms and is so ridiculous.

（外）孩兒。今日是個喜慶日子。閒言閒語， LI ANDAO [*speaks*]: My dear, today is an auspicious day.
　　　　　　　　　　略渾融些罷。 Let's avoid all nonsense and try to find some compromise?
（旦）別樣事渾融得。這朝廷恩典，怎麼渾 FLYING CLOUD [*speaks*]: We could try to compromise with
　　　　　　　　　　　　融的。 regard to other things. When it comes to imperial honor,
how could a compromise be found!

[*YZJ* 209–210, scene 42, "Investiture Completed" ("Gaoyuan")]

In response, Wandering Cloud contends that she and Huo had met and committed themselves to marriage before Flying Cloud came into his life. Therefore,
she should be the one to receive the official honorific. Just as the tension quickly
mounts and no proper solution seems possible, an official arrives to announce the
imperial edict that Huo had been granted two official positions—one as the aca-
demician at Hongwen Hall (thanks to his examination success) and the other as
the governor-general of Helong. The senior men in the two families then decide
that Wandering Cloud should enjoy the official honorific and corresponding status as wife of the Optimus and Flying Cloud as wife of the governor-general, even
though the Optimus and the governor-general were actually the same man. This
proposal sounded agreeable to all parties involved, and the play ended there, without mentioning whether the court approved the solution negotiated within the two
families.

It is striking that, in this concluding scene, which woman would be recognized
as the only official wife by the court remains an unsolved question. Such an ambiguous ending would be unsettling because an official could take as many concubines as he could afford, but he would break the law if he claimed more than one
wife. The one-wife principle is at the core of the Confucian teachings about ethical
values, frequently invoked in the classics to illustrate the importance of maintaining social order. *Swallow's Letter* deviates from the typical romantic plot of *chuanqi*
drama, where a scholar is matched to a single beautiful woman or else his two
women work out a harmonious relationship.[22]

The audience certainly noticed this exceptional ending, too. There were speculations among some literati that this plot parodied the life of the iconic Donglin official Ni Yuanlu (1593–1644), who had spoken out most vigorously against the eunuch
faction and convinced the Chongzhen emperor to punish them.[23] Ni enjoyed the
highest reputation within the Eastern Grove–Restoration Society community. The
emperor admired his talents, personality, and character. Over the course of several
years, Ni received steady promotions to prestigious and powerful positions. In 1636,

the emperor seemed ready to appoint Ni to one of the most influential official posts, that of grand secretary. Feeling threatened by Ni's ascendance, the Eastern Grove's political rivals submitted a memorial to the emperor, which accused Ni of illegally obtaining an honorific for a woman he had established as his second wife, when in fact he had not really divorced his first wife as he had claimed.[24] Unwilling to stir up more factional confrontations, the emperor made an ambiguous gesture by ordering Ni to retire without, however, meting out any serious punishment for the potential violation of the law against having two official wives.

According to an account provided by his family, Ni Yuanlu had first married a daughter of the prestigious Chen family, but he soon divorced her at his mother's request because the daughter-in-law was said to be unfilial and disrespectful. But his wife's name still appeared on his exam records when he passed the provincial-level examinations. By the time he obtained the highest degree, the *jinshi* title, he had remarried. Because his first wife's name could not be deleted from the provincial-exam record, now his full exam records included the names of both his ex-wife, Chen, and of his second wife, Wang. This dual record was naturally a serious concern for Ni. But following the ill-conceived advice from a colleague who then was serving as the president of the Board of Personnel and convinced him it would not be a problem, Ni decided to request the honorific for his second wife, Wang. This request planted the seed for the later controversy stirred up by his factional enemies.[25]

The biographical accounts composed by Ni's sympathizers skirt the question of whether he had indeed obtained a title for his second wife illegally. Some speculated that Ni could have been pressured by his mother to divorce his first wife, but he might not have wanted to completely sever ties with her, or perhaps he even had hoped for a reunion after his mother's death![26] Although it was unwise for Ni to hide these complications and allow a messy domestic situation to arise, they agreed that he had not committed any serious misconduct. Ni's case thus has remained one of the mysteries of late Ming political history.

This mixture of facts and imagination existed in an environment of political distrust and social voyeurism. An official document issued to and preserved in the Ni family genealogy contradicts the claim by Ni's son, showing that when Ni passed the civil service examinations, his first wife, Chen, received the official recognition and an honorific.[27] A messy situation surfaced years later, when Ni received a promotion and requested an official honorific for his second wife, even though his mother allegedly kept the first—and divorced—wife in the same household.[28] The confusion caused by the attempt of the family to cover up the domestic problems allowed the factional enemies to sensationalize the case and turn it into a scandal. For instance, in 1641, many officials in the Eastern Grove–Restoration Society camp advanced to key government positions. Their political rivals created and disseminated a list called "The Twenty-four Noxious Vapors" (*ershisi qi shuo*).[29] Each of the officials on this list was assigned a sensational epithet to represent one specific evil force/energy that threatened the political order. Among them, Ni Yuanlu represented the element of promiscuity (*yin qi*).[30] He was nicknamed on this list as "Fake Jiang Shi" (*jia* Jiang Shi), one of the legendary "Twenty-four Fil-ial Exemplars" (*ershisi xiao*), hinting at the previous accusation that he divorced his official wife on the false grounds that she was unfilial, but that in fact he sim-ply wanted to make another woman his wife.[31] About a year later, in 1642, Ruan Dacheng composed the *chuanqi* drama *Swallow's Letter*.

Artistically, the play was applauded as a masterpiece, as evinced by its instant pop-ularity in literati circles. However, as noted previously, Ruan's political reputation made a political reading of this play inevitable. Many early modern literati and mod-ern scholars have closely scrutinized *Swallow's Letter* and analyzed what they see as evidence of parody,[32] while others have argued against reading this play as satire, sug-gesting that our interest in political history has led to misinterpretations of it. How-ever, as shown above, there is another way to think about how the unusual overlap of the details of the last scene of *Swallow's Letter* with Ni's case might suggest insinua-tion by Ruan's dramatic design. Such cues might in turn have invited some Eastern Grove–Restoration Society members to read and react to it politically. The ending of *Swallow's Letter* resembles Ni's biography too closely to be dismissed as pure coinci-dence. The arrangements made by the seniors at the end of *Swallow's Letter*, giving one woman the title associated with the protagonist's success in the civil service examinations and the other the honor associated with the promotion, remind one of the important role played by Ni's mother in his domestic life. It is thus unsurprising that some literati suspected personal parody in the last scene, whereas the modern audience may simply see in it "a high-water mark of Ming comedy."[33]

10.7 SPONTANEITY IN THEATER

Our examination of Ruan Dacheng and *Swallow's Letter* has highlighted two fac-tors that could help predict the audience's political interpretation of a drama: the identity of the playwright and the broader resonance of the textual details of a *chuanqi* drama. Sometimes, however, when a *chuanqi* drama was being performed, the question of whether the audience read its text and author's intentions politi-cally might be less important in igniting political sentiments than the excitement stirred up in the highly charged atmosphere of the performance itself.

Take *Swallow's Letter* again as an example. No official accusations or organized public condemnation was directed at this play. On the contrary, the play and the performance by Ruan's family troupe enjoyed remarkable acclaim for its artistic refinement and commercial success. We know of only one instance of public con-frontation in conjunction with the performance of *Swallow's Letter*. On the evening of the Moon Festival in 1642, a group of Restoration Society scholars assembled some of the most famous courtesans at a banquet in the Nanjing pleasure quar-ters. The host, Mao Xiang (1611–1693), a popular figure within the Society circle, planned to have *Swallow's Letter* performed at this gathering to celebrate his union with Dong Xiaowan (1623–1651), who had been an elite courtesan before overcom-ing barriers to become Mao's concubine. One particular scene in *Swallow's Letter* performed at this banquet, which depicted the reunion of the protagonist Huo and the courtesan Xingyun (Wandering Cloud), indeed seemed to be a wonderful choice for this occasion. To make this celebration perfect, Mao Xiang even booked Ruan Dacheng's renowned family troupe to perform the play.

One of the most memorable events in late Ming political history unfolded at this very moment: as the actor and actress were mesmerizing the audience with their beautiful singing and movement, the aroma of wine and courtesans' fragrance at the banquet stimulated the scholars' minds. Old friends coming from other parts of the empire to take the civil service examinations had arrived just in time to join the gathering. Their reunion elicited tears of joy. As the friends recalled memories of their heroic struggle against the "evil men," the audience's reaction to the *Swallow's Letter* performed by Ruan's troupe gradually changed. "The performance was remarkable. During the course of each act, the audience applauded the singers while at the same time generating their own chorus of condemning the playwright." It was reported that the performers returned home and described to Ruan how the crowd had insulted him.[34]

As this incident shows, spontaneous reactions during a *chuanqi* performance could also play a critical role in making a play politically significant. When Mao Xiang and his Restoration Society friends engaged Ruan's troupe to perform *Swallow's Letter*, at the beginning of the performance, Ruan's identity and the possible insinuation embedded in the playtexts appeared not to concern them. It seemed that many of these culturally refined and economically privileged men simply wanted to have a good time. They expected to be entertained by the best dramatic performance in town, rather than commiserating about the eunuch faction or Ruan's purported parody of a certain Eastern Grove official. It was the other factors at play in the gathering—drinking, singing, chatting, and joking—that excited the audience to respond to the play in an unexpected manner, which eventually turned this banquet into a political event and made it extremely difficult for future audiences to separate the performance of this play from late Ming political historiography where Confucian moral judgment sided against Ruan Dacheng. It was the writings by those who had participated in the banquet and survived the Ming-Qing regime change that consolidated the memory of the incident as a political event, a famous act of "condemnation during performance" (*mazuo*).[35]

CONCLUSION

This chapter has shown that the classification of a drama as political was fluid in the seventeenth century. The identity of the playwright, the play's contents, and the audience reaction to it were all subject to change in different contexts and gave political meaning to one another. This means that, in the Confucian tradition, the readers and audiences of *chuanqi* drama would be most heavily influenced by the moral judgment in the political historiography. This fluidity in turn determined that, ultimately, whoever dominated the compilation and transmission of historical records would have more control over the perceptions of a *chuanqi* drama and its author. The party with a louder moralistic voice, both at the time and in historical records, determines the fate of a play, sometimes in perpetuity. Modern readers of these plays must become familiar with these factors to assess their artistic value.

When Li Yu wrote "Forgo Satire," parts of which have been quoted earlier in this chapter, he was aware of all these interpretive habits and tendencies among the readers and audience of *chuanqi* drama. He also recognized that politically minded authors had exploited these interpretive habits and tendencies:

> They cast persons they were fond of as heroes and heroines and cast those they were angry with as shady and clownish characters. They attributed unheard-of base behavior to a particular person, had actors perform and perpetuate it, to the extent that their version became a closed case, which even the most exemplary conduct of that person's descendants could do nothing to alter.
>
> [*XQOJ* 20; trans. Pollard, 37]

Another important lesson here is that drama perpetuated the Confucian moral-political system, not by imposing it on the audience but by working with the audience's (often liberal) interpretations and reactions. In this cultural context, politics made the best material for drama precisely because arbitrary understanding and moral judgment were always part of the political dynamics. This was true even in the case of drama on current affairs, whose main appeal was supposedly its goal of presenting "facts." As scholars have pointed out, many plays in this genre fabricated sensational details and incorporated vulgar rumors.[36] Ostensibly produced to condemn the evil men in politics, such as the eunuch faction, by portraying them as morally corrupt and even deviant, these plays satisfied the audience's expectations for entertainment but failed to deliver truths about political figures or events. This complicated relationship among politics, moralism, and drama also explains why an artistically sophisticated and entertaining play such as Kong Shangren's (1648–1718) *The Peach Blossom Fan* (*Taohua shan*) can readily replace facts in people's understanding of the political history of the Ming-Qing dynastic transition with its vivid representations of some colorful political figures, including that of the "small man" Ruan Dacheng (☞ chap. 12).

Judging might not have been Kong Shangren's intention, however. As Wai-yee Li eloquently points out, aesthetic mediation in *Peach Blossom Fan* "renders both political engagement and the escape from politics compelling yet elusive," but in the meantime, aesthetic pleasure itself is "a problematic proposition" because the danger of mixing aesthetics and politics always looms.[37] Weaving *Swallow's Letter* seamlessly into the plot of *Peach Blossom Fan*, Kong's employment of the dramatic device of a play within a play tellingly reveals that the brutal exercise of casting and defying judgment—the most traumatic aspect of the literati experience of the dynastic transition—continues for both playwright and audience. *Peach Blossom Fan* gives Ruan a stage on which to talk about his *Swallow's Letter* as a value-neutral artwork. Meanwhile, by showing how theater itself ultimately becomes the symbol of a morally corrupt and doomed regime, *Peach Blossom Fan* also exposes the impossibility of a nonpolitical interpretation of *Swallow's Letter* in the context of seventeenth-century history. The precarious political environment in the early Qing and the dramatists' struggle to stage the "unstageable world" manifested this phenomenon in an even more extreme manner.[38]

Ying Zhang

NOTES

1. Ayling Wang, "*Shishiju* as a Public Forum: *The Crying Phoenix* and the Dramatization of Contemporary Political Affairs in late Ming China," in *1616: Shakespeare and Tang Xianzu's China*, eds. Tian Yuan Tan, Paul Edmondson, and Shih-pe Wang (London: Bloomsbury Arden Shakespeare, 2016), 72. It must be noted that the meaning of this term for modern scholars varies. For more information, for example, see Paize Keulemans, "Onstage Rumor, Offstage Voices: The Politics of the Present in the Contemporary Opera of Li Yu," *Frontiers of History in China* 9, no. 4 (2014): 165–201; Gao Meihua, "Mingdai shishi xinju" (New Ming Dramas on Current Affairs), Ph.D. dissertation, Guoli Zhengzhi daxue, 1991; and Li Jiangjie, *Ming Qing shishiju yanjiu* (Ming-Qing Dramas on Current Affairs) (Jinan, China: Qilu shushe, 2014). Finally, for an in-depth discussion of how such *shishiju* plays continued and became more complicated to stage immediately after the fall of the Ming, see Guojun Wang, *Staging Personhood: Costuming in Early Qing Drama* (New York: Columbia University Press, 2020).

2. This Grand Secretary is Yan Song (1480–1567).

3. Keulemans, "Onstage Rumor, Offstage Voices," 178.

4. As Alison Hardie points out, political dramas of the Ming-Qing transitional period provided outsiders to government politics with information about political events. See Alison Hardie, "Political Drama in the Ming-Qing Transition: A Study of Four Plays," *Ming Qing yanjiu* XVII (2012), 31.

5. Translation by Ian Johnson and Wang Ping, *Daxue and Zhongyong: Bilingual Edition* (Hong Kong: Chinese University of Hong Kong Press, 2012), 47.

6. Ying Zhang, "The Politics and Practice of Moral Rectitude in the Late Ming: The Case of Huang Daozhou (1585–1646)," *Late Imperial China* 34, no. 2 (2013): 52–82.

7. For example, see Zhao Qian, "Li Yu 'Jiegou lun' kaolun" (An Examination of Li Yu's "Treatise on Structure"), master's thesis, Qinghai shifan daxue, 2015, 21–24.

8. Ying Zhang, *Confucian Image Politics: Masculine Morality in Seventeenth-Century China* (Seattle: University of Washington Press, 2016), esp. chap. 1.

9. For a brief review of the subjects of drama on current affairs, see Ayling Wang, " 'Yong dangshi shoubi, pu dangqian qingshi': Lun Ming mo Qing chu shishiju zhong zhi xianshi yishi yu lishi shuxie" (Using Contemporary Forms to Document Contemporary Affairs: An Examination of the Political Awareness and the Writing of History in Plays on Contemporary Affairs from the late Ming and early Qing Periods), in *Zhonghua wenhua de chuancheng yu chuangxin: Jinian Mou Fuli jiaoshou lunwenji* (The Transmission and Transformation of Chinese Culture: A Festschrift in Memory of Professor Mou Fuli), ed. Wang Chengmian (Hong Kong: Chinese University of Hong Kong Press, 2009), 264–267.

10. The two references to the Song dynasty appear in scene 2, "Composition under Duress," where a main character introduces his family background; and scene 29, "Fake Announcement" ("Jiabao"), where a character mentions the location of the civil service examinations.

11. Authenticity was a central intellectual, social, and cultural issue in the late Ming era. *Green Peony* constructs its storyline around this question. For example, toward the end of the play, in scene 25, the two cheaters who faked their literary talents were exposed in a new essay contest titled "On the Authentic".

12. Lu Shiyi, *Fushe jilüe* (A Brief Account of the Restoration Society), cited in Zhang, *Confucian Image Politics*, 92–93.

13. Lin Zhiying, "Yi ju wei ge: Chuanqi *Lü mudan* de xiezuo yu Wu Bing de gaibian" (Weaponizing Drama: The Composition of *Green Peony* and Wu Bing's Rewriting), *Qinghua xuebao* (The Qinghua Review) 42, no. 4 (2012): 699–731. For a biographical review of Wu Bing and this play, see Jing Shen, *Playwrights and Literary Games in Seventeenth-Century China: Plays by Tang Xianzu, Mei Dingzuo, Wu Bing, Li Yu, and Kong Shangren* (Lanham, MD: Lexington Books, 2010), esp. 123–126.

14. Translation by this author. The translations of the titles of scene 2 and 3 are adopted from Cyril Birch, *Scenes for Mandarins: The Elite Theater of the Ming* (New York: Columbia University Press, 1995), 186–187.

15. Lin, "Yi ju wei ge."

16. Chen Shude, "Cong Ming mo juzuo fengqi bian Ruan Dacheng 'Shichao si zhong' zhi ying-she dongji" (A Discussion of the Motivations for Insinuation Found in Ruan Dacheng's Four Plays in Light of the Trends in Late Ming Drama), *Yishu xuebao* (Taiwan Journal of Arts) 65 (1999): 171–185.

17. Chen, "Cong Ming mo juzuo fengqi," 177.

18. Cited in Chen, "Cong Ming mo juzuo fengqi," 176–178.

19. Shen, *Playwrights and Literary Games*, 39–41.

20. Chen, "Cong Ming mo juzuo fengqi," 179.

21. The flowery headdress here symbolizes the imperial honorific for the wife of an official.

22. Shen, *Playwrights and Literary Games*, 262.

23. Cheng Huaping, *Ming Qing chuanqi biannian shi gao* (A Preliminary Annalistic History of the Chuanqi Drama of the Ming and the Qing Dynasties) (Jinan, China: Qilu shushe, 2008), 236.

24. Zhang Tingyu et al., *Ming shi* (History of the Ming) (Beijing: Zhonghua shuju, 1974), 6840.

25. Ni Huiding, *Ni Wenzhenggong nianpu* (Chronological Biography of Ni Yuanlu) (Beijing: Zhonghua shuju, 1994), Appendix. Ni Huiding mentions neither of his father's wives in the main text of the chronological biography.

26. Yang Shicong, *Yutang huiji* (Collected Writings from Jade Hall), in *Ming Qing shiliao cong-bian chu ji* (Collections of Ming-Qing Historical Sources I), ed. Shen Yunlong (Taipei: Wenhai chu-banshe), vol. 3, 1602–1603.

27. "Chifeng Wenzheng gong pei Chen tai gongren" (Title Conferment to Lady Chen, wife of Ni Yuanlu), in Ni Ming et al., *Guyu Ni shi zupu* (The Genealogy of the Ni Family of Guyu) (Shang-hai Library), vol. 1, 87.

28. Ni Yuanlu's letter to his mother about the issue of the honorific hints that he and his mother had kept something secret from other family members. Perhaps out of concern for social and cultural custom, they failed to offer a clear explanation about (or even announce) the divorce to protect the family's reputation. See Liu Heng, *Zhongguo shufa quanji Mingdai bian Ni Yuanlu juan* (Complete Collections of Chinese Calligraphical Works, the Ming Dynasty, Ni Yuanlu) (Beijing: Rongbaozhai chubanshe, 1999), 224–225.

29. Traditionally, the Chinese have used the calendric system of Twenty-four Solar Terms (*ershisi qi*), with each term marking one point in the seasonal changes of a year. These terms deter-mined the timing of agricultural—and later, cultural—activities throughout the year.

30. Xia Xie, *Ming tongjian* (Comprehensive Mirror of the Ming) (Changsha, China: Xuelu chu-banshe, 1998), 2449.

31. Jiang Shi's story was widely circulated as one of the "Twenty-four Filial Exemplars" in pre-modern China. In this story (also called "The Fountain Bubbled and the Carps Leaped"), Jiang Shi and his wife served his mother filially.

32. Cheng, "Cong Ming mo juzuo fengqi," 180.

33. Birch, *Scenes for Mandarins*, 223.

34. Cited in Kang Baocheng, "*Yanzi jian* chuanqi de bei bayan yu bei shangyan—jian shuo wenxue de 'ce bu zhun' yuanli" (Boycotting and Performing *The Swallow's Letter*: Exploring a The-ory of Uncertainty in Literature), *Xueshu yanjiu* (Scholarly Research) 8 (2009): 1–16.

35. Guo Yingde, "Yishi yu xiangzheng: Qing Shunzhi shi qi nian Mao Xiang Dequantang yeyan yanju shulun" (Ritual and Symbolism: Mao Xiang's Banquet at the Dequantang in Shunzhi 17 [1660]), *Lingnan Journal of Chinese Studies* 6 (2016): 63–88.

36. Wang, "Yong dangshi shoubi," 267.

37. Wai-yee Li, *Women and National Trauma in Late Imperial Chinese Literature* (Cambridge, MA: Harvard University Asia Center, 2014), 553.

38. Wang, *Staging Personhood*.

PRIMARY SOURCES

LMD   Wu Bing 吳炳. *Lü mudan* 綠牡丹 (*The Green Peony*). Shanghai: Shanghai guji chubanshe, 1985.

XQOJ   Li Yu 李漁. *Xianqing ouji* 閒情偶寄 (*Leisure Notes*). Shanghai: Shanghai guji chubanshe, 2000.

YZJ   Ruan Dacheng 阮大鋮. *Yanzi jian* 燕子箋 (*The Swallow's Letter*). Shanghai: Shanghai guji chubanshe, 1986.

SUGGESTED READINGS

TRANSLATIONS

Birch, Cyril, trans. "Bigamy Unabashed: Ruan Dacheng's *The Swallow Letter*." In *Scenes for Mandarins: The Elite Theater of the Ming*, introd. and trans. Cyril Birch, 219–248. New York: Columbia University Press, 1995.

Birch, Cyril, trans. "A Quiz for Love: Wu Bing's *The Green Peony*." In *Scenes for Mandarins: The Elite Theater of the Ming*, introd. and trans. Cyril Birch, 183–218. New York: Columbia University Press, 1995.

Pollard, David, trans. "Li Yu on the Theater: Excerpts from *Pleasant Diversions*." *Renditions*, 72 (2009): 30–70.

ENGLISH

Hardie, Alison. "Political Drama in the Ming-Qing Transition: A Study of Four Plays." *Ming Qing yanjiu* XVII (2012): 1–34.

Keulemans, Paize. "Onstage Rumor, Offstage Voices: The Politics of the Present in the Contemporary Opera of Li Yu." *Frontiers of History in China* 9 (2014): 165–201.

Shen, Jing. *Playwrights and Literary Games in Seventeenth-Century China: Plays by Tang Xianzu, Mei Dingzuo, Wu Bing, Li Yu, and Kong Shangren*. Lanham, MD: Lexington Books, 2010.

Wang, Ayling. "*Shishiju* as a Public Forum: *The Crying Phoenix* and the Dramatization of Contemporary Political Affairs in Late Ming China." In *1616: Shakespeare and Tang Xianzu's China*, ed. Tian Yuan Tan, Paul Edmondson, and Shih-pe Wang, 64–75. London: Bloomsbury Arden Shakespeare, 2016.

Wang, Guojun. *Staging Personhood: Costuming in Early Qing Drama*. New York: Columbia University Press, 2020.

CHINESE

Chen Shude 陳樹德. "Cong Ming mo juzuo fengqi bian Ruan Dacheng 'Shichao si zhong' zhi yingshe dongji" 從明末劇作風氣辨阮大鋮「石巢四種」之影射動機 (A Discussion of the Motivations for Insinuation Found in Ruan Dacheng's Four Plays in Light of the Trends in Late Ming Drama). *Yishu xuebao (Taiwan Journal of Arts)* 65 (1999): 171–185.

Cheng Huaping 程華平. *Ming Qing chuanqi biannian shi gao* 明清傳奇編年史稿 (*A Preliminary Annalistic History of the Chuanqi Drama of the Ming and Qing Dynasties*). Jinan, China: Qilu shushe, 2008.

Guo Yingde 郭英德. "Yishi yu xiangzheng: Qing Shunzhi shi qi nian Mao Xiang de quantang yeyan yanju shulun" 儀式與象徵：清順治十七年冒襄得全堂夜宴演劇述論 (Ritual and Symbolism: Mao Xiang's Banquet at the Dequantang in Shunzhi 17 [1660]). *Lingnan Journal of Chinese Studies* 6 (2016): 63–88.

Li Jiangjie 李江杰. *Ming-Qing shishiju yanjiu* 明清時事劇研究 (*A Study of Ming and Qing Dynasty Plays on Contemporary Affairs*). Jinan, China: Qilu shushe, 2014.

Lin Zhiying 林芷瑩. "Yi ju wei ge: Chuanqi *Lü mudan* de xiezuo yu Wu Bing de gaibian" 以劇為戈—傳奇《綠牡丹》的寫作與吳炳的改編 (Weaponizing Drama: The Composition of *Green Peony* and Wu Bing's Rewriting). *Qinghua xuebao (The Qinghua Review)* 42, no. 4 (2012): 699–731.

II

A Much-Desired Match

Playwriting, Stagecraft, and Entrepreneurship

A master of comedy, the writer and entrepreneur Li Yu (1611–1680) defied the social conventions of his day. From shockingly graphic descriptions of anomalous genitalia in his fiction to the flamboyant exhibition of his theater troupe, Li Yu proved himself an inveterate entertainer committed to making people laugh in a historical moment defined by loss and nostalgia. Theatricality was the defining feature of his life and work. In his work, Li's flair for the theatrical is manifest in the inventiveness of the *chuanqi* plays he wrote over the course of his life: these plays dramatize the horror and shock of hilariously mismatched young lovers, women taking charge of their own marriage arrangements rather than men pursuing women, or the supernatural transformation of a kind (but physically disgusting) young man. Perhaps nowhere is this flair dramatized so extravagantly as in the theatrical tour-de-force of a troupe of actors performing scenes of one play within another that led to the (presumed) real death of the woman in the leading role.[1]

Li Yu conceived of role-play in writing and onstage as a way to expand the experiential possibilities of a single, finite, and even disappointing life. He developed a distinctive authorial persona that plays up his ingenuity by interrupting readers of his fiction and essays with instructions to put down the book and try to guess what will happen next, and chiding them when they fail to guess correctly. He was obsessed with improving the ability of theatrical performance to captivate and entertain audiences, and toward the end of his life, he published a comprehensive guide to playwriting and performance that touched on all aspects of the art of the theater. In addition to writing and directing plays, Li Yu's entrepreneurial experiments involved a dizzying array of arenas: he published and sold his own books, compiled anthologies, designed gardens, managed a touring theater troupe starring his concubines, and traveled around the country mingling with and entertaining high-ranking officials and influential literary figures. This chapter will introduce Li Yu's life and his dramatic theory from *Leisure Notes* (*Xianqing ouji*) before delving into one of his signature plays, *A Much-Desired Match* (*Yizhong yuan*).

11.1 A VERY THEATRICAL ENTREPRENEUR

Like many men of his generation, Li Yu had pursued the conventional path of a student aspiring to an official position through the examination system during the last decades of the Ming dynasty, and it was not until after the fall of the Ming in 1644 that he began to seek other ways to make a living. The wrenching transition between the Ming and the Qing dynasties left many influential cultural figures dead or forced them into reclusion from official life. During those early years of the Qing, many men refused to serve the new government out of loyalty to the Ming dynasty. Some joined the Ming resistance in the south; others lived in Buddhist temples. Some took up tutoring jobs or started business ventures, while others began to sell their writing or paintings openly for the first time—something that had long been anathema for a proper literatus (☛ chap. 4). Li Yu occupied a moderate position during a time of political upheaval and partisanship: he was not an outspoken Ming loyalist (*yimin*), but neither did he serve the Qing in any official capacity. Instead, harnessing continued elite interest in writing, reading, and watching plays, he sought to make a living from his involvement in the world of theater. He was not alone in this; what set him apart from his contemporaries was his particularly entrepreneurial approach.

Li Yu was one of the most prolific authors of his day, and theater was the bedrock of his protean career: ten of his plays are extant today, many of them in high-quality editions, and his name was attached to many others, either as author or commentator.[2] He designed his plays with performance in mind, imagining a broad audience that included illiterate persons. Nevertheless, unlike many playwrights of his day whose works survive largely in manuscript, Li Yu also wrote for the broad readership enabled by print. He oversaw the publication of his plays, producing woodblock imprints of individual plays as he completed them, and later as collections of five and ten plays. Li Yu hired talented woodblock carvers to produce his illustrated plays (☛ chap. 4). These carefully edited, beautifully crafted volumes catered primarily to a readership that was concentrated in urban centers, but they transported the sumptuousness of theater to readers in all corners of the empire. His fine editions sold well, and—although we do not have any sales records—it seems that the publication of a new play every other year or so brought in enough income to support him and his family.

Like most *chuanqi* plays, Li Yu's plays were romantic comedies structured around the meeting of a promising young scholar and a sweet young beauty, their subsequent separation and misadventures, and a happy final reunion. More than any of his contemporaries, Li was devoted to making audiences laugh, and he painted even the usually earnest young lovers and their strict parents with comic strokes. Li Yu's plays also stand out for their delight in overturning commonsense understandings or clichéd plots. For example, his first play, *Women in Love* (*Lianxiang ban*), published in 1651 when he first moved to Hangzhou, offered a new twist on the usual scholar-beauty romance, exploring what would happen if a woman rather than a man were to fall in love with an archetypal young beauty. *Women in Love* retains its ability to challenge social convention even today, as evidenced by the marketing of its 2010 Beijing performance as a "lesbian" play. With this play, Li Yu inverted the common theme of jealousy among women in polygamous families by having his female protagonists marry the same man in order to maintain their romantic relationship with one another. This play was followed by *Mistake with a Kite* (*Fengzheng wu*), an uproarious comedy of errors that culminates in the pairing of two couples: one beautiful and elegant, and the other ugly and vulgar. The comedy derives from the fact that the two women live in the same household, so that time and again, the suitors mistakenly communicate with the wrong woman. As was typical, only in the final moments of the play are the couples appropriately paired and married.

Li Yu's third play, *A Much-Desired Match* (*Yizhong yuan*), which was published in the mid-1650s, and which will be the focus of this chapter, dramatizes the trials of talented aesthetes trying to make a living in a late Ming Hangzhou that runs on deception. The conceit of the play is that two gifted women painters associated with the West Lake of Hangzhou (☛ chap. 4), Yang Yunyou (d. 1627) and Lin Tiansu (roughly contemporary), are to be matched with the renowned male painters whose work they forge to make a living: Dong Qichang (1555–1636, style name Sibai) and Chen Jiru (1558–1639, style name Meigong). Dong and Chen are overwhelmed by high demand for their paintings, and in a shop, they find excellent forgeries of their own works, painted by local women. The two men respond to this discovery by resolving to find and marry the forgers. Lin is found quickly through her servant, but Yang proves eminently difficult to locate, and hilarity ensues as she undertakes two sham weddings to fake "Dong Qichangs" and commits murder before marrying the real Dong in the final scene.

All four protagonists were historical figures, recently deceased at the time of this play's writing, and for many they came to symbolize attachment to a lost late Ming world in which the real Dong and Chen were illustrious cultural figures. Although the four were acquainted with one another in life, the marriages that Li Yu works out in the play are purely fictional, meant to improve upon the historical version of events by bringing them more in line with the happy endings of romantic comedy. A feminist reading of this new outcome is also possible: the female leads—talented, resourceful, clever, and witty—are the stars of the show, and the play is written to correct their stories in particular, for Li Yu insists that they deserve a better fate than they received in history. As Lin Tiansu, the future bride of Chen Jiru, tells Yang Yunyou, the eventual wife of Dong Qichang:

(小旦) 從古以來"佳人才子"的四個字再分不開。是個佳人一定該配才子，是個才子一定該配佳人。若還配錯了，就是千古的恨事！如今世上的才子只有兩位：第一個是董思白，第二個是陳眉公。若論佳人也只有兩位：第一個是你，那第二個也就要數着我了。

SECONDARY YOUNG FEMALE *as* LIN TIANSU [*speaks*]: Since ancient times, "scholars and beauties" (*caizi jiaren*) have never been separated. If there is a beauty, she will surely be matched with a scholar, and if there's a scholar, he will surely be matched with a beauty. It's a matter of eternal regret if they happen to be mismatched! Nowadays there are only two scholars in the world: the first is Dong Sibai, and the second is Chen Meigong. As for beauties, there are also only two: the first is you, and the second one, well, that's none other than me.

[*YZY* 8.3431, scene 28, "The Fake Marriage" ("Kuanghun")]

On the whole, *A Much-Desired Match* serves as a dramatized rewriting of history, meant to give these talented women a happier ending than they had in life. The fact that Li Yu asked Huang Yuanjie (c. 1620–1669), a contemporary woman making a living as a writer, painter, and tutor near West Lake, to write a preface and add commentary to the play suggests that this compensatory gesture may be an earnest one. Nevertheless, the humorist Li Yu subjects his revived female protagonists to many detours and trials along the way.

A central problem of *A Much-Desired Match*—the role of art in an increasingly commercialized age—was the conundrum at the heart of Li Yu's own cultural production. These early plays, both on stage and in print, were instant hits. They were so popular that by 1662, Li moved to Nanjing, the center of drama printing at that time, to combat the unauthorized reproduction of his works. In 1668, he built Mustard Seed Garden (Jiezi yuan) just inside the city wall in southeastern Nanjing. He printed and sold his works, edited collections, and letter-writing paper out of this garden residence, and Mustard Seed Garden soon came to operate as his brand name.

During this period, Li Yu also organized a household troupe of several talented young women he had been given as concubines, who learned to enact his plays. They performed for guests at his residence in Nanjing and accompanied him on long journeys he took around the empire to seek patrons to financially support his cultural work. More than any literatus before him, Li Yu aimed to design cultural products that would cater to a broad range of consumers by mixing literary and popular styles. Li recorded his methods of playwriting and his technical expertise regarding performance, and he is best known today for the fruits of those efforts: his comprehensive treatise on drama was published in a wide-ranging collection of essays on the arts of living titled *Leisure Notes* (1671). This text was already influential at the time of his death in 1680. The sections on drama were extracted and published separately in 1925 and are today considered a milestone in the history of Chinese dramatic theory.

As this chapter will show, taken together, Li Yu's play *A Much-Desired Match* and his theorization of theater in *Leisure Notes* dramatize the role of art in a fast-paced commoditized economy. The expansion of the market from the sixteenth century onward led to increased demand for books and works of art, and literati and artists alike responded to that change by developing their crafts in new directions. For Li Yu, this meant conceiving of his role broadly and boldly experimenting with expanding the parameters of literati cultural production into new territory. With *Leisure Notes*, it is in this entrepreneurial spirit that he offers a vision of what theater could be: an all-encompassing, dynamic art form that provides a fully immersive aesthetic experience that anyone could enjoy. The creation of such an immersive experience requires being attuned to a more general audience than self-appointed literati aficionados.

In *A Much-Desired Match*, Li Yu exploits the comic potential that results when an increased demand for paintings by famous artists is accompanied by a decrease in the ability of purchasers to appreciate the art. Theater, he seems to suggest, is the best medium in which to offer a critique of the unsustainable demands of the art market, with its outdated claims of authenticity. Theater, after all, makes art of the inauthentic. It is here, at the intersection of the medium of theater with the medium of painting, that Li Yu makes a strong case for theater being the truest of all art forms in the rapidly changing world in which he lived.

11.2 *LEISURE NOTES:* TOWARD A COHERENT, UP-TO-DATE, AND ACCESSIBLE THEATRICAL EXPERIENCE

Since the twentieth century, scholars have been most interested in Li Yu's comprehensive treatise on drama, as presented in *Leisure Notes.*[3] Two sections on playwriting ("Ciqu bu") and directing ("Yanxi bu"), along with a third section on the selection and training of female performers ("Shengrong bu"), conceived of the theater in a newly comprehensive way, departing from standard methods of dramatic composition as well as of stage presentation. Li Yu revolutionized received understandings of drama by challenging the dominance of the arias, the general indifference to dialogue, and the tendency to prioritize lyricism over stagecraft. For him, the value of theater far exceeded the narrow category of its poetry-like aspects. He sought instead to identify a broad range of constituent elements that together produced the theatrical experience and then theorize how they might be regulated and altered. He analyzed concerns that we associate with playwriting, like structure, plot development, and dialogue, and he also addressed issues that today are often left to other theater professionals, such as makeup, stage lighting, and actors' understanding of the significance of their lines.

In the groundbreaking conceptualization of theater in *Leisure Notes*, Li Yu prioritizes the structure of a play over the quality of its verses; he treats the writing of spoken dialogue as a literary art, and he offers extensive insights on the training of actors. A comment on playwriting in *Leisure Notes* offers a good example of the sort of imaginative maneuver at the heart of Li Yu's innovative dramatic theory:

> Li Yu may hold the brush in his hand, but his mouth is onstage. His body assumes all the movements of actors onstage, and his spirit circles round the four directions, examining plot elements and trying out sounds and tunes. If it's good, he immediately writes it down, if not, he puts down his brush.
>
> [*XQOJ* 48, "In Writing, Distinguish between the Verbose and the Laconic" ("Ci bie fanjian")]

This comment relates to writing plays rather than performing them, but it serves as a good example of the kind of thinking Li Yu engaged in as he reimagined theater's potential. We see the playwright imagining himself performing the work onstage, even as his spirit soars throughout the four directions, considering the plot and the aural effect of the play's performance as he gives it shape with his brush. He also shifted the focus away from the literary elements of a play, arguing instead that the performed play was the proper object of aesthetic contemplation.

In addition to its fame for such positive innovations, however, Li Yu's dramatic theory has also gained some notoriety: the third section on the selection and training of actresses, "On Voice and Appearance" ("Shengrong bu"), discusses the practice of purchasing women as concubines who might also be taught to perform in plays. Such a practice was not unusual, but writing about it certainly was. This section, despite its assumption that some women are persons to be bought and sold, includes some suggestions that seem to have liberating potential for women, such as an argument for women's literacy, alongside comments that would today be considered overtly sexist, such as scrutinizing skin tone or having a woman walk on a raised platform so that when she averts her eyes, an observer might still be able to catch her gaze.

This section has been a source of discomfort from Li Yu's day to the present, but for different reasons. In the book's opening pages, Li Yu apologized to his contemporaries for his inability to find a low-cost substitute for human performers. *Leisure Notes* was marketed as a budget guide to the good life, with inexpensive alternatives suggested for everything from paintings to antiques, but in the theater, he explained apologetically, there was no good substitute for living actors. By the twentieth century, however, the difficulty was not in the expense involved in purchasing female actors, but rather in the centrality of indentured labor to the Chinese theater of earlier periods. In the changed climate of the modern Chinese nation, the traditionally low social status of actors as people who could be bought and sold was seen as a backward custom no longer compatible with Chinese dramatic practice or social vision. Reformers worked to disassociate acting as a profession from prostitution. What is more, this period of reform was associated with women claiming their right, as citizens, to participate in the public theatrical world, both onstage alongside male actors and in the audiences of public theaters. However, it was in the name of equal rights that women fought for these changes, making Li Yu's treatise obsolete, which obviously denied women autonomy. In this changed environment, Li's treatise continued to be discussed, but it was often approached as though the section on female actors did not even exist.

Li Yu's nonchalant commodification of women is disturbing, but it does not render his discussion of women performers irrelevant to today's readers. We have very few records of the lives of such women, not least because of their low social status (➤ chaps. 2 and 3) and, as Li Yu's impassioned argument for women's literacy suggests, their customarily limited access to writing and print. By writing in some detail about these women actors and drawing upon his own experience with training his concubines to perform his plays in the Kun style (➤ chap. 8), Li Yu left behind a record of these women that is valuable for theater historians in its technical detail and to social historians in the rare glimpse that it offers into the lived experience of performers. Li Yu may not have considered his concubines as equally deserving of personhood, but for the scholar today, the details he provides for the elite theater practitioner can also be interpreted as an important record of the lives of purchased women performers in late imperial China.

We now turn to the opening sections of *Leisure Notes* to explore in detail some of the major tenets of his drama theory. Li Yu opens *Leisure Notes* with a series of essays on the "structure" (*jiegou*) of drama. He sought to convince aspiring playwrights of the value of an original plot, plainly presented and clearly developed. At the heart of this theory is the notion of a single "foundational element" (*zhunao*)—summed up as "a single person and a single event" (*yiren yishi*) [*XQOJ* 8, "Establishing the Foundational Element" ("Li zhunao")]—at the heart of every good play. His first three plays can be understood in this way, as answering new, but simple questions: What if a woman fell in love with another woman (*Women in Love*)? What if a young person depended on the unruly medium of a kite to carry a love letter (*Mistake with a Kite*)? And what if a famous painter could marry a talented woman who could help him double his production (*A Much-Desired Match*)? While the reader or audience member, encountering such plays for the first time, cannot surmise precisely how these plots will develop, anyone can imagine some of the novel twists of plot that may be generated from such a premise. This foundational element guides the development of all aspects of the plot, even as it provides internal coherence for the play. Its simplicity is particularly well suited to the context of performed plays, where the audience must be able to easily identify characters (who were often performed by the same actors) and follow the storyline. Li Yu likens a play that is not governed by such a guiding principle to an ill-conceived monstrosity:

> Consideration of structure should precede selecting tunes, choosing rhymes, or picking up a brush. When the Creator endowed us with form, just as the semen and blood were beginning to congeal, and before the fetus was formed, he first established the complete form of the body, making it so that a drop of blood was endowed with all the features of the five organs and the skeleton. Now suppose that he had not had a complete idea before he began, but rather had—from the top of the head to the bottom of the feet—proceeded to create us step by step. If that had been the case, a body would contain countless scars where it had been cut off and then continued, which would obstruct the flow of blood and *qi*.
>
> [*XQOJ* 4, "1. Structure" ("Jiegou diyi")]

Here, Li Yu takes the physical body as a model for the composition of a play: just as the body develops according to a preestablished form, so a playwright needs to have a sense of the shape of the whole play in mind before he begins to write. This analogy conceives of the play as a living thing that must be well ordered if it is to thrive.

Li Yu was not the first to praise plays for their novelty (*xinqi*) or freshness (*xinxian*); avoiding clichés in description and in plot had been praised in the earliest commentaries on drama. He did take this preference further than any of his predecessors, however, insisting that all elements of a plot be brand new. Audiences at the time were accustomed to watching plays with which they were already familiar, and the common practice of performing "select individual scenes" (*zhezixi*) from multiple plays in a single evening demonstrates the degree to which basic knowledge of plots and characters was assumed. In addition to these conventions of familiarity in performance, most playwrights adhered to a model of composition that leaned heavily on existing literature. Almost all *chuanqi* plays were reworkings of popular old *chuanqi* tales (prose stories in classical Chinese) (☛ chap. 9; *HTRCFiction*, chap. 2), so there was very little precedent for making up an entirely new story. Nevertheless, the brevity of the tales that often served as inspirations for playwrights meant that there remained ample opportunity for freshness, even when the core idea was borrowed from earlier material. Ming playwrights frequently developed new characters, devised extensive subplots, and even changed the story so much that the original tale was barely recognizable. These changes, to them, constituted writing a new play.

While earlier critics tended to praise plays as fresh for offering a new take on a familiar story, Li Yu's narrower conception of novelty dismissed all previously used plotlines: "If the story has already appeared on the stage, and a thousand or ten thousand people have already seen it, it is no longer strange in the least, so why transmit it?" [*XQOJ* 9, "Avoiding Clichés" ("Tuo kejiu")]. Li Yu posits that no previously existing material is strange enough to be worthy of the name of the genre *chuanqi*, which, rendered literally, means "to transmit the strange."

Li Yu generally followed this rule in his own practice, and most of his plays revolve around a central theme or problem that is fundamentally new. The one exception is *Mirage Tower* (*Shenzhong lou*), which weaves together material from two Yuan *zaju* plays, *Liu Yi Delivers the Letter* (*Liu Yi chuan shu*) and *Scholar Zhang Boils the Sea* (*Zhang Sheng zhu hai*), in a transformative way.[4] In addition, Li Yu developed at least four *chuanqi* plays—*As Heaven Would Have It* (*Naihe tian*), *A Couple of Soles* (*Bimu yu*), *Woman in Pursuit of Man* (*Huang qiu feng*), and *The Ingenious Finale* (*Qiao tuanyuan*)—from his previously published *huaben* short stories (☛ *HTRCFiction*, chap. 9).[5] Yet even as Li Yu insists on absolute novelty, he remains highly attuned to the imminent obsolescence of all plays:

> It is not just that the works done by previous writers are considered old these days, but even for those plays that I have written with my own hand, if I look at yesterday's work today, there is also some distance from it. Yesterday's has already been seen, but today's has not, so I know that what I have not yet seen is new, while what I have seen already is old.
>
> [*XQOJ* 9, "Avoiding Clichés"]

This conception of theatrical production links it to the commercial market. In the midst of complex and rapidly evolving audience tastes, Li proposes that what lends a play value is the simple fact of its not having been previously seen. On the one hand, such a stance offers the playwright a livelihood and attributes a certain value to his works; on the other, it compels him to continuously produce new plays for audience consumption, calling into question older modalities of aesthetic appreciation. Li Yu was constantly under pressure to increase the pace of his creative output, and he depicts a similar dynamic in the lives of the artists in *A Much-Desired Match*.

Li Yu's focus on structure and novelty in playwriting can be linked to his connection to the market. Related to the market, too, is his interest in increasing the accessibility—that is, the comprehensibility—of his plays in performance. While almost all Ming *chuanqi* plays had sought balance in the proportion of lively, humorous scenes to drawn-out, emotive ones—a measure that distinguishes comic scenes from those steeped in gravitas (☞ chap. 7)—Li Yu allowed comedy to seep into scenes and roles from which it would normally be barred. In a particularly audacious affront to the standards of the *chuanqi* genre, Li Yu even wrote a clown role-type as the male lead (that character is eventually transformed onstage into a *sheng*-type character when his face paint is washed off). Such humor in his plays is often visible: actors in comic roles (*huamian*) wear makeup or clothing to accentuate their incongruities, such as ugliness marked by an exaggerated birthmark painted on an actor's face. Li Yu fully embraced physical comedy as well: in his plays, misunderstandings frequently come to blows.

The novel subject material of Li Yu's plays meant that he had to ensure that crucial elements of the plot were clearly conveyed to the audience. As a consequence, he promoted shorter plays and discouraged traditional practices like performing individual excerpted scenes from new plays, emphasizing that the full arc of a play be performed instead. The performance of a full play would also showcase his skill in structuring plays, an element that was lost when individual scenes were performed. All *chuanqi* plays are significantly longer than four-act *zaju* plays, with most extant *chuanqi* plays comprising between thirty and fifty scenes (☞ Introduction). Li Yu's longest plays have only thirty-six scenes, and six of them have exactly thirty. Despite this relative brevity, he recognized that the performance of a complete play was often not feasible because few people are dedicated enough to stay awake appreciating plays until dawn. Consequently, in addition to limiting the number of scenes, Li Yu designed a method for adapting the length of his plays to suit a single evening's performance: he instructed actors to replace cut scenes with summaries, thereby shortening the play without obscuring the plot.

Another strategy that Li Yu used to ensure that audiences understood the plot was to insist on the centrality of spoken parts (*binbai*) to the art of *chuanqi*. Whereas sung arias involved dense language, frequent poetic allusions, and drawn-out syllables, spoken parts, including recitative verse and especially dialogue, could convey details in a way that could be comprehensible even to illiterate members of the audience. Most drama criticism before Li Yu had little to say on dialogue, and the earliest printed plays often went so far as to omit it entirely (☞ chaps. 2 and 5). Li Yu's plays are full of speech, and the theory he develops in *Leisure Notes* attempts to raise its status from mere "talk" to that of "literary composition" (*wenzhang*). He saw dialogue as a way to translate difficult arias, a step that was necessary because "arias can only transmit sound, they cannot convey the story" [*XQOJ* 49, "In Writing, Distinguish between the Verbose and the Laconic"]. Li Yu's theorization of speech in plays was a significant development of the notion of "naturalness" (*bense*, literally "original color") valorized in previous drama criticism and practice (☞ Introduction, chap. 7). With a broad focus that encompassed composition on the page and a newly articulated training process for actors, Li Yu made plays more accessible for the uninitiated and illiterate.

So far, the discussion of Li Yu's theorization of theater has focused on three major aspects of playwriting: structure, novelty, and accessibility. The next section examines an excerpt from Li Yu's essay on prologue scenes alongside the opening scene of his play *A Much-Desired Match*. The prologue scene and related essay provide a concrete example of one of the core structural features of the *chuanqi* genre. They also showcase Li Yu's distinctive voice, which oscillates between bombastic claims and droll self-effacement. Li's discussion of the function of an opening scene will also underscore the seriousness of purpose behind his discussion of the mechanics of plays: his literary creations appear flippant only because they are meticulously crafted to appear this way.

11.3 *A MUCH-DESIRED MATCH*: HOW TO READ AN OPENING SCENE

The first scene of a *chuanqi* play is particularly difficult to understand for two reasons (☛ chap. 7). First, it offers a synopsis of the entire plot, describing, often obliquely, the characters who will star in it and the challenges they will face. Second, it is written entirely in verse, which readers and audiences must decipher without the aid of spoken dialogue or "extrametrical syllables" (*chenzi*). Let us first examine what Li Yu proposes opening scenes should accomplish in his essay "Prologues" (*jiamen*, literally "house door") in *Leisure Notes*:

> Even before the prologue (*jiamen*), there is a brief opening song (*qu*), such as "West River Moon" ("Xijiang yue") or "Butterflies Enamored of Blossoms" ("Die lian hua"). This has never had a fixed standard, and people have used it however they like. The song has never had anything to do with the topic at hand; it's been nothing other than conventional lines encouraging people to have a drink, forget their cares, and join in the festivities. In my opinion, the opening scene (*kaichang*) of a play (*ciqu*), just like the introductory remarks (*maotou*) in an ancient-style essay or the broaching of a topic (*poti*) in an examination essay, should attempt to "reveal the mountain upon opening the door"; it should not "borrow a hat to cover its head." That is, it should sum up the general meaning and significance of the whole work and integrate it with the prologue lyric that follows. First, it should merely hint at what is to come, then it should state it clearly: the hinting is like the "broaching of a topic" [in an examination essay], while the clear statement is like the "carrying forward of the topic." Only if this standard is established will *chuanqi* be a literary form with a foundation. When examination essays are read in the examination halls, examiners can take or leave those essays that do not seem striking until the second or third line. However, if, from the moment the essay is opened, it can capture examiners' eyes and keep them from wandering in the slightest: that is the sort of skill that indicates a sure pass. I hope that whenever talented people pick up the brush to write, they will always think of it this way, and not just when they're writing plays.
>
> [*XQOJ* 60–61, "Prologues"]

The first scene of a play, then, typically consists of three parts: declaimed lyrics, the plot summary set to another tune title, and the closing poem (not mentioned in this excerpt). Li Yu elaborates on its purpose with a multilayered analogy to the civil service examination essays, the successful passing of which was the goal of most educated men in late imperial China. As such, preparation for crafting examination essays—referred to as "contemporary essays" (*shiwen*), or "eight-legged essays" (*bagu wen*) (☞ *HTRCProse*, 14.1) for their highly regulated eight-part structure—occupied much of students' time and energy. Prior to Li Yu, playwriting was often considered an escape from the grueling process and stilted form of the examination essays: he is among the first to suggest that thinking of dramatic composition in terms of the eight-legged essay would allow writers to apply compositional skills from other contexts. Examination success is also a crucial part of *chuanqi* narratives, as most of the talented male protagonists pass with distinction before they are reunited with their paramour. The comment that accompanies this passage praises Li Yu's own writing for always adhering to this advice:

(末上)	ADDITIONAL MALE *as* TROUPE LEADER *enters [and declaims]*:
【西江月】	*To the tune "Xijiang yue"*
才子緣慳夙世，	Talented men, destiny unfulfilled in a former existence,
佳人飲恨重泉。	Beautiful ladies swallowing resentment in the Shades below.
黃衫豪客代稱冤，	A bold fellow decked out in yellow will air grievances on your behalf,
筆俠吟髭奮撚。	A brush-wielding gallant fiddles vigorously with his poet's beard.
追取月中簿改，	He implores the Old Man in the Moon to alter the marriage register,
重將足上絲牽。	And hitch once again these lovers' ankles with red thread.
戲場配合不由天，	Here on the stage, love-matches depend not on Heaven;
別有風流掌院。	Quite a different romantic is in charge.
【前詞】	*Reprise*
試考會真本記，	If you examine the original "Tale of Oriole,"
崔、張未偶當年。	You will find that Cui [Yingying] and [Scholar] Zhang did not end up married at that time.
西廂也屬意中緣，	*The Story of the Western Wing*, then, is also a "much-desired match,"
死後別開生面。	As it gave Cui and Zhang new life after their deaths.
作者明言虛幻，	The author has clearly stated that this staged tale is an imaginary one,
看官可免拘牽。	In hopes that the audience will not be misled.
從來無謊不瞞天，	There has never been a lie that does not hide the truth from Heaven,
只要古人情願。	So long as the ancients wish it so.
【慶清朝慢】	*To the tune "Qing qing zhao man"*

董子、陳生，	Master Dong and Scholar Chen
齊名當世，	Enjoyed equal fame in their time,
文詞翰墨兼長。	Excelling at literary composition and painting alike.
有女雙耽畫癖，	There were two girls who devoted themselves to painting,
各倣才郎。	Each imitating a talented man.
瞥見情留尺幅，	A glimpse of affection left on a small painting,
分頭擬效鴛鴦。	And each followed the example of mandarin ducks in love.
風波起，	A storm brewed:
一投陷穽，	One was caught in a snare,
一遇強梁。	The other encountered a lout.
從奸黨，	Meeting a gang of brigands,
隨豪客，	Following a charlatan,
周旋處，	Round and round they went,
大節保無傷。	Chastity preserved unscathed.
賴有江生仗義，	Thanks to Scholar Jiang's loyalty and righteousness,
徹底劻勷。	They had someone looking out for them.
救出男粧女士，	He rescued the woman dressed as a man,
便充佳壻代求凰。	And then passed her off as a good son-in-law, standing in to seek a wife.
逢良友，	A meeting of friends,
齊歸趙璧，	Both delivered intact to their rightful mates,
各自成雙。	Each turned into a happy pair.
名士逃名，偶拉同心友。	Famous gentlemen flee their fame, and by chance meet like-minded friends.
才女憐才，誤落奸人手。	Talented women fall for talent, and mistakenly end up in villains' hands.
兩番嫁壻，都是假姻緣。	On two occasions married off, both false "marriage destinies."
一旦逢親，纔完眞配偶。	Only when he meets his bride is our true love-match complete.

[YZY 8.3235–3236, scene 1, "The General Idea" ("Dayi")]

Before we return to Li Yu's essay "Prologues" to evaluate whether he follows his own advice in this first scene of *A Much-Desired Match*, let us examine how the scene works. It opens with a parallel reference to an unidentified romantic pair (the scholar and beauty that typify the *chuanqi* genre), inviting readers and listeners to wonder who they are and what destinies had been left unfulfilled in their previous lives. At this point, the fact that these are plural is detectable only in translation: the idea that this play features not one but two sets of lovers will be revealed later. It may also refer to the universal types (that is, to all would-be scholars and beauties in the world). The "bold fellow decked out in yellow" (*huangshan haoke*) was originally a character from the Tang dynasty *chuanqi* tale "The Tale of Huo Xiaoyu" ("Huo Xiaoyu zhuan"), who compelled the fickle scholar Li Yi to return to face Huo, the lover he had abandoned.

Here, Li Yu has taken on this role, promising to bring a pair of departed lovers back from the grave and change their fate, revising Heaven's judgments. In *Leisure Notes*, Li Yu calls playwriting the "boldest (*zui haodang*) of all literary forms" [*XQOJ* 48, "Aim for Likeness in Language" ("Yu qiu xiao si")], praising its unique ability to allow him to transform himself instantly into a high official, a rustic recluse, a gifted poet, or even an immortal. Paired with the more obvious self-reference of the "brush-wielding gallant" in the following line, as well as the statement in the final couplet that the "romantic" (*fengliu*) Li Yu has coopted control over assigning fates from Heaven, this opening verse uses the *mo* role-type in his capacity as troupe leader-cum-announcer to explain the playwright's accomplishments and goals to the audience.

The second stanza engages much more explicitly with the concept of revision and the power of plays to change fate. Whereas in *The Peony Pavilion* (*Mudan ting*), it is "love" (*qing*) that conquers death (☛ chap. 9), here, it is the writing and revision process. Similarly, Yuan playwright Wang Shifu had engineered a happy ending for the ill-fated couple of the Tang tale "The Tale of Oriole" ("Yingying zhuan") in his *The Story of the Western Wing* (*Xixiang ji*) (☛ chap. 1). In a highly self-reflexive vein, Li Yu alerted readers to take his works for the fictional accounts that they were, as is evident from this first stanza; but it is worth noting that these warnings did not stop later readers from assuming that the marriages that Li Yu describes in the play actually took place (☛ chap. 10).[10]

Does Li Yu's prologue scene succeed, given the standards he outlines in *Leisure Notes*, as introduced at the beginning of this section? In his essay, he criticizes the opening lines of most plays for being overly general: "Conventional lines encouraging people to have a drink, forget their cares, and join in the festivities." He uses the phrase "borrowing a hat to cover its head (*jiemao fuding*)" to suggest that the same clichéd lines are expected to serve this purpose for any play. Li Yu proposes that the verses should rather "reveal the mountain upon opening the door;" that is, they should display the full significance of the play right from the start, in a single panoramic view.

The opening song of the first scene of *A Much-Desired Match* first refers to Li Yu's ability as the author to offer an alternative version of events from those that transpired in the real world, and it also recounts the play's major themes. The reprise offers a specific example of such a revision of fates from *The Story of the Western Wing*. Rather than explicitly describing the contents of the play to come, these verses refer to it obliquely from several different angles that nevertheless relate specifically to this play.

According to Li Yu's essay, a prologue should provide a succinct plot summary. In the passage cited previously, under the tune title "Qing qing zhao man," we learn the names of the three friends, as well as all the main events of the play: Two girls imitate the style of two famous painters, Dong and Chen. The latter see the paintings and seek to "imitate mandarin ducks" (*nixiao yuanyang*) (a common metaphor for romantic love). The first stanza ends with the double separation that comprises the bulk of the action of the play: Lin Tiansu, disguised as a man, is captured by a band of brigands and made to work as their secretary, while Yang Yunyou is abducted by a lecherous monk and taken by boat to Beijing. The second stanza credits a third man, Jiang Huaiyi, with bringing both matches to completion against these considerable odds: first rescuing Lin, and then deceiving Yang one more time to get her married to Dong. This prologue thus does offer a succinct summary of the plot.

The closing poem condenses the plot even further: the first two lines are roughly parallel, the first told from the men's perspective, contrasting what they seek (to escape fame) with what they get (like-minded friends). The second is told from the women's perspective: they seek talent, only to end up in separate, seemingly hopeless situations. Although this opening scene places approximately equal emphasis on each couple, the play itself focuses primarily on the relationship between Dong Qichang and Yang Yunyou, played by the *sheng* and *dan*, respectively. Accordingly, the last two couplets focus solely on the story of Yang and Dong: It is Yang who undergoes two false marriages, first to "Natural Eunuch" Huang (Huang Tianjian), who has lost his penis to syphilis, and then to Lin Tiansu—both of whom are disguised as Dong Qichang—before finally meeting Dong for the first time, and marrying him, in the final scene of the play. It is this series of Yang's comic mismatched marriages for which the play is best remembered. As for Li Yu's ambitious proposal for prologues, it is for readers to judge whether this opening scene—across centuries and languages—is able to "capture [your] eyes and keep them from wandering in the slightest," as he said it should.

11.4 LOVE, ART, AND THEATER IN A WORLD FULL OF FRAUDS

The remainder of this chapter examines how *A Much-Desired Match* dramatizes the comic side of an exuberant art market as characters work to deceive others and discern the truth for themselves. One of the innovations of *A Much-Desired Match* is its challenge to audience assumptions about the role of paintings in theater. It was common for *chuanqi* plays to feature a central object that would journey throughout the duration of the play, connecting characters in distant places and moving the plot forward. Whereas portraits had long been important as tropes in drama texts and as props in performances, they were usually treated as a singular object within the world of the play. *The Peony Pavilion*, for example, expends a significant amount of dramatic energy on the single self-portrait at the heart of its plot: the female heroine Du Liniang's singular self-portrait plays a crucial role in depicting her authentic self—one that is truer than the emaciated physical form that is reflected in the mirror—and it is the first version of her with which the scholar Liu Mengmei falls in love (☞ chap. 9).

By contrast, in *A Much-Desired Match*, paintings proliferate on the stage, robbed of the potential for significance as authentic vehicles of the emotions of those who produced them. Instead, as men fall in love with women by seeing their imitation paintings that are almost indistinguishable from their own works, they epitomize the commodification of art and love alike. It is only Yang's inscription on her "Dong Qichang" painting that suggests its questionable provenance, and this, as described in scene 3, results from a momentary lapse in concentration. Paintings in *A Much-Desired Match* are not a means to find true love, instead serving the pragmatic function of an artist finding someone who can help him double his output. By depicting a large number of paintings, and by choosing to feature recently deceased, famous, and prolific painters, Li Yu's play asks readers and viewers to think about what love looks like in an increasingly market-driven culture.

Scene 5 dramatizes the moment when Dong and Chen encounter the masterful forgeries of their styles that inspire them to locate the women who painted them. At this point, the audience has watched each female lead sign Dong's and Chen's names to their own paintings and send them to be sold at the shop of Monk Vacuity (Shikong heshang) on the shore of West Lake. As Dong Qichang, Chen Jiru, and Jiang Huaiyi arrive at the shop, Lin Tiansu's maid has just left, after delivering Lin's "Chen Jiru" fan painting:

（生、衆行上）YOUNG MALE *as* DONG QICHANG *together with* COMPANIONS *enter, walking, [and sing]:*

【太平歌】*To the tune of* "Taiping ge"

依湖岸，Here along the lake's shore,

訪古問招提，To find relics of the past, just ask at a local temple.

蚤早不覺行來蕭寺裏。Before we know it, we've arrived at a Buddhist temple.

（作進店介）老上人請了。DONG QICHANG *acts out entering the shop [and speaks]:* Venerable One, greetings.

（淨）請了。阿彌陀佛，要買甚麼骨董？你看玉器、窰器、銅器、犀角杯、珊瑚枕、伽楠香的扇墜，蜜蠟金的念珠，樣樣都有，隨你要那一件，取出來看就是。COMIC *as* MONK VACUITY [*speaks*]: Greetings. Amitabha Buddha—may Buddha preserve us! What sort of antiques would you like to buy? Let's see: I have jade pieces, earthenware pieces, bronze pieces, rhinoceros horn cups, coral pillows, agarwood fan pendants, amber rosaries, all sorts of things. I'll take out anything you'd like to have a closer look at.

（生、衆）DONG QICHANG, *together with* COMPANIONS, [*sing*]:

貧兒不識金和貝，Poor scholars like us cannot appreciate such costly wares,

只恐怕值多還少同猜謎，I'm afraid it's a guessing game to us whether they're worth a little or a lot,

空勞你慧口辨高低，In vain would we trouble you, Wise One, to further assess their value,

做彌勒笑人癡。For a Maitreya you'd be, laughing at having made fools of us.

（外）有名人書畫，借幾幅看看。EXTRA MALE *as* JIANG HUAIYI [*speaks*]: If you have calligraphies or paintings by famous people, we'd like to see a few.

（淨）這等，還是要古人的今人的？若要古
　人的，有羊眞孔艸、蕭行范篆；宋徽宗的
　鷹，蘇東坡的竹，馬麟、黃筌的花卉，米元
　章、倪雲林、王叔明、黃大痴的山水。若要
　論今人，一發說不得許多。如今極貴重的莫
　過于董思白、陳眉公這兩個大名公的字畫
　了。貧僧這邊要大幅就大幅，要單條就單
　條，要扇面就扇面，任憑取看就是。

（生、小生微笑介）

（外）這等，就是陳、董二公的畫，借來看
　　　　看罷了。
（淨取畫，付介）這是董思白的。（衆展看
　　　　介）
（小生、外）果然畫得好！無筆墨之痕，有
　　　生動之趣，眞是化工手筆。

（淨取扇付介）這是陳眉公的。（衆展看
　　　　介）
（生、外）好！結構不凡，點染自異，不枉
　　　名手。

（淨）何如？小店的物事再沒有不好的。列
　　位請坐了細看，貧僧去泡茶來。（下）

（外）可是二位的眞筆？

（生）畫倒像是眞的，只是落款的字太作意
　　了些，覺得有幾分可疑。

（小生）小弟這柄扇子也是這等，還要細
　　　看。
【賞宮花】
（生）
難評是與非，教人信又疑！

MONK VACUITY [*speaks*]: In that case, do you want [something] ancient or modern? If you want [something by] the ancients, I have Yang's regular script and Kong's grass script, Xiao's running script and Fan's seal script.[7] I have eagle paintings by Song Emperor Huizong, bamboo by Su Dongpo, plants and flowers by Ma Lin and Huang Quan, landscapes by Mi Yuanzhang, Ni Yunlin, Wang Shuming, and Huang Dachi.[8] If you want something contemporary, there are more than I can mention. At the moment, none are more highly valued than the calligraphy and paintings of the two famed masters Dong Sibai and Chen Meigong. Here at this poor monk's, if it's a large painting that you want, you'll get a large painting; if it's a hanging scroll, you'll get a hanging scroll; if it's a fan painting, you'll get a fan painting, I'll take out whatever you'd like to see.

DONG QICHANG *and* SECONDARY YOUNG MALE *as* CHEN JIRU *smile*.

JIANG HUAIYI [*speaks*]: All right then, why don't we take a look at the Chen and Dong paintings?

MONK *gets a painting, hands it over,* [*and speaks*]: This is Dong Sibai's. *They spread it out and look at it.*

CHEN JIRU *and* JIANG HUAIYI [*speak*]: It's painted well after all! There are no brush traces, and it has a lively gusto to it: truly the work of a naturally marvelous talent.

MONK *gets the fan, hands it over* [*and speaks*]: This is Chen Meigong's. *They open it and look at it.*

DONG QICHANG *and* JIANG HUAIYI [*speak*]: Bravo! The composition is extraordinary, and the details are unique. It doesn't do wrong by the famous masters.

MONK [*speaks*]: What do you think? There's nothing in this shop that's not first rate. Please, gentlemen, have a seat and examine them carefully while I go brew some tea. *Exits.*

JIANG HUAIYI [*speaks*]: Could they be authentic works of yours?

DONG QICHANG [*speaks*]: The painting does seem authentic enough, but the characters of the inscription look somewhat contrived. I think it's a little suspicious.

CHEN JIRU [*speaks*]: Likewise for this fan of mine. It requires a more thorough examination.

To the tune of "Shang gonghua"

DONG QICHANG [*sings*]:

It's hard to judge the true and the false, they make one believe—and also doubt!

且喜得有一首詩在上面，待我看，是幾時做的？（念前詩介）呀！這一首詩並不是我做的！（沉吟，大笑介）是了！是了！不消說得，這畫是婦人的畫，詩也是婦人的詩，假冒賤名的，被小弟看出來了。

（外、小生）怎見得？

（生）這詩上的話，明明說出來了。這一幅畫與這一首詩，分明是個貧士之女，家無四壁，被淒風苦雨吹逼不過，寫來寄感慨的。若不看詩，那裏辨得出？

（外、小生細看介）
是不差。難道世上有這等聰明女子？

（生）
假筆眞情現，
難道我男子效蛾眉？

（嘆介）同是一般的技藝，我享這樣的榮華，他受那般的貧困，豈不可憐！

（生）
爲甚的世上侏儒同怨飽，
閨中曼倩獨啼饑？

（小生）你的单條還有詩可辨，我這一幅便面，竟無隙可尋。

【降黃龍】
（小生）
假筆眞情現，
心迷，
若說是眞的呵，
我禿筆枯毫，
醉後狂時，
怎寫得恁般嬌媚？

DONG QICHANG [speaks]: Fortunately, there's a poem inscribed on it. Let me look and see when it was written. *Recites the poem from earlier.* Aha! This poem was most certainly not written by me. *Recites in a low voice, laughs heartily.* I've got it! I've got it! It hardly needs to be said that this painting was painted by a woman, and the poem is a woman's poem. She tried to pass it off as mine by using my name, but I have seen right through it.

JIANG HUAIYI and CHEN JIRU [speak]: How can you tell?

DONG QICHANG [speaks]: The words of this poem say so very clearly. The painting and the poem were obviously done by the daughter of some destitute scholar. With nothing but four bare walls to call home, overcome by the bleak winds and dismal rains pressing in on all sides, she wrote this to express her indignation. If I hadn't seen the poem, how would I have been able to tell the difference?

JIANG HUAIYI and CHEN JIRU *inspect it carefully.*

DONG QICHANG [speaks]: Not bad, indeed. Do you really think there's a woman of such keen talent in this world?

DONG QICHANG [sings]:
This borrowed brush reveals genuine feelings,
Could it be that I, a man, have been imitating a painted brow [a woman] all along?

DONG QICHANG sighs [and speaks]: The artistry is exactly the same: what a shame that I enjoy glory while she suffers in poverty.

DONG QICHANG [sings]:
Why is that the dwarfs of this world all resent being kept overstuffed,
While the Manqians of the inner chambers alone cry out with hunger?[9]

CHEN JIRU [speaks]: Still, your hanging scroll has a poem that allows you to identify it. On this fan painting of mine, there's not a telltale seam to be found.

To the tune of "Xiang huanglong"

CHEN JIRU [sings]:
This borrowed brush reveals genuine feelings.
My mind is bewildered:
If it's authentic,
How did I, with my dried-up, bald brush,
While tipsy or mad,
Paint in so delicate and enchanting a way?

若說是假的呵，	And if it's fake,
又與我的懶雲怪石，	Why are the idle clouds and strange rocks,
偃竹欹松，	The bent bamboo and leaning pine,
又纖毫無異。	So absolutely indistinguishable from mine?
好教我狐疑，	It really gives me pause,
難道是自避嫌名，	Could it be that someone was avoiding their own name,
却倩他人書諱？	And so put down mine instead?
終不然又有個貧家女士，	After all, it's not as if there could be *another* woman scholar from a poor family,
盜把名題。	Who surreptitiously inscribed *my* name.

[YZY 8.3262–3265, scene 5, "Encounter with the Paintings" ("Huayu")]

Monk Vacuity runs a successful business based entirely on lies—we know from a previous scene that he is no monk at all, but a wanted criminal in disguise. He begins by reciting some of the valuable items for sale in his shop, a list that includes some of the most sought-after commodities of the day, including imported rhinoceros horn, which would be carved into exquisite vessels; and agarwood, a rare fragrant resin typically imported from Southeast Asia. When the gentlemen protest that they do not have the means to purchase such pricey things, they affect superior taste by preferring the loftier realms of painting and calligraphy, distinguishing themselves from the crass merchant who would be eager to ostentatiously purchase expensive things. The monk is quick to respond: he claims to possess paintings by all the most famous painters, past and present. We are not supposed to take the monk at his word, however. The way he describes the paintings suggests that he does not perceive any significant differences among them: any painting is as good as the next.

After listing the names of famous painters, he discusses their sale in terms of medium alone: "If it's a fan painting that you want, you'll get a fan painting [. . .]." This mode of marketing shifts the focus from the paintings themselves to the objects that they constitute, equating all paintings of similar size and shape. That Dong and Chen themselves cannot even tell whether a painting is their own suggests that they too have come to think of paintings as commodities. This conception of painting also resonates with the requests for paintings in other scenes, where the point is to own a "Dong Qichang" painting rather than to actually appreciate art. In scene 2, a series of runners arrive at Dong Qichang's residence, carrying various media that their masters have requested be embellished with his painting or calligraphy, and in scene 21, infatuated idlers in the capital carry similar objects to Yang requesting inscriptions. The lack of understanding of the paintings themselves is made explicit in the latter scene: Yang mocks one of the onlookers by painting him as a monkey, but he misinterprets this as a demonstration of her favor, noting that she completed his painting first.

The fact that "Dong" and "Chen" paintings are in such high demand is the initial reason for these painters' incognito excursion to West Lake. Given the contrast in characterization between the monk and the two male leads, it is difficult to notice at first the striking parallels among them: when we meet them in scene 5, all three have sloughed off their names to "hide their tracks" (*biji*). Near the end of Jiang Huaiyi's monologue at the beginning of this scene, he mentions that Chen and Dong are visiting the lake to "flee fame" (*taoming*), using a word that literally means to "flee from one's name." That same expression—"Fleeing Fame"—is the title of scene 2 of the play, where Dong and Chen first discuss their plan to tour West Lake incognito. To do so, they change their clothes and remove the banner emblazoned with Dong's surname on their boat.

If Dong Qichang is running from his name, many others prove happy to take it on—first when Yang borrows his name to sign her painting, and later as she marries two fake "Dong Qichangs." In the excerpt given previously, Dong encounters one of these paintings in the very first shop he enters. His friends praise "his" painting ("There are no brush traces, and it has a lively gusto to it: truly the work of a naturally marvelous talent"), and he is initially unsure whether he painted it or not, noting vaguely that it "seems authentic." But after careful scrutiny of the poem inscribed on the painting, Dong deduces that it must have been painted by an impoverished woman. Yang's inability to complete the painting without revealing something of her true self speaks to her depth of feeling: the sincerity of her misery breaks through her disguise. Although Dong resolves to find and marry the artist, this proves difficult given the sheer number of false "Dong Qichangs" that populate the play. By the play's end, there have been, quite uproariously, "Dongs" everywhere—in addition to Yang Yunyou, "Natural Eunuch" Huang, Monk Vacuity, and Lin Tiansu all "play" Dong. After marrying a fake Dong Qichang for the second time, Yang exclaims:

（旦）如今董來董去，只是董個不了。 YOUNG FEMALE as YANG YUNYOU [*speaks*]: Lately, there are Dongs coming and Dongs going. It's just been endless Dongs!

[*YZY* 8.3431, scene 28, "The Fake Marriage"]

Playing with the homophones of "movement" (*dong2*) and "understanding" (*dong3*) relative to Dong's last name (*dong1*), this proliferation of "Dong Qichangs" underscores the breakdown of the idealized relationship between artist and discerning connoisseur (the *zhiyin*), and points to the increasingly commercialized nature of this relationship: true connoisseurs are hard to come by, but so are true artists.

In contrast to the revelation of her own internal state on the surface of Yang Yunyou's "Dong Qichang" painting, Lin Tiansu's painting does not reveal even a hint of its provenance ("there's not a telltale seam (*xi*) to be found"). The word *xi*, meaning "seam" or "gap," here refers to a clue that would lead to the actual artist responsible for the painting. It is a testament not only to her skill, but also to her deep involvement in the world of commerce that Lin Tiansu (who, as we learn in scene 3, sells her body as well as her paintings) is able to paint *exactly* as Chen Meigong does—so much so that he believes that he painted it himself. Nevertheless, unlike with Dong and Yang, Lin and Chen's romance proceeds quickly and seamlessly—she is easy to find, on the one hand because of her status as a courtesan, but on the other because her maid, dressed in the secondary comic role (*fujing*), comes right out and says, "That is a 'Chen Meigong' landscape painted by the young lady of my household with her very own brush, how could it not be authentic" [*YZY* 8.3261, scene 5]?

Lin Tiansu is fully embroiled in the marketplace of forged paintings and disguised people: for her, if a painting passes as a "Chen Meigong" landscape, then that is precisely what it is. And what better proof could one have than for Chen Meigong himself to try to remember exactly when he painted it? Lin's skill at seamless transformation is showcased elsewhere in the play in the context of cross-dressing. In scene 13, when she dresses in male attire to return home to bury her parents, Chen is worried that it will be obvious that she is a woman. After she has fooled Jiang into believing that she was her brother paying a visit, she explains how she accomplishes such a seamless physical transformation:

（小旦）須要自家認定，我是個鬚眉如戟的丈夫，把那些男子反當做婦人看待，自然氣雄胆壯，不露纖弱之容。

SECONDARY YOUNG FEMALE as LIN TIANSU [*speaks*]: I need only firmly believe myself a valiant man with halberd-like beard and brow, regarding myself as one of those men who plays a woman, and as a matter of course my spirit grows mighty and my courage magnificent, revealing nothing of my slender fragility.

[*YZY* 8.3316, scene 13, "The Send-off" ("Songxing")]

Here again, we see that Lin is able to fully transform herself into another role: into Chen through her painting, and into a young male scholar through her costuming. In *Leisure Notes*, Li Yu identifies the art of presenting a seamless story as a key element of good playwriting, and, as noted previously, he envisions himself as fully embodying all the perspectives of the theater within himself as he works out a play. In this light, Lin's seamless presentations of artifice are not dismissed as forgery or deception. Rather, they celebrate play-acting and valorize the role-play that is central to Li Yu's conception of playwriting.

Whereas Lin revels in the possibilities of role-playing and forgery, Yang Yunyou spends the play desperately trying to figure out how to see through such disguise and dissimulation in order to locate the real Dong Qichang. Yang's father, a poor scholar named Yang Xiangxia, is a cranky, lazy, and unlikeable man who lives off his daughter's forged paintings. He readily entrusts Monk Vacuity with the task of marrying off his daughter, and Monk Vacuity dupes him with a "fake within the fake" (*jiazhong zhi jia*) scheme, which combines a "fake body"—that of the impotent and thus ostensibly harmless "Natural Eunuch" Huang—with a fake name—that of Dong Qichang. Once his hair has grown out, Monk Vacuity plans to marry Yang himself in a double windfall: attaining at once a beautiful woman and the income from her paintings.

Yang Yunyou responds to the monk's proposal on behalf of Dong Qichang with trepidation and suspicion. Her father, by contrast, having already received a deposit in silver from the monk, is quick to accept the proposal, and makes every sort of excuse for him: "And besides, what can you tell about people based on their external appearance? You must ascertain what is in their hearts" [YZY 8.3279, scene 7]. Yang Xiangxia's appeal to matters of the heart is clearly self-interested, suggesting that the language of authenticity has been coopted by the selfish schemers.

Once Yang Yunyou has been carried off on the boat with "Natural Eunuch" Huang posing as Dong Qichang, she decides to test whether he is truly "Dong" by requesting his advice on her painting. Huang wonders aloud at length how he might avoid exposing his ignorance, deciding first to offer a critique. He says that the plum blossoms she painted look rather "stark" (lengjing) without leaves. She counters that plum blossoms are unique in that their flowers and leaves never appear simultaneously, gesturing to those blooming along the shore as evidence. Disconcerted by his error, Huang offers the excuse that he was dazzled by her beauty and decides to try praising her instead in another attempt to conceal his ignorance:

（丑轉介）夫人的畫，筆筆都是古人，如今的作者那裡畫得出？便是古人復生，遇此丹青也應嘆賞！

CLOWN as "NATURAL EUNUCH" HUANG turns [and speaks]: Every brushstroke of your painting resembles the ancients, what painter of our day could accomplish this? If the ancients were reborn today, even they would express their admiration upon encountering this painting!

（旦）既然如此，請問一問，不知奴家的筆意，像那一位古人？

YOUNG FEMALE as YANG YUNYOU [speaks]: If that is the case, might I ask which of the ancients my humble style resembles?

（丑）待待待我想來。（背介）這樁苦事是我自家惹出來的了，沒原沒故說甚麼古人，就貼張招子到肚裡去，也尋不出這個人來。（悶想，忽笑介）妙妙妙！有一個古人就在口頭，為甚麼不講？（轉介）夫人，我肚裡的古人極多，想來都不相合。只有一代名公的畫，極像你的筆仗。

"NATURAL EUNUCH" HUANG [speaks]: Let—let—let me think a moment. In an aside: I brought this unpleasant assignment upon myself, for no good reason mentioning these "ancients." Even if I were to put a sign up in my belly, I would still not be able to find a single "ancient." "NATURAL EUNUCH" HUANG acts out thinking in a dejected fashion, and then suddenly laughs: Yes, yes, yes—I've got it! One of the ancients is on the tip of my tongue, why not tell her? Turns: Lady, there are so many ancients in my belly that I can't keep them straight when I try to think of them. However, there is a famous gentleman from one dynasty whose paintings very much resemble your own.

（旦）是那一個？

YANG YUNYOU [speaks]: Which one might that be?

（丑）叫做張敞。

"NATURAL EUNUCH" HUANG [*speaks*]: His name is Zhang Chang.

（旦驚介）張敞雖是個古人，不曾聞得他會畫。請問相公，出在那一本書上？

YANG YUNYOU *starts* [*and speaks*]: Although Zhang Chang is an ancient figure, I have not heard that he could paint. May I ask you in what book this is recorded?

（丑）這是眼面前的故事，要查甚麼書本，那一個不說張敞畫梅，張敞畫梅？

"NATURAL EUNUCH" HUANG [*speaks*]: It's from a story that's right in front of our eyes, what need would there be to look it up in a book? Who doesn't say "Zhang Chang paints temples," "Zhang Chang paints temples"?

（旦大笑介）張敞所畫的是眉眼之眉，不是梅花的梅。你認錯了。

YANG YUNYOU *laughs heartily* [*and speaks*]: What Zhang Chang painted are the eyebrows of his wife, not an actual painting. You've got it wrong.

（丑）他是個聰明的人，或者兩樣都會畫也不可知？

"NATURAL EUNUCH" HUANG [*speaks*]: He was a clever man; how do you know he couldn't have painted both?

（旦背介）這等看起來，畫畫的事是一竅不通的了。但不知寫作何如？待我把兩樁技藝都考他一考。

YANG YUNYOU, *in an aside*, [*speaks*]: It seems that he is completely ignorant of painting, but I'm not sure how his writing is. Let me test him in both of these arts at once.

[*YZY* 8.3326–3327, scene 14, "The Fool Revealed" ("Luchou")]

With humor that would be comprehensible to audiences of varying levels of education (Li Yu claims that the target audiences for his plays always include illiterate women and children), this encounter showcases Yang's ability to slowly expose the ignorance of "Natural Eunuch" Huang, who knows nothing of art or books. The only historical name Huang can think of is that of Zhang Chang, an official during the Western Han (206 BCE–9 CE) who was supposed to have lovingly drawn his wife's eyebrows for her. Later, the four-character expression, "Zhang Chang paints eyebrows" (*Zhang Chang hua mei*) came to indicate devotion between spouses. "Eyebrows" and "plum blossoms" have the same pronunciation (*méi*), but are written with different characters, so the misunderstanding assumes both illiteracy and a basic misunderstanding of a well-known expression (I have translated the first *méi* as "temples" here to allow a similar misunderstanding between the words "temples" and "eyebrows" in English). It is Li Yu's initial description of Huang that causes the commentator, Huang Yuanjie, to remark that of all playwrights, Li Yu alone excels at writing the comic roles as well as the more serious leads [*YZY* 8.3273, scene 6]. This comment would have been inspired by lines like this one: "He was a clever man; how do you know he couldn't have painted both?" Li Yu's fool earns his laughs as well: Li shows Huang thinking quickly, drawing on his available skills, and developing his social position. Ultimately, Yang excuses him from writing a poem. The fact that Huang is implicated in the ruse but not its mastermind relieves him of the burden of representing villainy. He will soon cooperate with Yang in a plot to kill the monk.

The second fake "Dong Qichang" that Yang Yunyou encounters is none other than Lin Tiansu. Lin has already passed a test similar to those designed by Yang, but her success ultimately reveals the ignorance of her examiners. In that test, bandits who are looking for a secretary capture Lin, who is traveling in male attire. These bandits have been repeatedly disappointed by the incompetence of the scholars they have captured, so they decide to test their new captive. Once again, the humor hinges on their misunderstanding of a common expression. One of them proposes a test based on his misunderstanding of the expression "A single character is worth a thousand pieces of gold (*yizi zhi qianjin₁*)." Mistaking the final character, "gold (*jīn₁*)," for a homophonous unit of measurement, "catty (*jīn₂*)," he suggests weighing the scholar to see how many characters he knows because "each character weighs a thousand catties (*yizi zhi qianjin₂*)" [*YZY* 8.3338, scene 15]. His fellow bandit explains his mistake by pointing out that even a cursory knowledge of characters would result in an inordinately heavy person. Without mentioning the mistaken character, he explains that this common expression posits the figurative value of education and is not meant to be taken literally.

This quantification of literacy resonates as well with the description of paintings being evaluated without discussion of their artistic quality. Dismissing this initial idea, the bandits are then inspired by the common expression that "scholars have bellies full of ink (*duli you moshui de, jiushi xiucai*)." One of the bandits brings a rope and proposes to hang their captive upside down from a tree to determine what is in his belly. They finally choose a test that also serves as a knowing wink at the readers or audience of this play: because "all the famous scholars can perform plays these days (*wende jinlai de mingshi dou hui chuanxi*)," the new captive is asked to sing some lines from a play. Lin passes the test easily [*YZY* 8.3339, scene 15].

In scene 28, determined not to end up with another fake Dong Qichang, Yang Yunyou subjects a disguised Lin Tiansu to her own sequence of tests in composition, calligraphy, and painting. Lin passes all three of these tests, proving that she is a brilliant and talented individual. Although she remains apprehensive, Yang is convinced that she has finally met a true scholar, and she is eager to consummate the marriage. As she begins undressing Lin, she starts noticing feminine characteristics, and Lin finally reveals her identity and the scheme, explaining to Yang that she must marry Dong because there are only two beauty-scholar pairs in the world. Dong Qichang is finally made whole again: body, mind, and name in one person. With this reconstitution, the grand reunion that concludes every *chuanqi* play is made possible.

However, careful viewers of the play should know that we cannot take Lin Tiansu at her word. Her claim that there are only two ideal pairs of lovers in the world suggests that once Yang Yunyou has found the real Dong Qichang, a happy ending for all will ensue. Yet even during the celebration of the final scene, each person seems to be celebrating not an ideal union of scholar and beauty, but the achievement of something that they themselves have long desired. In fact, at the very moment that all should be in agreement, the new husband and wife cannot agree on who will paint the future "Dong" paintings. For his part, the real Dong Qichang is celebrating that there will never be an "authentic" Dong painting again:

（生）	DONG QICHANG [sings]:
【六么令】	*To the tune of "Liu yao ling"*
有了這床頭捉刀，	Now that I have someone to "hold a sword at the head of the dais,"
再去作眞本蘭亭，也覺徒勞。	It would be a fruitless endeavor to try to produce any more authentic "Orchid Pavilions."
從今玉管不親操，	Beginning today, I will no longer hold my own brush;
都交付女英豪。	I'll hand them all over to this lady champion.
（合）	ALL, *together,* [sing]:
做一對，	A fine pair they'll make:
懶夫勤婦全偕老，	Lazy husband and industrious wife, growing old together.
懶夫勤婦全偕老！	Lazy husband and industrious wife, growing old together!
（旦）	YANG YUNYOU [sings]:
【前腔】	*Reprise*
才疎技少，	My talent is meager, and my skills are few,
只好做針指餘工，	I can only do a little needlework and
箕帚微勞。	Take care of the sweeping.
怎敢把文房杵白也親操？	How could I dare to take up the tools of the study myself?
徒傷手，慮貽嘲。	That would only harm my hand and bring ridicule on you.
（合）	ALL, *together,* [sing]:
做一對，	A fine pair they'll make:
巧夫拙婦全偕老，	Clever husband and doltish wife, growing old together.
巧夫拙婦全偕老！	Clever husband and doltish wife, growing old together!
（末）	ADDITIONAL MALE *as* YANG XIANGXIA [sings]:
【前腔】	*Reprise*
年來攪擾，	This past year, I've caused you such trouble.
未結婚親，	Before you were even married,
雨露先叨。	You granted me favor.
幸將骨肉報瓊瑤，	What good fortune that I can now repay your generosity with my own flesh and blood.
慚翁婿，	Ashamed is your father-in-law,
媿蘭椒。	Undeserving of your kindness.
（合）	ALL, *together,* [sing]:
做一對，	A fine pair they'll make:
寒冰暖玉全偕老，	Cold ice and warm jade, growing old together.
寒冰暖玉全偕老！	Cold ice and warm jade, growing old together!
（老旦）	OLD FEMALE *as* MAID [sings]:
【前腔】	*Reprise*

雖則是危途共保，	Though it's been a perilous path we've shared,
感娘行福分如天，	I feel that my mistress's fortune is like the sky,
携上雲霄。	And she'll carry me along into the clouds.
烏鴉怎入鳳凰巢？	How does a crow end up in a phoenix's nest?
便做個康成婢也福難消！	It's because when a servant girl is blessed with abundance, blessings are hard to disperse!
（合）	ALL, *together*, [*sing*]:
做一對，	A fine pair they'll make:
梅香小姐同偕老，	Plum Fragrance and her mistress, growing old together.
梅香小姐同偕老！	Plum Fragrance and her mistress, growing old together!

[YZY 8.3443–3444, scene 30, "Encountering the Real One" ("Huizhen")]

A "substitute brush" (*daibi*)—that is, a "ghostpainter"—is at the center of this love story, and as it concludes, each character paints a different picture of the happy ending they envision. The expression that Dong uses, "holding a sword at the head of the dais" (*chuangtou zhuodao*), is a reference to an anecdote in *A New Account of Tales of the World* (*Shishuo xinyu*) (☞ HTRCProse, chap. 8), in which Cao Cao had someone stand in his place to receive an envoy from the neighboring Xiongnu out of concern that he did not look imposing enough. The envoy, however, saw through the ploy and reported that the true hero was the man "holding the sword at the head of the dais."[10] This then became a synonym for ghostwriting.

In the midst of this scene, titled "Encounter with the Real One" ("Huizhen"), Dong further declares that there will never be another authentic (*zhenben*) "Dong Qichang" painting produced, borrowing the term "Orchid Pavilion," a frequently copied work attributed to famed calligrapher Wang Xizhi of the Eastern Jin (265–420 CE). The scene title harkens back to the "The Tale of Oriole," referenced in the opening scene: another title for that story is "The Tale of Encountering a Realized One" ("Huizhen ji"); it also resonates with its homonym *huizhen*, or "to paint a portrait." For her part, Yang Yunyou seems thrilled to take refuge in a traditional wifely role, authenticity having been finally secured in the person of Dong Qichang himself. Her father and maid (the former maid of Monk Vacuity) both sing for themselves, pleased with the lifelong security that they will gain as a result of this happy match. A much-desired match, to be sure—but for different reasons.

Returning briefly to the opening scene, we find a foreshadowing of this play's unique take on romance in the bustling art marketplace of the late Ming era. Two terms are used in the opening scene for the activity of imitation. The first instance—in "There were two girls who devoted themselves to painting, seeking to imitate (*fang*) these talented men"—describes the forgery of paintings, and as such carries the potential for judgment, as paintings are judged superior when they are "true traces" (*zhenji*) of a painter's brush. Here, this imitation is attributed to the women's obsession (*pi*), generally a positive trait in the late Ming vocabulary of personality. The second instance—in "A glimpse of affection left on a small painting, and each followed the example (*nixiao*) of mandarin ducks in love"—refers to mandarin ducks, a common image for a loving couple. In this second case, imitation describes that which every pair of lovers does, especially in the context of romantic *chuanqi* plays (namely, to imitate the loving pairs that nature provides as models). The only way to be truly in love is to copy previous examples. When we have finished laughing, this art-market-inspired, brand-new play asks us to reconsider the value of imitation.

With *A Much-Desired Match*, Li Yu mobilizes theater, which foregrounds the art of impersonation and role-play, to comment on authenticity in a world that runs on forgery and deception. Whereas paintings, with their claims to present traces of a particular painter's brush, invite judgments as to whether they are authentic or forged, plays offer even their authors an opportunity to escape themselves. Although Li Yu as a playwright was obsessed with making sure that his performance of each role represented in a play was seamless, he was creating a cultural product that was eminently reproducible: in both the printing and the performance, a Li Yu play—and any play that resembled it—featured his name. *A Much-Desired Match* reveals that compared to this ability of theater, painting was at a marked disadvantage. Painting was unable to duplicate itself and increase its production without fundamentally severing the implied relationship between artist and connoisseur. Theater did not pose such difficulties, so it was the ideal medium for a bold and irreverent cultural entrepreneur like Li Yu. Through his work in the theater, Li Yu expanded the parameters of cultural production to resonate within a rapidly changing world of partial truths and multiple perspectives.

S. E. Kile

NOTES

1. This play (*Bimu yu*) is the first of Li Yu's plays to be translated into English. See *A Couple of Soles: A Comic Play from Seventeenth-Century China*, trans. Jing Shen and Robert E Hegel (New York: Columbia University Press, 2019).

2. For scene summaries of *The Ingenious Finale* (*Qiao tuanyuan*), *The Mistake with a Kite* (*Fengzheng wu*), and *As Heaven Would Have It* (*Naihe tian*), see Eric Henry, *Chinese Amusements: The Lively Plays of Li Yu* (Hamden, CT: Archon, 1980), 177–244.

3. Translations of selections from this work are available in English. See David Pollard, trans. "Li Yu on the Theatre: Excerpts from *Pleasant Diversions*," *Renditions* 72 (2000): 30-70; David Pollard, trans. and ed. *The Chinese Essay*, London: Hurst and Company, 2000, 93–99; and Faye Chunfang Fei, ed. and trans., *Chinese Theories of Theater and Performance from Confucius to the Present* (Ann Arbor: University of Michigan Press, 1999), 77–87.

4. Huang Lizhen, *Li Yu yanjiu* (A Study of Li Yu) (Taipei: Guojia, 1978), 157. For an English translation of the first, see David Hawkes, trans., *Liu Yi and the Dragon Princess: A Thirteenth-Century Zaju Play by Shang Zhongxian* (Hong Kong: Chinese University Press, 2003); for the second, Allen A. Zimmerman, trans., *Scholar Zhang Boils the Sea*, in *The Columbia Anthology of Yuan Drama*, eds. C. T. Hsia, Wai-yee Li, and George Kao (New York: Columbia University Press, 2014), 371–402.

5. The source for the first is "A Hideous Fellow Who Is Timid With Pretty Women Ends Up with Gorgeous Wives" ("Chou langjun pajiao pian deyan"). An English translation is found in Li Yu, *Silent Operas*, trans. Patrick Hanan (Hong Kong: Renditions, 1990), 1–42. The second is from "Tan Chuyu Expresses His Love in a Play; Liu Miaogu Dies to Preserve her Chastity When the Aria Ends" ("Tan Chuyu xili chuanqing Liu Miaogu quzhong sijie"). An English translation is found in Li, *Silent Operas*, 161–201. The third, from "A Widow Hatches a Plot to Receive a Bridegroom;

Beautiful Women Unite to Seize a Brilliant Poet" ("Guafu sheji zhui xinlang zhongmei qixin duo caizi"), comes from *Silent Operas, Second Collection: Priceless Jade* (*Wushengxi erji Liancheng bi*); and the last comes from "The Female Chen Ping Saves Her Life with Seven Ruses" ("Nü Chen Ping jisheng qichu") and "Tower of my Birth" ("Shengwo lou"). The English translations for these are found in Li, *Silent Operas*, 76–96, and in Li Yu, *A Tower for the Summer Heat*, trans. Patrick Hanan (New York: Columbia University Press, 1992), 221–259.

6. See Chen Yinke, *Liu Rushi biezhuan* (Alternative Biography of Liu Rushi) (Shanghai: Shanghai guji chubanshe, 1980), 371.

7. Here, the monk refers to the early historical painters Yang Xin (370–442), Kong Linzhi (369–423), Xiao Sihua (400–455), and Fan Ye (398–445).

8. These are all historical Song and Yuan dynasty painters: Song Emperor Huizong (Song Huizong, 1082–1135); Su Dongpo (Su Shi, 1037–1101); Ma Lin (thirteenth century); Huang Quan (903–965); Mi Yuanzhang (Mi Fu, 1051–1107); Ni Yunlin (Ni Zan, 1301–1374); Wang Shuming (Wang Meng, 1308–1385); and Huang Dachi (Huang Gongwang, 1269–1354).

9. "Manqian" is the style name of Dongfang Shuo, a witty personality who served the court during the reign of Emperor Wu of the Western Han (Han Wudi, r. 141-87 BCE). Dongfang warned a group of dwarfs working in the stables that the emperor planned to execute them. When questioned, Dongfang explained that he and the dwarfs, despite differences in physique, received the same rations. As a result, he reasoned, the dwarfs had well beyond the sustenance they needed, while Dongfang did not have enough. Here, the women are analogized to Dongfang—understood as being worthy of more recognition—while Dong equates himself with the dwarfs, as he is famous. For a translation of the biography of Dongfang Shuo, see Burton Watson, *Courtier and Commoner in Ancient China: Selections from the History of the Former Han* (New York: Columbia University Press, 1974), 80–81.

10. Liu Yiqing, "Rongzhi" ("Appearance and Manner"), in *Shishuo xinyu* (*A New Account of Tales of the World: Shih-shuo hsin-yü*), trans. Richard B. Mather (Ann Arbor: Center for Chinese Studies, University of Michigan, 2002), 330.

PRIMARY SOURCES

XQOJ   Li Yu 李漁 (1611–1680). *Xianqing ouji* 閒情偶寄 (*Leisure Notes*). In *Li Yu quanji* 李漁全集 (*The Complete Works of Li Yu*), vol. 3. Hangzhou, China: Zhejiang guji chubanshe, 1992. Modern typeset edition based on the Yishengtang edition.

YZY   Li Yu 李漁 (1611–1680). *Yizhong yuan* 意中緣 (*A Much-Desired Match*). In *Li Yu quanji* 李漁全集 (*The Complete Works of Li Yu*). Ed. Helmut Martin, vol. 8. 3223–3446. Taipei: Chengwen, 1970. Facsimile reproduction of Yishengtang edition of *Liweng chuanqi shizhong* 笠翁傳奇十種 (*The Ten Plays of Liweng*).

SUGGESTED READINGS

TRANSLATIONS

Chang, Dongshin, trans. "Act Ten from *The Loving Perfume Companion*, Li Yu (1611–1680)." In *Homoeroticism in Imperial China: A Sourcebook*, ed. Mark Stephenson and Cuncun Wu, 97–107. New York: Routledge, 2013. [Translation of Scene Ten of Li Yu's first play, *Women in Love*.]

Chang, Dongshin, trans. "Xiang yong" (Poems on Fragrance): A Translation of a Scene from Li Yu's *Lianxiang ban* (*The Fragrant Companion*)." *CHINOPERL* 30 (2011): 239–257. [Translation of Scene Six of Li Yu's first play, *Women in Love*.]

Fei, Faye Chunfang, ed. and trans. "Li Yu: From *Li Liweng on Theater*." In *Chinese Theories of Theater and Performance from Confucius to the Present*, trans. and ed. Faye Chunfang Fei, 77–87. Ann Arbor: University of Michigan Press, 1999. [Translated excerpts from *Leisure Notes*.]

Li Yu. *A Couple of Soles: A Comic Play from Seventeenth-Century China*. Trans. Jing Shen and Robert E. Hegel. New York: Columbia University Press, 2019. [First complete translation of a Li Yu play in English.]

Pollard, David, trans. and ed. *The Chinese Essay*, 93–99. London: Hurst and Company, 2000. [Translated excerpts from *Leisure Notes*.]

Pollard, David, trans. "Li Yu on the Theatre: Excerpts from *Pleasant Diversions*," *Renditions 72* (2000): 30–70. [Translated excerpts from *Leisure Notes*.]

ENGLISH

Hanan, Patrick. *The Invention of Li Yu*. Cambridge, MA: Harvard University Press, 1988.

Henry, Eric P. *Chinese Amusements: The Lively Plays of Li Yu*. Hamden, CT: Archon Books, 1980.

Shen, Jing. *Playwrights and Literary Games in Seventeenth-Century China: Plays by Tang Xianzu, Mei Dingzuo, Li Yu, and Kong Shangren*. Lanham, MD: Lexington Books, 2010.

Sieber, Patricia. "Seeing the World through *Xianqing ouji* (1671): Visuality, Performance, and Narratives of Modernity." *Modern Chinese Literature and Culture* 12, no. 2 (2000): 1–43.

CHINESE

Chen Duo 陳多, ann. *Li Liweng quhua* 李笠翁曲話 (*Li Yu's Remarks on Drama*). Hunan, China: Renmin wenxue, 1980.

Huang Guoquan 黃果泉. *Yasu zhi jian: Li Yu de wenhua renge yu wenxue sixiang yanjiu* 雅俗之間: 李漁的文化人格與文學思想研究 (*Between Elegant and Popular: A Study of Li Yu as a Cultural Personality and His Literary Thought*). Beijing: Zhongguo shehui kexue, 2004.

Huang Lizhen 黃麗貞. *Li Yu yanjiu* 李漁研究 (*A Study of Li Yu*). Taipei: Guojia, 1978.

Huang Qiang 黃強. *Li Yu yanjiu* 李漁研究 (*A Study of Li Yu*). Hangzhou, China: Zhejiang guji chubanshe, 1996.

Wang Xueqi 王學奇, Huo Xianjun 霍現俊, and Wu Xiuhua 吳秀華, eds. *Liweng chuanqi shizhong jiaozhu* 笠翁傳奇十種校注 (*The Ten Plays of Liweng, Edited and Annotated*). Tianjin, China: Tianjin guji chubanshe, 2009.

12

The Peach Blossom Fan and *Palace of Everlasting Life*

History, Romance, and Performance

As historical plays, *The Peach Blossom Fan* (*Taohua shan*, hereafter *Fan*) and *Palace of Everlasting Life* (*Changsheng dian*, hereafter *Palace*) are both concerned with events that had happened in the past. Their approaches to representing the past, however, differ in significant ways. This chapter examines the two plays' treatment of history as a subject for moral meditation (as seen in *Fan*) or as a romanticized object (as explored in *Palace*). *Fan* (1699) centers around the love story between the renowned scholar Hou Fangyu (1618–1655) (➤ Introduction) and the famed courtesan Li Xiangjun (1624–1653). The romance is set against the background of the transition from the Chinese Ming dynasty (1368–1644) to the Manchu Qing dynasty (1644–1911), a momentous and protracted political transition that consumed playwrights in China, in Japan, and even as far away as the Netherlands.[1] Meanwhile, *Palace* (1688) depicts the romance between Emperor Xuanzong (Li Longji, 685–762) and the Prized Consort Yang (Yang Yuhuan, d. 756), one of the most controversial episodes in the distant Tang dynasty (618–907). Thanks to their unswerving love for each other, even when parted by death, the couple is happily reunited in the heavenly realm. These two plays offer themselves as interesting examples of how drama as a form of historical writing represents, re-creates, and transmits actual historical knowledge (➤ chap. 10), but also refashions the collective memory of the period depicted with an unrelenting emphasis on romance as a central force in history.

Moreover, written after more than a century's worth of literati experimentation with the long drama form (➤ chaps. 8, 9, 10, and 11), both plays evince a high degree of self-reflexivity with regard to the music, singing, and performers at the core of Chinese song-drama. The theme of performance-within-a-play figures prominently in both plays. "Performance" in this chapter refers to music played by an orchestra, music accompanied by dance, singing in theater, singing as storytelling, and plain storytelling, with each type potentially overlapping with each other. Thus, "performance," used in the word's broadest sense, helps bring out the cumulative effect of the many moments of performance scattered throughout each play. As shown in this chapter, the vantage point of performance highlights the contrast between the two plays: in *Fan*, the female lead's training in theatrical performance teaches her the language of love, but in the long run, such playacting exposes the nature of romance as nothing but meaningless role-playing. Yet at the same time, it is also performance—most notably, singing and storytelling—that functions not only as an effective medium of political criticism, but also enables the marginalized members of the society to gain a voice and some political influence. In contrast, in *Palace*, performance—particularly music and dancing—serves more as a language of love than as a means of political critique. In short, performance aestheticizes the historical figures and the events surrounding them in order to champion love as a form of eternity. In other words, with minimal attention to political undertones, *Palace* transformed historical figures into the stuff of romantic legend, whereas *Fan* wanted to be read as a serious meditation on actual events. Ultimately, *Fan* and *Palace* converge on the use of performance—particularly storytelling—as a form of mediated history.

12.1 KONG SHANGREN AND HONG SHENG: *CHUANQI* PLAYS AS ALTERNATIVE HISTORY

The use of drama as a form of mediated history is related to the two playwrights' interest in studying historical changes and understanding an individual's position against the background of historical developments. Kong Shangren (1648–1718) was a sixty-fourth-generation descendant of Confucius who was trained in the curriculum for the civil service examinations and was interested in a wide range of subjects, such as ritual, music, warfare, and agriculture. While serving in a government post from 1686 through 1690 in Yangzhou, a hub for the many literati who still felt loyal to the fallen Ming dynasty, Kong befriended many of these Ming loyalists. He also visited various famous historical sites associated with late Ming figures and events in Yangzhou and adjacent areas.[2] In combining site visits with what we might call "oral history," Kong prepared himself for the composition of *Fan*. From 1698 to 1699, Kong worked through three drafts and finally completed the play.

To realize his goal of making history come alive, Kong Shangren sought to reconcile the demands of historiography with the needs of dramaturgy. To underscore the play's status of a historical lesson in dramatic form, Kong included in the play's printed edition a detailed bibliography titled "Textual Sources for *The Peach Blossom Fan*" ("*Taohua shan* kaoju"), exemplifying his emphasis on historical credibility [*THS* 15–21]. However, in Confucian historiography, historians could adopt either a straightforward style (*zhibi*) or the more highly regarded form of indirect writing (*qubi*)—particularly with regard to sensitive matters—in order to not simply convey the facts of a story, but also point to their moral significance. Similarly, in political communication with authority figures—most notably, with the emperor—it might be foolhardy to point to problems too directly (☞ chap. 10). Wit might be an effective way to offer political criticism and moral guidance. One particular character in the play, the Master of Ceremonies at the Temple of Imperial Sacrifice (Taichang si) in Nanjing, highlights *Fan*'s dual sources of inspiration for the representation of history:

（副末）司馬遷作史筆，東方朔上場人，只怕
世事含糊八九件，人情遮蓋兩三分。

SECONDARY MALE *as* MASTER OF CEREMONIES [*speaks*]: In adopting the persona of a historian like Sima Qian as well as that of the court jester Dongfang Shuo, I am afraid that [the playwright] only indirectly conveyed the nature of most events, and in a handful of cases, covered up some underlying truth out of consideration for some people's feelings or image.

[*THS* 133, scene 21, "Solitary Chanting" ("Guyin")]

Sima Qian (145–90 BCE), author of *The Records of the Historian* (*Shiji*), was the most influential historian in Chinese history (☞ chap. 5). Dongfang Shuo (154–93 BCE), a Daoist magician and court entertainer, was known for his superb skill at jests and witticisms when giving political advice to the emperor. This observation thus draws attention to Kong's dual identity of historian and playwright in the creation of *Fan*. Like Sima Qian the Grand Historian, Kong employs the style of "concealment" (*hui*) and "indirect writing" (*qubi*) in his representation of history. Like the court jester, he also embeds "remonstration" (*jian*) in his commentary on the events (☞ Introduction). Thus, despite all the gesturing toward a factual basis for the play, historical factuality is not, and should not be assumed to be, the main point.

The interest of Hong Sheng (1645–1704) in the history of the Tianbao reign (742–755) is manifested through the three-stage process of the composition of *Palace*. In 1675, he wrote a play entitled *Pavilion of Deep Fragrance* (*Chenxiang ting*), based on a story about the Tang-dynasty poet Li Bo (701–762). It reflects Hong's feelings as a talented scholar who failed to be appreciated by his contemporaries and was languishing at the bottom of society. Indeed, Hong's life was full of misfortune: he tried to enter officialdom through the civil service examinations, yet he failed repeatedly, which caused him a great deal of disappointment and sorrow. At the age of twenty-four (in Chinese years), he moved to Beijing to study at the Imperial Academy, but he fell on hard times and was reduced to extreme poverty. His personality contributed to his hardships: he was reckless, aloof, and haughty, and he refused to conform to the social norms of the time. Four years later, Hong rewrote *Pavilion of Deep Fragrance* to center on the story of Li Mi (722–789), who assisted Emperor Suzong (r. 756–762) in achieving the revival of the Tang dynasty after its near-collapse in the wake of a series of rebellions. Entitled *Dancing to [The Melody of] the Rainbow Skirts* (*Wu nichang*), a shorthand reference to the famed "The Melody of Rainbow Skirts and Feather Robes" (*Nichang yuyi qu*), this version shifted the focus from personal misfortune to the rise and fall of a dynasty.[3] Hong Sheng subsequently revised *Dancing to the Rainbow Skirts* to focus on the romance between Emperor Xuanzong and the Prized Consort Yang. This new play, *Palace*, was finalized in 1688, and was so popular for a while that it was said to be the only music performed at lavish banquets in wealthy households, as well as in wine shops and music halls. It traveled as far as Vietnam.

For both playwrights, the very act of playwriting serves as a means of writing history. Interestingly, professional entertainers, empowered by the medium of performance, are given the voice to tell and interpret history in both plays. Those characters' performances of storytelling in turn form an analogy to the playwrights' writing of drama as history.

The form of *chuanqi* drama is conducive to representing historical events, while also drawing on the tools of literature to make history come alive. First, compared to historical genres such as biography, drama need not strictly adhere to historical facts, and it enjoys greater freedom to employ fictional elements for dramatic effect. Second, the rotation of aria, dialogue, and poetic recitation in a play helps to explore the protagonists' inner world without relying too much on portrayals of the outer world and overt actions of characters. Third, the sheer length of a *chuanqi* play, usually reaching as many as forty scenes, offers ample space for the playwrights to present historical processes in detail, while the episodic structure of the play allows the writers to depict characters and events from multiple perspectives (☞ chap. 5).[4] With those formal advantages, *Fan* and *Palace* enliven a version of the past both on paper and onstage, all while offering readers and audiences an interpretation of the recounted history. *Fan*, engaging the still-palpable recent past, is interested in drawing a historical lesson out of a love story and is concerned about the moral implications of historical judgment.[5] In contrast, in the case of *Palace*, the long interval between the events and the play's own time affords the playwright the freedom to aestheticize the imperial love story, while eschewing the sermonizing that had informed previous literary renderings of the narrative.

The varied treatment of romance in *Fan* and *Palace* is particularly important when considered as an early Qing response to the late Ming intellectual and literary discourse usually referred to as the "cult of *qing*" (love, passion, feelings, and sensibilities). Confucian orthodoxy considered moral cultivation to arise from the rigorous study of the Confucian classics and a strict adherence to the ethical principles prescribed in those texts. In the late sixteenth century, a new school of Confucianism began to challenge the validity and effectiveness of textual learning. Following the idea of Wang Yangming (1472–1529) that everyone is born with "innate knowledge of the good" (*liangzhi*), philosophers and writers looked to human emotions and desires as the new source of morality. In this new view, far from leading people astray, passion and romantic love were not just natural, they were where one could find one's own innate moral compass. So many *chuanqi* plays and short vernacular stories in the late-sixteenth and early-seventeenth centuries were so devoted to the celebrating love that modern scholars speak of a "cult of *qing*."[6]

Both *Fan* and *Palace* engage with the notion of love (*qing*). Indeed, both are compared to *The Peony Pavilion* (*Mudan ting*, hereafter, *Peony*), a late Ming play that, through its novel use of dreams, represents the summit of the cult of *qing* in *chuanqi* drama (☞ chap. 9). *Fan* features significant textual references to *Peony*, which indicates Kong Shangren's interest in drawing an analogy between his play and the classic. *Palace* was praised by its contemporary audience as "a lively version of *The Peony Pavilion*" (*yibu renao* Mudan ting).[7] Indeed, not only does *Palace* share the same theme of death-defying love with *Peony*, but Hong Sheng also felt a life-long passion for the works of *Peony*'s author, Tang Xianzu (1550–1616). However, as discussed next, the two plays' relation to *Peony* stand in stark contrast: while *Palace* offers an example of love made visible through dance and audible through music, *Fan* voices a harsh critique of indulgence in passion and emotion through singing and storytelling.

12.2 PEACH BLOSSOM FAN: "TALK ABOUT LOVE IS SIMPLY POINTLESS"

Invoking the theme of scholar-meets-beauty (*caizi jiaren*) romance within a larger scheme of dynastic transition, *Fan* breaks with the generic convention of the lovers' eventual happy union. While scholar-meets-beauty romances usually end with the talented scholar's success in the civil service examination and his subsequent blessed marriage with a beautiful maiden, Hou Fangyu (1618–1655) and Li Xiangjun (1624–1653) do not conform to their expected roles. Instead, when the couple is reunited after many personal trials and political tribulations, *Fan* arranges for a Daoist priest to awaken the couple to love's illusory nature at their reunion in scene 40. The couple then separates voluntarily to take refuge in religion. This deviation from generic conventions points to Kong Shangren's intention to uproot the belief in the validity of romantic love and subvert the discourse of passion. As the priest notes: "Talk about love is simply pointless" (*yanyu yinci tai xudao*—literally, "speaking amorous and obscene words without getting to the point") [THS 251].

The love story between Hou Fangyu and Li Xiangjun begins as many other scholar-meets-beauty-romances, and yet it gets entangled ever more deeply with political changes. Hou, the male lead, is a young scholar of considerable literary fame. When he comes to Nanjing to sit for the civil service examination, he learns about the beauty of the courtesan Xiangjun. Upon their first encounter, Hou and Xiangjun fall in love. As a token of his affection, Hou gives Xiangjun a palace fan inscribed with a poem that he composed for her. At their wedding as husband and concubine, Xiangjun receives a gift of 300 taels of silver. They learn from the intermediary Yang Wencong (1596–1646) that the gift is from the notorious official Ruan Dacheng (1587–1646), who was widely believed to have supported the ruthless Grand Eunuch Wei Zhongxian (1568–1627) (☛ chap. 10).

Now that the Wei Zhongxian clique has collapsed, Ruan is trying to court Hou because of Hou's status as a respected member of the Restoration Society (Fushe).[8] Xiangjun rejects the gift and denounces Ruan for his corruption and for his former association with the evil eunuch clique. Feeling humiliated, Ruan soon seizes an opportunity to frame Hou on trumped-up charges, claiming that Hou is conspiring to revolt with the military general Zuo Liangyu (1599–1645) to seize Nanjing for themselves. Hou is forced to leave Nanjing and seek refuge elsewhere, leaving Xiangjun behind (☛ HTRCProse, C15.4).

During their separation, Xiangjun demonstrates unswerving loyalty to Hou, even in the deteriorating political environment. After a peasant rebel army enters Beijing and the last Ming emperor commits suicide in 1644, Ma Shiying (1591–1646) and Ruan Dacheng help the prince of Fu (Fuwang) ascend the throne in Nanjing. Thus begins the Southern Ming regime (1645). Ma tries to abduct Xiangjun and marry her to an official as a concubine, but Xiangjun refuses to submit and attempts suicide. She hits her head against a pillar in an effort to kill herself, and her blood splatters onto the fan that Hou gave her. This particular scene is extremely dramatic and violent. It also takes a more "masculine" form compared to Consort Yang's more conventional way of suicide by women (i.e., hanging herself). In this sense, Xiangjun's suicide attempt is not only a form of self-empowerment—it is also a process of self-masculinization, which echoes her later engagement with music for political remonstration. The painter Yang Wencong transforms the bloodstains on the fan into a picture of peach blossoms. Hou receives the peach blossom fan and hurries back to Nanjing, only to find that Xiangjun has been brought to the Southern Ming court. Upon his return, Hou is arrested by Ruan Dacheng.

After the Manchu army captures Nanjing in 1645, both Hou and Xiangjun take refuge in the hills. They unexpectedly reunite at a grand ritual ceremony for the spirits of the recently deceased Ming emperor and the ministers who followed him in death. The Daoist priest hosting the ceremony challenges their obsession with romance and tears the peach blossom fan to pieces. The newly reunited couple is awakened to the futility of love in the face of the fallen empire. They part ways, and both convert to Daoism. Hence, as noted earlier, the last scene, titled "Entering the Way" ("Rudao"), depicts the joyful reunion between Hou and Li after a long separation, and yet the Daoist priest ends up convincing them of the illusionary nature of their belief in love. The priest challenges them thus:

（外）你们絮絮叨叨，說的俱是那裏話？當此地覆天翻，還戀情根慾種，岂不可笑！

EXTRA MALE *as* PRIEST [*speaks*]: What's the point of that trivial talk of yours? At this moment of earth-shattering changes, you are still obsessed with romantic feelings and amorous desires. Isn't it laughable!

（生）此言差矣！從來男女室家，人之大倫，離合悲歡，情有所鍾，先生如何管得？

YOUNG MALE *as* HOU FANGYU [*speaks*]: You are mistaken! The marriage of man with woman is the source of human ethics. The sorrows of separation, the joys of reunion, all these are the fruits of love. Why should you object to it?

（外怒介）呵呸！两個癡蟲，你看國在那裏？家在那裏？君在那裏？父在那裏？偏是這點花月情根，割他不斷麼？

PRIEST *angrily* [*speaks*]: Pshaw! Two piteous romantic fools! Just take a look: Where is the empire now? Where is the family now? Where is the emperor now? Where is the father now? And, now, you are incapable of uprooting this most trivial of feelings, romance?

[*THS* 250–251, scene 40, "Entering the Way" ("Rudao")]

The priest denies the very meaning of love in the face of the destruction of the state and suggests that they convert to Daoism to seek peace of mind. Hou attempts to argue for the legitimacy of romantic relationships by pointing out the importance of marriage among the cardinal relationships in the Confucian worldview. The priest counters that even the state and the basic social institutions such as the family are inherently illusory, never mind romantic feelings. Through the lovers' religious conversion, the playwright evokes a deep sense of disillusionment and heartfelt mourning for the end of an era. As such, according to Kong, the play is to "inspire the viewers to take heed [for the future], and thus offer a remedy for an age of decline" (*chengchuang renxin wei moshi zhi yijiu*) [*THS* 1]. That is, *Fan* intends to make the audience aware of the mechanisms of historical change. If the audience is fully cognizant of the nature of cause and effect, the playwright seems to suggest, they will not be condemned to repeat history.

12.3 *PALACE OF EVERLASTING LIFE*: "WITH NEW LYRICS, (THIS PLAY) IS ALL ABOUT LOVE"

In *Palace*, Hong Sheng depoliticizes the relationship between Emperor Xuanzong and the Prized Consort Yang to create an exemplary love story. For him, the couple represents "the intentness of feelings that is rarely found in imperial families" (*qing zhi suozhong, zai diwang jia hanyou*) [*CSD* 1]. The opening scene—a short prologue comprising only two tunes—articulates the play's central theme and outlines its main plot. The first song-lyric reads as follows:

（末）	ADDITIONAL MALE *as* TROUPE LEADER [*declaims*]:
【滿江紅】	*To the tune* "Man Jiang hong"
今古情場，	Ever since antiquity, on the stage of love,
問誰個真心到底？	How many could remain true till the end?
但果有精誠不散，	Those whose sincerity lasted beyond life and death
終成連理。	Were eventually united like intertwined branches.
兩心那論生和死。	Even life and death don't matter.
笑人間兒女悵緣慳，	It's laughable that lovers in this world sigh over the difficulty of destiny.
無情耳。	It is only because they do not know what love is.
感金石，回天地。	True love moves metal and stone, Heaven and Earth;
昭白日，垂青史。	It shines like the sun and is passed down in history.
看臣忠子孝，總由情至。	Loyal ministers and filial sons became such because of love.
先聖不曾刪鄭、衛，	Even the ancient sage [Confucius] did not delete the amorous music of Zheng and Wei [when he compiled *The Book of Songs*];
吾儕取義翻宮、徵。	So today people like me can use music to express the meaning of love.
借太真外傳鋪新詞，情而已。	In retelling the unofficial history of the Prized Consort Yang to compose new lyrics, (this play) is all about love.
	[*CSD* 1, scene 1, "Outlining the Play" ("Chuan'gai")]

An explicit statement of the play's agenda (☛ chap. 11), the prologue first comments on the rarity of true love in history and then defines what true love means and how it manifests itself. By describing the transgressive power of love, it prepares the audience for the play's supernatural framework and justifies the legitimacy of this approach. It moves on to point out the relationship between love and history (i.e., true love deserves a place in history, through which it achieves eternal renown). Even political loyalty and filial piety—the most basic and important human relationships in the Confucian world—are manifestations of deep love. The tune then turns to comment on the legitimacy of the literary expression of love, comparing the play to love songs found in the *The Book of Songs* (*Shijing*) (☛ Introduction, chap. 9). By compiling tunes and composing new lyrics, Hong Sheng claims that this play is meant to enunciate the meaning of love.

The play begins with Yang Yuhuan's entering the imperial harem and receiving the title of Prized Consort (*Guifei*) thanks to her extraordinary beauty. As she becomes the emperor's favorite concubine, her family members also benefit from imperial favor. Yang Guozhong, a cousin of the consort, rises to the highest position at court, the chancellor. In a dream, Yang visits the moon palace and observes celestial maidens performing the music of *The Rainbow Skirts*. The next day, she transcribes the piece from memory and dances to the music at her birthday banquet.

A rebel army led by General An Lushan (703–757) approaches the capital, forcing the emperor to flee westward with the consort. At Mawei Post west of Chang'an, the emperor's guards assassinate Yang Guozhong and demand the death of the consort because the troops attribute the cause of the rebellion to Yang Guozhong. The emperor is forced to consent, and Yang hangs herself. The Jade Emperor in Heaven learns about Yang's plight and allows her soul to return to the celestial realm. Before long, the imperial army crushes the rebellion and the emperor returns to Chang'an. He tries to find Yang's spirit with the help of a wizard, who discovers that it resides in one of the abodes of the immortals, Mt. Penglai. The wizard then builds a magic bridge leading to the Moon Palace. The emperor crosses the bridge alone to meet the consort, and they become husband and wife for eternity. Some may argue that the blissful celestial reunion is possible only because of the play's supernatural framework, which indicates that the playwright might be uncertain about the possibility of seeking refuge in *qing* in real life. While that is conceivable, Hong Sheng's celebration of love in the fictional world of theater is beyond doubt.

The distant past doesn't have the kind of direct connection to the present as the recent past does, so it possesses less potential to disrupt the newly established order. This may explain why *Palace* could largely eschew making explicit political judgments of the historical characters it portrays, thus breaking free of the moralistic paradigm in its interpretation of history. Even when it apportions praise and blame to the emperor and the consort, it explains it all away. Instead, it uses these characters to suit its artistic agenda, one that glorifies the power of love as transgressing the limits of the moralistic framework of historical accounts. *Palace*'s emphasis on romance forms a contrast to *Fan*'s interest in making sense of recent political changes. This difference explains the two plays' varied approaches to presenting the music and performances within each of them.

In the following section, we discuss the three functions of performance in the two plays: First, music functions as a form of self-expression by granting the female characters the language of love. However, in *Fan*, music—particularly musical theater—is also the medium through which the play reveals love's artificial and illusory nature. Second, as a medium of political remonstration, music transforms the female lead in *Fan* from a romantic protagonist into a political subject. Contrastingly, in *Palace*, music as the embodiment of lyricized love is devoid of any political function. Third, the two plays converge on their use of performance as a means to recapitulate and reflect on the past they depict. By granting a voice to the characters of professional performers—the storyteller and the music master in *Fan* and the imperial musician in *Palace*—they bring entertainers who were typically socially marginal figures to the center of historical representation. In doing so, the two plays draw attention to the nature of drama as a form of alternative history.

12.4 PEACH BLOSSOM FAN AND *PALACE OF EVERLASTING LIFE*: MUSIC AS THE LANGUAGE OF LOVE

In *Fan*, Li Xiangjun's study of *Peony* is one of the two defining events of the female lead's entrance into the play, the other being her receiving the name of Xiangjun ("Fragrant Princess"). While being named by a client highlights the young courtesan's status as a silent object, her training in theater and mastery of the classic romantic comedy *Peony* grants her a voice of self-expression for the first time. Scene 2 depicts Li's practice of singing tunes from *Peony* under the instruction of Sun Kunsheng, a music master skilled in the soft and elegant southern musical style. Through the memorization, practice, and singing of the very tunes sung by the female romantic lead of *Peony*, Du Liniang, Li learns about love. She acquires Du's language of self-expression and internalizes the same feelings and desires that Du expressed. Songs, in other words, provide Li Xiangjun with a romantic education and transform her into a desiring subject and a desirable lover. This scene of Li's encounter with *Peony* invites a comparison between the Hou-Li romance—even before it happens—and the amorous love story in *Peony*. Because Du Liniang is widely viewed as the most representative embodiment of love in *chuanqi* drama, *Fan*'s use of her as the model of romantic subjectivity for Li calls attention to the play's effect in invalidating the whole discourse of love.

In contrast to *Peony*'s use of songs to attest to the authenticity of love, *Fan* uses *Peony*'s lyrics to pit the play against its original message. For instance, the repeated interruption of Xiangjun's practice by her teacher Su Kunsheng, as well as his insistence that she perfect certain singing techniques, remind the audience of the artificiality of theater and foreground the constructed nature of the language of love. As we will discuss in the next section, in *Fan*, musical theater as a language of love turns out to be illusory, but it proves effective as a medium of political critique.

While the Li-Yang relationship in *Palace* is also subject to political and social disturbances, love persists because music is its unshakeable anchor amid chaos and change. The transmission of *The Rainbow Skirts*—including its recomposition by the consort and her addition of a dance to the music—aestheticizes the amorous history of the Tang court. The melody grants the love affair a prominent acoustic character by marking a milestone in the development of the relationship. Connecting the heavenly and human realms, it transcends the lovers' biological limits and symbolizes the possibility of eternal love.

The transmission of *The Rainbow Skirts* and the unfolding of the love story is essentially one. Originally a piece "long kept a secret in the Moon Palace" (*jiu mi yuegong*) [*CSD* 50], "the celestial melody is transmitted to make a fine story in the human realm" (*jing jiang tianshang xianyin liuzuo renjian jiahua*) [*CSD* 50]. The melody enriches, if not outright produces, the story, while the story relies on the transmission of the melody to develop. This inseparable unity is reinforced, as the consort is both the protagonist of the love story and functions as the human transmitter of the celestial music. Thanks to her heavenly origins—in her previous life, she was the Jade Goddess of the Penglai Island, a fabled abode of immortals—Yang is chosen to transmit *The Rainbow Skirts* to the world. The Moon Goddess Chang E summons Yang's spirit to the Moon Palace to view a performance of the melody, which proves to be a visual spectacle: heavenly maidens in white coats and red skirts, embellished with embroidered-cloud collars on their shoulders, ornamental chains and tassels around their necks, and flying ribbons, play the melody under osmanthus trees. Osmanthus flowers, known for their arresting fragrance, scent the performance. The enchanting smell renders Yang's viewing experience immersive—something that affects multiple sensory dimensions. Little wonder that such a performance profoundly affects the consort in her "heart and soul" (*xinpo*) and enables her to rediscover her musical talent, which takes the compatibility and mutual appreciation between her and the emperor to a higher level.

Just as Xiangjun learning *Peony* is a process that requires practice and adjustments, Yang has to learn and re-create *The Rainbow Skirts* in order to fully inhabit it. After viewing the heavenly performance in a dream, in scene 12, she transcribes the score from memory and, more important, she makes changes to improve it. Her standards are so high that "every character must fit perfectly according to the rules, and all sections must be in seamless harmony with one another" [*CSD* 56], suggesting her mastery of musical techniques and her refined taste. In the process, Yang demonstrates true understanding of the nature of music—she is inspired to put the final touches on the score based on the chirping of orioles. The completion of her composition is therefore both the result of human skill and the manifestation of harmonious interactions between human beings and the cosmos. The commentator Wu Ren (fl. 1694) noted that this episode is comparable to "the sage learning from the thousand things."[9] Yang's ability to take inspiration from nature reflects her true understanding of music because the musical ideal in Confucian thought was to epitomize the harmony between human beings and nature.

Yang's composition of *The Rainbow Skirts* enriches her character and marks the spiritual consummation of her relationship with the emperor. Before reading the score, he appreciated her effort as "a tasteful endeavor of a beauty" (*meiren yunshi*) [*CSD* 56]. What matters is the aesthetic value of the event—a beautiful woman engaging with music—rather than her competence or the quality of the composition. After reading the score, the music-loving emperor is in awe of the consort's talent; she is not just beautiful, but also has a spiritual core (*lingxin*) manifested through her musical aptitude. Just as important, Yang views composing *The Rainbow Skirts* as a chance to achieve victory over Consort Mei's *Dance of the Startled Swan* (*Jinghong wu*), the only thing that stands in the way of the emperor's undivided attention to Yang. Her attempt is successful: After seeing the score, the emperor declares that "*The Startled Swan* is no longer worth mentioning" [*CSD* 56]. In this sense, music equips the consort with an exclusive claim on love.

Music as an expression of romantic subjectivity is at its most powerful when the melody is literally embodied by the consort herself. In scene 16, her dance to *The Rainbow Skirts* marks the climax of merrymaking in the romantic relationship. According to the composer (i.e., the consort), the third section of *The Rainbow Skirts* is most suitable for and "mutually complementary with slow dancing and measured singing" (*jie yu manwu xiangsheng huange jiaochang*) [*CSD* 76] because of its rhythm, beat, and texture. At her birthday banquet, she dances to the music on top of a specially made jade plate, while Li Guinian and other court musicians play the third section of *The Rainbow Skirts*. The emperor is delighted and beats the drum himself to keep the beat for her. The performance, a collaboration among ingenious musicians, passionate lovers, and the state's highest political authority, marks the high point of aestheticism in *Palace*. The emperor praises Yang's performance as "the best [dance] in a thousand years" (*dushan qianqiu*) [*CSD* 76]. After that point, the consort is not only the transmitter and composer—she personifies the music through her body and has become the melody.

The unity between the melody and the consort is confirmed by their eventual return to the heavenly realm. Not only Yang has been enlisted as an immortal; *The Rainbow Skirts* is also included in the musical repertoire of the Harmonious Heaven (*juntian*), the center of the nine Heavens, which is most celebrated for the Grand Music (*guangyue*) performed there. In scene 50, the melody, in Yang's improved version, is performed upon her reunion with the emperor in the Moon Palace. As the background—the acoustic context—of the lovers' reunion and immortalization, the music evokes memories of the couple's happiest time in the imperial palace and marks the triumph of eternal love in the heavenly realm.

In the human realm, the expressive power of *The Rainbow Skirts* reaches even unintended audiences, represented by the young scholar and flutist Li Mo. Li Mo describes himself as learned in music and especially skilled at playing the iron flute. In scene 14, admiring the courtly production of the new melody, yet having no access to the "secret score" (*mipu*), he waits outside the palace walls to eavesdrop on the musicians rehearsing *The Rainbow Skirts*. He plays along on his flute to memorize the score by heart, claiming repeatedly that "these few notes

I have suddenly come to understand" [*CSD* 66]. The phrase rendered as "coming to a sudden realization" (*huangran xinling*) shows Li Mo's exceptional talent. More important, it indicates a kind of natural connection that he has with the music, through which the obscure scholar-musician becomes an "intimate friend" (*zhiyin*) to the consort and her persistent defender thereafter. It is Li Mo who learns the entire score from Li Guinian, the official court musician, after Yang's death, and he is the one responsible for its preservation in the human realm. Appearing at various critical moments of the melody's transmission—the preparation of its first performance in court and Li Guinian's postwar recounting of the Li-Yang love story on the street in scene 38—Li Mo bridges the temporal and spatial interval between past and present. Therefore, despite the fact that the actual *The Rainbow Skirts* had long been lost by Hong Sheng's time, it is portrayed as the medium through which love may achieve eternal acclaim. By contributing to the transmission of *The Rainbow Skirts*, though not its actual score, the playwright also draws a possible analogy between Li Mo and himself.

12.5 *PEACH BLOSSOM FAN* AND *PALACE OF EVERLASTING LIFE*: PERFORMANCE AS POLITICAL REMONSTRATION

As discussed previously, Li Xiangjun acquires the language of love through learning the tunes from *Peony*, thus forming her romantic subjectivity. Ironically, in scene 25, it is also her mastery of singing *Peony* that makes her appealing to the Hongguang emperor. Although the emperor's appreciation of her singing of the romantic classic saves her from personal humiliation—that is, being assigned by the vengeful Ruan Dacheng to assume the role of a clown in a play staged at court—her singing of *Peony* also implicates her in the destruction of the state. After all, in the playwright's view, the quick demise of the Southern Ming regime had everything to do with the decadent ruler's indulgence in entertainment and pleasure and indifference to matters of state.

Finding herself in a dire situation, Li Xiangjun is able to redeem herself by turning music from a language of love into a medium of political critique. *Fan* is indeed a play that discloses the danger of obsession with love by speaking the very language of love. For Li, it is her voice of moral and political criticism, expressed through theater, that ultimately defines her. She is not only a courtesan-turned-concubine; more important, she is a righteous subject of the Ming who dares to stand up to corrupt officials. When abducted into the Hongguang emperor's court and forced to entertain as a singing girl, Li turns singing into an opportunity to vent her pent-up anger by publicly denouncing Ma Shiying and Ruan Dacheng. She sings about her forced separation, first from her husband and then from her mother [*THS* 156]. Through her voice, the playwright made clear that treacherous and evil administrators like Ma and Ruan were more harmful to common people than bandits. When a member of the audience stops her from complaining, she concedes that "my own injustice is indeed not worth telling," and she turns to revealing the officials' misconduct in public affairs:

（旦）　　YOUNG FEMALE *as* LI XIANGJUN [*sings*]:

【五供養】　　*To the tune* "Wu gongyang"

堂堂列公，　　August high officials, the Southern Court depends on you,

半邊南朝，望你崢嶸，　　To revive the remaining half of the country.

出身希貴寵，　　But you only promote those with prominent family backgrounds.

創業選聲容，　　Upon establishing the court you only seek beautiful singers,

後庭花又添幾種，　　To fill the Emperor's Inner Court with entertainment.

把俺胡撮弄，對寒風雪海冰山，　　You have abused me and dragged me to this place of ice and snow.

苦陪觴詠。　　With great sorrow, I sing and pour wine, serving in your company.

[*THS* 157, scene 24, "Denunciation at the Banquet" ("Mayan")]

Rising above personal grudges, Li Xiangjun uses performance as an opportunity to voice criticism of Ma and Ruan for using the newly established Southern Ming dynasty as nothing but an opportunity for personal gain. Government posts are handed out based on connections, and powerful ministers are only concerned about currying favor with the emperor and indulging in pleasure. Those evil men are held responsible for the dynasty's impending destruction. It is particularly ironic that this astute and sober observation of the cause of crisis is not only made by a woman, but one from the lowest social background. Yet even the allegedly lowly courtesan possesses a more acute sense of right and wrong than her social superiors, as Li continues to sing:

（旦）　　LI XIANGJUN [*sings*]:

【玉交枝】　　*To the tune* "Yu jiaozhi"

東林伯仲俺，　　The Eastern Grove patriots won universal esteem.

青樓皆知敬重。　　Even we girls in the pleasure quarters know to respect them.

…　　…

冰肌雪腸原自同，　　With my body as pure as ice, and my heart as chaste as snow, I shall find sympathy.

鐵心石腹何愁凍。　　With my will of iron and stone, I have no fear of freezing.

…　　…

奴家已拚一死，　　I am not afraid of death,

吐不盡鵑血滿胸，　　But I shall never stanch the longings and sorrow in my breast.

吐不盡鵑血滿胸。　　I shall never stanch the longings and sorrow in my breast.

[*THS* 157, scene 24, "Denunciation at the Banquet"]

Pitting the evil officials—Ma and Ruan—against the respectable members of the Eastern Grove (Donglin) Party, Xiangjun demonstrates a sense of social responsibility and political courage. The tune then turns inward to focus on her body and inner feelings, with Li confessing her determination to remain chaste and pure, even if doing so costs her life. The song employs the well-known allusion of the cuckoo crying blood (*juanxie*) to describe the singer's unyielding resistance against the abuse imposed on her.[10] The allusion is familiar, but interesting nonetheless, because of the analogy between the bird and the courtesan: for the oppressed, singing is the last recourse, but also the most dramatic expression of sorrow. Echoing the bloodstains on the fan, the image of blood in this tune also suggests self-imposed violence. Music is thus unequivocally associated with violence brought about by political struggle and national crisis.

Compared to Li Xiangjun's mastery of theater, first as the language of romance and then as the medium of political remonstration, Liu Jingting is someone who has mastered the art of storytelling as a language of political critique from the beginning of the play. Through a skilled performance of storytelling, he turns the stereotypical view of entertainers as vulgar people without moral cultivation upside down, challenging the prescribed boundaries between the elite and lower classes. In fact, in *Fan*, it is those from the lowest class of Ming society who turn out to be the firmest and most reliable guardians of virtue and the most level-headed critics of contemporary politics amid degenerating social mores.

It is performance—or storytelling, in the case of Liu Jingting—that grants the entertainer a voice and agency in the political realm. As early as scene 1,[11] the male lead, Hou Fangyu, is awed by what he learns from fellow members of the Restoration Society about Liu's righteous action of giving up Ruan Dacheng's patronage. Hou notes: "I had no idea that there were heroic fighters among these kinds of people" [*THS* 7]. "These kinds of people" (*cibei*) here refers to professional storytellers and performers in general. Such people occupied the lowest rung of the social ladder in imperial Chinese society. Chen Zhenhui (1604–1656), a Restoration Society member, adds that Liu is "a famed gentleman in the realm of rivers and lakes" (*jianghu mingshi*) and should be properly addressed as "gentleman" (*xianggong*). After listening to Liu's performance of a drum ballad, Hou claims that Liu is truly "a kindred spirit of ours" (*wobei zhongren*), and "storytelling is merely his 'hobby'" (*yuji*, literally "extra skill") [*THS* 10].[12] In other words, he is not a professional of any kind, an identity that literati typically had looked down upon (☛ chap. 4).

Meanwhile, the literati do not seem to be fulfilling the social and political responsibilities expected of them. Faced with the imminent fall of the capital in the north, they believe that "people like us should simply appreciate the sight of spring" [*THS* 6]. Yet such escapist nonaction is only one of their problems. As the playwright goes on to show during the rest of the play, they also demonstrate a crippling lack of rational strategies in dealing with political foes. In scene 3, a Restoration Society member publicly humiliates Ruan Dacheng through verbal and physical abuse when Ruan attempts to join a ritual performance at the Confucius Temple. Later, in scene 4, associates of the Restoration Society relentlessly ridicule

Ruan for courting favor with Wei Zhongxian, even while watching a play that Ruan composed (☞ chap. 10) . These two incidents sow the seeds for Ruan's later retaliatory attacks. As the play shows, this kind of emotional response and obsession with presumed heroism does not save the empire from internal and external crises.

In contrast to the scholars' excessive emotionality and their political ineffectiveness, Liu Jingting and Su Kunsheng are not only heroic and highly effective, they are also cultivated in literati culture. Su Kusheng is responsible for teaching the female lead the language of love and that of late Ming literati culture through *Peony*, the quintessential romantic comedy. Liu Jingting is learned in Confucian classics, demonstrating a mastery of *The Analects* (*Lunyu*), one of *The Four Books* at the core of the examination curriculum, in his storytelling to scholars of the Restoration Society in scene 1. When challenged by the scholars about the suitability of the classic to the genre of storytelling, Liu states: "[Is it that] only scholars can talk about it, but this old man can't? I am determined to borrow an esteemed classic today by telling an episode [from *The Analects*]" [*THS* 7]. He goes on to tell a story based on the episode of Confucius editing the music of the state of Lu to restore the proper rituals.

By learning the Confucian classics as a storyteller, Liu challenges the notion that the Confucian tradition belongs only to students in the civil service examination system. Liu is soon joined by the students themselves. One of them compares his storytelling to "lectures on the examination essays" (*yingzhi jiangyi*), stating that the former is more thorough and exciting [*THS* 10]. Indeed, having heard this storytelling, Hou Fangyu claims that Liu's excellent character and broad-mindedness make him "one of us" [*THS* 10]. He further adds, setting aside Liu's own attitude, that storytelling is merely his "hobby" (*yuji*). However, it is precisely through the seemingly insignificant "hobby" that Liu gains agency by revealing Ruan Dacheng's treachery.

Unlike in *Fan*, music in *Palace* is devoid of the function of explicit political remonstration, which is in accordance with the play's agenda of depoliticizing the Li-Yang romance. The play takes pains to alleviate the love affair's political implications and portrays both the emperor and the consort in a positive light, emphasizing their adamant commitment to love and thus elevating private over public responsibilities.

Palace reevaluates the two famous historical characters against a new standard—that is, loyalty to romantic love. While the consort is conventionally deemed a femme fatale in history, *Palace*, in the voice of the local Earth God (Tudi shen), praises her as someone who is "martyred for the country" (*weiguo juanqu*) [*CSD* 150]. The deity further explains that it is "the heroic beauty's generous sacrifice of her life" (*kangkai jiaren jiang nan qing fu*) that ensured the emperor's safety [*CSD* 150]. In scene 33, her death, according to the Earth God, won the people's heart for the emperor and made the eventual revival of the dynasty possible. By highlighting the positive impact of Yang's death on the political situation, the play validates the significance of love. It is, after all, the consort's steadfast devotion to the emperor that makes her willing to meet her death. Love, in other words, is the source of political loyalty and heroism.

The heavenly judgment of the emperor's conduct is hardly concerned with his failure as a ruler. His inability to prioritize his responsibilities for the state over personal and emotional needs leads to the outbreak of the rebellion, which takes a great toll on the state and its subjects. In scene 44, acting as the judge of the emperor, the Weaving Maid in the Moon Palace refers to him as Li Sanlang (literally "third son of the Li family"), a nickname denoting intimacy and devoid of any deferential overtones. She attributes Yang's undeserved death to Li's "giving up their love lightly and breaking his vows first" (*qing qingduan shi xianhui*) and considers him "one of the heartless fickle men" (*boxing nan'er bei*) [*CHD* 195]. This observation turns out to be the play's most explicit criticism of the emperor—criticism that only targets Li's actions as a lover.

Yet, Li is soon forgiven even as a lover after the goddess's husband comes to his defense. The husband points out that the emperor did fight for Yang—even in the face of a national crisis—but the situation spun out of his control. The emperor was also deeply saddened by Yang's death and filled with regret. Thus, he deserves sympathy and forgiveness. The husband's reasoning convinces the Weaving Maiden of the emperor's devotion, so she immediately pardons him. Even though she recognizes the emperor's negligence of state affairs, credulity toward heinous people, and failure to heed good advice, the celestial judge lets love override duty. As such, the play clears the couple (especially the consort) from moral condemnation. They are not subjected to political remonstration as they have been in earlier versions of the story, but instead become the embodiment of eternal love.

Then who is to blame for the political upheaval? *Palace* adopts a binary characterization and attributes the social chaos to the antagonists in the play. An Lushan's rebellion is explained as being the combined result of his ungrateful and treacherous personality and Yang Guozhong's selfish quest for power. More important, the play considers the villains' viciousness and bad conduct nothing but a manifestation of their intrinsic evil. The Qing-dynasty scholar Wu Ren (b. 1647) commented on An Lushan's first appearance in scene 3, noting that the tune, sung by An himself, reveals his "domineering nature" (*bahu zhiben*).[13] An's evil nature is reinforced by his odd physique, to which the play makes repeated references. For example, An has such a large belly that it overhangs his knees. When the emperor asks him what the belly harbors, he responds: "Nothing but an innocent heart [full of loyalty to your majesty]" (*weiyou yipian chixin*) [*CSD* 20]. Traditional Chinese physiognomy considers features of physical appearance an index to one's personality, which explains the play's interest in the abnormal size of An's belly, a sign of his shameless obsequiousness. By demonizing those men, the potential blame for the emperor's failure to recognize villains, as voiced by Guo Congjin in scene 26, is downplayed significantly.

12.6 PEACH BLOSSOM FAN AND PALACE OF EVERLASTING LIFE: PERFORMANCE AS MEDIATED HISTORY

Both of these plays express their playwright's reflection on history, and both are self-reflexive, in that they contain retellings of the events depicted by the characters in the play. *Fan*, in particular, is said to be "the only play in the Chinese tradition to turn both history and the interpretation of history into part of the dramatic presentation," which emphasizes the presence of critical voices in the play that are generally not found in other historical plays.[14] In both cases, a character's narration of the past—a past within which he or she was a participant—accords with the playwright's attitude toward the related historical events. Interestingly, both plays assign the roles of the self-reflexive narrator to the professional entertainers in the story. In so doing, Kong Shangren and Hong Sheng draw an analogy between the storytelling of the past by performers in the play and their own storytelling of history in the form of song-drama.

At the end of *Fan*, Su Kunsheng and Liu Jingting are given the opportunity to recount what happened during the establishment and destruction of the Southern Ming court. Liu Jingting has turned into a fisherman who "weaves old stories about the rise and fall of the dynasty into idle talks about love" (*ba xie xingwang jiushi, fu zhi fengyue xiantan*) and Su Kunsheng, now a woodcutter, claims to have his "belly stuffed with the unofficial history of the Southern Dynasty" (*mandu nanchao yeshi*) [*THS* 255]. When they meet again in the mountains (sequel to scene 40), Liu Jingting performs a *tanci* ballad, summarizing the political situation of the late Ming. Following Liu's ballad, Su Kunsheng sings a set of northern tunes entitled "Mourning for Jiangnan" ("Ai Jiangnan"), which portray the deterioration of Nanjing after the fall of the Southern Ming. The set concludes: "The fragmented dream in the mountain feels most realistic. It is hard to get the past off one's mind. It is hard to believe the territorial map has already changed" [*THS* 260]. Reflecting on the recent changes, Su articulates the struggles of being caught between past and present, memory and reality. We can surmise that this discomfort was shared not only by recluses such as Liu Jingting, but also by those who had taken refuge in religion, such as Hou and Li.[15] Such emotional attachment to the past and denial of the new reality renders the storytelling of the "unofficial history of the Southern Dynasty" a kind of mediated history.

Similarly, in *Palace*, not only is the court musician Li Guinian given the voice to reconstruct the past, but his account of the past is also mediated in nature. In scene 38, in a performance of a string ballad named "Neglected Stories of the Tianbao Reign" ("Tianbao yishi"), Li recounts the imperial romance for the benefit of the commoners on the street. The reason behind Hong Sheng's choice of Li as the storyteller is twofold. First, as the leading court musician, Li learns the score of *The Rainbow Skirts* directly from the consort's maids. He thus belongs to a musical genealogy that can be traced to the consort, and ultimately to the Moon Goddess. At the consort's birthday banquet in scene 16, Li Guinian leads court musicians to play *The Rainbow Skirts*: he is joined by the emperor, who keeps the beat on the drum, while the consort dances on a jade plate. Li Guinian's role in this performance—one that marks the completion of Yang's re-creation of the celestial performance—renders him not only a witness, but a participant in and an embodiment of history. Second, Li Guiniang's string-ballad performance—which is depicted in an entire scene—forms an analogy to the playwright's own dramatization of the

Li-Yang love story, just like the one discussed previously in *Fan*. While Li Guinian's performance serves to transmit *The Rainbow Skirts* and the imperial romance, the play of *Palace* is yet another attempt of the telling and retelling in the long history of the Li-Yang love story.

Li Guinian's account of the past—encapsulated by the "Neglected Stories of the Tianbao Reign"—is mediated and personal: It is a story narrated from a third-person point of view, yet prominently marked by the narrator's feelings and personal experiences:

（末）	ADDITIONAL MALE *as* LI GUINIAN [*sings*]:
【梁州第七】	*To the tune* "Liangzhou diqi"
可哀落魄，	How pitiful my dire straits!
只得把霓裳御譜沿街賣，	I have no choice but to peddle the imperial score of *The Rainbow Skirts* on the street.
有誰人喝聲采？	Yet is there anyone to applaud and cheer for my performance?

[*CSD* 171, scene 38, "String Ballad" ("Tanci")]

Having gone from prestigious court musician to itinerant street singer in the distant Jiangnan area, Li imbues his version of the story with deep sorrow at his own unfortunate fate. For him, the past most immediately signifies his personal glorious feats. *The Rainbow Skirts'* falling into obscurity and lack of appreciation is even more striking than his personal plight.

As a witness to and participant from the past, Li Guinian's narrative is emotional and one-sided, thus open to opposition and criticism. Although only a very brief account, it engenders a spectrum of varied responses from the audience members present at Li's performance. An old man in the role of older mandarin, representing the orthodox school of thought, considers Yang a femme fatale while protesting Li Guinian's aestheticization of her relationship with the emperor. He regrets that the consort caused the emperor to neglect state affairs, which caused the disastrous rebellion. Another kind of voice embodied by Li Mo, the scholar-flautist, is both sympathetic to the story that Li Guinian tells and appreciative of the musician's talent and skills. For Li Mo, the past is an aestheticized object of admiration and emulation and the consort is the embodiment of this past. Determined to protect this embodiment from being tarnished, he convinces the old man that the rebellion resulted from the emperor's appointing the wrong frontier general and entrusting a treacherous minister with power, thus holding the emperor responsible for the disturbances. These two opposite views among the audience complicate the musician's version of history, just as Su Kunsheng's and Liu Jingting's dual accounts of the past in *Fan* call each other into question.

To further complicate the matter of how the past is interpreted, Hong Sheng depicts a type of audience that is simply ignorant about musical performance and, more important, indifferent to the past and uninterested in learning about it. A sojourning merchant in the audience tries to appreciate the imperial music master's performance only by comparing it to a form of local folk music. Attempting to imagine the consort's beauty, he refers to an old prostitute for a point of comparison, and he even makes a bawdy joke about being aroused by the amorous story. Both he and an old prostitute could not wait to hurry off to enjoy "drinking some strong alcohol and eating garlic buns" [*CSD* 175] at the end of Li's performance. The lower-class audience's sole interest in satisfying their appetite for strong-flavored food and drink encapsulates the utmost indifference to sophisticated musical skills and tragic romance. While it is true that the merchant (in the role of old man) and the prostitute (in the role of clown) are meant as comic relief, these two characters have larger implications. The misunderstanding, ignorance, vulgarity, and utter apathy that they demonstrate highlight in a dramatic manner the complexity involved in the process of remembering history. In the end, it is the appreciative voice that prevails, as it represents the play's lyricized vision of the tragic love affair.

CONCLUSION

Through *Fan* and *Palace*, two plays, which were completed within eleven years of each other and both engaged with the theme of romance in history, this chapter begins by questioning the representation of history in *chuanqi* drama. Due to the prominence of the theme of performance in both plays, the discussion looks at how this theme figures in the presentation of romance and history. Both plays intend to offer an alternative narrative of history. *Fan* is concerned with drawing a moral and political lesson from the recent past—part of the lesson being the danger of emotionality and indulgence in passion. By contrast, *Palace* celebrates the power of love by presenting an aestheticized and depoliticized version of the distant past. Accordingly, performance as an expression of love is ultimately shown to be ineffective in *Fan*, which highlights its validity and power as a medium of political remonstration. In *Palace*, performance of music not only communicates love, it also becomes the embodiment of love and proof of love's eternity. Despite those differences, both plays feature performances that recapture and reflect on the events being depicted. Those examples of performance-within-a-play call attention to the mediated nature of the presentation of history, which suggests a possible analogy between themselves and historical *chuanqi* plays as a kind of alternative history.

Mengjun Li and Guo Yingde

NOTES

1. For examples of Japanese plays engaging with this topic, see Satoko Shimazaki, "Fantastic Histories: The Battles of Coxinga and the Preservation of Ming in Japan," *Frontiers of Literary Studies in China* 9, no. 1 (2015): 17–53. For examples in the Netherlands, see Paize Keulemans, "Tales of an Open World: The Fall of the Ming Dynasty as Dutch Tragedy, Chinese Gossip, and Global News," *Frontiers of Literary Studies in China* 9, no. 2 (2015): 190–234.

2. A city of strategic importance and enormous wealth, Yangzhou carries a special weight in the history of the Ming-Qing transition. For instance, it was where the upright Ming official Shi Kefa

(1601–1645) committed suicide upon the arrival of the Manchu troops in May 1645; Shi's refusal to open the city gates to the Manchu troops led to a disastrous ten-day massacre, known as the Yangzhou Massacre.

3. Both *Pavilion of Deep Fragrance* and *Dancing to the Rainbow Skirts* were staged in Hong Sheng's time, but both are unfortunately lost to us.

4. Lynn A. Struve, "History and *The Peach Blossom Fan*," *Chinese Literature: Essays, Articles, Reviews* 2, no. 1 (1980): 57.

5. In *Fan*, Kong Shangren articulates that his aim was to "express thoughts derived from the rise and fall of an empire through a story of meeting and separation of a couple" [*THS* 1]. This chapter is mainly based on two modern reprints of the *Fan* and *Palace*: Hong Sheng, *Changsheng dian* (The Palace of Everlasting Life), ann. Xu Shuofang (Beijing: Renmin wenxue chubanshe, 1998) and Kong Shangren, *Taohua shan*, ann. Wang Jisi and Su Huanzhong (Beijing: Renmin wenxue chubanshe, 1961). All references will be to the latter edition unless otherwise noted. All translations of *Fan* and *Palace* are mine [MJL]. I consulted two existing complete translations of these two plays: *The Peach Blossom Fan*, trans. Shih-hsiang Chen and Harold Acton with Cyril Birch, reprinted with a new introduction by Judith Zeitlin (New York: New York Review Books, 2015); and *The Palace of Everlasting Life*, trans. Yang Xianyi and Gladys Yang (Beijing: Foreign Language Press, 1995).

6. For scholarly discussions on the "cult of *qing*," see Wm. Theodore de Bary, "Individualism and Humanitarianism in Late Ming Thought," *Self and Society in Ming Thought*, ed. Wm. Theodore de Bary, 145–247 (New York: Columbia University Press, 1970); Maram Epstein, *Competing Discourses: Orthodoxy, Authenticity, and Engendered Meanings in Late Imperial Chinese Fiction* (Cambridge, MA: Harvard University Asia Center, 2001); and Martin W. Huang, *Desire and Fictional Narrative in Late Imperial China* (Cambridge, MA: Harvard University Asia Center, 2001).

7. Hong Sheng mentions that Prime Minister Liang Qingbiao (1620–1691) touted *Palace* using this phrase in his preface (*liyan*) to the play [*CSD* 1].

8. In previous factional struggles at the Ming court, Wei ruthlessly persecuted members of the reformist Eastern Grove Party. Because the Restoration Society saw itself as the successor to the Eastern Grove Party, its members considered Ruan an enemy.

9. See comments in the upper margin in Hong Sheng, *Changsheng dian* (The Palace of Everlasting Life), in *Zhongguo shida gudian beiju ji* (Collection of Ten Great Classical Tragedies from China), ed. Wang Jisi (Shanghai: Shanghai wenyi chubanshe, 1982), vol. 2, 643.

10. Legend has it that an ancient emperor of the state of Shu transformed into a cuckoo after his death. The bird is said to cry sadly all the time, until blood comes out of its mouth, because of the emperor's longing for his country and his subjects.

11. The first scene of a *chuanqi* play is usually devoted to introducing the male lead. Liu Jingting's prominence in this scene indicates that this character's significance is comparable to the male lead in *Fan*.

12. This claim is not true historically; Liu Jingting was a renowned professional storyteller in real life.

13. See Hong, *Changsheng dian*, 617, the upper margin. Wu Ren's literary name is Shufu, and he is also known as Wu Wushan.

14. The critical voices in *Fan* are represented by liminal characters such as the Master of Ceremonies, Liu Jingting, and Su Kunsheng, who move in and out of the dramatic illusion and who are both actors and interpreters. Wai-yee Li, "The Representation of History in *The Peach Blossom Fan*," *Journal of the American Oriental Society* 115, no. 3 (1995): 421.

15. It is worth noting that historically, Hou Fangyu took the civil service examination under the Qing and regretted that later in his life.

PRIMARY SOURCES

CSD   Hong Sheng. *Changsheng dian* 長生殿 (*Palace of Everlasting Life*). Ann. Xu Shuofang 徐朔方. Beijing: Renmin wenxue chubanshe, 1998.

THS   Kong Shangren 孔尚任. *Taohua shan* 桃花扇 (*The Peach Blossom Fan*). Ann. Wang Jisi 王季思 and Su Huanzhong 蘇寰中. Beijing: Renmin wenxue chuban she, 1961.

SUGGESTED READINGS

TRANSLATIONS

Kong Shangren. *The Peach Blossom Fan*. Trans. Shih-hsiang Chen and Harold Acton with Cyril Birch, reprinted with a new introduction by Judith Zeitlin. New York: New York Review Books, 2015.

Hong Sheng. *The Palace of Everlasting Life*. Trans. Yang Xianyi and Gladys Yang. Beijing: Foreign Language Press, 1995.

ENGLISH

Li, Wai-yee. "The Representation of History in *The Peach Blossom Fan*." *Journal of the American Oriental Society* 115, no. 3 (1995): 421–433.

Lu, Tina. *Persons, Roles, and Minds: Identity in* Peony Pavilion *and* Peach Blossom Fan. Stanford, CA: Stanford University Press, 2001.

Sibau, Maria Franca. "Maids, Fishermen, and Storytellers: Rewriting Marginal Characters in Early Qing Drama and Fiction." *CHINOPERL* 35, no. 1 (2016): 1–27.

Strassberg, Richard E. *The World of K'ung Shang-jen—A Man of Letters in Early Ch'ing China*. New York: Columbia University Press, 1983.

Struve, Lynn A. "History and *The Peach Blossom Fan*." *Chinese Literature: Essays, Articles, Reviews* 2, no. 1 (1980): 55–72.

Zeitlin, Judith. "Music and Performance in Hong Sheng's *Palace of Lasting Life*." In *Trauma and Transcendence in Chinese Literature*, ed. Wilt L. Idema, Wai-yee Li, and Ellen Widmer, 456–487. Cambridge, MA: Harvard University Asia Center, 2006.

CHINESE

Chen Wannai 陳萬鼐. *Kong Shangren yanjiu* 孔尚任研究 (*A Study of Kong Shangren*). Taipei: Shangwu yinshuguan, 1971.

Hong Sheng 洪昇 (1645–1704). *Changsheng dian* 長生殿 (*Palace of Everlasting Life*). In *Zhongguo shida gudian beiju ji* 中國十大古典悲劇集 (*Collection of Ten Great Classical Tragedies from China*), ed. Wang Jisi 王季思. 2 vols. Shanghai: Shanghai wenyi chubanshe, 1982.

Meng Fanshu 孟繁樹. *Hong Sheng ji Changsheng dian yanjiu* 洪昇及《長生殿》研究 (*A Study of Hong Sheng and* Palace of Everlasting Life). Beijing: Zhongguo xiju chubanshe, 1985.

Wang Shih-pe 汪詩珮. "Zhuiyi, jiyi, yinyu: *Taohua shan* zhong de 'Zuozhe qiren'" 追憶，記憶，隱喻：《桃花扇》中的"作者七人" (Recollection, Memory, and Metaphor: The "Seven People Who Acted" in *Peach Blossom Fan*). *Xiju yanjiu* 戲劇研究 (*Journal of Theater Studies*) 19 (2017): 1–50.

Wang Yongjian 王永健. *Hong Sheng he Changsheng dian* 洪昇和長生殿 (*Hong Sheng and* Palace of Everlasting Life). Shanghai: Shanghai guji chubanshe, 1982.

Yuan Shishuo 袁世碩. *Kong Shangren nianpu* 孔尚任年譜 (*An Annalistic Biography of Kong Shangren*). Jinan, China: Qilu shushe, 1987.

PART III

Mid–Qing Dynasty

Zaju and *Chuanqi* Plays

13

Song of Dragon Well Tea and Other Court Plays

Stage Directions, Spectacle, and Panegyrics

Theatrical performances had long been part of Chinese court culture. The Office of Music Instruction (*Jiaofang si*) in charge of songs and theater for court performances was set up as early as the Tang dynasty (618–906). The Xuanzong emperor of the Tang (r. 712–756), whose romance with the Precious Consort Yang was depicted in *Palace of Everlasting Life* (🖝 chap. 12), established the famous Pear Garden (*liyuan*) conservatory for the training of musicians and dancers in his court.[1] Theater continued to flourish in the palace in later dynasties owing to the patronage of the imperial house, initially as short skits sandwiched among a number of other court entertainments such as dances and acrobatics, and later in the Ming and Qing dynasties as longer plays with more complex stories and full librettos.

Chinese court theater reached its height, in terms of scale and resources mobilized, in the Qing dynasty, particularly during the reign of the Qianlong emperor (r. 1736–1795). Drama was used for political and ritual purposes, as well as for entertainment. Performances took place on occasions such as imperial birthdays, weddings, state rituals, and seasonal festivals in the Qing court. The resulting plays are commonly referred to as "plays composed to answer an imperial order or official demand" (*chengying xi*).[2] These plays tend to be highly functional. As the modern drama scholar William Dolby aptly summarized, "the themes of the court plays suited the propaganda, self-confirmatory and entertainment purposes of the emperor."[3] The Qianlong court was especially well known for its extravagant theatrical productions, supported by official institutions in charge of drama, vast number of court musicians and performers, and grand theater stages.[4] The resulting form of theater was visually pleasing, with elaborate props, marvelous stage machinery, and exquisite costumes, and filled with spectacular features to impress and entertain the emperor and the imperial family. Traditionally, much scholarly attention has been devoted to the stagecraft and performance aspects of Chinese court theater. As a result, court plays are often perceived to lack literary value and thus are routinely ignored by scholars of Chinese literature.

Yet we should recognize that "court theater" is a generic term that comprises multiple forms of drama associated with courtly occasions. Textually, these court plays are rich, diverse, and complex. Abundant texts in varied forms were generated in the process of Chinese court theatrical productions: fully written-out copies submitted for censors' review; instructional texts used by performers; promptbooks or production notes to facilitate stage management; archived copies to serve as templates in preparation for future performances; and high-quality versions for reading purposes, in exquisite, handwritten manuscripts—or, less commonly, in printed editions, occasionally even in lavishly produced, multicolored versions presenting the various features (title, tune patterns, stage directions) of the drama texts in up to five colors.[5]

Reading these court entertainment texts presents several challenges, with which this chapter aims to engage. Our mode of reading Chinese dramatic texts in literary history has been very much guided by the conventions of canonical literati plays, such as those written by the famous writers Tang Xianzu (1550–1616) (☛ chap. 9) and Kong Shangren (1648–1718) (☛ chap. 12). Accordingly, modern histories of Chinese dramatic literature (*xiqu wenxue shi*) have often focused on the self-expression and literary merit of such literati-authored works. In contrast, we will see in this chapter that court theater presents a rather different literary world, one that was largely anonymous, in which individualized authorship is either unknown or at times generically attributed to the official in charge of overseeing the theatrical production rather than the creator of the actual literary text. Court plays typically were not created for self-expression, but primarily to fulfill the occasional, social, and ritual needs of the imperial house. Applying the same principles of literary aesthetics developed for literati plays to court entertainment texts is therefore mistaken. A fuller appreciation of Chinese court plays requires us to consider their functionalities, the specific occasions for which they were produced, and the performative and literary aspects displayed in these texts.

To illustrate the potential ways of reading court dramatic texts, we will look at one particular form of court drama, with a well-documented history of having printed reading texts and, in some cases, even records of individual authorship. This type of court drama resulted from the occasional need to provide playtexts for court imperial entertainment beyond the compounds of the imperial palace, such as when the sovereign was on tour. Like the custom of Queen Elizabeth I (r. 1558–1603) to go on royal progresses to the countryside in Tudor England, the Qianlong emperor's southern tours were distinctive features of his long reign in eighteenth-century China. He carried out a total of six such tours, in 1751, 1757, 1762, 1765, 1780, and 1784.[6] These were well-orchestrated political spectacles, with Qianlong performing a wide range of official duties and tasks, including inspecting hydraulic infrastructure, observing local customs, and interacting with the populace. During these extended tours, the sovereign was usually offered theatrical entertainment by his hosts at various stops along the way. This led to a form of local production of court drama in Qing China in which new, imperial theatrical entertainment had to be prepared by the local officials and hosts who sourced their so-called court playwrights locally.

For example, on the occasion of the first southern visit of the Qianlong emperor in 1751, Li E (1692–1752, *juren* 1720) and Wu Cheng (1701–1772) wrote two plays that were collectively titled *New Songs to Welcome His Majesty* (*Yingluan xinqu*).[7] Such plays performed outside the capital in southern China were often referred to as "plays to welcome His Majesty" (*yingluan xi*). In what I call "local court drama," we begin to see not only more visibly named authorship associated with the texts produced, but also diverse modes of aesthetics and dramatic representation. The set of court plays we are going to discuss in detail here is a particularly interesting example of this tradition.

13.1 CONTEXTUALIZING WANG WENZHI'S COURT DRAMA

In 1780, during the fifth southern tour of the Qianlong emperor to Hangzhou, an elite writer and retired official named Wang Wenzhi (1730–1802, *jinshi* 1760) was commissioned to compose nine plays for the occasion. In his *Notes on Songs* (*Quhua*), Liang Tingnan (1796–1861), an influential historian, dramatist, and scholar-official, gave an informative account of the context behind the production of these plays in which his uncle, Liang Sen (fl. 1770s), was involved. The tone of the passage cited here is noteworthy too, as it very vividly captures and engages with a series of literary tropes and ideals of governance and sovereignty commonly found in the court theatrical tradition:

> During the Qianlong reign, when His Majesty made his fifth visit to the south, my uncle Liang Sen was serving as an official in Central Zhejiang and received an assignment to dutifully undertake the task of organizing theatrical performance and elegant music [for the visit]. An order was issued in advance and a hefty sum was paid to engage the Junior Compiler Wang Wenzhi (*hao* Menglou) in composing nine new plays, all of which were written based on the local topography and scenery. These nine plays are respectively titled *Sannong deshu* (*The Three Harvests Receive Timely Rain*), *Longjing chage* (*Song of Dragon Well Tea*), *Xiangzheng bingjian* (*Auspicious Signs of Icy Silkworm Cocoons*), *Haiyu ge'en* (*Songs of Grace within the Seas*), *Dengran fajie* (*Lantern Lights in the Dharma-world*), *Geling danlu* (*Elixir Furnace at Geling Hill*), *Xianyun yanling* (*Immortal Wine to Extend Life*), *Ruixian Tiantai* (*Lucky Omens at Mount Tiantai*), and *Yingbo qingyan* (*Fairy Waves Clear and Peaceful*). Performers with the best skills were selected to play [the roles] and the plays were offered at the Temporary Palace at West Lake. Before each act was performed, a copy was first bound with yellow silk and respectfully presented for the viewing of His Majesty. These theatrical productions always received praise and rewards, and such bestowals were frequent. Nowadays when these "dharma tunes" (*faqu*)[8] are once again performed, we can still look up to the old times when the seas were peaceful, people were happy, and products were bountiful. The seventy-year-old Son-of-Heaven inspected the region to find out about local customs. Among the mulberry and hemp fields, His Majesty shared joys with the common people. Such airs of harmony and peace are rarely seen in a thousand years. This was truly a grand ceremony.
>
> [QH 265]

The nine plays that were created noticeably featured multiple felicitous messages (e.g., *Auspicious Signs of Icy Silkworm Cocoons*; *Lucky Omens at Mount Tiantai*) and blessings, such as for longevity (e.g., *Elixir Furnace at Geling Hill*, *Immortal Wine to Extend Life*), which were emblematic of the court dramatic style. The overall thematic scope of these plays was also tied closely to imperial ideology, showing a strong emphasis on building an image of a glorious and peaceful age through these dramatic representations—one that allowed people to "still look up to the old times when the seas were peaceful, people were happy, and products were bountiful." The concluding lines of Liang's account are particularly revealing about the interactions that these court dramas aimed to capture between the court and the local region, and also between the emperor and the common people. "To find out about local customs" fits with and reiterates the scheme and purpose of Qianlong's southern tours: "His Majesty shared joys with the common people" echoes and reenacts an ideal of kingship—a true and virtuous ruler shares his pleasure with his people, as discussed in *Mengzi* (1A.2, 1B.1, 1B.4).

13.2 WANG WENZHI'S AUTHORSHIP OF COURT DRAMA

It is worth noting that these were new plays, commissioned specifically for the occasion. In Liang's account, we are told that the local official engaged an elite scholar named Wang Wenzhi to carry out the task. This is very different from the common mode of production of dramatic entertainment in the palace, which was executed by an anonymous team and undertaken by the imperial theatrical institutions. The writer chosen for the task also merits special attention. This is no ordinary man or lowly playwright that one may usually associate with court entertainment. Perhaps better known as a poet and calligrapher[9] than as a dramatist, Wang Wenzhi was a member of the top national elite and highly successful (ranked third, *tanhua*) in the civil examination in 1760. Wang was first appointed junior compiler (*bianxiu*) and then promoted to reader-in-waiting (*shidu*) in the Hanlin Academy in the capital, where those who passed the civil examination with highest honors received training to reach the pinnacle of the political world. Wang later became the prefect of Lin'an in Yunnan. After retirement, one of his major hobbies was to maintain a private drama troupe for his own enjoyment. He frequently hosted theatrical performances in his residence for his friends, and even took his actors along on his travels.[10] Wang also participated actively in other drama activities in literati circles. For example, he wrote commentaries for literati friends and major playwrights such as Jiang Shiquan (1725–1785, *jinshi* 1757) and assisted his friend Ye Tang (1724?–1799?) in editing a significant anthology of musical arias in 1792 (☞ chap. 8).

In contrast to his fellow literati playwrights, however, Wang Wenzhi appears to have played a more active role than was typical for such court dramatic productions. One may not want to go as far as to call Wang a court playwright, but it is noteworthy that the nine plays produced on this occasion of Qianlong emperor's southern tour remain Wang's only extant dramatic works, and he was not known to have composed other plays in noncourt contexts. Another point of note in Liang Tingnan's account is that Wang was given a substantial monetary reward for the plays. We know of a few instances of imperial or regional patronage of literati playwrights, but it is rare to find financial transactions concerning their playwriting work explicitly mentioned. The fact that Wang Wenzhi was paid "a hefty sum" for composing these court plays and that he was very much a playwright-for-hire on this occasion again reminds us of the diverse and complex modes of playwriting, patronage, and authorship in the late imperial Chinese theatrical world.

13.3 TEXTS AND FUNCTIONS OF WANG WENZHI'S COURT DRAMA

In his colophon to the plays, Liang Sen, the official behind the orchestration of this court drama production in Hangzhou, provided additional information on subsequent circulation of the plays at the end of the emperor's southern tour: after sending off His Majesty, Liang Sen's friends copied the texts and committed them to print [*FXH* 63.499].[11] The full set of nine plays currently survives in at least three Qing dynasty editions: two stand-alone print editions (one of which was printed by Liang Tingnan) and the other as part of an anthology. Not sharing a common title among the various editions, the set of plays are alternately referred to as *New Songs to Welcome His Majesty* (*Yingluan xinqu*),[12] *Yuefu Songs to Welcome His Majesty in Zhejiang* (*Zhejiang yingluan yuefu*), or *Ci Lyrics to Welcome His Majesty in Zhejiang* (*Zhejiang yingluan ci*).[13] The nine plays are very short, each consisting of only a single act. Written in the style and tradition of court drama, they serve as a functional text for the occasion and are filled with panegyrics as well as visual spectacles.

List of plays in *FXH* edition	Title of the play (title in English translation)
#1. 《三農得澍》	*Sannong deshu* (*The Three Harvests Receive Timely Rain*)
#2. 《龍井茶歌》	*Longjing chage* (*Song of Dragon Well Tea*)
#3. 《祥徵冰繭》	*Xiangzheng bingjian* (*Auspicious Signs of Icy Silkworm Cocoons*)
#4. 《海宇歌恩》	*Haiyu ge'en* (*Songs of Grace within the Seas*)
#5. 《燈燃法界》	*Dengran fajie* (*Lantern Lights in the Dharma-world*)
#6. 《葛嶺丹爐》	*Geling danlu* (*Elixir Furnace at Geling Hill*)
#7. 《仙醞延齡》	*Xianyun yanling* (*Immortal Wine to Extend Life*)
#8. 《瑞獻天台》	*Ruixian Tiantai* (*Lucky Omens at Mount Tiantai*)
#9. 《瀛波清宴》	*Yingbo qingyan* (*Fairy Waves Clear and Peaceful*)

Interestingly, of these nine plays, four also appear as a separate set in a manuscript copy titled *Raising Silkworms* (*Sican ji*, hereafter *SCJ*). Several characteristics of the format of *SCJ* indicate that it might be a palace manuscript copy or one produced with this tradition in mind. For instance, all references to and words related to the emperor or imperial grace are raised to the top margin at the start of the next column of a vertical line of text, and all arias and prose dialogues are subsequently indented (i.e., positioned lower vertically) by two Chinese characters. In contrast, the printed editions of Wang's plays published and circulated outside the palace (e.g., *FXH*) do not reflect this practice. The observance of such a deferential typographic arrangement in the manuscript version suggests that these four plays might have been performed (or were intended to be performed) in the imperial palace in Beijing as well.

Furthermore, it is noteworthy that as indicated on its contents page, the four plays included in *SCJ* were arranged in a different order from that seen in the *FXH* edition with the complete set of nine plays:

Order in *SCJ* edition	Title of the play as on the contents page of *SCJ*	Order in *FXH* edition
1.	*Haiyu ge* (*Songs within the Seas*) [sic *Haiyu ge'en* (*Songs of Grace within the Seas*)][14]	#4《海宇歌恩》
2.	*Sannong deshu* (*The Three Harvests Receive Timely Rain*)	#1《三農得澍》
3.	*Geling danlu* (*Elixir Furnace at Geling Hill*)	#6《葛嶺丹爐》
4.	*Xiangzheng bingjian* (*Auspicious Signs of Icy Silkworm Cocoons*)	#3《祥徵冰繭》

No explanations were given as to why only four plays were included in this edition or why they followed a different sequential order, but such differences suggest that Wang Wenzhi's nine plays need not be considered as a fixed set to be performed (or necessarily even read) in its entirety or in a given order. Rather, they appear to be a group of nine plays that could be adapted for performance in various forms, either in whole or in part.

One may also speculate why only four of the nine plays (plays #1, #3, #4, and #6 in the *FXH* edition)[15] were selected for the palace manuscript version of *SCJ*. If printed editions of Wang Wenzhi's set of plays such as the set reprinted in *FXH* were produced with readers in mind, the palace manuscript version was almost certainly prepared for the purpose of court performance. It is interesting to note that play #2, *Song of Dragon Well Tea*, which is textually one of the most engaging plays in the set, was not included in the palace manuscript. This reminds us to consider how these court plays, even within the same set, may display varying qualities and degrees of suitability for different functions and occasions: some rely more on visual effects onstage, while others demand closer engagement with literary tropes and rhetorical strategies that are more appropriate to reading the play than just watching it being performed.

13.4 IN PRAISE OF THE OCCASION AND HIS MAJESTY: FUNCTIONALITIES OF COURT PLAYS

Those in charge of arranging performances of court drama were very clear about how to match theatrical programs with the needs of particular audiences and occasions because that was a main concern. Court playtexts themselves often indicate the event that gave rise to their initial performance and could later be modified to fit different audiences.[16] Wang Wenzhi repeatedly referenced the specific occasion for which his plays were written. For instance, play #7, *Immortal Wine to Extend Life*, begins with the following scene:

吾仙赤松子、　　　[IMMORTAL CHISONGZI *speaks*]: I am immortal Chisongzi;

吾仙張道齡、　　　[IMMORTAL ZHANG DAOLING *speaks*]: I am the immortal Zhang Daoling;

吾仙許邁，　　　[IMMORTAL XU MAI *speaks*]: I am immortal Xu Mai.

恭逢聖主五次南巡，萬靈呵護。[17] 吾仙籍隸杭州，敬向西湖虔迎法駕。　　　[*All three speak together*]: Respectfully, on the occasion of His Majesty's fifth southern tour, myriad deities guard and protect [His Majesty's arrival]. In the immortal register we belong to Hangzhou Prefecture and we hereby solemnly make our way to West Lake to piously welcome His Majesty's carriage.

[*FXH* 63.463]

Here, we see that the specific occasion—His Majesty's fifth tour to the south, in 1780—is visibly embedded in the text and explicitly celebrated.[18]

To create a grand spectacle befitting the imperial visit, these plays were embellished with large group scenes, multiple dramatis personae (many of whom are immortals or divine figures often accompanied by their attendants) and grand entrances of large groups of performers at once (e.g., twelve farmers in this play, some with rice carts and full bags celebrating a good harvest [*FXH* 63.471]). In addition, these local court dramas are designed around local scenery and folklore (e.g., local deities from Hangzhou). These figures gather either to welcome His Majesty or in preparation of the sovereign's imminent arrival. For example, in a scene in play #1, *The Three Harvests Receive Timely Rain*, we are told that the Dragon King in charge of the Eastern Sea (who would be in charge of local rainfall) has made his way to the Qiantang River, famous for its tidal bores generated by the funnel-shaped Hangzhou Bay, to prepare for the arrival of the emperor [*FXH* 63.386].

The plays also made full use of almost every opportunity to extol His Majesty's wide-ranging accomplishments.[19] Recurrent themes include timely rain for a bountiful harvest for the farmers,[20] peaceful times for the populace, and smooth seas for sailors. At first, these blessings appear to spring from the good deeds of the local deities, but later they are revealed to have been carried out under imperial command, thereby attributing them to His Majesty's benevolence.

Singing the praises of the emperor in Wang's play is at times even more overt. A good example of this type of panegyric is found in a scene in play #4, *Songs of Grace within the Seas*, where the Dragon Kings of the four quarters are invited to give a full account of the plenteous virtue and enormous achievements (*shengde daye*) of the emperor, who is eulogized as the Great Sage (*da shengren*), very much presenting the Qianlong emperor in the mold of an ideal, sage Confucian ruler. The Dragon Kings then go to great lengths to list His Majesty's multiple good qualities—namely, virtue (*de*); merit (*gong*); civil (*wen*) and martial (*wu*) talent; benevolence (*ren*); and filial piety (*xiao*) [*FXH* 63.430–433].

Such a direct and explicit approach to glorification may be one of the reasons why this play was placed first in the palace manuscript version. But lavish praise was not the only way to keep the emperor entertained. Wang Wenzhi also came up with several other ways to engage His Majesty in his court drama, both onstage and on the page.

13.5 PAGEANTRY, FORMULAIC SEQUENCES, AND VISUAL SPECTACLES

Qing court theater was filled with pageantry and spectacles, often presented in set dance routines or involving formulaic entrance and exit sequences. Wang Wenzhi's court plays very much followed this tradition. He created pageants with an aim of representing the loyalty and respect of "all under Heaven" (*tianxia*) for the emperor by introducing dramatis personae coming from all four corners of the world and eight quarters of the universe to pay tribute to him [*FXH* 63.437]. The entrances of these deities and their entourages were often accompanied by dance sequences, as demonstrated in the following stage directions in play #6, *Elixir Furnace at Geling Hill*:

（扮四青鸞、四白鶴上，繞場飛舞下；扮青龍、白虎、朱雀、元武四天將引六丁六甲神跳舞上）

Costumed as four blue phoenixes and white cranes, [performers in unspecified role types] enter, dance as if they were flying, then exit; costumed as the Four Heavenly Generals, namely Green Dragon, White Tiger, Vermilion Bird, and Dark[21] Turtle, [performers in unspecified role types] enter, leading the deities of the six Maidens and the six Generals,[22] and perform a dance sequence.

[*FXH* 63.451]

One of the most striking and unusual visual elements of Qing court theater was the graphic formation of large, auspicious Chinese characters or phrases by actors on the stage. Abundant traces of such visual performances can be found in the extant Qing palace playtexts. Graphic charts named "character models" (*ziyang*) were used to keep track of the positions that individual actors had to take in the construction of the characters, and are often found in playtexts designed to include information on blocking (*paichang ben*). For example, the blocking version of an anonymous court play titled *Auspicious Signs Celebrating Benevolence and Longevity* (*Xiangzheng renshou*) includes stage directions instructing actors to form the Chinese characters *fu* (fortune) and *shou* (longevity) through their collective movements and positions onstage at specific moments of the play. Furthermore, it also includes as an addenda large outlines of these two characters, in which the names of the actors are written in at the position that each is supposed to take. Annotation is provided above each character, stating that it is to be formed by twenty-four "longevity" pageboys (*shoutong*) (see figure 13.1).[23] Some scripts also contain

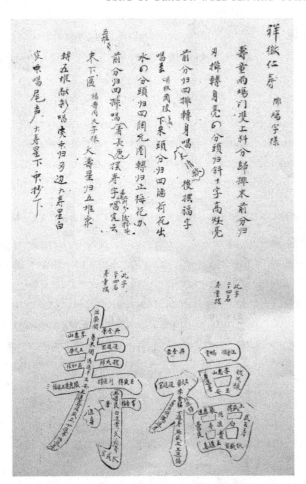

FIGURE 13.1 The character on the left means "longevity" (*shou*), which, according to the annotation in the small script above the character, is to be constituted by 24 pageboys; ditto for the character on the right, which means "fortune" (*fu*). From *Gugong zhenben congkan* (Collectanea of Precious Books from the Forbidden Palace) (Hainan: Hainan chubanshe, 2001), vol. 695, 146.

illustrations guiding actors to form other auspicious patterns, such as a bat[24] or a ligature composed of two *xi* characters signifying "double happiness."[25]

Apparently, a similar kind of pageantry characterized the theater performances orchestrated during Qianlong's southern tours. In the extant editions of Wang Wenzhi's drama, although they lack the kind of graphic markings or illustrations described here, they do contain very detailed stage directions. Recurrent stage directions using the basic formula of "*changshang she* [*XXX*]" (onstage, set up XXX) draw our attention to what was possibly meant to be the central attraction onstage. For example, play #4, *Songs of Grace within the Seas*, with a Buddhist theme, has stage directions requiring a replica of Mt. Sumeru, the sacred mountain that stands at the center of the universe, to be placed onstage [*FXH* 63.429]. In play #5, *Lantern Lights in the Dharma-world*, the stage directions describe a pagoda illuminated by lanterns being set up onstage [*FXH* 63.448]. The same play also concludes with the following stage directions:

（眾持燈排壽字緩下） *The many performers, holding lanterns in their hands, form the character "shou" (longevity), and gradually exit.*

[*FXH* 63.450]

This was very much in the style of graphic formation in court theatrical performances in the palace. For this kind of dramatic text, therefore, it is rewarding to pay close attention to the stage directions and use them as clues to imagine the visual spectacles intended to be part of the performance of the play.

13.6 ENGAGEMENT THROUGH LITERARY ELEMENTS

Given their strong emphasis on stage effects, court entertainment playtexts are not usually associated with the kind of literary qualities examined in earlier chapters in this volume. Nonetheless, in some court plays, especially those produced by literati writers in local regions to welcome His Majesty, one can find some examples where the playwright attempts to appeal to the emperor through literary means. For example, play #1, *The Three Harvests Receive Timely Rain*, cites a poem by the famous Song dynasty poet Su Shi (1037–1101), explicitly labeling it as a "poem by Su [Shi]" (☛ *HTRCP*, C13.2–3, C15.3):

翻翻聯聯銜尾鴉，	Flapping around and around, a flock of crows fly in sequence nose-to-tail,
犖犖确确蛻骨蛇。	Rugged and ragged, a snake in molting [reveals] its bones.
分疇翠浪走雲陣，	Paddy by paddy azure waves run [like] lines of clouds,
刺水綠針抽稻芽。	Pricking the water, green needles—rice shoots emerging.
西湖四月開桑麻，	At West Lake in the fourth month [the growing of] mulberry and hemp begin.
黿鳴窟中如打衙。	Calls of alligators from their caves are like the beating [of drums] at the Magistrate's Office.
天公憐我農人苦，	Lord of Heaven sympathizes with the hardship we farmers suffer,
喚取阿香推雷車。	He calls out Axiang to push the thunder cart.[26]

[*FXH* 63.382]

A closer reading, however, will reveal that Wang Wenzhi's citation is not quite the same as Su Shi's original poem. Important changes were made to two lines. Line 5 is completely changed from Su Shi's original, which reads: "At Dongting in the fifth month the sand is about to fly" (*Dongting wuyue yu fei sha* 洞庭五月欲飛沙 [*SSXJ* 80]). Wang silently modified the line, first by changing "Dongting Lake" to "West Lake" to match the locale of the emperor's visit, and also by altering the image of a drought-struck landscape, where the land is so dry that sand is about to fly, to fields of growing mulberry and hemp—a more upbeat image of burgeoning agricultural activity. This change in tone is even more striking in line 7. In the original poem, Su Shi complained about the Lord of Heaven "not seeing" the old man who was in tears (*Tiangong bujian laoweng qi* 天公不見老翁泣) because of the drought. Wang's rewrite transforms the line entirely, turning it into an affirmation and appreciation of the compassion of the Lord of Heaven (representing the emperor) toward the farmers—a more fitting stance for a celebratory court play.

Similarly, play #7, *Immortal Wine to Extend Life*, borrows from and also changes a poem by another well-known Song dynasty writer, Wang Anshi (1021–1086) [*FXH* 63.466]. While the Su Shi citation is marked in the text as a "poem by Su Shi" (*Su shi*), the latter is not explicitly labeled as a citation. One may read such intertextual relations between Wang's plays and the earlier poetic corpus as a kind of literary game, in which learned readers would have been expected to identify and engage with the original source and the changes made to it.[27]

In terms of engaging the reader through literary elements, the most interesting example among Wang Wenzhi's nine plays is play #2, *Song of Dragon Well Tea*. In quick succession, readers are introduced to a hodgepodge of Buddhist holy men (arhats), Daoist immortals, Buddhist monks, tea-picking men and women, tea-serving maids, and the Dragon King of Longjing and his daughters. A strong link is made between the characters in the play and the local region of Longjing (Dragon Well), an area southwest of West Lake renowned for its tea plantations. What may appear at first glance to be an assembly of random episodes turns out to be all part of a consciously constructed local tribute to the Qianlong emperor. For instance, the play begins with two arhats washing their alms bowls at the Dragon Well Pond. When Arhat Aṅgaja comes on stage, he delivers the customary self-introduction. But it quickly becomes clear why the playwright chose him to open the play: Arhat Aṅgaja introduces himself as originally numbered thirteenth among the sixteen arhats, but he was later redesignated as the first, a change initiated by none other than the Qianlong emperor himself. In 1757, during his second southern inspection tour, the Qianlong emperor visited the Shengyin Temple in Hangzhou where he was taken to view a set of Sixteen Arhats. He later renamed and reordered the images according to a scheme then popular in Tibet.[28]

In staging the sites associated with the Longjing area, the play not only presents its physical landscape, but also the textual space associated with this locale. For one, the playtext is filled with unmarked citations of poetic lines from earlier literary sources about West Lake. For another, a significant example of the use of famous sites in Longjing is Wisp of Cloud (Yipianyun), a rock named for its appearance. In the play, this locale is not only referred to by the actor in the play, but it is also actually staged as a physical object in the performance, as illustrated in the stage directions:

（場上設一片雲石，楊作見介）　*On the stage, set up the "Wisp of Cloud" rock. Yang acts out seeing it.*

[FXH 63.401]

In this scene, the Daoist immortal Yang Xi is strolling in the hills of the Long-jing region when he comes across the Wisp of Cloud. The visual dimension of such a stage property is not to be neglected, as it fits with the aesthetics of Chinese court theater, in its emphasis on creating spectacles onstage. Furthermore, specific aspects of the physical landscape being represented closely intersect with the literary space created in the play. Right after he sees the rock, Yang Xi then looks up and sees a poem written by the emperor, which he respectfully acknowledges and then reads aloud onstage [FXH 63.401]. The poem recited in the play is none other than an actual poem that had been written by the Qianlong emperor on this site during his previous visit in 1765.[29] Another of the emperor's poems, on brewing tea in Longjing, is also cited verbatim and introduced to the audience in the same manner in a later scene [FXH 63.408].[30]

It is perhaps not surprising that a prolific writer like the Qianlong emperor, who is known to have written more than 43,000 poems over the course of his life, also left behind a large corpus of poems about his visits to Longjing. His experiences there were first captured in a piece titled "A Poem in Thirty Rhymes to Record my Feelings on my First Tour of Longjing" ("Chuyou Longjing zhi-huai sanshi yun").[31] He even wrote sets of eight poems about Longjing for each of his four visits, including the one in 1780, when Wang Wenzhi's plays were performed for him. The emperor's poems led to the local canonization of the eight locales, on which the sets of poems focus, as the "Eight Scenic Sights of Longjing" (Longjing *bajing*). These sights included not only the Wisp of Cloud rock, but also the studio of Master Biancai Yuanjing (1011–1091) (Fangyuan an), who was the abbot of Hangzhou's Upper Tianzhu Monastery for seventeen years, as well as the Crossing-the-Stream Pavilion (Guoxi ting), famous for its commemoration of the much-celebrated friendship between Master Biancai and the poet Su Shi.

It should be clear from all this that Wang Wenzhi's play not only drew extensively from local folklore and tales, but also engaged actively with Qianlong's previous visits to Longjing and His Majesty's own writings on the cultural site. There is no doubt that the playwright had the emperor in mind when doing so, but it is also worth noting again the local patronage that our playwright-for-hire, Wang Wenzhi, received on this occasion. We can imagine that the local hosts also would have been pleased to be reminded that the region was graced and endorsed by His Majesty in words.

CONCLUSION

Let us return to the question with which we began this chapter: How do we read Chinese court drama, particularly local court drama? The set of nine plays by Wang Wenzhi that we have looked at in this chapter is only one of an enormous number of extant dramatic texts often classified under the umbrella term "Chinese court plays." But in actuality, "Chinese court plays" comprise a mixed and complex group of texts displaying a variety of qualities and characteristics.

Rather than to think of Chinese court theater as one homogenous type of theater, it is more useful and effective to consider it as a cultural milieu in which various types and forms of drama coexisted, including not only new plays produced specifically for court consumption on particular occasions, but also other forms of folk or literati drama previously composed for noncourt contexts and later introduced into the court and adapted for palace performance. This allows us to better appreciate the wide range of Chinese court theater produced over time, as well as the different audiences, readers, and agents involved in the creative process. It also encourages us to read the resulting dramatic scripts more closely and differentiate among them according to their purposes, functions, and specific historical contexts.

In many ways, Wang Wenzhi's set of nine court plays calls for this need to seek a pluralistic understanding of Chinese court drama. If Chinese court drama has long been known to be largely associated with the imperial palace, and therewith a mostly anonymous world of theatrical productions, the examples discussed here remind us of the need to consider court theater in broader terms geographically, following where such demands arose, and to rethink the role of literati writers such as Wang Wenzhi in such local productions. Court theater may be renowned for its staging effects and visual spectacles, but Wang's case also leads us toward exploring less-studied aspects of these court plays—their literary characteristics, poetic borrowings, and intertextual relations with other genres—all of which call for a more contemplative mode of closer reading than one usually gives to court drama. The two physical forms in which Wang's court plays survived in writing— one in its complete set of nine plays in print, and the other comprising only four plays in a court manuscript—also highlight the need to understand Chinese court drama as a wide spectrum of texts operating between their dual functions of reading text and visual performance, consumed both on page and onstage.

Tian Yuan Tan

NOTES

1. The term "Pear Garden" later became more broadly used, up to the present day, to refer to Chinese theater and its actors and troupes.

2. See Fu Xihua, *Qingdai zaju quanmu* (A Complete Catalogue of Qing *Zaju* Plays) (Beijing: Renmin wenxue chubanshe, 1981), *juan* 7–10, 351–620. The court plays by Wang Wenzhi discussed in this chapter are also included in Fu's catalog; see Fu, *Qingdai zaju quanmu*, 361–365. Qing court dramatic texts are now more readily accessible through various large-scale reprint projects such as *Gugong zhenben congkan* (Collectanea of Precious Books from the Forbidden Palace) (Haikou, China: Hainan chubanshe, 2000–2001), with volumes 660–696 on drama texts; and most recently, the 450-volume *Gugong bowuyuan cang Qinggong nanfu shengping shu xiben* (Playscripts from the Imperial Institutions Nanfu and Shengpingshu held in the Palace Museum) (Beijing: Gugong chubanshe, 2015–2017).

3. William Dolby, *A History of Chinese Drama* (New York: Barnes and Noble, 1976), 142.

4. A good example is the extant three-tiered Pavilion of Pleasant Sounds (Changyin ge) in the Palace Museum in Beijing. A picture of this three-tiered stage can be found on the official website of the museum (https://www.dpm.org.cn/explore/building/236437.html).

5. For a succinct introduction to the available color reproductions, see David L. Rolston, "Research Note: Recent Color Reproductions of Qing Dynasty Palace Multi-colored Play Scripts," *CHINOPERL* 34, no. 2 (2015), 188–193.

6. These were conducted to emulate earlier tours conducted by his grandfather, the Kangxi emperor (1654–1722, r. 1661–1722). A digitalization of four scrolls depicting these Qing inspection

tours can be accessed in "Recording the Grandeur of the Qing" (http://www.learn.columbia.edu /nanxuntu), a collaborative project of the Metropolitan Museum of Art, the Asia for Educators Program at Columbia University, and the Visual Media Center at Columbia University.

7. A reprint of these two plays is available in *Congshu jicheng xubian* (Sequel to the Assembled Collectaneas) (Taipei: Xinwenfeng chuban gongsi, 1988), vol. 162, 363–380. Li E's play is also included in Yao Xie's (1805–1864) *Fuzhuang jin yuefu xuan* (Contemporary *Yuefu* Plays Selected by Fuzhuang), in the "Quge" ("Songs in Streets and Alleys") section, held at the National Central Library in Taipei (no. 15181).

8. The use of the term "Dharma tunes" resonates with the court entertainment in the Tang dynasty, as this form of music was once performed in the Pear Garden conservatoire of Emperor Xuanzong.

9. Wang Wenzhi was considered one of the four great masters of calligraphy in the Qing dynasty, along with Weng Fanggang (1733–1818), Liu Yong (1719–1805), and Liang Tongshu (1723–1815).

10. This is highlighted in Wang's tomb inscription written by Yao Nai (1731–1815); see *Zhonghua dadian: wenxue dian: Ming Qing wenxue fendian* (Chinese Encyclopedia: Literature: Section on Ming and Qing Literature) (Nanjing, China: Jiangsu guji chubanshe, 2005), 633.

11. In this chapter, the text of reference for the plays will be to the more accessible reprints of them in Wang Wenzhang and Liu Wenfeng, eds. *Fu Xihua cang guben xiqu zhenben congkan* (Collectanea of Precious Books of Ancient Dramatic Texts in Fu Xihua's Holdings) (Beijing: Xueyuan chubanshe, 2010), vol. 63, 381–500. For Liang Sen's colophon, see p. 499. Parenthetical references will take the form of the page citations in the main text: *FXH*, 63.499.

12. Such titles are generic, so they can often be applied to more than one work. One may recall that the same title, *Yingluan xinqu*, was also used in naming the plays composed by Li E and Wu Cheng in 1751 mentioned previously.

13. The three titles derive, respectively, from (1) *FXH* 63.381–500; (2) a copy originally from the collection of Wu Mei (1884–1939), one of the most important drama critics of his time, now held at the Beijing National Library (no. 04367); and (3) Yao Xie's *Fuzhuang jin yuefu xuan* edition. It is noteworthy that in the *FXH* edition, the collective title *Yingluan xinqu* is adopted only later by the modern editors; it is not found in the original printing by Liang Tingnan, which simply introduces the set of nine plays as "*zaju*" [*FXH* 63.379].

14. The fourth character *en* (grace), being a reference to His Majesty, is moved to the top margin of the next line on the first page of the main text. The copyist apparently failed to notice this and recorded only the first three characters on the contents page as if they constituted the entire title.

15. For the reader's convenience, I refer to individual plays in this chapter using the "# number" format following their regular order of appearance when printed in an entire set of nine plays, as represented in the *FXH* edition.

16. For example, see Xiaoqing Ye's discussion of *Ascendant Peace in the Four Seas* (*Sihai shengping*), a court play commissioned for and containing specific references to the occasion of Earl George Macartney's mission to China in 1793. In later versions of the play, however, details related to the mission were removed and other modifications were made to reflect the different political realities during the Jiaqing and Guangxu reigns. See Xiaoqing Ye, *Ascendant Peace in the Four Seas: Drama and the Qing Imperial Court* (Hong Kong: Chinese University Press, 2012), 87–97.

17. A similar line appears in the next scene of the play with the introduction of another character. See *FXH* 63.465.

18. Similar references to this occasion can also be found in *FXH* 63.386 (play #1), 428 (play #4), and 491 (play #9).

19. Later, Qianlong's southern visit was not always portrayed in a positive light, such as in the Peking opera titled *Da Qianlong* (*Trouncing the Qianlong Emperor*), as discussed in Rudolf G. Wagner, *The Contemporary Chinese Historical Drama: Four Studies* (Berkeley: University of California Press, 1990), 254–258.

20. Praying for rain was part of the Qing court rituals that would be conducted by the emperor.

21. The name of the deity is Xuanwu 玄武, but here, the character *xuan* 玄 has been replaced with *yuan* 元 to avoid the taboo of mentioning the given name of the Kangxi emperor (Xuanye 玄燁).

22. The six *ding* (Maidens) and the six *jia* (Generals) correspond to two groups of spirits of the sexagenary cycle.

23. See *Gugong zhenben congkan*, vol. 696, 148. In another play, titled *Fortune, Prosperity, and Longevity* (*Fu lu shou*), we are informed that the Chinese characters should be formed by as many as thirty-two actors. See *Gugong zhenben congkan*, vol. 696, 274–275.

24. See *Myriad Flowers Offer Auspicious Omens* (*Wanhua xianrui*), in Wu Shuyin, ed., *Suizhong Wushi chaoben gaoben xiqu congkan* (Collectanea of Mr. Wu of Suizhong's Manuscripts and Draft Copies of Chinese Plays) (Beijing: Xueyuan chubanshe, 2004), vol. 26, 268. The Chinese term for "bat" is *bianfu* or *fu*, which is a homophone with *fu*, meaning "fortune."

25. For example, see *Gugong zhenben congkan*, vol. 696, 292, 295.

26. For the lines that are identical to Su Shi's original poem, the translation has been modified from Michael A. Fuller, *The Road to East Slope: The Development of Su Shi's Poetic Voice* (Stanford, CA: Stanford University Press, 1990), 181–182. The original poem is titled "On the Way to Wuxi, Composed on the Topic of the Watermill" ("Wuxi daozhong fu shuiche"); see *SSXJ*, 79–80.

27. Another example is the use of pastiche of Tang poems (*ji* Tang), a common feature found in much literati drama in late imperial China. This device was also occasionally used by literati playwrights, such as Jiang Shiquan, when they wrote for imperial events.

28. Marsha Weidner, ed., *Latter Days of the Law: Images of Chinese Buddhism, 850–1850* (Honolulu: University of Hawai'i Press, 1994), 264.

29. This is the third of a set of eight poems; see Gao Jin, Sa-zai, Agui, et al. comp., *Qinding nanxun shengdian* (Imperially Commissioned Great Canon of the Southern Tours), *juan* 9, 17a, *Siku quanshu* (The Complete Collection of the Four Treasuries) (hereafter *SKQS*) edition (Taipei: Taiwan Shangwu yinshuguan, 1986), 658.173.

30. Yu Minzhong, et al. comp., *Yuzhi shi sanji* (Imperial Poetry Collections: Third Collection), *juan* 22, 21a, *SKQS* edition, 1305.600.

31. *Yuzhi shi sanji*, *juan* 22, 1a–2a, *SKQS* edition, 1305.590–591.

PRIMARY SOURCES

FXH Wang Wenzhang 王文章 and Liu Wenfeng 劉文峰, eds. *Fu Xihua cang guben xiqu zhenben congkan* 傅惜華藏古本戲曲珍本叢刊 (*Collectanea of Precious Books of Ancient Dramatic Texts in Fu Xihua's Holdings*). Beijing: Xueyuan chubanshe, 2010.

QH Liang Tingnan 梁廷枏. *Quhua* 曲話 (*Notes on Songs*). In *Zhongguo gudian xiqu lunzhu jicheng* 中國古典戲曲論著集成 (*Assembled Treatises on Classical Chinese Drama*), vol. 8. Beijing: Zhongguo xiju chubanshe, 1959.

SCJ Wang Wenzhi 王文治. *Sican ji* 飼蠶記 (*Raising Silkworms*), Qing dynasty manuscript copy held at the Beijing National Library (no. A03425).

SSXJ Wang Shuizhao 王水照, ed. *Su Shi xuanji* 蘇軾選集 (*Selected Works of Su Shi*). Shanghai: Shanghai guji chubanshe, 2014.

SUGGESTED READINGS

ENGLISH

Chen, Liana. "The Empress Dowager as Dramaturg: Reinventing Late-Qing Court Theatre." *Nan Nü: Men, Women and Gender in Early and Imperial China* 14, no. 1 (2012): 21–46.

Idema, Wilt L. "Performances on a Three-Tiered Stage: Court Theatre during the Qianlong Era." In *Ad Seres et Tungusos: Festschrift für Martin Gimm*, eds. Lutz Bieg, Erling von Mende, and Martina Siebert, 201–219. Wiesbaden, Germany: Otto Harrasowitz, 2000.

Tan, Tian Yuan. "Sixty Plays from the Ming Palace, 1615–18." In *1616: Shakespeare and Tang Xianzu's* China, eds. Tian Yuan Tan, Paul Edmondson, and Shih-pe Wang, 96–107. London: Bloomsbury Arden Shakespeare, 2016.

Wu Xiaoling. "*Glowing Clouds in an Azure Sky*: A Newly Discovered Royal Pageant." Trans. Lindy Li Mark and Samuel H. H. Cheung. *CHINOPERL* 14, no. 1 (1986): 1–14.

Ye, Xiaoqing. *Ascendant Peace in the Four Seas: Drama and the Qing Imperial Court*. Hong Kong: Chinese University Press, 2012.

CHINESE

Chiu Hui-Yin 丘慧瑩. *Qianlong shiqi xiqu huodong yanjiu* 乾隆時期戲曲活動研究 (*A Study of the Theatrical Activities during the Qianlong Era*). Taipei: Wenjin chubanshe, 2000.

Li Zhenyu 李真瑜. *Mingdai gongting xiju shi* 明代宮廷戲劇史 (*A History of Ming Dynasty Court Theater*). Beijing: Zijincheng chubanshe, 2010.

Luo Yan 羅燕. *Qingdai gongting chengying xi jiqi xingtai yanjiu* 清代宮廷承應戲及其形態研究 (*A Study of Qing Dynasty Court Plays and Their Forms*). Guangzhou, China: Guangdong gaodeng jiaoyu chubanshe, 2014.

Tan, Tian Yuan 陳靝沅. "Guanyu Ming Qing gongting yanju yanjiu de jidian sikao" 關於明清宮廷演劇研究的幾點思考 (Reflections on the Study of Late Imperial Chinese Court Theatre). In *Ming Qing gongtingshi xueshu yantaohui lunwenji (di yi ji)* 明清宮廷史學術研討會論文集（第一輯）(*A Conference Volume of Essays on the Historiography of the Ming and Qing Courts*), ed. The Palace Museum, 467–77. Beijing: Zijincheng chubanshe, 2011.

Zhu Jiajin 朱家溍, and Ding Ruqin 丁汝芹. *Qingdai neiting yanju shimokao* 清代內廷演劇始末考 (*Research into the Beginnings and End of Theater Performances at the Qing Dynasty Inner Court*). Beijing: Zhongguo shudian, 2007.

The Eight-Court Pearl

Performance Scripts and Political Culture

In 1644, the armies of the Manchu-Qing regime (1636–1911) swept south through the Great Wall at Shanhai Pass to claim the capital of Beijing, the seat of power of the toppled Ming dynasty (1368–1644). During the subsequent consolidation and expansion of the Qing Empire throughout the territories of the former Ming (and eventually well beyond), the alien dynasty entered a fraught pattern of relations with the majority Han people whom it had conquered. The Manchu-Qing—with considerable Han collaboration—retained political and military dominance; cultural dominance, however, largely still resided with the Han elite, especially epitomized by the cultural production of the lower Yangzi River Delta region, or Jiangnan. One such field of cultural production was drama, both in its written and performed expressions. Playwrights might hail from anywhere within the empire, but by the mid-1600s, the elite-recognized—and hence most exalted—genre of opera was Kunqu, which had its origins in the preeminent Jiangnan city of Suzhou (☞ chap. 8).

The Qing court openly acknowledged Kunqu as the most sophisticated genre within a hierarchy of many regional musical styles, although inside the private quarters of the imperial palace and in the villas of the Manchu nobility, taste in dramatic performance could be much more eclectic. Indeed, drama performance became a site of contestation for cultural supremacy between the Qing court and Han men of letters. On the one hand, Manchus were wooed by the siren call of opera, generating imperial alarm about Manchu assimilation to Han customs. On the other hand, partly due to active patronage by the Qing court, opera flourished in the commercial playhouses, native-place lodges, and private homes of urban centers, especially in Beijing. Over the course of the Qing era, the political capital and the epicenter for theater became one and the same city.

As evidence of this, a new "fanzine" literature (*huapu*) of the most accomplished actors in the capital developed in the second half of the eighteenth century. This literature predominantly focused on male youths cross-dressing to perform the young ingénue roles. These guides to the star "boy actresses" have preserved not just the names of the players, but also the popularly performed plays and scenes from longer *chuanqi* dramas. These catalogs of mid- to late-Qing commercial performance reveal that commercial theater troupes in the capital thrived off of the past repertoire of great dramatic works from the thirteenth through the late seventeenth centuries, although typically the text of the original "playwright" was bowdlerized, truncated, or performed as excerpted scenes when mounted onstage.

Nevertheless, despite the many adaptations of old plays, mention of brand-new plays is frequently scattered throughout the pages of these records. More important still, the last century and a half of the Qing era has left behind a trove of performance scripts, ranging from actors' part scripts to full production texts (featuring arias, scores, spoken dialogue, choreography, and costume notes). Much of this textual material was never intended for posterity; it is only happenstance that has preserved it in the archival record. And yet, the fact that so many of these ephemera have survived speaks to the incredible lure of dramatic performance through the end of the Qing dynasty (and beyond).

This chapter delves into this substratum of dramatic textual production by focusing on one anonymous, early-nineteenth-century history play with the title *The Eight-Court Pearl* (*Bachao zhu*). *Eight-Court Pearl* is a hand-copied, five-book opera script (of seventy-three full manuscript pages) recorded in the second decade of the 1800s and attributed to the Hechun Troupe, one of the most famous theatrical companies operating in Beijing over the first half of the nineteenth century. I read this script as being representative of a much larger corpus of new—often-anonymous—plays crafted in the eighteenth and nineteenth centuries, many of which have simply dropped out of the archival record.

After introducing what can be known about the provenance of the script, this chapter addresses the script in relation to dramas written by named authors, and especially the history plays of the Suzhou School dramatists such as Li Yu (1591?–1671?) (☞ Introduction), as well as other textual antecedents. It then turns to look at this "below-the-radar" play for what it can tell us about how such works captured the restive mood and political concerns of urban audiences at the time.

As literature, *Eight-Court Pearl* is utterly insignificant—it is not even a complete play. But if we read this script as a window onto the political culture of early nineteenth-century Beijing, it may not be so trivial. Indeed, the Qing court was wise to be concerned about drama as a carrier of subversive messages. *Eight-Court Pearl* refracted a growing incidence of popular unrest at the doorstep of the Qing palace and presaged much larger conflagrations to come. More intriguing still, the ghost-writer for this script may have been someone in the Manchu princely household who acted as the guarantor for the Hechun Troupe.[1] If so, that makes the play's politics even more interesting; it complicates our understanding of Manchu-Han tensions in the early decades of the nineteenth century, suggesting that dissatisfaction with the political status quo was not confined to Han subjects of the Qing. Rather, by the early 1800s, even Manchus in noble households were discomfited by social injustice and disillusioned with the ability of the state to rectify official malfeasance.

14.1 *EIGHT-COURT PEARL*: THE SCRIPT

Only a handful of clues survive to piece together the provenance of *Eight-Court Pearl*. The manuscript is housed in the library of the Chinese National Academy of Arts (Zhongguo yishu yanjiuyuan), having entered the archive in 1952 as part of a large purchase of hand-copied scripts (including more than 700 booklets) that had been in the collection of a former palace eunuch by the name of Geng Yuqing. Yuqing is likely the courtesy name for Geng Jinxi,[2] a eunuch who served as an actor in the court in the last years of the Qing and who had studied the martial male (*wusheng*) role type as a youth with Yang Longshou (1854–1900), the maternal grandfather of the eminent twentieth-century Peking opera female impersonator Mei Lanfang (1894–1961) (🖝 Visual Resources).[3] Perhaps not surprisingly, the Geng scripts entered the archive shortly after Mei Lanfang had been appointed the inaugural director of the academy. The bulk of the manuscripts in this Geng Script Collection (*Geng jucang*) emanated from the Office of Ascendant Peace (Sheng-ping shu), the Qing palace agency responsible for court entertainment from 1827 through 1924.[4] An additional handful of these scripts, including *Eight-Court Pearl*, are labeled as the property of the Hechun Troupe.[5]

Eight-Court Pearl was copied out over fifteen days dating to the first half of January 1819. The relation that recording might have to literary creation or performance is unclear; it is quite possible that the copying of the text was in preparation for a commissioned performance, perhaps at the home of a wealthy patron.[6] Each bound volume of the script bears the name of the Hechun Troupe (figure 14.1).[7] The troupe commenced performing in Beijing in 1803, and although it was commercial, it was loosely affiliated with the household of Aisin Gioro Mianke (1763–1826), the holder of the title of Prince Zhuang (Zhuang qinwang) at the time and the heir to one of the original eight "Iron Hat" (*tiemao*) princely households.[8]

Presumably, the prince acted as guarantor for the commercial troupe, meaning that the troupe had to register with his household, which was then responsible for the troupe's conduct in the capital, although evidence suggests that such princely oversight had waned considerably by the early nineteenth century.[9] The Hechun Troupe disbanded in 1833, but shortly thereafter it reconstituted itself and continued to perform in the city's commercial playhouses for another twenty years.[10] I will return to the Zhuang princedom and the possible connection of its household members as ghostwriters for the Hechun Troupe later in this chapter. For now, suffice to say that the Hechun Troupe was one of the most renowned opera companies in the capital for half a century.

The Hechun Troupe was also one of the so-called Hui troupes, or Huiban, whose performance experimentations in the capital seeded the eventual development of Peking opera (*jing ju*) (🖝 Introduction). Commentators at the time singled out the Hechun Troupe in particular for its fight scenes, claiming: "The Hechun Troupe is known for its 'stunts.' Every day at noon they perform plays from the various novels such as *Romance of the Three Kingdoms* [🖝 HTRCFiction, chap. 4] or *The Water Margin* [🖝 HTRCFiction, chap. 6] and these are called the 'middle-scroll' scenes" [Yang Maojian, *Menghua suobu*, QYLS 352]. And again, "the Hechun Troupe . . . excels at stage combat and tumbling. It is the best of the four [Hui] troupes when it comes to the 'middle-scroll' scenes" [Yang Maojian, *Chang'an kanhua ji*, QYLS 319].[11] These scenes featured martial arts combat as their main attraction, as opposed to excerpts with more lyrical dramatic content.

The Hechun Troupe was also known for its eclectic musical range, performing the earthier "high melody" (*gaoqiang*, a localized version of Yiyang melody) and "Qin melody" (*qinqiang*) operas, along with the more sophisticated Kun opera. As one source asserted: "Today's *gaoqiang* preserves the music of the Jin and Yuan [dynasties]. The Hechun Troupe still practices this. They also often perform *qinqiang*" [Yang Maojian, *Chang'an kanhua ji*, QYLS 319]. Leaving aside the claim for the antiquity of these melodies, this observation about the troupe's musical choices accords well with the mix of arias found in *Eight-Court Pearl*, some of which feature Kun opera tune titles and others that were to be sung in more popular musical genres.[12] These characteristics of the troupe ensured that, as one observer put it, "the theater troupes of the capital are named Sixi, Chuntai, Sanqing, and Hechun. All four are equally famous, but the Hechun troupe is the only one that is not liked by the elite. . . . But the petty urbanites of the city love to watch that troupe" [Luo-mo'an laoren, *Huaifang ji*, QYLS 595]. We can be fairly certain, then, that *Eight-Court Pearl*, in terms of both aesthetic characteristics and dramatic arc, captured the sensibilities of middlebrow urban audiences.

The title of the play refers to a precious pearl (passed down over the course of eight reigns) that is an heirloom of the Ren family; the pearl would seem to loom large in the plot—hence the title—although because the script is incomplete, it is hard to know its full significance in the drama. The play lampoons those who abuse access to power and showcases vigilante action as a solution to the injustices that ensue from official corruption and overweening wealth.

The plot of the script weaves together several main threads that shuttle back and forth between the urbane city of Hangzhou (☞ chap. 4) and a backwater prefectural city in Shandong province during the final decades of the Ming dynasty. The first of these threads follows the attempts by an evil fox spirit, disguised as a beautiful woman, to prey upon the unsuspecting Zhu Xian, the newly chosen winner of the county-level examination in Hangzhou. When his cousin, Fang Ju, comes to his rescue, the demon turns her wrath against him, too.

A second plot thread traces the depredations of the fictional Wei Chuan, the adoptive son of the notorious real-life eunuch Wei Zhongxian (1568–1627) (☞ chap. 10), who first steals the eight-court pearl from Ms. Cong (Cong shi), the attractive wife of Ren Kui, who has been forced to pawn the jewel to pay for medicine for her mother-in-law. Wei Chuan's good-for-nothing friend, Hu Tong, eggs him on, saying:

（仝）如今我有上好的主意。珠子到手，岂可还他？叫他到王府去取良子。他若不来，宝珠千岁进贡。他若来时，就留在府中，千岁做个戏妾，岂不美哉？

HU TONG[13] [*speaks*]: I have a really swell idea. Now that the pearl is in your hands, how can you return it to her? Have her come to your residence for the silver. If she doesn't come, the pearl is a gift to you, my liege. If she does, then my liege can detain her to keep as your playmate. Wouldn't that be sweet?

（川）好，会办事。我进京对爹爹說放你出
任为官。

WEI CHUAN[14] [*speaks*]: Excellent! You do know how to get things done. When I get to the capital, I will tell Daddy to appoint you to an official post.

[*BCZ* 5a][15]

When Wei Chuan then tricks Ms. Cong into entering his household so that he can possess her, it turns out that she has martial abilities and is able to fight her way to safety. Wei then turns his designs to the beautiful younger sister of Fang Ju. These two threads get woven together when Ms. Cong resorts to begging to secure the money to attend to her ill mother-in-law and retrieve the family heirloom. Zhu Xian generously comes to her aid. This exchange is witnessed by the Fox Spirit, who thereafter disguises herself as Ms. Cong and visits him at night. The Fox Spirit convinces Zhu Xian's mother to let her spend a night under their roof and then reveals her true vixen nature after a careless drink of wine:

（旦狐）妙吓，且喜被我赚入祝府。此是天
助助吾也。吓，什么东西这等异香？哦，原
来一壶美酒。我自出母胎何曾享受此物。今
夜樂饮一壶。

YOUNG FEMALE *as* FOX SPIRIT [*speaks*]: Wonderful! I'm delighted to have tricked my way into the Zhu household. Heaven assists me! Oh, what is that strange fragrance? Ah, it's a bottle of luscious wine. I've never once tasted this. Tonight, I will indulge a drink.

（旦狐）
【红纳祅】
好良宵，
看将来天輻揍。

FOX SPIRIT [*sings*]:
To the tune "Hongna'ao"
What a lovely night;
From the looks of things, heaven is causing everything to fall into place.

怎知我娟仙兒用机谋，欺藐他肉眼，

Who would have thought that I could so connive to trick their mortal eyes,

凡胎难猜透。
夺取他元陽，
夺取他元陽，
我登仙列宿 . . .

Making it hard for them to guess my disguise?
Once I've snatched away his pure yang essence,[16]
Once I've snatched away his pure yang essence,
I will ascend the ranks of the transcendents and be listed among the immortals . . .

我今不与祝贤暗中偷，
怎能勾織女会牵牛 . . .

. . . If tonight I do not secretly lie with Zhu Xian,
Then let not the Weaving Maid ever join in union with the Cowherd.[17]

（白）吓，怎么横身酸麻、头昏眼花 . . .
（团介，变狐形，上桌伏介）

Speaks: Ah, how comes it that my body aches and goes limp? My head swoons and my eyes blur . . .
She circles around and dons a fox mask, jumping onto the table and crouching.[18]

[*BCZ* 8b–9a]

A third plot strand features several martial good fellows who prevent rich bullies in the prefecture of Liaocheng in Shandong from abducting the sister of the local scholar Lan Cong. The scholar ends up taking the blame for the ensuing melee and is imprisoned; meanwhile, his martially adept sworn brothers plot to free him from the prison, and a crony of the bullies is sent to the jail to poison Lan Cong. Book 5 of the script comes to an end with Pi Deng, the principled jail warden, preventing the plotted assassination. In the closing coda, Pi Deng sings:

（皮）	PI DENG[19] [*sings*]:
【江頭金別】	*To the tune* "Jiangtou jinbie"[20]
有俺皮登在此，	With me, Pi Deng, here,
要害藍老爺的性命，	should anyone try to harm Master Lan,
萬萬不能也。	I won't let 'em, no way, no how!

[*BCZ* 73b]

To the extent that there is organization to the plot, it follows a billiard-ball-type trajectory, in which one martial hero meets up with another, who then moves the dramatic action forward until a new conflict ensues, often climaxing in a fight scene. None of these various threads are brought to conclusion by the end of book 5. The full play must have been even longer, but we cannot know if the version left to us is truncated because it was never finished or because the remaining scenes were not preserved. Indeed, we do not know if the script was ever performed, although as the first page of the script in figure 14.1 shows, someone has used red ink to punctuate the black text of the arias and to circle the tune titles and costume notes for emphasis, which would suggest preparation for singing and acting. And someone, purporting to be affiliated with the Hechun Troupe, took the time to write out what does exist of it.

The plot of *Eight-Court Pearl* weaves social commentary into raucous, sometimes suggestive entertainment. More important, it smacks of anticorruption sentiment, largely directed (as I will explore further shortly) against Heshen (1746–1799), the powerful late-eighteenth-century Manchu grand councillor and former imperial guardsman—and reputed lover—of the Qianlong emperor (r. 1736–1796). The barbed wit of the opera opens a space for resistance against abusive political power. While not fully oppositional—the veiled attacks on Heshen would surely have been possible only after he had been purged from office—the urban, commercial stage at the very least provided an arena in which actors and audiences could give vent to an after-the-fact, politically charged resentment. This entertainment aesthetic was a key attraction of the mid- to late-Qing commercial playhouses.

Meandering as the plot of *Eight-Court Pearl* is, several features distinguish the script as tapping into popular currents of urban discontent. First, the play is set in the late Ming dynasty and features as its main villain the fictional Wei Chuan, presented in the script as the adopted son of the notorious real-life chief eunuch, Wei

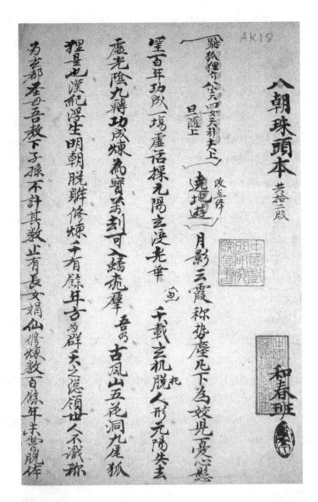

FIGURE 14.1 The opening page of book 1 of the partial script for *The Eight-Court Pearl*, held in the Traditional Drama Library (Xiqu yanjiusuo) of the Chinese National Academy of Arts, Beijing. Courtesy of the Zhongguo yishu yanjiuyuan.

Zhongxian. It is modeled on a pattern of Ming history plays by the mid-seventeenth-century Suzhou dramatists that use the preceding dynasty to critique current politics. Already in the early Qing era, the dramas of the Suzhou School playwrights had a political bite to them. *Eight-Court Pearl* was crafted in that tradition.

Second, the script opens with a scene in which the natural and social orders of the world are out of whack. A fox spirit schemes to come down into the human realm to acquire sufficient human essence to perfect her demon nature and acquire everlasting life. This theme paralleled contemporary interest in "literature of the strange" (*zhiguai*), which recorded tales about anomalies of nature that were also read at the time as political and moral allegory.

Third, the solution to the problems of social and phenomenological dysfunction posed by the play is vigilante action, in which protagonists use martial prowess—either individually or in groups—to fight corrupt people in positions of power. True, no direct reference to Heshen is found in the play, or in the tales of the strange that were much in vogue at the height of his power. But I will try to show parallel concerns expressed in writings by elite commentators and by the text of *Eight-Court Pearl*, which point to a general mood of disaffection with officialdom and disenchantment over the state's inability to enact justice.

14.2 SUZHOU SCHOOL HISTORY PLAYS AND OTHER TEXTUAL ANTECEDENTS

The structural model upon which *Eight-Court Pearl* is based comes from *chuanqi* dramas written in the mid-seventeenth century, a style that has especially come to be associated with the plays of a coterie of early Qing dramatists centered in the preeminent Jiangnan city of Suzhou. Many of these dramatists chose playwriting as a conscious rejection of politics during the traumatic Ming-Qing dynastic transition. Instead, they poured their passion for social justice into crafting historical dramas that frequently were set in the Ming dynasty. Reflecting their regional origin, these plays were written to be performed in the Suzhou-identified Kun opera genre. But these dramas—or rather, scene selections from them—quickly became popular in commercial performance throughout the Qing Empire. By the eighteenth century, highlighted scenes from these multiscene dramas had become standard fare for performance by troupes in commercial playhouses in major urban centers, including, perhaps above all, Beijing. As evidence, about one-quarter of the 500-plus scenes collected in the late-eighteenth-century drama anthology *A Patchwork Cloak of the Whitest Fur* (*Zhuibaiqiu*) were drawn from these Suzhou School plays.

The most representative and prolific of these mid-seventeenth-century Suzhou playwrights was Li Yu (c. 1591–c. 1671), the author of forty-two plays (and not to be confused with another Li Yu, the subject of chapter 11). Li Yu's playwriting career spanned the Ming-Qing dynastic transition, with his four most famous plays written in the late Ming and the remaining works in the first decades of the Qing. Li Yu never held office under either the Ming or the Qing dynasty. His father had been a retainer in the household of the late Ming official Shen Yongmao (1560–1638), whose own father, Shen Shixing (1535–1614), had served a stint in the post of grand secretary under the Wanli emperor.

Li Yu's inherited servile status made him ineligible to sit for the exams in spite of his prodigious literary ability. The wealthy and powerful Shens—natives of Suzhou—were renowned for their private troupe of actors. Having been raised in such an environment would explain Li Yu's intimate familiarity with drama ["Qianyan," *LYXQJ* 1–3]. After the fall of the Ming, Li Yu relied on writing plays for a living. Li's plays, in particular, seem to have exerted a strong influence on the script of *Eight-Court Pearl*. Rather, if there is a literary prototype toward which *Eight-Court Pearl* is gesturing, it is works such as Li Yu's *A Handful of Snow* (*Yipengxue*) and *Biographies of the Pure and Loyal* (*Qingzhong pu*, hereafter *Biographies*), both of which chronicle the abuses of righteous men at the hands of unscrupulous power brokers at court.

Li Yu's *Handful of Snow* relates the tragedy that ensues from the political and personal struggle to gain possession of a jade cup so rare as to have been named "A Handful of Snow." The cup belongs to Mo Huaigu, a Ming official. This information is leaked to Yan Shifan (?–d. 1565), the son of the notoriously corrupt Yan Song (1480–1567), the most powerful official at the time (☞ chap. 10). Yan Shifan covets the cup and will stop at nothing to get it. Tang Qin, a once-starving scroll mounter who had been taken in by Mo Huaigu, acts as go-between, trying to get Mo to make a gift of the cup to Yan. Unwilling to part with his treasure, Mo supplies Yan with a fake, but Tang exposes the substitution. Mo Huaigu is forced to flee for his life, but his servant, Mo Cheng, and concubine, Xueyan, forfeit their lives to save their master—but not before Xueyan wreaks vengeance on Tang. By the mid-Qing, the scenes featuring Xueyan's revenge and Mo Cheng's sacrifice had become perennial favorites on the commercial stage, at salon performances in the homes of the wealthy, and at court (☞ Visual Resources).[21]

With certain key substitutions, echoes of the plot of *Handful of Snow* can be discerned in *Eight-Court Pearl*: the coveted rare object is now the pearl rather than the jade cup; the greedy villain is Wei Chuan, in place of Yan Shifan; and the figure of the scoundrel go-between is captured in *Eight-Court Pearl* in the character of Hu Tong, a friend of the Hangzhou licentiate Zhu Xian, who double-crosses Zhu to assist Wei Chuan in stealing not only the pearl, but also other men's wives. Even the opening setting of Hangzhou in *Eight-Court Pearl* recalls the earlier work, for Mo Huaigu, the protagonist in Li Yu's drama, hails from Hangzhou. Substitution here may be key, for it was this type of mixing and matching—the bricolage assemblage of plot elements from dramatic works of the past—that enabled commercial troupes (equipped with less literacy than literati playwrights) to create the building blocks of their own scripts.

The second of the Li Yu plays that hovers in the wings of *Eight-Court Pearl* is *Biographies*, set in the late Ming era, at the time of the persecution of the Eastern Grove (Donglin) partisans by Wei Zhongxian (☞ chaps. 10 and 12). It centers on the historical martyrdom of the outspoken scholar–official critic Zhou Shunchang (1584–1626) and the local riot in Suzhou that his death provoked. The main protagonist of *Biographies* is Zhou Shunchang, but the play also features five commoner heroes who lead civic unrest against official wrongdoing. The opening aria sets the theme:

【滿江紅】	*To the tune* "Man Jiang hong"
璫焰燒天，正亘忠良灰劫。	When eunuch arrogance engulfs heaven in flames, the good and loyal are ever reduced to ashes.
看幾許驕驄嘶斷，杜鵑啼血。	How many proud stallions have whinnied themselves hoarse, the cuckoo keening until it spits up blood?
一點忠魂天日慘，	We present one loyal soul tragically sacrificed in broad daylight
五人義氣風雷掣。	And the five righteous men whose fury thundered with sincerity.

[*LYXQJ* 1291]

Later abridged versions of the play picked up on the phrase "five righteous men" as an alternative title.[22] It was the scenes of the five rioters that had the greatest staying power in the later performance repertoire and that also seem to echo through the exploits of the many martial good fellows in *Eight-Court Pearl*. *Biographies* was an overtly political drama that castigated the abuses of men who wielded usurped power. *Eight-Court Pearl*, its latter-day imitator, likely would have also tapped into the audience's resentment against abuse of power in more recent times.

These plays trafficked in melodrama, by which I mean the caricatured depiction of heroes and villains. This characteristic was further accentuated by Chinese opera stage conventions, with clowns and rogues depicted in tofu-patch white-face[23] and characters with integrity made up so as to accentuate a stylized—yet more naturalistic—attractiveness (the tofu-patch makeup is shown in figure 14.2). Indeed, the mix of dialogue, recitative, and aria (which carried the drama's over-the-top emotional content) approximates the literal meaning of melodrama (drama with music), and so I borrow this term from the Western theatrical tradition to characterize Qing dramatic production. Historical melodrama was a central attraction of the mid- to late-Qing commercial stage.

The melodramatic quality of such plays seems to have increased from the late Ming into the Qing, although how much this had to do with changing playwright sensibilities versus the movement of drama from page to stage is hard to gauge. To take Li Yu's *Handful of Snow* as an example, the play, completed in the late Ming

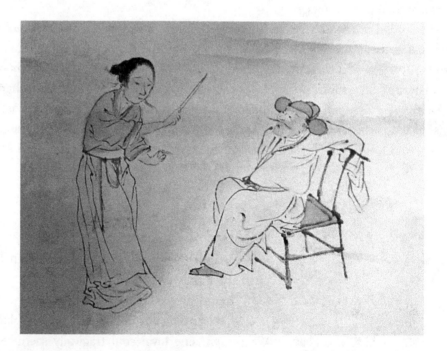

FIGURE 14.2 Anonymous Qing dynasty painting of the scene "Stabbing Tang Qin" ("Ci Tang"), the commonly used title for slightly modified performance versions of the scene "Exterminating the Villain" ("Zhu jian"), in Li Yu's *Handful of Snow*. Reproduced in Wang Wenzhang, ed., *Kunqu yishu tupu* (A Pictorial Catalog of the Art of Kun Opera), Beijing: Wenhua yishu chubanshe, 2017, 63.

era, shows much greater nuance of characterization than the works he penned during the Qing period. Mo Huaigu, the protagonist of *Handful of Snow*, is a decidedly ambiguous figure: he is shown to be a bad judge of character in befriending Yan Shifan and the duplicitous Tang Qin; and he is willing to let his faithful servant and loving concubine sacrifice their lives so as to retain his ownership of the precious jade cup. It is the servant and concubine—supporting characters—who act with greater righteous conviction. Indeed, the concubine, Xueyan, might be read as a cipher for the jade cup (even the meaning of her name—"Snow Beauty"—echoes that of the cup); she destroys her object-self in the act of seeking justice on behalf of her lord-owner. In the Qing performance script tradition, however, Mo Huaigu largely drops out of the narrative, with the most frequently performed scenes in the *Patchwork* anthology and other hand-copied scripts featuring either Xueyan or Mo Cheng, thereby having the effect of accentuating the gulf between virtue and vice.

To the extent that can be assessed from its incomplete text, the script of *Eight-Court Pearl* inherited the trend toward caricature and melodrama. The characters neatly separate into heroes and rogues. Fang Ju, for instance, one of the martial heroes, turns out to be the human manifestation of a black tiger spirit, and thus his righteous spiritual powers make him an effective foil against the scheming Fox Spirit. The women, too, neatly fall into three categories: evil and sexually avaricious; old, infirm, and ineffective; or young, beautiful, and prey to the villains (even if sometimes martially savvy). Paired with this moralism, however, is also a strain of fatalism. Heaven seemingly visits disaster upon good people for no rhyme or reason. This anxiety is voiced in the scene in the Zhu residence immediately following the Fox Spirit's revelation of her animal-spirit nature:

（丫）东厢房失火了。	MAID [*speaks*]: The eastern chamber has caught on fire!
（夫）这还了得。看任大娘可在里面。	MADAM[24] [*speaks*]: How terrible. See if Madam Ren is inside.
（小生）吓，怎么没有火？母亲，这是个什么东西？	SECONDARY YOUNG MALE *as* ZHU XIAN [*speaks*]: Ah, how is it that there is no fire? Mother, what is this?
（夫）阿呀，	MADAM [*speaks*]: Aiya,
（夫）	MADAM [*sings*]:
厢房内火光腾腾，	In the chamber a fiery glow rises up,
厢房内火光腾腾。	In the chamber a fiery glow rises up.
唬得母子神不定，	It scares us out of our wits.
张牙舞抓人惊怕。	That creature with bared teeth and outstretched claws is frightful.
好教人辨不出是何鬼怪精。	We cannot make out if it be ghost, goblin, or sprite.
（夫）什么妖精？	MADAM [*speaks*]: What demon is this?
（小生）孩儿认不出。	ZHU XIAN [*speaks*]: Mother, I don't know.

（夫）家院，与我打。　　　　　MADAM [*speaks*]: Servant, go beat it for me.

（院）小人不敢进去。　　　　　SERVANT [*speaks*]: I dare not go inside.

（夫）这便怎么好？　　　　　　MADAM [*speaks*]: What are we to do?

　　　　　　　　　　（夫）　　MADAM [*sings*]:

这纔是闭户紧关门，　　　　　　Here we shut our doors and lock our gates,

　　果然祸從天降生。　　　　　And yet calamity rains down from heaven.

這堂堂相府鬼弄人。　　　　　　A demon terrorizes us even in our stately home.

　　（夫）唬唬飛我也。　　　　MADAM [*speaks*]: How frightening!

（小生）母亲，不必驚怕，表兄家中有照妖　　ZHU XIAN [*speaks*]: Mother, fear not. My cousin has a
鏡。孩兒前去借来，将此孽畜化为灰烬也。　　demon-reflecting mirror at home. I will go borrow it from
　　　　　　　　　　　　　　　　　　him and reduce this beast to ashes.

[*BCZ* 9a-9b]

When Zhu Xian returns with the demon-reflecting mirror, it does not work, and he falls down in a stupor. His mother calls for a doctor, and the scene comes to a close with the servant reiterating:

（院）正是，闭门家里坐，祸從天上来。　　SERVANT [*speaks*]: Truly, this is a case of shutting your
　　　　　　　　　　　　　　　　　　doors and sitting at home, but calamity descends from
　　　　　　　　　　　　　　　　　　heaven.

[*BCZ* 9b]

The moralism and fatalism of melodrama took on special poignancy, I suggest, during the Jiaqing reign (1796–1820). In February 1799, just weeks after the death of the retired Qianlong emperor, Grand Councillor Heshen was arrested and ordered to commit suicide for his crimes against the state. According to some accounts, he had amassed a personal fortune of over 80 million taels of silver, an amount exceeding the surplus of the state treasury at the time.[25] Heshen's corruption, which had been the subject of official remonstrance and much sotto voce complaint during his rise to power, could be aired in public after his fall.

In popular perception at the time, what made Heshen's misdeeds possible was his close relationship with the Qianlong emperor. Anecdotes about his vices became the stuff of notational jottings and urban lore in the first decades of the nineteenth century. The Manchu courtier Zhaolian (1776–1829), for one, took great relish in cataloguing Heshen's foibles in his 1815 publication *Miscellaneous Notes from the Whistling Pavilion (Xiaoting zalu)*. Zhaolian offers several anecdotes that present Heshen as lacking in the proper decorum for an official. In one, he tells that Heshen once grabbed the hand of an elderly colleague in the Grand Council in jest and asked, "How do you keep your hands so soft?" The reply: "I don't let them touch bribe money."[26]

Of note here is that at least two stories circulated in early nineteenth-century accounts that linked Heshen's extravagance to pearls, the coveted item in the Hechun Troupe script. The contemporary commentator Jiao Xun (1763–1820) recounts that Heshen took daily medicinal pills made of fresh pearls encrusted in gold—a sign of his extravagance.[27] Another tale claims that he pilfered from the imperial storehouse an exquisite snuffbox made of a giant pearl.[28] At the time that Heshen's property was confiscated, it was said that he had accumulated more than 200 court rosaries and strings of pearls.[29] One source for these stories may have been the Jiaqing emperor's edicts indicting Heshen for his crimes, which were then distributed in digest form in the *Imperial Gazette* (*Dibao*) and became the stuff of further embellishment in commonplace literati jottings and street gossip.[30] Given all this, I think it is not too far-fetched to speculate that the character Wei Chuan in *Eight-Court Pearl* (with his designs on Lady Cong's pearl) would have been viewed by audiences at the time—if they ever had the chance to view it—as a ringer for Heshen.

Of course, Heshen was only the most visible example of rapacious officials in the late eighteenth and early nineteenth centuries. If we believe the moralizing accounts of the time, just about everyone in an official position was on the take. This perception, too, is reflected in *Eight-Court Pearl*. With one exception, all the officials featured in the play are shown to be corrupt and greedy. In contrast, most of the protagonists are presented as the sons of upright officials who have suffered impeachment or worse at the hands of Wei Zhongxian and his henchmen. As a result of such persecution, the sons have had to lie low and live by their wits and martial skills.[31] The character Yan Xiu's entering couplet perhaps best captures this sentiment. At his first entrance, Yan Xiu intones:

（顏秀上白）	YAN XIU[32] *enters and declaims:*
恨权奸掌朝綱，	How I hate those villainous men of power who dominate the court;
欺君误国見豺狼；	Deceiving the ruler and failing the state, they are no better than jackals and wolves.
但得風雨迎曉日，	If only wind and rain should yield to brighter days,
定杀佞臣姓名揚。	I shall kill those sycophantic ministers and so make a name for myself."

[*BCZ* 28b]

The contrast with the opening poems of the greedy men of power in *Eight-Court Pearl* could not be clearer. When they enter the stage, they sing:

（张廷照、佟高、付欠上全唱）	ZHANG TINGHAO, TONG GAO, and FU QIAN *enter and sing*[33]:
一声雷鸣震天中，	One shout and our voices thunder in heaven;

費盡田產圖受用。	We do all we can to buy up land for our private pleasure.
四方遊人如蜂擁，	We roam the four directions like a swarm of hornets;
这富贵天涯吹送。	As wealth and riches flow in from around the realm.

[BCZ 43b]

The image of officials that emerges from the script is decidedly dark and cynical.

Narrative fiction of the Ming-Qing era often alerted readers to problems in the social realm by openings in which animals took the form of humans, and in that guise wreaked havoc on the world. Foxes in Qing tales and anecdotes also symbolize the attractions and dangers of sexual desire. Whether or not a man succumbs to the temptation of the fox is a mark of his moral fiber.[34] While they long predate the production of *Eight-Court Pearl*, these tales of the strange reached a high point in the late eighteenth century in the writings of the eminent court official Ji Yun (1724–1805). Ji's anecdotes are didactic, often with foxes held up as a mirror to the human world. As Rania Huntington explains: "The society drawn here consists of a tiny elite of transcendent foxes (the officials); a larger group of foxes living out their lives in human form and aspiring to the elite (the literati); and ordinary, four-footed foxes burying in the ground and eating poultry (the peasants)."[35] This parallel hierarchy of foxes and humans is amply reflected in the structure of *Eight-Court Pearl*. The fox that preys upon the examinee student Zhu Xian is hoping to become a transcendent; and the transcendent leader of the foxes who eggs her on is as debauched as the human officials in the play. By invoking the fox lore, *Eight-Court Pearl* situates itself in the complex of contemporary texts about a moral order gone awry.[36]

14.3 VIOLENCE AS THE SOLUTION

The solution to endemic corruption in the worldview of *Eight-Court Pearl* is vigilantism. This was not merely brave talk; it both reflected real-world tendencies and had real-world repercussions. Indeed, in 1813, just a few years before the recording of *Eight-Court Pearl*, sectarian rebels in north China had banded together, infiltrated the capital city, and attacked the imperial palace.[37] Although the rebels were quickly suppressed, the Jiaqing emperor (r. 1796–1820) was spooked by the incident. His suspicion was directed especially against commercial opera. Within a few months of the uprising, the emperor issued an edict proscribing the performance of martial plays in the capital. "Performing plays among the populace," the edict reads, "has never been forbidden. But often there is a fondness for performing various plays about bravos who like to fight. The ignorant commoners mistake robbers and thieves for heroes and insubordination for righteousness. . . . It does great harm."[38] The emperor's concerns were not unfounded, for the rebels had included, among others, an owner of one of the city playhouses and several actors.[39] The fortunes of the Hechun Troupe, which excelled at martial plays, turned sour in the years immediately following the 1814 edict. Indeed, the troupe's creation of new multibook plays (such as *Eight-Court Pearl*) may have been one tactic to rekindle its livelihood after the emperor's attempt to suppress plays with martial content.[40]

All of this points to what might be called a growing culture of violence—both real and representational—that infused urban life in the early-nineteenth-century capital. It is not that we have not seen this before. Historians have long noted growing social unrest in China beginning in the late eighteenth century. But we find in the partial script of *Eight-Court Pearl* an example of urban audiences becoming ever more enamored of vigilantism as a response to official corruption.

14.4 WHO WERE THE DISAFFECTED?

It is tempting to link the urban appeal of the Hechun Troupe and its martial plays such as *Eight-Court Pearl* to growing Han alienation from Qing rule in the early decades of the nineteenth century. As the massive Qing Empire came to be challenged by domestic and foreign stresses, long-suppressed (or newfound) Han resentment at Manchu rule came to be expressed more openly. As such, the enthusiasm for such plays may also have foreshadowed the popular embrace of the Nian Rebellion (1851–1868) and Taiping Civil War (1850–1864) of the mid-nineteenth century, in which class warfare was harnessed to anti-Manchu hostility. The partial script of *Eight-Court Pearl*, however, suggests that that may not be all there is to the story. What, after all, should we make of the patronage of the Hechun Troupe by a Manchu princely household?

Members of the Zhuang Princedom had a lengthy history of involvement in drama, beginning with the first Prince Zhuang, Yunlu (1695–1767). Under the Qianlong reign, Yunlu, the emperor's uncle, had been made editor-in-chief of the *Great Compilation of Musical Scores from the Southern and Northern Arias in All Nine Modes (Jiugong dacheng nanbeici gongpu)*, a massive court-sponsored compilation of drama prosody. Yunlu was also closely involved in overseeing the creation of grand drama (*da xi*) for court spectatorship during the mid-Qianlong years, including *Annals of the Tripartite Division (Dingzhi chunqiu)*, based on the Three Kingdoms story cycle (☜ chap. 16).[41]

Other than the princely household patronage of the Hechun Troupe, which likely commenced circa 1803,[42] I have found no direct connection of Mianke, the titleholder to Prince Zhuang in the early nineteenth century, with drama creation or performance, although we know that by this time, Manchus living in the capital were so thoroughly besotted with opera that they were willing to risk their careers to flout edicts proscribing their attendance at commercial playhouses. Indeed, the Prince Zhuang of the subsequent generation, Imai (1814–1860), Mianke's thirteenth son, forfeited his branch of the family's princely title in perpetuity and was demoted from First Degree (*qinwang*) to Second Degree (*junwang*) Prince upon being caught participating in an orgy of opera performance and opium smoking at a nunnery in the outskirts of Beijing in 1838.[43]

Mianke's twelfth son, Yigeng (1809–1848), was a noted historian, writer, and storyteller.[44] He specialized in a signature Manchu genre of storytelling known as "bannermen tales" (*zidishu*), which was popular in Beijing and northeast China during the eighteenth and nineteenth centuries. A subset of these tales related the hardships of life in the banners, the Qing administrative system that regulated jobs, salary, and life in general for all Manchus (as well as some Han and Mongol subjects) in service to the imperial household in Beijing.[45] Yigeng, who also went by the pseudonym Master Helü (Helü shi), served as an imperial guardsman for six years, from 1831–1838.[46] He is most noted for his *Collected Writings of the Studio of Exquisite Dreams* (*Jiameng xuan congzhu*), an assortment of historical anecdotes about the Manchu nobility and notes on Manchu rituals, titles, and language. He is the known author of at least sixteen bannermen tales, most of which provide brief vignettes of contemporary life among the bannermen, with titles such as "On Imperial Guardsmen" ("Shiwei lun"), "The Lament of the Old Guardsman" ("Lao shiwei tan"), or "Master Helü's Own Lament" ("Helü zitan").[47]

The scholarship on Yigeng's bannermen tales reads them as barely veiled autobiographical records. Even if not transparently autobiographical, these narratives nevertheless reveal a sardonic and moralizing take on the foibles of the bannermen: they put on airs (with pretensions to the literary skills of Han men of letters); they flaunt their wealth (when they have it); they neglect their official duties as guardsmen (to pursue pleasures and entertainment such as opera); and they fall on hard times as they grow old (forced to pawn their belongings to make ends meet).

Yigeng was not alone among Manchu noblemen in voicing such concerns. His elder kinsman Zhaolian complained that the protocols for guards had become lax in his day, with men shirking their duties and, on occasion, even falling asleep on their watch in front of the palace gates.[48] Lower-ranking bannermen had even more reason to be disgruntled. The Manchu-language diary of Mucihiyan, a low-ranking bannerman in the nineteenth-century capital, reveals that many Manchus were caught between a rock and a hard place, not permitted to engage in work outside the imperial household but also insufficiently compensated by the banner bureaucracy to make ends meet. As the research of Bingyu Zheng illustrates, Manchus choosing to violate the injunctions against visits to playhouses was about more than getting furtive entertainment thrills; it was also a crucial method for forging vital survival networks for straitened bannermen. The boogeymen in Mucihiyan's diary are not Han; his Manchu supervisors are the ones who make his life miserable.[49]

Yigeng's vignettes of bannermen culture in his tales further call attention to the vicissitudes of life at court even for Manchus in the Aisin Gioro clan, the clan of the royal succession. The career trajectories of Mianke and Yigeng were no exception in this regard. Mianke, in his thirty-eight years of service, rose to the prestigious post of Chamberlain of the Imperial Bodyguard of the White Banner (*zheng baiqi ling shiwei nei dachen*), although he served at the whim of three successive emperors and on multiple occasions—in 1801, 1806, 1815, and 1823—was demoted or impeached for seemingly minor infractions: a servant being caught riding a horse onto the imperial path; an underling having commandeered the boat of a Han commoner; or dereliction of duty for having failed to notice rotting wood and cracked paint in the imperial tombs.[50] Yigeng lost his "top-rank official cap" (*toupin dingdai*) in 1828 on account of his deceased father's infractions and then was further humiliated at his brother's loss of the family's princely title in 1838, thereafter turning his talents to writing and storytelling.[51] Might the father, Mianke, have dabbled in ghostwriting for the Hechun Troupe when he was out of favor and down on his luck in January 1819? We can never know. But even if Mianke had no hand in the writing of *Eight-Court Pearl*, the fact that his household served as the guarantor of the Hechun Troupe suggests that even some imperial kinsmen sanctioned the sentiments in the play.

We can know, however, that the banner guardsmen of early-nineteenth-century Beijing, not unlike Mianke's sons (the writer Yigeng and the wastrel opera enthusiast Imai), as well as the plaintive diarist Mucihiyan, were intimately entangled with opera performance in the Qing capital. If they had money, they commissioned plays for private family performance by their own troupes.[52] Men like them also made up a large proportion of the literate (but not necessarily literary) cohort of operagoers in the city. Surely they populated the middlebrow audiences for the Hechun Troupe's martial-themed plays, which were snubbed by many Han men of letters in favor of more song-laden, romantic operas. And they, too, so it seems, reveled in the jabs at abuse of power and the vigilante solutions to the problem in plays like *Eight-Court Pearl*, not because they were anti-Manchu, but rather because they were anticorruption (even if some of them, on some level, may have been party to that self-same corruption). Resentment of abuse of power was a sentiment that seemed to animate Manchu and Han opera audiences alike in the early-nineteenth-century capital.

Indeed, the moralizing seen in Manchu-authored writings from the early nineteenth century, such as Zhaolian's *Miscellaneous Notes from the Whistling Pavilion* and Yigeng's *Collected Writings of the Studio of Exquisite Dreams* and his storytelling tales reveal a strain of critical Manchu self-reflection and anxiety about the downward slide of the bannermen and court politics in general. If this current of self-critique falls out of the record for much of the rest of the nineteenth century, it resurfaces in the politically engaged works of early-twentieth-century Manchu writers such as the amateur-turned-professional Peking opera star Wang Xiaonong (1858–1918), who quit his post as a Qing official to write and act in new Peking operas advocating constitutional monarchy; and the leftist writer Shu Qingchun, better known by his pen name, Laoshe (1899–1966), who wrote plays and semiautobiographical novels mocking the habituated airs of now-destitute Manchus.[53]

CONCLUSION

Eight-Court Pearl may not be great dramatic literature. The script, modeled on mid-seventeenth-century history plays, is derivative. Nevertheless, reading such performance scripts from the Qing dynasty can open an important window onto the political culture of Beijing in the early nineteenth century. The plot—with its focus on a world rife with abuse of power and its veiled finger pointing at Heshen, the most notorious of corrupt officials at the turn of the nineteenth century— offers insight into why such plays might have been so appealing to urban audiences. Changing the system was unthinkable beyond taking matters into one's own hands. Vicarious enjoyment of such vigilante action sold well in the commercial playhouses of the capital.

What is perhaps more surprising, given the tenuous associations between the Hechun Troupe and the Zhuang princely household, is that those with considerable access to power seemed equally drawn to the martial exploits of *Eight-Court Pearl* and other similar operas. This Manchu elite embrace of a populist sensibility anticipates the Qing court's patronage of more popular opera styles in the second half of the nineteenth century. While some powerful figures at court may have seen in this dramatic material simple solutions—and clear-cut, moralistic divisions between right and wrong—at a time of existential crisis, other Manchus, along with some of their fellow Han opera enthusiasts, seem to have sympathized with the veiled critique of the social and political order. Together, the ever-widening acceptance of such populist plays paved the way for the ascendancy of Peking opera to the status of national opera in the twentieth century.

Andrea S. Goldman

NOTES

1. Beginning in the mid-eighteenth century, all commercial opera troupes were at least nominally sponsored by or registered with a princely household, which acted as a guarantor for the company.

2. The given name is also rendered as Jingxi.

3. See the record of the 1950 interview with Geng Jinxi in Zhu Jiajin, *Gugong tuishilu* (A Record of Leisure in the Imperial Palace) Beijing: Beijing chubanshe, 1999), 419. See also You Fukai, "Wan Qing neiting xiban 'putian tongqing ban' chutan" (A Preliminary Discussion of the Late Qing Court Opera Troupe 'All Under Heaven Celebrates'), *Yishu pinglun* (Art Criticism) 22 (2012): 1–43.

4. In 1827, the Daoguang emperor eradicated the Nanfu agency that was formerly responsible for palace entertainment, in its stead establishing the scaled-down Shengping shu. Many noneunuch actors were dismissed from service at the time. The Shengping shu continued to serve the Qing court's entertainment needs even after the fall of the dynasty and up until the former child emperor Puyi and his staff were evicted from the palace in 1924. For more on the Shengping shu, see Ye Xiaoqing, *Ascendant Peace in the Four Seas: Drama and the Qing Imperial Court* (Hong Kong: Chinese University Press, 2012).

5. According to the Account Book (*zhangben*) of the Zhongguo yishu yanjiuyuan, the entire lot was acquired for 3.3 million yuan old scrip (equivalent to 330 yuan new scrip) in 1952, shortly after the founding of the institution; based on the Account Book and personal communication with Dai Yun and Liu Xiaomin, librarians and researchers at the Zhongguo yishu yanjiuyuan.

6. Copying of the first book of the script began on January 1, 1819; the fifth book was completed on January 15. The opening aria tune title has been crossed out and replaced by another, livelier tune, hinting strongly that someone was preparing the script for production. The opening tune title is "Roaming the Earth" ("Rao di you"), a standard opening aria in southern tune suites. The title was crossed out and replaced by the new tune title, "Painting the Lips Red" ("Dian jiang chun"), another common opening aria, but in the northern tune style. On the significance of the tune titles, I have benefited from consultations with the Chinese opera scholars Lu Yingkun and Wu Xinmiao (personal communication).

7. The script bears three seals in addition to the name of the troupe. The two red ink seal stamps are of the Zhongguo yishu yanjiuyuan and its Xiqu yanjiusuo (Traditional Drama Institute). A third seal stamp, in black ink, reads "Jingting," and this is likely the seal of the previous collector, who perhaps was associated with Geng Yuqing.

8. The Qing organized its military and administrative structure around banners, for a total of twenty-four, with eight each designated as Manchu, Mongol, and Han banners. The eight Iron

Hat princes were the most powerful noble houses among the Manchu banners, given this inherited distinction because they were the descendants of the founding dynastic princes. See Mark C. Elliott, *The Manchu Way: The Eight Banners and Ethnic Identity in Late Imperial China* (Stanford, CA: Stanford University Press, 2001).

9. Dai Yun, "Xunzhao Hechun ban de zuji" (Tracing the Footsteps of the Hechun Troupe), *Xiqu yishu* (Theater Arts) 30, no. 3 (2009): 33–39; Andrea S. Goldman, *Opera and the City: The Politics of Culture in Beijing, 1770–1900* (Stanford, CA: Stanford University Press, 2012).

10. Dai, "Xunzhao Hechun ban de zuji," 33–39; Goldman, *Opera and the City*.

11. Performances in playhouses in the mid-to-late Qing were made up of sets of scenes from longer *chuanqi* dramas. The parts of the "scroll" scenes consisted of connected scenes from the same longer drama, loosely rendering the full storyline—or at least a significant section of it—from the longer narrative of the play. Typically, a day's lineup included a "beginning scroll," a "middle scroll," and a "final scroll," with shorter one- or two-scene selections interspersed between the parts of each scroll. This terminology may have been inspired by painted handscrolls, which were unrolled and viewed one section at a time (David Rolston, personal communication).

12. Some of the tune titles in *Eight-Court Pearl* are simply listed as "*bangzi*," a designation for a popular northern musical style distinguished by the rhythmic hitting of a wooden block to keep the tempo and composed of parallel rhyming couplets. *Bangzi* is often loosely rendered in English as "clapper opera."

13. In hand-copied performance scripts, the role types of the characters are not always identified. But Hu Tong is likely played by a supporting male (*fu*).

14. As indicated previously, no role type for this character is indicated in the script.

15. These performance scripts are written with a mix of traditional, simplified, and "alternative" characters. To the best of the ability of contemporary Chinese software, I have captured the mix of characters in the Chinese rendering of the text here and throughout the rest of this discussion.

16. "Pure yang essence" is a literary phrase for semen. The Fox Spirit needs semen to complete her cultivation as an immortal.

17. According to legend, the Weaving Maid and the Cowherd are immortals who fall in love against the wishes of the Queen Mother of the West. As punishment, they are sent down to Earth as lowly mortals. After their return to immortality, they become star-crossed lovers who see each other only once a year, on the seventh night of the seventh month, when magpies create a bridge across the sky that allows them to meet.

18. In palace scripts, the designation of animal plus *xing* (or likeness) can indicate that the actor dons a mask and full body animal costume (David Rolston, personal communication). This may be indicated in the minimal stage directions given in this passage here.

19. No role type is indicated for this character.

20. This tune title is likely an orthographic corruption of either "Jiangtou jingui" (The Golden Cassia at the Riverhead) or "Jiangtou songbie" (Parting at the Riverhead).

21. These were some of the few scenes from the original drama that transitioned from *kunju* to *pihuang* performance in the commercial marketplace. The Traditional Drama Library of the Zhongguo yishu yanjiuyuan alone holds more than five versions of this drama, including a late Ming woodblock thirty-scene edition; a nineteenth-century manuscript edition of "Stabbing Tang Qin" ("Ci Tang"), Xueyan's revenge scene, for performance in Kunqu; a single-role Kunqu script (with choreography notes); a Qing court edition rendered into the Peking opera genre, likely created for the viewing pleasure of the renowned theater aficionado Empress Dowager Cixi; and a 1917 edition labeled as *cai xi* (short for *dengcai xi* or "lantern plays"), possibly indicating that it was for performance with lanterns before the now-deposed emperor still living within the imperial palace.

22. The earliest extant version of this play has thirty-five scenes. An abridged nineteenth-century Kunqu manuscript of the play housed in the Traditional Drama Library of the Zhongguo yishu yanjiuyuan and titled *Wuren yi* (Five Righteous Men) comprised sixteen scenes. Versions of this play have also been rendered in Peking opera and other regional musical genres.

23. The tofu patch refers to the white square of face paint that covers the eyes and nose of actors playing the clown and *fu* (usually villain) roles.

24. Zhu Xian's mother is identified by the character *fu*, scribal shorthand for *furen*, or "madam."

25. David S. Nivison, "Ho-shen and His Accusers: State and Ideology in the Eighteenth Century," in *Confucianism in Action*, eds. David S. Nivison and Arthur Wright (Stanford, CA: Stanford University Press, 1959), 211.

26. Zhaolian, *Xiaoting zalu* (Miscellaneous Notes from the Whistling Pavilion) (Beijing: Zhonghua shuju, 1997, reprint), 103.

27. Zhaolian, *Xiaoting zalu*, 212; and Jiao Xun, *Yishu* (Reminiscing Over Letters), cited in Xiao Yishan, *Qingdai tongshi* (A Survey History of the Qing Dynasty) (Shanghai: Shangwu yinshuguan, 1928), vol. 2, 194.

28. This anecdote, based on the observation of Sun Shiyi (1720–1796), is recounted in Xiao Yishan, *Qingdai tongshi*, 193–194.

29. Feng Zuozhe, *Heshen qi ren* (On Heshen) (Beijing: Zhongguo kexue chubanshe, 2008), 196.

30. For more on the *Dibao* as a source of gossip, see Emily Mokros, *The Peking Gazette in Late Imperial China: State News and Political Authority* (Seattle: University of Washington Press, 2021), especially chapter 3, "State News in the Marketplace."

31. The list of these characters includes Fang Ju, Xiong Zhang, and Yan Xiu.

32. No role type is indicted in the script, but Yan Xiu is probably played by a martial male (*wusheng*).

33. The tune title is not denoted in the script.

34. See Xiaofei Kang, *The Cult of the Fox: Power, Gender, and Popular Religion in Late Imperial and Modern China* (New York: Columbia University Press, 2006).

35. Rania Huntington, *Alien Kind: Foxes and Late Imperial Chinese Narrative* (Cambridge, MA: Harvard University Asia Center, 2003), 80.

36. Another text from the mid-seventeenth century that opens with the theme of a demon gone awry is the anonymous *Taowu xianping* (A Frivolous Account of a Monster), a novelistic account of the rise and fall of Wei Zhongxian.

37. On the Tianlijiao uprising, see Susan Naquin, *Millenarian Rebellion in China: The Eight Trigrams Uprising of 1813* (New Haven, CT: Yale University Press, 1976).

38. Cited in Dai, "Xunzhao Hechun ban de zuji," 35.

39. Dai, "Xunzhao Hechun ban de zuji," 35.

40. Dai, "Xunzhao Hechun ban de zuji," 35.

41. Zhaolian, *Xiaoting xulu* (Supplementary to Miscellaneous Notes from the Whistling Pavilion), 378.

42. Dai, "Xunzhao Hechun ban de zuji," 33–34.

43. On this incident, see Goldman, *Opera and the City*, 92–95; and Kang Baocheng, "Zidishu zuozhe "Helü shi" shengping, jiashi kaolüe" (A Brief Study of the Life and Pedigree of Zidishu Author, Master Helü), *Wenxian* (Documents) 4 (October 1999): 139. See also Chongyi, *Dao Xian yilai chaoye zaji* (Assorted Notes About the Court and Society Since the Daoguang and Xianfeng Eras) (Beijing: Beijing guji chubanshe, 1982), 19–20.

44. I have retained the Chinese romanization for Yigeng (rather than Manchu pronunciation) since international library catalogs follow pinyin romanization for his name.

45. On Yigeng's dates, see Elena Suet-Ying Chiu, *Bannermen Tales (Zidishu): Manchu Storytelling and Cultural Hybridity in the Qing Dynasty* (Cambridge, MA.: Harvard University Asia Center, 2018), 237; cf. Kang Baocheng, "Zidishu zuozhe "Helü shi" shengping, jiashi kaolüe," 135–136, which speculates that Yigeng was Mianke's eldest son.

46. Yigeng, "Shiwei suoyan" ("Random Words of an Imperial Guardsman"), in *Jiameng xuan congzhu* (Collected Writings of the Studio of Exquisite Dreams), in *Jindai Zhongguo shiliao congkan* (Collected Publications of Modern Chinese Historical Sources), ed. Shen Yunlong (Taipei: Wenhai chubanshe, 1970, reprint), vol. 522, 439.

47. See Chiu, *Bannermen Tales*, 236–257; and Kang, "Zidishu zuozhe 'Helü shi' shengping, jiashi kaolüe," 129–130.

48. Zhaolian, *Xiaoting zalu*, 102. See also Chiu, *Bannermen Tales*, 247.

49. Bingyu Zheng, "Managing Daily Life in Nineteenth-Century Beijing: A Bannerman's Diary," 2018 Association for Asian Studies paper.

50. As cited in Kang, "Zidishu zuozhe "Helü shi" shengping, jiashi kaolüe," 133–134.

51. See Chiu, *Bannermen Tales*, 237–238.

52. On the importance of the princely households to the cultivation and perpetuation of troupes that performed combined Kun-Yi opera, see Lu Yingkun, *Beijing gaoqiang yanjiu* (A Study of "High Melody" Opera in Beijing) (Beijing: Zhongguo renmin daxue chubanshe, 2017), 33–35.

53. On the Peking opera plays of Wang Xiaonong, see Joshua L. Goldstein, *Drama Kings: Players and Publics in the Re-creation of Peking Opera, 1870–1937* (Berkeley: University of California Press, 2007), chap. 3; and Rebecca E. Karl, *Staging the World: Chinese Nationalism at the Turn of the Twentieth Century* (Durham, NC: Duke University Press, 2002), chap. 2.

PRIMARY SOURCES

BCZ   Anonymous. *Bachao zhu* 八朝珠 (*The Eight-Pearl Court*). 1819. Manuscript in the Geng Yuqing 耿玉清 collection. Zhongguo yishu yanjiuyuan 中國藝術研究院 (Library of the Chinese National Academy of Arts), Beijing.

LYXQJ Chen Guyu 陳古虞, Chen Duo 陳多, and Ma Shenggui 馬聖貴, ed. and ann. *Li Yu xiqu ji* 李玉戲曲集 (*The Collected Plays of Li Yu*). 3 vols. Shanghai: Shanghai guji chubanshe, 2004.

QYLS   Zhang Cixi 張次溪, ed. *Qingdai Yandu liyuan shiliao* 清代燕都梨園史料 (*Historical Materials on the Qing-Dynasty Theater in Beijing*). Beijing: Zhongguo xiju chubanshe, 1988.

SUGGESTED READINGS

ENGLISH

Chiu, Elena Suet-Ying. *Bannermen Tales (*Zidishu*): Manchu Storytelling and Cultural Hybridity in the Qing Dynasty*. Cambridge, MA: Harvard University Asia Center, 2018.

Elliott, Mark C. *The Manchu Way: The Eight Banners and Ethnic Identity in Late Imperial China*. Stanford, CA: Stanford University Press, 2001.

Goldman, Andrea S. *Opera and the City: The Politics of Culture in Beijing, 1770–1900*. Stanford, CA: Stanford University Press, 2012.

Mackerras, Colin P. *The Rise of Peking Opera, 1770–1870: Social Aspects of the Theatre in Manchu China*. Oxford, UK: Clarendon Press, 1972.

Ye Xiaoqing. *Ascendant Peace in the Four Seas: Drama and the Qing Imperial Court*. Hong Kong: Chinese University of Hong Kong Press, 2012.

CHINESE

Dai Yun 戴雲. "Xunzhao Hechun ban de zuji" 尋找和春班的足跡 (Tracing the Footsteps of the Hechun Troupe). *Xiqu yishu* 戲曲藝術 (*Theater Arts*), 30, no. 3 (2009): 33–39.

Feng Zuozhe 馮佐哲. *Heshen qi ren* 和珅其人 (*On Heshen*). Beijing: Zhongguo kexue chubanshe, 2008.

Fu Jin 傅謹. *Xiban* 戲班 (*On Theater Troupes*). Beijing: Beijing daxue chubanshe, 2010.

Lu Eting 陸萼庭. *Kunju yanchu shigao* 崑劇演出史稿 (*A Draft History of Kun Opera Performance*). Shanghai: Shanghai wenyi chubanshe, 1980.

Lu Yingkun 路應昆. *Beijing gaoqiang yanjiu* 北京高腔研究 (*A Study of "High Melody" Opera in Beijing*). Beijing: Zhongguo renmin chubanshe, 2017.

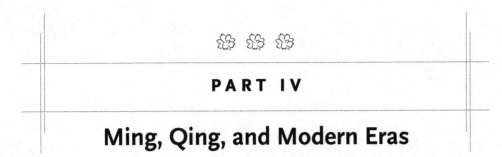

PART IV

Ming, Qing, and Modern Eras

Ritual Plays

Mulian Rescues His Mother

Play Structure, Ritual, and Soundscapes

One of the major contributions of Buddhism to Chinese family life consisted of expanding the repertoire of the ritual actions that sons, daughters, and later descendants could undertake to improve the fate of their deceased parents, grandparents, and other ancestors. On the one hand, according to the Buddhist notion of karma, it was believed that one's actions in this life owed something to one's conduct in previous lives, but they could also shape one's future existence in the human or one of the other five realms (two kinds of hell and an animal realm on the lower end and two kinds of godly realms on the higher end, with the human realm sandwiched in between). On the other hand, the benefits of good karmic acts were not limited to oneself—one could seek to generate merit on behalf of other beings—relatives, strangers, animals, or orphaned ghosts—with the assistance of Buddhist deities and clergy to help them attain a better current, posthumous, or future life. Specifically, as a filial descendant, one could sponsor certain rituals at certain times of the year to rescue souls that were languishing in one of the many Buddhist hells and deliver them to a less painful form of existence. The exemplary filial son in Chinese Buddhist lore is a merchant-turned-monk by the name of Mulian, who went to great lengths to rescue his deceased mother from the depths of hell and whose heroic exploits eventually gave his name to a memorable subgenre of Chinese drama, the "Mulian Rescues His Mother from Hell" plays (*Mulian jiumu*).

According to the play, Mulian was a filial son by the name of Fu Luobo (Turnip), who treated his parents very respectfully. But when Mulian went on a business trip, his mother, Madam Liu Qingti, started to live a sinful life behind her son's back. Heaven condemned Madam Liu to die abruptly and be banished to the lowest of all the many fearsome hells. Once Mulian found out that his mother was suffering in the underworld, he was heartbroken. He became a monk and eventually was admitted to the ranks of Buddha's immediate disciples. Empowered by the Buddha with two magic tools, Mulian was able to enter and tour the different levels of hell to search for his deceased mother. Eventually, following the Buddha's instructions, Mulian organized the grand Yulanpen Ceremony to collectively deliver the souls of the deceased from hell and to release his mother from her reincarnation as a dog. Thanks to the superior power of this particular ritual of salvation, she attained rebirth as a human being, and Mulian's family was happily reunited.

Compared to the other plays discussed in this anthology, Mulian drama is notable for its distinctive performance context. Typically, the play has been embedded in a body of Chinese ritual practices pertaining to the salvation of the souls of ancestors, the deliverance of the orphaned souls of strangers, rites of exorcism, and the celebration of the birthday of a deity. Similar to other Chinese opera performances, the performance of Mulian plays offers pleasure and amusement to the audience, a point also borne out by historical documents. However, as this chapter will argue, staging a Mulian play is not primarily intended for pleasurable entertainment or aesthetic delight. Rather, on a communal scale, Mulian plays have been performed as ritual operas in Chinese memorial rites held during the Ghost Festival, either as part of the Buddhist Yulanpen Festival or the parallel Daoist Zhongyuan Festival observed on the fifteenth day of the lunar Seventh Month, as well as on other festive occasions. On a smaller scale, the Mulian story has also been performed by Daoist priests as a form of operatic ritual at private funeral services conducted for an individual. As such, these plays are closely connected with the idea of ritual efficacy designed to benefit dead people and living communities alike.

The inspiration for the Mulian plays came from a variety of earlier Buddhist texts about Mulian (Mahāmaudgalyāyana in Sanskrit), one of the Buddha's two chief disciples.[1] Two Chinese sutras tell the story of how Mulian's quest for his mother resulted in the establishment of the Ghost Festival; however, it was most likely another genre, the so-called transformation texts (*bianwen*) (⟿ *HTRC Fiction*, chap. 3), a Tang-dynasty Buddhist "show-and-tell" sort of performance geared toward illiterate lay audiences, that made Mulian a household name in medieval China. With at least one version accompanied by now-lost pictures, Mulian transformation texts popularized the idea that offerings presented directly from the descendants to their ancestors were not as efficacious as those given on behalf of the ancestors to the community of Buddhist monks at the end of their summer retreat. It also provided a very vivid map of all the different hells and portrayed salvation as a collaborative effort between the Buddha, his monk-cum-disciple Mulian, devoted Buddhist laypeople, and the mother herself.

The earliest record of a performance of a Mulian play dates to the twelfth century, when people were said to have attended Mulian shows in the lead-up to the Ghost Festival in the Song-dynasty capital of Kaifeng. However, the first extant and most influential dramatic version of the story was written by the Ming dynasty literatus Zheng Zhizhen (1518–1595). Not only did Zheng compose a full-length Mulian play entitled *Mulian Rescues His Mother: An Exhortation to Goodness* (*Xinbian Mulian jiumu quanshan xiwen*), but shortly after its completion, it appeared in print in 1582. A sprawling compendium of all manner of religious-themed stories woven around the core plot of Mulian, the play runs to more than 100 scenes spread across three volumes. For many of the stories included in the plot and subplots of the play, Zheng's version became the authoritative rendering that exerted a profound influence on late Ming, Qing, and even modern retellings of these tales. At the same time, as we shall see, the performative context also shaped the enactment of the play in major ways.

Given the importance of Zheng's adaptation of the Mulian story, this chapter will analyze his version of the play and what it can tell us about the structure of Ming drama, the soundscape of exorcism, and beliefs about the ritual efficacy of

Chinese drama. To situate Zheng's version of the Mulian story, the discussion begins by explicating the context and iconography of hell found in the "Mulian Transformation Text." The next section examines how Zheng rewrote and restructured the Mulian story to make it conform to the ideological and compositional requirements of late Ming *chuanqi* drama. The final section of the chapter discusses the ritual features when the play was staged for religious purposes. As we will see, in Chinese rites of exorcism, Mulian drama used special sonic effects to accrue blessings to the community in which such plays were being performed.

15.1 THE ICONOGRAPHY OF HELL

With the greater penetration of Buddhism into popular strata of Chinese society in the Tang dynasty, depictions of hell assumed ever-greater prominence in visual and literary sources. In the late seventh century, a school of painters began to specialize in what were called "the transformation of hells" (*diyu bianxiang*). The founder of that lineage had a near-death experience and was said to have toured various hells. His firsthand experience became the basis for his tableaux of hell, which adorned major temples in the capital of Chang'an. However, it was the talent of his student, Wu Daoxuan (also known as Wu Daozi, fl. 713–755), which became synonymous with the highest achievement in the rendering of such images. Folklore reported that one of Wu's murals of hell was so fearsome that "everyone in the capital saw it and they all feared punishment and cultivated goodness; butchers and wine sellers in the two markets did not do any business."[2] And when a Tang Chan Buddhist master wanted to describe the idea of fear, he invoked such paintings as the most fear-inducing sight imaginable:

> When you all see that there is danger—when you see various things endangering your life, a tiger or knives and swords—you immediately become uncontrollably frightened. What is this like? It is just like the world's master painter, one who normally paints transformation scenes of hell, who, after painting tigers and knives and swords, looks closely at them and himself becomes frightened.[3]

The form that most likely popularized such images and notions of hell were the transformation texts told by itinerant storytellers via images and prosimetric narratives. Found among the large cache of texts preserved near Dunhuang, a desert oasis along the Silk Road, such transformation tales addressed themselves to unlettered audiences. As it happens, one of the most famous transformation texts is the one of the eleven devoted to Mulian, with the full title "The Transformation Text on Mulian Rescuing His Mother from the Underworld, with Pictures, One Scroll, with Preface" (anonymous, late ninth to early tenth centuries, hereafter "Transformation"). Originally, this text was accompanied by about twenty pictures, which most likely depicted the various major stations of Mulian's underworld journey: the river at the entrance of hell; the court of King Yama, one of the major kings of Hell; and several infamous hells, such as the Knife Hill–cum–Sword Forest Hell, the Copper Pillar–cum–Iron Bed Hell, and the dreaded Avici Hell. While the pictures have been lost, the text itself offers vivid images of the various courts of hell that Mulian traverses.[4] It was no coincidence that such lore had grown around Mulian, who was, as an early Chinese Buddhist put it, "best at shamanic travel [among Buddha's disciples]. He often rode the spiritual penetrations along the six paths of rebirth, viewing the good and evil retribution suffered by sentient beings and returning to explain it to humans."[5] In "Transformation," most narrative attention is lavished on the two lowest registers of existence—that is, the hungry ghosts and the hell dwellers—as the text lays out the cosmography of the netherworld in excruciating detail. When Mulian secured a magic tool from the Buddha to open the doors of the heinous Avici Hell, the horrors that await him are described as follows:

> Mulian walked forward and came to a hell. When he was something over a hundred paces from it, he was sucked in by the fiery gases and nearly tumbled over. It was the Avici Hell with lofty walls of iron, which were so immense that they reached to the clouds. Swords and lances bristled in ranks, knives and spears clustered in rows. Sword trees reached upward for a thousand fathoms with a clattering flourish as their needle-sharp points brushed together. Knife mountains soared ten thousand rods in a chaotic jumble of interconnecting cliffs and crags. Fierce fires throbbed, seeming to leap about the entire sky with a thunderous roar. Sword-wheels whirled. . . . Iron snakes belched fire. . . . Copper dogs breathed smoke. Metal thorns descended chaotically from midair, piercing the chests of the men. Awls and augurs flew by every which way, gouging the backs of the women. Iron rakes flailed at their eyes. . . . Copper pitchforks jabbed at their loins. Thereupon, they were made to crawl up the knife-mountains and enter the furnace coals. Their skulls were smashed to bits, their bones and flesh decomposed; tendons and skin snapped, liver and gall broke. Ground flesh spurted and splattered beyond the four gates; congealed blood drenched and drooked the pathways, which run through the black clods of hell. With wailing voices, they called out to heaven—moan, groan. . . . There were more than several ten thousand jailers [that is, demon-bailiffs] and all were ox-headed and horse-faced.
>
> [*DHBWJ* 726; trans. Mair, 627]

Echoes of such earlier imagery can be found in later descriptions of dramatic renditions of the Mulian story. Typically, Mulian plays were performed at night and lasted into the morning, thus making night itself part of the atmospheric charge of the performance. In his oft-cited work *Dream Memories of Tao'an* (*Tao'an mengyi*), Zhang Dai (1597–1684), a well-known theater aficionado, describes how the stage setting of an elaborate performance of a Mulian play that he witnessed evoked the cosmography of hell (☞ *HTRCP-CCC*, L37). According to Zhang, after being regaled with some magnificent eye-catching acrobatics (☞ Introduction), the audience found itself surrounded by vividly frightful scenes from the pantheon of the netherworld:

There were heavenly gods and earthly spirits, ox-headed and horse-faced [demon-bailiffs from hell], the spirits of Ghost Mother and Death Star, [the attendants of hell known as] yakshas and rakshas, [the tools of tortures found in the various hells such as] saws, grind-stones, and three-legged cauldrons, the gleaming iciness of Knife Hill, the Sword Forest of King Yama's hell, the blood oozing from the Iron Walls [of the Avici Hell]—everything was as vivid as the "Transformation Images of Hell" painted by Wu Daozi.

[*TAMY* 78, "Mulian Performance" ("Mulian xi")]

Thus, Mulian drama would come to incorporate aspects of the earlier literary and visual traditions, but as we shall see, it also offered new immersive ways to experience the story of Mulian. Dramatic renditions could tell a tale of filial devotion in hellish realms, but by virtue of enlisting actors—and at times the audience—in the representations of ghosts and ghostliness at nighttime, the netherworld unfolded before the audience's very eyes and ears. This liveness, the very immediate presence of such spectral forms, could collapse the spatial boundaries between the narrated "hells there" and the context of "our lives here." Most important, perhaps, as this chapter will show, the amalgam of the spectral and the theatrical united actors and audience into a mode of ritual action designed to keep these spectral presences at bay and bring peace and prosperity to the community.

15.2 ZHENG ZHIZHEN'S *MULIAN RESCUES HIS MOTHER*: EXHORTATION TO GOODNESS

As noted previously, we know that a Mulian play was performed as early as the twelfth century in Kaifeng, the imperial capital of the northern Song dynasty (960–1126). The memoir *The Eastern Capital: A Record of a Dream of Splendor* (*Dongjing Menghua lu*), written not long after the fall of Kaifeng in 1127 by one of its former residents (*HTRCProse*, C12.2), documents the practices associated with important holidays. Thus, in the winter, New Year's festivities started with purifying activities of an exorcistic nature and culminated in the grand Lantern Festival on the fifteenth day of the first lunar month, which inaugurated a new agricultural season. In the summer, the Ghost Festival on the fifteenth day of the seventh month marked the beginning of another period of renewal. As ghosts of all sorts were believed to have been released from hell and roam the world during the seventh month, they needed to either be kept in check (hungry ghosts) or promoted (ancestral ghosts) through different kinds of offerings to ensure the continued harmony of the earthly realm. The Ghost Festival is among the earliest holidays that we know to have been celebrated with specific theatrical entertainments:

The Ghost Festival took place during the fifteenth day of the seventh month. For several days prior to the festival the markets sold [ritual] items [to be offered to] the netherworld . . . They also sold printed texts of *The Scripture*

on Mulian, the Most Honorable One . . . After the seventh night, performers
from the entertainment quarters performed the variety play *Mulian Rescues
His Mother.* It was performed until the fifteenth day to an ever-growing number of viewers.[6]

[*DJMHL* 8.211–212]

During the seven days leading up to the Ghost Festival, professional actors
regaled audiences from all walks of life with the Mulian story. Printed scriptures
and paper offerings were sold at market. Evidently, the Buddhist scriptures were
printed and sold for public consumption; but, as with all known play titles from the
northern Song period, no playtext of the Mulian drama survives today. Although it
is hard to know for certain, a full written text of the play likely did not exist at this
early juncture. Given that a majority of the performers in those days were illiterate, the contents of the play, the associated performing skills, and the specific staging techniques would probably have been passed from generation to generation,
mainly through oral transmission. Hence, Mulian theatricals were part of a folk
tradition that was performed on festive occasions in various local villages and provincial towns, as well as in the imperial capital.

It was not until the end of the sixteenth century that Zheng Zhizhen composed
the first full-text version of a Mulian play—*Mulian Rescues His Mother: An Exhortation to Goodness* (hereafter *Exhortation*)—which was published in 1582 in Huizhou
(Anhui province), one of the major centers of publishing during the late Ming
period (1550–1644). A native of Qimen county in the Huizhou region, Zheng was a
Confucian scholar who had received formal education in the Chinese classics and
traditional learning. Similar to the social identity of a majority of the authors of
late Ming drama, Zheng was not a professional playwright per se. According to
one of the prefaces to *Exhortation*, Zheng had repeatedly failed the imperial civil
examination, and then he decided to retreat to his personal artistic world and
devote himself to literary writing.[7]

Two points deserve special attention here. First, one particular preface highlights that Zheng lived a leisurely life after failing the civil examinations and wrote
Exhortation for his own amusement. However, we should not necessarily take
this claim at face value. "Devoting oneself to one's literary interests" is a standard
euphemism used by a cultural elite who, for a variety of reasons, did not hold office
and was otherwise engaged in writing popular literature, including drama and fiction. Because fiction and drama were believed to reach even uneducated men and
women, such writers thought it was a particularly effective way to live up to the
Confucian ideal of providing a moral education for the public. As Zheng Zhizhen
noted in his own preface to the play, "If goodness is commended, people will love
to do it. If evil is reproached, people will be frightened and avoid doing it."[8]

Second, Zheng's motive for composing *Exhortation* was also driven by more
practical reasons. He likely aspired to produce a "marketable version" of the Mulian
play that could be commercially printed in the flourishing publishing industry of
Huizhou or staged with the patronage of the wealthy Huizhou merchants, who

advocated traditional Confucian ethics of filial piety and female chastity. Thus, whereas previous extant versions of the Mulian story had a strong Buddhist flavor, Zheng combined Confucian ethical values and the Buddho-Daoist world of spirits, gods, and demons in new ways. Rather than relying on Buddhist or Daoist definitions of what constituted good and evil behavior, Zheng emphasized that the violation of Confucian ideas such as filial piety, female chastity, and widow fidelity would result in punishment in hell. In addition, aware that for sixteenth-century audiences, the breaking of vegetarian vows on the part of Mulian's mother would have been insufficient cause to merit her banishment to the depths of hell, Zheng added more grievous acts to the roster of Madame Liu's sins, such as killing dogs to feed monks, burning down the vegetarian halls of the monks, burning monks to death, and violating the deathbed instructions of her husband. Conversely, in the heavenly part of the other world, it was Confucian exemplars such as good officials, filial sons, and chaste women who occupied the highest ranks, ahead of Buddhist monks and Daoist priests.[9] Most interesting, perhaps, is that Zheng mapped some of story elements onto the local landscape in Huizhou. It is in Zheng's native village of Qingxi, for example, that Mulian finds the canine incarnation of his mother.[10] So prominent and pervasive did Mulian performances become in the Huizhou region that a modern proverb notes, "[E]ven dogs can howl out the three volumes of the Mulian song-drama."[11] How did Zheng structure the story so that it became a mainstay of theatrical performances not only in Huizhou, but in the other southern regions like Jiangsu, Jiangxi, Fujian, Hunan, and Sichuan? A closer look at the structure of the play will shed some light on this question.

15.3 *EXHORTATION*: STRUCTURE AND PLOT

The publication of the three-volume *Exhortation* marks a crucial landmark in the evolution of the Mulian plays in Chinese drama. Written as a *chuanqi*, the play consists of 104 scenes in three separate volumes (*juan*) with 34 scenes in volume 1, 36 scenes in volume 2, and 34 scenes in volume 3.[12] Through the voice of an actor appearing in the opening scene of volume 3, the author introduces his mode of composition: "Having searched for facts and consulted earlier narratives, I composed these arias for dramatic performance" [*MLJM* 3:322]. What I have translated here as "earlier narratives" (*chenbian*) may imply that there were, perhaps, short local performances and rearranged scenes staged at local theaters. Using these earlier versions as the basic skeleton, Zheng Zhizhen produced an original full-length edition through restructuring the plot of the narrative, enriching the scenes with new subject matter, adding new arias, and incorporating a variety of folk songs, comic skits, stories of immortality, independent morality tales, and other short performances into the three-volume framework.

Compared with other works of Ming drama, *Exhortation* is explicit about how its structure relates to the intended performance of the play. The opening scene ("Kaichang") of volume 1 announces: "We are going to present the *Exhortation* in three volumes; tonight, we shall perform Volume 1" [*MLJM* 1]. In the last scene of volume 3 (entitled "The Great Yulanpen Ceremony" ["Yulan dahui"]), the two concluding lines read: "The Mulian play is now completed after this three-night performance. The merits of the fellow believers will continue to flourish for thousands of generations" [*MLJM* 3:499]. Analyzed from this point of view, the tripartite structure of *Exhortation* is designed specifically for a three-day performance. In the ideal conception of the performance, it would take three days to complete the whole play, with one volume being mounted each day.[13]

Volume 1 introduces the story of the virtuous Fu Xiang, the subsequent business trip of Mulian, and his mother's sinful transgressions at home during Mulian's absence. This volume starts with the Fu family joyfully celebrating the Lunar New Year and ends with Mulian returning home and reuniting with his mother. The plot is organized in a tripartite structure—the family gathering at New Year's, Mulian's journey, and the family reunion. As with other Chinese plays, such a structure of union, separation, and reunion conforms to a sensibility of Chinese drama—that is, the interweaving of the sorrow of parting and the joy of reunion (*beihuan lihe*).

Mulian's father, Fu Xiang, is a virtuous believer in Buddhism. Both Fu Xiang and his wife, Liu Sizhen (Mulian's mother, also known as Liu Qingti and Madam Liu in the play), practice charity and provide generous alms to Daoist priests and Buddhist monks and nuns. The original name of Mulian is Fu Luobo before he converts and becomes a close disciple of the Buddha at the end of volume 2. The family lives a harmonious and religious life. However, the situation changes after Fu Xiang dies. Instigated by her brother Liu Jia, Liu Sizhen breaks the Buddhist precept of vegetarian fasting, surreptitiously consuming all kinds of meats—a strictly prohibited and unacceptable behavior for a devout Buddhist. More shockingly, she insults and expels monks by burning their lodges. Meanwhile, during Mulian's business trip, he encounters a group of bandits in the Diamond Mountain. In this desperate moment, Guanyin (Avalokiteśvara, the goddess of mercy), transforms herself into the bandits' confidant, not only saving Luobo, but also converting the ten bandits, who become sworn brothers of Luobo and are hitherto referred to as Ten Friends. Learning about the sinful transgressions of his mother from Guanyin, Luobo promptly returns home. The final scene, "Mother and Son Reunited," closes the volume with a happy reunion between Luobo and Liu Sizhen, highlighting the virtue of filial piety.

In Chinese dramaturgy, the dramatic closure of the first volume is known as "Minor Finale" ("Xiaoshousha"). In the famous treatise *Leisure Notes* (*Xianqing ouji*) (☞ chap. 11), the drama critic and playwright Li Yu (1611–1680) discussed this feature in the following manner:

> Minor finale: In the final scene of the first half (of the play), the plot development is to be suspended, and the music briefly halted. This is called "Minor Finale." . . . This will lead people (i.e., audience/reader) to speculate about what will happen next and how the situation will be resolved.
>
> [*XQOJ* 68, "The Minor Finale" ("Xiaoshousha")]

The dramatic design of the "Minor Finale" ends the first day's performance of *Exhortation* with a temporary happy conclusion, leading the audience to ask:

What will happen next to this family? Will Luobo discover the sinful behavior of Madam Liu? Given the filial character of Luobo, can such a harmonious relationship between mother and son be sustained?

The performance resumes on the second day. The plot of volume 2 is structured as two parallel journeys: the descent of the deceased Madam Liu into hell and the pilgrimage of Luobo to "the West" (meaning India) to seek help from the Buddha to rescue his mother. Such a story cycle reveals another tripartite structure—family union, Mulian's and Madam Liu's journeys, and Mulian's reunion with the Buddha.

The first scene of volume 2 presents a pleasant and delightful family gathering, at which Luobo greets his mother by offering her a cup of the wine of longevity. The sunny and lively spring scenery establishes a contrast with the impending somber and dreadful journeys to be embarked on by both the mother and her son. To cover up her transgressions, when her son is away in the garden, Madam Liu orders her maid to bury the bones of the poultry and the other animals she has been eating. One day, as Madam Liu has a fierce confrontation with Yili, a loyal servant of Luobo, regarding her meat eating, the ground in the garden bursts open, exposing all the bones that were previously buried there. Faced with such an ominous revelation, Liu makes a false vow to Luobo: she swears that if she has committed any transgressions, she will die bleeding from all seven of her orifices and will subsequently descend to hell to be punished by eternal suffering. At that very moment, Mulian's mother faints, with blood pouring out of her eyes, nose, and mouth. After she dies, her soul is captured by the "ghost guard" (i.e., demon-bailiff) and sent to hell. While mourning for his mother's death at home, Luobo is tested by Guanyin, who sends a rude Daoist priest to provoke his anger and a beautiful young maiden to seduce him, but the virtuous Luobo passes both of these trials. Subsequently, Guanyin informs him that his mother is currently suffering in hell. The only way to rescue her is to seek help from the Buddha in the West.

The first scene of volume 2, titled "Presenting the Wine of Longevity," is a continuation of the last scene of volume 1. At home, Luobo presents seasonal wine to his mother in spring. This first scene of volume 2 also resonates with the harmonic and lively theme presented in the first scene of volume 1 ("Longevity Greeting in Lunar New Year"); thus, the two volumes (and the first two days of the performance) are connected, maintaining a continuous flow. At the end of volume 2, after overcoming all the dangers and challenges of the road, Luobo arrives in the Western Paradise and is united with the Buddha and his Ten Friends. This happy reunion marks the second "Minor Finale" of the play. A similar structure repeats in volume 3.

In volume 2, determined to start the difficult journey to the West, Luobo proposes to call off his engagement with his fiancée, Cao Saiying. Taken to the underworld by the demon-bailiffs, Madame Liu is escorted past the Mountain of Gold Money, the Mountain of Slippery Oil, and the Home Gazing Terrace, and then is made to cross the Naihe Bridge, the boundary between the earthly realm and the netherworld. In Luobo's pilgrimage, on the other hand, Guanyin subdues the White Ape to protect him. At the Dark Pine Forest, she turns herself into a beautiful woman to test his moral resolve. With the help of the White Ape, Luobo is able to pass the Mountain of Flames and cross the Icy Pond and the Sand River. In the final scene, after he arrives at his ultimate destination, he becomes a disciple of the Buddha and joins with him and his Ten Friends. The performance of the second day concludes with this union between Mulian, Buddha, and the Ten Friends.

Volume 3 starts with a religious scene, in which the Buddha gives a lecture about Buddhist sutras to Mulian and the Ten Friends. The setting and characters of the first scene of the volume ("Lecturing about the Way") present a continuation of the last scene of volume 2. As it happens, in the following scene, Hell observes its own version of the Lantern Festival. When practicing meditation, Mulian is able to see that his mother is suffering in the underworld. Having received two magic tools—a staff and a pair of sandals—from the Buddha, Mulian descends into hell to save his mother. The play then depicts the horrific scenes that Mulian witnesses on his tour through the ten courts of hell, all the while highlighting the theme of karmic retribution—sinful actions of the past sow the seeds of present fruits of sufferings. In the Tenth Hall, Mulian learns from the King of the Turning Wheel (of Rebirth) that Madam Liu has been reincarnated as a dog. Assisted once again by Guanyin, Mulian locates his mother's canine reincarnation in Qimen county. When he follows the dog into a nunnery, Mulian runs unexpectedly into his former fiancée, Cao Saiying, who resolved to stay true to him in the name of female chastity. In the final scene, all the major characters of the play show up to participate in the grand Yulanpen Ceremony. They join together to perform the ritual of salvation in the Ghost Festival in order to deliver the soul of Madam Liu into human form. This finale ends the play with a joyful religious reunion on the fifteenth day of the seventh month. Thus, the volume as a whole begins with the Lunar New Year and ends with the Ghost Festival, two major holidays of renewal.

The final scene of volume 3 concludes the whole play with the grand scene "The Great Yulanpen Ceremony." This is the dramatic design that Li Yu dubs the "Grand Finale" ("Dashousha"):

Grand Finale: The concluding scene of the whole play is named "Grand Finale." The major difficulty of this scene is not to reveal any trace of wrapping up, and yet to present the happy feelings of a reunion. For example, in cases where there are five key characters scattered in different directions— East, West, South, and, North—they should be brought together in this finale.
[XQOJ 68–69, "The Grand Finale" ("Dashousha")]

In the concluding scene, all the major characters are assembled from various directions to participate in the Yulanpen ritual during the Ghost Festival, including Fu Xiang, Luobo, Yili, Cai Saiying, the Ten Friends, and other monks. They join together to perform this rite of salvation in delivering the soul of Madam Liu and other orphaned spirits from damnation. The three-day performance ends with this grand finale and a happy family reunion. The structural design of *Exhortation* is illustrated in figure 15.1.

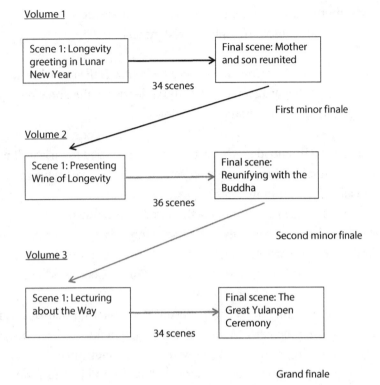

FIGURE 15.1 An overview of the scenes in the earliest extant Mulian playtext (1582) that illustrates the progression through two "Minor Finales" ("Xiaoshousha") to the "Grand Finale" ("Dashousha").

15.4 MULIAN PLAYS AND SONIC FORCE IN PERFORMANCE

After the three-volume *Exhortation* was published in 1582, it became a model for later versions of the play. The moral lessons imparted by the three-volume play center on karmic retribution, filial piety, and female chastity. Nonetheless, when a Mulian play is put onstage, particularly when performing rituals of exorcism or salvation, its interpretation can take on additional functions. The modern drama scholar Piet van der Loon made the following observation about performing Mulian plays in a ritual context:

[Their objective] was not to retrace in a realistic fashion the life of the virtuous Mu-lien or of the Goddess of Mercy, Kuan-yin. Nor were they staged to give lessons in morality or to inculcate religious precepts by threatening people with the punishment of their sins. Their principal preoccupation was not even with the ancestral cult. No, they performed a direct and spectacular action, which served to cleanse the community of all impurities, which drove away the menace caused by the malevolent forces of contagion, and which pacified the dissatisfied souls of those who had suffered violent and premature death. In fact, the essential part of the ritual was precisely those dramatic elements which could be taken as simple embellishments of Mu-lien or other legends . . . the story was merely a convenient framework for a scenic performance, which could itself equally unfold in an independent fashion.[14]

In his *Commentaries on Songs from the Remote Mountain Hall* (*Yuanshantang qupin*), the famous drama critic Qi Biaojia (1602–1645) describes the sonic contours and duration of Mulian play performances as follows:

> [The playwright] has no idea what music [should be used for arias]. [The sound of the music] does nothing more than imitate blind beggars who go from door to door calling and singing. Nothing can be done about [its being performed] since the uneducated masses are mesmerized by Buddhism. The play consists of one hundred and nine scenes [*sic*]. It takes three days and nights to complete a performance of the whole play, and this causes a clamor that stirs up villages.
> [*YSTQP* 114, "Exhortation to Goodness" ("Quanshan")]

While many other late Ming literati were devout Buddhists, Qi Biaojia was not one of them. In comparing the performance of the troupe to the voices of beggar-singers, Qi is condescending in his attitude toward this religious play. The last phrase he uses — "hongdong cunshe" — is translated as "creating a big sensation in the village community." In fact, *hongdong* may also suggest "fashioning a bustling atmosphere" or "stirring up sound and excitement." In an entry in his diary from the year 1639, Qi Biaojia complained that a Mulian play performed in a neighboring village was so "noisy" that he could not sleep.

To understand how it was possible for late-sixteenth and early-seventeenth-century Mulian plays to create such a sonic spectacle, we should look at the performing environment of Chinese drama in rural villages. A late-Ming painting called *A Painting Scroll Showing the Prosperity of Nanzhong* (*Nanzhong fanhui tu*) shows a drama performance in the countryside (see figure 15.2).[15]

A stage is erected outside a temple next to rice paddy fields and a waterwheel. On this makeshift theater made of timber or bamboo, the troupe performs on a red carpet, a device commonly used to demarcate theatrical space. Unlike today's customary theatrical practices, the orchestra is visible to the spectators, not in a sunken pit. Made up of people of all genders and all ages, the attendees talk to one another and move around freely in the open space between the temple and the stage as they watch the performance. There is thus no clear demarcation between audience and nonaudience, participants and bystanders, and theatergoers and religious worshippers. This mode of outdoor rural performance represents the predominant setting of staging drama in premodern China. Besides entertaining the members of the communities during a temple fair, the main purposes of this kind of performance were to please the deities on their birthdays, to appease orphaned souls, and to celebrate annual festivals to bring blessings and good fortune to the village community.

In the memoir *Dream Memories of Tao'an* referenced previously, Zhang Dai witnessed a Mulian play performance and its sound effects in the countryside in Zhejiang province. A notable troupe from Huizhou (in Anhui province), the birthplace of

FIGURE 15.2 Staging Chinese drama in a rural village.

Mulian performances, was hired to perform a three-day Mulian play on a big stage erected on a martial training ground. All kinds of costly and large paper offerings were exhibited around the stage, and the audience was, as noted earlier, surrounded by frightful and vivid scenes from the pantheon of the netherworld. After some spectacular acrobatics, for which Mulian plays were famous, the play took a somber turn:

> The audience was very uneasy; under the light of the lamps, their faces took on the ghastly look of ghosts. During the performance of scenes like "Summoning the Evil Ghosts of the Five Directions" ("Zhao wufang e'gui") and "Madam Liu Flees the Stage" ("Liu shi taopeng"), over a myriad people shouted all at once. Jolted by the fear that perhaps pirates had suddenly landed, local magistrate Xiong sent out a yamen officer to investigate.[16]
>
> [*TAMY* 78, "Mulian Performance" ("Mulian xi")]

These two scenes are not part of Zheng Zhizhen's play per se, but most likely harked back to earlier popular Mulian-related performance traditions. However, thanks to modern fieldwork and documentaries about the Mulian play tradition, we can form an idea of how a scene like "Madam Liu Flees the Stage" might have been put on in late Ming China.[17] According to one modern account, while facing her trial in hell, Madam Liu is able to escape, run around, hide, jump down off the stage, and dash around among the spectators. A demon-bailiff also jumps off the stage to look for the fugitive. At this point, spectators participate in this game of tracking her down. Led by the demon-bailiff, the audience shouts together while searching for Madam Liu, who represents all the evil spirits and natural disasters that may jeopardize the survival of the community. The spatial scope of this communal hide-and-seek is not limited to the stage area, but usually extends to the whole village. With the support of the audience (expressed in their voices, movements, and actions), Liu is finally found, captured, and brought back to the stage, and the trial scene resumes. Throughout the pursuit, the members of the audiences all shout, and their voices can be heard from miles away.[18]

So why did people shout all at once when troupes staged such scenes? Were they applauding, screaming "bravo" or "encore" to show their appreciation? Alternatively, were they angrily yelling at the actors while hurling stones at the stage? No, the forceful sounds—shouting and screaming—produced by the villagers were instrumental in achieving the exorcistic function of the Mulian play. "Noise" was a key factor in this collective ritual action; it served as a powerful "weapon" in driving out evil spirits, orphaned souls, and pestilence beyond the confines of the community (☞ chap. 16).

15.5 THE SOUNDSCAPE OF EXORCISM

Why is such clamorous sound crucial in such ritual-theatrical performances? It would appear that such scenes symbolically reenacted rituals connected to the Great Exorcism (*Da nuo*). The *nuo* exorcism dates back at least to the Zhou dynasty (1045 BCE–256 BCE) and was often associated with New Year's festivities. Its most noticeable feature, as noted in one version of the *Zhuangzi* (c. 369 BCE–286 BCE), is making a forceful sound by "drumming, screaming, and shouting" (*jigu huzao*).[19] Other ancient classics also described how an exorcist led hundreds of officials to perform the annual ceremony of exorcism. In one such performance, according to *The History of the Later Han* (*Hou Hanshu*), a special percussion instrument—the "*tao*-drum"—was used to produce a clamorous sound:

> One day before the *La* Festival, there is the Great Exorcism, which is called the expulsion of pestilences. In this ceremony, one hundred and twenty youths aged ten to twelve are selected from among the palace nobility. They all wear red headcloths, black tunics, and hold large "*tao*-drums." The exorcist covers his head with bear fur, wears a mask with four eyes of yellow gold, a black shirt and a red skirt . . . . With one hand he holds a halberd and with the other, he brandishes his shield . . . and the Supervisor of the Retinue leads them to expel evil demons from the Palace.[20]

The main purpose of hitting the "*tao*-drum" was not to create a festive atmosphere for the upcoming Lunar New Year. Rather, it aimed to create sound rhythms that had the magic power to ward off demons, epidemics, and evil spirits from the Inner Palace.[21]

Ritual performances during the history of Chinese exorcism share a number of common elements, and sound has been a key feature in this symbolic structure.[22] The Mulian play experienced by Zhang Dai should be viewed as an enactment of such a common ritual pattern, manifesting unique yet shared sonic features. Similar to other rites of exorcism, "noises"—hitting drums and cymbals, the shouts of the audience, exploding firecrackers—are not something extraneous or detrimental to the performance of the Mulian play taking place. On the contrary, these sonic devices are integral, functional, and vital to the ritual, engendering immediate meanings in the specific context. As "tens of thousands of people shout together," music and sound are intentionally organized in the event, where opera and exorcism have been synthesized into one entity and are enacted together by the troupe and the audience. To the audience-participants, performing this seasonal ceremony guarantees a peaceful, orderly, and flourishing life for the community.

In short, the episode "Madam Liu Flees the Stage," witnessed by Zhang, is an essential and integral component of performing the Mulian play in the community. The primary purpose was not necessarily to convey the moral values of Confucianism or Buddhism, nor was it to entertain the participants-audience on the spot. Rather, a rite of exorcism was carried out through a mass performance in the process of "Searching for Madam Liu." The noise produced by the masses was crucial to "cleanse the community of all impurities, which drove away the menace caused by the malevolent forces of contagion."[23] No wonder, then, that every time a Mulian play was performed, it caused enough commotion in the village (*hongdong cunshe*) for people in neighboring villages to lose sleep.

CONCLUSION

Mulian drama serves as an ideal illustration of the complexity and multiplicity of Chinese traditional plays. From *Exhortation*, we can observe the various dimensions of collaboration in the productions of Chinese drama, such as literati culture and folk tradition, literary writing and popular performance, ritual efficacy and theatrical amusement, Confucian moral values (such as filial piety) and Buddhist philosophical teachings (such as karmic retribution). Since the twelfth century, Mulian plays have been enacted in a wide range of theatrical forms; however, the first full text appeared only in the late sixteenth century. In other words, Mulian plays had been performed for centuries before the first published text appeared. Hence, Zheng Zhizhen composed *Exhortation* based on a preexisting body of written and oral materials that circulated in the region, and he gave it a popular Confucian twist. Viewed in this light, Zheng's compositional practice is a creative process of reinterpreting, compiling, and rewriting.

However, as is often the case with theatrical materials, the performance context is just as important as the text itself when it comes to the meanings given to a particular story cycle. On the one hand, it may not have been Zheng's original intention for his work to be performed as part of a ritual of exorcism where thousands of people participated, shouting loudly while chasing the sinful Madam Liu. On the other hand, excerpts of *Exhortation* were also performed in commercial venues, showcasing the sophisticated theatrical performances of individual artists. But even there, the performance context could reshape Zheng's work.

Among the most famous scenes that defied Zheng's editorial intervention was "Longing for Worldly Pleasure" ("Sifan"). A staple of Kunqu theater as well as

Beijing opera, in this short play, a Buddhist nun rebels against the pious life that her parents expect of her. While Zheng sought to tone down her rants against piety in general and Buddhist practice in particular, the extant scripts of this scene give full rein to the young woman's rejection of Buddhist practices and filial piety. Hence, the cultural meanings of the Mulian drama are rich, multifarious, and contextual, and are deeply embedded in various types of theatrical expressions, staging practices, and performance contexts.

Sai-shing Yung

NOTES

1. On Mulian in early Buddhist literature, see "Mahāmaudgalyāyana," in *The Princeton Dictionary of Buddhism*, ed. Robert E. Buswell, Jr., and Donald S. Lopez, Jr. (Princeton, NJ: Princeton University Press, 2014), 498–499.

2. Stephen F. Teiser, *The Ghost Festival in Medieval China* (Princeton, NJ: Princeton University Press, 1988), 194.

3. Stephen F. Teiser, "'Having Once Died and Returned to Life': Representations of Hell in Medieval China," *Harvard Journal of Asiatic Studies* 48, no. 2 (1988): 462.

4. Teiser, *The Ghost Festival in Medieval China*, 168–195.

5. Teiser, *The Ghost Festival in Medieval China*, 168.

6. With minor modifications, I used the translation appearing in Stephen Teiser, "The Ritual behind the Opera: A Fragment Ethnography of the Ghost Festival, A.D. 400–1900," in *Ritual Opera, Operatic Ritual: "Mu-Lien Rescues His Mother" in Chinese Popular Culture*, ed. David Johnson (Berkeley and Los Angeles: University of California Press, 1989), 200–201.

7. Zhu Wanshu, "Notes on Compilation, " *MLJM*, 3–5.

8. Guo Qitao, *Ritual Opera and Mercantile Lineage: The Confucian Transformation of Popular Culture in Late Imperial Huizhou* (Stanford, CA: Stanford University Press, 2005), 115–116.

9. Guo, *Ritual Opera and Mercantile Lineage*, 118–127.

10. Guo, *Ritual Opera and Mercantile Lineage*, 125.

11. Guo, *Ritual Opera and Mercantile Lineage*, 2.

12. Such a division of volumes and counting of scenes are based on the Gaoshi shanfang edition, which forms the basis for *MLJM*. A Fuchuntang edition published in Nanjing also consists of three volumes, but it has a different way of counting the number of scenes. See https://www.wdl.org/en/item/7110/ (accessed on April 13, 2021).

13. For a scene-by-scene summary of all three volumes, see Guo, *Ritual Opera and Mercantile Lineage*, 108–114.

14. Piet van der Loon, "Les origines rituelles du théâtre chinois" (The Ritual Origins of Chinese Theater), *Journal Asiatique* (Asiatic Journal) 265 (1977): 161–162. For the translation of this passage, see Stephen Teiser, "The Ritual behind the Opera," 207.

15. Liao Ben, *Zhongguo xiqu tushi* (An Illustrated History of Traditional Chinese Theater and Drama) (Zhengzhou, China: Henan jiaoyu chubanshe, 1996), 503.

16. I use the translation by David Johnson, with minor changes. See David Johnson, "Actions Speak Louder than Words: The Cultural Significance of Chinese Ritual Opera," in *Ritual Opera, Operatic Ritual*, 9.

17. See Zhu Hengfu, *Mulian xi yanjiu* (A Study of Mulian Plays) (Nanjing, China: Nanjing daxue chubanshe, 1993), 118–134; Hou Jie, "Mulian Drama: A Commentary on Current Research and Source Materials," in *Ethnography in China Today: A Critical Assessment of Methods and Results*, ed. Daniel Overmyer (Taipei: Yuan Liou Publishing, 2002), 23–48.

18. Mao Limei, "Yiyang qiang Mulianxi" (Mulian Plays in the Yiyang Musical Style), *Minsu quyi* (Folk Arts) 78 (July 1992; special issue on Mulian plays, vol. 2): 16–17.

19. Li Fang et al., comp., *Taiping yulan* (The Imperial Reader of the Taiping Era) (Beijing: Zhonghua shuju, 1998 [1960]), vol. 3, 2405–2406. The passage does not appear in the standard version of the *Zhuangzi*. In the same section of the *Taiping yulan*, there is another entry quoted from Lian Pin's "Danuo fu" ("Rhapsody on the Great Exorcism"), which also mentions a similar ritual practice of drumming and shouting in the Great Exorcism. See Li, *Taiping yulan*, vol. 3, 2406.

20. Fan Ye, *Hou Hanshu* (The History of the Latter Han) (Beijing: Zhonghua shuju, 1965), 7.3a, 287 and 4a, 291. I use the translation by Derk Bodde, *Festivals in Classical China: New Year and Other Annual Observances during the Han Dynasty 206 B.C.–A.D. 220* (Princeton, NJ: Princeton University Press, 1975), 78–79, with minor revisions. For a similar account in the *Zhou Li* (Rites of Zhou), see Ruan Yuan, ed., *Shisan jing zhushu* (Commentaries and Subcommentaries on the Thirteen Classics), "Xia Guan, Sima" part 2, 31.12a.

21. For a discussion on the ethnography of drumming in the Chinese rite of exorcism, see Yan Changhong and Pu Hengqiang, *Zhongguo gu wenhua yanjiu* (A Study of Ancient Chinese Culture) (Nanning, China: Guangxi jiaoyu chubanshe, 1997), 209–232.

22. Rong Shicheng (Yung Sai-shing), *Xiqu renleixue chutan: Yishi, juchang, and shequn* (The Anthropology of Chinese Drama: Ritual, Theater, and Community) (Taipei: Maitian, 1997).

23. Loon, "Les origines rituelles du théâtre chinois," 161–162.

PRIMARY SOURCES

DHBWJ   Wang Chongmin 王重民, et al., ed. *Dunhuang bianwen ji* 敦煌變文集 (*A Collection of Transformation Texts from Dunhuang*). Beijing: Renmin wenxue chubanshe, 1957.

DJMHL   Meng Yuanlao 孟元老. *Dongjing menghua lu zhu* 東京夢華錄注 (Annotated Edition of *The Eastern Capital: A Record of a Dream of Splendor*). Ann. Deng Zhicheng 鄧之誠. Beijing: Zhonghua shuju, 1982.

MLJM   Zheng Zhizhen 鄭之珍. *Xinbian Mulian jiumu quanshan xiwen* 新編目連救母勸善戲文 (*Mulian Rescues His Mother: An Exhortation to Goodness*). Ann. Zhu Wanshu 朱萬曙. Hefei, China: Huangshan shushe, 2005.

TAMY   Zhang Dai 張岱. *Tao'an mengyi* 陶庵夢憶 (*Dream Memories of Tao'an*). Taipei: Kaiming shuju, 1957.

XQOJ   Li Yu 李漁. *Xianqing ouji* 閒情偶寄 (*Leisure Notes*). In *Zhongguo gudian xiqu lunzhu jicheng* 中國古典戲曲論著集成 (*A Compendium of Classical Chinese Drama Criticism*), vol. 7. Beijing: Zhongguo xiju chubanshe, 1959.

YSTQP   Qi Biaojia 祁彪佳. *Yuanshantang qupin* 遠山堂曲品 (*Commentaries on Songs from the Remote Mountain Hall*). In *Zhongguo gudian xiqu lunzhu jicheng* 中國古典戲曲論著集成 (*A Compendium of Classical Chinese Drama Criticism*), vol. 6. Beijing: Zhongguo xiju chubanshe, 1959.

SUGGESTED READINGS

TRANSLATIONS

Berezkin, Rotislav, introd. and trans. "A Local Drama from Shaoxing: *Record on Rescuing Mother (Jiumu ji)*." In *Chinese Folk and Popular Literature*, ed. Victor H. Mair and Mark Bender, 303–308. New York: Columbia University Press, 2011.

Mair, Victor H., trans. "Transformation Text on Mahâmaudgalyâyana Rescuing His Mother from the Underworld, with Pictures, One Scroll, with Preface." In *The Shorter Columbia Anthology of Traditional Chinese Literature*, ed. Victor H. Mair, 607–642. New York: Columbia University Press, 2000.

Scott, A. C., ed. and trans. "Longing for Worldly Pleasures." In his *Traditional Chinese Plays*, vol. 2, 14–39. Madison: University of Wisconsin Press, 1969.

ENGLISH

Bereskin, Rostislav. *Many Faces of Mulian: The Precious Scrolls of Late Imperial China*. Seattle and London: University of Washington Press, 2017.

Goldman, Andrea. "The Nun Who Wouldn't Be: Representations of Female Desire in Two Performance Genres of 'Si fan,'" *Late Imperial China* 22, no. 1 (June 2001): 71–138.

Guo, Qitao. *Ritual Opera and Mercantile Lineage: The Confucian Transformation of Popular Culture in Late Imperial Huizhou*. Stanford, CA: Stanford University Press, 2005.

Johnson, David, ed. *Ritual Opera, Operatic Ritual: "Mu-Lien Rescues His Mother" in Chinese Popular Culture*. Berkeley, CA: Chinese Popular Culture Project, 1989.

Judd, Ellen R. "Ritual Opera and the Bonds of Authority: Transformation and Transcendence." In *Harmony and Counterpoint: Ritual Music in a Chinese Context*, ed. Bell Yung, Evelyn S. Rawksi, and Rubie S. Watson, 226–246. Stanford, CA: Stanford University Press, 1996.

Teiser, Stephen F. *The Ghost Festival in Medieval China*. Princeton, NJ: Princeton University Press, 1988.

CHINESE

Chen Fangying 陳芳英. *Mulian jiumu gushi zhi yanjin ji qi youguan wenxue zhi yanjiu* 目連救母故事之演進及其有關文學之研究 (*The Evolution of the "Mulian Rescues His Mother" Story Cycle and Related Literature*). History and Chinese Literature Series. Taipei: National Taiwan University, 1983.

Liu Zhen 劉禎. *Zhongguo minjian Mulian wenhua* 中國民間目連文化 (*Popular Chinese Culture Surrounding Mulian*). Chengdu, China: Bashu shushe, 1997.

Mao Gengru 茆耕茹. *Mulian ziliao bianmu gailue* 目連資料編目概略 (*An Overview over Research Materials on Mulian*). Taipei: Caituanfaren Shihezheng minsu wenhua jijinhui, 1993.

Tanaka Issei 田仲一成. "Xinjiapo Puxian tong xianghui feng jia pudu Mulian xi chutan" 新加坡莆仙同鄉會逢甲普度目連戲初探 ("A Preliminary Examination of the Mulian Plays of Universal Salvation in the Native Place Association of Puxian in Singapore"). In *Fujian Mulian xi yanjiu wenji* 福建目連戲研究文集 (*A Collection of Research Essays on the Mulian Plays of Fujian Province*), 66–86. Fuzhou, China: Fuzhou sheng yishu yanjiusuo, 1991.

Zhu Hengfu 朱恒夫. *Mulian xi yanjiu* 目連戲研究 (*A Study of Mulian Plays*). Nanjing, China: Nanjing daxue chubanshe, 1993.

16

The Story of Hua Guan Suo

Chantefable and Ritual Plays

In Chinese traditional drama, the story is performed with a complex mixture of songs, dialogue, dramatic action, and narrative verse. Arias to set melodies allow emotional intensity and lyrical expression; dialogue and dramatic action enact the central conflict; and verse declamations in third-person narrative introduce a situation, summarize the story, or pass final judgment. These key elements, with the exception of dramatic action, also featured in storytelling genres that developed in the entertainment quarters of urban areas from the Song era (960–1279) onward. A similar format of narrative in verse, dialogue, and dramatic action can be found in plays of exorcism known as *nuoxi*, performed during the New Year festivities. In these plays, masked actors enact the role of powerful deities and perform ritual plays to expel the demons of misfortune from the community. Up to the present day, narrating a story through the medium of song, verse, and prose remains a significant aspect of three performance types in China: professional storytelling, regional opera, and ritual plays of exorcism.

16.1 GENRES

This chapter features excerpts from two different but related genres that rely primarily on narrative to tell the story: *shuochang cihua* (prosimetric stories, here translated as "chantefable") and plays of exorcism. A chantefable is an oral, written, or printed narrative comprising verse, prose, and dramatic dialogue. From the tenth and eleventh centuries CE, stories in chantefable style were related by professional storytellers in urban theater stalls, and by itinerant storytellers traveling through villages. They were also performed in plays of exorcism. In this case, the Master of Ceremonies relied on a manuscript of the text to relate the story. The plays of exorcism discussed here derive from ancient ceremonies of exorcism (*nuo*) performed at royal courts and in the countryside since the Zhou dynasty (ca. 1046–256). By the early centuries of the common era, the imperial military forces became involved in a new form of exorcism rite known as "military *nuo*" (*jun nuo*). Thousands of cavalry performed spectacular feats of military prowess during the *nuo* festivities in order to demonstrate the awesome power of the ruler. Masked players took on the spirits of past heroes and engaged in battles that symbolized the victory of good over evil. In this way, the plays carried out two main functions: they exorcised the forces of misfortune at the lunar New Year and entertained both the deities and the crowds with spectacular battle scenes relating to historical events.[1]

The *nuo* plays discussed in this chapter evolved from the more elaborate type of *nuo* festivities that first appeared during the Song era in marketplaces, regional centers, and villages. They represent the type of Chinese drama performed by mostly amateur players at the regional level over the last millennium. This type of play did not include arias to set melodies and relied to a greater extent on third-person narrative forms than did the more musically demanding plays of the elite. Chantefable stories and *nuo* plays thus demonstrate the permeability of narrative and dramatic modes in some types of Chinese theater. In addition, the examples given here highlight the importance of playmaking in offering imaginative reconstructions of historical eras—in this case the fall of the Han and the rise of the Three Kingdoms (220–265), a time of civil war when China was divided into three rival kingdoms. The Three Kingdoms saga is one of the preeminent story cycles in the Chinese tradition (➤ *HTRCFiction*, chap. 4, *HTRCFiction—LC*, L03.07, L03.08). A blend of history and fiction, these tales present a dazzling array of formidable warriors and clashing personalities. Three Kingdoms plays and storytelling tackle issues of loyalty and treachery, of humanity and brutality. When performed by Chinese troops garrisoned in border regions, the plays became a powerful symbol of Han Chinese authority over so-called barbarous tribes.

In this chapter, we focus on the fictional character of Hua Guan Suo, who is claimed to be the second (or sometimes the third) son of Guan Yu, a historical figure who died in 219 CE.[2] Guan Yu was the foremost general on the side of Shu-Han during the Three Kingdoms era. After his death, he was venerated as a powerful deity.[3] Storytellers, playwrights, and novelists commonly wrote sequels to the stories of popular figures by inventing tales about their sons or disciples. This could well account for the origin of the legendary story of Hua Guan Suo, whose name reflects his adopted father (Suo), his teacher (Hua), and his birth father (Guan). Stories about a figure called Guan Suo probably first appeared in the eleventh century, long after the Three Kingdoms era. At this time, loyalist troops of the Song dynasty sought to ward off the Jurchen invaders, an early Manchu people. The likely military provenance of the tale accounts for the constant focus on costume, weaponry, and spectacular feats of battle prowess.

16.2 THE CHANTEFABLE *THE STORY OF HUA GUAN SUO*: REGIONALITY

The Story of Hua Guan Suo (*Hua Guan Suo zhuan*) is the only extant complete rendition of the story of this legendary figure. The regional affiliation of this text is quite complex.[4] The tale was probably first transmitted orally in the Wu-speaking regions of the Yangzi River delta. The final folio of this chantefable text has the publishing label of the Yongshun shutang publishing house and a date based on the reign era that equates in Western chronology to 1478. Another member of the chantefable corpus, *The Story of Xue Rengui*, has a publishing label of Yongshun shutang and a title page with the words "Newly printed in Beijing." This appears

to indicate either that Yongshun shutang is a Beijing publisher or that this edition
was reprinted in Beijing from a text derived elsewhere. This chantefable is part of
a corpus of thirteen prosimetric narratives and one play excavated from a tomb in
the burial grounds of the Xuan family in Jiading County (formerly part of Suzhou
prefecture) during the mid-1960s. It is the only one of the corpus to have illustrations at the top of each folio, a format known as "picture above, words beneath"
(*shangtu xiawen*) (👉 chap. 4).[5] Pictorial formats of this type were characteristic of
Jianyang publishing in the southern province of Fujian.

Linguistic evidence also points to a southern origin. The verse style of *The Story
of Hua Guan Suo* is said to be based on the rhyming patterns of the Wu-speaking Suzhou region rather than those of the Beijing region, and Chinese characters are used to represent sounds that reflect typical Wu speech patterns.[6] In the
twentieth century, a ritual play script about Hua Guan Suo from the Wu-speaking Guichi region of Anhui contains verse material very close to that found in the
fifteenth-century chantefable of Hua Guan Suo. This indicates that whatever the
actual place of origin, *The Story of Hua Guan Suo* could be read aloud or acted
out in Wu regional speech. The tale may have originated within the Wu-speaking region, but plays about this hero were transmitted to provinces in south and
southwest China such as Guizhou, Jiangxi, and Yunnan, where they continued to
be performed well into the twentieth century. The ready diffusion of this tale in
various textual and performance traditions throughout the vast Chinese empire
helps to account for wide divergences in the treatment of the central themes, as
we discuss next.

16.3 CENTRAL THEMES

Stories about the collapse of the social order at the end of the great Han dynasty, the
emergence of rebel leaders and powerful hegemons, and the subsequent tripartite
division of the country were endlessly recycled in storytelling, opera, and village
plays throughout the imperial era. The chantefable of Hua Guan Suo stands out
for its divergence from what became known as the mainstream storyline popularized in the famous Ming novel *The Romance of the Three Kingdoms* (hereafter *The
Romance*). Whereas *The Romance* traces the fortunes of the three sworn brothers
Liu Bei, Guan Yu, and Zhang Fei, the chantefable focuses on Hua Guan Suo, the
fictional son of Guan Yu. *The Romance* draws on historiography and performance
genres to delineate the outbreak of civil war in the waning years of the Han dynasty,
the usurpation of the throne by the talented but unscrupulous Cao Cao, and the
rise of numerous pretenders to the throne, including Liu Bei, a distant scion of the
house of Han. The chantefable, by contrast, relates the tale of the purely legendary Hua Guan Suo, who grows up with no knowledge of his natural father. As a
young adult, he journeys to seek recognition from Guan Yu, who is renowned for
his superb fighting skills and sense of honor (👉 chap. 3). Despite his small size,
Hua Guan Suo proves himself to be a match for his father in military prowess. He
takes part in the campaign against non-Chinese tribes in Yunnan and is instrumental in avenging his father's untimely death at the hands of enemy forces.

The chantefable story thus revolves around the father-son relationship rather than the cause of empire as in earlier *zaju* theater and *The Romance*. However, paradoxically, the chantefable begins with a bizarre rendition of the famous oath of brotherhood. In the conventional story, the brothers swear an oath of loyalty to each other and to serve the failing Han dynasty. In the chantefable version and related ritual plays, Liu Bei approves the slaughter of the families of his two sworn brothers to ensure that they can dedicate themselves entirely to his service. It is intriguing that a narrative that begins with an extreme form of sworn brotherhood based on the slaughter of one's wives and children should culminate in a story exemplifying a son's filial piety, as Guan Suo destroys those who betrayed his father. While no hint of this surprising twist to a familiar legend can be found in earlier *zaju* theater, plain tales (*pinghua*), or the contemporaneous *Romance*, this unusual version was transmitted in village plays of exorcism well into the twentieth century. As we discuss later in this chapter, the military context in which the story of Hua Guan Suo developed could help to account for the striking brutality of this tale.

16.4 ORIGINS AND HISTORICAL DEVELOPMENT

While some scholars argue for the indigenous origins of prosimetric (verse and prose) storytelling, it is likely that the translation of Buddhist sutras from Indian languages into stories related in verse and prose during the Tang dynasty provided an important impetus to the popularity of this form. In the early stage of the development of Chinese opera, playwrights incorporated elements of popular storytelling genres into their plays. For example, *zaju* employs a third-person narrative to introduce a new character, to offer recapitulations of the plot, or to offer a final judgment or commentary at the denouement.[7] The guides to the Song-era capitals contain references to stories or possibly texts (*huaben*) for both prosimetric and dramatic performances. Both genres are said to draw on a shared storehouse of thematic material relating to historical heroes, battles, stories of romance, the supernatural, criminal acts, and court cases. This suggests the perceived commensurability of Song era prosimetric and dramatic traditions, which relied on similar story material and competed for audiences in the urban entertainment quarters.

The fifteenth-century corpus of texts found at Jiading County is among the earliest extant examples of the chantefable genre. The texts contain an abundance of characters used for their phonetic value, simplified forms (borrowed from cursive script), and formulaic verse drawn from storytelling, opera, and ritual theater.[8] It is important to bear in mind that the rendition provided here is based on the modern reconstruction and does not reflect the original printed edition, which abounds in vernacular character forms used in handwriting. The phonetic renditions of the original assisted reading and recitation by the less educated, including the villagers who performed the plays of exorcism. The nonstandard characters could be understood as an accommodation to the reading practices of a popular audience, as distinct from a highly literate market.

16.5 AUTHORSHIP

Chinese vernacular texts can rarely be attributed to known authors, and *The Story of Hua Guan Suo* is no exception. This chantefable may have been compiled by writers known as *cairen* (men of talent) who compiled popular texts for publishing houses (☞ chaps. 2 and 7). The author or compiler of this text was familiar with storytelling conventions and may have had access to the earlier *Plain Tale of the Three Kingdoms* (*Sanguo zhi pinghua*) or similar materials. Occasionally, the chantefable echoes lines in the earlier prose account (one example is discussed next). The unknown author was also familiar with dramas about the Three Kingdoms heroes.

The earlier Yuan era play, *In a Dream Guan and Zhang, A Pair, Rush to Western Shu* (*Guan Zhang shuang fu Xi Shu meng*) (☞ chap. 3), for example, contains many parallels with the same treatment of this scene in *The Story of Hua Guan Suo*.[9] The play depicts the ghosts of Guan Yu and Zhang Fei returning in a dream to their sleeping sworn brother, Liu Bei, who is unaware of their deaths. Guan Yu reports that he was betrayed by Liu Feng, who is an adopted son of Liu Bei. When his calls for help go unanswered, Guan Yu is executed by the forces of the kingdom of Wu. Zhang Fei reports that he has been killed by a disloyal subordinate. The brothers remind Liu Bei of their sworn oath and call for vengeance against those who have betrayed them. In the chantefable Guan Yu (but not Zhang Fei) returns as a ghost to see Liu Bei. He explains in detail how Liu Feng killed the couriers bearing messages calling for aid. Liu Bei devises a gruesome death for Liu Feng and calls on Hua Guan Suo to lead the campaign of vengeance against the Wu forces. In this way, Hua Guan Suo fulfills his role as a filial son worthy of his illustrious father. One can assume that the unknown author of this text was very familiar with both chantefable storytelling and dramatic performances of stories of the Three Kingdoms.

16.6 PERFORMATIVE ASPECTS

The Story of Hua Guan Suo is narrated primarily in verse or song (*chang*) style, with seven syllables to a line. The first four syllables (two plus two) form a meaningful unit, followed by the final three syllables. Most couplets form a complete semantic unit. Even lines tend to conform to a loose rhyming pattern based on nasal-finals (*n* and *ng*). This is the staple form of prosimetric genres in the Chinese tradition. The verse sections combine third-person narrative (the dominant mode) and first-person narrative, where the narrator slips unannounced into the first person. The continuous shifts between third and first person enlivens the style and adds a dramatic quality to the narrative style. Occasionally, one can also find verse segments with lines of ten syllables. This poetic mode is identified in a cartouche either as *zan1 shi zi* or as *zan2 shi zi*. The first *zan* (*zan1*) can be translated as "augmented line" and the second (*zan2*) as "song of praise," a term associated with invitation to the deities in Buddhist rituals and storytelling.[10] Here, we will translate this mode as "Ten Beats to a Line." The augmented line length allowed a range of special poetic effects. In this particular chantefable, the main function of the "Ten

Beats to a Line" is to profile the physical attributes, battle attire, and amazing prowess of the leading protagonists.[11] In plays of exorcism, the same mode is deployed for the spectacular entry of the competing warrior and the evocation of spiritual or demonic power.

The verse style used in chantefables is highly formulaic, in line with the oral tradition on which it is based. This vernacular style was easier to learn than the elaborate arias to set melodies found in operatic-style drama and could be readily adopted by illiterate or semiliterate villagers engaged in the New Year plays of exorcism.

Chantefable stories often begin with a verse prelude summing up preceding historical events. *The Story of Hua Guan Suo* begins with a prelude that comprises a list of items of popular knowledge and beliefs. The narrator begins with the mythic founding of the cosmos and legendary sage rulers and then proceeds to list the earliest dynasties and the key events leading to the breakdown of the social order, which is where the story proper begins. The prelude reflects popular understandings of the past as a constant shift between periods of chaos and periods of peace and stability. Similar preludes in verse can be found in fiction and drama relating to the Three Kingdoms story cycle and in village ritual drama.[12]

As we discuss next, the opening segment of *The Story of Hua Guan Suo* of the fifteenth century has striking textual parallels with a play of exorcism performed in Anhui province in the twentieth century. In the Anhui ritual play, the prelude was recited, chanted, or sung in solemn mode by the Master of Ceremonies, who read from a script. The intention was to alert the audience to the causes of social breakdown, while at the same time encouraging them to anticipate the grand finale, which will see the restoration of good government and favorable harvests.

16.7 EXAMPLE OF A PRELUDE

自從盤古分天地，	In the beginning Pan Gu parted Earth from Heaven,
三皇五帝夏商君。	Next came the Three Sovereigns, Five Emperors, and the courts of Xia and Shang.
周朝伐紂興天下，	The house of Zhou punished the last Shang king and conquered all under Heaven,[13]
代代相承八百春。	Zhou rule passed on from age to age, in all eight hundred years.
周烈王時天下亂，	But by the reign of King Lie [r. 375 BCE to 369 BCE], the world fell into chaos,
春秋列國互相吞。	In the Spring and Autumn era [722 BCE to 481 BCE], rival states devoured each other.
秦皇獨霸諸侯城，	Until the Qin Emperor alone became master of the feudal kingdoms [in 221 BCE],
焚典坑儒喪聖文。	He burnt the classics and buried the scholars; the sacred texts were lost.

西建阿房東填海，　　In the west he built the Epang [Afang] palace; to the east he reclaimed land by the sea,

南修五嶺北長城。　　In the south he stationed troops on the Five Peaks; to the north he built the Great Wall.[14]

欲傳世世為天子，　　He wished to reign forever as Son of Heaven,

游至沙丘帝業崩。　　But at Sandy Knoll the imperial project perished with his death [210 BCE].

[MCSCC 1]

At this point, the prelude refers to one of the most significant events in ancient Chinese history—the remarkable rise of the prince of the state of Qin to become the first emperor of a unified empire, only to be followed by the precipitous decline and fall of the dynasty under his hapless heir. The narrator then goes on to recount the emergence of the great Han dynasty, the interregnum when a usurper took the throne, the bloody extirpation of the usurper, and then the continuation of the Han royal house by an imperial descendant. The storyteller further relates that the era of peace under the Han came to an end when the Yellow Turban rebels led a major uprising. It is at this time of imperial breakdown that the central characters in the chantefable make their first appearance:

劉備據了西川主，　　Liu Bei occupied the Western Rivers as overlord,

漢裔金枝玉葉人。　　A scion of the Han, he was a jade leaf on a golden bough.

軍師便有諸葛亮，　　For Commander-in-Chief, he had Zhuge Liang,

武勇關張是好人。　　For bravery in battle, Guan Yu and Zhang Fei, both good men.

都在青口桃源洞，　　At Qingkou in Peach Springs Cave,[15]

關張劉備結為兄。　　Guan, Zhang, and Liu Bei vowed to be brothers.

三人結義分天下，　　The three men swore an oath to jointly rule the empire,

子牙廟裏把香焚。　　At the temple of [Jiang] Ziya they lit sticks of incense.

（白）關、張、劉備三人結為兄弟。在姜子牙廟裏對天設誓。宰白馬祭天，殺黑牛祭地。只求同日死，不願同日生。哥哥有難兄弟救，兄弟有事哥哥便從。如不依此願，天不遮地不載,貶陰山之後,永不轉人身。

[NARRATOR] *in plain speech*:[16] The trio, Guan, Zhang and Liu Bei, were joined in sworn brotherhood. In the temple of Jiang Ziya [the God of War], they swore an oath and slaughtered a white horse as sacrifice to Heaven and a black ox as sacrifice to Earth. "We seek only to die on the same day, not to be born on the same day. If the elder is in trouble, the younger will rescue him. If the younger has a problem, the older will come to his aid. If anyone breaks this pledge, may he have no refuge beneath the heavens, nor any place to live on earth; may he be banished behind the Mountain of the Underworld, never to regain human form."

[MCSCC 1–2]

The oath of brotherhood is not recounted in the official historical records. However, by the Yuan era, it had become a fixed element in historical narratives such as the plain tale (*pinghua*) version of The Three Kingdoms, and in drama (*zaju*) such as *Liu, Guan, and Zhang: The Tripartite Oath of Brotherhood in the Peach Orchard* (*Liu Guan Zhang: Taoyuan san jieyi*, hereafter *Tripartite Oath*). As discussed next, the chantefable rendition adds a particular twist to the conventional tale, involving the brothers' slaughter of each other's families. This could well be due to the provenance of the story of Guan Suo among military men in the turbulent years when China was under foreign rule, that is, from the Southern Song to the end of the Yuan era (i.e., the mid-twelfth to fourteenth centuries).

16.8 THE OATH OF BROTHERHOOD

The fifteenth-century chantefable, while derivative of the earlier Three Kingdoms story cycle dating back to the third century CE, incorporated elements from a much more recent period of dynastic breakdown and civil war. Stories about a figure called "Guan Suo" (but not "Hua Guan Suo") emerged around the time of the fall of north China to the Jurchen invaders in the eleventh and twelfth centuries (☞ chap. 2). Loyalists, rebel leaders, brigands, and fighting men readily adopted the nickname of "Guan Suo." Even professional wrestlers in the Southern Song capital assumed the moniker "Rivaling Guan Suo" to boast of their strength. Around this time, one also finds quasi-fictional texts relating stories about a band of twelve men who formed an oath of brotherhood and took part in repressing a rebellion. One such text, *Neglected Events of the Reign Period of Proclaiming Harmony* (*Xuanhe yishi*, c. thirteenth century), records that one of the twelve sworn brothers, a certain Wang Xiong, bore the nickname "Rivaling Guan Suo."[17] During the era of Mongol rule, a Song loyalist called Han Lin'er (fl. 1355–1366), the leader of the Red Turbans (*hongjin*), carried out a blood sacrifice and swore an oath to Heaven and Earth before he mounted his uprising. The term *hongjin* subsequently appeared in numerous vernacular texts, including this chantefable tale. At one point, Hua Guan Suo captures troops who wear "turbans red as if dyed with blood" [*MCSCC* 9] and welcomes them into his army as sworn brothers. Over the centuries, storytellers absorbed material from contemporaneous events to form a distinctive variant of the well-known story of the Three Kingdoms, a story that reflected its likely emergence during the years of foreign rule from the Southern Song to the end of the Mongol Yuan. A striking example is the brutal finale to the oath of brotherhood in the chantefable story. Liu Bei encourages his newly sworn brothers to kill their wives and children in order to be free to serve him with the utmost loyalty. Note that in the excerpt here, Guan Yu is referred to as "Lord Guan," reflecting his celebration in the pantheon of Chinese deities:

（劉備道）我獨自一身，你二人有老小掛心，恐有回心。

LIU BEI *speaks*: I am without family, but you both have dependents to worry about. I'm afraid you may go back on your pledge.

（關公道）我壞了老小,共哥哥同去。   LORD GUAN *speaks*: I will destroy my family, young and old, and follow my elder brother.

（張飛道）你怎下得手殺自家老小？哥哥殺了我家老小，我殺了哥哥底老小。   ZHANG FEI *speaks*: How could you raise a hand against your own household? Elder brother, you kill my family and I will kill yours.

（劉備道）也說得是。   LIU BEI *speaks*: You have spoken well.

[*MCSCC* 2]

The Ming period *zaju* drama referred to above, *Tripartite Oath*, does not contain any mention at all of the families of the sworn brothers. The oath of brotherhood concludes with an order from the emperor to quell the rebellion of the Yellow Turbans. The brothers then express their utmost loyalty to the reigning emperor. This play was part of the repertoire performed in the palace before the emperor, which no doubt accounts for the expression of dedication to the throne.[18]

The chantefable rendition belongs to a completely different milieu—one that put a premium on the fierce bonds of loyalty between bands of warriors. The story of Hua Guan Suo may reflect the kind of play that was performed on festival occasions in military garrisons where troops were stationed far away from their families. The idea that one's close male allies ("sworn brothers") were more important than one's wife and children can also be found in the contemporaneous novel *The Romance of the Three Kingdoms*. For example, when the family of Liu Bei falls into enemy hands, Zhang Fei blames himself and prepares to cut his own throat. But Liu Bei seizes his sword, saying: "There's an old saying, 'Brothers are like arms and legs; wives and children are merely garments that can always be mended. But who can mend a broken limb?" (chap. 15). In a later chapter, an admirer is unable to find fresh game to offer hospitality to Liu Bei and kills his wife, slicing flesh off her arms, to offer him a meal. Liu Bei is shocked when he finds her corpse in the kitchen (chap. 19). These instances of macho barbarity in *The Romance* hint at darker currents in the cult of the sworn brotherhood that may well have emerged from actual practice among military men.

In the next segment of the chantefable story, we learn that Zhang Fei does not have the heart to kill Guan Ping, Guan Yu's elder son, and he also allows the wife, Hu Jinding, to get away. As we learn later, she is pregnant and will give birth to the son who will be called Hua Guan Suo, after his natural father (Guan Yu) and his teacher, Master Huayue and adopted father, Master Suo:

張飛當時忙不住,   Zhang Fei set off at once in a terrible hurry,
青銅寶劍手中存。   Grasping his bejewelled bronze sword in his hand.
來到蒲州解梁縣,   He arrived at Puzhou in Xieliang County,
直到哥哥家裏去。   And went directly to the home of his sworn brother.
逢一個時殺一個,   When he came across one he killed one,

逢着雙時殺二人，	When he met up with two he killed two.
殺了一十單八口，	He killed altogether eighteen souls,
轉過關平年少人。	Then he turned to the young boy, Guan Ping,
叫道叔叔可憐見，	Who called out, "Uncle, take pity on me,
留作牽龍備馬人。	Spare me to groom and saddle your horse!"
張飛一見心歡喜，	On seeing him, Zhang Fei rejoiced,
留了孩兒稱我心。	"It pleases me to spare this child."
走了嫂嫂胡金定，	He allowed Hu Jinding, his [sworn] brother's wife, to flee.
當時兩個便回程。	Then the two men set off on the road to return.
將身回到桃源鎮，	On reaching Peach Spring town,
弟兄三個便登程。	The three brothers renewed their journey once again.
前往興劉山一座，	They came to a hill they called "Raising the Liu [Royal House],"
替天行道作將軍。	Here they became warriors carrying out justice on Heaven's behalf.

[MCSCC 2]

"[Carry] out justice on Heaven's behalf" was also the rallying cry of the heroes of the Water Margin (*Shuihu*) saga, a story cycle about the historic rebel leader Song Jiang (fl. 1121) and his band of some thirty-six bandit-rebels (☞ *HTRCFiction*, chap. 6, *HTRCFiction-LC*, 03.09, 03.10). There are numerous echoes of the Water Margin story in the chantefable of Hua Guan Suo.[19] These two story traditions flourished during the years leading to the collapse of the Northern Song dynasty and the ascendancy of the Jurchen Jin dynasty in northern China during the mid-twelfth century.

16.9 *THE STORY OF HUA GUAN SUO*: AN EXAMPLE OF "TEN BEATS TO A LINE"

Plays of exorcism typically feature a violent confrontation between an exorcist-warrior and a demonic force that needs to be expelled from the community. The poetic mode known as "Ten Beats to a Line" is here deployed to set up the moment of battle between the forces of good and evil. As the name implies, this mode comprises ten syllables to a line in the pattern of six syllables (three plus three) plus four syllables. The first six syllables detail the costume and weapons, while the final four syllables focus on the dazzling or fearsome nature of the weaponry. The descriptions given here are highly reminiscent of the costumes, masks, and headdresses worn by the amateur actors in twentieth-century plays of exorcism and were probably familiar to readers of this chantefable from local exorcism plays.[20] In a declamation of the "Ten Beats to a Line" on stage, the actor takes on the spirit of a formidable warrior (or, in some cases, a demon). He parades around the stage, striking fear or evoking admiration in the audience, before finally taking up his battle stance. The dramatic effect is greatly enhanced by his gorgeous costume and the ferocious stare etched onto his face mask.

In *The Story of Hua Guan Suo*, the hero is likened to the Taoist deity Hua Guang [*MCSCC* 13], known for his white face, shiny appearance, and magical use of fire weapons. Hua Guang is said to have been born with three eyes; the third eye is in the middle of his forehead. The association between Hua Guan Suo and Hua Guang (possibly due to confusion between the names) could account for the references given here to brightness, fire, and the Sun. Note that the *shiman dai* (a belt engraved with a Man warrior wrestling with a lion) refers to the "lion-king" of the southern Man population of Yunnan. This signals to the reader or audience the role of Hua Guan Suo in helping to subjugate the southern tribes of Yunnan, as related in the final section of the chantefable:

【攢十字】	"Ten Beats to a Line"
戴一頂，四縫盔，爭光火強，	On his head a four-seamed helmet, shining brighter than fire,
穿一副，黃龍甲，耀日爭光。	Girded with a coat of mail like yellow dragon-scales, glowing brighter than the Sun.
披一領，茜羅袍，得紅血染，	His silken gown of madder red, as if dyed with crimson blood,
繫一條，獅蠻帶，獸口生雲。	Cinched with a belt inscribed with a southern tribesman wrestling a lion; clouds stream from the monster's open jaws.
彎一張，黃樺弓，鞘長弝短，	Hanging by his side a yellow painted bow, with long tips and a short grip,
插一弧，狼牙箭，點點金星。	In his quiver are wolf-teeth arrows poison-tipped, glistening like golden stars.
懸一條，竹節鞭，馬龍擺尾，	Dangling down is a "bamboo-notched" whip, waving its tassel-tail like a dragon-steed,
背一口，乾武劍，亮徹如銀。	Armed with a Heavenly battle-sword, gleaming sharp like silver.
撚一條，黃龍槍，兵如猛獸，	Flicking his yellow dragon-spear, this warrior fierce as a wild beast,
騎一匹，乖劣馬，搶出壯門。	Mounting a spirited horse, he bursts out through the gate.

[*MCSCC* 6]

16.10 A PLAY OF EXORCISM FROM QINGXI VILLAGE, GUICHI (ANHUI PROVINCE), TWENTIETH CENTURY

The chantefable of Hua Gua Suo has close links with ritual plays of exorcism that are still performed today in rural China. Two regional traditions will be discussed here: the first from Anhui province, near the coast; and the second from Yunnan province, in the southwest. The extract discussed next comes from a ritual play script collected in 1956 in Qingxi village, Guichi, Anhui, by Wang Zhaoqian.[21] Guichi is part of the Wu-speaking area of coastal China. It is located close to the southern bank of the Yangzi River. Troops were garrisoned there during the twelfth-century resistance to the marauding Jurchen armies, which suggests the possibility that the Guan Suo plays at Guichi developed from performances of military exorcism plays (*jun nuo*) for military audiences.[22]

These plays continued into the twentieth century. Wang Zhaoqian recounts that in 1956, he viewed a performance of the story of Hua Guan Suo in Qingxi village. In subsequent decades, however, ritual performances were suppressed by the authorities. For instance, during the Cultural Revolution (1965–1976), most of the masks, costumes, props, and scripts were burned.[23] In 1984, Wang revisited the area and found that only three families could still perform the play of Hua Guan Suo. He collected from villagers a script about the story of the birth and childhood of Hua Guan Suo, which will be discussed here. This twentieth-century script displays striking parallels with the fifteenth-century chantefable rendition. In particular, the play begins with a prelude very similar to that found in *The Story of Hua Guan Suo*. The prelude presents collective wisdom about the reasons behind war, disaster, and chaos and culminates in a striking reminder about the purpose of the ritual—to expel the forces of evil and ensure peace and prosperity (➤ chap. 15).

Guichi local gazetteers confirm that plays of exorcism date to at least the sixteenth century. Festivities involved a "parade of the gods" (with statues taken from the temple and carried around the village), lantern displays, and simple plays accompanied by cymbals and drums.[24] During the Qing dynasty (1644–1911), four leading Guichi families organized their own performances of ritual plays.[25] In the twentieth century, the practice continued only in more remote or supposedly "backward" areas. Plays of exorcism were performed only by male villagers, and roles were passed down from father to son. The ritual aspect of these plays lies in the belief that once men put on the appropriate masks and costumes, they could invoke the divine spirits they are portraying to enter their own bodies. The idea is to channel the forces of *yang* (the male force) to expel the forces of *yin* (female) from the village.[26] The performance relied heavily on the Master of Ceremonies, a village elder who would recite the narrative verse and organize the sequence of play events and choreography (➤ chap. 12).[27] It was thus not essential for the villagers to memorize large portions of the script, but rather to learn how to enact their role on the stage site, which could be in the temple or on open ground (➤ Introduction).

In Guichi, the verse material is sung in a slow, solemn style known locally as "exorcism mode" (*nuoqiang*), which was also used for funeral laments.[28] The narration proceeds in couplets comprising lines of seven syllables with regular end-rhymes. The first line of the couplet ends in a syllable with a deflected tone, and the second ends in a syllable with a level tone. When an important role made an appearance, incense was lit and firecrackers set off, filling the stage area with smoke. Booming drums and clashing cymbals accompanied the stylized sequences of the masked players. Here are excerpts from the verse prelude as declaimed by the Master of Ceremonies and the following scene of the oath of brotherhood:

自從盤古分天地， In the beginning Pan Gu parted Earth from Heaven,

三皇五帝到如今。 The Three Sovereigns and Five Emperors followed down to the present.

周朝法律興天下， The court of Zhou set up the law and established all under Heaven,

代代相傳八百春。 Zhou rule passed on from age to age, in all eight hundred years.

周烈王時天下亂， But by the reign of King Lie, the world fell into chaos.

春秋列國互相吞。 In the Spring and Autumn era, rival states devoured each other.

秦王獨霸諸侯國， Until the Qin Emperor alone became master of the feudal kingdoms.

焚典坑儒滅聖經。 He burned the classics, buried the scholars, and destroyed the sacred canon.

[AGNJX 338]

The narrative continues to recount the breakdown of the Qin polity and the emergence of the new Han dynasty under Liu Bang. The story proper begins with the declining years of the Han. In the extract given here, Zhang Fei explains how, after the oath of brotherhood, he slaughtered the family of his sworn brother, Guan Yu, with the exception of the pregnant Hu Jinding:

及今献帝昏愚弱， In the present day the Emperor Xian is stupid and weak,

曹操專權起霸爭。 Cao Cao has monopolized power, warlords contend with each other,

吾兄玄德遵遺詔， My brother, Xuande [Liu Bei], is carrying out the imperial command.

要除奸黨立乾坤。 To get rid of the traitorous band and set the world to rights!

（張白）俺家姓張名飛，表字翼德，乃亳州人氏。只因黃巾作亂，天下不得太平。今往桃園，結義兄弟三人，替天行道。在家牽掛，恐有回心散約，彼此換殺老小。關家一十八口，俱被我殺了。今有胡氏嫂嫂，身有懷孕三月，立誓在前，一刀不傷二命是自放他殘生。 ZHANG [FEI] *speaks*: My name is Zhang Fei, styled Yide. I come from Haozhou. It is because the Yellow Turban bandits are causing chaos that there is no peace under Heaven. Now I am traveling to Peach Gardens, the three of us will swear an oath of brotherhood to carry out the Way on behalf of Heaven. But we are burdened with families, it is feared we will go back on our pact. So we have each killed each other's families, both young and old. In the Guan household I have killed eighteen in all. Now Mistress Hu, my brother's wife, was three months pregnant. I swore an oath that I would not kill two with the same sword, and so I have spared her life.

[AGNJX 339]

It is remarkable that in the twentieth century a village play could continue to transmit a tale that so thoroughly offends the Chinese value of love of family. However, it appears that the mutual slaughter of each other's families had become a fixture in Guan Suo plays of exorcism, which required acts of violence and sacrifice to exhibit the visible potency of the exorcist-warrior.[29]

As we discuss in the next section, the story of Hua Guan Suo traveled with military garrisons and migratory populations to the southern and western reaches of the empire, where the demons to be subdued were the so-called barbarous southern tribes.

16.11 GUAN SUO PLAYS IN XIAOTUN VILLAGE, CHENGJIANG (YUNNAN PROVINCE), TWENTIETH CENTURY

Xiaotun (literally "small garrison") is a village located on a high plateau on the left bank of the Yangzong River to the south of modern-day Kunming, in Yunnan province. According to the villagers, their forebears arrived in the fifteenth century, when the Ming government established permanent garrisons to pacify the local Miao (Hmong) population. Local records attest that the new arrivals came from the eastern provinces of Jiangsu, Anhui, and Jiangsu.[30] Over the generations, the Chinese soldiers intermarried with the Miao population. The chief function of the Guan Suo plays in Xiaotun was to expel the demons of famine and pestilence in an area known for its poverty and frequent outbreaks of epidemics. However, the words of the plays also remind the population of the role that their forebears played in pacifying the indigenous population of the region.[31]

Due to its remoteness and inaccessibility, Xiaotun was able to maintain its tradition of Guan Suo plays into the mid-twentieth century. However, the village did not escape the wrath of the Cultural Revolution, when most local temples were destroyed and the ritual plays were forbidden to be performed. Manuscripts of play material from before 1949 no longer survive, but new scripts have been compiled in recent years based on the memories of participants who learned their roles in the 1940s.[32] The plays tend to be short and involve two masked warriors engaged in combat. The masks are made of paper-mâché, on which is inscribed the facial markings of dramatic roles such as male lead and female lead. The main heroes are played by "old male leads" (laosheng). As with the Anhui plays, drums and cymbals accompany the performance (☛ Visual Resources).

The Guan Suo cycle of plays performed in Xiaotun derive ultimately from the ritual plays of the eastern provinces, such as Anhui. However, there are significant differences between the Anhui and the Yunnan performances of Guan Suo plays. First, the Xiaotun Guan Suo plays have been relatively untouched by regional operatic traditions, whereas Anhui plays include songs sung to local opera tunes. Second, the Guan Suo plays are the only type of theatrical performance carried out by the Xiaotun villagers, so they play a central role in the village's ritual life. The plays are performed to venerate Guan Suo himself, who is regarded as a deity and has a dedicated temple in the village. The majority of plays are thus not about Guan Suo, but rather about the heroes of the Three Kingdoms era. Given Guan Suo's claimed participation in the campaign to subdue the southern tribal lands, one could say that the implicit focus of the plays in Xiaotun is the conquest of this "barbarian" region by Han Chinese.[33]

The Guan Suo plays are enacted every year at the lunar New Year by village men. The first stage takes place at the local temple. The deity (Guan Suo) is invited to attend the performance and extend his blessings. A rooster is killed. Drops of its blood are splattered on the masks used in performance and poured into a cup, which is passed around for the actors to sip. The rooster is then cooked and eaten. The next stage is a parade through the village in full costume, with the figure playing Liu Bei knocking on the doors of each household to offer blessings and exorcise demons. When the troupe reaches open land by the riverside, the audience will gather around on all sides and the play will begin.

The first item is the Roll Call of Generals. Other plays about the Three Kingdom heroes will be performed over the ensuing days, concluding with a ceremony at the temple to Send Off the Deity.[34] Next is the opening section of the Roll Call, where Liu Bei awards titles to his five "tiger generals."[35] The solemn formality of this opening piece celebrates the importance of imperial power in ensuring peace and stability. The Six Ministries referred to here are Administration, Finance, Rites, War, Punishments, and Public Works. Liu Bei (in the role of *laosheng*), wearing a yellow dragon robe and holding a royal tablet, is at center stage. He recites the verse given here. Next to him is Zhuge Liang (also in the role of *laosheng*), wearing a dark red Taoist gown and holding his horsetail whisk. The generals are lined up on either side of these two figures:

（老生）　OLD MALE *as* LIU BEI [*declaims*]:
君王駕坐金鑾殿，　The monarch takes his seat in the golden phoenix palace,
眾臣朝王喜盈盈。　The assembled court rejoices together with the monarch.
嘹亮笙簫通帝座，　Clear and loud, pipes and flutes resound around the imperial throne.
歌舞齊聲鬧沉沉。　The sounds of song and dance swell in solemn crescendo.
五府六部文和武，　Officers of the Five Garrisons and Six Ministries, both civil and military,
衣冠濟濟上朝廷。　Their robes and caps in strict array, arrive at court.
王開金口親封贈，　The monarch opens his golden mouth to personally award the honors.
風調雨順國太平。　Wind and rain come in due season and the kingdom is at peace.

[QIU 605]

16.12 COMBAT SEQUENCES

A typical sequence in the Xiaotun plays comprises a "sung" section alternating with scenes of combat. Each general introduces himself by declaiming a self-description in "Ten Beats to a Line." After each couplet, he moves in an arc around the stage three or four times. The "Ten Beats to a Line" section presented next is very similar to that found in the Ming-era chantefable. The lines describe the warrior's headdress, costume, and weaponry, together with symbols projecting spiritual power. After reciting the final couplet, the actor comes to a halt and adopts a ferocious stance, his weapon at the ready, as if awaiting combat. This example illustrates how the "Ten Beats to a Line" poetic mode can be deployed to convey the menacing nature of the warrior or demon combatant. In this scene, two men bearing flags enter the stage area as Zhang Qian, a fictional character who appears here as a blend of a local bully and crude buffoon, makes his own entrance:

（淨）	COMIC *as* ZHANG QIAN [*declaims*]:
戴一頂紫金盔，絨纓蓋頂，	Wearing a helmet of spun gold, with knitted tassels on top,
穿一件青花袍，龍鳳裝成。	Robed in a white gown marked in blue with a dragon and phoenix.
繫一根青絲帶，繡上五才，	Cinched with a belt of black hair, embroidered with the Five Talents,
披一幅青絲甲，龍虎相爭。	Girded with a black coat of armor, inscribed with tussling dragons and tigers.
騎一匹青龍馬，江場大戰，	Riding a green dragon courser, he battles it out on the banks of a river,
使一條紫金槍，殺氣騰口。	Wielding a spear of spun gold, killing airs emerge from his mouth.

[*QIU* 609]

CONCLUSION

Third-person narrative has been a feature of Chinese drama from its earliest days. It was retained in numerous dramatic forms in the later imperial period because it contributed important functions to performance. For example, narrative verse is deployed to commence proceedings with solemnity, to introduce characters, to summarize plot details, and to pronounce a parting judgment. The declamatory verse style could be recited in regional vernaculars, thus allowing ready comprehension by diverse audiences. With its formulaic language and regular septasyllabic lines, narrative verse was easy to learn and to extemporize. These features, borrowed from the Chinese oral tradition, account for the popularity of the prosimetric form in storytelling and drama.

In certain types of regional theater, particularly plays of exorcism, narrative verse remained the dominant performance medium well into the twentieth century. The prelude segments, recounting the course of Chinese history, allowed audiences to readily acquire folk wisdom about the reasons behind the rise and fall of dynasties and the shifts between periods of chaos and stability. The lessons about good governance and the fragility of the social order were not lost on even illiterate audiences. The "Ten Beats to a Line" verse sections, familiar to the audience from Buddhist folk genres, gave a quasi-religious aura to the warrior protagonists of these stories.

Anne E. McLaren

NOTES

1. The Song thinker Zhu Xi (1130–1200) observed that "exorcism, though an archaic ritual, is very close to play" (*nuo sui guli er jin yu xi*), quoted in Qitao Guo, *Exorcism and Money: The Symbolic World of the Five-Fury Spirits in Late Imperial China* (Berkeley, CA: Institute of East Asian Studies, 2003), 36.

2. The historical Guan Yu had only two sons, Guan Ping and Guan Xing. In the chantefable, Guan Suo is twice said to be the second son of Guan Yu, and Guan Xing is not mentioned at all. For discussion of this point, see Anne McLaren, "Chantefables and the Evolution of the *San-kuo-chih yen-i*," *T'oung Pao* LXXI, no. 4–5 (1985): 212–214. The earliest edition of *The Romance of the Three Kingdoms* (*Sanguo yanyi*, c. 1522) contains no mention of this legendary hero, but most later editions relate either the story of Hua Guan Suo's early life or the story of Guan Suo in Yunnan.

3. Barend J. Ter Haar, *Guan Yu: The Religious Afterlife of a Failed Hero* (Oxford: Oxford University Press, 2017).

4. This is a short title. The original is divided into four sections, each with its own title.

5. Anne McLaren, *Chinese Popular Culture and Ming Chantefables* (Sinica Leidensia vol. 41. Leiden, Netherlands: Brill, 1998), 59–60.

6. Inoue Taizan, Ōki Yasushi, Kin Bunkyo, Hikami Tadashi, and Furuya Akihiro, *Ka Kan Saku den no kenkyū* (A Study of *The Story of Hua Guan Suo*) (Tokyo: Kyūko shoin, 1989), 59–83.

7. Ye Dejun presents numerous examples in his *Song Yuan Ming jiangchang wenxue* (Prosimetric Literature of the Song, Yuan and Ming Eras) (Shanghai: Zhonghua shuju, 1957), 43–44. See also J. I. Crump, *Chinese Theater in the Days of Kublai Khan* (Tucson: University of Arizona Press, 1980), 127–129.

8. The corpus is known as the Ming Chenghua era (1465–1487) *shuochang cihua* (see *MCSCC*). A facsimile of the original text, together with a complete English translation, are provided in Gail Oman King, ed. and trans., *The Story of Hua Guan Suo* (Tempe: Center for Asian Studies, Arizona State University, 1989). Inoue et al., *Ka Kan Saku den no kenkyū*, includes a facsimile of the original along with a modern critical edition of the text.

9. For more detail, see McLaren, "Chantefables and the Evolution of the *San-kuo-chih yen-i*," 214–217. For a translation of this play, see Wilt L. Idema and Stephen H. West, ed. and trans., *Battles, Betrayals, and Brotherhood: Early Chinese Plays on the Three Kingdoms* (Indianapolis: Hackett Publishing, 2012), 296–315.

10. In Buddhist precious scrolls *(baojuan)* of the Ming and Qing eras, one finds *zan shi zi* (in the sense of "augmented line") and *zan* (in the sense of invocation to the Buddhist deity). See Lu Yongfeng and Che Xilun, *Wu fangyan qu baojuan yanjiu* (A Study of the Precious Scrolls in the Wu Dialect Region) (Beijing: Shehui kexue wenxian chubanshe, 2012), 225–227, 231, 233, 240, 243. The compiler of this chantefable uses the two forms of *zan* interchangeably. On the absorption of Buddhist elements into exorcism rituals, see Guo, *Exorcism and Money*, 34.

11. In another chantefable, the same poetic form is used to describe battle formations in terms of traditional cosmology; see McLaren, *Chinese Popular Culture*, 109–110.

12. McLaren, *Chinese Popular Culture*, 107–108. In an early edition of *The Romance* (c. 1548), the text proper is preceded by a similar prelude in verse entitled "Zongge" ("Summative Song").

13. The Xia is held to be the earliest Chinese dynasty, although it is not attested in the archaeological record. The Shang is the first historical Chinese dynasty (ca. 1600 BCE–1028 BCE). The Zhou dynasty ruled ca. 1027 BCE–256 BCE.

14. These lines set out the vast extent of the Qin empire. The expression *xiu* (to build) is believed to be an error, used instead of *shu* (to garrison), a term found in the official history. Here, the chantefable follows the same line found in the earlier *Plain Tale of the Three Kingdoms* (*Sanguo zhi pinghua*, 1.1b).

15. In drama (*zaju*) and plain tales (*pinghua*) of the Yuan era, the reference here is to Tao Yuan (Peach Garden), not Tao Yuan (Peach Springs). The chantefable narrator refers to Peach Springs four times. This is another sign that this chantefable draws from an oral tradition that is distinct

from that deployed by the author of *The Romance*. Ter Haar notes the existence of a Daoist tradition based around Peach Springs Cave (see *Guan Yu*, 139–140). Another example of divergence could be the line about the sworn brothers jointly ruling the empire (as previously discussed). In the mainstream tradition, Guan Yu and Zhang Fei pledge fealty to Liu Bei as their leader.

16. The printed Ming chantefable includes indications of the mode of delivery in cartouches in the manner of printed dramatic texts. The types of delivery include speech (*bai* and *shuo*), singing (*chang*), and "Ten Beats to a Line" (*zan shi zi*). Manuscripts often replicate such markers, but less systematically. One can assume that these modalities were treated somewhat differently by the Master of Ceremonies or the performer, and were understood differently by the reader. I think we can assume the following: The prose sections (*bai* and *shuo*) would have been declaimed clearly (as in the staging of Chinese drama). The verse sections (*chang*) would have been declaimed, or even given a melodic effect, to accentuate the use of verse, rhythm, and rhyme. The "Ten Beats to a Line" in plays of exorcism was declaimed in a histrionic manner to convey the aroused passions of warriors engaged in mortal combat [*QIU*, 604].

17. The title *Proclaiming Harmony* refers to the Xuanhe era (1119–1125), which is a reign period of the Northern Song dynastic era. In a later iteration of this same tale, *The Record of the Water Margin* (*Shuihu zhuan*), Wang Xiong becomes Yang Xiong, but he retains the same nickname.

18. For a translation, see Idema and West, *Battles, Betrayals, and Brotherhood*, 1–39.

19. For more details, see McLaren, *Chinese Popular Culture*, 242–243.

20. For photos of masks and costumes used for Guan Suo plays, see Yunnan sheng qunzhong yishuguan (Yunnan Province Fine Arts Academy of the Masses), *Yunnan minzu minjian yishu* (The Folk Arts of the Yunnan Nationalities) (Kunming, China, Yunnan Renmin chubanshe, 1994), 224–225.

21. *AGNJX*, 337–374.

22. Inoue et al., *Ka Kan Saku den no kenkyū*, 75.

23. *AGNJX*, 3.

24. *AGNJX*, 526.

25. *AGNJX*, 533.

26. *AGNJX*, 605.

27. *AGNJX*, 607.

28. *AGNJX*, 610.

29. For more on this point, see Ter Haar, who notes that early legends about Guan Yu portrayed him as a demon: "As a former demon, Lord Guan was capable of using physical force to combat a variety of enemies, from demons to barbarians," (*Guan Yu*, 150).

30. *QIU*, 589. Guan Suo was established as a cult figure in Yunnan at the time of the Ming invasion; see McLaren, "Chantefables," 168. Guan Suo plays were brought into Xiaotun from a neighboring village in the Qing era to help combat an epidemic; see *QIU*, 594.

31. On the role played by the Yunnan Guan Suo plays in consolidating imperial authority in the late imperial era, see Sylvie Beaud, "How the North Tried to Pacify the South through Ritual Practices: On the Origins of the Guan Suo Opera in the Nineteenth Century," ed. Victor H. Mair and Kelley Liam, *Imperial China and Its Southern Neighbours* (Singapore: Institute of Southeast Asian Studies, 2015), 316–337.

32. *QIU*, 602–603.

33. Beaud suggests that the Xiaotun population, a mixture of Han and indigenous groups, sought to claim Han identity through the adoption of Guan Suo as a symbol of "central authority" ("How the North Tried to Pacify the South through Ritual Practices," 331).

34. *QIU*, 599–601.

35. This event is briefly related in *The Romance* (chap. 37) and in *The Plain Tale of the Three Kingdoms*.

PRIMARY SOURCES

AGNJX Wang Zhaoqian 王兆乾, ed. *Anhui Guichi nuoxi juben xuan* 安徽貴池儺戲劇本選
(*A Selection of Scripts from the Nuoxi Plays from Guichi Village, Anhui Province*). Taipei:
Shihe Zheng Minsu wenhua jijin hui, 1995.

MCSCC Zhu Yixuan 朱一玄, ed. *Ming Chenghua shuochang cihua congkan* 明成化說唱詞話
叢刊 [*The Collected Chantefables from the Ming-Dynasty Chenghua Reign (1464–1487)*].
Zhengzhou, China: Zhongzhou guji chubanshe, 1997.

QIU Qiu Kunliang 邱坤良. "Guan Suo yishi yu Guan Suo xiju—yi Yunnan Chengjiang
xiao tun 'wan Guan Suo' wei li" 關索儀式與關索戲劇—以雲南澂江小屯玩關索為
例 ("Guan Suo Ceremonies and Guan Suo Plays—The Example of Playing Guan
Suo in Xiaotun, Chengjiang, Yunnan Province"). In *Minjian xinyang yu Zhongguo
wenhua guoji yantao hui lunwenji* 民間信仰與中國文化國際研討論文集 (*International
Conference Proceedings on Folk Belief and Chinese Culture*), 587–620. Taipei: Center for
Chinese Studies, 1994.

SUGGESTED READINGS

TRANSLATIONS

Idema, Wilt L., and Stephen H. West, ed. and trans. *Battles, Betrayals, and Brotherhood: Early
Chinese Plays on the Three Kingdoms*. Indianapolis: Hackett Publishing, 2012.
King, Gail Oman, ed. and trans. *The Story of Hua Guan Suo*. Tempe: Center for Asian Studies,
Arizona State University, 1989.

ENGLISH

McLaren, Anne E. "Chantefables and the Evolution of the *San-kuo-chih yen-i*." *T'oung Pao* LXXI,
no. 4–5 (1985): 159–227.
McLaren, Anne E. *Chinese Popular Culture and Ming Chantefables*. Sinica Leidensia vol. 41. Leiden,
Netherlands: Brill, 1998.

CHINESE

Yunnan sheng qunzhong yishuguan 雲南省群眾藝術館 (Yunnan Province Fine Arts Academy
of the Masses). *Yunnan minzu minjian yishu* 雲南民族民間藝術 (*The Folk Arts of the Yunnan
Nationalities*). Kunming, China: Yunnan Renmin chubanshe, 1994.

ACKNOWLEDGMENTS

Throughout this project, it took a global village to conceive, nurture, and complete *How to Read Chinese Drama: A Guided Anthology*. We gratefully acknowledge the Chiang Ching-Kuo Foundation for International Scholarly Exchange for supporting the conference entitled "A Gateway to Chinese Theatre, or How to Read Chinese Drama," held in Columbus, Ohio, in summer 2017. Not only were the beginnings of many chapters included in this volume first presented there, but the substantive and lively discussions that preceded and followed each presentation proved to be a major inspiration for us.

Our largest debt goes to our contributors. They believed in the need for this volume as much as we did. In the interest of clarity, they graciously worked through multiple rounds of revisions with good cheer and great patience. When prompted, they entertained our many queries, large and small. Together, they egged us on with their collective enthusiasm for wanting to make this volume available for their own and everyone else's classrooms.

We are much indebted to Zong-qi Cai for his vision for the "How to Read Chinese Literature" (HTRCL) series. In summer 2016, he spearheaded a meeting of HTRCL editors in Beijing that helped us think through the conception of our volume. In the course of executing this project, we were fortunate to draw on Zong-qi's unfailing support. We always marveled at how he answered our questions with superluminal speed, as though ours were the only project on his hands.

It has been a pleasure to work with Christine Dunbar and Christian P. Winting at Columbia University Press, and with Ben Kolstad and his team at Knowledge Works Global. All three peer reviewers offered valuable insights and thoughtful suggestions. To the one who disclosed his identity, David L. Rolston, we are particularly grateful. He went above and beyond in offering more overall comments, detailed criticisms, and stylistic improvements than anyone could ever ask for in their wildest peer review dreams. His boundless knowledge and painstaking attention to detail have enriched everyone's chapters. As editors, we are particularly thankful for his many incisive suggestions for the Introduction.

In terms of the preparation of the apparatus for *How to Read Chinese Drama*, we have benefited from the assistance of many talented graduate students. We want to take this opportunity to acknowledge the contribution of the late Zhang Xiaohui (then a PhD candidate at the University of Illinois, Urbana-Champaign), who put together a very useful stylesheet and guide to common formatting errors, which he first shared with us at the "A Gateway to Chinese Theater" conference. We are deeply saddened that he did not live to see the published work.

We are also much indebted to the thoughtful, meticulous, and timely work of Erxin Wang (a PhD student at The Ohio State University), who brought her knowledge of early modern literature and her editorial acumen to bear on her compilation of the Thematic Contents, Chronology of Events, and Glossary-Index. We also thank Hui Yao (a PhD candidate at The Ohio State University) for putting her expertise in modern drama and visual culture in the service of creating the Visual Resources section.

For assistance with formatting and editorial matters, we are grateful to the ingenuity of Hunter Klie (PhD student, The Ohio State University) in devising and implementing the bilingual format; the keen eye of Amanda Etchison (BA Chinese/Journalism, The Ohio State University) in proofreading the chapters prior to peer review, and the early formatting assistance provided by Anzia Mayer (MA Chinese, The Ohio State University).

For her additional editorial feedback and scholarly input, we thank Wenbo Chang (Georgia Institute of Technology), the coeditor of *How to Read Chinese Drama in Chinese: A Language Companion*.

We also wish to acknowledge the support of The Ohio State University. In terms of logistical and fiscal support for the "A Gateway to Chinese Theater" conference, we express our thanks to David Liu (Department of East Asian Literatures and Languages) and Nathan Lancaster (then at the East Asian Studies Center). In addition, I (Patricia) thank my chair, Mark Bender, for his support of the project and the Division of Arts and Humanities for granting me a semester of special research assignment for its development and for a collaborative award (with Maria Palazzi, Marjorie Chan, and Leigh Bonds) for the creation of a prototype for "The Digital Chinese Theater Collaborative." I am also grateful for successive classes of undergraduate students enrolled in my Chinese 4404 "Chinese Drama" course for feedback on how to teach Chinese drama, while continually pointing to new ways to connect traditional theater to contemporary culture. And I thank the graduate students in my Chinese 6452 "Late Imperial Literature" survey courses and my Chinese 8897 "Theater, Media, and History" seminar for their engagement with and feedback on individual chapters (circulated with the permission of the authors) and on an early draft of the Introduction.

On a personal note, I (Patricia) also wish to acknowledge the inspiration of my son, Colin Reano-Sieber, who grew alongside this project, reveling in pretend play (bye bye Ultima Thule, hello Oort Cloud); and the support of my husband, Ronald M. Reano, who kept it real between pandemic stacks of laundry, daily outdoor fun, and backyard photographs of the Andromeda Galaxy. Colin's and Ron's boundless sense of adventure and our love for each other nurtured the work represented here.

In the years that it has taken for this book to materialize, both my (Regina's) kids started college only to be locked down together with John and me in a tiny apartment in Spain for a long stretch. The conversation, cooking, curiosity, and good cheer of all three made this unexpected experience interesting, entertaining, and infinitely happy.

In this spirit of exploration and fortitude, we dedicate our joint labors on this edited volume to Colin, Clara, and Antonio.

CONTRIBUTORS

Andrea S. Goldman is associate professor of late imperial and modern Chinese history at the University of California, Los Angeles, specializing in opera history, urban history, and gender history. Her book *Opera and the City: The Politics of Culture in Beijing, 1770–1900* (2012) uses opera as a lens through which to observe court and city dynamics in Qing-dynasty Beijing. In 2014, *Opera and the City* received the Joseph A. Levenson Award for the best monograph on China (pre-1900 category) from the Association for Asian Studies. Goldman's current work in progress explores the transnational reconstruction of masculinity in China circa 1900–1950 through intertwined biographies of a French Sinophile opera aficionado and a renowned early-twentieth-century cross-dressing actor of the female ingenue (*dan* 旦) role type.

Guo Yingde (PhD, Beijing Normal University, 1989) is professor of traditional Chinese literature and Chinese classical drama at Beijing Normal University. He has published more than twenty books and more than 200 academic papers. His books include *Ming Qing chuanqi zonglu* 明清傳奇綜錄 (Survey of Ming-Qing Chuanqi Drama) (1997), *Ming Qing chuanqi shi* 明清傳奇史 (History of Ming-Qing Chuanqi Drama) (2012 [1999]), *Zhongguo gudai wenti xue lungao* 中國古代文體學論稿 (Essays on Literary Genres in Ancient China, 2005), and *Tanxun Zhongguo quwei: Zhongguo gudai wenxue de lishi wenhua sikao* 探尋中國趣味：中國古代文學的歷史文化思考 (In Search of Chinese Flavors: Exploring the History and Culture of Ancient Chinese Literature) (2017).

Hui Yao is a PhD candidate in the Department of East Asian Languages and Literatures at The Ohio State University. She received her master's degree in East Asian languages and civilizations from the University of Pennsylvania. Her research interests include modern Chinese literature, wartime cinema, and the interplay among cinema, traditional theater, and spoken drama. She is currently working on her dissertation on Republican director Fei Mu through the lens of translation studies and media studies. She coauthored (with Patricia Sieber et al.) "In Search of Pure Sound: *Sanqu* Songs, Genre Aesthetics, and Translation Tactics," in *The Journal of Chinese Literature and Culture* 8, no. 1 (April 2021): 161–202. She compiled the "Visual Resources" list for *How to Read Chinese Drama: A Guided Anthology*.

Wilt L. Idema taught at Leiden University from 1970 to 1999, and at Harvard University from 2000 to 2013. His research has mostly focused on the vernacular traditions of late imperial China, such as drama, fiction, and prosimetric narrative. Together with Stephen H. West, he has published extensively on early Chinese drama, including *Chinese Theater 1100–1450: A Source Book* (1982); *The Moon and the Zither: The Story of the Western Wing* [1991; revised edition *The Story of the Western Wing* (1995)]; *Monks, Bandits, Lovers and Immortals: Eleven Early Chinese Plays* (2010); and *The Orphan of Zhao and Other Yuan Plays: The Earliest Known Versions* (2015).

S. E. Kile is assistant professor in the Department of Asian Languages and Cultures at the University of Michigan, and a specialist in Ming and Qing literature and culture. His research foregrounds the operations of gender and performance, as in the article "Transgender Performance in Early Modern China," *differences* 24, no. 2 (2013): 130–149 (Chinese version: 鄺師華. "Zaoqi jindai Zhongguo de kuaxingbie biaoyan" 早期近代中国的跨性别表演," in *Zhongguo xing/bie: lishi chayi* 中国性 / 別：歷史差異, 2015). He has also addressed contemporary interpretations of premodern same-sex romance in "Sensational Kunqu: The April 2010 Beijing Production of *Lianxiang ban* (*Women in Love*)," *CHINOPERL* (2011). He is currently finishing a monograph that theorizes early modern mediation and entrepreneurship through the cultural production of Li Yu (1611–1680) entitled *Master Medium: Li Yu's Technologies of Culture in the Early Qing*.

Shiamin Kwa is associate professor of East Asian languages and cultures and comparative literature at Bryn Mawr College. She has written on Xu Wei's plays in *Mulan: Five Versions of a Classic Chinese Legend* (2010), *Strange Eventful Histories: Identity, Performance, and Xu Wei's* Four Cries of a Gibbon (2012), and in *A Companion to World Literature* (2020).

Joseph S. C. Lam is professor of musicology at the School of Music, Theatre, and Dance at the University of Michigan. A musicologist and sinologist, he specializes in the music and culture of the southern Song (1127–1279), Ming (1368–1644), and modern China (1900–present). Lam's recent publications include "Eavesdropping on Zhang Xiaoxiang's Musical World in Early Southern Song China," in *Senses of the City*, edited by Joseph Lam, Shuen-fu Lin, and Christian de Pee (2017); "Zhang Dai's (1597–1680) Musical Life in Late Ming China, in *Ming China*, edited by Kenneth Swope (2019); and "Huaigu yinyue lilun yu shijian di yige chubu tian" (A Proposal on Music of Reminiscence: Theory and Practice), in *Yinyue yishu/Musical Art* (2019/2). His latest monograph is *Kunqu, A Classical Opera of Twenty-first Century China* (University of Hong Kong Press, 2022 forthcoming).

Ling Hon Lam is associate professor in the Department of East Asian Languages and Cultures at the University of California, Berkeley. His research and teaching interests cover premodern drama and fiction, sex and gender, media culture, and critical theories. He is the author of *The Spatiality of Emotion in Early Modern China: From Dreamscapes to Theatricality* (2018). His other publications include "The Matriarch's Private Ears: Performance, Reading, Censorship, and the Fabrication of Interiority in The Story of the Stone," *Harvard Journal of Asiatic Studies* (2005), "Reading off the Screen: Toward Cinematic Illiteracy in Late 1950s Chinese Opera Film," *Opera Quarterly* (2010), and "Bao-yu's Multimedia Classroom: Reading, Performance, and the Vicissitudes of the Voice from *The Story of the Stone* to Its Film Adaptations" in *Approaches to Teaching The Story of the Stone* (2012). He is currently working on the historical ontology of media in early modern to twentieth-century China.

Mengjun Li is assistant professor of Chinese at the University of Puget Sound. She teaches courses on Chinese literature and cinema, as well as the Chinese language at various levels. Her research interests include traditional Chinese fiction and drama, print culture, and popular culture of the twentieth century. Li has published two articles on the production of vernacular novels in the seventeenth century: " 'Carving the Complete Edition': Self-commentary, Poetry, and Illustration in the Early-Qing Erotic Novel *Romance of an Embroidered Screen* (1670)," in *East Asian Publishing and Society* (2017); and "Genre Conflation and Fictional Religiosity in *Guilian meng* (Returning to the Lotus Dream)," in the *Journal of Chinese Literature and Culture* (2019). She is currently finishing a book manuscript tentatively titled *Formularized Genius: Negotiations of Genre and Desire in Traditional Chinese Fiction*.

Regina Llamas is associate professor in the humanities at IE University in Spain. She holds a BA from Beijing University in Chinese language and literature and a PhD in East Asian languages and cultures from Harvard University. Her earlier work, both in English and Spanish, focused on southern Chinese drama, dramatic historiography, modern ethnography and dramatic performance, and the later Qing commentarial dramatic tradition. She is currently working on a monograph on the historiography of Chinese drama and how the discipline was formed. She is the author of *Top Graduate Zhang Xie: The Earliest Extant Chinese Southern Play* (2021). Other recent works include "Xu Wei's *A Record of Southern Drama*: The Idea of a Theater in Seventeenth-Century China," in *1616 in China and England*, ed. by Tian Yuan Tan, Paul Edmonson, and Shi-pe Wang (2016); and "A Reassessment of the Place of Shamanism in the Origins of Chinese Theater," in *Journal of the American Oriental Society* (2013).

Anne E. McLaren is professor of Chinese literature at the University of Melbourne, Australia. She has published widely in the field of Chinese popular culture at the regional and village levels, including fiction, oral traditions, theater, and the performing arts. She has a particular interest in the transformation of oral traditional material into literary genres. Her publications include *Chinese Popular Culture and Ming Chantefables* (1998) and *Performing Grief: Bridal Laments in Rural China* (2008). She has also published numerous studies on the early development of the Ming novel *The Three Kingdoms*. A recent publication deals with a new genre of theatre known as *tanhuang*, which emerged in the late imperial era ("Selling Scandal in the Republican Era: Folk Opera in Performance and Print," in *CHINOPERL*, 2019). She is currently engaged in a book-length project on the folk epics of regional China.

Patricia Sieber is associate professor in the Department of East Asian Languages and Literatures at The Ohio State University. Her research interests encompass Chinese drama, song culture, translation studies, and gender studies. She is the author of *Theaters of Desire: Authors, Readers, and the Reproduction of Early Chinese Song-Drama* (Palgrave Macmillan, 2003) and coeditor (with Guo Yingde, Wenbo Chang, and the late Xiaohui Zhang) of *How to Read Chinese Drama in Chinese: A Language Companion* (under advance agreement with: Columbia University Press) and (with Li Guo and Peter Kornicki) of *Ecologies of Translation in Early Modern East and South East Asia, 1600–1900* (Amsterdam: Amsterdam University Press forthcoming). She guest-edited a special issue on "The Protean World of *Sanqu* Songs" for *The Journal of Chinese Literature and Culture* (April 2021); and is currently working on two book-length studies on literary translator P.P. Thoms (1790–1855) and on Yuan-dynasty *sanqu* songs. Her essays on Chinese drama and song culture have appeared in *Modern Chinese Literature and Culture, Journal of Chinese Literature and Culture, Monumenta Serica, Journal of Chinese Religions*, and *Ming Studies*, among others.

Tian Yuan Tan is Shaw Professor of Chinese at the University of Oxford. His main areas of research include Chinese literary history and historiography, text and performance, and cross-cultural literary interactions. He is the author of *Songs of Contentment and Transgression: Discharged Officials and Literati Communities in Sixteenth-Century North China* (2010), *Kang Hai sanqu ji jiaojian* 康海散曲集校箋 [A Critical Edition of the *Sanqu* Songs by Kang Hai (1475–1541) with Notes and Two Essays, 2011], coauthor (with Paolo Santangelo) of *Passion, Romance, and Qing: The World of Emotions and States of Mind in* Peony Pavilion (2014), and coeditor (with Maghiel van Crevel and Michel Hockx) of *Text, Performance, and Gender in Chinese Literature and Music: Essays in Honor of Wilt Idema* (2009), (with Xu Yongming) of *Yingyu shijie de Tang Xianzu yanjiu lunzhu xuanyi* 英語世界的湯顯祖研究論著選譯 (An Anthology of Critical Studies on Tang Xianzu in Western Scholarship, 2013), and (with Paul Edmondson and Shi-pe Wang) of *1616: Shakespeare and Tang Xianzu's China* (2016).

Erxin Wang is a PhD student in the Department of East Asian Languages and Literatures at The Ohio State University. She received her master's degree in East Asian languages and cultures from Washington University in St. Louis. Her research interests include early modern Chinese theater and fiction, transgender performance, and intellectual history. She is the translator of Ye Ye, "Yuan-Ming *Sanqu* Songs as Communal Texts: Discovering Their Literary Vitality from a New Research Perspective," *The Journal of Chinese Literature and Culture* 8, no. 1 (April 2021): 113–138 and of Shih-pe Wang, "Plays within Songs: *Sanqu* Songs from Literary Refinement (*ya*) to Popular Appeal (*su*)," *The Journal of Chinese Literature and Culture* 8, no. 2 (Nov 2021) (forthcoming). She compiled the Thematic Contents, Chronology of Historical Events, and Glossary-Index for *How to Read Chinese Drama: A Guided Anthology*.

Shih-pe Wang is professor of Chinese literature at National Taiwan University (NTU) and currently serves as vice president for student affairs. Her major research field is classical Chinese drama in general and Kunqu in particular. She is the author of *Qian Jia shiqi kunju yiren zai biaoyian yishu shang yinying zhi tantao* 乾嘉時期崑劇藝人在表演藝術上因應之探討 (The Actors' Performance of Kunqu in the Qianlong and Jiaqing Periods of Qing Dynasty, 2000) and a coeditor (with Tian Yuan Tan and Paul Edmondson) of *1616: Shakespeare and Tang Xianzu's China* (2016). Recent journal articles include "Plays within Songs: *Sanqu* Songs between Literary Refinement (*ya*) and Popular Appeal (*su*)," *The Journal of Chinese Literature and Culture* 8, no. 2 (2021) (forthcoming); "Yi Yuanju wei fa: Zailun *Mudanting* zhi jingdian xing" 以元劇為方法：再論《牡丹亭》之經典性 ("Taking Yuan Drama as a Method: Reexamining the Canonical Nature of *The Peony Pavilion*"), *Taida zhongwen xuebao* 臺大中文學報 (Bulletin of the Department of Chinese Literature, National Taiwan University), 2018; "Qianji yu mingcong: Qing zhongye *Leifengta* chuanqi bianyan xinlun" 潛跡與明蹤：清中葉《雷峰塔》傳奇演變新論 ("Hidden Traces, Obvious Tracks: A Reexamination of the Development of the *chuanqi Thunder Peak Pagoda* in the High Qing)," *Minsu quyi* 民俗曲藝 (Journal of Chinese Ritual, Theatre and Folklore), 2018.

Stephen H. West is Louis Agassiz Professor of Chinese, Emeritus, University of California, Berkeley, and Foundation Professor, Emeritus, Arizona State University. He is the author or coauthor of several translations and studies of Yuan drama. He is a specialist in the urban literature of the twelfth to thirteenth centuries and early Chinese performing literature. His latest work, coauthored with Ruth Dunnell and Yang Shaoyun, will be a full translation and annotation of the Daoist Qiu Chuji's journey to the western slopes of the Hindu Kush, his return, and his death.

Sai-shing Yung obtained his BA and MPhil degrees from the Department of Chinese, University of Hong Kong, and his PhD from Princeton University. Specializing in traditional Chinese drama, he is currently teaching at the Department of Chinese Studies, National University of Singapore. His research interests include late Ming drama, social history of Cantonese opera, Chinese sound culture, dialect-cinema of Hong Kong, and cultural cold war in Asia. His major publications include *The Anthropology of Chinese Drama: Ritual, Theater, and Community* (in Chinese) (2003); *Cantonese Opera from the Gramophone: A Cultural History (1903–1953)* (in Chinese) (2006); *From Red Boat to Silver Screen: Visual and Sonic Culture of Cantonese Opera* (in Chinese) (2012); and the edited book *A Study on the Taiping Theatre Collection* (in Chinese) (2015).

Gillian Yanzhuang Zhang is a PhD candidate in the Department of History of Art at The Ohio State University. She specializes in early modern Chinese art and material culture (ca. 1500–1850), with an interest in questions of media, artistic hierarchy, and circulation of images across centuries and cultures. From August 2019 to July 2020, Zhang was a predoctoral fellow at the Smithsonian Institution's National Museum of Asian Art. Her publications include the book *Siyu: Xiqiao cansi ye koushu shi* 絲語：西樵蠶絲業口述史 (The Language of Silk: An Oral History of the Silk Industry in the Xiqiao Region, 2012) and "Making a Canonical Work: A Cultural History of the *Mustard Seed Garden Manual of Painting* (1679–1949)," *East Asian Publishing and Society* (2020). Currently, she is writing her dissertation entitled "Image-Making and Intermediality in China's Long Eighteenth Century (1683–1839)."

Ying Zhang (PhD, history and women's studies, University of Michigan, 2010) is associate professor in the Department of History at The Ohio State University. Her research explores the history of Confucianism, gender and family, and political culture in premodern China. She has authored *Confucian Image Politics: Masculine Morality in Seventeenth-Century China* (2017) and *Religion and Prison Art in Ming China (1368–1644): Creative Environment, Creative Subjects* (2020).

VISUAL RESOURCES

CHAPTER 1, CHAPTER 4

WANG SHIFU, *THE STORY OF THE WESTERN WING* (*XIXIANG JI*) 西廂記

Hou Yao 侯曜, dir. *Xixiang ji* 西廂記 (*The Story of the Western Wing*, titled *Romance of the Western Chamber* in the film). Minxin Film Company (aka China Sun Film Company), 1927; Cinema Epoch, 2007. DVD (French intertitles and Chinese and English subtitles).

Adapted from the popular scholar-and-beauty story, this 1927 silent film offers its audience a transmedial experience, with extensive, Beijing opera–style martial scenes, extreme close-ups, and a wide range of shot/reverse shot editing. Student Zhang's psychological dream in the film also implies a crisis of male masculinity among intellectuals.

CHAPTER 2

ANONYMOUS, *A PLAYBOY FROM A NOBLE HOUSE OPTS FOR THE WRONG CAREER* (*HUANMEN ZIDI CUOLISHEN*) 宦門子弟錯立身

Ke Jun 柯軍 and Shi Hongmei 史紅梅. *Huanmen zidi cuo lishen* 宦門子弟錯立身 (*A Playboy from a Noble House Opts for the Wrong Career*). Beijing: Beijing wenhua yishu yinxiang chuban she, 2003. DVD (Chinese).

Produced by Beifang Kunqu juyuan 北方昆曲劇院 (Northern Kunqu Opera Theater), this performance claims to have "completed" the playtext and highlights its metatheatrical dimension by adding two plays-within-a-play onstage. The production team consulted historical materials to reconstruct Song *zaju* 雜劇 performances and Jurchen dances within the story. This play commemorates the 850th anniversary of the establishment of Beijing, back then known as Zhongdu 中都 (Central Capital), capital of the Jin dynasty, as the national capital. Modern diction is added to the play to attract a younger audience.

CHAPTER 3

GUAN HANQING, *THE PAVILION FOR PRAYING TO THE MOON* (*BAIYUETING*) 拜月亭

Shan Wen 單雯 and Zhang Zhengyao 張爭耀. *Yougui ji* 幽閨記 (*The Story of the Secluded Boudoir*, titled *The Inner Quarters* in the film). Nanjing, China: Jiangsu Sheng Kunju yuan, 2018. DVD (Chinese with English subtitles).

With a prelude and five scenes, this 2018 Kunqu performance claims to be a full-scale play (*benxi* 本戲) of *The Story of the Secluded Boudoir*, a *chuanqi* 傳奇 adaptation of *The Pavilion for Praying to the Moon* (*Baiyueting* 拜月亭). It also includes arias from iconic scenes (*zhezixi* 折子戲) such as "Under the Same Umbrella" ("Ta san" 踏傘) and "Sending for a Doctor" ("Qing yi" 請醫).

GUAN HANQING, *THE INJUSTICE TO DOU E* (*GANTIAN DONGDI DOU E YUAN*) 感天動地竇娥冤

Zhang Xinshi 張辛實, dir. *Dou E yuan* 竇娥冤 (*The Injustice to Dou E*). Changchun Film Studio, 1959; Guangzhou, China: Guanzhou yinxiang chuban she, 1997. DVD (Chinese).

This Puzhou opera film (Shanxi-based *Puju* 蒲劇) was made in 1959 as part of a series of celebrations commemorating the 700th anniversary of Guan Hanqing's dramatic compositions ("Jinian Guan Hanqing xiju chuangzuo qibainian" 紀念關漢卿戲劇創作七百年). With Puzhou opera's energetic singing style accompanied by the lively rhythm of wooden clappers, this opera film highlights Dou E's resistance to sexual aggression, the unjust murder charge itself, and the oppression by a repressive government in general. The film helped to canonize Guan as the "father of Yuan *zaju* drama."

CHAPTER 5

JI JUNXIANG, *THE ORPHAN OF ZHAO* (*ZHAO SHI GU'ER*) 趙氏孤兒

Chen Kaige 陳凱歌, dir. *Zhao shi gu'er* 趙氏孤兒 (*Sacrifice*). 2010; Los Angeles: Indomina Media, 2012. DVD (Chinese with English subtitles).

Adapted from the Yuan *zaju* 雜劇 play *The Orphan of Zhao*, this film changes the murder of a loyal family into a political conflict between two parties at the court of Lord Ling. Other key plot details are altered as well, with Cheng Ying assuming center stage. The English title *Sacrifice* implies that the orphan of Zhao is sacrificed in the course of Cheng Ying's attempt to avenge the death of his own child.

CHAPTER 6

XU WEI, *THE FEMALE MULAN JOINS THE ARMY IN PLACE OF HER FATHER* (*CI MULAN TIFU CONGJUN*) 雌木蘭替父從軍

Bu Wancang 卜萬蒼, dir. *Mulan congjun* 木蘭從軍 (*Mulan Joins the Army*). Xinhua Studio, 1939; Fuzhou, China: Fujian Sheng yinxiang chuban she, 2005. DVD (Chinese).[1]

This film was made in Shanghai during its "Orphan Island" (*gudao* 孤島) period (1937–1941), when the Chinese sections of the city were occupied by the Japanese army. Inspired by the Mulan story, it frames the backdrop as an unjust war and transforms Hua Mulan's filial love into a patriotic passion. With the national defense message and the combination of singing, comedic elements, and romantic love, the film gained immediate popularity in Shanghai, Nanjing, and Hong Kong. Its premiere in Chongqing, however, led to an incident in which the film print was burned because the audience believed that the director and the film studio had collaborated with the Japanese.

CHAPTER 7

NINE MOUNTAIN SOCIETY, *TOP GRADUATE ZHANG XIE* (*ZHANG XIE ZHUANGYUAN*) 張協狀元

Lin Meimei 林媚媚 and Yang Juan 楊娟. *Zhang Xie zhuangyuan* 張協狀元 (*Top Graduate Zhang Xie*). In *Kua shiji qianxi kunju jingying da huiyan* 跨世紀千禧崑劇菁英大匯演 (*Celebrating the Millennium: Performances from the Kunqu Masters*). Taipei: Guoli chuantong yishu zhongxin choubei chu, 2001. CD-ROM (Chinese).

Performed by the Yongjia Kunju Transmission Institute (Yongjia Kunju chuanxi suo 永嘉昆劇傳習所), with six actors playing twelve characters, this performance revels in metatheatricality. The actors state onstage that they are shorthanded and announce as they assume a new character that they are changing. The actors who play comic roles at times act as props and set pieces, all the while commenting on the play and explaining the theatrical conventions to the audience.

GAO MING, *THE LUTE* (*PIPA JI*) 琵琶記

Zhang Jingxian 張靜嫻. "*Pipa ji*: Chikang" 琵琶記·吃糠 ("Eating Husks," in *The Lute*). In *Kunqu baizhong, Dashi shuoxi* 昆曲百種, 大師說戲 (*One Hundred Pieces of Kunqu, Master Performers Talk about Their Scenes*). Changsha, China: Hunan dianzi yinxiang chuban she, 2014. DVD (Chinese).

This lecture features the eminent Kunqu artist Zhang Jingxian explaining and demonstrating her acting in the iconic scene of *The Lute* entitled "Eating Husks." Zhang adopts an acting style of "plain drawing" (*baimiao* 白描) to express Zhao Wuniang's 趙五娘 muted grief and her emotional and practical dilemmas through her intimate conversation with the husks. Zhang stresses hand gestures instead of water sleeves (*shuixiu*, 水袖) to highlight the bitterness of everyday life.

CHAPTER 8

LI RIHUA, *THE SOUTHERN STORY OF THE WESTERN WING (NAN XIXIANG)* 南西廂

Liang Guyin 梁谷音. "*Xixiang ji*: Jiaqi" 西廂記·佳期 ("Happy Time," in *Story of the Western Wing*). In *Kunqu baizhong, Dashi shuoxi* 昆曲百種, 大師說戲 (*One Hundred Pieces of Kunqu, Master Performers Talk about Their Scenes*). Changsha, China: Hunan dianzi yinxiang chuban she, 2014. DVD (Chinese).[2]

This lecture features Liang Guyin, a veteran female Kunqu performer. She discusses her creation of Crimson (Hongniang 紅娘) in the scene "Happy Time" in *Southern Western Wing*. Giving a line-by-line demonstration and interpretation of her eye expressions, kinetic movements, and the use of her sash as a prop, Liang reveals how she learned the scene from her teachers' oral transmission and how she personalized it with her own artistic touches.

CHAPTER 9

TANG XIANZU, *THE PEONY PAVILION (MUDAN TING)* 牡丹亭

Wang Shiyu 汪世瑜 and Pai Hsien-yung 白先勇 (aka Bai Xianyong), dir. *Qingchunban Mudan ting* 青春版牡丹亭 (*The Youth Edition of The Peony Pavilion*). Performed by Shen Fengying 沈豐英 and Yu Jiulin 俞玖林. Hangzhou, China: Zhejiang yinxiang chuban she, 2007. DVD (Chinese with English subtitles).

Premiered in 2004, this nine-hour youth edition of *Peony Pavilion* highlights the romantic love between Du Liniang 杜麗娘 and Liu Mengmei 柳夢梅, with twenty-nine scenes instead of the original fifty-five. The concept of a "youth edition" targets university students with a young, beautiful cast and special attention to the costumes, music, and stage setting. Its popularity, both domestically and internationally, has contributed to the revival of Kunqu in contemporary times.

Buxiu de jujiang: Jinian Tang Xianzu, Shashibiya, Saiwantisi shishi 400 zhounian 不朽的巨匠: 紀念湯顯祖, 莎士比亞, 塞萬提斯逝世400周年 (*The Grand Masters: Commemorating the 400th Anniversary of the Deaths of Tang Xianzu, Shakespeare, and Cervantes*). Beijing: Guojia tushuguan, 2016. DVD (Chinese).

Held by the National Library of China (Zhongguo guojia tushuguan 中國國家圖書館) on July 29, 2016, this event included lectures and performances commemorating Tang Xianzu 湯顯祖, Shakespeare, and Cervantes. Young artists in Beifang Kunqu juyuan 北方昆曲劇院 (Northern Kunqu Opera Theater) performed "Breaking off the Willow Branches" ("Zheliu" 折柳) in Tang's *The Purple Hairpin* (*Zichai ji* 紫釵記). The Kunqu director Cong Zhaohuan 叢兆桓 introduced Tang's theatrical concepts to the audience, most of whom were college students. The recording of this event has been added to the National Library Open Course website.

CHAPTER 10

RUAN DACHENG, *THE SWALLOW'S LETTER (YANZI JIAN)* 燕子箋

Lin Jifan 林繼凡. "*Yanzi jian*: Goudong" 燕子箋·狗洞 ("Doghole," in *The Swallow's Letter*). In *Kunqu baizhong, Dashi shuoxi* 昆曲百種, 大師說戲 (*One Hundred Pieces of Kunqu, Master Performers Talk about Their Scenes*). Changsha, China: Hunan dianzi yinxiang chuban she, 2014. DVD (Chinese).

This lecture features the famous *chou* 丑 (clown) actor Lin Jifan demonstrating his performance of "Doghole." It is a scene where the cunning scholar Xianyu Ji 鮮於佶, who fraudulently gained the position of top graduate, faces a second test. Lin combines a "cold" acting mode to portray Xianyu's condescending attitude toward the doorkeeper with a "hot" one to demonstrate his amusing desperation when he fails to write anything and flees through a doghole.

CHAPTER 11

LI YU, *MISTAKE WITH A KITE (FENGZHENG WU)* 風箏誤

Qian Zhenxiong 錢振雄 and Kong Aiping 孔愛萍. *Fengzheng wu* 風箏誤 (*Mistake with a Kite*). In *Moling lanxun, Moling lanyun* 秣稜蘭薰, 秣陵蘭蘊 (*The Orchid Disposition of Nanjing*). Yilan, Taiwan: Guoli chuantong yishu zhongxin, 2002. DVD (Chinese).

This performance of rearranged scenes (*zhezixi* 折子戲) from *Mistake with a Kite* was performed by Jiangsu Provincial Kunqu Troupe (*Jiangsu sheng Kunjuyuan* 江蘇省昆劇院) in 1999, the second time they visited Taiwan. The four scenes—namely, "Composing a Poem on the Kite" ("Tiyao" 題鷂), "Mistake with the Kite" ("Yaowu" 鷂誤), "Startled by the Ugly One" ("Jingchou" 驚醜), and "Being Dispatched to Take the Civil Service Exam" ("Qianshi" 遣試)—feature a series of humorous events precipitated by misunderstandings around the identities of two young men and two young women.

CHAPTER 12

KONG SHANREN, *THE PEACH BLOSSOM FAN (TAOHUA SHAN)* 桃花扇

Tian Qinxin 田沁鑫, dir. *1699 Taohua shan: Zhongguo chuanqi dianfeng* 1699 桃花扇: 中國傳奇巔峰 (*The Peach Blossom Fan (1699): The Pinnacle of Classical Chinese Theater*). Performed by Shan Wen 單雯 and Shi Xiaming 施夏明 (youth version). Nanjing, China: Jiangsu wenhua yinxiang chubanshe, 2006. DVD (Chinese with English subtitles).

This Kunqu play is directed by eminent spoken drama director Tian Qinxin and performed by the Jiangsu Kunqu Troupe 江蘇昆劇團. Forty-four scenes are presented in six acts, with some excisions and minor plot adjustments. In the middle of the stage stands a movable decorated pavilion that is used at specific moments in the performance. A duplicate of the Ming painting *Bustling Scene in the Southern Capital* (*Nandu fanhui tu* 南都繁會圖) is printed on a big screen in the background to reconstruct the prosperity of Nanjing in the Ming dynasty, where the story is set.

HONG SHENG, *PALACE OF EVERLASTING LIFE (CHANGSHENG DIAN)* 長生殿

Cao Qijing 曹其敬, dir. *Changsheng dian* 長生殿 (*Palace of Everlasting Life*). In *Shanghai kunju tuan jiantuan sanshi zhounian jinian* 上海昆劇團建團30周年紀念 (*The Thirtieth Anniversary of the Establishment of the Shanghai Kunqu Opera Troupe*). Performed by Cai Zhengren 蔡正仁, Zhang Jingxian 張靜嫻, etc. Guangzhou, China: Guangzhou Qiao jiaren wenhua chuanbo youxian gongsi, 2008. DVD (Chinese).

This performance is a full-scale play with four "books" (*ben* 本, a large chunk of the overall story, usually containing a series of scenes) that lasts for ten hours. In each book, the Emperor Xuanzong (Li Longji 李隆基) and the Prized Consort Yang (Yang Yuhuan 楊玉環) are played by a different pair of performers. This is an all-star performance that allows different Kunqu masters to demonstrate their unique interpretations of these roles.

CHAPTER 13

QING COURT THEATER

Bertolucci Bernardo, dir. *The Last Emperor*. Columbia Pictures, 1987; Optimum Releasing, 2004. DVD (English).

This film creates a narrative using interspersed flashbacks to narrate the life of Puyi 溥儀, the last emperor of China. One scene in the film shows a court performance during Puyi's wedding. It presents the three-tiered Pavilion of Pleasant Sounds (Changyin ge 暢音閣), one of the grand stages where court plays were performed.

Bo Xiaolin 薄曉琳. "Theater and Music to Extol the Good Times" ("Xiyue shengping" 戲樂升平). In *The Forbidden City 100* (*Gugong 100* 故宮100). Beijing: Zhongguo guoji dianshi zong gongsi, 2011. DVD (Chinese).

This six-minute video is one episode of *The Forbidden City 100*, a documentary about the history and culture surrounding the Forbidden City. It introduces one of the court stages, the Pavilion of Pleasant Sounds (Changyin ge 暢音閣), including its architecture and stage design.

CHAPTER 14

LI YU, *A HANDFUL OF SNOW* (*YIPENG XUE*) 一捧雪

Zhou Xinfang 周信芳. "*Yipeng xue*: "Shentou," "Ci Tang" 一捧雪·審頭刺湯 ("Interrogating the Cut-off Head" and "Stabbing Tang Qin," in *A Handful of Snow*). Shanghai: Xinhui jituan Shanghai shengxiang chuban she, 2002. DVD (Chinese).

This performance highlights two iconic scenes in the play *A Handful of Snow*, a tragedy instigated by the obsession with an antique jade cup by the same name. This performance is part of the "Remastered Classics of Chinese Beijing Opera" (*Zhongguo jingju yinpeixiang jingcui* 中國京劇音配像精粹) project (No. 344). The original audio is taken from the 1962 performance by Zhou Xinfang 周信芳, Liu Binkun 劉斌昆, Li Yuru 李玉茹, and Li Tongsen 李桐森, with contemporary stand-in performers.

Wu Zuguang 吳祖光, dir. *Mei Lanfang de wutai yishu* 梅蘭芳的舞臺藝術 (Mei Lanfang's Stage Art, Master of Beijing Opera). Shanghai: Zhongguo changpian Shanghai gongsi, 2012. DVD (Chinese).

Produced in 1955, this film is a product of "Commemorating Mei Lanfang's 50 Years on Stage" ("Jinian Mei Lanfang wutai shenghuo wushi zhounian" 紀念梅蘭芳舞臺生活五十周年). It consists of a short documentary entitled *Mei Lanfang's Artistic Career* (*Mei Lanfang de yishu shenghuo* 梅蘭芳的藝術生活) and four of Mei's representative rearranged scenes excerpted from different plays, including "The Broken Bridge" ("Duanqiao" 斷橋); "Draft a Memorial" ("Xiuben" 修本) and "The Golden Palace" ("Jindian" 金殿) from *A Sword Called the Edge of Universe* (*Yuzhou feng* 宇宙鋒); "Decisive Battle on Jiuli Mountain" ("Jiulishan huizhan" 九裡山會戰) and "Farewell to the Concubine" ("Bieji" 別姬) from *Farewell My Concubine* (*Bawang bieji* 霸王別姬); and "The Drunken Beauty" ("Guifei zuijiu" 貴妃醉酒).

CHAPTER 15

ZHENG ZHIZHEN, *MULIAN RESCUES HIS MOTHER: AN EXHORTATION TO GOODNESS* (*XINBIAN MULIAN JIUMU QUANSHAN XIWEN*) 新編目連救母勸善戲文

Wong Hok-Sing 黃鶴聲 (aka Huang Hesheng), dir. *Guanyin de dao, Xianghua Shan da he shou* 觀音得道, 香花山大賀壽 (*The Enlightenment of Guanyin, The Great Celebration of Birthday at the Fragrant Flower Mountain*, aka *Night of the Opera Stars*). Performed by Lee Bo-Ying 李寶瑩 (Li Baoying) and Chan Ho-Kau 陳好逑 (Chen Haoqiu), 1966; Hong Kong: China Art F. E. Video Production Co., n.d. VCD (Cantonese with complex character Chinese subtitles).

This film documents the performance of a ritual play adapted from "Celebrating the Birthday of Guanyin" ("Guanyin shengri" 觀音生日), in Zheng Zhizhen's 鄭之珍 *Mulian jiumu quanshan xiwen* 目連救母勸善戲文 (*Mulian Rescues His Mother: An Exhortation to Goodness*). It features the famous "Eighteen Transformations of Guanyin" ("Guanyin shiba bian" 觀音十八變). Conventionally, this unique title is performed by the troupes to celebrate the birthdays of the patron deities of Cantonese opera, such as Huaguang Xianshi 華光先師 and Tian Dou Xianshi 田竇先師. The earliest record of this ritual play dates back to 1900.

CHAPTER 16

ANONYMOUS, *GUAN SUO RITUAL PLAY* (XIAOTUN VILLAGE, YUNNAN) 關索儺戲

Zhang Yimou 張藝謀, dir. *Qianli zou danji* 千里走單騎 (*Riding Alone for Thousands of Miles*). 2005; Culver City, CA: Sony Pictures Home Entertainment, 2007. DVD (Chinese and Japanese with English subtitles).
This film tells the story of a Japanese father traveling to Yunnan to record the local villagers' "Yunnan mask play" (*Yunnan mianju xi* 雲南面具戲) *Riding Alone for Thousands of Miles* for his dying son. The production team intended to use the Guan Suo plays preserved in Xiaotun 小屯 village and invited the Guan Suo play performer Li Bencan 李本燦 as a consultant. The actual performance recorded in the film ended up being staged by performers of Guizhou *dixi* (地戲, "ground drama"), which allegedly had the same origin as Guan Suo plays.

NOTES

For samples of online resources, search with the name of a play, title of a specific scene, or performers' names on websites like YouTube, CCTV *Kongzhong juyuan* 空中劇院 (CCTV Sky Theater), and Bilibili.com. For example, see "*The Lute*: Cai Bojie" (Chinese with English subtitles), Confucius Institute at the University of Michigan YouTube Channel, May 3, 2019, https://www.youtube.com/watch?v=4Zp6eXoikTQ.

1. For the English subtitles of this film, see Christopher Rea, trans., *Hua Mu Lan*, Modern Chinese Cultural Studies YouTube Channel, June 11, 2020, https://www.youtube.com/watch?v=B99xRkrwdTs.

2. For the English translation of this lecture, see Josh Sternberg, trans., "Lecture 11: Given by Liang Guyin 'The Tryst' 佳期 (Jiaqi)," from *The Western Chamber* 西廂記 (*Xixiang ji*)," in *Kunqu Masters on Chinese Theatrical Practice*, edited by Josh Sternberg (London: Anthem Press, 2021 forthcoming).

GLOSSARY-INDEX

This index does not contain thematic entries, as they are already provided in the thematic table of contents beginning on page ix.

Guo Moruo 郭沫若 (1892–1978),
chap. 1 32

guoqu 過曲 (standard vocal compositions
composed according to distinctive
song patterns), chap. 8 197

Guoxi ting 過溪亭 (Crossing-the-Stream
Pavilion), chap. 13 320

H

Haiyan 海鹽 (a county in Zhejiang
province), Introduction, chap. 8
19, 196

Haiyu ge'en 海宇歌恩 (*Songs of Grace
within the Seas*), chap. 13 311, 313–314

Han Chulan 漢楚蘭 (character in
*Moonlight and Breezes in the Courtyard
of Purple Clouds*), chap. 2 60, 64–66

Handan meng ji 邯鄲夢記 (*The Dream of
Handan*), chap. 9 222

Han Jue 韓厥 (character in *The Orphan
of Zhao*), chap. 5 130, 132–134, 143–144

Han Lin'er 韓林兒 (fl. 1355–1366),
chap. 16 374

Han Wudi 漢武帝 (Emperor Wu of the
Han [r. 141–87 BCE]), chap. 5, chap. 11
129, 283

hangdang 行當 (theatrical role),
Introduction 13

haose huangyin loumian zei 好色荒淫
漏面賊 (a depraved and shameless
gangster), chap. 3 95

he 喝 (shouting), chap. 3 82

Hechun 和春 (Hechun Troupe, active in
Beijing, ca. 1803–1853), Introduction,
chap. 14 20, 326–328, 330, 337–339,
341–342

Hejin 河津 (place name, in Shanxi
province), chap. 9 221

Helü shi 鶴侶氏 (Master Helü),
chap. 14 340

"Helü zitan" 鶴侶自歎 ("Master Helü's
Own Lament"), chap. 14 340

Heshen 和珅 (1746–1799), chap. 14 330–
331, 336–337, 341

hen diedie 狠爹爹 (vicious father),
chap. 3 89

henqie 狠切 (savage), chap. 3 89

henxin 狠心 (brutal), chap. 3 89

hongdong 鬨動 ("fashioning a bustling
atmosphere" or "stirring up sound
and excitement"), chap. 15 360

hongdong cunshe 鬨動村社 ("great
commotion in the village"), chap. 15
360, 363

Hongguang 弘光 (an emperor of the
Southern Ming and the name of his
only reign period [r. 1644–1645]; see
also Fuwang), chap. 12 296

hongjin 紅巾 (Red Turbans), chap. 16 374

Honglou meng 紅樓夢 (*Dream in the Red
Chamber*, also translated as *Story of the
Stone*), chap. 1 47

Hongniang 紅娘 (Crimson, character
in *The Story of the Western Wing*),
Introduction, chap. 1, chap. 4, chap. 8
15, 31, 115, 194

"Hongniang qing yan" 紅娘請宴
("Crimson Delivers an Invitation to
the Banquet"), chap. 4 115

Hong Sheng 洪昇 (1645–1704), chap. 12
286–287, 289, 291–292, 301–302

Hongtong 洪洞 (place name),
chap. 4 112

Hongwu zhengyun 洪武正韻 (*Correct
Rhymes of the Hongwu Reign*, 1375),
Introduction 17

Hongzhi 弘治 (an emperor of the Ming
dynasty and the name of his only
reign period [r. 1488–1505]), chap. 1,
chap. 4 31, 102, 122

Hou Fangyu 侯方域 (1618–1655),
Introduction, chap. 12 2, 285,
289–290, 298–299

Hou Hanshu 後漢書 (*The History of the
Latter Han*), chap. 15 362

hou huayuan 後花園 (rear garden),
chap. 9 216

Hou Yao 侯曜 (1903–1942), chap. 1 32

jing jiang tianshang xianyin liuzuo renjian jiahua 竟將天上仙音，留作人間佳話 ("the celestial melody is transmitted to make a fine story in the human realm"), chap. 12 294

jingju 京劇 (literally "capital opera," alternatively translated as "Peking opera" and "Beijing opera"), Introduction, chap. 14 20, 327

"Jingmeng" 驚夢 ("Interrupted Dream"), chap. 4, chap. 9 121, 223

jingshi 京市 (capital), chap. 2 70

jingshu 經書 (classics), chap. 4 109

Jingting 敬亭 (a seal stamp on the script of *The Eight-Court Pearl*), chap. 14 342

Jiugong dacheng nanbeici gongpu 九宮大成南北詞宮譜 (*Comprehensive Formulary of Northern and Southern Arias in Nine Music Modes*, 1746; also translated as *Great Compilation of Musical Scores from the Southern and Northern Arias in All Nine Modes*), chap. 8, chap. 14 196, 339

jiu mi yuegong 久秘月宮 ("long kept a secret in the Moon Palace"), chap. 12 294

Jiushan shuhui 九山書會 (Nine Mountain Society), chap. 7 172

ju 具 (able), Introduction 16

juren 舉人 (degree for examinees who have passed the provincial examination), chap. 13 310

juzuo jia 劇作家 (dramatist), chap. 8 192

juan 卷 (scroll; volume), chap. 1, chap. 15 37, 355

juanxie 鵑血 (cuckoo blood), chap. 12 298

juese 角色 (theatrical role), Introduction 13

junchen zaju 君臣雜劇 (*zaju* dramas about lords and ministers), chap. 2 54

jun nuo 軍儺 ("military *nuo*," a type of exorcism rite), chap. 16 367, 378

juntian 鈞天 (the Harmonious Heaven), chap. 12 295

junwang 郡王 (second-degree Manchu prince), chap. 14 339

K

kaichang 開場 (opening scene), chap. 11, chap. 15 266, 355

Kaifeng 開封 (place name, present-day Kaifeng), Introduction, chap. 3, chap. 9, chap. 15 12, 21, 85, 217, 350, 353

kan'ai 堪愛 (how lovely), chap. 8 207

kanguan 看官 (readers), chap. 4 115

kangkai jiaren jiang nan qing fu 慷慨佳人將難輕赴 ("the heroic beauty's generous sacrifice of her life"), chap. 12 299

Kangxi 康熙 (an emperor of the Qing dynasty and the name of his only reign period [r. 1661–1722]), chap. 13 321, 323

Kano Naoki 狩野直喜 (1868–1947), chap. 5 142

"Kao Hong" 拷紅 ("Interrogating Crimson," a rearranged scene), chap. 8 196

ke1 科 (stage directions), chap. 4, chap. 5 113, 131

ke2 客 (retainer), chap. 5 128

Kong Linzhi 孔琳之 (369–423), chap. 11 283

Kong Shangren 孔尚任 (1648–1718), Introduction, chap. 4, chap. 10, chap. 12, chap. 13 15, 113, 253, 286, 288–289, 301, 310

ku 哭 (public wailing to mourn someone), chap. 3 82, 94

Kuanggushi Yuyang sannong 狂鼓史漁陽三弄 (*The Mad Drummer Plays the Yuyang Triple Rolls*), chap. 6 152

"Kuanghun" 誆婚 ("The Fake Marriage"), chap. 11 259

"Kuijian" 窺簡 ("Peeking at the Letter"), chap. 4 120

yu meng er yu jue 愈夢而愈覺 ("the more one dreams, the more one becomes awake"), chap. 9 222

"*Yuming tang chuanqi* yin" 玉茗堂傳奇引 ("Preface to Tang Xianzu's *Chuanqi* Drama"), chap. 9 233

yu-mo 魚模 (rhyme class), chap. 2 60

"Yu qiu xiao si" 語求肖似 ("Aim for Likeness in Language," the title of a section from Li Yu's *Leisure Notes*), chap. 11 269

yushui zhi huan 魚水之歡 (the harmony/joy of a fish playing with water; an euphemism for lovemaking), chap. 8 208

"Yutai kuijian" 玉臺窺簡 ("Espying the Missive at the Jade Terrace"), chap. 4 115

Yutang huiji 玉堂薈記 (*Collected Writings from Jade Hall*), chap. 10 255

Yuyao 余姚 (a town in Zhejiang province, China), Introduction, chap. 8 19, 196

"Yuyun youhui" 雨雲幽會 ("The Secret Tryst," an act in *The Story of the Western Wing*), chap. 4 110

yuan 怨 (to lament), chap. 3 82

yuan 圓 (a unit of currency), chap. 14 342

yuanben 院本 (farces; farcical skits), Introduction, chap. 3 5, 98

Yuankan zaju sanshi zhong 元刊雜劇三十種 (*Thirty Yuan-Printed Zaju Plays*, 1914), Introduction, chap. 3, chap. 46, 79, 107

Yuanqu xuan 元曲選 (*Select Yuan Plays*, 1615–1616), Introduction, chap. 2 7, 68

Yuanshantang qupin 遠山堂曲品 (*Commentaries on Songs from the Remote Mountain Hall*), chap. 15 360

"Yuanyu 冤獄 ("Unjust Imprisonment"), chap. 3 99

Yuan Zhen 元稹 (779–831), chap. 1, chap. 8 33–35, 38, 40, 194, 199

yue 樂 (music), Introduction 18

Yue 越 (place name, present-day Zhejiang province), Introduction 19

Yue 岳 (family name), chap. 4 108

Yue Fei 岳飛 (1103–1142), chap. 5 148

Yuefu shiji 樂府詩集 (*The Poetry Collection of the Music Bureau*), chap. 6 166

yuehu 樂戶 (the hereditary ranks of musician households), Introduction 21

Yueshu 樂書 (*The Book on Music*), chap. 9 217

"Yuexia jiaqi" 月下佳期 ("The Happy Tryst on a Moonlit Night," an illustration title in *The Reprinted, Original Yuan Edition of The Story of the Western Wing with Annotations and Phonetic Glosses*; also translated as "Happy Time in a Moonlit Night," a scene from *Southern Western Wing*), chap. 4, chap. 8 115, 209

yuezhe, shengren zhi suo le 樂者，聖人之所樂 ("music is what the sages take pleasure in"), Introduction 18

Yunlu 允祿 (1695–1767), chap. 8, chap. 14 202, 339

Yunlüe 韻略 (*Treatise on Rhymes*), chap. 7 190

Yunyan guoyan lu 雲煙過眼錄 (*Records of Clouds and Mist Passing before One's Eyes*), chap. 4 122

Z

za 雜 (mixed), chap. 3 83

zaju 雜劇 (literally "variety plays" or "wide-ranging plays," the dominant form of northern style drama during the Yuan but a dramatic genre that flourished through the Qing), Introduction, chap. 1, chap. 2, chap. 3, chap. 5, chap. 6, chap. 8, chap. 11, chap. 13, chap. 14, chap. 16 3, 5–10, 13–14, 16, 18–20, 22, 31, 39, 41–45, 48–50, 53–56, 58, 65, 67, 78–84, 90, 97–98, 127–130, 147, 155, 194–195, 200, 203, 264–265, 322, 370, 374–375